BOOKS BY

KENNETH TYNAN

TYNAN RIGHT & LEFT

TYNAN

RIGHT & LEFT

PLAYS

FILMS

PEOPLE

PLACES

AND

EVENTS

BY KENNETH TYNAN

ATHENEUM

1967

NEW YORK

For permission to reprint most of what follows, the author is grateful to the editors of eleven publications, three of them English—THE OBSERVER, THE QUEEN and PUNCH—and eight American, as listed below. The author's thanks are also due to Robert Bolt, for permission to reprint his comments on *A Man for All Seasons;* to Jean-Paul Sartre, for "An Interview with Sartre"; and to Truman Capote and Joseph M. Jenkins, for their comments on *In Cold Blood.*

ESQUIRE, for "The Rising Costa del Sol," first published in *Esquire* as "The Eclipse of the Fun"

HARPER'S BAZAAR, for "The Charleroi Adventure" and "Cyril Connolly," first published in that magazine

HARPER'S MAGAZINE, for "Command Performance," copyright © 1960 by Harper's Magazine, Inc. Reprinted from the October 1960 issue of *Harper's Magazine* by permission

HOLIDAY, for "An Audience of Critics," © 1964, The Curtis Publishing Company; "Barcelona," © 1959, The Curtis Publishing Company; "George Cukor and the Girls," © 1961, The Curtis Publishing Company; "Joan Littlewood," © 1964, The Curtis Publishing Company; "Memoir of Manhattan," © 1960, The Curtis Publishing Company; "Miles Apart," © 1962, The Curtis Publishing Company; "Non-Conformists of San Francisco," © 1961, The Curtis Publishing Company

THE NEW YORKER, for "Theatre in Paris," © 1966 The New Yorker Magazine, Inc.; reprinted by permission

PLAYBOY, for "The Bogart I Never Knew," "Papa and the Playwright" and "The Royal Smuthound," which originally appeared in that magazine

SHOW, for "Orson Welles," reprinted with permission from the October 1961 issue of *Show* magazine

FOREWORD

Most of the pieces here assembled were written in the past ten years. They are the work of a drama critic at large not only in theatres but in cinemas, books, cities and the lives of other people. Much of my adult life has been spent in covering last week's plays for next week's readers; but between the fall of one curtain and the rise of another, a good deal of time elapses, and over the years I have been encouraged by a number of beguiling editors to look at the other performing arts, to report public spectacles and events, to visit places that attracted me, to meet people who appealed to my talent-snobbism, and even to read a few books.

This book is, in part, the result of those excursions. It records the fingerprints (and the bruises) left by many aspects of mid-century cultural life on the mind of a mid-Atlantic cultural journalist. In other, less lapidary words, here are some of the things—on stage and off—by which I've been pleased, provoked, disturbed and enthralled since my thirtieth birthday, a decade ago.

'Forty—sombre anniversary to the hedonist...' Thus Cyril Connolly in *The Unquiet Grave*. It is sombre, too, for the critic. (What has he learned? What, if anything, has he *changed*? What achievement is really commemorated in those files of autumn-tinted clippings?) As I shamble aghast into the prime of life, I wonder what kind of dossier the Greatest Critic of Them All is compiling for me, Up There:

Occupation. Opinion-monger, observer of artistic phenomena, amateur ideologue. Latterly, Literary Manager of National Theatre of Great Britain, under direction of Laurence Olivier. Describes relationship with Olivier as akin to that of 'a tugboat nudging an ocean greyhound into harbour'. Defines drama criticism as a 'self-knowing account of the way in which one's consciousness has been modified during an evening

vii

in the theatre; and the greater the self-knowledge, the better the critic. At any level, criticism must be accurate reportage of what has taken place outside you; at the highest level, it is also accurate reportage of what has taken place within you.' Has summarised the nature of good drama as follows: 'If a play does anything—either tragically or comically, satirically or farcically—to explain to me why I am alive, it is a good play. If it seems unaware that such questions exist, I tend to suspect that it's a bad one.' Attributed aphorisms:

1. 'A critic is a man who knows the value of everything and the price of nothing. Hence he should not work for a subsidised theatre unless it has a strict accountant.'

2. 'A good drama critic is one who perceives what is happening in the theatre of his time. A great drama critic also perceives what is *not* happening.'

Hobbies. Travel, sex, watching bullfights, eating highly-spiced food, talking to gifted and/or funny people. (Evidence both of intense curiosity and of jaded palate.)

Philosophical beliefs. Sun-worshipper, mainly from the shade. Empirical neo-Marxist, dabbler in Zen Buddhism, and (lately) devout exponent of ideas about human and animal behaviour expressed in Konrad Lorenz's book, *On Aggression.* Shuns metaphysics, and declares that 'the exercise of reason is dull only to primitive and uninstructed people'. When told by an admirer: 'I read you religiously,' is alleged to have answered: 'Please read me agnostically.'

Political beliefs. Socialism—always provided (*a*) that it leaves room for the gay, irreverent spontaneity of Zen, and (*b*) that it takes into account the basic doctrines of Lorenz: namely, that human beings are animals in whom love is inseparable from aggression, and territorial (not class) allegiances are ultimately paramount.

Moral beliefs. Professes to act on principle of 'Do as you would be done by', but denies that this is evidence of virtue: 'for anyone tinged with sado-masochism, as most intellectuals are, that isn't a moral precept, it's pure wish-fulfilment.' (Has described those who read his reviews as 'part working-class, part intelligentsia—half Ad-mass, half sad-mas.') Yet a moralist, all the same. Is on record as having said: 'If the artist is to give the chaos of events any meaning, he must place them in a structure of ideology, which implies a morality. This is true of all works of narrative art.' Detests compromise of any kind, but not because he is brave or principled. Explains that he is too guilt-ridden to be corruptible: he cannot permit himself the moral leeway that more innocent hearts could survive untainted.

Psychological diagnosis. Possesses a Super-Ego of tremendous (though only sporadically exercised) power, in the form of reproving conscience that drives him to periodic bouts of self-punishing work; and an equally powerful Id, which insists on immediate sensual rewards. Caught between these mighty adversaries, his Ego is ground to dust, like a neutral principality in a polarised world. When working or satisfying his appetites, he knows precisely who he is; but with the cessation of these pursuits, his identity tends to blur and disappear. Can seldom banish from his mind the fact of approaching mortality. This may account for his instinctive sympathy with Socialist-maternal ideal of equality and mercy rather than with Conservative-paternal ideals of hierarchy and authority. Characteristic sample of conversation: 'When I'm unhappy, I can't work. When I'm happy, I don't need to work. When I don't need to work, I'm unhappy.' Favourite quotations include wide variety of stoical pronouncements on the necessity of facing death with grace and defiance (sign over his desk reads: 'Be light, stinging, insolent, and melancholy'), plus a single sentence culled from published works of psychiatrist named Dr Bergler: 'Every writer without exception is a masochist, a sadist, a peeping Tom, an exhibitionist, a narcissist, an "injustice collector" and a "depressed person constantly haunted by fears of unproductivity".' Laughs surprisingly often, all things considered.

Literary diagnosis. Regarded by many fellow-journalists as a snob, and by many academic critics as a charlatan. (Trapped, once again, between Id and Super-Ego.) Not very artistic, except perhaps in temperament. Probably best summed up as a student of craftmanship, with a special passion for imaginative craftsmen who put their skills to the service of human ideas.

Conclusion. Still unreached. To assist interim judgment, a selection of relevant documents is appended.

K.T.

CONTENTS

I: THEATRE

Titus Andronicus, BY WILLIAM SHAKESPEARE, AT THE STOLL;
Cymbeline, BY WILLIAM SHAKESPEARE, AT STRATFORD-ON-AVON

Having closely compared Peter Brook's production of *Titus An-dronicus* with Peter Hall's production of *Cymbeline,* I am persuaded that these two young directors should at once go into partnership. I have even worked out business cards for them:

> Hall & Brook, Ltd, the Home of Lost Theatrical Causes. Col-lapsing plays shored up, unspeakable lines glossed over, unactable scenes made bearable. Wrecks salvaged, ruins refurbished: un-popular plays at popular prices. Masterpieces dealt with only if neglected. Shakespearean juvenilia and senilia our speciality: if it can walk, we'll make it run. Bad last acts no obstacle: if it peters out, call Peter in. Don't be fobbed off with Glenvilles, Woods, or Zadeks: look for the trademark—Hall & Brook.

The present examples of Hallage and Brookery come unmistakably from the same firm. In each case the director has imposed on a blood-stained, uneven play a unifying conception of his own. Messrs Brook and Hall have swathed in 'atmosphere' pieces of work which otherwise would be tedious. They have punctuated drab texts with ritual proces-sions, barbaric music and extravagant scenic effects, thereby distracting attention from lines and situations that would be absurd without such adornment. And, by an odd coincidence, they have both been craven in the same way. Asked to produce Tamora's lost sons, Titus replies: 'Why, there they are both, baked in that pie': Mr Brook deletes the last four words. Similarly, when Caius Lucius exclaims: 'Soft ho! what trunk is here without his top?' Mr Hall deletes the last three. This is in-excusable cowardice. Those who devote themselves to making silk purses out of sows' ears are in duty bound to go the whole hog.

Two years ago Mr Brook's production crowned a Stratford season

3

which had already seen Sir Laurence Olivier's triumphant Macbeth. After that banquet, *Titus* came as an unexpected *bonne bouche*, and also as a neat bit of directorial do-it-yourself, since Mr Brook was responsible both for the music, growling and pinging, and the décor, stately and arcane. The same production, having lately visited and apparently dumbfounded such exotic cities as Zagreb and Warsaw, is now installed at the Stoll as an established classic. This is going altogether too far. While I admire the skill with which Sir Laurence and his director have made the play palatable, I wish they had collaborated on something nobler than a versified atrocity report. They have done superbly something that was not worth doing at all; and I am sure that London would have preferred to see its greatest actor in the highest reaches of his art, not splashing about in its shallows.

I agree that he splashes tremendously, making crested waves of mere ripples; no one can rival Sir Laurence when it comes to transports of rage, moans of grief, guttural crows of triumph and Senecan doughtiness of soul. Yet on Monday night he was well below par. His voice seemed constipated, a crafty squawk instead of a terrible bellow; he rushed and gabbled, betraying all the signs of an over-tired actor who is addressing a foreign audience and counting on their inability to understand what he is saying.

This symptom was noticeable in many of his colleagues: I have never heard a Shakespeare play so unintelligibly raced. There were two shining exceptions: Maxine Audley and Anthony Quayle as Tamora and Aaron, who ran away with the evening by the simple expedient of not running at all. Sir Laurence's London appearances are rare, and this one is not to be missed; but I hope that no one will go expecting to see him, or his author, at anything like their best.

Mr Hall tackles *Cymbeline*, a slightly better play, with similar aplomb and comparable success; which does not mean that I think his production should forthwith be sent on an extended tour of Eastern Europe. What he has done is to weld all the play's manifold facets—its jokes and beheadings, its Roman armies and Renaissance villainies—into the same experience; and he has achieved this by throwing over the whole production a sinister veil of faery, so that it resembles a Grimm fable transmuted by the Cocteau of *La Belle et la Bête*.

He creates, in short, an ambience in which the ludicrous anomalies of the plot are believable and even lovable. Lila de Nobili helps him, with a cobwebby, tree-shaded, magic-prone Gothic setting that takes us straight into the world of momentous fantasy where alone the play can flourish. Posthumus (Richard Johnson) is a perfect white-clad knight;

the Queen (Joan Miller) an Arthurian enchantress. Helmets gleam and threaten from high hillsides, and all the costumes are silvery, bulrushy or glaucous green. All but for the Romans, who wear crimson and gold: the massed advance of those embossed and glittering shields makes a stunning visual impact.

I was prepared to be entranced by Peggy Ashcroft's Imogen until I began to be obsessed by this actress's ocular mannerisms. We all know that she blinks: it was my misfortune to discover that her blinks coincide with the words she intends to emphasise. Having spotted this trick, I watched only for her blinking, and am thus in no position to assess her performance. Otherwise, my admiration for Mr Hall's production is boundless, and I was as appalled as he must have been by the off-stage engineer who prefaced every musical intervention with thirty booming seconds of gramophone hum.

(1957)

Epitaph for George Dillon, BY JOHN OSBORNE AND ANTHONY CREIGHTON, AT THE OXFORD UNIVERSITY EXPERIMENTAL THEATRE CLUB

The world premiere of *Epitaph for George Dillon*, written four years ago by John Osborne and Anthony Creighton, began sluggishly. It is high-tea-time in a dim London suburb. Dad stares bleakly at the sauce-bottle, Mum resists the temptation to throw it at him, daughter Josie jives in tartan slacks and daughter Norah plods cheerily towards bureaucratic oblivion. Aunt Ruth, a handsome Communist crossed in love, is admittedly 'different': otherwise, this is a family of conventional squalor. Then, at the end of the act, a lodger arrives, his name George Dillon. Picking up a portrait of Mum's dead son, he murmurs: 'You stupid-looking bastard.' At this point the undergraduate audience, steeped in Mr Osborne's *Look Back in Anger*, nodded and said to itself: 'Jimmy Porter, as I live and suffocate.'

In part they were right. In many ways George is a first sketch for Jimmy. His origins are blatantly autobiographical: like Mr Osborne he is young, an actor, a playwright and a vegetarian. He has a talent for rhetorical derision and is so touchy that he can interpret the offer of a cigarette as a calculated insult. He specialises, as an actor, in 'scornful parts'. He can spot phonies a mile off, and shoots as soon as he can see the whites of their sepulchres. He deflates with savage jabs a flushed young man, highly reminiscent of Colin Wilson, who asserts that 'the really smart thing is the spiritual thing'.

Victorian heroes were annoyed because they could not marry the squire's daughter: George, like Jimmy, is annoyed because he could, and did. Like most contemporary red-brick intellectuals, he regards the upper classes neither with envy, as an outsider, nor with guilt, as a renegade, but with frank and total boredom. His problem is an intelligence that will not let him sleep: he analyses himself as lethally as he analyses his enemies. Having floored them with a left hook, he follows through with a moral haymaker that inexorably connects with his own jaw. In two respects he resembles Lucky Jim: he puts on comic voices when telephoning, and he has an inexplicable sexual success with every woman he meets. Otherwise he seems identical with Jimmy.

Yet, as the house slowly realised, he is vitally different, and in the difference lies the virtue of this engrossing play. Aunt Ruth sees in George the lover she has just left, a brilliant young sponger: George sees in Ruth the wife he has just abandoned, an older woman who sought to enslave him. Haunted by these ghosts, they can never come together, and the duologue in which they discover this is more adult than anything in *Look Back in Anger*.

Psychologically, too, there is a basic split between George and Jimmy. Jimmy has a big talent which he chooses to leave idle: George has a small talent which he believes to be big. He has all the symptoms of genius, the high temperature, the glandular swellings, the bursts of extravagant gaiety: but he lacks the genuine disease. His plays are accepted, but only after a clever manager has dirtied them up for twice-nightly repertory. He thinks himself big with art, but it is a hysterical pregnancy, not uncommon among adolescent girls.

Here and there one discerns ambivalence, and suspects that Mr Osborne thought rather more highly of George's gifts than Mr Creighton. But the final curtain leaves no room for doubt. The idol of this *drame à clef* has feet of clay, and knows it. He is the sick sad oyster that could not produce the pearl. A little thoughtful snipping and rewriting should certainly bring the play to London.

(1957)

Shadow of Heroes, BY ROBERT ARDREY, AT THE PICCADILLY

We read non-fiction as well as fiction. On the radio we listen as attentively to feature programmes as to plays. On screens of all sizes we watch documentaries. Why, then, should we not have documentary drama? That is the question posed by Robert Ardrey's *Shadow of Heroes*, which is a sort of illustrated lecture on the Hungarian revolt of 1956. The events covered by the play, which begins in 1944, are nearly all authenticated. Where they are not, Mr Ardrey tells us so through his narrator, who is Emlyn Williams in a tweed overcoat and muffler.

Cards are on the table throughout. Nobody pretends that Alan Webb *is* Janos Kadar; in Brechtian style, he is said to 'speak for' Kadar, just as Mogens Wieth 'speaks for' Lazlo Rajk, whom Kadar betrayed, and Peggy Ashcroft for Mrs Rajk. By thus warning us not to identify the players with their roles, Mr Ardrey hits two bull's-eyes with one shot. He reinforces our faith in his impartiality, and at the same time insures his cast against any inadequacies of performance—in this case a necessary step, since West End actors are seldom at their happiest when playing people to whom politics are a matter of life or death. Miss Ashcroft gets sincerely worked up, though there is not in her soul the iron that must have existed in Julia Rajk's; and Mr Webb, whom I certainly never expected to see as a leader of the revolutionary proletariat, does surprisingly well. But I doubt if I should let either of them off so lightly without Mr Ardrey's crafty *caveat*.

What gives the play its power is its use of drama as a living newspaper: the idea is old and neglected, and it was thrilling, last week, to see it revived. No theatrical technique is more intimately, immediately striking, and no better subject for it could be imagined than the story of postwar Budapest. These are events through which, however vicariously, we have all lived: the Russian conquest of Hungary (Hitler's last surviving ally), the steady hardening of Stalinism, the false dawn that followed Khrushchev's repudiation of his unmourned boss, the splendour of the students' revolt, the week-long October triumph of students and workers, and the misery of their mechanised defeat.

Mr Ardrey, though he never entered Hungary, conducts us through the shifting sands of this desperate epoch with the assurance of a native guide. Peter Hall's direction, on a stage naked except for a rostrum and a collection of dun, portable screens, flows as atmospherically as lightning. A masterly, controlling tact is everywhere perceptible: the crowd never screams, the recorded sound never deafens. As here presented, Mikoyan bears an unfortunate resemblance to Groucho Marx, and what little we see of Imre Nagy suggests nobody more formidable or exotic than Colonel Pickering. It does not matter. We are mesmerised by the potency of fact; so much so that I for one left the theatre filled with a phantom hope that someone, some day, might give us a similar treatment of Suez.

To anyone planning such a play I cannot extend any firm prospect of West End production; but I can counsel the putative author to learn from Mr Ardrey's example. He must first make sure that the dialogue he invents rings as true as the dates and facts on to which it is pinned. (In this respect Mr Ardrey wavers: most of what he invents sounds plausible but novelettish.) Secondly, he must study the special change that comes over facts in the theatre. They come to be equated with truth. So willingly does a theatre audience suspend its disbelief that it accepts facts not just as aspects of the truth but as the whole of it. No documentary playwright has room for all the facts. He must select, and selection means slanting: which is why all factual plays sound like propaganda plays, unless they are written by intellectual eunuchs, in which case they are plain dull. Mr Ardrey's piece is far from dull. It is honest propaganda, and as such it deserves honest probing.

First of all, for its omissions. It correctly states that the official 're-habilitation' of the executed Lazlo Rajk was made the excuse for a vast anti-Russian demonstration; but, in making Rajk his hero, Mr Ardrey forgets to point out that during his lifetime he was universally detested as the organiser of the secret police. Another curious gap is Mr Ardrey's failure to introduce to us any of the revolutionary leaders. The Hungarian uprising was pledged, as the Petofi Club voted on 23 October 1956, 'to ensure the development of Socialist democracy' and to assert 'the legitimate aspirations of the working class'. From Mr Ardrey's account you would never guess that a single Socialist took part in this predominantly Socialist revolt. He tells us at great length what it was against; but we hear little about what it was for.

Mr Ardrey, who is American, has just sent me a document listing the sources from which he drew his information. In it he says that he refrained, 'as a matter of taste', from mentioning that Kadar was castrated during his imprisonment in 1951—'a point . . . known to all students of the Hungarian uprising'. My sources—equally Hungarian and equally anti-Stalinist—deny this charge with open derision. Whom are you going to believe? In the answer to that question lies the challenge of plays like this. They urge us to find out for ourselves. Fiction dictates its own terms. Fact must meet us on ours. We cease to be mere tasters, and become judicial participants. *Shadow of Heroes* is an ailing play, but all lovers of a truly contemporary drama will wish for more like it.

(1958)

Pericles, BY WILLIAM SHAKESPEARE, AT STRATFORD-ON-AVON

Johnson thought *Pericles* a 'mouldy tale', though it is hard nowadays to see why. Today the epic is back in vogue: no longer, either in the novel or the theatre, do we reject as inartistic a series of imaginary events whose only common denominator is that they all happen to the same person.

Whoever wrote the play's first two acts was plainly a sloppy poet (e.g., his constant use of 'the which' to pad out the pentameter), but I don't doubt that, were he alive today, his scripts would be all over the wide screens. There is even, as they say, a picture in *Pericles*, assuming that the censor could be soothed. The fulcrum of the action—Pericles's flight from Antioch on discovering incest at court—would need what is known as a little fixing, and the brothel in Mytilene would automatically become a sort of wild teashop, but the rest is (almost literally) plain sailing. Before long the 'working title' would be abandoned, and an item would appear in *Variety*: 'De Mille rumoured dickering with Kirk Douglas for lead in upcoming blockbuster, "Around the Med. in Eighteen Years".'

But there is more to the play than crowd-catching melodrama. From the moment in Act III when Shakespeare announces his presence with: 'Thou god of this great vast, rebuke these surges', we are in another world. The verse, hitherto skipping, begins to stride; the characters, so many antique court cards, take on a third dimension. The brothel interludes are as good as anything in *Measure for Measure*, and, outside *Lear*, Shakespeare never wrote a father–daughter scene as moving as the mutual recognition of Pericles and Marina: after this, the old voyager's rediscovery of his wife seems almost perfunctory.

Daughters, in the later plays, are the thing: sometimes long-lost, like Marina and Perdita: sometimes, like Imogen and Cordelia, estranged from father: sometimes banished with him, as Miranda was: and once, in the case of Goneril and Regan, dedicated to his destruction. The climax of *Henry VIII* is the birth of a royal princess whose father, like Prospero, Lear and Pericles, has no male issue. Nor, at the time of his death, had Shakespeare. His only son died in 1596, and his daughters, Susanna and Judith, both survived him. To Susanna he left the bulk of his estate, while Judith got nothing. Was there no sibling rivalry here, no paternal preference? Were there no rows and reconciliations? We can only guess in the dark. My own conjecture is that Shakespeare was latterly much obsessed with his girls, which may explain why the greatest play-doctor in the history of drama chose the story of Pericles to revamp, and why he did it with such passion.

The Stratford production is pictorially magnificent, a restless Oriental kaleidoscope in which the crowds move horizontally and the stage lifts vertically. Tony Richardson, directing Shakespeare for the first time, deploys a visual imagination of Reinhardtian fertility: the action flows like a stream over rapids, accompanied by music that twangles and bubbles, disguising the bad bits and enlivening the good. The chorus, Gower, is Shakespeare's tribute to the earlier poet from whom he got his story: Mr Richardson brilliantly makes him a Negro fabulist, telling the strange tale to a bunch of credulous sailors.

In every respect save one Mr Richardson's Stratford début is as impressive as Peter Brook's, twelve years ago. The exception is in the matter of acting. There is nothing wrong with Richard Johnson's patient Pericles, Geraldine McEwan's sweetly candid Marina, or Patrick Wymark's oafish brothel-keeper. Nor is there anything memorably right: never do we feel that the text has been creatively pointed, jabbed into new life. And where it most matters, in the third-act storm where Shakespeare comes up like thunder, the lines are lost in mechanical uproar: I listened in vain for: 'The seaman's whistle is as a whisper in the ear of death.' 'More matter, with less art': Gertrude had Polonius's number, and Mr Richardson's too. He will be a superb director when he gets the balance right.

(1958)

Phèdre, BY RACINE, AT THE THÉÂTRE NATIONAL POPULAIRE

I am glad to announce that Jean Vilar and I have both overcome our resistance to Racine. M. Vilar, a Corneille man, has hitherto kept Racine off the stage of the Théâtre National Populaire: but he has now changed his mind, and in so doing has shown me that the pompous monotony and narrow sensibility which have put me off former productions of the plays existed not so much in the text as in the actors.

Up to now I have always regarded *Phèdre* as a disappointing sequel to *A Midsummer Night's Dream*. M. Vilar has made me realise that it is in fact a high tragedy with a correspondingly high melting-point: that is to say, it remains cold and unyielding unless subjected to the fire of a great performance. At the T.N.P. it is plunged into a blast furnace. Making the stiff lines bend to her passion, forcing the frozen vowels to cry with her pain, Maria Casarès gave me at last a hint of what Rachel must have made of the part. Never once does she generalise; this is a particular woman devoured by a particular obsession; yet in the specific instance she implies, as the best acting always does, the general application. If you have ever looked within yourself and hated what you saw, you will repond to Mme Casarès: at her best, she speaks for all of us at our worst.

Cocteau was right to cast her as Death in his film of *Orphée*. 'Loosed out of hell to speak of horrors' is precisely how she comes before us, haggard with bewilderment and terror, her great eyes staring and her hands uncontrollably shaking with fright. I have never seen the imminence of suicide more powerfully conveyed. 'C'est Vénus toute entière à sa proie attachée': with the line the actress became a vulture, and one felt the claws. The confession of love to her stepson was crowned by a single syllable: 'Donne', whereat she seized his sword in a frenzy of self-destruction that shocked the whole audience.

I do not know which to praise more: the stunned, stumbling walk that preceded her prayer to 'Implacable Vénus', or the helpless fervour, shamed beyond shame, with which it was delivered. 'Que fais-je? Où ma raison se va-t-elle égarer?' told me more about the fear of madness than any Lear I have ever heard, and when the poison was swallowed, and the queen quietly dead, one felt not only that a great storm had passed, but that a close friend had been horridly destroyed. It says much for Alain Cuny's resplendent Thésée that he held the stage for the remaining ten lines of the play without making anybody restive.

(1958)

Decade in Retrospect: 1959

I offer no prognosis, since the patient's condition is still desperately enfeebled, but I do not think it deniable that at some point in the past ten years the English theatre regained its will to live, emerged from its coma, and started to show signs of interest in the world around it.

Assuming that it gets the proper nourishment, it may walk again. If my optimism sounds hesitant, I ask you to remember that as recently as five years ago all the symptoms presaged disaster.

The early fifties saw the withering of the vogue for verse drama that had flowered, with so much acclamation, in the previous decade. It is absurdly easy, now that the boon of hindsight is ours, to explain why *The Cocktail Party* and the charming inventions of Mr Fry were so zealously over-touted. They gave us access to imagined worlds in which rationing and the rest of austerity's paraphernalia could be forgotten; they also reminded us that words could be put to other public uses than those of military propaganda, news bulletins and government regulations.

But as the economy revived, everyday reality became less obnoxious; and it was clear, soon after the new decade began, that audiences were ready for plays about the facts of contemporary life. This readiness amounted before long to a positive hunger. Terence Rattigan responded to it with his best plays, *The Deep Blue Sea* (1952) and *Separate Tables* (1954); Graham Greene contributed *The Living Room* in 1953; and their matinée Doppelgänger was N. C. Hunter, the author of *Waters of the Moon* and *A Day by the Sea*.

At the same time, the flood of interpretative energy that had poured since the war into productions of the classics had begun to dry up, or at least to seek diversion; in the last six years there have been few revivals worthy of mention in the same breath as Peter Brook's *Measure for Measure* and *Venice Preserv'd*, Tyrone Guthrie's *Tamburlayne*, and Douglas Seale's tripartite *Henry VI*, all of which were staged between 1950 and 1953. On both sides of the footlights one felt a movement toward something fresher, something that was connected more intimately —more journalistically, perhaps—with daily experience.

I do not wish to make extravagant claims. The movement was, and is, a minority affair, operating within an art that exerts, at best, no more than a minority appeal. The face of the West End has not been lifted overnight, detective stories and inane light comedies are as prevalent today as they were ten years ago, and our musicals (apart from *The Boy Friend*, a deliberate exercise in nostalgia) sound archaically quaint besides such post-1950 Broadway products as *Wonderful Town*, *The Pajama Game*, *My Fair Lady*, *West Side Story* and *Gypsy*. The quality of the bad shows is as low as ever. It is the quality of the good ones that has risen.

The breakthrough took place in the spring of 1956. Much as I wince at images of purulence, there is no doubt that the English Stage

Company's production of *Look Back in Anger* lanced a boil that had plagued our theatre for many years. Good taste, reticence and middle-class understatement were convicted of hypocrisy and jettisoned on the spot; replacing them, John Osborne spoke out in a vein of ebullient, free-wheeling rancour that betokened the arrival of something new in the theatre—a sophisticated, articulate lower-class. Most of the critics were offended by Jimmy Porter, but not on account of his anger; a working-class hero is expected to be angry. What nettled them was something quite different: his self-confidence. This was no envious inferior whose insecurity they could pity. Jimmy Porter talked with the wit and assurance of a young man who not only knew he was right but had long since mastered the vocabulary wherewith to express his knowledge.

Osborne's success breached the dam, and there followed a cascade of plays about impoverished people. Such plays had existed before; the novelty lay in the fact that the emphasis was now on the people rather than on their poverty. For the first time it was possible for a character in English drama to be poor and intelligently amusing.

Writers like John Arden, Doris Lessing, Alun Owen and Willis Hall had their works performed at the Court, and with three plays— *Chicken Soup and Barley*, *Roots* and *The Kitchen*—Arnold Wesker came closer than any other English dramatist to demonstrating that Socialist realism was not a dogmatic formula but a uniquely powerful means of conveying sane theatrical emotion. (The last act of *Roots* is as moving as any piece of native writing I have seen on the West End stage.)

Meanwhile, after years of neglect and discouragement, Theatre Workshop was coming into its own. Joan Littlewood's craggy determination to create a people's drama bore fruit at last with Shelagh Delaney's *A Taste of Honey* and Brendan Behan's two adventures in dialogue, *The Quare Fellow* and *The Hostage*. Rowdier and less cerebral than what was going on at the Court, Theatre Workshop's productions nevertheless made a more thorough conquest of the West End. Last summer, at the Criterion and Wyndham's (the respective homes of Miss Delaney's first play and Mr Behan's second), I saw in the audience young people in flimsy dresses and open-necked shirts whose equivalents, ten years ago, would have been in a cinema, if they were indoors at all. What is more, they were cheering at the end.

How has this upsurge of—we must face the phrase—proletarian drama come about? Primarily, of course, because two theatres with liberal policies were available to give it a hearing; without the Court and Theatre Workshop it would never have happened. But what external influences can one detect? Not many, I would say, from France. Messrs

Beckett and Ionesco have left their fingerprints on Harold Pinter and the mortally funny N. F. Simpson; otherwise, France is nowhere. (On the strength of his new play, *One Way Pendulum*, I suspect Mr Simpson to be the possessor of the subtlest mind ever devoted by an Englishman to the writing of farce.)

And Germany? The key name, of course, is Brecht, but the paucity of good translations, coupled with the short supply of managements who are willing and able to stage his work in the manner to which it is accustomed, has inevitably limited his impact. The brief London visit of the Berliner Ensemble recruited a multitude of admirers, but it has not, as far as one can tell, inspired any plays. We argue about Brecht's virtues and vices as an embodiment of 'committed art'; we contrast him with Shaw, whom Lenin acutely called 'a good man fallen among Fabians'; but we have borrowed little from his style beyond a few directorial tricks. Either we should perfect our German, or his translators should learn English.

In my view, the strongest and most unmistakable influence on our drama in the last ten years has been transatlantic. For the first time in its history, the English theatre has been swayed and shaped by America— by which I mean Hollywood as well as Broadway. The young people who are moulding the future of the London stage were all growing up at a time when the talking picture had established itself not merely as a viable medium of entertainment but as a primary (perhaps *the* primary) form of art. They cut their teeth on the films of Welles, Wyler, Wilder and Kazan, and on the plays (later adapted for the screen) of Arthur Miller and Tennessee Williams. Some of them prefer Williams, others Miller, but you will find very few who dislike both.

If latter-day English drama is serious in intent, contemporary in theme, and written in rasping prose, Broadway and Hollywood are part of the reason. The results, for good playwrights who are inimical to realism, have not been altogether beneficial. John Whiting appears to have abandoned the theatre; Peter Ustinov's development seems to have been arrested since *Romanoff and Juliet*; and sabre-toothed satire, which is nearly always stylised, has been represented in London only by Nigel Dennis's *Cards of Identity* and *The Making of Moo*, neither of which ran very long. ('Satire,' as George Kaufman said, 'is what closes on Saturday night.') It would be sad if a healthy and belated faith in realism were to lead to a rejection of all those non-realistic forms towards which satire naturally inclines.

My hope for the sixties is the same as my hope for the fifties—that before they are out I shall see the construction of the National Theatre.

Or, rather, of two National Theatres, equal in size and technical facilities. One of them would focus its attention on old plays, the other on new ones. The talent is demonstrably there. All it needs is financial succour, official status, and a permanent address.

A Broadway Bulletin: 1960

Returning, after two winters in New York, to the old grey parish of tall taxicabs, warm Coca-Cola and streets that curve, I should no doubt be a mine of classified information about the differences between the English and American theatres.

I ought to be bristling with antitheses, concerning the deep-seeking realism of American acting as opposed to the elegant superficiality of the English approach; and my homecoming conclusion should be something to the effect that one goes to Broadway for substance and to London for style. Had I spent only two weeks in New York, I would be delighted to generalise along these lines. After two seasons, however, it becomes more difficult.

In my absence, the drama of earthy social comment, which Broadway derides as a hangover from the thirties, has belatedly caught on in the West End; while in New York, the citadel of materialism, there has been an increasing emphasis on fable and fantasy. Frank Loesser, the author of *Guys and Dolls*, has recently turned out a pastoral operetta set in a timeless rustic community called Greenwillow; and last year's Pulitzer Prize for drama went to a verse play based on the Book of Job. What has happened is a process of exchange. We have adopted some of Broadway's discarded aspirations, and Broadway has adopted some of ours.

The result, on the whole, has been our gain. I say this with a distinct twinge of embarrassment; as a visiting reviewer in New York, it has not been easy for me to be candidly critical of the 1959–60 season—universally regarded as the drabbest in decades—without feeling rather like a week-end guest who responds to his host's hospitality by sneering at the linen. All the same, I do not think it deniable that English intellectuals are more interested in the theatre than they were five years ago, whereas American intellectuals are just as disenchanted as they always were. Professor Lionel Trilling has lately said that the theatre repels him except when he goes 'to the opera, or to a musical show, or to a good stylish performance of, say, Wycherley—the idea is to stay strictly away from serious plays of contemporary life. . . .' What with Osborne, Wesker, Lessing, Arden, Delaney and Behan, I doubt whether many English intellectuals would echo so lofty a condemnation.

Artistically—ever the frailest of adverbs in a society that ties to art's tail the clanking tincan of commercialism—there is little to choose between the aims of Broadway and London. Ethnically, Broadway has an enviable advantage. Nowhere, outside Israel, has the theatre opened its doors so widely to Jewish talent, which has produced a large part of what is durable in the American dramatic tradition; the musicals that continue to dazzle us flow almost exclusively from Jewish minds and pens. In addition, the insurgent Negroes are gaining fresh power with each generation, and have already established their artistic independence in works like Lorraine Hansberry's *a raisin in the sun*. Only two factors constrict and distort the American theatre—economics and ideology.

The economic argument is ancient and familiar. Since it costs about five times as much to stage a play in New York as it does in London, the management must be roughly five times as sure that the production will be a success. Hence the Broadway compulsion not to present a play that the audience *might* want to see, but to present one that it already wants to see, and has probably seen, in varying guises, many times before.

'Nowadays,' Arthur Miller said to me recently, 'plays are written, cast and directed by the audience.' For this reason, he said, he had decided to withhold his next play from the Broadway marketplace. He added that the seed of this decision had been planted long ago, during the pre-Broadway tryout of *Death of a Salesman*, when he had heard a middle-aged spectator remark to his wife: 'Do you suppose they're liking it?' The question was not whether he, the individual observer, was liking it, but whether it was going to be a hit, and therefore officially likeable.

The ideological problem that hinders the American theatre can be simply stated. Materialism is out; metaphysics are in. Or, to phrase it more modishly, the thirties are out; and Samuel Beckett's *Endgame* and Archibald MacLeish's *JB* are overwhelmingly in. According to plays like these, it is not within the power of social and political change to heal the eternal sickness of the individual soul. What is spiritual in man precedes, outweighs and will outlast what is earthbound and temporal. This governing postulate is embraced even by people of allegedly radical sympathies. I read in a Greenwich Village magazine that '*Death of a Salesman* offers nothing but a bland uplift. It tells the Broadway audience what they want to hear, that the liberal leftwing philosophy of the thirties was true after all. It has all of the answers, so it doesn't really ask any of the questions.'

The author dismisses Arthur Miller's play in order to exalt Tennessee Williams's *Suddenly Last Summer*, which he sees as a dark, visionary statement—akin to *Medea*, *King Lear* and *Moby Dick*—of the essential destructiveness of God. He scorns 'the fatuous liberalism and optimism of the old-fashioned "humanist" and "free-thinker" '; and, like many of his compatriots, he implicitly endorses the notion that mankind is at the mercy of an implacable, superhuman force for which the shorthand is God.

To stress man's submissiveness to divinity at the expense of his aspirations to humanity is always a conservative attitude, and the Broadway theatre is thoroughly conservative. It plays safe, obeying the precepts of uncontroversial suaveness that were bequeathed to the entertainment industry by Senator McCarthy.

Off Broadway, as one might expect, people have fewer qualms. The past year has given us three lively young playwrights—Jack Richardson, Edward Albee and Jack Gelber—who seem happily unafraid of treading on authority's toes. *The Connection*, Mr Gelber's play about dope addicts, is a work of startling novelty, pitched somewhere between *Waiting for Godot* and *The Lower Depths*. Its characters see themselves neither as martyrs nor as heroes, but merely as absentees from the daytime universe; their relationship to society is one not of enmity but of truancy.

In dialogue of wry, laconic candour, they debate their plight. The junkie seeks euphoria; the average citizen seeks happiness. How do these goals really differ? If the aim of life is pleasure, why is it more desirable to achieve it by pumping dollars into a bank account than by injecting dope into a vein? If, alternatively, the aim is spiritual enlightenment, how can we be sure that the insights of heroin are less reliable than those of mystical exaltation? In its oblique way, Mr Gelber's play comes nearer to being a genuine piece of social criticism than anything New York has seen for years. *The Connection*, you might say, connects.

So do certain night-club performers; the comedian Mort Sahl can still be deviously beastly to Vice-President Nixon, though he usually takes care to launch a glancing blow at Senator Kennedy in the next sentence. And there is always Lenny Bruce, a pallid, lissom young man with eyes of extraordinary deadness, who delivers fantastically outspoken harangues in an idiom that I can only describe as jazz-Jewish. Wickedly, he will disclose a Madison Avenue plot to bump up cigarette sales by starting a whispering campaign to the effect that cancer is an unbeatable status symbol ('I was in Nassau last month. Practically *everybody* had cancer'); and he is unnervingly virulent in his assaults on brainless evangelists, Governors of Southern States, and racists of all kinds.

Yet even Mr Bruce, who is as close to a genius as any comedian I have ever seen, takes his final stand on spiritual grounds. He is apt to recite to his audiences snatches of the Sermon on the Mount, and to inform them that Christ would not have killed Caryl Chessman or stubbed out a lighted cigarette on the neck of a Southern Negro. In so far as he is a philosopher, Mr Bruce's position is not far from that of Billy Graham, whom of all people he professes to despise. Believe nothing you hear about American materialism; in many ways America is the most ambitiously mystical country on earth.

If we are looking for energy, charm, attack or brilliance of timing—in fact, for any of the executive skills of theatre—America is still headquarters. In other departments it is temporarily lagging. 'It costs so little,' the old song used to wheedle, 'and it means so much.' The trouble with Broadway is precisely the reverse.

Billy Liar, BY KEITH WATERHOUSE AND WILLIS HALL, AT THE CAMBRIDGE; *The Lion in Love*, BY SHELAGH DELANEY, AT THE BELGRADE, COVENTRY; *The Happy Haven*, BY JOHN ARDEN, AT THE ROYAL COURT

In quantity, the past week has been a bright one for supporters of the new movement in our theatre; three plays by gifted young authors cropped up on successive nights. Quality, however, is another matter; and it is here that my lips purse and the brooding begins.

We have irrevocably (and healthily) renounced the 'gentleman code' that cast its chilling blight on so much of twentieth-century English drama. No longer are we asked to judge characters by the exquisiteness of their sensibilities, or by the degree to which, in moments of crisis, their behaviour is consonant with Bloomsbury standards of tact, good form and discreetly muted sentiment. Yet to these standards, rarefied and bloodless though they were, the audience assented, and in part aspired; they formed a shared territory of belief upon which communication of a sort was possible.

Now, dive-bombed by Mr Osborne and undermined by Miss Littlewood, they have been laid low. And the question arises: With what are they to be replaced? The old code, so to speak, has been cracked: where and what are the new assumptions which, jointly held by author and audience, will enable a new kind of communication to be achieved and sustained? For without some common ground, some area of truce wherein the playwright's convictions (moral, social or political) coincide with those of his spectators, drama quickly languishes; it may, in such circumstances, provoke a scandal, or bask in a fleeting *succès d'estime*, but it is very unlikely to take root.

The present state of the English theatre is one of deadlock. Its audience is still predominantly conservative, wedded by age and habit to the old standards; its younger playwrights, meanwhile, are predominantly anti-conservative, irretrievably divorced from the ideological *status quo*. Obviously, they need a new audience; but in order to attract it they will have to define and dramatise the new values for which they severally stand. We know what they are *against*—the human consequences of class privilege, the profit motive, organised religion, and so forth—but what are they *for*?

Most of them are Socialists of one shade or another; but it is significant that Arnold Wesker, their foremost advocate of affirmation, concluded his trilogy with a play that affirmed nothing but the futility of Socialism. The only general assumption on which Mr Wesker, his colleagues and their audiences seem to be substantially agreed is that the lower strata of English society deserve a more central place on the English stage.

But this is an extremely tricky area of agreement; because English audiences (outside the Royal Court and Theatre Workshop) instinctively associate the lower strata of society with the lower strata of comedy. Give them half a chance, and they'll laugh their heads off; and this creates a great temptation to play into their hands—as, for all its merits, *Fings Ain't Wot They Used T'be* unquestionably does. The point is that it takes a stiff injection of social comment to persuade your average playgoer to accept shows of this genre on any level other than that of farce. *Roots*, which was thus inoculated, is Mr Wesker's best work. *Billy Liar*, adapted by Keith Waterhouse and Willis Hall from Mr Waterhouse's exuberant novel, lacks any such injection. The broader implications of the book are skirted or ignored; it is presented in terms of pure farce. The first-night audience accordingly treated it as such, and understandably found it wanting.

The eponymous hero is a provincial adolescent in a ferment of furtive rebellion against everything that surrounds him; no explanation of his mutinous tendencies is offered beyond the fact that he has a bellicose and hard-cursing father. An undertaker's clerk and something of a psychopath, Billy lives a multitude of secret lives. At the slightest provocation he lapses into mimicry; an industrial dynast, an Augustan fop and a legless war hero are among his pet characterisations. His conscience is a vacuum. Three adoring girls are vying for his hand; by some miscalculation, he is betrothed to two of them, and much of the action concerns his efforts to relieve his official fiancée of her engagement ring in order to transfer it to her importunate successor.

He invents elaborate lies, most of them totally unnecessary, to greet anyone who telephones or knocks at the door; and he delights in spreading palpably false reports about pregnancies and amputations. When his grandmother dies—a garrulous old complainer whom in life he detested—he suffers a single, momentary pang of sorrow. Alone in a moonlit garden, he has been idly imitating bird-calls and playing about with a bamboo stick, which he uses first as an outsize cigarette-holder and then as a drum-major's baton; suddenly remembering the corpse upstairs, he curbs his fantasies, and begins, solemnly and in pure bugle tones, to hum the Last Post.

It is an unforgettable moment—the high point of the play, and also of Albert Finney's performance. This stocky, surly young maestro sometimes mugs as exorbitantly when playing Billy himself as he does when playing Billy imitating someone else; all the same, Mr Finney is a true fascinator, as Richard Burton was at his age. What mars the evening (apart from the adaptors' absurd decision to restrict the action to one suburban villa instead of letting it roam) is the fact that Billy Liar, as here presented, is no more than an opportunistic splicing of Jimmy Porter, minus the passion, and Lucky Jim, minus the moral awareness. The result is a ramshackle piece of purely whimsical entertainment, and Lindsay Anderson rightly directs it as such.

Shelagh Delaney's second play, *The Lion in Love*, has many of the negative merits of the new school. Though it deals with a Lancashire family in a state of constant emotional upheaval, it wastes no time on sentimental agonies or grand romantic outbursts. Everything is compressed, slimmed down to the hard bone of fact. Dad, a congenital bolter, leaves home for the umpteenth time, and for the umpteenth time slinks back. Banner, his son, returns rich from the prize-ring, spends all he has, and departs, almost unnoticed, for Australia. Peg, Banner's sister, is picked up by a lively young Glaswegian and whisked off to London. There are no emotional explosions; the tone throughout is cool and casual. It is also flat.

Miss Delaney prattles on like a primitive, filling her pages with traditional North Country tags, mottoes, quips and insults—the small change of Lancashire conversation, though possibly silver-sounding to Southern ears. Apart from an odd phrase here and there (e.g., the description of council houses as 'brick boxes with eyes in them'), the writing leaves no mark on one's memory. The last act is a riot of loose ends, and no hint of underlying philosophy is vouchsafed beyond the assertion that everyone is out for himself.

John Arden's *The Happy Haven* is an elephantine comedy of humours about an old people's home, run by a smug, adenoidal doctor who discovers a chemical formula for rejuvenation and wants to try it out on his patients. Already embarked on their second childhood, which seems to embody all the worst, most bitterly competitive features of their first, they shrink in horror from the idea of being young again. Eventually, they manage to pump the doctor full of his own elixir, whereupon he dwindles into a teddybear-clutching schoolboy. End of joke.

Mr Arden fails not merely because his wit is elephantine, but because his play has no anchor in normality. The characters are all unhinged, and there is no one to act as a bridge between ourselves and the grotesques across the footlights. The acting, meanwhile, is first rate; nobody could improve on the unctuous breeziness, the glottal wheedling, of Peter Bowles as the medical superintendent.

(1960)

The Caretaker, BY HAROLD PINTER, AT THE DUCHESS

With *The Caretaker* Harold Pinter has begun to fulfil the promise that I signally failed to see in *The Birthday Party* two years ago.

The latter play was a clever fragment grown dropsical with symbolic content. A befuddled young lodger, lazing in a seaside boarding-house, was visited and ultimately kidnapped by a pair of sinister emissaries from the Outside World; the piece was full of those familiar paranoid overtones that seem to be inseparable from much of *avant-garde* drama. In *The Caretaker* symptoms of paranoia are still detectable—one of the characters is a near-zombie whose individuality has been forcibly effaced by a brain operation—but their intensity is considerably abated; and the symbols have mostly retired to the background.

What remains is a play about people. They are three in number, and all male. One is the mental *castrato* I have already mentioned; a sad, kindly fellow, he inhabits a suburban attic that is crammed with cherished objects of no conceivable use, among them a rusty lawn-mower and a disconnected gas-cooker. (Cf M. Ionesco's *Le Nouveau Locataire.*) He offers a bed to a mangy, homeless old tramp, who spends most of his time raging about imagined insults and planning abortive trips to Sidcup, where he has left his references and proofs of identity in charge of a quondam friend. The triangle is completed by his host's brother, a talkative, ambitious young man who owns both the attic and the crumbling house beneath it. Eager to obtain a job as caretaker, the tramp tries flattering the brothers, and even attempts to play one off against the other. He succeeds only in antagonising both, and ends up evicted.

Now it may very well be that there are symbols here. The two brothers may represent the bifurcated halves of a schizoid personality; alternatively, the landlord may stand for the Super-Ego, the tenant for the Ego, and the tramp for the Id. Either way, I am not particularly concerned. What holds one, theatrically, is Mr Pinter's bizarre use (some would call it abuse) of dramatic technique, his skill in evoking atmosphere, and his encyclopaedic command of contemporary idiom.

To take these qualities in order: where most playwrights devote their technical efforts to making us wonder what will happen *next*, Mr Pinter focuses our wonder on what is happening *now*. Who are these people? How did they meet, and why? Mr Pinter delays these disclosures until the last tenable moment; he teases us without boring us, which is quite a rare achievement. It is reinforced by his mastery of atmosphere. There is a special belt of English suburbia, spectral in its dusty shabbiness, that exists in no other Anglo-Saxon country. America has tenement drama, penthouse drama and drama set in the exurbanite strongholds of the middle class; but London is unique in the *déclassé* decrepitude of its Western suburbs, with their floating population, their indoor dustbins, their desolate bed-sitters, their prevalent dry rot—moral as well as structural—and their frequent, casual suicides. Mr Pinter captures all this with the most chilling economy.

We come finally to his verbal gifts; and it is here that cracks of doubt begin to appear in the façade of my enthusiasm. Time and again, without the least departure from authenticity, Mr Pinter exposes the vague, repetitive silliness of lower-class conversation. One laughs in recognition; but one's laughter is tinged with snobbism. Towards the end of the evening I found myself recalling an experimental play I had seen some ten years before. Its origins were Dutch, and it took place in a snowbound hut on top of a mountain; the *dramatis personae* were The Mother, The Daughter and Fate, who emerged from a wardrobe in the second act and delivered a baleful tirade about death. Rain, meanwhile, splashed into a bucket through a hole in the roof. When the harangue was done, the Mother lifted her eyes and said, more aptly than perhaps she knew: 'Only the drip speaks.'

Mr Pinter's play likewise has a bucket and a leaky roof; and it occurred to me, as the curtain fell, that what I had been watching was nothing more than an old-fashioned *avant-garde* exercise, galvanised into a semblance of novelty by the author's miraculous ear for colloquial eccentricities. Instead of The Brother, The Other Brother and Everyman, the characters were called Aston, Mick and Davies; and instead of declaiming, they chatted.

Yet the quality of the chat is consistently high. Mr Pinter is a superb manipulator of language, which he sees not as a bridge that brings people together but as a barrier that keeps them apart. Ideas and emotions, in the larger sense, are not his province; he plays with words, and he plays on our nerves, and it is thus that he grips us. Three remarkable actors embody his vision. Donald Pleasence, as the wild Welsh tramp, has the showiest part and gives the most spectacular performance; but I felt that he was carried, like a drunk between two policemen, by the muscular playing of his colleagues—Alan Bates, as the heartless, garrulous brother, and Peter Woodthorpe, as the stolid, pathetic one. The direction, an object lesson in the organisation of nuances, is by Donald McWhinnie.

(1960)

The Life of Galileo, BY BERTOLT BRECHT, AT THE MERMAID;
Candida, BY GEORGE BERNARD SHAW, AT THE PICCADILLY;
Tamburlaine the Great, BY CHRISTOPHER MARLOWE, AT THE
OXFORD UNIVERSITY DRAMATIC SOCIETY

Is it churlish to confess that one went in some trepidation to see the Mermaid Theatre's production of Brecht's *Life of Galileo*? Not really; for the play demands of its interpreters a special, cool, expository style that English actors do not normally associate with historical drama. Or, for that matter, with drama of any kind.

Most plays follow the pattern of the sexual act; they begin evenly, work up to a climax of emotion, and then subside; and the actor's job is to make the audience feel exactly what the characters on stage are feeling. Acting thus becomes a form of love-making, and is accounted successful when the spectator proclaims himself (or herself) ravished, overwhelmed or taken by storm. In costume pieces, the wooing tends to be noisier and more importunate; and if the period is Renaissance, it is likely to border vociferously on rape.

To break up the clinch, along comes Brecht, bearing a bucket of cold water in the shape of a play about the Italian Renaissance in which nobody rants, or raves, or even raises his voice. The nearest approach to a climax—Galileo's recantation before the Inquisition—takes place offstage.

The usual theatrical priorities are reversed; we see a lot of Galileo's working life and little of his private life. By persisting in heresy, he brings about the collapse of his daughter's plans for marriage; most playwrights would wallow in a situation like that, but Brecht treats it curtly, almost parenthetically. He pays us the compliment of assuming that we are more interested in learning why Galileo was persecuted than in feeling persecuted ourselves. Instead of empathy, he offers analysis; each scene is a statement, not an attempt to communicate emotion. Never are we allowed to feel: 'This is happening to me.' Instead, we murmur to ourselves: 'This need not have happened to him.' We are fully aware of the facts, and this enables us to pass judgment on his judgment.

Meanwhile, our sense of detachment is reinforced by the projected captions and choral interludes that preface every scene. Throughout the evening, Brecht keeps reminding us that life is indivisible; science, politics, economics and ethics are all roped together for the upward climb; and if one of them slips, the rest are imperilled. When Galileo caves in before the ecclesiastical politicians, the future of mankind is plunged into jeopardy. The impression left by the piece is one of quiet, thoughtful magnificence.

How can an English company cope with a play in which personalities are subjugated to ideas? To my astonished pleasure, the Mermaid actors cope very well indeed. The translation (by Charles Laughton) is full of vivacity, and the director, Bernard Miles, has wisely aped the Berliner-Ensemble's original production. He cannot match the expensive simplicity of Caspar Neher's copper settings; and the carnival scene has lost much of the grotesque flamboyance it had in Berlin. Mr Miles himself plays Galileo; gawkily to begin with, but gaining strength with the great affirmation: 'Truth is the daughter of time, not of authority.' Thereafter he is first-rate, grey-haired and defeated, appealing always to our comprehension, and never to our sympathy.

Some day I should like to hear a debate between Brecht and Arthur Koestler. In *The Sleepwalkers*, Mr Koestler deplores the present rift between reason and faith, which he blames on the intransigent pride of Galileo; Brecht, on the other hand, wholeheartedly approves of the rift, but reproves Galileo for not having been proud or intransigent enough to provoke it. Who is right? And to what degree? The fact that I am bothered by such questions is proof that I have lately seen a play by Brecht. Go thou, and be bothered likewise.

High on the list of the great *cliché* plots is the one about the stripling—sometimes a son, sometimes a quasi-lover—who threatens to disrupt a conventional marriage (e.g. *Young Woodley, Love in Idleness, Tea and Sympathy, Hamlet* and *Oedipus Rex*). Another popular item concerns the renowned thinker who is unable, for all his wisdom, to make his home life run smoothly (e.g. *Escapade,* Anouilh's *L'Hurluberlu, The Master Builder* and *King Lear*). *Candida* is Shaw's attempt to combine both themes. Morell, the sensible Christian Socialist, vies for the love of his relentlessly complacent wife with Marchbanks, the juvenile apostle of poetic unreason.

The play wears badly, partly because the serious lines sound solemn and partly because the comic lines are couched (as often in Shaw) almost exclusively in terms of rebuke—by which I mean the sort of brisk, hygienic one-upmanship that nannies use to remind adults that their true home is the nursery. Very little about *Candida* interests me except the flagrant lie on which it is founded—namely, that Morell the 'pig-headed parson' and Marchbanks the 'wretched little nervous disease' are two different people. In fact, they represent different sides of the same person. Morell is the tireless lecturer, crusader and member of committees; Marchbanks is the gushing, puritanical infant, forever in bodiless love with a maternal, pre-Raphaelite goddess. Morell wrote the plays of George Bernard Shaw, and Marchbanks wrote his letters to Ellen Terry and Mrs Patrick Campbell. Together, they add up to the exuberant, infertile figure of G.B.S. in whose collected works there is no line less credible than Candida's claim to have borne children. Defining 'wicked people', Marchbanks observes: 'They have the power to ask love because they don't need it; they have the power to offer it because they have none to give.' I cannot imagine a better description of Shaw's letters to Mrs Pat.

Frank Hauser's production of *Candida* is unquestionably furtive. The furniture hugs the walls, and the actors hug the furniture, with the result that the centre of the stage is seldom occupied except *en passant*. Jeremy Spenser, when fully audible, is a fine, urgent Marchbanks; Michael Denison plays Morell with the beaming aplomb of a younger John Clements; and students of the play will know what I mean when I say that Dulcie Gray, who is cast as Candida, would make an unforgettable Prossy.

Tamburlaine the Great, cut and directed by John Duncan, is the most accomplished thing the O.U.D.S. has done for years. The lawn is alive with swirling soldiers, who stop dead in their tracks the instant anybody speaks; when the speech ends, they zoom about again, coming to rest in starkly stylised postures as soon as the next syllable has been uttered. The total effect is like a highly organised version of the game

known as 'Statues', overlaid with what I take to be an intimate knowledge, on the director's part, of the Japanese cinema.

The supporting cast, studded as it is with constantly repeated names
like Usumcasane, Theridamas, Mycetes, Celebinus and Callipine, got
blurred in my mind, rather as if they were a horde of pills and wonder
drugs bent on decimating one another:

> Young Streptomycin, take a thousand horse
> And storm the gates of Sulphacetamide!
> But who comes here? The currish Pentathol
> Doth spur his steed across the grassy plain
> With Formalin and mighty Dexamil.
> Beard'st thou me here, thou bold Barbiturate?
> Sirrah, thy grandam's dead—old Nembutal.
> The spangled stars shall weep for Nembutal,
> As Jove himself did cry for Chlorophyll.
> She'll serve thy turn, and that of Ephedrine.
> Is it not passing brave to be a king,
> Aureomycin and Formaldehyde,
> Is it not passing brave to be a king
> And ride in triumph through Amphetamine?

(1960)

A Man for All Seasons, BY ROBERT BOLT, AT THE GLOBE

In *A Man for All Seasons*, Robert Bolt has chopped the later career
of Sir Thomas More into a series of short and pithy episodes, each of
which is prefaced by a few words of comment and explanation, addressed
directly to the audience. Changes of scene are indicated emblematically,
by signs lowered from the flies; and the style throughout inclines rather to
argument than to emotional appeal. There is no mistaking whose influence has been at work on Mr Bolt; the play is clearly his attempt to do
for More what Brecht did for Galileo.

In both cases, the theme is persecution, and the author's purpose is
to demonstrate how authority enforces its claims on the individual conscience. More was a victim of the Reformation; Galileo, a century later,
fell foul of the Counter-Reformation; and both men, being contented
denizens of our planet, were extremely reluctant to embrace martyrdom.
Each found himself the servant of two masters. Galileo had to choose
between science and the Pope, More between the Pope and the King; and

each of them, after years of hair-splitting and procrastination, ended up by choosing the Pope—Galileo because he feared for his body, More because he feared for his soul. According to Brecht, Galileo was disloyal to the new science, and is therefore to be rebuked; according to Mr Bolt, More was loyal to the old religion, and is therefore to be applauded.

It is hereabouts that the two playwrights part company. I have no idea whether Mr Bolt himself is a religious man, but I am perfectly sure that if someone presented him with irrefutable evidence that every tenet of Catholicism was a palpable falsehood, his admiration for More would not be diminished in the smallest degree, nor would he feel tempted to alter a word of the text. The play's strongest scenes, all of which occur in the second half, are those in which More, employing every resource of his canny legal brain, patiently reminds his inquisitors that silence is not to be equated with treason, and that no court can compel him to reveal or defend his private convictions. His position, in short, is that he takes no position; and I have no doubt that we are meant to draw an analogy between More and those witnesses who appear before the Un-American Activities Committee and take the Fifth Amendment.

As a democrat, I detest such coercive investigations into a man's innermost ideas; as a playgoer, however, I feel entitled to know what his ideas are, and how he arrived at them. Here, where Brecht is voluble, Mr Bolt is mum. If, upon completing *Galileo*, Brecht had suddenly learned that his protagonist's hypotheses were totally untrue, he would either have torn up the manuscript or revised it from start to finish. From Mr Bolt's point of view, on the other hand, it matters little whether More's beliefs were right or wrong; all that matters is that he held them, and refused to disclose them under questioning. For Mr Bolt, in short, truth is subjective; for Brecht it is objective; and therein lies the basic difference between the two plays.

Compare them, and it soon becomes obvious that Mr Bolt's method is the more constricting. Since there can be no battle of ideologies, he must reduce everything to personal terms; the gigantic upheavals of the Reformation dwindle into a temperamental squabble between a nice lawyer who dislikes divorce and a lusty monarch who wants an heir. Our attention is focused on the legal stratagems whereby More postponed his martyrdom, and distracted from the validity of the ideas that got him into trouble to begin with. The play contains some muscular period writing, especially in the scene where More deliberately insults his old crony, the conformist Duke of Norfolk, in order to absolve him from the responsibility of breaking off their friendship; and it is history's fault, not Mr Bolt's, that his hero came to grief so much less dramatically than

Brecht's. (More's fate was sealed by a perjured witness; whereas it was Galileo himself who laid low Galileo.) At bottom, however, *A Man for All Seasons* is not so much a play as an essay in hagiography. Mr Bolt looks at history exclusively through the eyes of his saintly hero. Brecht's vision is broader: he looks at Galileo through the eyes of history.

The direction, by Noel Willman, skips swiftly around a permanent setting (by Motley) of impenitently Swedish-modern design. Leo McKern plays the Chorus, a bellicose, time-serving oaf whom the programme labels, somewhat rudely, 'The Common Man'. Beery and button-holing, Mr McKern gives a reekingly good account of a highly tendentious role.

Where More himself is concerned, Mr Bolt has indulged in a lot of simplification. He has banished More the scurrilous pamphleteer, More the earthy pleasure-lover, and More the vernacular comic, whom C. S. Lewis has called 'our first great Cockney humorist'. What remains is More the gentle reasoner, and this Paul Scofield plays to the hilt, at once wily and holy, as unastonished by betrayal as he is by fidelity. He does the job beautifully; but where, in this obsequious piece of acting, is the original Scofield who burst upon us, some twelve years ago, like exquisite thunder? Perhaps time has tamed him, or security, or something unassertive in his cast of mind. It is true that he has never given a bad performance; but it was not in negatives like this that we formerly hoped to praise him. We were looking for greatness. The power is still there, though it has long been sleeping; may it soon revive and transfix us.

(1960)

The above review provoked a comment from Robert Bolt which was published in the next edition of *The Observer*. It ran:

'Mr Tynan's certainly fair and probably generous notice of my play raises incidentally a philosophic question of practical importance. I am grateful for the comparison he drew between *A Man For All Seasons* and *Galileo*—indeed I impudently challenged it by misquoting Brecht's most celebrated line at the climax of my own play. It is where the plays diverge that Mr Tynan makes the proposition which I want to query: "For Mr Bolt, in short, truth is subjective; for Brecht it is objective; and therein lies the basic difference between the two plays."

'I only roughly understand what is meant by "objective truth". It is presumably a truth which remains true regardless of who does or doesn't hold it to be true. It seems a very religious concept. But in the present context Mr Tynan's point is clear enough: "If, upon completing *Galileo*, Brecht had suddenly learned that his protagonist's hypotheses were totally untrue, he would either have torn up the manuscript or revised from start to finish." Is this Mr Tynan's guess, or did Brecht himself say he would? For what it means is that the worth of this play about Galileo is conditional upon the correctness of Galileo's hypotheses. I don't believe this, and I don't believe Mr Tynan does, really. Thus:

'The difference between the hypotheses of modern cosmology and the hypotheses of Galilean cosmology is already quite as sharp as the difference between the Galilean and the Aristotelian. If the Galilean hypotheses were "true" and showed the Aristotelian to be "untrue" then by the same token the Galilean are now shown to be untrue. If the Galilean hypotheses are untrue then, according to Mr Tynan, *Galileo* should be torn up or rewritten. In fact, Mr Tynan and I both think it a great play.

'Or, if this comparative view of the truthfulness of successive hypotheses is insufficiently "objective" for Mr Tynan, let us anticipate the dawning of that day when every feature of the Galilean cosmology has been discarded in favour of others. (I take it Mr Tynan does not deny the possibility of such a thing. If he does, he has a kindred spirit, not in Galileo but the Cardinal Inquisitor.) If that day is tomorrow, will Brecht's absorbing, profound and illuminating play at once become boring, superficial and dull? It will continue to be as absorbing, profound and illuminating as it in fact is. But where can these virtues now reside? What is it that is left when the "objective" truth of Galileo's beliefs is removed from the play *Galileo*? Just Galileo. And that is what Brecht's play is about, as mine is about More.

'There are many differences between the two plays (apart I mean from the obvious one in sheer stature), but the *basic* difference is this. Both men were passionately and to their core convinced. Both were required by Authority to deny themselves. One complied; the other refused.

'Brecht's play shows the frightful price which may have to be paid for that compliance—the reduction of the man in his own estimation to a status where he has only the right to scratch himself and eat. My play shows the frightful price which may have to be paid for that refusal to comply—the end of life on any terms at all.

'Both plays are about uncommon individuals but both are also about organised society. As the essence of organised society, I have taken, quite overtly I think, the structure of the Law. An act of perjury in a trial for High Treason seems to me not altogether undramatic but in this case it has a wider significance, too. More, as Mr Tynan emphasises, put his trust in the Law, that is, in organised society; this act of perjury, engineered by the Court, showed how the appointed guardians of society were ready to crack it open and let in anarchy to maintain their own advantages. As for the passive bulk of society, those with no immediate responsibility for what is done, I don't think my portrait of the Common Man is "rude" or "tendentious"; he is not actively malignant; under similar circumstances could either Mr Tynan or myself be sure of doing better?

'Here is the practical bearing of all this: Any society needs a conservative and a radical element. Without the first it flies apart, without the second it putrefies. The conservative can be taken for granted, for it only needs acceptance and a good working substitute for acceptance is sloth. But the radical rejects the *status quo*, and unless this is done in the name of a definite vision of what an individual human person is, and is not being allowed to be, rejection degenerates to a posture, no less complacent than the Establishment itself. I think this is our present position. Much ink, perhaps some blood, will flow before we arrive at a genuinely modern, genuinely credible vision of what a human person is. But I think that any artist not in some way engaged upon this task might just as well pack up and go home. The personal is not "merely" personal.'

I replied as follows:

Mr Bolt's dissenting gloss on my review of *A Man for All Seasons* is a healthy phenomenon; it is always cheering when a playwright shows that he cares more about the ideas he is expressing than about the number of paying customers he can induce to listen to them. But while I respect Mr Bolt's motives, I cannot swallow his conclusions; they seem to me to be founded on premises that expose, quite poignantly, the limitations of our Western approach to historical drama.

Mr Bolt surveys his chosen slice of the Tudor era with the right end of the telescope firmly clapped to his eye: what he sees is Sir Thomas More, in dominant close-up, with everything else out of focus. A hint, now and then, is lightly dropped that More's obduracy was not only a crafty individual challenge to Tudor law but a social and political threat to the whole process of the English Reformation. Once dropped, however, these hints are rapidly swept under the carpet and forgotten. Mr Bolt is primarily absorbed in the state of More's conscience, not in the state of More's England or More's Europe.

Brecht, on the other hand, though he gives us an intimate study of Galileo's conscience, takes pains to relate it at every turn to Galileo's world and to the universe at large. In short, he uses the wrong end of the telescope as well. He naturally worries about 'what an individual human person is'; but he also worries about the society into which that person was born, and the contributions he made (or failed to make) towards improving it. Brecht's play deals with Galileo *and* the postponed dawn of the age of reason. Mr Bolt's play deals with More, *tout court*.

As to the matter of 'objective truth': what concerns Brecht is Galileo's contention that the earth revolved around the sun, and I am not aware that anybody has yet disproved it. If they had, I have no doubt that Brecht would have written a different play, possibly based on the arrogance of scientists who fail to verify their hypotheses, or on the ways in which hubris can stunt the growth of enlightenment. 'The truth,' as he never tired of insisting, 'is concrete'; Galileo is in possession of a useful, concrete, revolutionary truth, which authority compels him to deny.

Does Mr Bolt seriously think that Brecht would have devoted the same attention to a man who held that the earth was a saucer-shaped object created in the seventh century A.D.? That, too, would have constituted a heresy, and the Church would unquestionably have silenced anyone who sought to spread it. Under pressure, the heretic might well have recanted, and thereby reduced himself, as Mr Bolt says of Galileo, 'in his own estimation'. But what about the estimation of history? Heartless though it may sound—and the theatre, where suffering is feigned, is the last stronghold of permissible heartlessness—I must confess that I am more interested in a persecuted scientist whose beliefs are demonstrably true than in one whose beliefs are demonstrably false.

Mr Bolt makes no such distinctions. For him, the mere fact of belief is enough, and Sir Thomas's martyrdom would have been just as tragic if the point at issue had been his refusal to admit that two plus two equalled four. We are expected to sympathise with him simply and solely because he declines to reveal his convictions. It is here that Mr Bolt and I part company. There may be evidence of temperamental bias in my preference for oppressed heroes with whose opinions I agree; but I don't think I am acting unfairly when I demand that heroes should define their opinions, regardless of whether I agree with them. Brecht tells us precisely what Galileo asserted, and why he asserted it; and the play grows out of the explanation. Mr Bolt tells us nothing about More's convictions or how he came to embrace them. In the second act Norfolk asks him whether he is willing to abandon all he possesses because of 'a theory'—namely, the idea that the Pope is St Peter's descendant.

'Why, it's a theory, yes; you can't see it, can't touch it; it's a theory,' More replies. 'But what matters to me is not whether it's true or not but whether I believe it to be true, or rather not that I *believe* it but that *I* believe it. . . . I trust I make myself obscure?'

That is as close as we get to knowing what More believes, and why. It is not, in an age as pragmatical as ours, nearly close enough. By way of a footnote; I concede that people like Mr Bolt and myself might easily behave, in comparable circumstances, as corruptly and boorishly as the character played by Leo McKern. What is 'rude' and 'tendentious' is that a character who is the essence of boorish corruption should be labelled 'The Common Man'.

Chicken Soup With Barley, BY ARNOLD WESKER, AT THE ROYAL COURT; *Rhinoceros*, BY EUGÈNE IONESCO, AT THE STRAND

Arnold Wesker's *Chicken Soup with Barley* is the first of his three plays about the members, friends and connections of the Kahn family; the other two—*Roots* and *I'm Talking About Jerusalem*—will follow at intervals of a month.

The action of the trilogy takes place between the middle thirties and the late fifties, and has as its background three wars—the Spanish Civil, the Second World, and the Cold. Its purpose is to show the ways in which these huge disturbances impinge on a Jewish working-class household, altering their habits of work and thought, and thus determining the course of their lives.

The theme is a vast one, and Mr Wesker is splendidly equipped to handle it. Like many Jewish writers, he thinks internationally, yet feels domestically; and it is this combination of attributes that enables him to bring gigantic events and ordinary people into the same sharp focus. The function of drama, in Mr Wesker's view, is not just to tell a story, but to interpret history.

The subject of *Chicken Soup with Barley* is the erosion of political certainties, and their replacement by apathy. We begin in 1936; the Fascists are marching on the East End, and the Kahns are on fire with Communist zeal—all of them, that is, except Harry the *paterfamilias*, whose ardour tends to evaporate when violence impends. His sister Cissie is a union leader, and his daughter Ada a schoolgirl militant, but Harry himself skulks and evades, for which he is reviled by his wife Sarah, who is as instinctively Communist as she is instinctively maternal. The Spanish war is on, and the conflict with Fascism is imminent; for the moment, all the issues are clear.

In the subsequent acts—set in 1946–47 and 1955–56—a fog of doubt descends; and black and white blur into grey. Fascism has been defeated, and a Labour Government has pushed through a minor social revolution; but the Kahns still find themselves living in an acquisitive, competitive jungle. One of their former comrades has become a respectable shopkeeper, and blushes to recall the pinkness of his past. Cissie, the workers' champion, slips into embittered retirement; Ada, deciding that the real enemy is not capitalism but industrialisation, moves into the country to practise handicrafts *à la* William Morris; and Harry's son Ronnie, a Socialist poet in the making, is shattered by the suppression of the Hungarian revolt. Harry himself, meanwhile, has suffered two strokes and subsided into a state of passive acceptance; convinced that he has nothing to live for, he gradually loses the will to live. Only Sarah— ignorant, intuitive, tea-brewing Sarah—survives with undiminished idealism; and it is she who brings down the curtain by pleading with Ronnie: 'If you don't care, you'll die!'

Mr Wesker's socialism is more emotional than intellectual; he is concerned less with economic analysis than with moral imperatives. His rhetoric sometimes rings hollow, and what distinguishes his style is not so much its subtlety as its sturdiness. All the same, nobody else has ever attempted to put a real, live, English Communist family on to the stage; and the important thing about Mr Wesker's attempt is that they *are* real, and they *do* live.

Some of the performances leave room for qualms. Kathleen Michael, for example, seldom conveys the intensity of feeling that keeps Sarah going, and the cast as a whole could do with a little more Jewish dynamism, not to mention a little more Jewish wit. But considering the talent on hand, I have no major quarrels with John Dexter's direction. Although the Kahns bicker incessantly, they differ in one vital respect from the theatrical characters to which we are inured. They are not arguing about a way of earning, or a way of spending, or a way of making love. They are arguing about a way of life.

Some years ago, Eugène Ionesco and I locked horns in a controversy on the subject of social drama, which I liked and he detested. In support of his antipathy, he said that he could take any 'social play' that had ever been written, and diametrically reverse its meaning simply by changing a few words here and there. That, according to M. Ionesco, was enough to demonstrate the futility of the form. I did not believe him at the time, but I believe him now, since I have recently seen *Rhinoceros*, in which he proves his point up to the hilt. This is M. Ionesco's first attempt at a 'social play', and the number of interpretations to which it is susceptible is roughly equal to the number of people in the audience.

A couple of rhinoceroses are heard thundering through the streets of an unnamed European city. They swiftly multiply, and before long it is obvious that the inhabitants themselves are turning into rhinos, some of the unicorn, others of the bicorn variety. In other words, they are turning into faceless conformists; by surrendering to the herd instinct, they are consenting to the destruction of the human ego. The hero, a tipsy little clerk, looks on in horror while all his chums desert him in favour of inhuman, thick-skinned, hard-hoofed anonymity.

But what is the rhinoceros meant to symbolise? Communism, unquestionably; but also Nazism, Socialism, Calvinism or any other ism that appears to threaten one's selfhood. You can change the meaning of *Rhinoceros* merely by switching a few words; and however you switch them, its development is monolithically unsurprising. M. Ionesco is right: there is nothing worse than a bad social play.

Ostensibly, his piece is a defence of individualism against creeping totalitarianism. In fact, it is a concealed attack on reason as a guide to political conduct, and on the very notion that logic may be used as a means of social persuasion. M. Ionesco is begging us to leave people alone to work things out for themselves, and the more alone the better—if ninety-nine per cent of the world voted for the abolition of capital punishment it would presumably be the part of the true individualist to vote for its retention rather than conform.

The play is directed, dashingly and unmistakably, by Orson Welles. I had been warned to expect a display of trickery; instead, I saw much less trickery than M. Ionesco's stage directions call for. I also saw a group of actors on whom a unified style had been emphatically—and no doubt painfully—imposed. The overlapped dialogue, the whirligig moves, the boisterously assured utterance—these are Mr Welles's trademarks, and the production as a whole is exactly what we have come to expect of him: a carefully orchestrated battle of egos, performed by actors who have learned from their director that being inhibited gets you nowhere in the theatre.

Laurence Olivier, as the last exemplar of individualism, is not so much miscast as undercast. Wearing an inexplicable Apache wig, and behaving with a determined kind of boyish, hangdog charm, Sir Laurence skitters gracefully around the stage, rolling his eyes and trying hard to seem humble and insignificant. The task is not an easy one; there is never any doubt that with one breath, one vocal blast, one surge of his enormous humanity, he could blow the part to smithereens, and with it the play. He controls himself quite splendidly; one merely laments the waste of his time.

(1960)

Roots, BY ARNOLD WESKER, AT THE ROYAL COURT; *Improvisation,*
or The Shepherd's Chameleon AND *Victims of Duty,* BY EUGÈNE
IONESCO, AT THE ARTS

The miraculous thing about *Roots*—part two of Arnold Wesker's
trilogy—is that its author has managed to build an intensely moving
play out of the raw materials of old-fashioned kitchen comedy, if not of
outright farce. Ignorant rustics, pap-fed on pop songs; baths taken in
the kitchen; the domestic row in which Mum won't address Dad except
through a third person; the family high tea, complete with trifle, mayon-
naise bottle and uncomfortably brilliantined yokels; the arty daughter
with ideas above her station; the wife who tells her ailing husband that
he has indigestion between the shoulderblades—mention any of these
inventions to your average playgoer, and he will instantly assume that
there's fun in the offing; the kind of fun, as it happens, that ruined the
Abbey Theatre.

And indeed, Mr Wesker does want us to smile; but he makes sure
that condescension, in our smiling, is replaced by compassion, and that
we are always aware of the sad, hard facts underlying the behaviour we
find so hilarious. Taken separately, the details he accumulates are frequently comic; his achievement is to have set them in a context of such
tangible reality that sympathy banishes belly-laughs. It is Chekhov's
method, applied not to the country gentry but to the peasants at the gate.

Like N. F. Simpson, Mr Wesker can amuse us with the vacuous
redundancies of everyday chit-chat; unlike Mr Simpson, he draws our
attention to the causes of mental apathy—among them television, the
Light Programme and the popular Press—as well as to its effects. Mum
squabbles with Dad over the use of an electric cooker; but we know
what Dad earns, and realise that for him electricity is a luxury. And the
comedy of a chronic stomach-ache wanes when we learn that it can cost
a man his job.

Above all, Mr Wesker shows his mastery in the way he handles
Beatie, the heroine. Long absent in London, Beatie has fallen in love
with Ronnie Kahn (the East End poet of *Chicken Soup with Barley*);
she comes home bursting with his ideas about the necessity of convincing
ordinary people that art is intended for them, and not merely for the
intellectually privileged. She postures and proselytises, like a hot-
gospeller among Eskimos, while her relations look on, impassively bewildered. The rules of conventional dramaturgy demand that she should

get her come-uppance; in the final scene, she is jilted by Ronnie, and all seems set for her to abandon her pretensions and return to the simple life. We expect capitulation. Instead, Mr Wesker gives us triumph. By losing Ronnie, Beatie finds herself, and proclaims, now with unassailable certainty, that she has been right all along. Her astonished cry of self-discovery brings down the curtain on the most affecting last act in contemporary English drama. It would be wrong to describe *Roots* as a Socialist play, but if anyone were to tell me that a Tory had written it, I should be mightily amazed.

Among living playwrights Mr Wesker has few peers when it comes to evoking an atmosphere of family cohesiveness; his characters belong together, even when they are not on speaking terms with each other. Under John Dexter's direction, the Royal Court team performs in a spirit of what might be called unromantic realism, though it is in fact—to revive an unfashionable word—nothing more or less than naturalism.

Joan Plowright's Beatie seemed to me a touch too pawky, suggestive less of rural Norfolk than of urban Lancs. One suspected at times that Miss Plowright thought Beatie rather a silly girl; and by imitating Ronnie as if he talked like a well-bred phoney, she made it hard to believe that the two had ever met. All the same, she grips one's attention throughout, and rises glowing to the challenge of the final scene.

In *Improvisation, or The Shepherd's Chameleon*, the first half of the double bill at the Arts, M. Ionesco rails against those who question the validity of his dramatic method. 'The critic', he asserts, 'should describe, and not prescribe.' In *Victims of Duty*, the second half of the bill, he shows us the kind of play that the critics are presumably trying to keep him from writing. It deals with a persecuted little man (Chaplinesque) who is forced by a mysterious detective (Kafkaesque) to uncover the secrets of his past. After about fifteen minutes, caprice takes over—the concept of art as the product of accident, the theory that communication can be achieved only by sacrificing integrity.

'It is in my dreams, my anguish, my dark desires, my inner contradictions,' says M. Ionesco in the curtain-raiser, 'that I reserve the right to find the stuff of my plays.' I do not doubt that *Victims of Duty* is stuffed with dreams, anguish and the rest; but I reserve the right to deny that the result is more than a cloudy and befuddled *mélange*. When you've seen all of Ionesco's plays, I felt at the end, you've seen one of them.

For a professed enemy of didacticism, he is strangely didactic himself. In *The Shepherd's Chameleon* he appears as a harassed author whose creative flow is interrupted by three pedants who seek to baffle him with talk of Brecht and science; and the play embodies his protest against their attempts to label him and define the nature of his art. Yet in these matters M. Ionesco himself is the supreme dogmatist. In his view of drama there is no room for rational qualms or for the ambiguities he so much despises in Brecht; either a playwright is a total individualist, utterly unconcerned with ideology, or he is not a playwright at all.

Or so M. Ionesco insists. It is probably unfair to take his absolutism quite seriously; more charitably, perhaps, one should regard him as a brilliant improviser, raging against the world of ideas into which fame had dragged him, and determined to place his work beyond the reach of criticism—and also of thought. One can't help feeling that he ought to follow Ring Lardner's example and stay out of critical debates. I mention Lardner because he wrote, in the twenties, a number of short nonsense plays that easily outdo M. Ionesco in the extravagance of their non-sequiturs, and contrive to be shatteringly and disturbingly funny without claiming to have been born out of private agony.

(1960)

I'm Talking About Jerusalem, BY ARNOLD WESKER, AT THE ROYAL COURT

As a rule, Harold Pinter's characters live immured in a room, vaguely intimidated by the world outside, fearful of direct communication with each other, and therefore talking about everything except what most deeply concerns them. As representatives of our way of life, they precisely complement Arnold Wesker's characters, who rush out to grapple with the world, bent on communicating with each other and anyone else who will listen, and seldom talking about anything but their deepest concerns.

Yet what do they accomplish? *I'm Talking About Jerusalem*, the last instalment of Mr Wesker's trilogy, suggests that his answer is: almost nothing. The members of the Kahn family end up with their hopes baffled and their ideals defeated. The world outside has let them down; they feel alienated and rejected. No doubt they will 'carry on', but their passion for causes has abated, and they are no longer quite sure where they are going. One more disastrous adventure, you feel, and the path might well lead straight to Mr Pinter's room. Mr Wesker's conclusion, in short, is not very far from Mr Pinter's starting-point: that there is something in our society that is irrevocably hostile to the idea of human brotherhood.

At the beginning of *Chicken Soup with Barley* the Kahns, like Lincoln Steffens, 'have seen the future, and it works'. By the end of *I'm Talking About Jerusalem*, twenty-three years later, they have decided that it doesn't. Their early allegiance to Communism has long since disintegrated; and although Beatie Bryant emerges from *Roots* with a new sense of purpose and identity, we are not told exactly what she is going to do with it.

This last play deals with a frustrated attempt to translate Socialist theory into practice. Ada Kahn and her husband Dave, haters of mass production and readers of William Morris, move out of the East End into a lonely Norfolk cottage, where Dave proposes to manufacture furniture of his own design, thereby—as he hopes—reviving the tradition of pride in craftsmanship that industrialisation has stifled.

The first two acts, in which he and his wife are struggling to establish themselves, pleasantly remind us that Mr Wesker is one of the few Western dramatists who can write about political idealists without mockery or condescension. The moving-in process, accompanied by the forebodings of Ada's mother and the soaring enthusiasm of Ronnie Kahn; Dave's momentary qualms when a wartime chum turns out to have developed into a cynical 'realist'; the family game wherein Ada and her young son pretend to be lumps of clay into which Dave, mimicking the Deity, solemnly breathes life—all this is lovingly observed, and lambently acted, especially by Frank Finlay as the cynic. Mr Finlay's assault on Dave's ideals—and, by extension, on his own past—is an unforgettable set piece, full of implied self-hatred; even his laughter sounds like a kind of weeping.

In the third act the dream fades. Dave's prices are too high to compete with factory products, the bank refuses him a loan, and he is forced to go back to the city, while Ronnie looks on, tearfully wondering what went wrong. Two full-blooded minor characters, Aunt Cissie and Aunt Esther, barge amusingly in; but the play as a whole tails off into something between a whimper and a shrug. An experiment in medievalism has collapsed, and everyone behaves as if it were the end of the world. Nobody points out to Dave or Ronnie that the failure of a privately owned furniture business can hardly be equated with the failure of Socialism; all that happens is that Ronnie, after a bout of weeping, brings down the curtain by bellowing to the fields: 'We're bloody mad to cry!' One can only agree. This final outburst of affirmation comes across as an empty gesture, utterly devoid of intellectual substance; and its effect, I am afraid, is to strengthen John Whiting's recent animadversions on the new movement in our theatre. Mr Whiting conceded that it had a heart: 'All the throbbing emotionalism proves it.... It is that little tiny head that worries me.'

It worries me, too. All the same, I part company with Mr Whiting when he derides Beatie Bryant (and through her, Mr Wesker) because she 'seems to see art as an educative influence, something which uplifts, does you good. Nonsense! Some of the best art teaches nothing and can do irreparable harm, if not actually deprave.' I will not embarrass Mr Whiting by asking him to give examples, but I do beg him to ponder the following remarks of John Berger's:

> ...why should an artist's way of looking at the world have any meaning for us? Why does it give us pleasure? Because, I believe, it increases our awareness of our own potentiality.... The important point is that a valid work of art promises in some way or another the possibility of an increase, of an improvement. Nor need the work be optimistic to achieve this; indeed, its subject may be tragic. For it is not the subject that makes the promise, it is the artist's way of viewing his subject.

Mr Wesker's view of his subject is blurred, at the end, by sentimentality and intellectual flabbiness, for which I have chided him. But he cannot legitimately be condemned for having tried to 'do us good'. I have been emotionally enlarged, and morally roused, by the experience of hearing Mr Wesker talk about Jerusalem. This is not, perhaps, what Mr Whiting means by art; but it is what most of us mean by theatre.

(1960)

Platonov, BY ANTON CHEKHOV, AT THE ROYAL COURT; *The Playboy of the Western World*, BY J. M. SYNGE, AT THE PICCADILLY

If anyone still lives who needs proof of Chekhov's genius, let him go and see *Platonov*. This is the master's first play, composed when he was twenty-one, discovered in manuscript after his death, and now presented in Dmitri Makaroff's adaptation by the English Stage Company. It makes a singular impression; as if a Russian novel of country life had been dramatised by Georges Feydeau and then handed over to Chekhov for total rewriting.

'*Quel ennui!*' we hear quite early on; and later: 'How stale the air is in Russia!' As in *The Cherry Orchard*, an estate is in jeopardy. People on all sides are busy destroying each other, as Trigorin destroys Nina, out of idleness. Neglected wives, retired military men, bankrupt landowners, grasping merchants and envious peasants crowd the stage, most of them either drunk or listless, and many of them both.

Here are the theatrical first-fruits of Chekhov's lifelong curiosity about the symptoms and causes of human boredom. Drunk or sober, the characters address each other with disastrous candour. They change the subject on impulse, almost by free association, and they have the Chekhovian (or perhaps the Russian) habit of taking calamities lightly and trivialities tragically. With them, elation and suicidal gloom are split seconds apart.

In the midst of this provincial desolation squirms Platonov, who must be regarded as one of the great comic creations of the last hundred years. He is a school-teacher of considerable intellect and high physical attractiveness. He decided long ago to concentrate on developing the latter attribute, and he has regretted his decision ever since. Whenever he deceives his wife, he is stung by an attack of remorse so savage that it can be alleviated only by deceiving her with someone else. The more he hates himself, the more cynical he becomes; and the more cynical he becomes, the more he hates himself.

In the course of the play Platonov meshes limbs with a sexy widow and an idealistic young wife; he also insults a local blue-stocking so challengingly that she mistakes insult for love. His three liaisons ultimately collide, and in their collision, which involves a great slamming and locking and bursting open of doors, resides what we may call the Feydeau element of the plot.

It is here that Rex Harrison, as Platonov, comes into his own. Edgy and tentative in the first, expository act, he now expands and relaxes. This bearded satyr, febrile and wild-eyed, rides a perfect switchback from euphoria to misery. He makes the farce funny, by impeccable timing; and touching, an instant later, by his ability to convert querulous complaints into emotional assets. We almost pity the cad, leering and whining though he usually is. He even looks Slavic; I shall not soon forget the scene in which he rises at dawn with a hangover, automatically downs a vodka, and pauses shortly thereafter, stricken by a genuine uncertainty, to ask himself: 'Did I have a drink just then?'

George Devine and John Blatchley directed, and the five elaborate sets are by Richard Negri. It is an indication of the production's general success that it ends, in the midst of laughter, with a thoroughly convincing death. A death, moreover, that happens on a hot, rainy morning. In Chekhov's plays even the weather is Chekhovian.

The Playboy of the Western World is excellent company once in a while, but it is possible to have too much of a good Synge. In the past four years I have seen the play five times, including the musical comedy version and the one presented by the Berliner Ensemble, who changed the title to *The Hero of the Western World* and linked Christy Mahon's Ireland to Mike Hammer's America by means of a front-cloth covered with Mickey Spillane dust-jackets. (Message: in decadent societies, murderers are idolised.)

In short, I have lately had a basinful of Synges' sorcery; and for this reason I smile less readily than I once did at his quips about Irish parents, Irish tippling, Irish priests and Irish braggartry. The play's basic idea—that a reputation for patricide can transform a weakling into a sex-symbol—still tickles me, slightly, as a pleasantly amoral conceit; but of the outrage that swept through that first Dublin audience I feel not a spark.

Even the style is beginning to defeat me. I concede its soft lyricism; but where is its hard meaning? Synge is often praised for his mastery of cadence, and for the splendour of his dying falls. Dying they may well be, but they take an unconscionable time doing it. Synge seldom lets a simple, declarative sentence alone. To its tail there must be pinned some such trailing tin can of verbiage as—to improvise an example—'the way you'd be roaring and moiling in the lug of a Kilkenny ditch, and she with a shift on her would destroy a man entirely, I'm thinking, and him staring till the eyes would be lepping surely from the holes in his head'. Nor can I bring myself to devote my full attention to a play in which all the characters are numskulls—and quaint, pastoral numskulls at that.

Writers like O'Casey, Behan and J. P. Donleavy have ruined my taste for Synge; and that taste, once lost, is not easily recovered. I acknowledge a handful of magical speeches and an uproarious duologue about skulls and bones at the opening of the last act. For the rest, put me down as a saturation victim. As Pegeen Mike, Siobhán McKenna gets her arms akimbo and her voice bountifully throbbing. All she lacks is tenderness; instead of a nice girl pretending to be a termagant, she gives us a real termagant.

(1960)

Chin-Chin, BY FRANÇOIS BILLETDOUX, AT WYNDHAM'S

The excellent new issue of the theatre magazine *Encore* contains a long and fascinating letter from Peter Brook about Jack Gelber's off-Broadway play *The Connection*. Mr Brook's conclusion is as follows:

> *The Connection* proves to me that the development of the tradition of naturalism will be towards an ever-greater focus on the person or the people, and an increasing ability to dispense with such props to our interest as story and dialogue. I think it shows that there is a supernaturalistic theatre ahead of us in which *pure behaviour* can exist in its own right, like pure movement in ballet, pure language in declamation, etc.

In its miniature, unconsidered way, *Chin-Chin* is a move in the direction of Mr Brook's prophecy. Written by a young Left-Bank author called François Billetdoux, and cleverly adapted by Willis Hall, it consists of eleven short glimpses of a ripening acquaintanceship between two people who have nothing in common save grief. There is hardly any plot; the essential action has taken place before the curtain goes up. The dialogue is spare, elliptical, capricious in its sudden changes of tone. Much of it resembles two non-matching monologues forever interrupting each other, zipped into a semblance of unity merely by force of circumstance. Each of the two characters (there are only three speaking parts) tries and fails to break out of self-pity into the other's distress. They stand for no one but themselves, they seek to prove nothing, and they do not demand our sympathy; we can watch them or not, as we wish.

This detached attitude towards the audience is both unfamiliar and uncongenial to many playgoers, who like to be told whether what they are seeing is meant to be comic or serious. Much of M. Billetdoux's play is extremely funny, and much of it is sad, but neither the laughter nor the tears are signposted for us. To speak quite strictly, they are unintentional. The author is showing us 'pure behaviour' as he has selectively recorded it; and he is inviting us to smile or weep as we would at reality itself. If, like almost everyone, you have been brought up on plays that devote their energy to evoking positive emotional responses, you quit Wyndham's Theatre disappointed, feeling that you have had a pretty thin evening; no climaxes, no quotable wit, and no clinching resolution. Yet as time passes, you may find (as I did after seeing the play in Paris last summer) a strange thing happening. You cannot get that couple out of your mind.

They are both expatriates in Paris. One is a prim Englishwoman, by name Pamela Puffy-Picq. The other is Cesareo Grimaldi, an Italian building contractor in his forties. What brings them together is the fact that their respective spouses, who are both French, have run off with each other. The distracted Grimaldi arranges to meet Mme Puffy-Picq, in hopes of learning something about the man for whom his wife has left him. And thus begins a weird experiment in *camaraderie*.

Where background and temperament are concerned, he and Pamela are poles distant. She never dreams; he always does. He drinks; she doesn't. He is an idealist; she is a realist. Yet they are forced into a kind of intimacy, since each is now the other's closest link with the happily married past. It is not that they particularly like each other; they can simply see no alternative, having lost what they most cherished. There is no sex in the relationship. Grimaldi makes a futile attempt to introduce it, but he passes out before laying a hand on her. They go through all the pains and none of the pleasures of marriage; the rows, without the rewards. They wander from bar to bar, silently aware that whatever gave their lives meaning has irretrievably departed. By now Pamela is drinking, too, and Cesareo moves into her flat, thereby appalling her teenage son, who packs his bag and goes off to live with father.

The beleaguered couple spend most of their time indoors, with the blinds drawn, the bottles emptying, the funds dwindling, and all ties with the world severed. Only by night do they dare to venture out. On one such jaunt, they stand and look up at the apartment block wherein their ex-beloveds have set up house, but neither has the courage to go inside. Returning, they stumble over Pamela's son, drunk in a gutter; without a qualm, they steal his wallet and go on their purposeless way. You feel they will survive, as far as anyone can survive unloved.

I don't wish to make extravagant claims for this wry little piece; but I do ask you to approach it on its own terms, and to judge it, like a Japanese watercolour, as much by what it omits as by what it includes. Perhaps it omits too much; one would like, for instance, to know something more about Pamela's husband than that he is a doctor. All the same, I can think of very few playwrights who would be capable of treating a situation like this with so little sentimentality, so much candour, and such an immense faith in what is, after all, the basic assumption of drama: 'that man is passionately interested in man'. (Acknowledgments, once more, to Mr Brook.)

Celia Johnson, who is Maudie Littlehampton transposed into three dimensions, has just the right nervy niceness for Pamela, and the right rebuking stare, spectrally disquieted and British to the core. This lovely actress is partnered by Anthony Quayle, who plays bull to her china-shop, giving a doughty, craftsman's performance that lacks nothing except the authentic flavour of Italy. From Italian lips the words flow; from Mr Quayle's they have to be pushed. The settings are properly un-obtrusive, with one riveting exception—the scene outside the apartment building, which has inspired Sean Kenny to design a tower on stilts that would be the envy of Le Corbusier. Howard Sackler directed.

(1960)

The Duchess of Malfi, BY JOHN WEBSTER, AT THE ALDWYCH

With a rattle of skeletons and a fanfare of maniacal screams, the Stratford-on-Avon company has opened its first London season. *The Duchess of Malfi* is a play for which exaggerated claims have sometimes been made; as a traumatic experience, branding the mind with panic, it is not to be compared with Alfred Hitchcock's grisly masterpiece, *Psycho*, and G. H. Lewes was right, though turbid in utterance, when he con-demned 'the irredeemable mediocrity of its dramatic evolution of human passion'.

Webster is not concerned with humanity. He is the poet of bile and brainstorm, the sweet singer of apoplexy; ideally, one feels, he would have had all his characters drowned in a sea of cold sweat. His muse drew nourishment from Bedlam, and might, a few centuries later, have done the same from Belsen. I picture him plagued with hypochondria, probably homosexual, and consumed by feelings of persecution—an in-tensely neurotic mind, in short, at large in the richest, most teeming vocabulary that any age ever offered to a writer.

One imagines his contemporaries dismissing him as 'that charnel-house poet', much as we nowadays dub Beckett the dramatist of the dust-bin. And although we cannot call him the inventor of the sick joke (a field in which Kyd, Marlowe and Shakespeare were all ahead of him), he certainly rolled back the frontiers of the new genre—as witness the scene in which Duke Ferdinand extends a hand for his sister to shake, omitting to warn her that it has lately been severed from a corpse. In the whole of Webster's work, scarcely an act is committed that is not moti-vated by greed, revenge or sexual rapacity.

Yet his characters die superbly, asserting their selfhood to the last breath—even the least of them, such as the Duchess's maid, who expires with a sudden, plaintive cry of: 'I am quick with child!' Webster's people are most themselves when the knife, noose or potion is nearest; you might say that his plays come alive the closer they get to death. *The Duchess of Malfi* is an intricate tale of the vengeance sought and obtained by two brothers—one ducal and incestuous, the other ecclesiastical and more normally lecherous—on their widowed sister, who has offended by remarrying beneath her.

The present production, by Donald McWhinnie, is a forthright, noisy affair, played all out for melodrama; effective enough in its way, but far from the subtle, imaginative interpretation of which I for one went in hopes. Peggy Ashcroft's Duchess is more ripely moving than her Haymarket performance of fifteen years ago; but I wished, as I listened to Eric Porter's strangled ranting, that Gielgud were still playing Ferdinand, still imparting the same thrill of finality to the line: 'I will never see thee more.' There are no blatant weaknesses in the cast, and nothing is lacking in the production, save finesse and originality.

(1960)

Hamlet, BY WILLIAM SHAKESPEARE, AT STRATFORD-ON-AVON

I begin to grow testy with the new regime at Stratford. It has now given us a *Hamlet* as paltry and undercast as any I recall from the days before Sir Barry Jackson took over the theatre. In that unreformed era, when a dozen productions or more were rushed on to the stage every season, much expense was spared, and niceties of interpretation often went by the board; all the same, one could count on a certain basic professional assurance, which made up in heartiness what it lacked in subtlety. From this *Hamlet* even that is often missing. The production moves uneasily, as if mired in sloth and indecision, and seems no less tentative when it is trying to be conventional than on the few occasions when it ventures into originality.

Much of the casting is incomprehensibly wayward. Gertrude (Elizabeth Sellars) could pass for Hamlet's younger sister, and the Ghost, wailing in the shadows, sounds less mature than either of them. Geraldine McEwan is at once a passionless Ophelia and a glum reminder of our theatre's perennial deficiency in girls with a natural talent for emotional acting. In a context like this, Noel Willman's Claudius is something of a relief; at his first entrance, Mr Willman strikes a note of

decent banality from which he never afterwards departs. To establish
that he is a crafty fellow, he keeps his eyes roving from side to side, like
air-pockets in a pair of spirit-levels; and he clinches the case against
Claudius by eating grapes. It is a rule of Shakespearean production that
men who eat grapes are definitely voluptuaries and probably murderers.

Remains Ian Bannen, an honourable actor whose Hamlet is just
what one would expect of a born Horatio. I can best describe Mr
Bannen's performance as apologetic, though in a rather special sense:
what we see is not Hamlet apologising for his shortcomings as a hero, but
Mr Bannen apologising for his shortcomings as Hamlet. We watch the
actor shrinking from the role, bashfully grinning even when death is upon
him; his relationship to the part is that of a sturdy bird-dog to a soaring
eagle. Like his dad, this Hamlet moans and irrationally whimpers. The
idea (or so I guess) is to show us a man whose emotional development
ceased at puberty; tied to his mother, he is scared of growing up; and the
trunk into which he absurdly hops to deliver the 'rogue and peasant
slave' soliloquy is doubtless meant to signify the womb.

So far, so good: a timorous Hamlet is perfectly acceptable. But a
slow-witted Hamlet is inconceivable, and it is here that Mr Bannen dis-
qualifies himself. He makes the prince a plodder, depressive and numb of
brain, and thus brings the play to an early standstill, since its motive
force derives entirely from the restless intellectual energy of its protagonist. To play Hamlet without a racing mind is like entering for the
Mille Miglia without a racing motor.

The acting as a whole is based on the false assumption, all too
common in Shakespearean performances, that you begin with the lines
and then endeavour to pump feeling into them. In fact, the lines are
the end of the process. The actor must first earn the right to speak
them. In every scene, sometimes in every speech, he must ask himself
exactly what the character is seeking to achieve; having singled out an
objective, he must narrow it down by patient experiment until it becomes
so specific that the lines as written are the only possible means of
expressing it.

No such discipline is visible in Peter Wood's production, which consists in the main of a series of readings, some noisier than others. The
play is subjected to a number of niggling cuts and minor textual eccentricities; and there are some weird discrepancies between what Shakespeare prescribes and what Mr Wood provides. 'Up, sword', says Hamlet,
with nothing in his hand but a dagger; and no sooner have we heard a
cannon's boom than Hamlet identifies it as the bray of 'kettle-drum and
trumpet'.

Little else in the evening is worthy of memory. The English theatre has plenty of classical actors: what it needs is a few more classical directors. Apart from Tyrone Guthrie and Peter Brook, the front rank is unoccupied.

(1960)

A Gap Defined: 1960

Permit me, in a thin week, to pursue a general topic. To begin with a postulate: theatre sustains itself by a process of cross-fertilisation to which all of its species contribute. From this it follows that a weakness in any particular species, however humble, will sooner or later be transmitted to the rest. Not at all frivolously, I am going to suggest that our theatre as a whole has been infected, and injured, by our weakness in the tiny, ancillary department of satirical cabaret.

Where else but in a small room, late at night, before an audience more notable for its mind than its money, can the true satirist—whether writer or performer or both—practise his art and polish his weapons? In such an atmosphere he need not restrict himself to the hints and nudges that masquerade as satire in West End revues. He can be outrageous and uninhibited; he can pierce to the quick of the ulcer without bothering to administer sedation; he can speak freely on any subject from the Cuban revolution to the Immaculate Conception.

Cabaret of this sort is not only satirical in itself, but the cause that satire is in other theatrical forms. The London stage has always excelled in turning out samples of complacent, self-congratulating and fundamentally inoffensive wit; and it has lately been exploring the comic potentialities of surrealism. But whenever it attempts satire, in the full, corrosive sense of the word, it looks blundering and amateurish. It is out of practice. It has no training-ground, no source.

Compare, for instance, the German theatre in the twenties, nourished by the stinging, acidulous wit of the Berlin *Nachtlokalen*, on which Brecht and Weill founded their method and based their style. In Paris, meanwhile, one has the *chansonniers*, which have always been outposts of opposition to whatever regime chanced to be in power, and which have reserved their right to dissent, even under de Gaulle. The French theatre has many failings, but it has never wanted for satirists.

Since the war, however, the prime incubator of nonconformist night-club wit has been America. Adolph Green and Betty Comden, who wrote the lyrics of *On The Town* and *Wonderful Town*, made their reputations in the *boîtes* of Greenwich Village; and Abe Burrows, the co-author of *Guys and Dolls*, started his career as a cabaret parodist. More recently, a new group, higher of brow and redder in tooth and claw than its predecessors, has taken control. It is led, of course, by Mort Sahl, an avid sceptic who might be defined as a liberal nihilist; he is quoted, I see, as having said that, whereas the last presidential election produced a bumper crop of male children christened Dwight or Adlai, the present one should yield an even larger number named Undecided.

There is also Lenny Bruce, to whom nothing either human or in-human is alien. This cool iconoclast includes among his pet targets the bomb, sexual hypocrisy, racial intolerance, the profit motive and organised religion; as an ice-breaker, he sometimes uses a routine in which a Madison Avenue publicist telephones the Pope, addressing him as Johnny, urging him to 'wear the big ring' when he visits America and assuring him that: 'Nobody knows you're a Jew.' By way of finale, he often employs a Negro associate, to whom he explains that in the great big yonder racial barriers will collapse and we shall all be united—Negroes, Italians, Jews, Puerto Ricans, Germans, everyone. 'And then,' he adds, his eyes shining, 'we'll all go out and beat up the Polacks.'

Messrs Sahl and Bruce rose to fame from a cellar-club in San Francisco called 'the hungry i'; at the same time, a similar haunt in Chicago was fostering the talents of Mike Nichols and Elaine May, in whose work delicate verbal surgery replaces the machine-gun of Sahl and the cobra-fangs of Bruce. Mr Nichols is blond and reflective, Miss May dark and intense. Their act is an unnerving display of mutual empathy, since much of their material is improvised; Odets, Wilder, Joyce, Pirandello and Dostoevsky are some of the authors whose styles I have heard them simulate, impromptu and by audience request.

Among their contemporaries and competitors are such unsettling wags as Shelley Berman, Jonathan Winters and Bob Newhart, all cabaret-bred; and a new generation of satirists is in active training. For proof, consider a sketch I saw last spring in a Chicago dive known as 'The Second City'. It showed Richard Nixon coming down to breakfast wearing his new, liberal mask, to which his daughter reacted with a scream of: 'Momma, *who's* that *man*?'

We, meanwhile, have strip-joints with acres of gooseflesh, and clip-joints with sequinned, androgynous floorshows.

As a nation we are not devoid of satiric gifts. Our suburbs and provinces abound in fledgling Jimmy Porters and Billy Liars, fast-talking, quick-thinking young intellectuals who specialise in informed derision;

but there is nowhere for them to develop their skill. We lack a place in which intelligent, likeminded people can spend a cheap evening listening to forthright cabaret that is socially, sexually and politically pungent. Lacking it, we have a theatre in which lumbering charades are gravely acclaimed for their unsparing mordancy. Thus is the great name of satire neglected, degraded and traduced.

Romeo and Juliet, BY WILLIAM SHAKESPEARE, AT THE OLD VIC

'This is as't should be'—*Romeo and Juliet*, IV, 2.

In the past half-century nothing has plagued the English classical theatre more than the problem of coping with its permanent responsibility, its matrix and its millstone—the works of William Shakespeare.

Fashions in Shakespearean production have succeeded each other as swiftly as Picassovian phases. Modern-dress enthusiasts have vied with platform-stage purists; the plays have been staged as Jacobean masques, neo-Victorian extravaganzas, exercises in Tudor rhetoric, expositions of Freudian dogma, and Ruritanian charades. Contemporary scholarship, with its heavy emphasis on the conventional element in Elizabethan drama, has not gone unnoticed; and it is nowadays an axiom, even among non-experimental directors, that the production style (sometimes known as the chosen convention or the overall concept) takes precedence over everything else. Individual characterisation—that square old Bradleyan obsession—has sharply declined in status; nobody has any ideas on the subject beyond a vague and unquestioned assumption that all Shakespearean characters are 'larger than life'.

Last Tuesday at the Old Vic a foreign director approached Shakespeare with fresh eyes, quick wits and no stylistic preconceptions; and what he worked was a miracle. The characters were neither larger nor smaller than life; they were precisely life-size, and we watched them living, spontaneously and unpredictably. The director had taken the simple and startling course of treating them as if they were real people in a real situation; and of asking himself just how those people, in that situation, would behave.

It sounds obvious enough; yet the result, in Franco Zeffirelli's production of *Romeo and Juliet*, is a revelation, even perhaps a revolution. Nobody on stage seems to be aware that he is appearing in an immortal tragedy, or indeed in a tragedy of any kind; instead, the actors behave like ordinary human beings, trapped in a quandary whose outcome they cannot foretell. Handled thus realistically, it is sometimes said, Shakespeare's essential quality gets lost. I passionately demur. What gets lost is not Shakespeare but the formal, dehumanised stereotype that we have so often made of him.

It is likewise urged that Signor Zeffirelli robs Shakespeare of his poetry; but this argument is valid only if one agrees with those blinkered zealots who insist that poetry is an arrangement of sounds, instead of an arrangement of words. Last Tuesday I heard every syllable; meaning and character were wedded, and out of their interaction poetry arose. The production evoked a whole town, a whole riotous manner of living; so abundant and compelling was the life on stage that I could not wait to find out what happened next. The Vic has done nothing better for a decade. A young English director of my acquaintance made a true comment in one of the intervals. 'Every director in the audience,' he said, 'is biting his nails and wondering why he never thought of this before.'

It is hard to know where to begin the catalogue of particular praise. The sets (also by Signor Zeffirelli) are spaciously atmospheric, composed of peeling, flaking walls that serve equally well for interiors or exteriors. Children scuffle in the alleys and vendors bawl their wares. We are unmistakably in Verona, or anyway in Italy; the director has even taught his English cast how to shrug. The rival factions are gangs of dawdlers with time on their hands; captives of the streets, like the boys in Fellini's film, I Vitelloni. Mercutio (electrically played by Alec McCowen) is their unquestioned idol, an intense, fierce, sourly witty young man, always conscious of his intellectual supremacy. His death comes as a chilling shock, since Signor Zeffirelli has caused it to occur by accident. His bout with Tybalt, a basically playful affair, is already over when the mortal thrust is delivered; it is a chance and unintended stroke, yet it kills him, whereafter the feud between the families takes on a new dimension of seriousness. They have squabbled immemorially, but this is their first murder, and it tilts the action towards tragedy.

Romeo, meanwhile, is an idler lured out of sulks into love. His meeting with Juliet at the Capulets' ball is staged with marvellous tact. A crowd has gathered to hear someone sing; around the fringe of it the lovers tentatively edge, ending up together, quietly pressing palm to palm. The balcony scene is heartrendingly good. Here, as everywhere else in the production, grace is subordinated to circumstance, the ideal to the real. Instead of leaping balletically up a conveniently placed creeper, John Stride (as Romeo) has to concentrate prosaically on climbing a highly uncooperative little tree. Judi Dench, a calm, wise little Juliet, awaits him aloft; their encounter is grave, awkward and extremely beautiful.

Romeo's departure for exile is staged with even greater earthiness. The bedroom setting is dominated by a lofty four-poster, in which the couple lie; and no doubt is left in one's mind that it is sheer, newly-wedded exhaustion, more than anything else, that delays Romeo's leave-taking.

The latter part of the evening suffers from some damaging excisions. One of them is superbly economic—the almost filmic cut from Juliet's feigned death to Romeo in Mantua, declaiming: 'Then I defy you, stars.' Many of the others, however, are confusing, especially in the last act, which looked slightly under-rehearsed. But the major fault hereabouts lies with the play. It lets the director down. In the world of tangible, credible reality that he has created, magic potions have no place.

(1960)

Meeting Zeffirelli

Ask a literate English director about his forthcoming classical production and he will probably expound to you the theme of the play, his concept of the author's purpose in writing it, and the convention in which he has decided to stage it. If he is a good talker, the play will take shape in your mind like a palace; order and harmony will emerge from what, beforehand, may well have seemed to you a text of chaotic dissonance.

You marvel at the structure that has thus been conjured up, marking the splendour of its proportions, the felicity of its general statement. Only later, if at all, does it occur to you that it is a structure without people. I do not mean without *characters*: the director will undoubtedly have explained how the major characters contribute to the grand design. What I mean is that it contains nobody living. It is a structure into which, in the course of rehearsals, actors will somehow have to be fitted.

I exaggerate, of course, but I exaggerate a truth. As a breed, English directors are nervous of actors, and not without reason. Shakespeare, the fountainhead of our classical theatre, was also the inventor of the star system, and the era of actor-management that his works inaugurated was flourishing quite happily until a few years ago. No wonder, therefore, that our directors, precarious in their new-found hegemony, should tend to emphasise form, pattern and overall concept—anything to keep the classical actor in a decently subordinate position, anything to postpone the nightmare in which he reasserts his power and once again takes over. The result of these stratagems has been a spate of disciplined, stylised productions, based on hard reading and scholarly authority, in which the recognisably human element has been held down to a minimum.

Now along comes Franco Zeffirelli, a thirty-six-year-old Florentine, with a production of *Romeo and Juliet*—his first of a classical play in any language—that has packed the Old Vic at every performance since it opened last October, and will run throughout the season, if not beyond. Zeffirelli's deepest heresy is that he trusts actors; he believes that they come first, and agrees with Joan Littlewood that the stage is theirs by right of promogeniture.

He rehearsed for more than five weeks and spent, by Old Vic standards, a small fortune. 'You can't force an actor', he says. 'He doesn't play with his technique, he plays with his own human qualities. My job is to offer many different solutions to him, and then to choose the right one. It may be comic or tragic, but it must be the right one *for him*. It must become part of his own blood and flesh.' And if it does not, the solution must be modified to fit him.

Slight and willowy, with eyes as sharp as a fly's, Zeffirelli began his theatrical career as an actor under the direction of Luchino Visconti, for whom he also designed scenery and supervised lighting. In the cinema, he was Visconti's assistant director on *La Terra Trema*, perhaps the crowning achievement of neo-realism, in which the cast was drawn entirely from Sicilian fisherfolk. After more films with Visconti, he moved on to opera in Milan, Paris, Amsterdam, Tel Aviv, Dallas and London, where his Covent Garden productions of *Cav.* and *Pag.* and *Lucia di Lammermoor* were critically cheered for their insistence on *verismo*, which may best be defined as an unqualified conviction that the roots of art lie in actual human behaviour. Zeffirelli often embarks on a production with an image at the back of his mind; always, however, it is something concrete, such as a black-shawled Sicilian woman running down a snow-white village street—the image that set the tone for his *Cavalleria*. Apart from this key symbol, nothing is fixed until Zeffirelli knows his actors inside out. He is a pure empiricist, and this is one of the many ways in which he differs from his English *confrères*.

He thinks, moreover, that it helps directors to have had acting experience. In this connection, he cites De Sica's film *Umberto D*; Louis Jouvet's epoch-making production, with designs by Bérard, of *Les Fourberies de Scapin*; and Eduardo de Filippo, 'a great, great genius', who writes, directs and stars in the plays that are performed by his own Neapolitan company.

Zeffirelli has never seen Roger Planchon and his troupe, but I have a suspicion that he might approve of them, partly because M. Planchon is an actor who urges his colleagues to collaborate with him on the script, but mainly because, like Planchon, Zeffirelli is unable to work fruitfully with people he cannot love. (He once abandoned a highly paid production for no saner reason than that he could not establish a loving relationship with the cast.) Above all, he detests directors who seek to impose preconceived ideas on their actors. The Germans, he feels, are the worst offenders in this respect, from Reinhardt to Brecht; in the work of the Berliner Ensemble he discerns 'great thought, great care, but not enough love'.

When directing, Zeffirelli spends most of his time on the stage, listening to the actors, aping their follies, spurring them to improvise and laying down broad pathways of characterisation within which they are free to ramble. Towards the end of the rehearsal period, he slips into the stalls—'to see if I like it or hate it. I laugh or I curse. Just as if I had paid to sit there.' Sometimes he inspires loyalty to an embarrassing degree, as with the Old Vic last summer: 'At first the actors were a bit suspicious—it was like fitting them into a new suit. But then came too much enthusiasm and participation. I had to control a flood.'

For Zeffirelli, that flood is the source of everything valuable. He has no patience with the idea that human behaviour in Shakespeare's plays is different in kind from what it is today; hence the arched eyebrows of the traditionalists at his earthy, informal portrait of Verona in *Romeo and Juliet*, and hence the complaint that he has deprived the warring households of their rightful aristocracy. Zeffirelli's answer is that Shakespeare wanted to give his audience a trip to Italy ('He was a frustrated traveller'), and that someone had to fill in the details. 'Take the Montagues, for instance. They are a noble, military family who have gone to seed. They are in decline. They produce only students—Romeo learns verses and Benvolio carries books. The Capulets are a rich merchant family, full of social climbers, men of wealth as well as men of action. The play has only one aristocrat, and that is Escalus. But anyway, in the English theatre you don't need to emphasise upper-classness. In fact, you need to underplay it. In Italy or America it would be different. You would have to build up the formal dignity.'

Zeffirelli was quite well aware that there was verbal music in *Romeo and Juliet*. He deliberately chose to soft-pedal it in order to stress other elements that seemed to him more important. 'With Racine, of course, I would use another method. He is a musical author. But British civilisation is based on facts, the evidence of facts—it is a sort of dialogue between facts and ideas.'

Small things—fleeting gestures, revealing inflections, poses casually struck—are Zeffirelli's raw material; in them resides the life of the production. He is not, however, an advocate of modern-dress Shakespeare. 'What matters is modernity of feeling, modernity inside. The verse must always have an intimate rhythm, the rhythm of reality. It must never become music.' He was much impressed by Marlon Brando's Antony ('a great symptom') in the film of *Julius Caesar*, although in general he has many reservations about the deep-analysis school of American acting: 'It is all right for actors when they are climbing, learning their job, but for mature actors it is—well—unprofessional.'

By temperament and in practice, Zeffirelli is a realist, but his definition of realism is very far from rigid. In the case of *Romeo and Juliet*, it simply means that he approached the text on the assumption that it could have been spoken by real people in a real human context; and that many sacrifices were worth making in order to get it spoken that way. Nobody, least of all Zeffirelli, would claim that this was the only way to handle the English classics; but its value as a corrective could be enormous. Applied to Restoration comedy, for instance, it might yield surprising results. I have often felt that there was more of the tape-recorder in Congreve and Wycherley than we commonly suppose.

A possible analogy might be with Goldini, who is one of Zeffirelli's passions. Nothing annoys him more than the suggestion that Goldoni's style is artificial. 'You don't know Goldoni in England,' he says. 'All you know is *Arlecchino* as the Piccolo Teatro play it, in the Commedia dell' Arte manner. It is really very ironic. Goldoni spent his life fighting the Commedia dell' Arte, yet outside Italy everyone calls him a Commedia dell' Arte writer. Actually, he wrote realistic, middle-class plays, full of the small facts of life, but always with a touch of madness about them. He reminds me of Chekhov with a dash of Pirandello.'

Zeffirelli is that comparative rarity, a realist who loves the past. He is fascinated by dead worlds—Shakespeare's Verona, Goldoni's Venice—and wants to recreate them, using the theatre to confront us with history. As he puts it: 'If only I could be back in London, say, at ten-thirty a.m. on January 26 1749! We have all felt this, or something like it. Well, I would like to bring back that moment, with all its strangeness and awkwardness.'

When I asked Zeffirelli what Shakespearean play he would like to direct next, his answer was *Hamlet*. He went on to discuss the protagonist with the solicitous, slightly gossipy familiarity of one who had known the boy all his life:

'Hamlet, you see, is not healthy. He has very little time to spend on this earth and he must express himself very quickly. He has great gifts of intuition and fantasy, but he has not developed enough to know about affection and love. He is a boy taken just in the moment when his affections should move away from his mother, but he dies too soon. He is all ideas and broken feelings, jumping like a monkey from one thought to the next, but he cannot go beyond the dreams and fantasies of adolescence. His destiny is to die soon. The whole arc of his life is different from other people's. Also he is a coward. His palms are wet.

'On the visual side, I see him living in a hard world—with no elasticity about it—a closed world, with high walls, no windows, lots of storms. Like a prisoner in a tower. But all that comes later. The first thing is to get the core of the character. Just the core. Then everything follows.'

But how, I wondered, could Zeffirelli reconcile realism with the Ghost? 'That's easy,' he said seriously. 'I believe in ghosts.'

(1960)

Crystal Balls: 1960

Today—there being no new West End shows to discuss—we improvise. The theme is prophecy. Basing our predictions on current and recent form, let us look ahead at next season, and at some of the plays that our more prominent contemporaries may have in store for us (Any resemblance to the plays they actually write, living or dead, is purely uncanny.)

As my imagination sees it, the season begins with a new comedy by T. S. Eliot, two years in the polishing and completed just too late for Edinburgh. Entitled 'The Tradesmen's Entrance', it represents Mr Eliot's first attempt to deal with the aspirations of the proletariat. Hard on its heels comes Graham Green's 'The Purifying Agent', a thriller with mystical overtones, set in Hull, about a Middle-European spy who finds himself hounded by Heaven as well as by M.I.5. Both are respectfully received, but neither rivals in popular acclaim the latest work of Lionel Bart, who follows up the success of *Oliver!* by turning *Bleak House* into a new Cockney musical called *Bleak!*

From across the Channel we have 'Cirque d'Automne', a sour yet fragrant tragicomedy in which M. Anouilh recaptures the creative mood, redolent of anguish and provincial railway stations, that moved him to write *La Sauvage* and *Eurydice*. 'Cirque d'Automne' has to do with a travelling circus that is stranded in Perpignan on New Year's Eve; its central characters are a philosophic ring-master, a pretty trapeze *artiste* of all too pliable morality, and the latter's drunken catcher, who wants—as he puts it—'to drop everything'. Translated as 'Autumn Circus', the play instantly runs into copyright trouble with the legal advisers of Miss Dodie Smith. Litigation of a similar kind also awaits the season's first transatlantic hit —a satirical farce adapted from episodes in the career of the inspired clown who founded *The New Yorker*. Terence Rattigan's lawyers immediately move into action against its title, 'Ross'.

Meanwhile, Tennessee Williams enters the lists with a romantic dithyramb in one act, unearthed from some forgotten bottom drawer. Its hero is a sensitive cadet who runs away from West Point to become a hungover beach-comber in Ischia; and it is called 'A Year of Dry Mornings'. From Arthur Miller, no play emerges; although there is strenuous controversy in the pages of *Encore* about a lecture he delivers to the Yale Drama School on the theatrical implications of Bertrand Russell's latest book, 'The Ethics of Catastrophe', and Aldous Huxley's new collection of apocalyptic essays, 'The Ending Revel'. In other quarters, pious attention is paid to Sir Michael Redgrave's autobiobiography, 'Aloof in the Theatre'.

But even when we have saluted 'The Undertaker' (John Osborne's blistering attack on Martin Luther) and 'Falling Over Backwards' (Arnold Wesker's biographical play about Ezra Pound), no doubt remains that the most vociferously debated theatrical offering of the season is Harold Pinter's smash hit, 'The Area'. In accordance with the pattern set by Mr Pinter's previous plays, it begins as follows:

Scene: A room. A camp-bed, unmade, centre. ALF, reading a telegram, wanders up and down. TAFF, wearing a cap and a Manchester United rosette, sits on the bed, dismantling a tin-opener. No doors, left, right or centre.

ALF: What you want to do, see, you want to watch out for that lot, or they'll have you round the twist. Right round the twist, they will, and then where are you? Up the wall, that's where you are, that's where they'll have you, if you don't watch out for them. See, I know that lot. I've had my eye on the lot of them. What I mean, I've seen them bellocking up and down Ladbroke Grove the minute the shops are shut. I know that sort inside out. They'll play Old Harry with you, that lot will. Not a spark of respect from top to bottom.

TAFF: You mean Old Nick.

ALF: What do you mean, I mean Old Nick?

TAFF: They'll play Old Nick with you. That's what you call proper usage.

ALF: What's that got to do with it, then?

Silence.

You're a bit of what they call a live wire, aren't you? You don't want to come the idiomatic over me, if that's what you think you're doing. I've bought and sold better men than you with one hand held behind my back, any day of the week, right, left and centre, until it's coming out of my ears. You want to be bloody careful, mate, I'm warning you.

TAFF: That tin of Heinz vegetable salad wants seeing to. Got a bit of rust on it.

ALF: You can whistle for your Heinz vegetable salad when that lot comes round after you. They'll give you Heinz vegetable salad all right, that lot will. What you want to do, see, you want to watch out for that lot. . . .

A Winter Journey: Stockholm, Warsaw, East Berlin

Never believe them when they tell you that Stockholm is the Paris of the north. After twenty-four hours in this icy city, where night falls while you are paying your luncheon bill, the truth dawned on me, about ten times as brightly as the day had: Stockholm is the Stockholm of the north, and other vaunts should be abandoned forthwith.

Winter here is a black season in which the spirit does penance and goes to bed early. Yet the Swedish climate, so unnerving to foreigners, explains in part the strength of the Swedish theatre. It splits the year up into artistic compartments. The winter is too dark for filming, and the summer nights are too white for plays; theatre and cinema thus become seasonal arts and you can practise both of them with equal devotion.

One result of this is that the company at the Royal Dramatic Theatre is full of faces one remembers from Ingmar Bergman films. Another, rather more important, is that Swedish directors bring to their movies experience gained in the theatre. The two forms are constantly enriching each other. Bengt Ekerot, who directed the world première of O'Neill's *Long Day's Journey Into Night*, played the role of Death in Bergman's *The Seventh Seal*. Alf Sjöberg divides his time between mounting plays at the Royal Dramatic Theatre and making films like *Miss Julie* and *Frenzy*. Bergman himself broke into the cinema with his script for the latter; since then he has spent his summers filming and his winters staging. These three are generally regarded as Sweden's best *metteurs-en-scène*; for purposes of comparison, ask yourself how many of their English counterparts work regularly—or at all—in films. The Swedish performing arts are homogeneous in personnel, flexible in technique, contemporary in outlook and international in scope, to an extent that would scarcely be possible in a bigger country with a strong and ancient theatrical tradition of its own.

State patronage of the drama goes back in Sweden to the latter part of the eighteenth century, and nowadays, despite the fact that there are fewer Swedes than there are Londoners, every town larger than a village has its subsidised playhouse and its devoutly attentive audience. But Sweden's real luck consists in never having had a Shakespeare or a Racine; its only classic—Strindberg—is a modern, for whom no traditional style exists to inhibit adventurous directors. Being thus uncommitted, it has been able to pick and choose, selecting what it needed from the production methods of Russia, France and Germany. In consequence, the Swedish theatre today is perhaps the most eclectic in Europe, with all the variety and lack of identity that that implies.

The great event in Stockholm last week was Ingmar Bergman's first production at the Royal Dramatic Theatre. For his *rentrée* to the capital he chose *The Seagull*, and handled it with a scrupulous, balanced, detailed realism that must have surprised anyone who knew him only by his films; the first act was a foundation stone of Chekhovian lyricism, with the spectators at Constantin's play standing around their wicker chairs, so many statues in a grey garden under a storm-swollen sky; and the last act, an elegy in a forlorn house with a leafless branch swaying in the wind outside, came closer to perfection than I had ever expected to see it. In the middle scenes the pace occasionally dragged. But the acting was discreetly superb—I single out Trigorin (Ulf Palme), a powerful presence, muted and gutted by too much worldliness; Masha (Christina Adolphson), skinny and self-conscious; and a Constantin who was petulant rather than knowingly pathetic.

Above all, I remember the moment in the last act when Bergman showed us Chekhov's Nina, as opposed to the hysterical chit we normally see; Christina Schollin, when she made her final entrance, had changed from child to woman. She still bore the scars of her affair with Trigorin, but one knew that she would survive them, and then go on, thus fledged, to become a good actress. Like everyone else in the cast, she had aged two years since we last saw her. Many directors overlook this lapse of time. Bergman did not.

At the same theatre I saw Jean-Paul Sartre's *Les Séquestrés d'Altona*, all four hours of it, magnificently directed by Alf Sjöberg with the benefit of three months' rehearsal. I don't wish to dwell on the play itself, for unless the English managers run mad *en bloc* we should be seeing it in London before the season ends. Enough to say that it concerns, and lacerates, a hard-faced Hamburg family who have done well out of the war; led by father, a shipping magnate now dying of cancer, they cooperated with the Nazis and felt no particular qualms; but the time is near when they must come to terms with the skeleton in their cupboard—Franz, the elder son, a former Nazi officer who has locked himself up in an attic room for thirteen lunatic years, the self-appointed keeper of the family conscience. He sucks them all into his raging guilt—his incestuous sister Leni, his flabby brother Werner, his idealistic sister-in-law Johanna, and even father himself, with whom, in the end, he commits suicide. As the curtain falls, Leni replaces him in the penitential garret. Clearly, symbolism is involved; M. Sartre, who often writes French like a German, has here transposed a French problem—guilt arising out of the Algerian War—into German terms, and I am not altogether sure that Leni, who takes over the responsibility for the future, is not meant to represent Leninism.

However this may be, the human relationships are what count on the stage, and Sjöberg clarifies their complications with a sure hand that touches every stop from downright naturalism to upright rhetoric. The cast play together like demons. Max von Sydow, as Franz, is a little too demonic, whirling about in a double-jointed fury that sometimes borders on self-indulgence; but the girls are blazingly good, especially Gertrud Fridh, who sees Leni as a mischievous troll, not unlike Hilda in *The Master Builder*. Meanwhile Lars Hanson, the doyen of the Swedish theatre and by common consent the finest Strindberg actor alive, is giving a performance as the father that must, if the delicate use of gigantic power is any criterion, be called great. The old man's gait is a stiff-backed shuffle; his face is a fixed mask of patient courtesy, and his voice has in it a soft huskiness that horribly suggests the cancer at his throat; yet merely by narrowing his eyes a fraction he can become impermeable granite.

Sjöberg, the orchestrator of these pedigree performances, told me afterwards that he approached *Altona* as he would approach any other good play. All drama, he said, had to do with an exchange of masks—with an attempt, conscious or not, on the part of one character to take on the image of another. Thus Franz, like Hamlet, tries and fails to assume his father's image; thus Nina is tempted to become Arkadina, and Constantin to become Trigorin; thus Bolingbroke aspires to be king, while Richard tries hard to be Bolingbroke; thus Miss Julie and her valet, in Strindberg's play, change places and social roles; thus Oedipus, who wants to achieve a truthful vision of life, ends up as blind as Teiresias, the eyeless prophet he scorned. I am not yet convinced that Sjöberg's theory is watertight, but I am quite certain that our theatre needs more minds like his. Even one more would do.

No plush in the Warsaw theatres, no gilt or cupids, no fancy prosceniums, and indeed one should not expect them. The departing Germans left behind them a wilderness, destroying all but four per cent. of the original buildings; out of ancestral piety the Poles reconstructed the main thoroughfare, Nowy Swiat, just as Canaletto had painted it, and painfully erected a perfect replica of the Old City, stone by stone and façade by façade—a labour of restoration without parallel in our time.

But elsewhere in the rebuilding, beauty perforce retired in favour of function, and the new theatres went up like concert-halls, aptly matching the concert-hall attentiveness of Polish audiences. They went up in large numbers, these lofty machines for staging plays and keeping spectators warm; apart from three children's theatres and as many devoted to satire, Warsaw today has eleven legitimate playhouses, several of which operate on more than one stage.

A little of their architectural anonymity has rubbed off on the productions. Since the death, some years ago, of the veteran Leon Schiller, no director of the first magnitude has arisen; men of talent abound, but none of them has developed a markedly individual style. (Some curious conventions universally prevail: the use, for instance, of follow-spots to pick out the stars, and the tradition, even in realistic plays, that all drinks served on stage must be imaginary.) The most admired of the younger players, Gustaw Holoubek, is a dry, alert, Brechtian performer of racing intelligence, and I can understand why Jan Kott, the foremost Polish critic, describes him as 'the most modern actor I have ever seen'; but what in Holoubek is deliberate restraint becomes in others a sort of non-committal aridity, and I felt a pervasive coolness, a failure to project specific emotions, that even my ignorance of the language could not wholly explain.

Technically, the general standard of performance is on a par with that of the very best German *Stadttheater*; but one is always conscious that in Warsaw a play is primarily a statement to be made, and only secondarily an emotional experience to be shared. According to a famous Polish philosopher, sentimentality lies not in feeling moved but in *liking* to feel moved. I can think of no vice that the Warsaw theatre is less likely to encourage. In the productions I saw, it was through décor that individuality most strongly asserted itself; through sculptured objects, abstract panels, mobile screens and dangling traceries, usually shown in silhouette against an enveloping sky—usually, too, designed by Jan Kosinski, an emperor in a field where most of his English colleagues are forced to behave like cringing suppliants.

The great thing about the Polish theatre, however, is not how it looks but what it acts. This seesaw country offers a variety of plays unequalled behind the Iron Curtain and certainly unapproached in Britain. In recent seasons Warsaw has seen works by Beckett, Brecht, Miller, Williams, Osborne, Ionesco, Wilder, Anouilh, Delaney, Sartre and the best contemporary Russians, plus a lavish sampling of the classics from Sophocles to Shaw. For anyone who speaks Polish, Warsaw is the ideal place to take a rush course in world drama. I append my notes on the principal theatres:

(a) The Polski, Poland's Comédie Française, where everyone applauds after familiar arias, dramatic points melodramatically made, and the heroic expression of noble sentiments. Here I sat through four hours of Schiller's *Don Carlos*, a Spanish tragedy composed of themes borrowed from *Hamlet* and *Phèdre*, with clever settings, a forthright and flamboyant *jeune premier* (Stanislaw Jasiukiewicz), and a rare display of honeyed crooning by Nina Andrycz as a distracted queen. In private life Mme Andrycz is the wife of Poland's Prime Minister, which may account for the fact that she behaves on stage less like an actress playing a part than a hostess holding a reception.

On the same theatre's second stage I saw *The Apple Cart*, a slick production that began with the gates of Buckingham Palace parting to disclose an anteroom, photographed in monochrome; through a hole in the photograph one looked out on a prospect of photographed garden. Andrzej Munk, the director, came to the theatre by way of the cinema; a similar progress has been followed by Andrzej Wajda, who lately absented himself from the movies to direct *Two for the Seesaw* at a tiny theatre-in-the-round.

(*b*) The Dramatyczny (Dramatic) Theatre, probably Warsaw's best. This is one of three playhouses built into the huge, wedding-cake, presentation-clock Palace of Culture that was Russia's gift to the Poles. Here I saw Dürrenmatt's *The Visit* performed with much stricter fidelity to the text than the romanticised London production, from which one would never have guessed that the heroine was meant to have an artificial arm and a wooden leg.

Two nights later there was *Le Diable et le Bon Dieu*, with Mr Holoubek in the exorbitant role of Goetz. Sartre's play is a full-scale assault on idealism. Goetz, a mercenary warrior in sixteenth-century Germany, has dedicated his life to absolute evil; when he tries to follow absolute good, nothing results but greater evil. Finally, realising that both courses are impracticable, he declares: 'I accept my share of evil to inherit my share of good', and takes command of a peasants' army. The conclusion is scarcely novel, but the path whereby Sartre reaches it is full of philosophical surprises; beside this master of dialectic, Shaw looks like a children's conjurer attempting to challenge Houdini.

I have left until last the new Polish plays, of which I saw two. One of them, staged at the Contemporary Theatre, was Leon Kruczkowski's *The First Days of Freedom*, a turgid tract with a war-time background. A broad-minded Polish officer, liberated from a Nazi prison camp, offers protection to a German girl who has been raped by one of his compatriots; in a moment of crisis she betrays him, and he is forced to shoot her. The liberal, in other words, must act illiberally for the sake of the greater good. The Warsaw intellectuals interpret the play as a Stalinist apologia it is also transfixingly trite, and a powerful incitement to slumber.

Kartoteka (The Card Index), at the Dramatic Theatre, is a much safer guide to the attitudes of the Polish *avant-garde*. Tadeusz Rosewicz, the author, has clearly learned from Kafka, Beckett and Ionesco. His hero, a classically alienated young drifter, sprawls on a bed in a gutter. He is visited by people from his past—an uncle, a faded ex-mistress, his parents, his wife—and figures symbolic of the present, including a conformist writer who sits up and begs like a dog. None of them can persuade him to get out of bed; since Poland's apparent rebirth in the autumn of 1956, there are no causes worth fighting for, no aims worth attaining. When a reporter asks him what his ambitions are, he bleakly replies: 'You came too late.'

The bitter hilarity of this piece is echoed in the work of Slawomir Mrozek, the most highly regarded of the younger Polish playwrights. Mrozek's *Police*, written in 1958, deals with a Ruritanian police-state in which authority has become self-defeatingly efficient. The people conform so sincerely that *agents-provocateurs* are beaten up by angry crowds whenever they shout anti-Government slogans. There is even an old lady who implores the security officials to search her house at least once a month because it makes her feel wanted. Mr Mrozek goes on to show us what happens when the police, threatened with redundancy, employ one of their own agents to throw a bomb at a general.

Plays of this kind are rare in Poland, and getting rarer. In the past twelve months, the censorship has stiffened, morally as well as politically; *The Hostage*, as I write, has been banned because its setting, a brothel, offends the Catholic Church. To mix a metaphor, the thaw is over and the heat is on.

Revisiting the Berliner Ensemble—a journey all theatre fanatics should make at least once a year—I find few changes. The round, red neon sign still twirls like an antic halo on the roof of Brecht's little playhouse by the Spree. Inside, the great revolving stage still spins for Mother Courage, of which role, last week, I saw Helene Weigel give her four-hundredth performance since the Ensemble was founded twelve years ago.

When I say that this piece of acting is earthy, you may imagine something plodding and laborious; but Frau Weigel's earthiness is light and springlike, even skipping and so utterly devoid of personal assertiveness that the life of the character appears to derive from the wares she handles and the trade she plies.

Her performance, in short and as ever, is devotedly Brechtian; it is not as an individual, separable from history and social circumstance, that we recognise Mother Courage, but as the owner of a broken-down canteen wagon at a particular time in a particular place. She works, therefore she is. Her function determines her loyalties, her friendships, her loathings and her blind, unwitting drive towards calamity; it is her love of bargaining, not any lack of maternal affection, that causes the death of her elder son, who is executed while she haggles over the amount of money necessary to save him. What Brecht prescribed, his widow, Frau Weigel, embodies: the maxim that there is no such thing as a character ungoverned by a social context.

A night or so later, I found the same tenet crisply enshrined in the great scene of the Pope's dressing in *The Life of Galileo*. At first, clad in his underwear and thus reduced to the stature of natural man, he is disposed to be lenient towards the heretics; but as the robes of authority ritually swathe his person, he becomes gradually aware of his social responsibilities, and ends up by turning Galileo over to the Inquisition.

A few of the company's best young actresses have lately drifted away, and their absence is sharply felt; otherwise, nothing crucial has changed, least of all in the theatre canteen, where one cannot distinguish the actors from the stagehands, the musicians, the electricians and the visiting journalists. When the Ensemble arrived in London in 1956 the press photographers flocked around the make-up girls and completely ignored the leading performers, who looked too much like ordinary human beings to be acceptable as celebrities. Last week the Ensemble embarked on a short tour of Eastern Germany, lending its home base— the Theater Am Schiffbauerdamm—to a guest company from the Deutsches Theater. The atmosphere backstage was radically different. The actors behaved like actors, the stage staff like stage staff. I suddenly thought of a remark that was once made to me by one of the Ensemble's younger directors: 'Working with Brecht,' he said 'makes you a connoisseur of reality.'

Little, then, has altered—some would say too little. In the past two years, the Ensemble has staged only two new productions. The first of them, which opened in the spring of 1959, was Brecht's *Resistible Rise of Arturo Ui*, a blank verse, comic strip exposition of Hitler's climb to power, set against a background of Chicago in the twenties; Arturo Ui— in other words Al Capone—represents the Führer. The performance of Ekkehard Schall as Ui-Hitler, dapper and dangerous, vulgar of mind yet physically Chaplinesque, driven half mad by the very idea of being contradicted, is at once hysterically funny and utterly repulsive; this is a model piece of Brechtian acting.

Ui was succeeded last April by *The Threepenny Opera*; its director, Erich Engel, was responsible for the original production, which was presented at the same theatre in 1928. The customers are pouring in—rather, one suspects, to hear Weill's score than Brecht's acid lyrics. Some of the show's essential bite gets lost in nostalgia; and one winces at the cuts that have been allowed to disfigure the last scene. Peachum's bitter reminder that real life contains few happy endings has been replaced by a naïve quatrain (composed, it is said, by Herr Engel himself) which knocks the rich but carefully avoids knocking reality.

A thought by way of postscript: could it not be argued that the whole of that Brechtian drama is a gigantic tribute to motherhood, and a blanket assault on matrimony? I am thinking not only of *Mother Courage, Frau Carrar*, and *Die Mutter*, but also of plays like *The Caucasian Chalk Circle*, in which the central relationship is between Grusha and the child she adopts; not to mention the *Good Woman of Setzuan*, who is far more of a mother than a mistress. Conversely, Brecht's fathers are always corrupt; Galileo, for example, prevents his daughter from marrying and turns her into a spy and informer. Brecht's male protagonists are usually drunks, cynics or compromisers; his heroines, such as St Joan of the stockyards and Simone Machard, are mostly instruments of salvation.

Did Brecht, as rumour insists, spurn his father and worship his mother? If so, it supports the old hypothesis that men who adore their mothers lean towards the Left, while those who idolise their fathers lean towards the Right. Mercy moves Left, and Authority moves Right. Brecht drove a car that was steered by Marx and fuelled by Freud; perhaps that is why, more than any other playwright of the century, he continues to hypnotise us.

(1961)

Beyond the Fringe, AT THE FORTUNE

The curtain rises on what might be a crypt, or perhaps an efficiently looted wine-cellar. It is anyway the kind of place into which the late Tod Slaughter used to lure his leading ladies, preparatory to hurling them down a disused sump. On the righthand side of the stage a flight of stone steps leads up to some sort of battlement. To the left of centre, and partly hidden beneath the platform, is a grand piano. Somewhere to the rear a flying buttress is distinctly visible.

Strewn (it is the only word) about the stage are three young men. One of them is gawky and angular, with large feet and carrot-coloured hair; he has wild eyes, and might just possibly be a Jew. (Later in the evening he is to deny this. 'I'm not a Jew,' he explains, 'I'm Jew-*ish*. I don't go the whole hog.') His real name is Jonathan Miller; I do not know what his other name is. Of his two companions, one looks like a well-kept minor poet, all lanky elegance and clearly as sly as they come. Like his friends, he is wearing casuals, ideal for lounging around crypts. To avoid confusion, we will call him Peter Cook.

The remaining member of the trio, better known (though only slightly better) as Alan Bennett, has spectacles, flaxen hair and the beginnings of a lantern jaw. With his kindly, puzzled face, he resembles a plain-clothes friar, badly in need of a tonsure. What he and his companions are doing in the cellar is immediately obvious: they are doing nothing. A right crew, one murmurs to oneself, of layabouts. Half a minute passes in silence, which worries them not at all. They shift easily, not uneasily, in their semi-sleep.

All of a sudden, there enters a smaller young man with twinkling dark eyes and twinkling dark hair, later identified as Dudley Moore. Seating himself at the piano, he plays the national anthem, and briskly departs. The others, who have leapt to attention, lapse once more into inattention. Idly, and a little querulously, they discuss the mystery pianist, and his habit of coming in every few minutes to play the national anthem. It emerges that he belongs to the Moscow State Circus. They resolve to win him over to the Western way of life by teaching him to blow a raspberry whenever Mr Khrushchev's name is mentioned. Soon afterwards the musician reappears; and before long all four of them are busily engaged in blowing rhythmic raspberries at Mr Macmillan. Plainly, someone has bungled, though in what way I cannot now remember.

The entire scene lasts only a few minutes; I have described it at such length and in such detail because it is the exordium of *Beyond the Fringe* which I take to be the funniest revue that London has seen since the Allies dropped the bomb on Hiroshima. Future historians may well thank me for providing them with a full account of the moment when English comedy took its first decisive step into the second half of the twentieth century.

The show began as a late-night experiment at last year's Edinburgh Festival, since when it has been shrewdly revised and much expanded. Only four men are involved, and they are the authors of all they perform. The set is unchanged throughout. Among other marvels, Mr Miller gives us a hearty, broadminded vicar, exhorting his lads to 'get the violence off the streets and into the churches where it belongs'; a squirming teacher of linguistic philosophy, frenetically distinguishing between 'why-questions' and 'how-questions'; and an implacable African politician, whom Mr Miller mocks with the probing intensity that an equal deserves. More seriously (the show is nothing if not morally committed), he appears as a condemned man, persistently asking the question we would all ask in that extremity: 'will it hurt?'

Mr Moore satirises folk-singers, fashionable composers, and the collaboration of Peter Pears and Benjamin Britten; during the interval, he crops up in the orchestra pit, tinkling away like a local incarnation of Erroll Garner. Mr Cook, meanwhile, qualifies at least thrice for the revue anthologies: once as a Beaverbrook journalist, nervously protesting that he has not ditched his liberal principles, and proudly declaring that he still dares, when drunk, to snigger at his employer; again as the Prime Minister, casually tearing up a letter from an old-age pensioner; and again as a Pinteresque outcast who would have liked to be a judge, if he had only had enough Latin. 'The trappings of extreme poverty', says Mr Cook in this characterisation, 'are *rotten*.'

Mr Bennett, in manner the mildest of the quartet, is perhaps the most pungent in effect. His man-to-man chat about Dr Verwoerd ('a bit of a rough diamond') and his opponents ('crypto-Socialists') in the Foreign Office is wickedly accurate; and one will not readily forget the oleaginous blandness with which Mr Bennett delivers a sermon on the text: 'My brother Esau is an hairy man, but I am a smooth man.'

I have omitted the collective numbers, among them a devastating attack on civil defence, and the only successful parody of Shakespeare that I have ever heard. Certainly, *Beyond the Fringe* lacks a great deal. It has no slick coffee-bar scenery, no glib one-line blackouts, no twirling dancers in tight trousers, no sad ballets for fisherwomen clad in fishnet stockings, no saleable Kitsch. For these virtues of omission we must all be grateful; but it can be justly urged against the show that it is too parochial, too much obsessed with BBC voices and BBC attitudes, too exclusively concerned with taunting the accents and values of John Betjeman's suburbia. *Beyond the Fringe* is anti-reactionary without being wholeheartedly progressive. It goes less far than one could have hoped, but immeasurably farther than one had any right to expect.

(1961)

Parenthesis on Tragedy

Tragedy has been dying for a long time now; the process was already far advanced when Nietzsche wrote *The Birth of Tragedy*; and the form has since had numerous obituarists. One of the most persuasive is George Steiner, whose post-mortem, *The Death of Tragedy*, appeared earlier this year. Mr Steiner points out that three principal mythologies —Greek, Christian and Marxist—have shaped 'the imaginative habits and practices of Western civilisation'. Of these, he concludes, none is 'naturally suitable to a revival of tragic drama. The classic leads to a dead past. The metaphysics of Christianity and Marxism are anti-tragic. That, in essence, is the dilemma of modern tragedy.'

A look at the postwar landscape suggests that Mr Steiner is right. Tragedy—the re-enactment of stories wherein men pass through anguish and are destroyed by forces they neither comprehend nor control— barely exists, except in pinchbeck *simulacra*. *Death of a Salesman*, for example, is not a tragedy; its catastrophe depends entirely on the fact that the company Willy Loman works for has no pensions scheme for its employees. What ultimately destroys Willy is economic injustice, which is curable, as the ills that plague Oedipus are not. Radical social reforms are inimical to the tragic sense, since they offer alternatives to defeat; hence the classic Marxist position, implied in the title of Vishnevsky's celebrated play, *The Optimistic Tragedy*.

There is today hardly an aspect of human suffering (outside the realm of medicine) for which politics, psychiatry and environmental psychology cannot offer at least a *tentative* solution. Powerfully helped by the rationalist crusade against belief in the supernatural, the assumption that man is capable of moulding his destiny has become the *idée reçue* of modern drama—the essential common ground between playwright and audience. In serious plays of the more ambitious sort, the result has been that protagonists who survive, such as Galileo and Luther, have tended to replace protagonists who don't.

Comedy, meanwhile, has occupied the territory that tragedy has vacated. Instead of the cosmic imprecations of Oedipus and Lear, we have the macabre clowning of Ionesco and Beckett, both of whom employ farcical devices to express a view of life as grimly deterministic as any Greek's. Venereal disease, in Ibsen a tragic and doomed affliction, becomes outrageously funny on the lips of Lenny Bruce, the sourest of the new American comedians. 'Sick' humour invites us to laugh at subjects like racial persecution, physical disabilities and mental deformity. In *Amédée* Ionesco uses a corpse as his principal comic prop; and *Beyond the Fringe* jests ferociously about nuclear war. Comedy on one level or another has distinguished all the productions I best remember from Theatre Workshop and the Royal Court: Behan, Delaney, Frank Norman, Nigel Dennis, N. F. Simpson and the early Osbornes.

What with Harold Pinter, Keith Waterhouse and Willis Hall on the sidelines, I think it safe to predict that satire, irony, gallows-humour and other mutations of the comic spirit will be the guiding forces of our theatre in the coming years. Tragedy, with its traditional respect for hierarchies and its passion for bloody *dénouements*, has little to say to a rebellious generation obsessed by the danger of imminent mega-deaths.

(1961)

Camelot, BY ALAN JAY LERNER AND FREDERICK LOEWE, AT THE MAJESTIC THEATRE, NEW YORK
An Evening with Mike Nichols and Elaine May, AT THE GOLDEN THEATRE, NEW YORK

Here and there, gold shines amid the Broadway dross. There is more than a trace of it in *Camelot*, which has been generally sniffed at. A famous American critic told me that he had found it 'about as exciting as a Christmas card arriving three days after New Year's Eve'; and when the curtain rose on a vista of snow-spangled trees and a faery castle, I sighed inwardly, knowing what to expect. Yet in time my interest deepened. The show is unabashed pantomime; but it is adult pantomime of an unusually sympathetic kind, through which there runs a vein of quite sensible idealism. We are to watch an earthly paradise destroyed by malice and by that archaic code of honour which Falstaff refuted.

Arthur, the young king, sets out to create a civilisation without wars or the provincial loyalties that provoke them; the Round Table is an assembly of chivalric equals, bound by oath to the preservation of peace through justice.

All goes well with this primitive United Nations (the analogy is clearly intentional) until Lancelot, the perfect knight and model of chivalry, falls in love with Guinevere. Though agonised, and tempted to violence, the king decides to take no action; but his hand is forced by the machinations of Mordred, who rouses the knights against Lancelot, and eventually, wearily, Arthur consents to war. On the eve of battle, however, he instructs his youngest follower to desert, so that the pacific dream of Camelot may not be wholly forgotten. The tale, drawn from T. H. White's *The Once and Future King*, is shrewdly retold by Alan Jay Lerner; the book and lyrics are garnished with whimsy, but rarely to excess; and there is much honesty in the playing. Since last we saw her, Julie Andrews has matured, with no loss of tenderness; and Richard Burton, of the furrowed face and accusing eyes, makes a peerless king. His singing is bold rather than beautiful, but his stage presence has that intangible quality of weight, as distinct from bulk, by which great actors always reveal themselves. This is a majestic performance. The show is sabotaged by the ineffable banality of Frederick Loewe's score, all sugar and fatty degeneration. Extending Bertrand Russell's civil disobedience campaign to the arts, I suggest that we should all lie down outside Mr Loewe to be carried away, limp, in police wagons.

The only successful Broadway show that is quiet and small is *An Evening with Mike Nichols and Elaine May*. Mr Nichols is slim, blond and unconcerned, possessed of a freezing, fading smile; Miss May is hopeful and vulnerable, the eager epitome of virginal insecurity. Together, they work like cat and mouse. I think of Miss May as an edgy Englishwoman, wearing her husband's hat to commit adultery; as a Tennessee Williams heroine instructing her lover to 'come here and shave my legs'; and as a gushing starlet who mindlessly remarks: 'The Bible is something we could all do a lot of with more.' And I recall Mr Nichols as a Southern playwright, as a name-dropping interviewer ('Russell's not like a lot of your philosophers. By that I mean he's not pushy'); and as a little boy, confined to bed with a cold, who challenges his sister to join him in the Pirandello game. They begin by playing house, which swiftly leads them into mutual accusations of indolence and drunkenness; before long, the game becomes reality, and we see the grown-up Nichols and May clawing at each other in what appears to be genuine antagonism. A ripple of consternation unsettles the audience. Suddenly:

'What are we doing?' says Miss May. 'We're doing Pirandello,' says Mr Nichols: and both beamingly bow.

(1961)

Othello, BY WILLIAM SHAKESPEARE, AT STRATFORD-ON-AVON

Franco Zeffirelli's production of *Othello* had a nightmare opening performance—four and a quarter hours of slowly mounting (and elaborately mounted) confusion. The Moor lost his beard half-way through a crucial scene; Iago was so stricken with *trac* that towards the end he and the text were virtually strangers, and lines like 'Why did he did so?' alternated with grosser oddities, such as the Ancient's startling announcement, early in the last act, that Cassio had died.

Meanwhile the workers backstage, unaccustomed to scene changes more complicated than those required by a permanent set, were fighting an unequal battle with the multitude and the magnitude of Zeffirelli's designs.

There were pillars, grilles and battlements to be flown in and out; gigantic doors, thunderously embossed, to be erected; vast waterfalls of stone steps to be mantled and dismantled. Not since the heyday of Charles Kean and his Shakespearean spectaculars has more been asked of an English stage staff in a classical production; and the result, inevitably, was a long, glum, attention-destroying pause after nearly every scene. As the sixth or seventh monumental vista appeared out of the womb of darkness, peopled by actors robed and grouped to resemble a recently cleaned Veronese picture, a left-wing friend sitting beside me grumbled in a whisper that this was the kind of thing that had ruined the Soviet theatre. Given the use of Zeffirelli's décor, a respectable opera company could send two productions out on tour, and still have enough left over for the Verdi *Otello*.

Much that went wrong last Tuesday will assuredly be righted—the flyaway whiskers, the scrambled words, the bungled scene-shifting. Sheer volume of scenery does not in itself offend me, as long as it is not allowed to impede the action; nor do I count it against Zeffirelli that he has chosen for *Othello* a style more ceremonial and stately than he employed in his fiery resurrection of *Romeo and Juliet* at the Old Vic. What is incurable at Stratford has to do with congenital miscasting; or, more precisely, with a misconception on Zeffirelli's part of the capacities of his two leading players.

The production was reverently designed as a showcase for classical actors. The result is more of a showing-up: the actors are dwarfed by the production. Ian Bannen's weedy, snickering Iago has some effective moments, notably when imparting intimations of homosexuality; bussing Roderigo, draping Desdemona's handkerchief over his head like a bridal veil, stroking Othello's hair as he lies in his fit; but these details are never made part of a coherent psychological pattern. This Iago is all warts and no face. His voice, light in tone and thin of texture, combines with that of John Gielgud, as Othello, to reduce the great jealousy scene, which Shakespeare scored for brass, to a viola duet.

Gielgud himself is quite simply over-parted. In his hands Othello dwindles into a coffee-stained Leontes; instead of a wounded bull, dangerous despite its injuries, we have an heraldic eagle with its wings harmlessly clipped. From some of the quieter passages ('Here is my journey's end', for example), Sir John extracts a wonderful music of resignation; but his voice has no body, no nakedness, no explosive power, and few more blatant falsehoods have ever been uttered on the English stage than when this Othello declares that he lacks 'those soft parts of conversation that chamberers have'.

Physically, the performance is jerky and puppetlike, laced in with knots of inhibition that persist even in the throes of epilepsy; one gets few whiffs of grandeur. It is really ironic. The theatrical Establishment predicted that Gielgud the classicist would burst through the limitations of Zeffirelli's realism. Instead, Zeffirelli's classicism has exposed the limitations of Sir John's. One's main regret, in fact, is that the director has failed to extend the actor's range. Whether intentionally or not, Newton Blick's Brabantio looks intensely Jewish; this is a performance not to be missed by anyone who wonders how Shylock might have reacted if Jessica had married a Negro.

(1961)

The Connection, BY JACK GELBER, AT THE DUKE OF YORK'S; *The Devils*, BY JOHN WHITING, AT THE ALDWYCH; *The Changeling*, BY THOMAS MIDDLETON, AT THE ROYAL COURT

It has been a week of violence in the theatre, of physical agonies both subtle and strident. In John Whiting's *The Devils* we had a man's bones crushed in torture, a burning at the stake, and the forcible administration of a clyster in the cloister. The screams of flagellated madmen rang through *The Changeling*, by Middleton and Rowley, which also involved three murders, one suicide and the amputation of a finger from a corpse. Finally, in *The Connection*, Jack Gelber invited us to witness a heroin injection and a bursting boil.

Mr Gelber alone succeeded in rousing the audience to reciprocal violence. He was recently quoted as having said, *à propos* of his play: 'The conflict of attitudes between audience and players—rather than the conflict on stage—is the focal point.' It was bitterly focal last Wednesday night. The galleryites were first baffled, next nettled, and ultimately driven to riot by the gall of an author who had paid them the compliment of assuming that the behaviour of human beings in a desperate extremity would be enough to ensure their attention, if not their respect.

The play deals with junkies, who tend to be self-absorbed and arrogant; the gallery interpreted their arrogance and self-absorption as deliberate insults. The life of a junkie alternates between long periods of nervous depression and short, sweet sessions of peace, induced by shots of heroin; the gallery saw nothing in this beyond a conspiracy to bore them, a plot to deprive them of plot. The last straw was Mr Gelber's refusal to sentimentalise his characters, to allow them the faintest vestige of self-pity; the tramps in *Waiting for Godot* were at least pathetic, whereas these people didn't seem to care whether they were loved, loathed or even tolerated. Forbidden to condescend, unwooed by charm, asked merely to observe, the gallery rebelled.

In a sense one cannot blame it. *The Connection* was born in a small, off-Broadway theatre that ideally suited its intimate, close-up technique; it is a true minority play, making special demands that far outstrip the normal capability of a West End audience. It fits into the Duke of York's about as snugly as a Bartok quartet would fit into Harringay Arena.

Reduced to essentials, it is a play about people who do not want to be in a play at all; lost people, with no interest in being found. They are vagrant addicts, gathered together at the behest of a writer named Jaybird and a manager named Jim Dunn, both of whom explain from the stage that the aim of the exercise is to give the assembled junkies free rein to improvise on a chosen theme. They will be paid in heroin, and the experiment will be filmed by a professional cameraman and his assistant, who promptly materialise from the auditorium. But the cast will not cooperate; they are interested in nothing except the whereabouts of Cowboy, their 'connection', the source of the next and all-important fix. The author tries to talk them into behaving as characters in plays are supposed to behave; the cameraman begs them to act like actors; but life is not so easily cajoled into becoming art. The junkies go their own way—Sam the rambling raconteur, Solly the stoic philosopher,

Ernie the unemployable musician, and Leach the nagging hypochondriac, plagued by an obdurate boil. They communicate with each other only under pressure, as if confined by mutual disenchantment in separate cells of the same prison.

The play the gallery saw last Wednesday was not exactly the play I admired in New York a year ago; some of the actors had grown self-indulgent, especially in the matter of pauses. Nor was it the play that Mr Gelber wrote; soon after the gallery butted in, several members of the cast panicked, and the number of lines they added to the text would probably equal the number they omitted.

Even so, I doubt if I shall ever forget Garry Goodrow as Ernie, wincing beneath the intrusive glare of the cameraman's spotlights. For sheer, microscopic realism, Mr Goodrow and his principal colleagues—Warren Finnerty, Jerome Raphel, James Anderson and Carl Lee—make up an ensemble that has no rival in England.

The subject of *The Devils* is the contagious hysteria that broke out in 1632 among the Ursuline nuns of Loudun and led, eventually, to the incineration of Urbain Grandier, a local priest whom they falsely accused of having lured them to traffic with Satan. Most of the girls were impoverished noblewomen with a great deal of repressed sexuality and no particular talent for religion; their prioress, the youthful Sister Jeanne, was further handicapped by physical deformity. Grandier, a notorious lecher, obsessed all of them, though they had never met him, and their frustrations boiled over when he refused Sister Jeanne's invitation to become their spiritual director. The prioress yelled rape; her flock followed suit; and their erotic fantasies were mistaken for diabolic possession. After savage but unavailing torture, Grandier went to the stake, still asserting his innocence. Whenever a theatrical character is put to death in circumstances of appalling injustice and ferocity, it is an even chance that the play is about religion.

Mr Whiting tells his ghastly tale in a series of brief, pointed scenes that add up to a mosaic of martyrdom. His style is laconic, darkly tinged with misanthropy; language like this has too long been absent from our stage. Those aphorisms steeped in vinegar, those phrases with tails like scorpions, could have come from only one pen; and there are speeches of the most limpid tenderness to soften the prevalent mood of Swiftian distaste.

Yet somehow the last act, for all its piling up of agony, fails to agonise; we end up impressed but unmoved, reflecting how much more powerfully Arthur Miller handled a similar theme in *The Crucible*.

What goes wrong? For one thing, Mr Whiting's sense of humour, which tempts him to make anachronistic jokes, and spurs Max Adrian to play the exorcist as a lightweight comic caricature. For another, Mr Whiting's conception of Grandier, which will astonish anyone familiar with Aldous Huxley's version of the story. Mr Huxley's Grandier is sharp-tongued, egotistical and highly contentious; Mr Whiting's, by contrast, is a colourless fellow, weary of life, anxious to embrace the hereafter, and replete with enough wry, rueful wisdom to sink a masterpiece. Nor are matters helped by the fact that he and Sister Jeanne never set eyes on each other; it is good history, and may have appealed to that part of Mr Whiting's temperament which has always shrunk from emotional confrontations, but it leaves one feeling theatrically cheated.

In one of his Hamburg essays, Lessing remarks: 'The first tragedy that deserves the name of Christian has beyond doubt still to be written. I mean a play in which the Christian interests us as a Christian. But is such a piece even possible? Is not the character of a true Christian something quite untheatrical?' He was thinking primarily of Christian meekness and humility, and the dramatic convention whereby all Christians are readymade martyrs; but he was also hinting that, unless one believes in an after-life of reward or retribution, one can never fully identify oneself with a protagonist of whose whole existence that belief is the motive force. Sooner or later, sympathy falters. Something of the sort happened to me in *The Devils*. Tiring of the tortures, and tiring of hating the torturers, I found myself with little left to feel, save perhaps a vague suspicion, finally mounting to certainty, that a squalid footnote to the history of superstition had been dignified beyond its deserts by an extremely gifted writer.

Tony Richardson, not formerly my favourite director, has done a firstrate job on *The Changeling*. The play is a Spanish tragedy, and to furnish it with sets and costumes Mr Richardson has cleverly consulted Goya. The great scenes stand up as firmly as ever. Beatrice, a hidalgo's daughter, hires a servant called De Flores to rid her of an unwanted suitor, only to discover, when the crime has been committed, that the murderer's fee is her virginity. She protests that her rank makes the liaison unthinkable, to which De Flores replies, in a speech that anticipates existentialism by several centuries:

> Pish! fly not to your birth, but settle you
> In what the act has made you; you're no more now.
> You must forget your parentage to me;
> *You are the deed's creature . . .*

Robert Shaw, bearded and facially scarred, plays the role with a kind of bruised devotion, looking like a cynical picador. One understands why Beatrice prefers his company to that of her pretty new husband; a villain who shares one's guilt is inevitably more attractive than a hero convinced of one's innocence. Mary Ure is a somewhat feeble Beatrice, tripping across the stage as if her surname was Lillie, and altogether resembling a meringue miscast as a hamburger. The subplot in the madhouse comes off surprisingly well, thanks to the leering earthiness of Norman Rossington and the busty insolence of Zoe Caldwell. Not since Peter Brook's *Venice Preserv'd* has a minor classic been so excitingly revived.

(1961)

The Dumb Waiter, BY HAROLD PINTER, AT THE THEATRE ROYAL, STRATFORD-ATTE-BOWE

The Pinter vogue continues to spread. Not since Christopher Fry in the late forties has an English playwright so powerfully influenced the style of his contemporaries. Mr Pinter has a whole school of dramatists speaking in his very accents; his is the new small talk, and very small, on lips stiffer than his, it can sound.

Its distinguishing features can be easily listed. First, the aimlessly iterated phrases: what I tell you three times is art. Next, the sudden use of an outlandish word in a sentence otherwise drab and demotic. (No wonder Coward is a Pinter admirer; he played similar tricks with upper-class idiom in the twenties.) And thirdly, a calculated gulf between the dramatic situation—usually one of undefined threat—and the language, numb and inexpressive, in which the characters respond to it.

The trouble with Mr Pinter's people is not that they cannot communicate with each other but that they leave the vital things unspoken, deliberately missing the points they are too scared to face or even to imagine; and what is left unsaid often erupts, at the end, into violence. Mr Pinter's ear ranks with Jenkin's and Van Gogh's among the great ears of history: his characters are robots whose conversation is so intimately real that it reconciles us to the frequent unreality of their behaviour. Menaced by nameless terrors, they chat idly about bus routes; but when he is writing at his best—as in *The Caretaker*—with a strict formal shape and a strong emotional impetus, they cease to be merely odd and become at once funny and frightening.

Last week brought a ham-fisted production of Mr Pinter's *The*

Dumb Waiter, listening to which with half an ear I suddenly realised that I knew the source of the Pinter style. Consider this colloquy between the two killers:

BEN: When he sees you behind him—
GUS: Me behind him—
BEN: And me in front of him—
GUS: And you in front of him—
BEN: He'll feel uncertain—
GUS: Uneasy.
BEN: He won't know what to do.
GUS: So what will he do?
BEN: He'll look at me and he'll look at you.
GUS: We won't say a word.'
BEN: We'll look at him.
GUS: We won't say a word.
BEN: He'll look at us.
GUS: And we'll look at him.
BEN: Nobody says a word.

And compare it with this:

SWEENEY: Nobody came
           And nobody went
           But he took in the milk and he paid the rent.
SWARTS: What did he do?
           All that time, what did he do?
SWEENEY: What did he do! What did he do?
           That don't apply.
           Talk to live men about what they do . . .
           I gotta use words when I talk to you
           But if you understand or if you don't
           That's nothing to me and nothing to you . . .

In *Sweeney Agonistes*, too, we note the same lurking violence ('I knew a man once did a girl in . . .'). Who would have thought that Mr Pinter shared a literary progenitor with Mr Prufrock!

(1961)

Luther, by John Osborne, at the Théâtre des Nations

Why, it was asked on all sides at the opening night of *Luther* in Paris, should John Osborne have wanted to write a play about the founder of Protestantism? I can think of a number of reasons that might have drawn the two men together across the centuries.

Luther in Christendom, like Mr Osborne in the microcosm of the theatre, was a stubborn iconoclast of lowly birth, resentful of authority and blind to compromise. Rather than retract a syllable of his writings he would defy the Pope; one is reminded of Mr Osborne's brushes with the Lord Chamberlain. To his surprise and alarm, Luther caused an international tumult with his attacks on indulgences, and was hailed as a popular hero by people of whose causes he thoroughly disapproved: is there not something here that might speak to the author of *Look Back in Anger*, embarrassed to find himself dubbed an apostle of social revolution when in fact, like Luther, he preached nothing but revolutionary individualism?

'In many ways, life began for Luther all over again when the world ... forced him into the role of rebel, reformer and spiritual dictator': thus Erik H. Erikson, the author of *Young Man Luther*, a psychiatric study that could have served as the germinal text for Mr Osborne's play. Dr Erikson, like Mr Osborne, seizes on the fact that Luther was plagued throughout his life by constipation, and habitually expressed himself in anal imagery. Oppressed and frequently beaten by his father, he became 'inhibited and reined in by a tight retentiveness'; the celebrated 'revelation in the tower', wherein he first felt himself flooded and illuminated by the Holy Spirit, took place while he was in the privy—'a revelation', Dr Erikson adds, 'is always associated with a repudiation, a cleansing...'

Once he had solved the riddle of the sphincter, his way was free to solve the problem of man's relationship with divinity. To some extent (for he was a great beer drinker) Luther made a god of his stomach, but to a much larger extent he made a stomach of his God. To break wind in the face of Satan and the Pope became an obsession with this superb vernacular poet; in Dr Erikson's words, 'a transference had taken place from a parent figure to universal personages, and ... a central theme in this transference was anal defiance'.

This aspect of Luther, the neurotic haunter of lavatories, is brilliantly conveyed by Mr Osborne, and as brilliantly linked with the

Luther we all know—the fractious, self-lacerating monk who refused to concede that the Church could wash away his guilt, and thus bequeathed to us the chronic Angst of Protestantism. Nothing is more typical of Luther than the fact, omitted by Mr Osborne, that he commissioned a series of woodcuts in which Rome was portrayed as a prostitute giving rectal birth to a swarm of misshapen demons; in this he is closer to Bosch than to Calvin. It was beguiling to observe, at last Thursday's première, that the lines by which a presumably sophisticated audience was most shocked were nearly all direct translations from the hero's own works.

In form, the play is sedulously Brechtian, an epic succession of *tableaux* conceived in the manner of *Galileo*; and the graph of its development is likewise Galilean—a rebel against papist dogma publishes heresies, and is asked by velvet-gloved officialdom to recant. The difference is that Luther rejects the demand; all the same, Mr Osborne's final scene is an obvious echo of Brecht's. The protagonist, having settled for domesticity, is seen smacking his lips over a good meal, conscious the while that he has betrayed the peasants who revolted in his name, just as Galileo betrayed the cause of scientific enlightenment. We are left with a powerful impression of a man who invented the idea of the individual conscience, responsible to no earthly authority, and was racked by his own invention, a man, as Cardinal Cajetan puts it, who hates himself and can only love others.

The language is urgent and sinewy, packed with images that derive from bone, blood and marrow; the prose, especially in Luther's sermons, throbs with a rhetorical zeal that has not often been heard in English historical drama since the seventeenth century, mingling gutter candour with cadences that might have come from the pulpit oratory of Donne. And it can readily swerve into comedy, as in the long harangue of the indulgence salesman, offering snake-bite remedies against the mortal nip of the serpent in Eden.

Always the play informs; one's reservation must be that it too seldom excites; the thrusting vigour of its style goes into exposition rather than action. Yet I count it (to burn a boat or two) the most eloquent piece of dramatic writing to have dignified our theatre since *Look Back in Anger*. The direction, by Tony Richardson, is simple and hieratic, and no finer Luther could be imagined than the clod, the lump, the infinitely vulnerable Everyman presented by Albert Finney, who looks, in his moments of pallor and lip-gnawing doubt, like a reincarnation of the young Irving, fattened up for some cannibal feast.

Julian Glover, Peter Bull and George Devine are the best of the lesser folk, and Jocelyn Herbert's décor is worthy, in its glowing restraint, of the Berliner Ensemble.

(1961)

Stop the World—I Want to Get Off, BY ANTHONY NEWLEY AND LESLIE BRICUSSE, AT THE QUEEN'S

One of the things that distinguish comedy today from comedy in the past is that today the comedians themselves tend to write it. Gone, increasingly, are the gagsmiths on whose lips the star would hang; instead of being spokesmen for committees, like Bob Hope or Jack Benny, the new clowns speak for themselves; and their craft, in consequence, has become more perilous and nerve-racked. In America, Mort Sahl, Lenny Bruce, Elaine May and Mike Nichols are of this breed; in England, Spike Milligan, and the four 'agile and mellifluous quodlibetarians' (to pluralise Max Beerbohm's phrase for Professor C. E. M. Joad) of *Beyond the Fringe*.

For this crack regiment Anthony Newley has now volunteered. In collaboration with Leslie Bricusse, he is responsible for the book, music and lyrics of *Stop the World—I Want to Get Off*, of which he is also, quite emphatically, the star. Nor, had the gallery booed, could he have exculpated himself by blaming the direction, since it was he who staged the show. He did not, of course, design it; after all, Sean Kenny was free, and it is universally agreed that the principal function of English stage design is to enable Mr Kenny to continue his momentous experiments in the use of surplus timber. Otherwise, the evening is Mr Newley's: his the laurels, his the thorns.

The verdict, I fear, must be thorns. From his past record (if not from his recent records) we know Mr Newley to be one of our brightest young performers, dapper and sly and capable of provoking a worried, modern kind of laughter. What perturbs me, in *Stop the World*, is the influence of those other Mr Newleys, the writer, the composer and the director: one man in his time plays many parts, but not all on the same night. The show concerns an average man named Mr Littlechap who marries the boss's daughter, gets rich, has affairs, enters politics, bags a peerage, and decides, as he dies, that he has led a selfish life. It all takes place in a circus tent, symbolising the human condition. To convey some idea of its quality, let me give you a list of the things without which, in the theatre, I can most easily do. They include:

(*a*) All plays in which circus tents symbolise the human condition (e.g.: *J.B.*).

(*b*) All protagonists with names like Mr Zero, Mr Adam, He, The Little Man and Mr Littlechap. To be theatrically interesting, Everyman must be Someone, not just Anyone.

(*c*) All mimes except Marcel Marceau. It was clear as soon as he shuffled in, pigeon-toed and baggy-trousered (a gait and garb that never varied), with a hopeless, prognathous grin on his white-painted face, that Mr Newley had been subjected to a massive overdose of Bip. When he spoke, one was startled; it was like being present at a miracle cure. In addition to walking without moving forwards, Mr Newley had the gall to end the show in the same foetal posture that M. Marceau adopts in the final moment of his most celebrated number—man's progress from birth to death.

(*d*) All plays in which the hero is represented as falling in love with the same eternal woman, who reappears throughout his life in various disguises (*vide* Terence Rattigan's *Who is Sylvia*?). In *Stop the World*, the Eve-figure has four identities; a Russian, a German, an American, and an Englishwoman called Evie. They are played by Anna Quayle, a Junoesque redhead who might, in happier circumstances, be extremely droll.

(*e*) All jokes about Russia that involve the mention of tractors.

(*f*) All puns except the very best. There is no excuse for horrors like 'a sour little Kraut' or 'the ig-Nobel Prize-winner'; and I hope I have now heard the last of the Steppes-steps homophone.

(*g*) All plays that carry political impartiality to the length of implying that there is no difference between Right and Left.

(*h*) All plays of which the director is also the protagonist.

(*i*) All plays of which the protagonist is also the author.

In sum, a sad, pretentious evening, visually monotonous and redeemed only by glimmers of potentiality from Mr Newley (that tinny, plaintive voice) and Miss Quayle. After this escapade, I hope Mr Bricusse will manage to persuade his talented partner to modify the demands of his ego. There were periods, especially in the second half, when one sensed an ominous coldness settling on the house; the audience, one felt, was sitting on its hands, while Mr Newley was sitting on the right hand of God.

(1961)

The Kitchen, BY ARNOLD WESKER, AT THE ROYAL COURT

Arnold Wesker has sometimes, and misleadingly, been likened to Clifford Odets; misleadingly, because his attitude towards working-class people is far less romantic (and hence less apt to plummet into disillusionment) than that of the young Odets, in whose hands the apathetic countryfolk of *Roots* would probably have been inspired by a fierce dedication to the cause of agrarian reform. A sounder transatlantic analogy would be with the early work of Eugene O'Neill; or so I decided after watching *The Kitchen*, the earliest known work of Mr Wesker.

As with O'Neill, the language is raw and demotic, engaged in a blindfold groping towards poetry; while from both writers one gets a sense of innocence betrayed, of outrage at the corrupting effect of mechanised urban life on human relationships and aspirations. O'Neill escapes to sea, Wesker to the countryside, but the lost paradise is not so easily regained; in *I'm Talking About Jerusalem*, mechanisation defeats idealism's attempt to return to simplicity.

The thronged, clangorous, ill-ventilated restaurant kitchen in which Mr Wesker's first play takes place is a metaphor for the dehumanising world of commercialism and mass-production; like O'Neill, he assumes that his audience is not shy of symbols. The mounting tumult that precedes the interval, with dishes flying, tempers fraying and cooks of half a dozen nations working and sweating together, is intimately reminiscent of the stokehole in *The Hairy Ape*, which O'Neill, the erstwhile sailor, knew at first hand, just as Mr Wesker, the former pastrycook, knows his kitchen. Instead of Yank, O'Neill's brutish protagonist, we have a mad-brained young German named Peter, who erupts in periodic outbursts of violence, the last of which moves him to slash his wrists with a meat-chopper. This final, self-destructive act is melodramatic and deplorably unmotivated; otherwise, Mr Wesker's play seems to me altogether more promising than *The Hairy Ape*, which was written (we may as well remember) when O'Neill was thirty-four, five years older than Mr Wesker is today.

The Kitchen achieves something that few playwrights have ever attempted: it dramatises work, the daily collision of man with economic necessity, the repetitive toil that consumes that large portion of human life which is not devoted to living. The vast, roaring stoves that dominate the bare stage also dominate the people who operate them; Cypriots, Cockneys, Germans, Italians, Frenchmen, Jamaicans and Irishmen, they are forced into uneasy fellowship by the fact of common employment.

In slack periods the truce is called off; usually the result is a quarrel, but sometimes peace breaks out, in such shapes as an impromptu dance, a sudden gesture of reconciliation, a fleeting awareness that a perspiring Jew and a perspiring German may have more in common with each other than with their employer. At one point Peter, the unbalanced hero, whom we are clearly to recognise as a frustrated artist, builds a triumphal arch out of pots, pans and a handful of flowers; having made this absurd and wonderful artifact, he challenges his colleagues to reveal their innermost dreams, to which they respond with visions that include money, sex, perfect friendship, dreamless sleep and a well-equipped radio workshop.

Inexorably, routine reasserts itself, and they swing back into the exhausting anonymous rhythms of their work. It is hard, taxing, complex work; and Mr Wesker never lets us forget, amid the clash of plates, and the cries of waitresses, that it is also, potentially, a minor form of art.

John Dexter's direction is flawless, rising at the end of the first half to a climactic lunch-hour frenzy that is the fullest theatrical expression I have ever seen of the laws of supply and demand. What mars the play is the fact that it gets nowhere; instead of ending, it stops; and this in turn is due to the fact that its central character is too vague and amorphous to provide a solid *point d'appui*. The youthful Olivier might perhaps have made something of Peter; as played by Robert Stephens, he is self-consciously histrionic, trapped in a quicksand and forever drawing our attention to the pathos with which he is sinking. The production lacks a centrepiece; instead of the *specialité de la maison*, we are fobbed off with spinach.

(1961)

A Breakthrough Breaks Down: 1961

In a week void of London *premières*, I scan the list of available productions and am shocked. So little, in ten years, seems to have changed. The Royal Court has arrived and survived, a beach-head for our splashing new wave; but one beach-head, it becomes chillingly clear, doesn't make a breakthrough.

A decade ago, roughly two out of three London theatres were inhabited by detective stories, Pineroesque melodramas, quarter-witted farces, debutante comedies, overweight musicals and unreviewable revues; the same is true today. The accepted new playwrights then were Fry, Eliot and Anouilh; of this threesome Anouilh is still represented on the playbills of London, and the other two have been replaced by Arnold Wesker (*The Kitchen*) and John Osborne (*Luther*).

As for Theatre Workshop, it is almost as if it had never been. Unknown in London ten years ago, and recently decapitated by the loss of Joan Littlewood, it has no West End memorial except what must by now be a fairly apathetic production of *Fings Ain't Wot They Used T'Be*. Theatrically, though not otherwise, Brendan Behan has been silent since *The Hostage*: Shelagh Delaney has not yet fulfilled the glowing promise of *A Taste of Honey*; and Alun Owen, all-conquering on television, failed to conquer Shaftesbury Avenue with *Progress to the Park*.

Harold Pinter's newest piece, *A Night Out*, was originally commissioned by, and performed on, television; and the flock of Pinter mimics—or *Pinteretti*, as I sometimes think of them—have made no impact at all on the theatre. Nor, if we are talking about public acclaim, has Mr Wesker, whom the West End persistently shuns. Our new school of regional actors has two leaders, of whom one, Albert Finney, can be seen in *Luther*, but only for a limited season, while the other, Peter O'Toole, is busy filming in Arabia.

Dispassionately eyed, the great proletarian upsurge of which we bragged so freely (and of which so many foreign critics wrote so enviously) looks very much like a frost. Its symbols are Willis Hall and Keith Waterhouse, the authors of *Billy Liar*—two working-class playwrights who owe their London success to a middle-class parlour farce.

Perhaps we expected too much; perhaps that is why the breakthrough broke down. In our rage against conventional theatre, we should have remembered the *caveat* of that incomparable critic, Trotsky:

> It is fundamentally wrong to oppose proletarian to bourgeois culture and art. Proletarian culture and art will never exist. The proletarian regime is temporary and transitory. Our revolution derives its historic significance and moral greatness from the fact that it lays the foundations for a classless society and for the first truly universal culture.

In other words, the worker's task is purely militant—to build a new society from which a new kind of art will emerge. Until then, we should not repine, we should even rejoice if working-class art shows signs of being influenced by the best of bourgeois culture. It was by publicly expressing sentiments like these that Trotsky hastened his expulsion from the Soviet Union. Too many of our younger playwrights have forgotten, in their passion for novelty of content, the ancient disciplines of style. Rightly determined to look beyond the drawing-room for their subject matter, they have poured the baby out with the bathwater. In the battle for content, form has been sacrificed.

What I look for in working-class drama is the sort of play that is not ashamed to assimilate and acknowledge the bourgeois tradition, which includes a multiplicity of styles, not all of them wholly despicable. Otherwise, the drift of writers towards television and the cinema will swell to flood proportions; dialogue composed in eavesdropped snippets will always be easier to write than dialogue orchestrated into acts. Moreover, I would remind aspiring prole satirists that the tone, background and terms of reference of *Beyond the Fringe*, the sharpest London revue I have ever seen, are entirely middle-class. To sum up, nothing is more crucially stupid than to deride the artistic achievements of a social class because one deplores its historical record.

Those achievements belong to the past. Between them and the work of people now living a link must be forged and maintained: between Strindberg and Osborne, Chekhov and Shelagh Delaney, Stanislavski and Joan Littlewood, Galsworthy and Wesker, Büchner and John Arden, and other such pairings. But these connections can rarely be made, since the opportunities for comparison so seldom arise. Lacking a National Theatre, London has no playhouse in which the best of world drama is constantly on tap, available for immediate ingestion by spectators of eclectic tastes. One function of such a theatre would be to bridge the gap between those elements of bourgeois theatre that lean towards the future and those elements of the new drama that extend a hand towards the past.

That is the ideal, and at present it is impracticable. One resorts to statistics. Last night the London theatre was to all intents and purposes cut off from history. Of thirty-four playhouses, only three were staging plays that were written more than ten years ago—*Dr Faustus*, at the Old Vic, *'Tis Pity She's a Whore*, at the Mermaid, and *The Rehearsal*, by Anouilh, at the Globe. This trio apart, the oldest play in London last night was Agatha Christie's *The Mousetrap*. I am all for modernity; but this is ridiculous.

The Blacks, BY JEAN GENET, AT THE ROYAL COURT

I cannot help suspecting that Jean Genet's *The Blacks* belongs to that large group of experimental plays which sound more like masterpieces in description than in performance.

It is based, like *Les Bonnes* and *Le Balcon*, on the recurrent Genetic idea that all human relationships are power relationships. There are those who dominate and those who are dominated; and the process whereby the two factions exchange roles corresponds to the systole and diastole of history. Life, in Genet's eyes, consists not so much of action and reaction as of crime and punishment, injury and revenge. From this harsh vision love is necessarily banished; it is a sign of weakness, a flag of surrender, an interruption in the deadly game.

Orphan, bastard, ex-convict and homosexual, Genet himself has a high stake in the game of retribution; he denies love with the cold, triumphant fury that distinguishes those to whom love has been denied. In Mr Clurman's phrase, he is 'a man who no longer permits himself the luxury of forgiveness'. All love corrupts, and to love one's enemy is at once a dereliction of duty and a form of suicide. Genet's plays are themselves acts of vengeance, directed against the bourgeois audience he detests.

His theme in *The Blacks* is the hatred of the Negro for the ruling Caucasian, which we may take to symbolise the hatred of all despised outsiders for the society that spurns them. A group of Negroes, wearing inelegant parodies of the evening clothes customary among whites, meet to re-enact the ritual murder of a white woman. The ceremony, we gather, is repeated nightly, and the participants take turns to impersonate the victim. The killer is ordered to exult in his blackness; he must feel no kinship with the slaughtered enemy, and the slightest hint that she attracted him, instead of inspiring total repulsion, is enough to brand him a traitor.

Meanwhile, overlooking the stage, there sits a tribunal representing colonial officialdom—a Queen, a Valet, a Judge, a Missionary and a Governor, all played by Negroes in deformed white masks. Ostensibly on hand to administer justice, they are finally brought down to face judgment themselves; their erstwhile 'inferiors' condemn them to death and carry out a mock execution. This completes the rite. It has all been a sham, a sort of rehearsal for revolution. But it has also been an elaborate diversionary tactic; for we learn that, even as we watched, a real murder was being committed off-stage—the murder of a Negro who betrayed the black cause.

Thus described, the play sounds like a masterpiece *maudit*; and so it might have turned out, in the hands of another writer. The subject cries out for the dry passion of a satirist, a Swift of the theatre, a dramatic vivisectionist; instead, it drowns in a flood of prose poetry. Genet's mind moves from image to image, never from idea to idea. His genius is anarchic, and resides in the phrase: as the anarchists of Catalonia resisted centralised authority, so Genet resists intellectual organisation. The images pile up, some of them memorable, others merely capricious; meanwhile, the argument stands still.

Since I have opted for a change of authorship, let me go further and call for a new production. Even in its present form, the piece would benefit hugely from direction that stressed its hieratic, ceremonial quality, which should suggest a Black Mass eerily tinged with voo-doo. In Roger Blin's staging it comes across as a slipshod prank, convey-ing no sense of danger. I am ready to believe that M. Blin's Paris pro-duction, which I did not see, was a great deal better. M. Blin does not speak recognisable English, which may account for his failure to realise that many of the West Indian and African members of his London cast were not speaking recognisable English either. Their accents have a muddying effect on dialogue that could scarcely be called limpid to be-gin with.

My familiarity with the text is mainly due to the fact that I have read the translation, a fluent effort by Bernard Frechtman, whose unseen collaborator, the Lord Chamberlain, has removed all the blatantly shock-ing words from what was expressly intended to be a blatantly shock-ing work.

(1961)

Let Coward Flinch

At a time when the talk is all of youth in the theatre, I should like to pose a question: Where are the *old* playwrights? Never, perhaps, in its history has our theatre been so thinly equipped with active, estab-lished dramatists past their thirties. We have Messrs Greene and Ratti-gan, of course, but most of their coevals and seniors are either inactive or unperformed, forced into silence by the swift, radical change in the theatrical climate. Shaw went on writing into his nineties, and Ibsen into his seventies; nowadays, 'too old at forty' is increasingly the rule. Where, for instance, is Mr Fry? And how is Mr Eliot? And who is N. C. Hunter?

I see that I have omitted Mr Coward. We know where he is, all right; he is rebuking history in the pages of *The Sunday Times*, wagging his finger at the theatre's 'new wave' and daring it to drown him. Last week, in the first of three articles, he accused the younger playwrights of having failed in the cardinal task of attracting large audiences—an ambitious charge, coming at a time when *A Taste of Honey* and *The Hostage* are prospering on Broadway, when *The Caretaker* and *Billy Liar* are coining it in London, and when it has just been announced that Mr Coward's latest play will shortly be withdrawn after a run of less than six months.

The bridge of a sinking ship, one feels, is scarcely the ideal place from which to deliver a lecture on the technique of keeping afloat. While flaying the new dramatists for boring their audiences with dirt, dustbins and Socialist dogma, Mr Coward observed that 'political or social propaganda in the theatre, as a general rule, is a cracking bore'. The exceptions, presumably, include such of his own works as *Peace in Our Time*, wherein a 'progressive' English intellectual eagerly collaborates with the Nazis, and *Relative Values*, which ends with a climactic toast to 'The final inglorious disintegration of the most unlikely dream that ever troubled the foolish heart of man—Social Equality'. ·

Mr Coward's second article, we were promised, would deal with 'the Scratch-and-Mumble School' of acting. Sentences at once began to form in my mind:

> Heretical though it may be to say so, I maintain that if a tax-ridden English playgoer coughs up a guinea for the privilege of occupying an orchestra stall, he is entitled to expect something slightly more glamorous than the spectacle of an extremely cross young gentleman, execrably attired, reeking of fried onions, and behaving like one of the less inhibited inmates of the London Zoo. ... Since I myself would never dream of embarrassing my underprivileged brethren by inviting them to discuss their squalid and monotonous problems under my roof, I see no reason why I should pay good money to hear the same problems discussed in the theatre. There are, I believe, Citizens' Advice Bureaux which exist for that very purpose.
>
> ... Nowadays, apparently, it is considered unpardonably right-wing for an actor to wear anything more seductive than a bedraggled T-shirt and a pair of inconveniently tight blue-jeans, while to speak

the Queen's English clearly enough to be understood by the honest souls in the gallery is proof positive that one has 'sold out' to the forces of reaction. . . .

I am senile enough to remember the time when West End actors were not ashamed to be better dressed than their audiences. . . .

It is doubtless too much to suggest that the ironing-boards which clutter up so many London stages might be used with advantage to give the actors' costumes a brisk pressing. . . . .

I feel now as I have always felt, that acting should be larger, and if possible prettier, than life. . . . It is both bigoted and snobbish to insist that the company of a vulgar, illiterate skivvy is preferable to that of a woman who, deprived of the benefits of a proletarian upbringing, has had to make do with elegance, breeding and wit. . . . Whatever may be the taste of the regimented hordes of playgoers outside London, Paris and New York, it is immensely gratifying to reflect that in these three cities at least there remains a hard core of loyal, middle-aged theatre-lovers who have had quite enough of the 'new drama', thank you very much, and frantically yearn for the day when the theatre will pull itself together and rise above it. . . .

And here I give in, because nothing of my invention could rival the following authentic excerpt from Mr Coward's opening blast:

'The first allegiance of a young playwright should be not to his political convictions, nor to his moral or social conscience, but to his talent.' This wins my medal for the false antithesis of the month; for what if the author's 'talent' is inseparable from his conscience and convictions, as in the best writers it is?

(1961)

Queen after Death, BY HENRY DE MONTHERLANT, AT THE OXFORD PLAYHOUSE

Talking about our younger playwrights in the new issue of *The Twentieth Century,* George Devine remarks: 'There's a movement away from modern dress naturalism. To begin with, they had to write what was close to them, from their own experience. Now they're starting to explore a much wider territory . . .' He cites John Osborne's *Luther,* and adds that Shelagh Delaney has plans for a play about Derby in the fifteenth century; he might also have mentioned John Whiting's *The Devils*, Peter Shaffer's long-gestated chronicle play about the Incas, and—upping the age-limit a little—Christopher Fry's *Curtmantle*.

If Mr Devine is right, and a resurgence of historical drama is imminent, we should all be grateful to the Oxford Playhouse for having chosen such a moment to present Henry de Montherlant's *Queen After Death*, one of the most numbing examples of the genre in modern dramatic literature, and an object lesson in how not to do it.

For Montherlant, history is dignified, and dignity is sententious; every speech comes tripping across the footlights with a ball and chain of pseudo-profundity attached to its ankle. The characters, so many robed machines for the production of densely scrambled platitude, exchange lectures on the state of their souls, the danger of love, the nature of power, the claims of justice, the necessity of duty, and other topics calculated to exploit the full capacity of the French language for exquisite, lapidary emptiness.

Quite often the people on stage seem to be engaged in earnest discussion of a play that is not in fact taking place. They express formal opinions; they swap sentiments, anecdotes and metaphors; but outside the printed text they have no existence at all. They are walking figures of speech, syntactical fictions. Stung by a crafty stroke of litotes, they may riposte with a shrewd oxymoron to the bread-basket; but it is all shadow-boxing, a sort of Tussaud tournament.

In English drama (I generalise), character reveals itself and is presented for judgment mostly in terms of class; in Continental drama (I generalise again), mostly in terms of temperament and ideas. But on bookshelves everywhere, accumulating dust and scholarly revaluations, one comes across a third kind of play, in which character consists merely in verbal gesture. It is to this category that *Queen After Death* belongs.

It was Montherlant's first dramatic attempt, written for the Comédie Française in the early years of the Occupation, and it is precisely the sort of play one would not expect from an eminent novelist; the theatre, he seems to have felt, was no place for the realistic disciplines of prose fiction. Alternatively, he may have been under the misapprehension that it was the Opéra, and not the Comédie Française, who had commissioned the piece; which would explain the fact that it reads less like a play in need of actors than a libretto in need of a composer. I have no doubt that a surge of Germanic orchestration would lift the words up to heights befitting, and falsely ennobling, their glacial pretentiousness.

The plot is basic, heroic enough to have entranced Corneille or Schiller, and brief enough to be summarised in the manner of a hastily

Englished opera-synopsis. Ferrante, the tyrannic king of Portugal, wishes that his Crown Prince son, Don Pedro, would marry the important Infanta of Navarra, who is maltreated by that son's refusal. (Aria: "Tis not the woman in me who is insulted, it is the Infanta.') It is transpired that Don Pedro has already himself a wife in secret, and pregnant for him, who is entitled Dona Inez. This news is rending the king choleric, whereabouts he ordains his son to break his contract and lose that wife. But Don Pedro would not lose her, and she him, and then the king causes her to be slain for reason of state. In that moment, with an irony of fate, nature cracked his heart (Aria: 'A king is like a huge tree'), so that he is dead afterwards.

Into this straightforward piece of *Realpolitik* Montherlant imports all sorts of tragic motives; it is a latterday French custom to unearth complex philosophical justifications for simple acts of cruelty or cowardice, with the result that villains, in the contemporary French theatre, often end up as unrecognised martyrs. The king, for instance, has Inez killed not because policy demands it but because he is a dying man, resentful of her youth and fertility.

But one's main objection to *Queen After Death* as a historical play is that it totally neglects historical circumstance. Its wordiness is modern wordiness, disguised in Renaissance trappings, and the result is that spurious brand of 'universality' which assumes that all human beings are always the same, whether ancient or modern, pagan or Christian, Negro or Caucasian, landlord or serf.

A play set in the past needs much fuller documentation than one set in the present; we cannot understand it unless we know the broad social context in which the action is laid. In the normal, conventional theatre, said Brecht, 'Thought determines Being'. In the epic theatre, on the other hand, 'Social Being determines thought'. Montherlant's play is a normal, conventional, and hence utterly frivolous treatment of a thoroughly epic theme.

(1961)

Ross, BY TERENCE RATTIGAN, AT THE HAYMARKET

I was out of the country when Mr Rattigan's *Ross* opened nine months ago, and though I saw it soon afterwards, no pretext for writing about it arose until last week, when Michael Bryant replaced Sir Alec Guinness as the scourge of the Turks. Ever since I heard Peter Sellers's impersonation of Sir Eric Goodness, a famous actor whose latest role is that of a Persian mystic named Smith, I have been unable to picture anyone else in the part; but Mr Bryant copes doughtily, and has the grace to seem decently embarrassed by Lawrence's last line—'God will give you peace'—and the bugle-call that accompanies it.

Reduced to essentials, Mr Rattigan's play is a Jack Harkaway adventure with a Freudian core. The villain is a bestial Turk who sprawls on a couch instead of sitting up like a gentleman; alone in the cast, and on top of his other vices, he sweats. Our side includes well-read General Allenby, perceptive Sir Ronald Storrs, and venal but lovable Auda Abu Tayi, a bloodthirsty sheikh with his heart in the right place. With one sickening exception (a public schoolboy gone rottten), T. E.'s mates in the RAF are likewise a first-rate crew—rough diamonds, perhaps, but one would thank one's stars for them in a tight corner.

In the middle of the picture is Lawrence, with his madcap dream, at which fools scoff, of a free, united Arab State. He's a queer one, is T. E., but you must admit the fellow's got guts; he's a man apart from other men, singled out by destiny, born to be fortune's fool. It turns out, early in the second half, that he knew all along about the Anglo-French agreement to carve up Arabia between them after the war. This would seem to invalidate everything he has so far professed, and to make him a cheat and a liar as well as a fool; but you must not imagine that he loses faith in his mission on grounds as rational as these.

Although it tells us nothing about Lawrence's childhood or upbringing, this is a psychological play. For the second time in his career (*Adventure Story* was the first), Mr Rattigan shows us a conquering hero who is stopped dead in his tracks by a revelation of sexual abnormality somewhere east of Suez. In the earlier work, Alexander the Great is stunned to discover that he has a mother-complex; in *Ross*, Lawrence the puritan learns, through being forcibly subjected to sodomy, that he is a non-practising homosexual. Guilt is the spur that has raised his clear spirit. He has done the right things for the wrong reasons. What shall it profit a man if he shall gain the world and lose his virginity? Convinced that his idealism is no more than a by-product of his perversion, Lawrence backs out of the limelight and espouses anonymity.

One would like to think that Mr Rattigan had read what Christopher Caudwell had to say about Lawrence's loathing of the Western way of life: 'He had desired to be just and friendly and brave and to hate pomp and ceremony and wealth, and to love the essence of a man simply as it realised itself in action ...' and about how he betrayed his ideal by bringing to Arabia 'the very evil he had fled':

Soon his desert Arabs would have money, businesses, investments, loud-speakers, and regular employment. But he could not realise this consciously, for he had never been fully conscious that it was bourgeois social relations he was fleeing.... He was in fact like a man who, fleeing blindly from a deadly disease to a healthy land, himself afflicts it with the plague.

But my main objection to *Ross* is not that its view of history is petty and blinkered; so, it might be urged, is Shakespeare's in *Henry V*. What clinches my distaste is its verbal aridity, its flatness of phrase, and—above all—its pat reliance on the same antithetical device in moments of crisis. For examples, see below:

1. 'I've an idea you don't care for authority, Ross.'
   'I care for discipline, sir.'
2. 'There's nothing in the world worse than self-pity.'
   'Oh yes there is. Self-knowledge.'
3. 'And so he will win his battles by not fighting them?'
   'Yes, And his war too—by not waging it.'
4. 'And is this only the beginning?'
   'It may be the ending, too.'
5. 'I think I must remind you that I have not yet offered you this appointment.'
   'No. Nor you have. And I haven't accepted it, either.'
6. 'Your man must believe in them and their destiny.'
   'What about your own country and *its* destiny?'
7. 'You're going to make it hard for me, are you?'
   'I see no reason to make it easy.'
8. 'You sicken me.'
   'I sicken myself.'

I will refrain from pressing the case, though it might be worth quoting, by way of conclusion, one spectator's comment on this most fashionable of chronicle plays. 'It was too episodic,' he said, 'to be really picaresque.' Non-commitment could hardly go further.

(1961)

The Lady from the Sea, BY HENRIK IBSEN, AT THE QUEEN'S

Listening to *The Lady from the Sea* one thinks of Melville's exalted hymn, in the first chapter of *Moby Dick*, to the lure of great waters:

Why did the old Persians hold the sea holy? Why did the Greeks give it a separate deity, and own brother of Jove? Surely all this is not without meaning. And still deeper the meaning of that story of Narcissus, who because he could not grasp the tormenting, mild image he saw in the fountain, plunged into it and was drowned. But that same image, we ourselves see in all rivers and oceans. It is the image of the ungraspable phantom of life. . . .

Ibsen's Ellida, the lighthouse-keeper's daughter, might echo all of this. Hydrophilia, fortified by more than a touch of narcissism, has long since claimed her for its own. Not a day of summer passes but she must take her ritual dip in the fjord, an undine restless for her native element. In imagination a sea-creature, she is in fact the second wife of a provincial doctor—one of those well-meaning fumblers whom Ibsen, most sadistic of theatrical matchmakers, delights to saddle with women they can neither comprehend nor satisfy.

In Dr Wangel's home Ellida feels superfluous, unwanted by her stepdaughters and unable to compete with her dead predecessor; she has come to despise her marriage as a squalid business arrangement, of no significance beside the pagan compact into which she entered, years before, with a mysterious, long-vanished sailor. His image has grown in her mind to obsessive proportions; and it is his return, almost as if she had telepathically summoned him, that precipitates the play's crisis. Speaking in terms of oracular starkness, he declares that he has come to claim his bride: Ellida must choose between her soul-mate and her legal husband.

But there is more to it than that. The choice is also between fantasy and reality. True, the sailor exists objectively; but so do the *revenants* in *The Turn of the Screw*; and I found my thoughts straying to that interpretation of James's novel which holds that the malevolent phantoms are projections of the heroine's repressed sexual desires. In Ibsen's play, it is not enough to regard the sailor merely as a symbol of Ellida's yearning for the sea; the basic symbol is the sea itself, which stands for all the elemental forces that bourgeois society frustrates and inhibits.

Not least among them is sex; we know that Ellida no longer sleeps with her husband. Emotionally stifled, and lacking other outlets for her energies, she almost literally *creates* the sailor, as an objective manifestation of her discontent.

If we miss the point, it may be because Ibsen compromised; in other words, he hesitated to introduce a wholly unreal character into an otherwise realistic setting. (A contemporary playwright would have no such qualms; e.g. the Match-Seller in Mr Pinter's *A Slight Ache*.) Hence the trouble he takes to deck the sailor's behaviour with the trappings of authenticity—a murder charge to account for his long absence, a newspaper report of Ellida's marriage to explain his sudden return. For me, the play's frailty lies here and not, as many critics have urged, in the *dénouement*. Ellida finally elects to stay with her husband, her reason being that he has allowed her, for the first time, to make a choice 'in freedom and on her own responsibility'. Being free to choose, she is able to reject. That, anyway, is her story, and one must admit that it constitutes a pretty feeble excuse for persisting in a marriage that has been unequivocally exposed as a sham. But what if she is rationalising? What if she is incapable of facing freedom and responsibility, and prefers the opportunities for neurotic self-indulgence that are offered by a life of irresponsible confinement? On that supposition, which nothing in the text contradicts, the play becomes an exercise in irony, with Ellida unmasked as a Nora who will never quit her doll's house. Or in this case, perhaps, her bird-bath.

Although it follows the conventional, affirmative reading of the last scene, the present production is a fine one, with settings by Motley that would not disgrace the Moscow Art Theatre. This is the only Ibsen play that Chekhov might have written, and Glen Byam Shaw has directed it with a Chekhovian feeling for its sunsets and nostalgias; the high mountain air we associate with Ibsen is here thickened by a river mist, intermittently pierced by the mournful hooting of steamers.

For Vanessa Redgrave, who plays Wangel's elder daughter, a Chekhov season must forthwith be mounted, with special emphasis on *The Seagull* and *The Three Sisters*. To witness the scene in which Miss Redgrave embraces her tutor's offer of financial help, rejects it upon learning that it involves marriage, and eventually, tentatively, reaccepts it, as her need to escape stagnation overrides her distaste for an unpropitious match, is to relive the painful, illusion-shedding transition that marks the end of youth. If there is better acting than this in London, I should like to hear of it.

As the mermaid manquée, Margaret Leighton is exquisitely distraught; a bit too actressy, now and then, a bit too conscious that this was one of Duse's greatest parts; but brilliant in many passages that call for controlled hysteria and/or abject melancholia.

(1961)

Altona, BY JEAN-PAUL SARTRE, AT THE ROYAL COURT

Jean Genet was once asked why he refused to meet Gide. He replied: 'A man is either a defendant or a judge. I do not like judges who lean over amorously towards the defendants.' Nor does M. Sartre; it is in remarks like this that one sees the link between M. Genet and his most voluble champion.

Altona is an act of judgment on the twentieth century, which might have been an admirable era (the closing lines tell us) if man had not been threatened by 'the cruel enemy who had sworn to destroy him, that hairless, evil, flesh-eating beast—man himself'. All the characters in the play are defendants, trapped inside the frame of the proscenium as securely as Eichmann within his glass cage in Jerusalem; their judge is the past, and its verdict is without mercy. Two death penalties are imposed, and one sentence of solitary confinement for life. The stage, as so often in M. Sartre's hands, becomes a place of moral inquisition, at once a court-room and a prison.

Ostensibly, the accused are members of a rich shipbuilding family in present day Hamburg; the guilt that enfolds and corrodes them is their complicity in the horrors of Nazism; but it is not only Germany that is on trial in this theatrical Nuremberg. It is also France. M. Sartre has said that he wanted to write a play about the French atrocities in Algeria, but gave up the attempt because 'no theatre in Paris would have produced it'. By further extension, *Altona* indicts all of us; our crime, as human beings, is that we have allowed crimes against humanity to be committed in our name.

The house of Gerlach is prospering under Adenauer as it prospered under Hitler and during the Allied occupation: every regime needs ships. Father, a sedate, implacable autocrat, is dying of throat cancer, and summons a family meeting to announce that Werner, his younger son, will shortly take over the business. Against his own will and the outspoken wishes of his wife, Johanna, Werner feebly consents; according to paternal dogma, mankind is divided into the weak and the strong, and Werner obediently takes his seat among the weak, ignoring Johanna's laments over his lost independence, and impervious to the jeers of his mischievous sister, Leni.

Such is the Gerlachs' downstairs world, an authoritarian encampment alive with mutual contempt. Upstairs their conscience rages, in the shape of Werner's elder brother, Franz, the firstborn, a former Nazi officer who has locked himself in his room for fifteen years, receiving no one but his sister Leni, with whom he has struck up an incestuous affair. Officially, Franz no longer exists: the family has procured a forged certificate of his death in South America, whither he is rumoured to have fled. In truth, he has gone profoundly mad; his sudden veerings of mood, coupled with his visions of small crustaceans, suggest a bad case of catatonic schizophrenia, complicated by *delirium tremens*.

Franz spends his time tape-recording messages for posterity, which he imagines as a race of crabs. He lives on champagne and oysters, whose shells he flings at a portrait of Hitler that hangs on the wall. His room is windowless, and he believes that the German people have been starved to the point of extermination by the victorious allies. Into this claustrophobic cell Johanna intrudes, spurred by a promise from old Gerlach that if she can persuade Franz to see him before he dies, he will release her husband from his commitment to shipbuilding. She attracts Franz, and thereby incurs the jealousy of Leni, who compels him to reveal that, so far from being a passive conniver at Nazism, he actually and willingly tortured prisoners.

This disclosure of active participation shocks Johanna into rejecting him; and we glimpse the point of one of Leni's earlier taunts: that Franz would be invulnerable if only he could bring himself to declare: 'I have done what I wanted, and I wanted what I have done.' Thus far, however, Franz cannot go; as M. Sartre might have said, men will confess to everything except their crimes. The play ends with Franz coming downstairs and shaming his father into a joint suicide. Leni replaces her brother in the attic, but there is no certainty about the future of Johanna and Werner. Although they quit the Gerlach mansion, they seem irreparably tainted by its freakish mystique.

This rich, cold, brain-twisting play makes one think of *Huis Clos*: the characters chase and torment each other behind closed doors, but the limits that confine them are not those of hell but those of bourgeois civilisation. In outline, *Altona* is the familiar story of a well-to-do household with a skeleton in its cupboard; in fact, it is a bourgeois drama dedicated to the demolition of the bourgeoisie. Its characters grate on each other as harshly as the oyster-shells that Franz scrapes together in his horrid distress. M. Sartre is hinting that the acquisitive way of life sets us one against another; that our corruption derives from a system in which, emotionally and economically, the fulfilment of individual desire takes automatic precedence over anything else.

The play's original title was *Les Séquestrés d'Altona*; in Justin O'Brien's resourceful adaptation *séquestrés* becomes 'people who live in private cells', estranged from each other and from the world at large. Their way of life forbids them to act as social beings. As M. Sartre once said, 'there is no love apart from the deeds of love; no potentiality of love other than that which is expressed in works of art'. The message of *Altona* is that beliefs count for nothing compared with acts. Old Gerlach, for instance, detested Hitler, but he still built ships for him. 'Could we have done more', asks Franz sardonically, 'if we had worshipped him?' We shall be judged by what we do, not by how we felt while we were doing it.

(1961)

One Over the Eight, AT THE DUKE OF YORK'S

As long ago as 1929 George Jean Nathan was complaining about the influence on the American theatre of the pixie mannerisms imported by English actors. 'What we need,' he said 'are (*sic*) more actors like Jack Dempsey, who tried the stage a little while ago. Jack may not be much of an actor, but his worst enemy certainly cannot accuse him of belonging to the court of Titania.'

Nathan took pains to define exactly what he was attacking: 'It isn't that the actors are biologically queer... it's that they possess or have acquired an air of effeminacy that, however hard or adroitly they try to conceal it, shows itself sooner or later during the course of a dramatic performance. . . .'

He was referring, of course, to the phenomenon we know as 'camp'. In the province of comedy, with which I am presently concerned, its distinguishing feature is a marked inclination towards the dainty, the coy and the exuberantly fussy. The ability to camp (let us drop those misleadingly inverted commas) is a useful, even a vital, part of comic technique, but it is not the whole of it; and in recent years, I disrespectfully submit, we have had excess of it, our appetite has sickened, and English high comedy has very nearly died.

When Nathan lodged his complaint, the process of enfeeblement was already well advanced; it was in the twenties that the habit arose of eviscerating Restoration comedies and capering through them as if they were sexless diversions for gentleman dancing-masters. And who, judging by the Wilde revivals of the past two decades, would ever guess that Oscar wrote his plays for performance by stolid, tweedy, Victorian actor-managers? High comedy in England is nowadays a hostage in the camp of camp; with each new season, its voice gets shriller, and its blood runs thinner.

These symptoms are nowhere more obvious than in the case of revue. I returned last week from New York, where several little revues are flourishing off Broadway. Each has its proper modicum of camp; but the best of them have something more—an earthy frankness, a robust yet subtle candour, of the kind that is inseparable from American-Jewish wit, surely today the sharpest on earth. By way of contrast, consider *One Over the Eight*, which exemplifies the atrophy of latterday English revue.

The expressions most frequently seen on the faces of the cast are two in number. The men register: 'How naughty I am!'; and the women: 'How naughty you are!' The atmosphere of arrested adolescence is overpowering. The dance routines are at once inventive and dull; boys in tight trousers smile and spin, sometimes accompanied by spinning girls, who might smile more convincingly if their clothes were more attractive. There is almost nothing in the show that could not have been written twenty years ago, apart from the odd reference to Mr Macmillan's Government, and a couple of sketches in which, following the current *avant-garde* trend, a voluble eccentric talks alarming nonsense to a captive audience of one. The barbs of the assembled satirists are mainly directed at the vocal solecisms of suburbia—those pseudo-genteel vowel sounds and mispronunciations which have been trampled to death in every revue since the war.

The star, Kenneth Williams, has a matchless repertory of squirms, leers, ogles and severe, reproving glares, and must be accounted the *petit-maître* of contemporary camp. As such, I salute him; but I wish there were more to English comedy than this. Most of the few good numbers, I should add, are by Peter Cook, and Tony Walton designed the pretty, slide-projected settings.

(1961)

Becket, BY JEAN ANOUILH, AT THE ALDWYCH

The Royal Shakespeare Theatre pursues its royalist course; after
The Hollow Crown, written by the monarchs of England, we have M.
Anouilh's *Becket*, which is about one of them. Not that one would
recognise Henry II from this Parisian portrait, any more than one would
recognise Joan of Arc in Shakespeare's termagant Pucelle; M. Anouilh
gives us the Plantagenet bully-boy who was half of Henry, but omits the
great judicial reformer who was the other.

More, perhaps, than any other sovereign of his century, Henry
deserved the title of intellectual. M. Anouilh ignores this altogether; indeed, in a foreword to the play, he explains that he never bothered to
find out what Henry and Becket were really like. What he sought to tell
was the story of a friendship sundered by the rival claims of Caesar and
God; and the obvious way to simplify the contest was to make the king a
man of passion and the archbishop a man of principle. It is the artist's
privilege thus to tamper with fact; all the same, one may regret that
M. Anouilh shied away from the harder task of showing a conflict between intellectual equals who differed only in their definitions of loyalty.

So much for the play M. Anouilh didn't write. The one he did write
is a clever, *insouciant* chronicle, glossed with neat jokes and flawed as an
entertainment only when it attempts high seriousness. This author's forte
is the sentimental-satirical, not the tragic; a master of pinpricks, he has
no gift for swordplay. His Becket is a Saxon who torments himself for
having collaborated with the Norman invader. Such intense self-disgust,
almost a century after the Conquest, strikes one as a trifle excessive;
something here smacks less of pre-Renaissance England than of postwar
France.

The early scenes sketch in the enigmatic relationship between Henry
and his favourite Saxon; exorbitant in all things, the king makes emotional demands on Becket that the latter, a worldly but passionless creature, cannot possible meet. Henry needs love, and Becket gives him companionship. M. Anouilh's study of a master increasingly dependent on
his servant, unable to comprehend that there are limits to what royalty
can command, and flying into tantrums whenever his whims are frustrated, provides the piece with its best and showiest moments, which Christopher Plummer takes in his swaggering stride. This is an actor of real
stage-seizing power, unafraid of the big gesture, and endowed with a
stabbing voice of kaleidophonic virtuosity.

One enjoys M. Anouilh when he is being sour (as in Henry's ran-
corous encounters with his wife and children) or wistful (as in the last
wintry meeting between the king and his erstwhile pal). It is when he goes
in for profundity that one wishes M. Anouilh would turn it up. He is
a quick but shallow thinker; the access of sanctity that overcomes Becket
on his appointment as archbishop, compelling him to take God's side
against the king, is something M. Anouilh's temperament cannot grasp
nor his talent express, except on the tritest level. In these mysteries he is
not so much a child (which would be tolerable) as a quiz kid. The
higher the play aims, the more abjectly it fails.

Becket, in short, is just what one would expect of an author who can
write, as M. Anouilh does in his preface: 'I suppose I am not very
serious; after all, I work in the theatre. . . .' By such wry disclaimers as
this does the secondrater declare himself.

Peter Hall's production is stronger and more unified in style than
the Broadway version I saw some months ago. Eric Porter, whom few
actors excel in the difficult art of conveying to an audience the specific
gravity of moral scruples, is a superbly worried Becket; Olivier, who
created the part in New York, was a much less convincing candidate for
martyrdom. Later, however, Sir Laurence took over the role of the king,
on which he worked the kind of magic that is the great actor's pre-
rogative: he imposed on a minor play a major act of reinterpretation.

His Henry was devoured by a passion that confused him even as it
consumed him: the actor implied what the character never suspected,
namely, that his attachment to Becket was homosexual. Hence the sulks
into which he is thrown by Becket's coolness; hence, too, the oafish
malice with which he steals his friend's mistress; he wants to deprive
Becket of a female bedfellow, and at the same time to be close to someone whom Becket has loved. When the girl kills herself, Henry is convulsed by a frenzy of guilt and begs permission to spend the night in
Becket's bed: in this scene Sir Laurence was so nakedly, pathetically vulnerable that one felt ashamed to be watching. And he made it quite clear,
by some interlinear stealth, that Henry raised Becket to the see of Canter-
bury in order to unsex him.

The keystone of this amazing performance fell into place just before
the final curtain. The penitent king, having undergone a ritual scourging,
quits the cathedral to acknowledge the cheers of his people. Sir
Laurence paused halfway to the door and, turning towards the martyr's
tomb, elaborately winked and blew in its direction a heartfelt farewell
kiss. These intimacies concluded, he swept out into history.

(1961)

O'Neill at Length

Shortly before Eugene O'Neill died in 1953, he destroyed all his un-finished work, including the scenarios and rough drafts of the massive nine-play cycle on which he had laboured for many years. By some over-sight, one script survived: an unedited version of *More Stately Mansions*, the sixth episode of the cycle, which was staged a few days ago in Stock-holm.

At regular intervals over the past nine years O'Neill's widow, Carlotta, has been releasing his unpublished manuscripts for production: but this must surely be Carlotta's final throw. Barring revelations from unsuspected safe-deposits, we have heard the last of 'the last of the O'Neills', as he tearfully called himself when his brother Jamie died of drink in 1923.

We can now, if we have strong wrists, survey the man as a whole: bound up in the 970 pages of *O'Neill*, by Arthur and Barbara Gelb, is all we know and rather more than we need to know. Few living people who ever shared a jar with this blackest of black Irishmen can have gone uninterviewed (or unquoted) by the assiduous Gelbs; slaves to a passion for background detail, they do not manage to get their hero born until page 55. Yet they win in the end, as sometimes happens with O'Neill's longer plays: the sheer weight of authentic, accumulated pain will not be denied.

What a death in life this biography records! Between the lines one can almost hear O'Neill moaning: 'If you don't pity yourself, no one else ever will.' His father a miserly matinée idol, wasting his talent on end-less tours of *The Count of Monte Cristo*; his mother a well-born morphine addict; his brother an alcoholic; his first son a wrecked intel-lectual who took a razor and killed himself; his second son a convicted junkie; his only daughter a mutinous beauty to whom he never spoke after she married Charles Chaplin; and his third wife (who bore him no children) the stormily beloved, indispensably protective Carlotta, whom he tried in a dark moment just before his death to dispatch to a mental home—add to this catalogue a taste for liquor, a dose of TB and a guilt-spawning Catholic upbringing, and you have the perfect blueprint for self-destruction.

O'Neill lived in a private hell which he threw open to the public, spreading its contagion to all who accepted the dangerous gift of his affection. For him the atomic bomb was 'a wonderful invention, because it might annihilate the whole human race'; despite his professed belief in the healing powers of Freudian theory and anarchist practice, his life in essence was a prolonged, undiscouraged courtship of suicide.

'Little subconscious mind, say I each night, bring home the bacon!': thus he described the birthpangs of a new play. His subconscious duly responded, as it usually did when addressed in his characteristic blend of fulsome rhetoric and dated slang; but how much of the bacon can we nowadays stomach?

His attitude towards women, who adored and disgusted him, is highly indigestible: 'he used to talk of girls as "pigs"', said one of his un-official fiancées; and the only women of whom he writes with un-qualified approval are those who openly admit that they are whores. In O'Neill's world, marriage never works: hence his lifelong adoration of Strindberg. When both his parents were dead, he borrowed their names —Ella and Jim—for use in *All God's Chillun Got Wings*, a play about a doomed alliance between Ella, a Caucasian, and a Negro called Jim. While he was writing it, brother Jamie died. At last, stripped of family constraints, he was free to develop as he chose. Almost alone among American writers, O'Neill improved as he got older.

It took him a long time to find himself; and the first self he found •was an eclectic mess. After years of hard-drinking vagabondage, he settled down during World War One in Greenwich Village: an artistic snakepit, full of half-digested European ideas but lacking the sense of discipline and continuity that shaped European art and saved it from the worst excesses of self-indulgence. Compare Paris in the great period of 1915–25 with Greenwich Village, where the style-setters were people like Mabel Dodge, Elizabeth Gurley Flynn, and Big Bill Haywood. In this pseudo-Bohemia, O'Neill formed an apocalyptic view of life later summed up by Heywood Broun as 'that of a saturnine sophomore'. He tried to graft European inventions—masks, symbolism, the Greek notion of fate, the Germanic trappings of expressionism—on to raw American experience, and he disastrously blundered.

Not until his fifties did this grievously haunted man overcome his personal shame and his artistic pretensions; when he did, he wrote the two autobiographical masterpieces by which his name will be durably remembered—*The Iceman Cometh* and *Long Day's Journey into Night*. Serious theatre in O'Neill's heyday was discernibly splitting into two branches—one rooted in naturalistic fact, and the other in fable and fantasy. In the nick of time, O'Neill chose American fact. It was a prosaic choice, but it made him a poet.

(1962)

Anatomy of the Absurd

In the modern world (said Mallarmé), a poet is like a sculptor who isolates himself to carve his own tomb. The remark recurred to me as I read Martin Esslin's *The Theatre of the Absurd*, an authoritative surview of the work, influence and antecedents of Beckett, Ionesco, Adamov and Genet.

Mr Esslin defines his subject as 'the lyrical, poetical theatre of the world within, the theatre of dream, mood and being'; and he cites a crucial passage from Camus:

A world that can be explained by reasoning, however faulty, is a familiar world. But in a universe that is suddenly deprived of illusions and of light, man feels a stranger.... This divorce between man and his life, the actor and his setting, truly constitutes the feeling of Absurdity.

By their repudiation of verbal logic, psychological consistency and any kind of ideological commitment, the dramatists of the Absurd try to shock us into awareness of our new and grievous plight—awaiting death in a universe without a God, ungoverned by reason and devoid of purpose. Towards the end of the book, Mr Esslin sums up his case:

Concerned as it is with the ultimate realities of the human condition, the Theatre of the Absurd, however grotesque, frivolous and irreverent it may appear, represents a return to the original, religious function of the theatre—the confrontation of man with the spheres of myth and religious reality.

These are large claims, and Mr Esslin works hard to substantiate them. With Beckett he succeeds completely: that bleak, denuded vision of man as a hungry biped condemned to die alone has a tragic honesty that Aeschylus would have recognised, if not comprehended. He defends Ionesco superbly as an antic poet of despair, and whets one's appetite for Adamov, the scope and size of whose output I had never before suspected: how has London dared to ignore *Le Ping-Pong, Paolo Paoli, Le Professeur Taranne* or the Adamov adaptation of Gogol's *Dead Souls*?

Tracing the forebears of the Absurd, Mr Esslin leads us back to the mime plays of antiquity; to the Commedia dell' Arte; to pantomime and vaudeville; to Lear and Lewis Carroll; to Jarry, Strindberg and the young, Rimbaud-impregnated Brecht; to the Dadaists and Tristan Tzara (who called one of his plays 'the biggest swindle of the century in three acts'); to the Surrealists and Artaud; to Kafka, and to Joyce.

All this is helpful and credible. But when Mr Esslin ropes in Shakespeare, Goethe and Ibsen as harbingers of the Absurd, one begins to feel that the whole history of dramatic literature has been nothing more than a prelude to the triumphant emergence of Beckett and Ionesco. Overstatement and Mr Esslin are not strangers. He thinks N. F. Simpson 'a more powerful social critic than any of the social realists'; and I wish I had an extra month of life for every playwright in connection with whose work Mr Esslin refers to 'the human condition'.

My present response to the Absurdists (apart from Beckett) is to enjoy their poetry while mistrusting their philosophy. How are we to judge what they write? According to Mr Esslin, by whether it 'springs from deep layers of profoundly experienced emotion' and 'mirrors real obsessions, dreams and valid images in the subconscious mind of its author'. If it fulfils these conditions (he continues), it will have a 'general, as distinct from merely private, validity'.

But what does 'valid' mean? A schizophrenic is as totally alienated from everyday reality as an Absurdist: do his perceptions therefore qualify as art? The man who reacts to the universe with a cry of impotent anguish is acceptable as an artist only if he can persuade us that he has sanely considered the other possible reactions and found them inadequate. Despair must speak from experience. When they wrote their first plays, Beckett, Ionesco, Adamov and Genet were all in their late thirties, which is the earliest reasonable age for wanhope. They are conceivably among the last and certainly among the most *outré* exponents of disillusioned Western individualism in the arts—an attitude summed up by the neurotic hero of Aldous Huxley's late novel, *Island*, who confesses, when faced with a workable contemporary Utopia, that he 'can't take yes for an answer'.

Adamov has recently changed his mind. He now maintains that 'the theatre must show . . . both the curable and the incurable aspect of things. The incurable aspect, we all know, is that of the inevitability of death. The curable aspect is the social one.' He has thus espoused Marxism, not in order to make men equally happy, but to give them equality of opportunity to contemplate their unhappiness:

When the material obstacles are overcome, when man will no longer be able to deceive himself as to the nature of his unhappiness, then there will arise an anxiety all the more powerful, all the more fruit-

ful, for being stripped of anything that might have hindered its reali-
sation.

This seems to me to get the priorities exactly right. What irks one
most about the Absurdists is their pervasive tone of privileged despair.

(1962)

Happy Days, BY SAMUEL BECKETT, AT THE ROYAL COURT

Samuel Beckett's new work, the latest bulletin from the Arctic lati-
tudes of his particular hell, the starkest portrait he has yet drawn of the
slow burial that begins with birth, is called *Happy Days*.

It is much too long, too full of infertile pauses, and should really
have been staged in one act, as a feminine counterpart to *Krapp's Last
Tape*. It is a dramatic metaphor extended beyond its capacities. That
said, I urge you to see it. But go early, and study the author's photograph that stares out of the programme.

Note the wrinkles between his eyebrows, converging in a crossroads
of anxiety; and the look on his face, at once accusing and aghast, as of
a man about to be struck by lightning, or a child who has been spat on
without warning. This head, one feels, has been cropped for execution,
and in its eyes the guillotine looms. This is our author, a prophet who
cannot help seeing beyond creature comforts to the engulfing grave.

He shows us Winnie, a middle-aged woman buried up to her waist in
a mound of sun-baked earth. Already death has half-claimed her; she
refers to the earth that is sucking her under, inch by inch, as 'the old ex-
tinguisher'. Yet she is jolly: despite her nostalgic chatter about the passing of 'the old style', she chuckles a lot, is grateful for the mercy of survival, and hails each new day as another free gift of happiness.

Her husband Willie lives in a burrow behind the mound from which
he sometimes emerges to scan a news-sheet or a pornographic picture, and into which he must always crawl backwards. With his bald
head and pointed skull, Willie represents the ageing phallus, just as
Winnie stands for the ageing breast. Now and then they share a laugh.
Winnie sees an ant bearing eggs, and Willie ventures a pun about
'formication'. 'I suppose some people might think us a trifle irreverent,'
his wife observes, 'but I doubt it. How can one better magnify the
Almighty than by sniggering with him at his little jokes, particularly the
poorer ones?'

But, of course, both she and Willie, and all mankind, are among the

Almighty's poorer jokes; the earth will inter our dreams as ineluctably as it rises around Winnie's neck. She mentions death's 'pale flag' and unexpectedly quotes 'Fear no more the heat o' the sun'; time and again the text refers back to Shakespeare and his contemporaries, the supreme poets of transience.

Brenda Bruce, peaked and wan but resilient to the last, sustains the evening with dogged valour, and ends up almost *looking* like Beckett; she is self-effacingly partnered by Peter Duguid, whose role is confined to a few shouts and murmurs, and a silent expedition on all fours.

Anyone disposed to scoff at the thought of an actress waist-deep in earth should know that Beckett has anticipated such mockery. Winnie describes a man and woman who once came to gape at her:

'What's she doing? he says—What's the idea? he says—stuck up to her diddies in the bleeding ground ... What does it mean? he says— What's it meant to mean?—and so on—lot more stuff like that— usual drivel—Do you hear me? he says—I do, she says, God help me—What do you mean? he says, God help you?'

Here Winnie gazes straight at the audience. 'And you, she says, what's the idea of you, she says, what are you meant to mean?'

Only those who are sure of the answer can afford to miss the play.

(1962)

The Broken Heart, BY JOHN FORD, AT THE CHICHESTER FESTIVAL THEATRE

Dear Sir Laurence:

I have now seen all but one of the three inaugural productions you have directed at the Chichester Festival Theatre, and I have to report a general feeling that all is not well with your dashing hexagonal playhouse. When you opened your season with *The Chances*, a flimsy Jacobethan prank by Beaumont and Fletcher, one shrugged and wrote it off as a caprice; but when *The Broken Heart*, a far more challenging piece, likewise fails to kindle one's reflexes, it is time to stop shrugging and start worrying. Something has clearly gone wrong: but how? Who put the hex on the hexagon? Does the fault lie in the play, in the theatre, or in you, its artistic director?

First things first. The play is Ford's best tragedy, and history rightly says that Ford is not bunk. It also says (and here you may not agree) that on this occasion he composed a series of agonised tableaux rather than a continuously developing action. Nearly all the principal characters are mismated or sexually deprived: we see them as if lit by magnesium flares, pleading, brooding, repining and expiring.

Young Orgilus yearns for Penthea, but cannot have her: during a feud between their two families she married someone else. Her brother Ithocles, who fixed the match and thereby drove Orgilus to despair, yearns just as vainly for Calantha, heiress to the throne of Sparta. At the end (forgive me this recapping) all four of them have died, the men by straightforward blood-letting and the girls by such recherché means as delayed-action heart failure and voluntary starvation.

Did you feel, as I did, a strange undertow of incest running beneath the text? Orgilus, for example, behaves like a cuckold when his little sister falls in love; and halfway through a scene between Ithocles and Penthea, who are twins, the latter's husband bursts in and accuses them of unnatural leanings. Whenever he writes about death or sin, Ford is marmoreal and unforgettable: his work is a scattering of noble fragments awaiting some genius of theatrical archaeology to reassemble it as a monument.

Given a script so awkwardly split between nobility and banality, did you find a production style that might weld it together? I think not. You went all out for anonymous rhetoric, 'fuyant le naturel'—as a French critic once put it—'sans trouver la grandeur'. A lot of vocal brandishing took place in a vacuum. 'Vehemence without real emotion', said G. H. Lewes, 'is rant; vehemence with real emotion, but without art, is turbulence.' One noted both kinds of vehemence in your *Broken Heart*.

When in doubt about the precise emotion behind a speech, have it delivered in tones of ungovernable rage: was this, as I suspected, your watchword? I liked your handling of Rosemary Harris, a calm, unpainted Penthea, looking at once ravaged and ravishing; and some of the crowd scenes had a solemn, collective splendour. But how do you account for Joan Greenwood's Calantha, a stoical heroine reduced to the stature of a baritone Joyce Grenfell? And Roger Furse's décor, three layers of gaudy wedding-cake propped up against the back wall? And your own performance as Miss Harris's enforced husband? Surely Bassanes is a stupid, self-deluding dotard at whose ridiculous jealousy we are supposed to laugh until, in the course of time, it becomes pathetic. You played him from the first as a sombre old victim bound for the slaughter, too noble and too tragic ever to be funny. Ford's tragedy was thus robbed of its essential comedy.

Most remarkable of all, you were indistinct: one lost more than half of what you said. And here begins my sad indictment of the peninsular Chichester stage. Shakespeare's actors performed on an out-thrust platform because they needed illumination from the sun's rays; the least desirable seats in the Globe Theatre—those occupied by the groundlings —were the ones nearest the stage. Proximity was a disadvantage. Nothing so quickly dispels one's sense of reality as a daubed and bedizened actor standing four feet from one's face and declaiming right over one's head. The picture-frame stage was invented in the seventeenth century to give all the spectators the same sightlines and the same viewpoint; but it encouraged expensive décor, and in the last fifty years we have been urged to revive the projecting stage, ostensibly for artistic reasons but actually because it cuts scenic costs to a minimum.

Chichester is a product of our gullibility: instead of letting the whole audience see the actors' faces (however distantly), we now prefer to bring them closer to the actors' backs. The Chichester stage is so vast that even the proximity argument falls down: an actor on the opposite side of the apron is farther away from one's front-row seat than he would be from the twelfth row of a proscenium theatre—where in any case he would not deliver a crucial speech with his rear turned towards one's face.

The more-or-less straight-edged stage (preferably stripped of its proscenium framing) remains the most cunning and intimate method yet devised for transmitting plays to playgoers: and it was on stages like this that you spent a quarter of a century polishing your technique. Alas, at Chichester your silky throwaway lines, flicked at the audience like legglances by Ranjitsinhji, are literally thrown away: they go for nothing and die unheard.

In a small theatre, where sound and sight present no problems, the promontory stage is perfectly viable. In a large theatre like Chichester's, it simply does not work, above all if the plays one is performing depend for their effect on verbal nuance. You might point out to the National Theatre Committee that, by recommending a stuck-out stage for the main playhouse and a proscenium for its junior partner, they have got things exactly the wrong way round.

(1962)

Plays for England, BY JOHN OSBORNE, AT THE ROYAL COURT; *Uncle Vanya*, BY ANTON CHEKHOV, AT THE CHICHESTER FESTIVAL THEATRE; *Cymbeline*, BY WILLIAM SHAKESPEARE, AT STRATFORD-ON-AVON

The pastime of sado-masochism—whereby one gains pleasure from dominating or being dominated—is deeply ingrained in English sexual life; so much so that the French call it *le vice anglais*. Whether it springs from faulty toilet-training or public-school brutality is not here our concern: the point is that it exists, that it inspires much of our pornography, and that it makes its first overt appearance on the English stage in *Under Plain Cover*, the second half of John Osborne's new double bill, *Plays for England*.

Mr Osborne's courage is doubly flabbergasting: not only does he state the facts about a sado-masochistic *ménage*, he also refrains from condemning it. The Turners, Tim and Jenny, are a provincial couple who never go out; they are much too absorbed in fetichist fantasies. They dress up in a variety of interchangeable roles—doctor and patient, strict master and meek housemaid, leather-clad motor-cyclist and docile Girl Guide. They are both obsessed with underwear, summed up in the wife's elaborate tribute to what she and her husband delight to call 'knickers'.

They persistently joke and improvise: when the wife, in her house-maid garb, threatens to hand in her notice rather than be chastised, the husband ripostes by declaring that the time is the thirties, and no other jobs are available. 'What a good idea!' she cries, bending to his inventive whim. Commodes, corsets and rubber in all its forms are among their other preoccupations, which they discuss as gaily as other couples discuss the garden, the curtains and the new car.

In the midst of a characteristically off-beat experiment, Tim asks Jenny whether she would like to have another baby. She says at once that she would. We suddenly realise that this is not only a thriving affair but a genuine, working marriage: an anal-sadistic relationship need not preclude love. This is perhaps the most audacious statement ever made on the English stage.

The *dénouement* is hasty and strained: Tim and Jenny are revealed to be brother and sister, the Press prises them apart and Jenny marries another, whom she swiftly deserts to rejoin Tim. Anton Rodgers and Ann Beach (particularly the latter) are superb as the mutually hypnotised couple. The script should immediately be sent to every *avant-garde*

writer, with special reference to Genet: what they leave opaque or translate into evasive poetic symbols is reduced by Mr Osborne to basic, un-
ambiguous sexual fact. The result is not, perhaps, a work of art; but as a
document it is unique and unmissable. It is also genuinely shocking.

It is preceded by *The Blood of the Bambergs*, a repetitive joke about
royal weddings. A prince is killed on the eve of marrying a princess in
Westminster Abbey: his place is taken by an Australian photographer,
who says he can feel 'the long, thrusting stimulus of the crown'. The
rest of the wit is on the same level of mechanical clumsiness. John Dexter
directs this half of the bill, leaving to Jonathan Miller the more rewarding
job of directing the other.

There is a tide in the affairs of men; and Chekhov's people have all
missed it. When the moment comes, the chance of a new life, their attention is somehow distracted, and the old life claims them again: they
meet each other always at the wrong time, too early or too late, so that
the splendid confrontation scenes beloved of other playwrights never take
place. Yet they might have done so, if only life were better organised;
and this 'if only', this constant, nagging sense that things might have
been otherwise, is what gives the plays their abiding power.

The eponymous anti-hero of *Uncle Vanya* discovers too late that
the intellectual brother-in-law he has spent his best years supporting is
a greedy old fraud; Astrov, the one-time idealist, falls in love with the
fraud's pretty bride when he is too far sunk in self-disgust to be capable
of love; and Sonya, the fraud's daughter, is too young for Astrov, who
has long since betrayed the ideals for which she loves him. One is always
aware of a discrepancy between what is and what might have been; and
by a sort of cruel kindness, Chekhov forces his characters, in the end, to
see each other as they really are.

Laurence Olivier's production, by far the best of the Chichester trio,
enshrines two superlative performances: his own as Astrov, a visionary
maimed by self-knowledge and dwindled into a middle-aged *roué*, and
Michael Redgrave's as Vanya, torn between self-assertion and self-
deprecation, and taking the stage in a tottering, pigeon-toed stride that
boldly amalgamates both. Joan Plowright (Sonya) drains every tear-duct
in the house with her final, defiant avowal of faith in the future, and
there are two definitive vignettes by Fay Compton and Sybil Thorndike.

Where Ilyena, wife to the fraud and mainspring of the action, should
be, we find a vacuum, inadequately filled by the artificial posing and
intoning of Joan Greenwood, who plays this vital and difficult part as
if she were the heroine in some cod production of Victorian melodrama.
Sean Kenny's setting, a timbered wall with a door and two windows, is

necessarily nondescript, since it must serve alike for outdoor and indoor scenes; the change from exterior to interior is cleverly managed by having light flow in through the windows instead of out.

Uncle Vanya works better on the Chichester stage than its two predecessors, mainly because it is written in easily comprehensible prose. All the same, I would rather have seen it at (say) the Haymarket; and I remain convinced that only those forms of theatre in which words are secondary—such as musicals, dance drama and Commedia dell' Arte—have much to gain from exposure to the three-sided stage.

Last Tuesday the shade of Brecht laid its hand on Shakespeare in William Gaskill's production of *Cymbeline*, a resplendent, panoramic achievement that would assuredly never have happened had Mr Gaskill not caught the Brechtian bug while directing *The Caucasian Chalk Circle*. The setting, which covers the stage floor and cyclorama and overflows beyond the proscenium, is of pure white netting; into and across it heavy objects of enormous sculptural beauty are lowered or shoved. The designer, René Allio, comes to Stratford from Roger Planchon's company in Lyons, where Brecht is the bible; and the costumes (also by M. Allio) have a thoroughly Brechtian look, worn and dignified by use. The stagescape is one of dazzling simplicity, before which events of extreme complexity are to unfold.

Of all our directors, Mr Gaskill is the best storyteller—lucid and unsentimental, never afraid of a leisurely narrative pace. He presents Shakespeare's ungainly fable as a tall tale told to a group of Jacobean stage-hands, who help between episodes to shift the scenery. As Cornelius, the narrator, puts it: 'Howsoe'er 'tis strange . . . yet is it true'; and we believe him.

We also believe everything that is said by Vanessa Redgrave, who plays Imogen with all her old sweetness and a doughty new strength. Whether bewailing her husband's departure ('I did not take my leave of him, but had/Most pretty things to say') or shocked by his imagined death ('I am nothing; or if not,/Nothing to be were better'), she radiates total candour. One rejoices when, in the last act, the estranged couple are fitly reconciled, and Miss Redgrave, looking as vulnerable as a baby giraffe, gently demands of her mate: 'Why did you throw your wedded lady from you?' The only smudge on this pristine performance is that whenever Miss Redgrave hits a high note, she cannot bear to leave it; which makes at times for vocal monotony.

Eric Porter's Iachimo, though not my idea of a practised seducer, brings to his role the zestful, squalid omniscience of a private detective: Imogen's left breast seems positively pox-raddled once he has described it as bearing 'a mole cinque-spotted'. Perhaps the subtlest acting comes from Clive Swift as Cloten, who turns the queen's loutish son into an epileptic young Blimp or pygmy Churchill.

The relationship between Cloten and his two attendants illustrates the care Mr Gaskill devotes to accuracy in matters of class distinction. Instead of sniggering at their master's eccentricities as if they had just met him for the first time, the courtiers treat Cloten with bored, habitual disdain: their compliments are a kind of poker-faced mockery. The Anglo-Roman war is staged in slow-motion choreography, like the battles in M. Planchon's production of *Edward II*; but Mr Gaskill's visual master-stroke is the dream wherein Posthumus, asleep in a pendent cage, imagines Jupiter descending on an eagle. The descent actually happens, and the bird has wings of gold. The effect, *mutatis mutandis*, is as grand as anything in *Ben Hur*.

(1962)

MARCEL MARCEAU, AT THE SAVILLE; EDITH PIAF, AT THE OLYMPIA IN PARIS

The late Ruth Draper, in her monologues, filled the stage with invisible people. Marcel Marceau fills it with invisible things; not objects merely, but natural forces as well; winds buffet him, the sea washes over him, and we feel their pressure as he does.

Revisiting Marceau after many years, one realises that his range of characterisation is extremely limited; and even within those limits the people he plays are mostly generalised. Bip, for instance, is not an independent creation; he is the early Chaplin pushed in the direction of goofiness, with a feckless smile and a face painted white. Nor has Marceau the gift of evoking unseen people around him; perhaps no mime ever had. We may shrewdly guess, if he looks upwards, that he is addressing someone tall; if downwards, someone small; but beyond such broad outlines as these the resources of his wordless art break down.

It is as a physical instrument that he earns our reverence, an incomparable machine for reacting to external circumstance. He becomes, in his finest numbers, almost impersonal; the escape from selfhood is complete, and he seems to move in a trance of anonymity, akin to those states of beatitude to which good Buddhists aspire. His body, to borrow a phrase from Jean-Louis Barrault, 'writes a silent sentence in space'. The imaginary objects or forces he encounters are not obstacles to be overcome; he and they exist not in opposition but in harmony; and this, too, is Buddhist. When he mimes a man walking into the ocean, what we see is not Marceau battling against the waves, but a statement of the relationship between a human body and the sea. As I watched him scaling a non-existent ladder, I recalled a fragment of doctrine I once gleaned from a book on Zen Buddhism: that when you climb a mountain, it is the mountain as much as your own legs that lifts you upwards. There is something very Zen about Marceau, not least when he takes a perfectly ordinary physical action, like running upstairs or walking against the wind, and shows us how strange and astounding it really is. One sees what P'ang-yun, the Zen poet, was getting at when he wrote:

Miraculous power and marvellous activity—
Drawing water and hewing wood!

And Marceau's effortless, self-erasing concentration on the physical task at hand exemplifies a favourite Zen dictum: 'In walking, just walk. In sitting, just sit. Above all, don't wobble.' After seeing Marceau at his best, one remembers the thing done—the ladder climbed, the tightrope walked—rather than the personality of the man who did it. To cite Buddhist scripture: 'The deed there is, but no doer thereof.'

Marceau is most like all of us when he is least like any of us. His masterpiece is still the brief, terrible item in which he marches, on behalf of us all, from birth to extinction; first unwinding from a foetal crouch, then discovering the use of his limbs, and striding across the landscape of youth, swinging his arms and immortally exulting: next faltering, aware of something leaden in his gait that cramps and bewilders him; and finally dwindling into the posture of astonished helplessness from which he began. Second only to this classic exposition of mortality is the number in which Marceau enters the domain of Pirandello; he plays a mask-maker who tries on one of his artifacts, an idiotically grinning mask of comedy, and cannot tear it off. It sticks like the shirt of Nessus; and a desperate struggle ensues between Marceau's face, fixedly beaming, and the rest of his body, increasingly anguished.

I would not give the impression that Marceau is good only when tragic. He can be brilliantly funny, swaggering in his sideburns like a zany Apache; trapped at a *soirée*, with a joke-teller on his left and a gloom-pedlar on his right, he puts his face through some memorable contortions; and he could satirise a matador with such skilled finesse that even the Spanish would fall about. But there is a distinction to be made between pantomime, in which gestures replace words, and mime, which tries to convey things inexpressible in words. Pantomime, according to M.

Barrault, is merely 'a *dumb* art; modern mime is a *silent* art'. Marceau the comedian is a bright pantomimic, adroit and unfailingly clever; but Marceau the pure mime is touched with greatness.

From one French soloist, all movement and no voice, I turn to another, all voice and no movement. Some five weeks ago, I heard Edith Piaf at the Olympia; she has since collapsed, but then she was packing the place, in the third month of her triumphant comeback after a long and disquieting absence. She seemed haggard as she appeared before us; a squat, diminished Colette, with thinning chestnut hair and a large, lost face that stared at us in a kind of horror, as if surveying itself in a mirror. Plain and devastated, it might have belonged to a model who had been Lautrec's mistress and inherited her lover's sorrows.

Planting herself behind the microphone, Piaf began to sing, with a rabid fury that left one scorched. There were no old songs; the repertoire scorned nostalgia. Much of it has vanished through the sieve of my memory, but I shall never forget the r's that she rolled, or the defiance she embodied, in a number called 'Je ne regrette rien'. Clenching her fists against fate, she repudiated the past. 'C'est payé, balayé, oublié—*je me fous du passé.*'

The slate was wiped clean, and she was beginning again; as the lyrics put it, 'je repars à zéro'. She walked off the stage to an ambush of cheers, looking like an exalted concierge. I thought, as she left, of Max Beerbohm's tribute to Dan Leno: 'So little and frail a lantern could not long harbour so big a flame.' But Max was writing an obituary; *chez* Piaf, the lantern survives, though the flame is temporarily dimmed. She must get well soon, and relume it.

(1962)

Afore Night Come, BY DAVID RUDKIN, AT THE ARTS; *Macbeth*, BY WILLIAM SHAKESPEARE, AT STRATFORD-ON-AVON

The latest product of the Royal Shakespeare Company's experimental workshop is David Rudkin's *Afore Night Come*. It starts deceptively mildly. We are in an orchard near Birmingham, where a group of casual labourers are gathering pears; the work is arduous and ill-organised, and they fall to wrangling among themselves.

One of them is a Brummagem Ted; another is a student with a newly polished accent; yet another is a sour joker ever ready to demonstrate exactly how commercial salesmen get seduced by lonely housewives. Hobnails, who drives the fruit to market, is a mental deficient, employed on sufferance. They and their chums are joined by a disruptive fellow-worker—a shambling Irish tramp who wears a folded dishcloth on his head against the heat, and dark glasses on his nose against the glare. He speaks poetically, works spasmodically and seems to care little for his job; and somebody soon points out that he took no part in the war.

Almost imperceptibly, menace tightens around him. No vote is taken, but we become aware that he is the chosen scapegoat. Knives are quietly sharpened; and in a climactic scene of shrieking horror, silently observed by three tall pear-trees, a ritual slaughter straight out of *The Golden Bough* is enacted by three labourers in black oilcloths, while a plane sprays insecticide over the infected orchard. The corpse is beheaded and impaled on a pitchfork, as in the celebrated and still unsolved 'witchcraft murder' which took place in the Midlands in 1945, and on which Mr Rudkin's play may well be based.

It is flawed by its limping reluctance to come to an end, and by a proliferation of symbolic references to Jesus Christ; all the same, it bears those signs of insolent originality at which the critic's soul quickens, recognising the rare but always familiar stigmata that betoken genius. In a green corner of the Black Country, Mr Rudkin discloses a pocket of primordial rustic violence that has been ignored and isolated by the industrial revolution. In this context the adjective 'black' acquires an ancient, satanic significance; the Irish victim fiercely berates the Black Country as 'the sphincter of the earth'. Not since *Look Back in Anger* has a playwright made a debut more striking than this.

Was it by chance, I wonder, that Peter Hall chose to offer us two plays about witchcraft in the same week? The other, *Macbeth*, once again repels an attempt to conquer it. The Royal Shakespeare team sets up an efficient base camp on the lower slopes of the play, and its push towards the summit carries it beyond the abyss in which the ill-fated Wolfit party so tragically perished, many years ago; but the peak, where storms rage in perpetual darkness, predictably defeats it.

Eric Porter, the leader of the expedition, brings intelligence and carefully husbanded resources to a role that responds to nothing less than free-spending genius. He surprises neither us nor himself; between what he feels and what he actually expresses there stands a censor, whose name may be self-criticism.

Seven years have passed since Olivier annexed the part and left us marvelling: When comes there such another? Without him, the play's faults obtrude—its narrative monotony, once Banquo is dead; its summary abandonment, halfway through the evening, of the relationship between Macbeth and his wife, who never meet after the banquet; and the near-sameness of its major supporting characters. Here, if anywhere in the upper reaches of dramatic literature, is a play in desperate need of a sub-plot. Banquo, Macduff and Malcolm are simply three just men put upon by a tyrant; the characterisation is not individual but ethical—that is, they are 'noble' and Macbeth is not.

With Duncan the production (by Donald McWhinnie) makes a bloomer long sanctified by tradition. Since the play is a study of regicide, we ought to feel that the sin Macbeth commits is something vast and mortal, not petty and sneaking. Ageing though he is, Duncan must have about him an air of magnificence, a quality capable of inspiring awe; only thus can we appreciate the magnitude of the crime. It should be as if Lear were assassinated. At Stratford we get the usual saintly old dotard. How this custom grew up I can explain only in terms of money and prestige: no actor powerful enough to play Duncan properly would dream of accepting so small a part.

Especially in the first half, Mr McWhinnie's production has many compensating (though mostly negative) virtues. The witches neither cackle nor wail; they utter their auguries and imprecations like people who expect to be believed and therefore need not overstate their case. Lady Macbeth (Irene Worth) is likewise restrained and credible: 'Unsex me here' is spoken not as a bombastic verbal gesture but as a straightforward request, addressed to a supernatural authority that is perfectly capable of answering it.

Mr McWhinnie's dry approach works well enough until half-time, after which the play needs an Olivier blood transfusion to keep our hearts pounding. We have here a director finely equipped to cool the excesses of rhetoric, but strangely incompetent when it comes to generating heat.

(1962)

Le Misanthrope, by Molière, at the Piccadilly

Perhaps because we see it so seldom, we forget how great a play *Le Misanthrope* really is. And when we do see it, it is apt to be so ornately tricked out with lace and ribbons that we respond more to the period than to the text; and instead of Alceste, in all his confounding complexity, we usually get some such flimsy replacement as the posturing mannikin that M. Barrault makes of the role.

Bernard Dhéran's production at the Piccadilly avoids the first of these perils by plumping for quasi-modern dress; the men wear tails and coloured waistcoats, the women Cardin gowns, in a setting of black drapes from which are suspended three glowing Lurçat tapestries.

As for Alceste, it cannot be said that Jacques François gives us the whole man, but he gives us more of him than I have ever seen in one performance. He has the key to the part, which is that Alceste is comic outside and tragic inside. Nearly everything he does is silly; nearly everything he feels is immensely serious, with implications that go far beyond the plight of a particular man rebelling against the hypocrisy of a particular epoch. His insistence on absolute candour is blind, humourless and therefore funny; as Mr Maugham said, in a quotation of which I never tire, sincerity in society is like an iron girder in a house of cards. In part, Alceste is an egoist fastidiously singling himself out ('Je veux qu'on me distingue') from the herd; and this is the aspect traditionally stressed by players like M. Barrault, whose attitude towards the role—one of tolerant amusement—is summed up in Philinte's: 'Le monde par vos soins ne se changera pas.'

This is what we may call the Establishment interpretation. But there is more to Alceste than that. The play is a comedy of principle; and its hero raises a question that returns every day to pester the conscience. How far should one accept the rules of the society in which one lives? To put it another way: at what point does conformity become corruption? Only by answering such questions can the conscience truly define itself. Alceste flouts custom by acting on his beliefs and speaking precisely as he thinks: he ends up in self-imposed exile. *Mutatis mutandis*, his problem is that of the republican when the national anthem is played; or that of the pacifist when asked to pay income tax. The road from Alceste's stand to the doctrine of civil disobedience is long and tortuous, but not impassable.

Socially then, the play is full of resonance; erotically, it is not less so. Alceste's devouring love for Célimène is the love, in all ages, of the intellectual perfectionist for the clever, disarming, imperfect doll; she lives in the world as it is, he in the world as it ought to be, and that way friction lies. Did we not say as much when Mr Miller married Miss Monroe? And was not a similar disparity noted between Molière himself and Armande Béjart, the pretty coquette he took to wife? The moment in the last act when Alceste begs his mistress to marry him, despite her newly proven inconstancy, rings piercingly true—as true, almost, as the moment immediately after, when she rejects him.

Madeleine Delavaivre is an admirable Célimène, sweet of tongue and passionately shallow. M. François clutches at the furniture, gnaws his nails, and twists his face into innumerable *moues* of outrage. At all of which we smile; yet, performing as he does with that peculiar, polite intensity which in French actors often blurs the boundaries between formal comedy and formal tragedy, M. François is also able to convey that there are qualities in Alceste without which civilisation would have little purpose and self-respect no name. Small wonder that the play has always had a good press: in his commitment to tell the truth, at no matter what cost in friendship or prestige, Alceste is the critical spirit incarnate.

(1962)

Blitz!, BY LIONEL BART, AT THE ADELPHI

Mawkish where it tries to be poignant, flat where it means to be funny, and secondhand where it aims at period authenticity, Lionel Bart's *Blitz!* is a misfire on the grand scale, despite the devoted salvage work of Amelia Bayntun and a supporting cast of between twenty-eight and ninety-seven players. (Amid so much smoke, it is hard to be sure.)

All the obvious gestures of verisimilitude are made. We hear Sir Winston exhorting and Vera Lynn consoling; while in the background, accompanied by sumptuous detonations, London is unquestionably burning. Yet all this seems utterly detached from what is going on in the foreground—a trite squabble between two East End families (one Jewish, one Gentile) that could have taken place at any time in the last fifty years. True, the Jewish girl is blinded in an air raid, but her face is miraculously unscarred and, after a brief lapse into drunkenness, her Gentile boy-friend comes to his senses and marries her; meanwhile, to preserve moral parity between the households, Mr Bart makes the girl's brother a deserter, who ultimately repents. An Irish trio, some homeless Indians and a couple of Chinese crop up in the crowd scenes to symbolise multiracial amity: and Mr Bart permits himself one 'daring' touch— a Negro spiv.

The songs are straightforward music-hall stuff, spiced now and then with hints that the composer-lyricist is aware, if only telepathically, of the achievements of composers whose work is less well known in England than his own; by a sort of osmosis, phrases and cadences from minor American musicals seep into his melodies; and there is one tune—a lively children's number called 'Mums and Dads'—that sounds exactly like a reject from *Oliver!*

In all, I cannot feel that Mr Bart's theme has inspired him; nor can I honestly say I am sorry. Twenty-two years have passed since the blitz began, and I see no fruitful point in being nostalgic about it: after all, nobody was writing musicals about trench warfare in 1940. A bookmaker repeatedly quoted by James Agate once said that Marie Lloyd had a heart as big as Waterloo Station. *Blitz!* is as big as Waterloo Station, but it has no heart.

It does, however, have Sean Kenny's scenery, and herein may lie its true significance. Belasco and Novello went pretty far in the direction of spectacular realism; but in *Blitz!* there are distinct signs that the sets are taking over. They swoop down on the actors and snatch them aloft; four motor-driven towers prowl the stage, converging menacingly on any performer who threatens to hog the limelight; and whenever the human element looks like gaining control, they collapse on it in a mass of flaming timber.

In short, they let the cast know who's boss. They are magnificent, and they are war: who (they tacitly inquire) needs Lionel Bart? I have a fearful premonition of the next show Mr Kenny designs. As soon as the curtain rises, the sets will advance in a phalanx on the audience and summarily expel it from the theatre. After that, the next step is clear: Mr Kenny will invent sets that applaud.

(1962)

Chips With Everything, BY ARNOLD WESKER, AT THE ROYAL COURT

A gauntlet of a play has been flung down on the stage of the Royal Court Theatre. Arnold Wesker's *Chips with Everything* is furious, compassionate and unforgiving: taking as its microcosm a squad of R.A.F. conscripts, it reveals the class system in action—the process of unnatural selection that divides people into Lenin's categories of 'who: whom'—and although it invites us to rage at the rulers and to pity the ruled, it denies us the luxury of catharsis.

Men are not born obedient. Servility is a reflex brought about by subtle and patient conditioning; and Mr Wesker explains how the habit is formed. To begin with, the airmen are sharply individualised: but after a sustained dose of indoctrination, they are barely distinguishable from the stereotypes of British war films and Whitehall farce. They have learned their place in the hierarchy, and may some day aspire to the ambiguous, compromised status of Corporal Hill, the N.C.O. in charge of their hut.

This last is a character beautifully observed, and as beautifully played by Frank Finlay. By birth a prole, he has gone over to the enemy, whose orders he carries out to the letter with wry, humourless gusto. Professionally bellicose on the parade ground, he relapses when off duty into immediate sympathy with the men he has just been bullying; and though he is unaware of the paradox, Mr Wesker sees to it that we are not.

On a slightly higher level of authority we meet the Pilot Officer ('I want a man clean from toenail to hair-root. I want him so clean that he looks unreal') and the P.T. instructor:

> I want your body awake and ringing. I want you so light on your feet that the smoke from a cigarette could blow you away, and yet so strong that you stand firm before hurricanes. I hate thin men and detest fat ones. I want you like Greek gods.

I wish I could quote more, if only to quell the prevalent rumour that Mr Wesker is a primitive who has no feeling for words. In fact, he uses them with a secure adroitness that betokens not merely a good ear but a shaping mind and a remarkable flair for character-revealing rhythms.

Almost everyone in the platoon springs to life in speech. There is Dickey, the underdog who talks like a technocrat ('We developed voluble minds in that technical college and we came away equipped with data'); and Smiler, an amiable boy whose face is fixed in a permanent, unintentional grin that lands him eventually in the guardroom, where his will is systematically broken by such questions as: 'Is your mother pretty? . . . Have you ever seen her undressed? . . . Have you seen her naked?' Finally, there is Pip, the banker's son whom Mr Wesker has significantly chosen as his hero.

Pip has rebelled against his own background and taken it upon himself to stir his working-class hut-mates out of their apathy rather as Beatie Bryant sought to awaken her family in *Roots*. He instructs them in the difficult habit of nonconformity: in an impressive monologue he describes how he first went into a workers' café and realised how different—how sadly and needlessly different—they were. 'You have babies, you eat chips, and you take orders': and he decides that something must be done about it.

At a Christmas party in the N.A.A.F.I. the officers urge the men to put on a show, expecting a spot of rock-'n-roll and a few obscene stanzas of 'Eskimo Nell'; in defiance, Pip gets a Scot to recite Burns, and an Englishman to chant the ballad of 'The Cutty Wren', the accompaniment to which begins with a spoon rapped on a bottle and swells until every man on stage is stamping and clapping and singing. It is an electrifying and entirely credible moment: folk art becomes, before one's eyes, a contemporary possibility.

Some of what follows is less believable. Pip refuses to take part in bayonet practice; in the course of disciplinary brain-washing it emerges that his motive for siding with the proletariat is nothing nobler than a desire to be 'a Messiah to the masses'; whereupon he surrenders his mission and agrees, after a sentimental scene with one of his disgruntled admirers, to become an officer. Truth is hereabouts tailored to fit an effective finale, in which the squadron parades for royal inspection and the audience remains seated throughout the national anthem. I query the resolution; but the dramatic knot is magnificently tied, and I shall not quickly forget the words in which the military Establishment rebukes the man who defies it: 'We listen but we do not hear, we befriend but do not touch you, we applaud but we do not act. To tolerate is to ignore.'

John Dexter's direction puts discipline to its right uses. Surveying Mr Wesker's working-class characters, one feels not only that this is how they were, but also that they could, in a better ordered society, have turned out very differently. In what is, Mr Wesker implies what might have been; and there are few theatrical gifts more basic than that.

(1962)

The Caucasian Chalk Circle, BY BERTOLT BRECHT, AT
THE ALDWYCH

In this month's issue of *Encounter* I am gravely chided. Nigel Dennis, a playwright and critic whose wit I revere, accuses me of judging plays by ideologies—by whether or not I agree with the attitudes they embody. Instead of allowing a play to impose itself on me (he declares), I impose on it my own criteria, moral and political, and if it fails to measure up to them, I condemn it. Why, he seems to be asking, can I not approach each new work as a separate experience, to be judged on its own terms without reference to mine?

The simple answer is that Mr Dennis claims more for criticism than I do. He expects of it absolute truth, whereas I aim only at a truth that is personal and relative. A play cannot be judged in isolation any more than a building can: it must be seen in relation to the landscape as a whole. If the latter is crowded with drama that conveys, openly or obliquely, a message of faith in conservative values, it is the job of the radical critic to act as a bulldozer, thereby making room for the outlawed opinions he prizes. In this way he performs the basic critical function of restoring the balance; and when his task is done, he must not repine if critics on the other side seek to tilt the opposite end of the seesaw.

'Beautifully written and constructed, though I detest the ideas it expresses' is legitimate appraisal, and so is: 'I like what the author has to say, but I deplore the manner in which he says it.' What is not legitimate is to ignore the ideas altogether. You cannot swallow Leni Riefenstahl's *Triumph of the Will* in toto without swallowing Nazism; and the same applies to Eisenstein's *Strike* and Socialism. The critic owes it to his readers to make his convictions clear where they are relevant to the work under review. If he fails to do so, he is guilty of withholding evidence; and if he has no convictions, he is less a critic than a mirror.

So much by way of preamble to the Royal Shakespeare's production of Brecht's *Caucasian Chalk Circle*. The subject is ownership. What belongs to whom? The prologue, set in Russia at the end of the last war, shows us two groups of peasants vying for possession of a fertile valley. A storyteller, urbanely played by Michael Flanders, is called in to persuade them that the land should be given to those who can use it best. From here we flash back to the exemplary tale of Grusche, a servant girl who looks after a highborn baby when its mother flees a palace revolution.

The telling is epic and episodic, Brechtian in the strictest sense, chopped up into significant fragments of action on the ceaselessly revolving stage. Through perils worthy of Pauline and peasant *tableaux* that would not have disgraced Brueghel, Grusche journeys with the child. Masks and billowing silken curtains, borrowed from the Chinese theatre, fill in the background. Hereabouts *naïveté* takes on an unlooked-for beauty; one feels reintroduced to innocence.

Brecht's bare, chapped, open-air poetry is given its full value. In the second half we follow the career of Azdak, the shady scribe who is appointed judge—emblem of the unjust man who subverts feudal justice, the coruscating twister who allies himself with the outlawed and the under-privileged. In its roistering ambiguities the part is almost Shakespearean; though one would hardly guess as much from the hectically scrambled delivery that mars Hugh Griffith's otherwise irresistible performance.

One blenches at lines like 'Do your stuff, flatfoot!' and at peasants who speak in the purest Mile End Cockney; but on the whole the production need not shrink from comparison with that of the Berliner Ensemble. Under-rehearsed though it is by continental standards, it towers over everything else in London, and I offer my felicitations to the director, William Gaskill, on a remarkable feat of generalship. To revert to my preamble: I endorse the play's message, but no message can confer greatness on a play unless a man of genius delivers it. The touchstone, in other words, is not what Brecht says but the fact that it is Brecht who says it.

(1962)

Journey to the Cradle

'Pom, pom, pom, pom,' Tyrone Guthrie sang softly—an Irish hymn, I believe—as our tourist bus moved out of Athens along the Eleusinian Way. A few rows behind him sat François Billetdoux, the author of *Chin Chin*, round-faced and beaming beneath a jaunty blue yachting-cap; nearby, Michel Saint-Denis sucked at his pipe and looked sagely avuncular.

There were some forty of us in all—playwrights, designers, architects, directors and critics, invited by the Greek Tourist Office to take part in a Unesco conference on 'mass spectacles' and their place in the theatre of the future. Today we were to witness a mass spectacle of the past: Euripides's *Bacchae*, staged in front of 14,000 pilgrims in the great auditorium at Epidaurus.

Not everyone listed in the conference brochure actually boarded the bus. Roger Planchon, the brilliant young cardinal-inquisitor who runs the Théâtre de la Cité de Villeurbanne, was among those absent; but then Planchon, like many Frenchmen, is a highly reluctant tourist; a few days later he turned down a trip to the Parthenon on the grounds that he had already seen it in a documentary film. 'They spent four weeks finding the best camera angles,' he blandly explained. 'How could I find better ones in two hours?' And thus he missed the orange-and-lemon light that falls at sunset on those delicately leaning pillars.

Except by a solitary Roumanian, the Iron Curtain countries were unrepresented in our debates: beneath the façade of international amity there lurked an unmistakable element of *colloque*-and-dagger. Politics and art are tightly enmeshed in Greece, and Leftish infiltration into the theatre is strictly proscribed: I discovered, for example, that the composer originally chosen to provide incidental music for *The Bacchae* had been summarily dismissed for criticising the regime. His replacement was

Hadjidakis, whose tunes have been ubiquitous in the Greek theatre since he wrote the theme-song for *Never On Sunday*.

The overland route to Epidaurus skirts the gulf of Salamis on its way to the Peloponnese. 'From that hill,' says our guide, a bright black-haired girl at once too sane to be a chauvinist and too Greek to be anything else, 'the arrogant Persian, Xerxes, saw the annihilation of his fleet, due to the witfull inspiration of the Athenians.' Beyond Corinth, we pass the gorge of Ayios Sostos, where in 1822 a thousand Greeks ambushed six times as many Turks and cut them to pieces. 'Greece,' says the guide merrily, 'is full of sophisticated death-traps.'

Her pride is infectious. One almost forgets that, apart from a handful of poets, a Cretan painter falsely styled El Greco, and a mild latterday Renaissance in the visual arts, this is a country with an unbroken tradition—nearly a thousand years old—of artistic sterility. Only the solace of a perfect climate has mellowed the militant nostalgia of Greek patriotism.

'Leave me alone!' cried Katina Paxinou, the obstreperous *doyenne* of Greek acting, when a friend of mine rashly remarked that the inhabitants of a certain Attic village reminded him of Bulgarians. 'Of course they remind you. Greece used to be everywhere. Greece was to Gibraltar. We once owned Sicily. When we were building the Parthenon the Bulgarians were apes in the trees, eating nuts. Don't talk to me—leave me alone!'

But even classical Athens has its detractors. Last year Robert Graves, under the direction of his daughter Jenny Nicholson, made a short 16 mm film in which he mischievously accused the Greeks of having fathered all the ills of contemporary civilisation. They invented athletics, he said, but also crooked athletics; drama, but also commercial drama. They divided the mind from the body by creating the concept of the intellectual, who could cerebrate in peace as long as there were four or five slaves to wait on him. More crucially, they upset the balance of the sexes by giving men the ascendancy over women; Delphi, according to Graves, has not been the same since Apollo took over. And if you want to know who invented brain-washing, you need look no further than the waters of Lethe.

Suddenly we debouch on to the Argive plain. The land flows down from a semicircle of mountains to the port of Argos; so that the valley resembles some god-sized enlargement of an ancient amphitheatre. To one side stands the wrecked acropolis of Mycenae, ruggedly upthrust and flanked by two bald peaks, on one of which there blazed the beacon fire that signalled the end of the Trojan war and warned Clytemnestra that her husband was homeward bound.

On these bleak hills no olive or cypress flourishes: this is Macbeth country, and the citadel, with its steep approach and massive gate, guarded by twin lionesses in stone, might well be Dunsinane. We clamber across the bedrooms and invade the burial-grounds of the House of Atreus, which destroyed itself thirty centuries ago and gave birth to that dramatised celebration of calamity that we nowadays know as tragedy. Through this gate came Agamemnon the victim and Orestes the avenger, prototypes of the two Hamlets, *père et fils*. We are all chilled and impressed, especially Guthrie, who strides in khaki through the ruins, tall and unfailingly inquisitive like Tati in *Les Vacances de M. Hulot*.

Thence, via the pretty port of Nauplia, to Epidaurus. A gigantic car park, with tourist buses snug as sardines. Green lawns and capacious snack-bars: 'A people's Glyndebourne,' says one of our number. A steady flood of shirt-sleeved ticket-holders moves towards the auditorium, which was built in the fourth century B.C. and excavated in 1910: not the biggest of existing Greek theatres, but assuredly the best preserved. Carved out of a hillside, it is part of a sanctuary once devoted to Aesculapius, the god of healing—which seems appropriate, for what is catharsis but healing by means of spiritual purgation?

Loudspeakers blare in four languages, bidding us leave our beer and sandwiches and occupy our seats. So I climb and elbow my way towards the two square feet of stone that are my allotted section of a semi-circular ridge. My seat, roughly halfway back, is in the twenty-second row, from which the faces down front seem doll-like, inexpressive ovals: I recall Guthrie's statement, in our *colloque*, that a spectator further removed from an open stage than the eighteenth row is exposed to appalling imperfections of sight and sound.

In an arc of some 200 degrees, the auditorium at Epidaurus steeply surrounds a circular acting area, which is backed by a gloomy setting of modern construction, representing the façade and portals of a palace. Beyond this there is a vista of pines and a prospect of jagged hills, behind which the sun sets, thereby enabling the play to begin: how the ancient Greeks survived a full, sunbaked day of drama, one play after another from dawn till dusk, is a matter of wonder. The cicadas rasp, and an owl sets up a mournful soprano hooting: both sounds are reproduced with dry, piercing clarity by the acoustics for which the place is famous. A gong is banged three times, the spotlights gild the apron stage, Dionysus enters, and the play begins.

For nearly all of us, *The Bacchae* was a disappointment. 'I enjoyed the occasion,' said Guthrie, 'more than the performance.' One heard a tame recital of a ferocious play: as always at Epidaurus, the text was translated into modern Greek.

What do you do if you are a Mediterranean with a large open-air arena at your disposal for festival purposes? If you are Spanish, you hire matadors and kill bulls; if you are Greek, you hire actors and kill kings. But where was the ritual majesty that one had expected?

Euripides's masterpiece, composed in his seventies, concerns a king half-appalled and half-attracted by the Dionysiac rites of the Bacchic women. Like a censor venturing into *Lady Chatterley's Lover*, he decides to sample their pleasures at first hand; but finally, as if dredging the depths of his subconscious, he encounters among their number his mother, who seizes and murders him.

This stark, outrageous tale was accompanied at Epidaurus by choric contributions from a group of young women about as capable of suggesting demoniacal possession as the senior class at Italia Conti. When Dionysus destroyed the palace of Pentheus, we saw nothing but a squirt or two of artificial smoke and a few projected flickers from a fire-machine. Venus suddenly gleamed in the western sky during the chorus's paean to Aphrodite, but this was surely an astronomical coincidence. The renowned Alexis Minotis directed the play and appeared as the king's grandfather; but the only tragic *frissons* were imparted by his wife, Katina Paxinou, who gave us a fully orchestrated rendering of maternal grief. Moaning and hoarsely sobbing, Mme Paxinou veritably sang the blues.

The Greek tradition of performing the classics *en plein air* is not, as we sometimes imagine, continuous since antiquity. In its present form it is relatively new; it was revived some thirty years ago after a lapse of sixteen centuries, during which time the auditoria were either unoccupied or unexcavated. Epidaurus is an experiment, and the Greeks know very little more than we do about amphitheatrical techniques.

Last Sunday, the National Theatre followed *The Bacchae* with the world première of Euripides's *Helen*—perhaps the only extant play to have languished unperformed for more than two millennia—and did it rather less than justice. Described in the programme as a tragedy (and directed as such), the piece is unmistakably a comedy, and a patriotic comedy at that. It declares that the Helen who went with Paris to Troy was a deceitful facsimile, devised by the jealous goddess Hera, while the real Helen was spirited to Egypt to await the return of Menelaus. The result is an ironic, tongue-in-mask satire on the theme of mistaken identity. Helen's honour is triumphantly saved: instead of cuckolding a Greek husband, she betrays an Egyptian wooer and sails happily home with her spouse. The style has the ornate elegance of mature Giraudoux.

As before, I sat twenty rows back, and pitied those who occupied the twenty-odd rows behind me. I also noticed that nobody except the chorus made any use of the forestage. Some kind of magnetic attraction tugged the players backwards, so that their faces should be visible to every spectator. This confirmed my suspicion that the proscenium stage —or, at least, a stage that draws a straight line between performer and audience—appeals to something deeply embedded in the psychology of acting.

On the whole, I doubt whether we have much to learn from the Greek theatre in its present revivalist phase. As audiences, we have lost our innocence. Last Sunday, when Helen and Menelaus were reunited after seventeen years' separation, 14,000 people burst into spontaneous applause. Their delight was moral, and reflected a simple, wholehearted approval of marital reconciliation. That simplicity, that naïve wholeness of response, is something we cannot hope to recapture. I state this as a fact, without nostalgia and without regret.

(1962)

The Merchant of Venice, BY WILLIAM SHAKESPEARE, AT THE OLD VIC

Received opinion declares that *Troilus and Cressida* is the most modern of Shakespeare's plays; but a case as strong could be made out for *The Merchant of Venice*. Quite nakedly, its protagonist is money— money lent, money invested, money exchanged for goods, money as an incitement to love.

For the first time in our theatre, capital takes the stage and rules the action; and where more aptly than in Venice, a great trading centre doomed to decline because it faced East when commerce was looking to the West? Later in the Shakespeare canon we shall see the Venetians fighting for their threatened prosperity, dispatching a Moorish general to safeguard their Eastern trade routes; but already, in *The Merchant*, they are feeling the pinch.

Antonio's melancholy is easily explained: he has incipient ulcers, brought on by worrying about the argosies on which his credit as an importer depends. It is he who finances the spendthrift young nobleman Bassanio in his shameless design to woo 'a lady, richly left'; meanwhile, the determination of the landed aristocracy to preserve its capital and keep out adventurers is the motive behind the casket test, prescribed by Portia's father in his will. Remains the Jew, heir and victim of a long

European tradition that forbade members of his race to own land or engage in trade, and hence drove them to seek wealth through usury.

Like a good Christian, Shakespeare pities Shylock the man but condemns him as a moneylender, because he commits the unnatural sin of making base inanimate metal breed. Here, as elsewhere, the playwright speaks for his age, giving magnificent utterance to a limited historic vision: it never occurs to him that Antonio, who invests for profit, is in no position to despise Shylock for expecting interest on his loans. A more modern viewpoint, however, breaks through in the trial scene, when Shylock hits on a potentially explosive argument:

> You have among you many a purchased slave,
> Which, like your asses and your dogs and mules,
> You use in abject and in slavish parts
> Because you bought them—shall I say to you,
> Let them be free, marry them to your heirs?
> Why sweat they under burdens? let their beds
> Be made as soft as yours, and let their palates
> Be season'd with such viands? You will answer,
> The slaves are ours:—so do I answer you:
> The pound of flesh, which I demand of him,
> Is dearly bought, 'tis mine, and I will have it.

For 'slave' read 'worker'; and you have a classic statement of the case against capitalism. It is logically unanswerable; and, needless to say, it goes unanswered. The Duke abruptly changes the subject; and before long the merchants, the landowners and the law, united in irresistible coalition, have brought the outsider to heel.

I offer these reflections to avoid dwelling too long on the mild disappointment occasioned by Michael Elliott's production. Lee Montague's Shylock is a niggling miniature, devoid of the suave malevolent grandeur that befits the king of the Rialto. Sheila Allen, with her towering presence, her soothing bass-clarinet voice, and her deeply concerned gravity in the advocate's role, is already halfway to Portia; all she needs is a rocket under her, to produce the missing spark of wit. As it stands, her performance is dreamily erotic, but it suggests the morning after rather than the night before.

(1962)

A Note on Satire

Satire is protest, couched in wit, against the notion that there is anything more important than the fact that all men must die. To quote from an American historian, Theodore Roszak:

> Man is the animal who cannot assimilate death; rather, he must eject the organic need to die which is in him. . . . Disassociation, or repression, is our way of asserting our independence of the body. And history is the course of repression. It is man's attempt to flee his mortality by investing his sensuous vitality in an enduring personal project that 'outlives' him. . . . That essentially is what the building of cities, the raising of pyramids, the conquest of empires is about. . . . Happiness would seem to have become an objective possibility for the human race. And yet the angry élites of the world and those who support them want us to turn our backs upon it. In their hands, real and urgent options become hopeless Utopias. . . . This is madness.

Or, to cite a parallel text by James Baldwin, culled from a recent *New Yorker*:

> Perhaps the whole root of our trouble, the human trouble, is that we will sacrifice all the beauty of our lives, will imprison ourselves in totems, taboos, crosses, blood sacrifices, steeples, mosques, races, armies, flags, nations, in order to deny the fact of death, which is the only fact we have.

The people who exalt abstractions, concepts, dogmas, ideals and ideologies above the five great human imperatives of birth, food, shelter, love-making and death—these are, and have always been, the satirist's *raison d'être* and his perpetual target.

(1962)

King Lear, by WILLIAM SHAKESPEARE, at STRATFORD-ON-AVON AND LATER IN LONDON

Lay him to rest, the royal Lear with whom generations of star actors have made us reverently familiar; the majestic ancient, wronged and maddened by his vicious daughters; the felled giant, beside whose bulk the other characters crouch like pygmies. Lay also to rest the archaic notion that Lear is automatically entitled to our sympathy because he is a king who suffers.

A great director (Peter Brook) has scanned the text with fresh eyes and discovered a new protagonist—not the booming, righteously indignant Titan of old, but an edgy, capricious old man, intensely difficult to live with. In short, he has dared to direct *King Lear* from a standpoint of moral neutrality.

The results are revolutionary. Instead of assuming that Lear is right, and therefore pitiable, we are forced to make judgments—to decide between his claims and those of his kin. And the balance, in this uniquely magnanimous production, is almost even. Though he disposes of his kingdom, Lear insists on retaining authority; he wants to exercise power without responsibility, without fulfilling his part of the feudal contract. He is wilfully arrogant, and deserves much of what he gets.

Conversely, his daughters are not fiends. Goneril is genuinely upset by her father's irrational behaviour, and nobody could fault her for carping at the conduct of Lear's knights, who are here presented as a rabble of bellicose tipplers. After all, what use has a self-deposed monarch for 100 armed men? Wouldn't twenty-five be enough? We begin to understand Regan's weary inquiry: 'What need one?'

Such is Mr Brook's impartiality, so cool the moral scrutiny he applies to the text, that we can laugh at Lear's crazy obtuseness without endangering the play's basic purpose, which is tragic; but generally tragic, not individually so. Mr Brook has done for *Lear* what he did for Alec Clunes's Claudius in *Hamlet* some years ago: he has taught the 'unsympathetic' characters to project themselves from their own point of view, not from that of the inevitably jaundiced hero.

Writing about this incomparable production, I cannot pretend to the tranquillity in which emotion should properly be recollected. To convey my impressions, I prefer to quote a slightly revised version of the programme notes I scrawled in the Stratford dark.

Flat white setting, combining Brecht and Oriental theatre, against which ponderous abstract objects dangle. Everyone clad in luminous leather. Paul Scofield enters with grey crew-cut and peering gait; one notes at once the old man's trick of dwelling on unexpected vowels and lurching through phrases as if his voice were barely under rational control.... Brook means us to condemn his stupidity, and to respect the Fool (Alec McCowen) who repeatedly tries to din his message into the deaf royal ears.... The knights are tight, and Goneril (Irene Worth) is right to be annoyed; but won't this wreck the scene in which Kent takes his revenge on Goneril's uppish steward? ...

Later: Kent certainly loses his laughs, but the scene reveals him as an unreflecting bully who is unable to give a coherent answer to Cornwall's patiently iterated question: 'Why art thou angry?' This is the alienation effect in full operation: a beloved character seen from a strange and unlovely angle.... Gloucester (Alan Webb), so often Lear's understudy and rival moaner, has taken on a separate identity: a shifty old rake and something of a trimmer, capable of switching his allegiance from Lear to Cornwall and back again....

Spurned by his daughters, Lear loses his wits purely in order to punish them: 'I shall go mad!' is a threat, not a pathetic prediction. 'Blow, winds' is an aria of fury, the ecstasy of vengeful madness; as Scofield howls it, three copper thunder-sheets descend behind him, rumbling and quivering....

Top marks for his drained, unsentimental reading of the lines about 'unaccommodated man'. (Lear by now is a rustic vagabond: cf. the classless derelicts of Samuel Beckett, and especially the crippled hero of *Endgame*.) High marks, too, for Brook's decision to stage Gloucester's trial in the same hovel where Lear has recently arraigned his daughters.

The blinding of Gloucester could hardly be more shocking. 'Upon these eyes of thine,' says Cornwall, 'I'll set my foot': and Brook, responding to the ghastly hint, gives Cornwall a pair of golden spurs with which to carry the threat into literal effect....

Am baffled as always by Edgar's inexplicable failure to reveal himself to his blinded father: Shakespeare is here milking a situation for more than it is worth....

And suddenly, greatness. Scofield's halting, apologetic delivery of 'I fear I am not in my perfect mind'; sightless Gloucester, sitting cross-legged on the empty stage while the noise of battle resounds in the wings; and the closing epiphany, wherein Lear achieves a wisdom denied him in his sanity—a Stoic determination, long in the moulding, to endure his going hence....

But even Brook is defeated by Edmund's tangled liaisons with Regan and Goneril: mainly because James Booth handles verse with the finesse of a gloved pugilist picking up pins, but also because the minutiae of sexual jealousy seem puny beside Lear's enormous pain.... Lighting deliberately bright throughout, even during the nocturnal scenes, as in the Chinese theatre; and no music except towards the end, when the text demands it....

This production brings me closer to Lear than I have ever been; from now on, I not only know him but can place him in his harsh and unforgiving world.

Last month, reviewing Peter Brook's bleak and beautiful production of *King Lear* before it moved from Stratford to London, I stressed its moral neutrality: the way in which, by presenting Lear as a cranky old despot who deserved a come-uppance from Goneril and Regan, Mr Brook had balanced the scales, so that the characters were neither 'bad' nor 'good' but equally entitled to our attentive concern.

They were not doomed by vice or predestinately driven: they were merely people, varying manifestations of 'the thing itself'. Not much nobility was permitted them; often they took the stage kneeling, grovelling, stumbling, squirming, wriggling about like worms, forced into graceless postures, slumped in the stocks, or shoved on their backs to be tortured.

I see now a clue to the nature of Mr Brook's cruel, unsparing egalitarianism; his production is amoral because it is set in an amoral universe. For him the play is a mighty philosophic farce in which the leading figures enact their roles on a gradually denuded stage that resembles, at the end, a desert graveyard or unpeopled planet. It is an ungoverned world; for the first time in tragedy, a world without gods, with no possibility of hopeful resolution. No Malcolm or Fortinbras is on hand to rebuild this ruined kingdom: Albany, the heir-apparent, resigns his inheritance to be shared between Kent, who promptly rejects it, and Edgar, who responds with a brief and highly ambiguous speech about obeying 'the weight of this sad time'.

Mr Brook never tries to compel our tears, though we may weep if we wish; as when Paul Scofield's growling king shares a bench with Alec McCowen's sniping fool, the latter anxiously gauging how close his master is to madness; or when Lear and Gloucester, respectively mindless and eyeless, meet at Dover and huddle together for comfort. But in general the tone is as starkly detached as Albany's, on hearing that Regan and Goneril are dead:

> This judgment of the heavens, that makes us tremble,
> Touches us not with pity.

The key to Mr Brook's approach may be found in an essay by Jan Kott, the Polish critic, comparing *Lear* to Beckett's *Endgame*; I have cited it before in these columns, and it is now available in *Shakespeare Notre Contemporain*, a collection of M. Kott's essays.

In brief, his argument is that Beckett and Shakespeare have more in common with each other than either has with the romantic, naturalistic theatre that historically separates them. For one thing, they have a sense of the grotesque, of the absurd discrepancy between the idea of absolute values and the fact of human fragility. Tragedy in the cathartic sense occurs only when there are fixed gods, fates, moral principles or laws of nature to which a man's acts can be opposed and by which they can be judged. Where no such absolutes obtain, the effect is not tragic but grotesque. It brings with it no consolation. 'Tragedy is the theatre of priests,' says Kott, 'the grotesque is the theatre of clowns.'

In *Lear*, he insists, the stage must be empty and sterile, a bare space of hostile earth. Gloucester's mock suicide is a tragic situation transmuted into farce; unless the gods exist, it is a comic irrelevance, a sacrifice made to a Godot who shows no signs of arriving. 'In both versions of *Endgame*, Shakespeare's and Beckett's, the Book of Job is played by clowns.' Shakespeare employs a quartet of near-buffoons—a madman, a fool, a blind man and a feigned demon. As for Beckett: 'The two couples—Pozzo blinded and Lucky struck dumb, Hamm who cannot rise and Clov who cannot sit—are drawn from the "endgame" of *King Lear*.'

Mr Brook, reversing the process, bases his *Lear* on Beckett. At times the measurements fail to tally; there is nothing remotely Beckettian, for example, in the Edmund–Regan–Goneril triangle or the battle scenes. But where the concept fits, as it mostly does, the production burns itself into your mind; you forget poor over-parted Edmund (James Booth), and remember only that you will seldom see such another Gloucester, and never such another Lear. Nor are you likely to emerge from a theatre with a sharper or more worrying sense of mortality.

(1962)

Giselle, AT COVENT GARDEN

Ballet is not my business, nor poaching my practice; but the sudden offer, in a week scarcely bulging with theatrical goodies, of two seats for *Giselle* was too tempting to decline: so much has been written about the purely dramatic impact of the Fonteyn–Nureyev partnership that I felt justified in trespassing.

Unlike many of my friends, I do not subscribe to the view that ballet, as a separate art form, is a passing fad. That it is young I admit (one can hardly do otherwise, since nothing in its surviving repertoire is much more than 130 years old); but this does not necessarily mean that the gods love it.

I do not underrate the arguments against it—that it is essentially a court entertainment which the nineteenth-century bourgeoisie adopted in order to raise themselves to the level of kings; that it got above itself when it claimed artistic independence and sought to be more than the handmaiden of drama and opera; and that it is out of all proportion for a single ballet company to consume (at a rough but conservative estimate) more than twice as much public money every year as the whole of the London theatre.

I also concede that *Giselle* itself is something of a hoax: where else but in the ballet world would you find a grown-up audience ready to believe that the betrayal of a village maid by a nobleman in mufti, played out to sweetly whimpering music in a pantomime setting of canvas cottages packed with scampering peasants, was an emotional experience comparable in intensity to *Hamlet*?

All the same, if faced with a question like: 'Must we scrap ballet?' I would certainly answer no. As practised in Britain, it blithely insults my intelligence and leaves my deeper sensibilities untouched; but it does appeal to my sense of occasion, which was profoundly stirred last Tuesday night. In her own way, that dark-haired woman, signalling madness while spinning so prettily, was every bit as poignant as Mary Pickford at her peak; as Stark Young said of another American actress, she was 'all music and security of outline, like a swan on water'; but what moved me more than anything else in her performance was the fact that I knew she was Margot Fonteyn.

As for Nureyev, I mistimed my emotional response, owing to the pressure of thrilled expectation in the house, and began to be moved just *before* he made his entrance. When he paced into sight, like a *dégagé* faun, I instantly recognised the physical ideal of romantic ballet and its audience: a frail, wild young animal, 'poetic' in the archaic sense of 'possibly prone to T.B.'

In the second act, down on one knee with his head cradled in his arms, he presented a perfect, fleeting image of contrition; and his face, which is that of a wide-eyed, mutinous orphan with a shock of ungoverned hair, reminded me throughout of the youthful Johnnie Ray, who had the same kind of delinquent pathos. Talent like this is born to flower in close-up; sooner or later Nureyev must surely migrate from the ballet to the cinema.

Meanwhile, I defy anyone not to be affected by the curtain-calls of *Giselle*; here, more than anywhere else, romantic ballet justifies its existence. Embracing bouquets, Dame Margot curtsies; Nureyev bows deeply from the neck, while the other men bow from the waist; Dame Margot proffers a bloom or two; Nureyev accepts them and kisses her hand; solo calls alternate with dual calls; and applause, the incessant obbligato, rhythmically swells and subsides. The more one claps, the more one's eyes mist with tears—tears of gratitude, perhaps, that art can be as undemanding, and at the same time as status-spawning, as this.

(1963)

Who's Afraid of Virginia Woolf?, BY EDWARD ALBEE, AT THE BILLY ROSE THEATRE, NEW YORK

The pride of the New York season, acclaimed alike by critics and civilians, is Edward Albee's *Who's Afraid of Virginia Woolf?* Every year there is at least one Broadway play to carp at which is tantamount to blasphemy; and this year Mr Albee's is it. Smiles freeze on hitherto friendly faces when I say that I found it too funny. 'You mean you think people destroying themselves are funny?' said one frozen face, to which I replied that I didn't and that that was exactly the point.

Mr Albee's piece is a marathon dissection of that familiar corpse, the married life of middle-class intellectuals; it is a microcosm of a microcosm, a cloistered game of ill-mixed doubles played out by a cast of four in three acrimonious acts. They are tipsy when it starts—just after a faculty party on a New England campus—and barely controllable when it ends; the action covers the small hours of their ripening intoxication.

The host is George, a middle-aged historian despised by his wife Martha, whose father founded the University; an adroit wielder of the castrating snippers, she enjoys reminding him that his academic life is a failure. No slouch where verbal sadism is concerned, he habitually retorts, with an eager, bonhomous smile creasing his face, that Martha is six years his senior, upset by the menopause, and therefore to be pitied. They sharpen their claws on two visitors—a square young biologist, ruthlessly bent on success, and his idiot bride, whom he married only because she developed a hysterical pregnancy.

Having humiliated each other to their mutual satisfaction, George and his wife turn their attention to a new game, which George calls 'getting the guests'. Before dawn breaks, the biologist has tried and physically failed to go to bed with Martha, and his bride, between vomiting fits, has learned from George that the reason for her hasty marriage is common knowledge. Another piece of bourgeois debris now comes crashing down: to compensate for their sterility, George and Martha have long since connived at a private pretence that they have a grown-up son. To revenge himself for Martha's attempted infidelity, George exposes this fantasy as an outright lie.

The false son, on whom the last act rests, is a strained and implausible gimmick; and the implied debate between humanism (the neurotic historian) and science (the heartless biologist) is too heavily loaded in the former's favour to be of much dialectical interest. What perturbed me most of all, however, was the author's respect for his audience; on the threshold of making them wince, he retreats and lets them off with a laugh. And the cast assists him, scoring quick comic points wherever the chance is offered, fearful (as Broadway actors too often are) of losing, even for a moment, the customers' rapt, approving attention. By signs like these we recognise a panicky theatre.

Mr Albee's text advances the great American art of insult; it is full of brilliant poetic invective and soaring cadenzas of spite, and it could not be better acted than by Uta Hagen, lecherously booming, and Arthur Hill as her blithely destructive mate; but it leaves one's heart unbruised and unmoved. It is too funny by half.

It also dwells on impotence, a long-established Broadway theme that has lately hardened (or softened) into an obsession. No serious play is complete without it. Mr Albee's scientist cannot make love to Miss Hagen; nor could Brick to his wife in *Cat on a Hot Tin Roof*; nor could Edward G. Robinson to his mistress in Paddy Chayefsky's *Middle of the Night*; nor could Jason Robards to his child-bride in Lillian Hellman's *Toys in the Attic*; nor could Paul Newman to Geraldine Page in *Sweet Bird of Youth*. In fact, since Stanley Kowalsky hit the sack with Blanche Dubois some sixteen years ago, the number of Broadway heroes who have proved their sexual prowess in the course of the action could probably be counted on the fingers of one hand.

(1963)

Mother Courage, BY BERTOLT BRECHT, AT THE MARTIN BECK THEATRE, NEW YORK

Brecht on Broadway: the very idea is as improbable as a fire-extinguisher on the burning deck. Yet it is now an accomplished fact. Jerome Robbins's production of *Mother Courage* opened here ten days ago to a critical reception that was seldom less than respectful and in some cases roundly enthusiastic.

The first outburst of vigorous, principled dissent has come from *Variety*, the soi-disant bible of show business, whose first and only commandment is, 'Thou shalt repay the investors with interest, or else.' Its reviewer found the play 'Sophomorically obvious, cynical, self-consciously drab and tiresome'; and he asked himself: 'Why should anyone think it might meet the popular requirements of Broadway—that is, be commercial?'

The question is practical and well worth posing; for the truth is that the more honestly Brecht is presented, the less likely he is to appeal to the middle-class, postprandial Broadway audience. They insist on clearly defined emotional climaxes, whether of laughter or tears; they like to be told how to feel; and the relaxed, ambiguous coolness of an authentic Brechtian production would leave them darkling in a twilight of boredom. They care little for a good tale told quietly, and even less for the aesthetic rewards to be gleaned from monochrome understatement. They would rather have Technicolor, however factitious its tints, than the earthy Brechtian shades of brown and beige; and their preference mars an otherwise honourable production.

While singing 'The Song of Fraternisation', Barbara Harris lets her voice pathetically quiver, thus defying the Brechtian precept that what makes a raped girl pitiful is not the way she sounds but the simple, concrete fact that she has been raped. As Mother Courage herself, a flinty peasant matriarch of the seventeenth century, Anne Bancroft is at once too young and too citified; although she ages effectively, and ends up looking not unlike Helene Weigel in the Berliner Ensemble production.

The difference has to do with emphasis. When Weigel says: 'Curse the war!' she shrugs the line off as if it were a mournful cliché; Miss Bancroft yells it, clenching her fists. Similarly, instead of the immobile, soundless cry, head flung back, with which Weigel reacts to the death of her son, Miss Bancroft stumbles halfway across the stage, emitting strangled yelps. Now and then she is even willing to sob, because that is what the customers demand.

I could snipe *ad infinitum* at Mr Robbins's production; he dispenses with the revolving stage that is essential for Mother Courage's wagon, he underlines the message by interlarding the scenes with slides depicting modern war, and he tolerates in Eric Bentley's adaptation such incongruously urban lines as 'Mother, may I smack him in the puss?' But he has obviously tried hard, and if he fails, the fault lies less with him than with the audience he is aiming to attract.

What they most enjoy—empathy, violence, loud colours and safe liberal exhortation—is precisely what Brecht spent the greater part of his life detesting. There is no room on Broadway for playwrights as simple and sceptical as this.

(1963)

Henry IV, BY LUIGI PIRANDELLO, AT THE CITIZENS' THEATRE, GLASGOW

Clichés breed on the wing, and soon lose touch with the good earth of fact. I instance the notion, widely received, that the new school of English actors is entirely made up of working-class realists whose horizon is bounded by pubs, slums and factory chimneys.

The reverse is the case: what attracts our young lions is not the mundane but the heroic, which they espouse as devoutly as Kean or Irving ever did. O'Toole gives us Lawrence, that latterday male St Joan, a militant ascetic betrayed by politicians, and then goes on to the poetic excesses of *Baal*; and now we have Albert Finney testing his strength on another diary of madness, Pirandello's *Henry IV*. The new men have their limitations, but they are limitations of talent, not of class.

Big actors will always be drawn to outsize drama; but how came Mr Finney to Glasgow? For the best of reasons: self-improvement. Seeking experience as a director, he offered his services to several repertory companies; one of them, the Citizens' Theatre, replied that they would gladly let him direct a couple of productions if he would first play the lead in *Henry IV*, which they had already scheduled for the spring. He agreed; and plunged into a play that was not of his choosing, and a part well outside his usual range. He behaved, in short, like a serious actor, and not like a star.

Pirandello's hero, middle-aged in the 1920s, is an Italian nobleman who has lived for more than two decades in a world of expensively preserved illusion. He suffered a kick from a horse while appearing in a local pageant as Henry IV, a contentious German monarch of the late eleventh century, with whom he has since identified himself. Hired servants in period costume keep up the pretence, which is rudely exploded when his former mistress and her new lover turn up with a doctor to cure him. We learn that his madness was feigned; that he donned it as camouflage, to conceal and contain the jealousy raging within him.

Stripped of his false *persona*, he murders the lover; after which he must needs return to insanity for good.

As so often in Pirandello, a superbly dramatic concept is flawed by sluggish exposition and a muddy garrulity of dialogue. Henry uses madness to stop the clock; by an act of will he fixes himself in time as a human being beyond the reach of change; instead of letting others define him, he defines himself, and must thus be approached on his own terms or not at all. We may see in him a symbol of the neurotic artist, who creates a private world in which to live, since he cannot bear the pressure of reality. But these are only afterthoughts: while the plot is unfolding, one curses Pirandello for having picked on a parallel as remote, obscure and needlessly intricate as the story of Henry IV. The same points, one feels, could well have been made without so much circuitous fuss.

But few actors could make them as Mr Finney does, seizing in every speech on the vital phrase, the essential gesture, that must be driven home. He is grotesquely miscast; too young, too moon-shaped of mien, and frankly inept at conveying the razor-edged intellect that underlies Henry's lunacy; but the thrust of his temperament carries him over these hurdles to hard-won triumph. His very presence, relaxed and watchful, the long arms dangling, the heavy head balefully swaying in search of opposition, imparts a sense of danger that is authentically feudal; and as he lopes crabwise around the stage, we are unnerved by the knowledge that at any moment he may do something violent and unpredictable.

This ability to arouse in one's audience the expectation of being astounded is not only cardinal to Henry; it is a hallmark of firstrate acting. I shall not quickly forget the fumbling convulsion of disgust—a sort of manual regurgitation—with which Mr Finney discards the sword he has just used to impale the hated lover. As for his voice, it is always pungent and frequently thrilling. Only a handful of living actors can make a whole audience gasp and recoil with a single syllable, and one of these is Mr Finney. 'My heart has changed towards her,' he says, explaining the revived affection he feels for his former mistress, whom he now sees reincarnate in her daughter; and then: '*Changed!*' he cries, rounding on the lover in a sudden volcanic access of point-blank fury. The house visibly quailed; even at the memory, hairs rise on the nape of my neck. Lillias Walker plays the mistress with the kind of casual, whiplash aplomb for want of which high comedy has languished in London these many seasons.

(1963)

Othello, BY WILLIAM SHAKESPEARE, AT THE OLD VIC

'All that's spoke is marr'd,' says Gratiano at the end of *Othello*; and as far as last Wednesday's protagonist was concerned, he never uttered a truer word. The right man to play the Moor need not boom as Robeson did, nor do I demand of him a musical voice; but he must be able to phrase the verse so that it makes emotional sense. He must respond to the driving flow of its rhythm:

> Like to the Pontic Sea,
> Whose icy current and compulsive course
> Ne'er feels retiring ebb, but keeps due on
> To the Propontic and the Hellespont . . .

Significantly, these indispensable lines are cut in Caspar Wrede's production; and the feeling they articulate is precisely what is missing from Errol John's performance in the central role. Mr John wreaks on the text the vengeance that Othello proposes for Desdemona: he chops it into messes. Other than the tint of his skin, this robust West Indian actor has few qualifications for the part; in fullness of years and majesty of presence he is equally deficient; but these faults would matter little if he had a commanding and well-commanded voice. Instead of which, he gives us a clipped, spasmodic tenor, raven-hoarse in moments of passion, and rendered monotonous throughout by its trick of ending every other phrase on an upward inflexion. 'Farewell the plumed troop' can be effectively delivered in many different ways; but a staccato mutter, I submit, is not one of them.

Iago, that early advocate of the hierarchic principle known as 'Buggins' Turn', is played by Leo McKern, squat and squalid as a poisonous bug, yet equipped with a mask of profound concern that would deceive a saint. This four-square performance keeps the evening on course, assisted by Catherine Lacey's Emilia (a sharp display of gipsy scolding) and a blushing, weak-willed Cassio from Eric Thompson. The rest is confusion, with Desdemona (Adrienne Corri) signalling good intentions like a tiny craft out of touch with its base.

Miss Corri bears the brunt of many directorial oddities. She is on hand when the Clown (normally deleted, to nobody's grief) makes a brief appearance inexplicably hung about with tabors, cymbals, a recorder and a syrinx, all of which he simultaneously plays, like a refugee from *An Evening of Renaissance Rubbish*. This zany interlude cleverly ruins

Othello's next scene: one expects the Moor to enter with a banjo, singing spirituals. Shortly afterwards Cassio presents himself to Desdemona, astonishingly clad in nothing but tights and shirt-tails:

DESDEMONA: How now, good Cassio! What's the news with you?
CASSIO: Madam, my former suit.
DESDEMONA: It's still at the cleaners.

Miss Corri doesn't actually utter that last line, though the situation cries out for it. Her martyrdom is sealed later on, when the décor compels her to undress in the castle courtyard and to go to bed on a marble sepulchre. Mr Wrede's production is gauche at best; at worst, it is permissive to the point of chaos. During the fiesta scene, a masculine voice rang out from the wings. 'Cassio!' it implored, 'Come and have a drink!' A theatre which tolerates *gaffes* like that will tolerate almost anything.

(1963)

The Wars of the Roses, BY WILLIAM SHAKESPEARE, AT STRATFORD-ON-AVON

By means of cutting, transposing and rewriting, John Barton—scholar in residence at the court of Peter Hall—has fashioned a trilogy out of the three parts of *Henry VI* and *Richard III*, and called it *The Wars of the Roses*.

The first two episodes were brought to blood-boltered life last Wednesday, respectively entitled *Henry VI* and *Edward IV*; and let me add to the confusion by suggesting that they might well be renamed *Henry V—Part II*, so long is the shadow thrown by the dead king. His coffin is the centrepiece of the opening scene; around it are grouped the men who will scheme and squabble, together with their wives and progeny, for the power that has passed into the hands of his power-hating son. While the sixth Henry shrinks from the arena, York and his dreadful sons will oppose the Lancastrian succession; Warwick will make and unmake kings, and finally undo himself; Joan of Arc will burn, Queen Margaret will rail, and before the two plays are done, nearly everyone on stage will have died a violent death, some of the supers several times over.

Yet not until next month, when the third play joins the repertoire, will the curse on the house of Lancaster work itself out; Henry VI's grandfather unseated an anointed king, and, as Peter Hall remarks in a programme note, 'the bloody totalitarianism of *Richard III* is the expiation of England'. Meanwhile, what we have at Stratford is gang warfare in armour, history seen as Lord Beaverbrook still sees it, in terms of the clashing greeds and temperamental incompatibilities of feudal potentates.

The great ones, almost to a man, are arrogant, savage and fickle; and so, aping them, are the common people, whose behaviour in Jack Cade's rebellion prompts the reflection that every government gets the country it deserves. Such is Shakespeare's impartiality that the embattled nobles all sound equally right; but such is his irony that we know they are all (apart from saintly Henry and Duke Humphrey, his peace-loving Protector) equally wrong. The higher the motives they profess, the more the corpses pile up.

Henry VI, with its string-pulling, power-balancing scenes in the council chamber, is a subtler diversion than *Edward IV*, which is mainly carnage and cutlery; as a whole, however, Mr Hall's dual production has nothing to fear from comparison with Douglas Seale's celebrated three-in-one presentation of the *Henry VI* saga at the Old Vic six years ago. Like his predecessor, Mr Hall has managed to reanimate petrified forests of genealogy, so that within half an hour one knows which cousin is on whose uncle's brother's side: and he is superbly aided by a thunderous iron-clad setting (by John Bury) that can swing in a few well-oiled seconds from indoor to outdoor, York to Lancaster, England to France.

Peggy Ashcroft, glottally rolling her 'r's', makes a balefully persuasive figure of Margaret, the Gallic she-wolf; and if I dwell on David Warner, it is not only because he plays the king, but because I have seldom witnessed such a finished performance by an actor who has barely started. Mr Warner is tall, lean and gangling; he cares about his subjects, whom he addresses in a vein of embarrassed regret, as befits a man who believes in peace yet cannot enforce his will. When he is murdered by Richard of York, he accepts the blade not only with forgiveness, but with a kind of wry affection for his assassin. I have seen nothing more Christlike in modern theatre.

(1963)

After the Fall, by Arthur Miller, at the ANTA Washington Square Theatre, New York; *Blues for Mister Charlie,* by James Baldwin, at the ANTA Theatre, New York

When eras are on the decline, all tendencies are subjective; but on the other hand when matters are ripening for a new epoch, all tendencies are objective.—Goethe.

In other words—to tidy up that gnomic generalisation—when a society has doubts about its future, it tends to produce spokesmen whose main appeal is to the emotions, who argue from intuitions, and whose claim to be truth-bearers rests solely on intense personal feeling.

By contrast, societies sure of the future tend to throw up spokesmen whose appeal is to the court of reason; whose private vision coincides with a public vision of man as a rational creature in control of his destiny. In the theatre, Brecht exemplifies the latter group; only primitive people, he felt, could fail to be excited by the application of reason to human affairs; and he had no time for plays that exalted subjective truth above historical truth.

One wonders what he would have made of the two extravagantly personal plays that dominate the current Broadway season: Arthur Miller's *After the Fall* and James Baldwin's *Blues for Mister Charlie.* Each is the work of a liberal conscience in headlong flight from reason; and each is blighted by an unstated, perhaps unconscious, assumption that American audiences are reachable only on the level of emotional assault. They can be hypnotised, browbeaten and breastbeaten; but they cannot be persuaded.

The hero (or monologist with interruptions) of Mr Miller's piece is a tinted blow-up of Mr Miller himself. By profession a liberal lawyer, he tells us the story of his life in a series of unchronological flashbacks linked by passages of self-flagellating narration. Played on a plaintive, cawing note by Jason Robards, Jr. he feels guilty about almost everything—his failure to appreciate his father (a weak man with two sons, as in *Death of a Salesman* and *All My Sons*); his failure to treat his first wife as a human being (he merely read her his 'classic' briefs); his failure to live up to his liberal beliefs (he felt relieved when a client subpoenaed by McCarthy committed suicide); his failure to cope with a sexy, celebrated second wife (Miss Monroe transposed into a pop singer); and his failure to feel guilty enough about all these failures. His capacity for self-accusation is endless, and the operative syllable is self: you get the feeling that if only Mr Miller's hero could expiate his multiple guilts, the future of Western civilisation would be assured.

The play would, in fact, be more convincing if Mr Miller had made it more explicitly autobiographical. The hero's desperate need for retributive judgment would make more sense if (like Mr Miller) he came from a strictly orthodox Jewish background; similarly, his tormented sense of responsibility for the McCarthy victim and the suicidal second wife would be more understandable if (again like Mr Miller) he had actually been a Communist sympathiser and the husband of Marilyn Monroe.

As it is, Mr Miller's fictional ego is too frail and trivial to bear the elaborate superstructure of atonement that he has imposed on it: he has neither turned himself into a symbol nor trusted himself as a fact. Eight years ago he wrote: 'I can no longer take with ultimate seriousness a drama of individual psychology written for its own sake, however full it may be of insight and precise observation.' He should have heeded his own words.

Mr Baldwin's play is likewise a monument to the fallacy that the flesh and blood of feeling can survive as drama without the muscle and bone of rational thought. *Blues for Mister Charlie* (Mister Charlie is Negro parlance for white man) presents the racial clash in tabloid terms, full of purple-hearted prose and gaudy stereotypes. Everything is italicised and spiked with exclamation marks; and the best scene is that in which Mr Baldwin, one-time boy evangelist, comes out into the open and frankly hits us with a Negro sermon.

The setting is a Southern town where a poor white storekeeper has murdered Richard Henry, a young Negro musician who has returned from a spell in New York infected with sassy notions of egalitarianism. Richard's father is a minister whose belief in non-violence is shaken by the death of his son; and on the sidelines we spot a number of other obligatory figures—among them the middle-class racist, the professional Uncle Tom, and the weak white liberal who befriends both sides.

Will the court find a white man guilty of shooting a nigger? Of course it won't; but what dismays one is the crude rejection of plausibility that precedes the acquittal. In the trial scene, a Negro lawyer interrogates the killer's wife in detail about her private life and the sexual advances that the murdered man is alleged to have made to her; in any Southern courtroom this would be unthinkable.

Mr Baldwin attributes the white-supremacy cult almost entirely to sexual envy: it is Richard's taunts about the size of the storekeeper's penis that drive the latter to kill him. Conceivably Richard is right:

Wayland Young, in his brilliant book *Eros Denied*, quotes a Negro sociologist from Brazil as saying that black and half-caste Brazilians 'have penises superior to those of other peoples both in size and in serviceability'. But Mr Baldwin prefers to have it both ways: while he derides the whites for believing the myth, he seems by implication to accept it himself. In other words, we are all equal, except that Negroes are probably better in bed. Thus—according to a militant Negro actress with whom I saw the play—Mr Baldwin neglects a crucial point: which is that the myth arose for no other reason than that sex was the only area in which the Negro was free. Here and elsewhere, the play creates an impression at which, had its author been white. Mr Baldwin would have been the first to scoff: namely, that Negroes are creatures of animal emotion, beyond the reach of reason.

Watching the production (and the righteous fury of players like Al Freeman, Jr., Diana Sands and Percy Rodriguez) was a formidable experience. Never before had I seen a Broadway theatre half-full of Negroes; and I remembered the Berlin opening of *The Diary of Anne Frank*, another occasion on which the emotion generated by the audience tripled the impact of a second-rate play. All the same, I cannot forgive Mr Baldwin for shunning so completely the rational approach. As E. H. Carr has said:

> It is only within the last 200 years at most . . . that social, political and historical consciousness has begun to spread to anything like a majority of the population. It is only today that it has become possible . . . to imagine a whole world consisting of peoples who have in the fullest sense entered into history and become the concern, no longer of the colonial administrator or of the anthropologist, but of the historian. This is a revolution in our conception of history.

And the key to that revolution—the force that makes it work—is not passion but reason.

(1963)

Conference at Edinburgh

Many people who should have turned up at the Edinburgh Drama Conference, jointly organised for the Edinburgh Festival Committee by the publisher John Calder and myself, were prevented by pressure of work; in most Western countries the theatre season begins in September. Others declined the invitation because the very idea of conferences repelled them; one such was John Osborne, who said that he hated discussing his work in public and felt no need to 'show the host to the congregation, in Edinburgh, or anywhere else'. Yet out of a chaos of language barriers and differing levels of intelligence, much emerged that was instructive, if not always reassuring.

We had dull days. The first afternoon failed because the chosen topic ('Who dominates the theatre—actor, director or playwright?') was too abstract; it caught fire only when Joan Littlewood made a fundamentalist plea for a theatre of communal celebration in which there were no distinctions between performers and audience.

Unanimity ruined the debate on censorship and subsidy; nobody defended the former or opposed the latter. Joan Plowright spoke for everyone when she said that subsidy was 'a recognition of the artist's right to fail, which is essential to his development. Millions of pounds are spent on the right of scientists to fail, and the creative artist should be accorded the same right that is granted to the man who experiments with nuclear warfare.'

Other sessions were notable less for what happened on the platform than for their private repercussions at parties and nocturnal *tête à têtes*. Tuesday's discussion of the relative importance of socially committed theatre and the 'Theatre of the Absurd' began with a shallow clash between Bernard Levin, who likened Brecht's mind to that of a nine-year-old child, and Wolf Mankowitz, who called Mr Levin a Fascist Jew; and despite pungent interventions by John Arden ('The god of the theatre is and always has been Dionysus') and Arthur Adamov ('The reason why Absurdist plays take place in No Man's Land with only two characters is primarily financial'), no real collision of intellect was achieved.

Late in the afternoon I attacked those Western playwrights who use their influence and affluence to preach to the world the nihilistic doctrine that life is pointless and irrationally destructive, and that there is nothing we can do about it. Until everyone is fed, clothed, housed and taught, until human beings have equal leisure to contemplate the overwhelming fact of mortality, we should not (I argued) indulge in the luxury of 'privileged despair'.

No sooner had I returned to my hotel than the telephone rang. It was Harold Pinter, wanting to know exactly what I meant by 'privileged despair'. I met him in the bar with Jack Gelber (*The Connection*) and Arthur Kopit (*Oh Dad, Poor Dad*); and constructive battle was joined. Pinter, gleamingly bespectacled, picked up a glass ashtray and said he could write a perfectly valid play about it without referring to social or economic conditions. I replied that unless the play told me who made it and how much he was paid, I would feel cheated.

Mr Kopit then intervened. He said he had lately written a comedy with a small cast which contained one episode that called for twenty-five extras. After consulting his agent, he had cut the crowd scene on the grounds that it 'destroyed the artistic unity'. Having heard the after-noon's arguments in favour of large, subsidised companies, he now realised that the reasons for which he had made the cut were not artistic but economic; the American theatre cannot afford twenty-five extras for a single scene. He determined to restore it to the script, and one felt that a blow for liberty had been struck.

One day that boded ill turned out superbly: the day devoted to nationalism in the theatre, which produced from Max Frisch a resolution urging the Rockefeller Foundation to set up an International Institute for translation, and from Wole Soyinka and Barry Reckord (two Negro playwrights) a furious reaction against the folksy exoticism of a poem sung by the Indian author, Habib Tanvir. Listening to their complaints, one saw that artistic differences were not only vertical (i.e., concerned with nationality) but also horizontal (i.e., concerned with class prosperity); and that the prime need of under-privileged countries was to shed the 'Uncle Tom' image bestowed on them by the wealthier parts of the world.

The third day provided the sharpest intellectual debate. Alain Robbe-Grillet (off-stage a deadpan joker who sported a conference badge labelled 'Henry de Montherlant', his least favourite author) defined cinema as an art in which everything was unreal—far more so than in the theatre—and in which one could never distinguish between fact and fantasy. In his new film, *L'Immortelle*, he said that it was up to the audience to decide which was which. Here Peter Brook jumped in to declare that this was mere solipsism; it might hold water philosophically, but it would not stand up to the Anglo-Saxon test of common sense, which the abstract French too often ignored. In fact, though not in theory, one knew the difference between dream and reality. This led to a fascinating exchange of definitions, from which it emerged that film, as a medium, was no more realistic than theatre was formal and artificial.

The last day, dedicated to the 'Theatre of the Future', gave us our notorious nude, who was towed across the musicians' gallery as part of a rehearsed 'Happening' conceived by a young San Franciscan director named Kenneth Dewey. It was hereabouts, in the course of this practical joke—a clumsy echo of *Hellzapoppin'*—that a gulf opened between the

American and Eastern European delegates. The latter had come prepared to discuss experimental theatre on a serious level; the Poles and Yugoslavs have staged all the off-beat plays in the Western repertoire, together with many of their own; but this confusion of jape with art, of accident with design, dismayed and deterred them, especially when they learned that Mr Dewey regarded the startled spectators as artists in their own right. (Even Ionesco was unsettled: art, he had pointed out earlier on, is an improvisation *which remains.*) Where was the line to be drawn? Why shouldn't a bar-room brawl qualify as theatre? 'Why indeed!' was the American reply. After the conference was over, a friend of Mr Dewey's named Alan Kaprow invited the audience to take part in a 'Happening' outside the McEwan Hall: it involved their climbing over piles of tyres surrounded by people hammering on oil-drums.

I witnessed this pitiful event from a balcony, with a group of embarrassed Eastern Europeans beside me. It was like watching children breaking up their nursery. A sophisticated Yugoslav said to me: 'I mistrusted you, Tynan, when I read that you had begun to praise social theatre. I thought you had gone over to Socialist realism. But now—' he gestured wanly towards the clamour below, 'I see what you are up against.' The East, in those words, moved sadly away from the West; the theatre of purposeful experiment from the theatre that denies all purpose. What we had seen was not the best of the American *avant-garde*; but it was not wholly untypical. 'The Nuremberg rallies,' said Mr Kaprow, 'were immoral, but they were great theatre—they were real Happenings.' I thought of something Christopher Caudwell wrote a quarter of a century ago about the decline of bourgeois art:

> On the one hand, there is production for the market—vulgarisation, commercialisation. On the other there is hypostatisation of the art work as the goal of the art process, and the relation between art work and individual as paramount. This necessarily leads to a dissolution of those social values which make the art in question a social relation, and therefore ultimately results in the art work's ceasing to be an art work and becoming a mere private phantasy.

The conference itself epitomised one of the contradictions of the West. Were the delegates addressing one another, with the audience as eavesdroppers? Or were they entertaining the audience, in order to sell tickets? The answer is that they were supposed to do both—to achieve a meeting of minds and at the same time a commercial success. They fell, not without honour, between these stools; as unsubsidised art, even at its best, inevitably must.

With that, for a year at least, I abandon weekly reviewing. I have prayed, season after season, for a national theatre; and the challenge of helping that enormous dream to take shape was something out of which I could not decently chicken. As from tomorrow, I am a bureaucrat, Laurence Olivier's Literary Manager; but I see no contradiction in this, no frontier irrevocably crossed.

It is the commercial theatre that sets up barriers between critic and artist, because in a theatre dependent on box office takings the critic's opinion may determine whether the artist thrives or starves. But in a non-commercial theatre, where profit and loss are not the first considerations, where actors and directors have security of employment, the relationship radically changes: critic and artist can work together in the common pursuit of perfection.

(1963)

An Audience of Critics

It all depends, I suppose, on whether you think of theatre as a business or as a public service. In New York (and in most of London and Paris) you go to the theatre to see a star or a hit or both; you are buying a seat for a luxury product which has proved its worth by making a fortune. But if you are a German playgoer (or his counterpart in Scandinavia and Eastern Europe) you are visiting a civic institution which you prize as jealously as any Chicagoan his White Sox. Your theatre is a part of your city's history, a place of public enlightenment where every change in actors or repertoire is your intimate concern. Your taxes subsidise the company (to the annual extent of some $3 per citizen), but you do not resent the burden, because you are fully aware that even if the theatre plays—as it usually does—to capacity, the cost of running the organisation and staging a dozen new productions each season cannot possibly be covered out of box-office receipts. Hence you are likely to boast of the fortunes you allow your theatre to *lose.*

In West Berlin and the Federal Republic there are 123 subsidised theatres which consume $70 million of public funds every year; in East Germany, with a much smaller population, there are eighty-six—annual consumption proportionately the same. It is from East Germany that German theatre takes its lead, but on one simple point of principle—that civilised people are entitled to the best of world drama—the two Germanys are united. The result is what must, for richness, variety and breadth of national coverage, be accounted the finest theatre in the occidental world.

Whenever I go to a play in Germany, I am struck by the intense, appreciative calm of the audience. After a production that seems to them too pompously traditional or too offensively experimental, they may hoot a tentative protest; but they always enter the theatre certain that they are about to see something worth the scrutiny of intelligent people. It may be Brecht or Beckett, Schiller or Arthur Miller; it may be eccentrically performed, like a ponderously mad *Macbeth* I saw last spring in Munich, with flying witches in fishnet tights, painted back-cloths of Highland cattle and Banquo's ghost zooming up through a spotlit trapdoor; but the text itself will never be negligible, and it will be assumed that you have come to learn something as well as to be entertained.

The audience files into a building that is bound to be spacious and likely to be new; more than a hundred theatres have sprung up in West Germany since the war. The customers leave their coats and hats in capacious, no-queuing cloakrooms; and before the performance you may see them *en famille* in the bar, sipping a beer, studying the programme and nibbling at a sausage. Once in their seats, they listen with the kind of devout attention that you associate with a concert rather than a play. Coughing is rare and rapidly stifled. When intermission comes, the audience quit their seats as swiftly and silently as quicksilver pouring off a corrugated roof. Hand in hand or arm in arm, they circle the foyer in clockwise motion until it is time to return. When the bell rings, they go quietly. I used to think they were too polite, too easily receptive; until I realised that for them the theatre is not an exceptional and costly after-dinner treat but a normal and cheaply available source of cultural nourishment, like a nocturnal combination of library and art gallery. It has always been there; it will always be there. The ticket-scalping frenzy involved in getting a seat for a Broadway hit would stagger a German; it would seem to him as ludicrous as the idea of art-lovers scratching each other's eyes out for a glimpse of the Venus de Milo. A masterpiece, by his definition, ought to be universally accessible; and it should remain so until everyone who wants to has seen it.

The indestructibility of German theatre was proved when it survived virtual decapitation in 1933. Germany in the twenties was the liveliest spawning-ground of theatrical experiment in Western Europe. Max Reinhardt, director of baroque spectaculars, was in his prime, together with his pupil and rival, Leopold Jessner; the strident expressionist plays of George Kaiser and Ernst Toller at first led the vanguard and then lost ground to the propagandist productions of Erwin Piscator, a dashing Left-winger who used film and cartoon to drive home his points, filling the Nollendorftheater with so much heavy machinery that the stage had to be reinforced with steel and concrete. Meanwhile, Bertolt Brecht, a fugitive from expressionism, joined forces with the composer Kurt Weill to create, in *The Threepenny Opera*, the first modern musical; after which Brecht went on to study Marx and to develop what he called 'Epic Theatre', a revolution in theatrical storytelling whose shock-waves are still changing the course of European drama.

This golden age—an arc-lit arena in which art and politics were one —was abruptly devalued by Hitler. Some of its leading figures stayed on in Germany, among them the director Jürgen Fehling, who later invited the club-footed Goebbels to attend his production of *Richard III*. But most of the great pioneers—actors, directors and playwrights alike— vanished into exile, there to remain for a dozen nail-biting years. Some found work in Hollywood; but many, when they returned, were discouraged and out of practice, having spent their best years in a twilight of penury. In 1945 German theatre had to recreate itself from scratch. The speed and assurance with which it did so make the Economic Miracle look like a confidence trick.

Foreign critics, faced with Germany's theatrical miracle, usually begin by applauding the high standards of acting and production, and then go on to deplore the lack of firstrate playwrights. After the Nazi blackout, I wonder what they expected. Under a dictatorship, the interpretative arts always suffer less than the creative. Even in exile, an actor or director can develop more easily than a playwright, who needs to see his work performed in his own tongue. Hitler forced German drama to skip a whole generation, and we cannot fairly pass judgment until the new crop of German writers—those born since 1930, whose formative years were not Nazi-blighted—have reached full maturity. When people bewail the dearth of German dramatists, I ask myself what they would be saying if Brecht were still alive. He died eight years ago, aged fifty-eight. Had he lived, his country would be envied everywhere as the home of the most influential playwright of the twentieth century.

The great tradition of German theatre stems, paradoxically, from the fact that a century ago Germany as a nation did not exist. The old Reich was split up into thirty-nine city-states, each of which sponsored a theatre to compete with its neighbours; and this provincial assertiveness grew stronger, if anything, when the country was unified. Later, as the population grouped itself around vast industrial centres, the princely state-theatres were reinforced by a flood of municipal playhouses, which now outnumber their aristocratic forebears five to one. Düsseldorf, Hamburg,

Munich and other big cities began to vie with one another; and all of them vied with Berlin. Hamburg was among the earliest civic trail-blazers; it was there, in the 1760s, that Gotthold Ephraim Lessing—a gifted playwright and incomparable critic—spent several abortive years trying to turn the excellent local company into the first effective German national theatre.

Court patronage begat civic patronage; and these in turn begat sub-scribers' organisations, of which the most powerful is the *Volksbühne* ('People's stage'), financed by the trade unions and founded at the end of the nineteenth century. Membership in the *Volksbühne* guarantees a certain number of cut-rate seats for several plays per season; but the seats are chosen by ballot and you cannot pick which plays you want to see. Limitation of choice is the penalty for slashed prices; but it is not a deterrent, as the figures demonstrate. At the Kammerspiele in Munich, thirty per cent of the audience belong to the *Volksbühne* or similar organisations; while at the Schiller Theatre in Berlin the percentage rises to forty-six.

From whatever source, subsidy is the ruling principle, based on the idea that a good theatre is not a luxury but a right. The Schiller Theatre, West Germany's best, runs two auditoriums and an experimental studio, receiving by way of civic allowance more than $1,800,000 a year. The Munich Kammerspiele, a charming flesh-pink interior seating only 750, gets half that amount and does not think itself especially favoured. In return for their donations, the city officials expect to see the finest avail-able actors in the finest castable plays. They do not expect to exercise artistic control. A few years back a German theatre announced that it was going to stage John Whiting's *The Devils*, an arraignment of papist witch-hunting in the seventeenth century. The Catholics complained and asked the local authorities to ban it. They were told that 'the repertoire is fixed not by politicians but by the artistic director'.

Those who fear that subsidy makes for a stale, conservative repertoire have statistics against them. During 1962–63, the plays most often per-formed in the two Germanys were both by living authors of liberal bent: Dürrenmatt's *The Physicists* and Max Frisch's *Andorra*. Last season, an analysis of performances at thirteen West German theatres produced these results:

Classical authors	33 per cent
Plays of the Ibsen-Hauptmann period	15 per cent
Modern light comedy	12 per cent
Other contemporary plays	40 per cent

Envious Anglo-Saxons tend to acclaim the German theatre because it enables actors to work together in permanent companies. With very few exceptions (notably Brecht's Berliner Ensemble) this envy is rooted in myth. Most German actors are engaged on a yearly basis. Promising new-comers may be persuaded to sign up for two or three seasons, but the top talents can seldom be pinned down for more than six months at a time. They prefer to switch from city to city, bringing each company they visit to the bar of their own immense accomplishment. Although they some-times abscond into TV they are rarely tempted into films; and this is what keeps the level of stage acting so high. The bulwark of German theatre is the low output, unattractive pay and paltry quality of German cinema.

Munich's Kammerspiele, founded fifty-three years ago, is a typical, upper-echelon West German theatre. Every season it puts on about ten new productions, each of which is rehearsed for five or six weeks. Some seventy actors are on its payroll. Around half of them, at any given time, will be under contract for a year or more, and will be paid a weekly salary ranging from $50 to $250.

The other half will consist of spear-toting walk-ons and itinerant guest stars, of whom the latter can earn up to $500 a week. Last summer their repertoire included four productions by Fritz Kortner, a stocky, white-haired dynamo in his seventies who played Hollywood Nazis dur-ing the Hitler years and returned to become the most discussed and exacting director in West Germany. He was represented in Munich by *Othello, Richard III*, Büchner's *Leonce and Lena* and *Zwiesprache*, a scab-tearing conversation piece about German affluence which he wrote himself. The same theatre also offered a French surrealist farce, a Vien-nese comedy by the ribald, untranslatable Nestroy (died 1862) and Edward Albee's well-known joust for mixed doubles, *Wer hat Angst vor Virginia Woolf?* Not a bad selection for the warm months in a southern city—for that is what Munich is, a quasi-Mediterranean complex of boulevards, overwhelmingly leafy.

Over Munich and every other theatrical centre in West Germany, Bertolt Brecht casts a long and dominating shadow, both as a playwright and as the founder, fifteen years ago, of the internationally acclaimed company of actors known as the Berliner Ensemble. Its home is in the Eastern zone of that bisected city, and there was a time, just after the Berlin Wall went up, when productions of his plays were anathema in the Federal Republic. But demand overrode disapproval; the modern German repertoire without Brecht is like Elizabethan drama without Shakespeare, and now, as before the Wall, his work is ubiquitously performed.

Not only his plays but his disciples have travelled westward. Several actors fledged by the Ensemble—and a couple of its best directors—crossed the border in pre-Wall days and stayed to spread the Brechtian word. Brecht is the great absentee landlord of contemporary German theatre.

Apart from Berlin (a special case, since it is not a part of the Federal Republic), the best West German theatres are those of Munich, Hamburg, Düsseldorf and Frankfurt. Many others aspire to join the élite: Darmstadt, Göttingen, Stuttgart, Bochum and Bremen are among the most recent contenders, in each case because a venturesome new director has applied a spur to the resident troupe. In Bremen (population 565,000: theatre subsidy—including opera—$1,200,000 a year) his name is Peter Zadek, who celebrated Shakespeare's quatercentenary by presenting *Henry V* in World War I costumes and ironically retitled it *Henry Hero*. In this production, Henry was a cynical, bullet-headed thug who delivered the exhortation on the eve of Agincourt not to his generals but to a French whore with whom he was in bed. The French leaders spent the night before the battle sipping wine around a Christmas tree beside which an English prisoner was being tortured. To make his attitude towards Shakespeare's warrior-king quite clear, Mr Zadek dropped in a backcloth adorned with painted heads of other Western heroes, ranging from Attila the Hun to Elvis Presley. This kind of anti-militarism is the norm in German theatre; in the arts at least, the reaction from Hitlerism is heartfelt and absolute.

Berlin, despite its geographical isolation, is the magnetic pole towards which all ambitions tend. This gleaming shopwindow of Western culture is dominated (dramatically speaking) by the Schiller Theatre, which stages in its three playhouses an annual total of twenty-five premières. Its prize possession is a fiftyish performer named Martin Held, who looks like a successful lawyer and, apart from Laurence Olivier, may very well be the finest middle-aged actor in Western Europe. (Like Olivier, Held played Archie Rice in John Osborne's *The Entertainer*.) In modern plays —as the capering Rag-picker in *The Madwoman of Chaillot* or the guilt-ridden schoolteacher in Max Frisch's *Andorra*—Held is unbeatable; no one excels him at revealing the chasms of desperation that lie beneath the wall-to-wall carpeting of contemporary middle-class life.

His youthful counterpart at the Schiller was Klaus Kammer, by general consent the successor to Gérard Philipe as Europe's finest *jeune premier*. A brilliant mime, with a range comprising Goethe and Kafka, Kammer had all the skills of theatre at his command when, early last May, word incredibly came that he had died in his garage of carbon monoxide poisoning. The car engine was running and the radio playing. He left a wife and two children; no one knows why (or even whether) he chose to die; but his death ripped an enormous hole in the fabric of German acting. His country cannot replace him—which is strange, because he was already thirty-five years old and past the age for Romeo; yet none of his juniors could play Romeo anything like as well. (Ekkehard Schall and Hilmar Thate of the Berliner Ensemble are both young and vastly gifted; but they are Brechtian actors, and one cannot be sure how they would look in plays by other authors, or from other periods.)

Kammer was romanticism incarnate, and he and Held exemplified German acting at its versatile best; serious, flexible, subtle and emphatic. French acting issues a statement; British acting proffers a hint; American acting unveils a neurosis. The Germans run everyone a close second; and, as Swift said, 'those to whom everybody allows the second place have an undoubted title to the first'.

If young actors of the top flight are rare, young directors are rarer. When the resplendent new *Freie Volksbühne* Theatre opened in Berlin eighteen months ago, the man chosen to run it was the veteran Erwin Piscator, now seventy years old. He brought off a scandalous success almost at once with his production of *The Deputy*, Rolf Hochhuth's bitter chronicle play attacking Pius XII for his failure to speak out against Hitler's decimation of the Jews; but it has since become obvious that Piscator's style—pugnacious, propagandist and openly Left-inclined —is not in tune with West German taste. He recently staged *The Merchant of Venice* (tactfully unperformed in Berlin since the war) as a parable of anti-Semitism. The Jews in their tenebrous ghetto were juxtaposed with the blond Venetians in their glittering *palazzi*; and the trial scene was preceded by a projected caption: 'Mercy for Antonio. No mercy for Shylock.' The décor, like the interpretation, was violently black-and-white; and the critics savaged both. In part they were justified; the production was based on an oversimplification and contained a good deal of cursory, skin-deep acting. All the same, the venom of the notices seemed excessive. Somebody, one felt, was protesting too much.

Siegfried Melchinger, professor of drama and contributor to the influential monthly *Theater Heute*, has written: 'The German-language theatre has many limbs but no head.' By this he means that it is split up into regional enclaves, each with a faithful band of local critics who tend to be ignorant of anything that happens outside their city limits. Decentralisation (i.e. the loss of Berlin as a capital city) has led to a lowering of critical standards. To this extent Mr Melchinger is right; but in a broader sense he is off the beam. The German-language theatre *has* a head. The trouble, from the West German viewpoint, is that it exists on the wrong side of the Berlin wall.

Foreigners can reach it by crossing the frontier at Checkpoint Charlie. After passport examination on the Eastern side—a slow process but a sure one, unless you are a spy—you go straight down the Friedrichstrasse for half a mile or so, turn right into a little square alongside the river Spree, and there it is—the Theater am Schiffbauerdamm, since 1954 the permanent home of the acting troupe known as the Berliner Ensemble, which Bertolt Brecht founded when he came home from exile in 1949. He chose the Schiffbauerdamm for sentimental reasons (it had housed his first success, *The Threepenny Opera*, in 1928), but he put it to rigorously unsentimental use. In this intimate, gilded playhouse, directing or codirecting the plays he had written in banishment, he created the crisp, effortless didactic style that has carried his company round the world (excluding America) and added the indispensable adjective 'Brechtian' to the lexicon of international theatre.

This stubby Marxist with his monkish tonsure and smelly cigars was a poet who believed that the exercise of reason could be made theatrically beautiful. He taught his designers to seek inspiration in the selective realism and sober colours (greys, browns and beiges) of Brueghel, Vermeer and Chinese art. Things worn and marked by use were to him the most beautiful, as he said in a moving poem to his wife, Helene Weigel, who has run the company since her husband's death in 1956. The cemetery in which Brecht lies buried is near the theatre and adjoins the apartment where he and Weigel lived. A jagged, asymmetrical gravestone bears his name, without dates or other legend.

Apart from *Mother Courage*—the tale of a woman who runs a mobile canteen in the Thirty Years' War and loses her three children because she loathes war less than she values profits—the major productions at present in the repertoire of the Ensemble are *The Life of Galileo* (Brecht's indictment of a great scientist who preferred security to integrity), *The Days of the Commune* (his analysis of the ideological softness that betrayed the Paris Commune in 1871), and *The Resistible Rise of Arturo Ui* (his comic-strip account of Hitler's accession to power, told in terms of Al Capone's Chicago, with Ekkehard Schall giving the performance of anyone's lifetime as the dapper gangster protagonist, a Chaplinesque puppet with a demon raging in his belly). The next Ensemble premiers—*Coriolanus* translated by Brecht—has been in preparation for many years. The most maddening thing about the Ensemble is the snail's pace of its perfectionism; its average output is barely more than one production a year.

What distinguishes it from other companies? When I took Laurence Olivier to see it last year, he murmured afterward in the theatre canteen: 'This isn't just a theatre—it's a way of life.' Lee Strasberg of the New York Actors' Studio saw it eight years ago. 'I expected something harsh and angular,' he said, 'but instead they're light, and elegant and poetic.' He added that their staging of Brecht's *Caucasian Chalk Circle* was one of the half dozen most beautiful productions he had ever witnessed anywhere.

Brecht's aim—as playwright and director alike—was always to be cool, clear and didactic. He wanted his actors neither to charm the audience nor to bowl it over with rhetorical power; he wanted them to address it on equal terms, as people talking to people, outlining a knotted human situation and explaining how it might have been unravelled. He thought the Marxist solution made more sense than any other; but always, at the heart of his doctrine, you arrive at a dual necessity—drama must teach, but it must also give pleasure.

As the commercial world understands it, theatre is whatever pleases those who pay to see it. As Brecht redefines it: 'The modern theatre must be judged not by its success in satisfying the audience's habits but by its success in transforming them . . . not by whether it interests the spectator in buying a ticket but by whether it interests him in the world.' The springboard of Brecht's theatre is what he calls 'pleasurable learning, cheerful and militant learning'. He enlists song, dance and argument to display things as they are and to suggest how they might be improved. Moreover, he invites us to submit his work to the ultimate test of truth, not of art. Artistically, his plays may be good or bad; what concerns him more is whether their conclusions are true or false.

History will judge the accuracy of Brecht's conclusions: it can hardly deny that he left as his monument the most exhilarating, mind-flexing body of work in the theatre of postwar Europe.

(1964)

The Marxist Magpie

Brecht probably wrote more than any other major playwright of the twentieth century; Shaw is the only serious contender who comes to mind, and his life was thirty-six years longer. The sheer bulk of Brecht's *oeuvre*—essays, reviews and treatises, as well as poems, *libretti*, plays and prose fiction—is stunning and still unmeasurable, since the East Berlin archives bulge with fragments as yet unpublished. His complete writings on theatre (of which John Willett has compiled, Englished and annotated a fascinating skimming*) are about to appear in a German edition running to six volumes.

Not the least remarkable aspect of his prodigious output is that it swelled rather than slackened during the Hitler years, when he was exiled and virtually unperformed. He was also cut off from practical contact with the theatre, which meant that many of the theories he launched were never tested in practice.

This led him at times into nonsense, as when he said (in 1940) that an actor using the alienation effect must 'discover, specify, imply what he is not doing', as well as what he actually *is* doing. 'Whatever he doesn't do must be contained and conserved in what he does': I have reread this sentence more than once, and—to lift a line from Garson Kanin—'I didn't get it the first time and I don't get it the *this* time.'

But the lapses are few and excusable. The rest of Mr Willett's anthology reveals on every page some bright new facet of the great Marxist magpie who brought science, poetry, politics, music, economics, dance and sociology to the service of his art, and compelled us by his example to redefine the form and function of twentieth-century drama. In 1926 he declares that he wants an audience with technical expertise and a sense of fun (*Spass*—a basic word in Brechtian lingo): 'We pin our hopes to the sporting public.' Next we encounter Brecht worshipping Shaw, 'who proved that the right attitude to any really important phenomenon is a casual (contemptuous) one, because it is the only one which permits complete concentration and real alertness'. He especially praises Shaw for his love of breaking up stock associations: 'We picture a usurer as cowardly, furtive and brutal. Not for a moment do we think of allowing him to be in any way courageous . . . Shaw does.' So (thereafter) does Brecht.

In 1927 he absorbs Marx and announces: 'When I read *Das Kapital*, I understood my plays.' The aesthete's opinion of theatre no longer interests him. Instead, he wants to hear from the sociologist, whose 'scale of judgment runs not from "good" to "bad" but from "correct" to "false" '. (This idea recurs throughout Brecht's work: he said later that a poet's words were not sacred unless they were true.) Where conventional theatre tries to unite the audience into an emotional entity, Brecht seeks to divide it, by forcing its members to react as individuals.

He cherishes reason as a source of delight as well as enlightenment, and in 1936 he admits that 'I cannot get along as an artist without the use

* *Brecht on Theatre.*

of one or two sciences'—nor can he wholly respect those artists who do. The craven bourgeoisie insists on confining science to the sphere of nature, 'not daring to let it loose on the field of human relationships'. Brecht begins to envisage a theatre as a sort of public laboratory where artists build working models of human behaviour to find out its causes and effects, just as scientists use models to study the behaviour of molecules.

Individual psychology now seems to Brecht a refuge for cowardly writers who would rather blame the psyche than society; he derides (1940) 'this rich inner life which for many intellectuals is merely a poor substitute for a rich outer life'. He draws a sharp distinction between bourgeois theatre, which seeks to make all human experience seem eternal, unchanging and unchangeable—the same emotions in varying social situations—and Brechtian theatre, which maintains that by changing the social situation you change the entire experience.

Brecht teaches himself to regard all human activities as bizarre and abnormal until he has thoroughly analysed the environment that fostered them. This is the scientific approach: 'The man who first looked with astonishment at a swinging lantern, and instead of taking it for granted found it highly remarkable that it should swing . . . was brought close to understanding the phenomenon by this observation, and so to mastering it.'

Knowledge breeds the desire to instruct; Brecht's didacticism, crude in the twenties, grows stronger with no loss of art in the thirties and forties. He writes an imaginary dialogue in which an actor complains: 'There's nothing an audience hates more than being sent back to school.' He replies: 'In that case your schools must be dreadful. If people hate them so much, abolish them!'

This exchange is part of *Der Messingkauf*, a four-handed conversation piece on the nature of theatre between a *dramaturg*, two actors and a philosopher (Brecht himself). It was drafted between 1937 to 1940; cleverly cut and reshuffled, it has recently joined the repertoire of the Berliner Ensemble. The full text was not available to Mr Willett; hence I offer my own version of some bits that he perforce omitted. *Spass* comes first:

> In the very nature of acting . . . there is an essential gaiety. If it isn't light-hearted, it becomes absurd. You can achieve every shade of seriousness by means of ease, and none of them without it. No matter how fearful the problems they handle, plays should always be playful. In the theatre we manipulate a pair of golden scales, meting out justice with elegance, indifferent to the earth that shakes

beneath our feet. It may seem offensive, in an age as violent as ours, even to debate an art so close to idle distraction. Tomorrow our corpses may be pulverised and scattered. But here, today, we busy ourselves with the theatre, because we want to evaluate our lives with its help. . . . The little knife must rest lightly in the surgeon's hand when his responsibility is so great. The world is surely out of joint, and it will take mighty upheavals to set it right. But among the many instruments that can serve this purpose, there is room for one that is slim and fragile, and insists on delicate handling.

Elsewhere in the same work, Brecht explains that he has come to the theatre to find out whether its skills can be put to his own particular purpose. The *dramaturg* asks him what that purpose is. 'I hardly dare to say,' he says humbly, 'You'll think it so banal and prosaic. I merely hoped to use your talents for a practical end—to try to discover the best way for people to live together.' The statement is simple, revolutionary and irrefutable: what else is theatre for?

'In times of upheaval, fearful and fruitful'—to return to Mr Willett's text—'the evenings of the doomed classes coincide with the dawns of those that are rising. It is in these twilight periods that Minerva's owl sets out on her flights.' Thus Brecht, though it sounds like Palinurus. In Mr Willett's book we follow the owl on a veering, crepuscular journey that begins in doubt and ends in wisdom.

Coriolanus, BY BERTOLT BRECHT AFTER SHAKESPEARE, AT THE BERLINER ENSEMBLE

'Naturally,' said Brecht in a note on his version of *Coriolanus*, 'we shall have to change the attitude of the plebs.' That is not all he changed, as I discovered in East Berlin a week ago, when the long-promised opening of *Coriolanus*—the Berliner Ensemble's first sortie into Shakespeare—at last took place.

First, the setting: a towering archway of Roman masonry that revolves to become the wooden stockade of Corioli. No togaed splendour in any of the costumes: this is tribal, barbaric Italy, five centuries ere the mightiest Julius fell. The plebs foregather, perhaps twenty in number, by no means a mob: for each of them a name has been invented. They are simultaneously one and many: this delicate balance is the sort of achievement that justifies nine months' rehearsal. Their protest against the patricians takes the form of a sit-down strike. The entrance of Coriolanus (a stubby, crew-cut figure played by Ekkehard Schall) brings them shuffling to their feet. Their reaction to his contempt, here and throughout, is not rage but passive resistance, a steady expressionless stare: they are used to it.

Between them and Coriolanus a necessary battle will soon be fought. First comes the unnecessary battle for Corioli, staged by the Ensemble at a pitch of audacity that is breathtaking even for them. The rival generals are shown as two elated young specialists, raptly playing the game of war. Corioli is conquered in three great flourishes of action, wordless except for deafening rhythmical chants of '*Cai-us Mar-cius!*' and '*Au-fi-di-us!*', yelled by the black-clad armies into the resonant concavity of their shields.

First the gates are stormed, with attack by siege ladders, counter-attack by vast nets of heavy rope, renewed attack by shield-plated phalanx. Next: battle in the open, with waves of soldiers clashing in the stylised manner of Chinese opera, knees akimbo and swords maniacally brandished. As they part, the mortally wounded slowly spin and fall. Finally: the generals meet in single combat, covered in blood yet *grinning* as they face each other, like two young Samurai delighting in their expertise.

Clearly we are not to look at these battles through modern eyes. The immorality of war is not the play's subject; nor is Coriolanus presented as a war criminal. Though given to fits of temper, he is not personally un-likeable. The hallmark of Brechtian theatre is that it judges men by their actions, not by their personalities. The animus of the production is not against Coriolanus himself but the social role in which he is cast.

The people are slow to rise against him. Appearing in the Forum to solicit their votes for the consulship, he eventually wins them over by singing a song of battle; we tend to forget that these are the same men he has just led at Corioli. The people's tribunes (played as sensible prag-matists, not heroic demagogues) persuade the plebs of their error; and Coriolanus is banished not by a roused and hysterical rabble but by solemn judicial process.

The production thus far is a masterpiece: politics and theatre ex-quisitely wedded. In the later acts Shakespeare lets Brecht down by stressing personal relationships (e.g., Coriolanus and Volumnia) in a way that goes against the Brechtian grain. Not that the production ignores the 'mother's boy' aspect of Coriolanus: Volumnia dresses him before the battle of Corioli (in lines lifted from *Antony and Cleopatra*), giving him a sword of robustly Freudian significance; and 'Boy!'—the taunt flung at him by Aufidius—is actually translated as 'Muttersöhnchen'. But the climactic scene with his mother is radically changed. Since private emotions cannot be permitted to alter the course of history, he remains unmoved by her pleas until—in a speech added by Brecht—she explains that the people of Rome, spurred on by their tribunes, have armed themselves against him. It is this news, and not filial duty, that halts him.

Thus Brecht makes his point: that the play's theme is the downfall of 'the individual who blackmails society with his indispensability'. But Shakespeare's play, no matter how you revamp it (and the liberties taken are many: not only *Antony and Cleopatra* but *Julius Caesar* and even the porter's scene from *Macbeth* are raided), is the work of a man who genuinely believed that heroes *were* indispensable. Brecht's anti-hero is historically convincing; but after the banishment, stripped as he is of emotional complexities, he becomes theatrically uninteresting, if not redundant. We already know about him all that we need to know.

Yet so much of a piece is this fantastic production that the falling-off in the second half is logically inseparable from the magnificence of the first. What we gain from the total experience immeasurably outweighs what we miss. Brecht's *Coriolanus* has left an indelible mark on Shakespeare's.

(1964)

The National Theatre: a speech to the Royal Society of Arts

On the north bank of the Thames, alongside Hungerford Bridge, there is a building originally intended for theatrical performance. Over the door you can still read its name: the Playhouse. It closed down as a commercial theatre many years ago and became a BBC studio. Directly opposite, on the south bank of the river, also alongside Hungerford Bridge, there is an empty site. On it, in the course of the next few years, the National Theatre will be built—a permanent, non-commercial home for the British theatre, whose doors (except during holidays, fires, floods, plagues and nuclear wars) will never thereafter be closed.

In this riverside confrontation there are the makings of a hopeful symbol. On the rich northern bank, we have the money-making theatre that the public failed to support; on the poorer southern bank, the non-money-making theatre that the public is paying to build. If this is a valid symbol, if the people of this country have really switched their allegiance from the commercial to the non-commercial theatre, then I find myself in the unwonted posture of arguing with the tide of accepted opinion instead of against it.

But of course it isn't as clearcut as that. Official opinion, in the course of the past hundred years or so, has slowly been coaxed, cajoled and pressured into taking the view that we ought to have a National Theatre. But even today, I am convinced that the great majority of people have only the vaguest idea of why we needed it. I doubt if they will actively attempt to sabotage the construction of the new theatre that Denys Lasdun, our architect, is designing—but then, they did nothing to sabotage the appalling Shell building that broods over the site like a bullet-riddled cenotaph. Apathy in these matters is no evidence of good judgment. Moreover, a few weeks ago I ran into outright hostility to the very idea of state-subsidised culture in a quarter where I had taken some kind of qualified sympathy for granted. I was talking to a well-known English novelist, who shall be Amis, about the National Theatre. He astonished me by saying that he objected on principle to all artistic ventures that were financed by the government. Art, he said, should rely on the laws of supply and demand: what the public wanted it would pay for out of its private pocket, and anything that could not pay its way was probably not good art. He challenged me to name a single great artist who did not prosper in his own lifetime. I whispered Mozart, whom he brushed aside as an exception; and I might have mentioned Brecht, who only achieved recognition when the East German government gave him a subsidised theatre to run.

Finally, my novelist chum told me that he would rather rely on the judgment of publishers who were profit-minded individualists than submit his manuscripts to a panel of faceless do-gooders employed by a Ministry of Culture. I tried to point out that public patronage was not intended to exclude private patronage—when suddenly I realised that we were arguing from different premisses. He was talking as a novelist, who needs only time, talent and a typewriter to produce a work of art. I, on the other hand, was concerned with the theatre, where, apart from this trio of prerequisites, a writer needs actors, directors, designers, carpenters, costumiers, wigmakers, stagehands, electricians and possibly singers, dancers and musicians as well, before his work can take on life and present itself for critical assessment. It costs infinitely less to publish a bad novel than to put on a bad play in the commercial theatre. And as soon as you begin to apply commercial criteria to the drama, you find that a play with two characters and one set, which runs for six months, must be considered 'better'—in inverted commas—than a play with fifty characters and twelve sets, which runs for a year: since the former will undoubtedly show a larger profit.

Ever since I had this unsettling chat, I have refrained from taking anything on trust when talking about the National Theatre. Hence the first question I'd like to deal with is: why do we need it?

Britain came late to the whole idea of state-aided theatre. One of the reasons for this is that our rulers have never officially concerned themselves with drama—and by rulers I mean royalty. Queen Elizabeth I enjoyed Shakespeare's plays, but she never paid for their upkeep. Louis XIV, by contrast, took Molière's actors under his fiscal wing and gave France the Comédie Française. Similarly, it was the rulers of the German city-states who founded the great German tradition of subsidised theatre; the provincial centres of German culture still compete with each other for theatrical supremacy.

Another reason for British backwardness is the lasting damage inflicted on the theatre by the Puritans in the seventeenth century. After their moral lacerations, acting came to be regarded as a form of clothed prostitution; and though Charles II subsidised actresses, he did not subsidise plays. Until Irving got his knighthood in 1895, acting remained a dubious profession, barely a stone's cast away from the brothel. And this mighty backlog of Puritan disapproval had to be dislodged before a British government could be persuaded to spend a penny of public money on an art so trivial. Nobody realised that the theatre had become trivial precisely because no public money had been spent to make it otherwise.

Twenty years ago a prominent American playwright summed up what he felt about the Broadway theatre: 'That the most exalted of the arts should have fallen into the receivership of businessmen and gamblers is a situation parallel in absurdity to the conduct of worship becoming the responsibility of a herd of water-buffaloes. It is one of those things that a man of reason had rather not think about until the means of redemption is more apparent.'

That was Tennessee Williams, talking about the American theatre in 1944. People in Britain have been arguing in the same way for more than a century, and elsewhere in Europe for more than three hundred years. The means of redemption became apparent a long time ago. The very idea that good theatre should be required to show a profit would seem indecent in Sweden, Denmark, Poland, Czechoslovakia, Hungary, Yugoslavia, Norway, Russia, Italy, both the Germanies and France. You might as well insist that public libraries should profiteer, or that the educational system should pay its way. Theatre in these countries is an amenity for which the state or the municipality—which are simply the individual writ large—must hold itself responsible. It is something the public needs and deserves, like art galleries, zoos and parks for recreation.

Henry James wrote in 1872: 'It is impossible to spend many weeks in Paris without observing that the theatre plays a very important part in French civilization; and it is impossible to go much to the theatre without finding it a copious source of instruction as to French ideas, manners and philosophy.'

The same could not have been said of the British or the American theatre in the late nineteenth century. In London and New York drama had been forced into the marketplace, there to compete with every other huckster. It had inevitably become a short-term art, dependent on quick financial returns, concerned only to produce what the public wants now—not what it might want over a period of five, ten or twenty years. It was compelled to concentrate on easily digestible, uncontroversial, ego-massaging, audience-ingratiating trifles—relieved on occasion by classical revivals tailored to fit star personalities. Box-office tyranny was absolute; and has remained so—apart from latterday trickles of patronage from bodies like the Arts Council—ever since.

Subsidy offers what commercialism negates: the idea of continuity, the guarantee of permanence. If a new production fails on first showing, it need not be lost for ever; it can be shelved for a while and then, if public opinion changes, be revived on the crest of a new wave. Subsidy also enables the theatre to build a durable bridge, with free passage for traffic in both directions, between the past and the present. If Broadway were subsidised, for instance, we should still be able to see Elia Kazan's productions of *A Streetcar Named Desire* and *Death of a Salesman*—they would still be on view, alternating with a dozen other plays, old and new, performed by permanent acting troupes. The plays of Chekhov and Gorki have been in the repertoire of the Moscow Art Theatre for sixty years, with occasional changes of cast. In this way each new generation of playgoers is kept in touch with history. The storehouse of past achievement is always open to the public, instead of being irrevocably burned down at the end of every season.

People sometimes fear that state subsidy may bring with it state control and censorship, and in totalitarian countries this has often been the case. The truth is that governments have two equally effective means of controlling their artists. One is by direct censorship. The other is more oblique but not less potent—it is censorship imposed by *withholding* subsidies, thereby enslaving the artist to the box-office and forcing him, unless he is a genius, to turn out lovable, undisturbing after-dinner entertainments.

What can happen to a theatre without subsidy was vividly animated for me at the Edinburgh Drama Conference. Ninety people attended it, speaking twenty-odd languages, and among them was a young American director who wanted to stage, on the last day of the conference, a 'Happening'. He explained it to me thus: 'You see, Ken, Broadway is like a jungle. If you want to experiment you have to go out into the streets.' He wanted to use the Conference audience in the following experimental way: 'First of all, there'll be no chairs in the hall. Not one. Just a couple of thousand used automobile tyres lying around on the floor. In the middle of the auditorium there'll be four monumental towers of gasoline cans. At the exits there will be four men in black sitting on motorcycles with the motors idling ominously. I shall then invite the audience to build a mountain of tyres in the centre of the floor. Next, and simultaneously, the lowest and the highest notes on the organ will be sounded, thereby creating a sense of unease. The cyclists, at this point, start to circle around the people building the mountain. The guys on the towers of gasoline cans will begin to strike them with hammers on the off-beat. The audience will then dismantle the mountain.' I asked him where they would sit. 'On the tyres, where else?' But (I pointed out) they had paid money and booked seats with numbers. . . .

At length I persuaded him to stage the Happening outside the hall in the courtyard, after the Conference was over. I stood on a balcony and watched it with a group of Eastern European directors—people who worked in theatres that subsidised experiment, and were not faced with the stark choice between commercialism and cut-price improvisation masquerading as art. Looking down, we felt like Louis XVI and his court with the revolutionary mob howling beneath. Except that this was not a genuine revolution; it was a gesture born of economic necessity. I learned afterwards what the young American was trying to do. He explained that he wanted to restore a sense of ritual and participation to the act of playgoing. But it was ritual without content, a party game instead of a communal festivity. It was do-it-yourself art—the only alternative, in an entirely profit-based society, to commodity art, art considered as a saleable product.

Subsidy is the missing link, the third force which can occupy and colonise the great intermediate area between minority theatre based on private whim and majority theatre based on private profits. This is precisely the area that the National Theatre exists to inhabit and develop; and our hope is that it will be the first, not of the few, but of the many— the beginning of a chain reaction that will set up a national grid of subsidised theatres in London and in every provincial centre.

In the British theatre as a whole, chaos still prevails. The notion that an ideal playhouse is a place where you can see a permanent company of first-rate actors appearing in a large and varied repertoire of firstrate plays is generally accepted; but the notion that such a playhouse must inevitably incur an enormous financial loss, even if it plays to capacity, is less widely embraced. The formation of the National Theatre company was a step towards sanity—towards placing the theatre on the same footing as art galleries and public libraries. The pioneers of the National Theatre movement—people like Shaw, William Archer and Harley Granville Barker—confidently expected that their battle would be won in time for the tercentenary of Shakespeare's death. That was in 1916, Victory was delayed until October 1963, when the National Theatre presented its inaugural production just in time for the quatercentenary of Shakespeare's birth.

There are many other serious legitimate theatres in Britain which are supported to a certain extent by public funds. The National Theatre gets more money than any of the others; but I should like to emphasise that none of them gets enough. To support our first year's operations, we received a Treasury grant of £130,000—only £50,000 more than the sum allotted the year before to the Old Vic. And the Old Vic employed a much smaller company at much lower salaries, and presented a much shorter list of plays. To keep our standards as high as our output, we shall need more money soon. The same applies to our friendly rivals, the Royal Shakespeare Company. I should like them to be able to compete with us on equal terms; because artistic competition usually makes for better art, whereas commercial competition seldom makes anything but money. The National Theatre and the Royal Shakespeare Company should be able to live side by side in the same kind of relationship as that which exists between the Comédie Française and Jean-Louis Barrault's Théâtre de France.

The tap of public patronage is not exactly gushing, but at least it has been connected. To borrow a dictum beloved of American Negro leaders: 'We ain't where we ought to be, and we ain't where we're going to be, but we sure ain't where we were.' The National Theatre, as a company, exists; the great *de facto* hurdle has been surmounted. It has acquired a brilliant architect in Denys Lasdun, and before long its permanent home will begin to creep up on the South Bank, mercifully obscuring at least part of the Shell penitentiary. What form the theatre will take is something on which I cannot pronounce. Anything I say here reflects personal bias, not official consensus. It is accepted that there should be two auditoriums; it is also accepted that if you try to cram more than a thousand people into a single auditorium, you are entering an area where audibility or visibility or both are sure to be imperfect. Neither on nor outside the Building Committee of the National Theatre is there absolute agreement as to how deeply the stage should project into the auditorium—how far, you might say, it should put its tongue out at the audience—but it is generally felt that actors and spectators should seem to be in one room, without the separating guillotine of the proscenium frame. Beyond this common ground, all is doubt and guesswork.

Speaking for myself and not for the National Theatre, I have two cherished hopes. One concerns the relative sizes of the two projected playhouses. Tradition, based on continental models and Harley Granville Barker's proposals, dictates that one should be large, reserved for the major classics, and the other small, devoted to experimental work. I believe this dichotomy to be artificial and archaic. It derives from the days when all reputable theatres had to be large in order to be commercial; and when plays of doubtful commercial value were forced into converted cellars, attics or church halls that could be cheaply rented. According to this viewpoint, there are two separate kinds of theatre: majority theatre, performed for money, and minority theatre, performed for kicks. This division, originally imposed by economic necessity, tends to survive in the minds and attitudes of those who are planning a theatre from which economic necessity has been removed. Instead of a big house holding a thousand and a little one holding three hundred or so, I would therefore propose two theatres much closer in relative capacity—eight hundred, let us say, and six hundred. Otherwise we may tend to perpetuate the class-conscious notion that there is one kind of drama for the many and another kind, implicitly superior, for the few. Any theatrical experience that cannot be communicated to six hundred people at a sitting is not, on the face of it, the sort of experience that a National Theatre exists to provide. I would hope, of course, for a third auditorium—a workshop or studio devoted to far-out experiment, such as the Schiller Theatre has in West Berlin—but the priority, in my mind, rests with the other two.

Next, there is the anguished question of how far the stage should jut out into the audience; and this is bound up with what we have just considered. The aim is to get as many people as possible as close as possible to the stage. Geometrically, this means that the larger the prospective audience, the more you have to push the acting area out into their midst. Reduce the audience, and at once you reduce the necessity of shoving out a peninsular stage—which even at its best imposes on the customers a number of dire deprivations, such as staring at an actor's rear view when most you need to look at his face and hear the words he is saying. I have heard it speciously argued that a projecting stage adds 'a third dimension' to acting. What a grotesque abuse of language! *All* live acting is in three dimensions, as opposed to screen and television acting, which has two; and I cannot understand how the ability to see one's fellow-spectators behind the actors materially adds to the sculptural roundness of the experience. If we erected a few rows of seats behind the actors on the stage of the Old Vic, would it really make the productions more three-dimensional? The truth, I suspect, is that *proximity* creates the illusion of an extra dimension. And in a theatre of reasonable size, you don't need a tongue-shaped stage to achieve proximity. It exists, after an improvised fashion, in that brilliant conversion job, the Mermaid Theatre in Puddle Dock, where the edge of the stage is straight.

All of us at the National Theatre worry about architectural problems, whether or not it is our business to do so. We also fret over our immediate task, which is to assemble the best available actors and put them into a snow-balling repertoire of the best available plays, ancient and modern, comic and tragic, native and foreign. But we have also stumbled across an additional problem. It has to do with re-education; slowly and patiently, we have had to set about re-educating actors, directors, playwrights and audiences alike. You would be surprised how hard it is, in a society where 'theatre' means 'theatre for private profit', to explain to people that *this* theatre actually belongs to them, and is not in any way stirred by the need or desire to show a profit. I have had to point out to playwrights that in our *modus operandi* they must take the long-term, not the short-term view; although we cannot offer them the quick financial gains of a West End run, we can offer them instead a repertory run that might last for decades. The base on which our enterprises rests can be simply stated; we are not selling a product, we are providing a service. Success at the box office is no longer the only criterion. We would rather have a first-rate work playing to less than capacity than a third-rate one filling the house. Instead of fearing criticism, we can learn from it without rancour, since we do not depend—as the commercial theatre must—on rave reviews for survival.

So far we have opened six productions in the space of five months. On the whole, the critics have applauded and the public has flocked. I don't doubt that this is partly due to the patriotic euphoria that clusters around the launching of any great national venture, and we are sure to run into an iceberg or two before long. But we have not fulfilled the cynical prophecy that the National Theatre would be a plush-lined museum; the names of Laurence Olivier, John Dexter and William Gaskill are not exactly renowned for reverent conventionality, and I am no conservative myself.

Equally, we have not established a 'style' of our own. This is because we never intended to. Good repertory theatres fall into two main categories. One is the kind that is founded by a great director or playwright with a novel and often revolutionary approach to dramatic art. He creates a style for his own special purpose. Examples of this process would include Stanislavsky's Moscow Art Theatre, Bertolt Brecht's Berliner Ensemble and Joan Littlewood's Theatre Workshop. The other category consists of theatres with a broader, less personal *raison d'être*: whose function—more basic though not more valuable—is simply to present to the public the widest possible selection of good plays from all periods and places. In this group you can place the Schiller Theatre in West Berlin; the Royal Dramatic Theatre in Stockholm; and the National Theatre in the Waterloo Road. Their aim is to present each play in the style appropriate to it—and that is an ambition by no means as modest as it sounds.

A year or so ago, I noticed that out of more than two dozen plays running in the West End, only three had been written before 1950. This is the kind of fantastic imbalance that the National Theatre exists to correct. By the end of our first year we shall have staged twelve plays—eight British, four foreign; nine by dead authors, three by living. Of these, roughly half will remain in next autumn's repertoire—some of them, hopefully, for periods of many years. In 1964–5 a dozen more productions have been chosen to join the list. Shakespeare is a necessity, though not in bulk; we are content to leave the lion's share of the bard to the Royal Shakespeare Company. To test the stamina of plays that were praised in the fairly recent past is part of National Theatre policy—hence our decision to revive Noël Coward's *Hay Fever*, directed by the author. Other productions in active preparation include Congreve's *Love for Love*, Strindberg's *Dance of Death*, *The Dutch Courtesan* by John Marston, Brecht's *Mother Courage* (which, apart from the Berliner-Ensemble's short but cataclysmic visit in 1956, has never been professionally performed in London), Chekhov's *Three Sisters*, a play by John Osborne based on Lope's *La Fianza Satisfecha* (a strange and startling moral fable), and *The Royal Hunt of the Sun*, by Peter Shaffer. The list is long and various, and only high subsidy makes it even conceivable.

You may ask whether the public wants the theatrical goods we have chosen for them and for which their taxes have paid. The answer is that it looks that way; up to last week the average attendance at the Old Vic was not far short of ninety per cent. And who are these playgoers? Where do they come from and what do they want? We have some information on this subject, derived from a questionnaire that we appended to the programme of Max Frisch's *Andorra*. Ten per cent of the audience, to date, have filled it in and returned it; and you may like to hear some of the results—bearing always in mind that the audience for a play like *Andorra* is likely to be younger and more experimentally inclined than the audience for an established classic.

The *Andorra* figures show that 35 per cent of the audience is either teaching or being taught. A further 24 per cent consists of clerical or other white-collar workers. Point three per cent (0·3%) are manual workers. The last figure is the most distressing, demonstrating as it does that live theatre is socially beyond the desires and financially beyond the means of working-class audiences. Something must be done to remedy this, the obvious course being to reduce the prices of admission, which would involve either an increase of subsidy or a lowering of artistic standards. The former would clearly be preferable. Encouragingly, fifty-five per cent of the audience is thirty-five years old or younger, which implies that we are not tailoring our programme to meet the demands of gerontophile nostalgia. Many of our spectators are addicts, obsessed with theatre to the point (in some cases) of mania. Thirty-seven per cent of them go to the theatre more than thirty times a year; and fifteen per cent more than fifty times. One realises that the theatre is kept alive by a hard core of absolute fanatics. Nine per cent of the audience, paying more than seventy-five visits a year, buy far more tickets than the thirty per cent who come fifteen times or less.

Geographically, the figures reveal an overwhelming majority of National Theatre-goers in London and the Home Counties—eighty-nine per cent, as against a tiny minority from the rest of Britain and the world. Obviously, we must tour as much and as widely as we can if we are to deserve the epithet 'National'. Replying to a question about the plays they would most like to see added to the repertoire of the National Theatre, the audience voted for Ibsen, Shaw, Brecht, Marlowe, Wilde, O'Neill and Jonson, in that descending order. Sixty per cent of them liked *Andorra* with only twenty-two per cent of hostility—not bad, considering that it was the first new play (and an awkward, foreign one at that) which the National Theatre had ever presented.

I have tried, in this headlong survey, to give some idea of the direction in which the National Theatre is moving. My conclusions, of course, are those of a navigator and not of a pilot. I once defined a critic as a man who knew the way but couldn't drive the car. As a back-seat driver at the National Theatre, I am putting that maxim to the test.

(1964)

The Royal Smut-Hound

For 'wind from a duck's behind', substitute 'wind from Mount Zion'.
Omit 'crap', substitute 'jazz'.
Omit 'balls of the Medici': 'testicles of the Medici' would be acceptable.
Delete 'postcoital', substitute 'late evening'.
For 'the Vicar's got the clappers', substitute 'the Vicar's dropped a clanger'.
Omit 'piss off, piss off, piss off', substitute 'Shut your steaming gob'.

These staccato commands are authentic and typical extracts from letters dispatched in recent years from the office of the Lord Chamberlain of Great Britain, second ranking dignitary of Her Majesty's Court. He is the official in charge of the royal household, responsible for receiving visiting potentates and for arranging all state ceremonies from christenings to coronations. He also appoints the Keeper of the Royal Swans. On no account must he be confused with the Lord *Great* Chamberlain—a lowly sixth in the dignitary ratings—who supervises royal openings of Parliament and helps the monarch (if the latter is male) to dress on coronation mornings.

Among the other duties of the Lord Small Chamberlain, as we may call him in passing, is that of censoring all plays presented for public performance in the United Kingdom; and it is this which explains the obscene correspondence that issues from his headquarters in St James's Palace. On royally embossed note paper, producers all over the country are gravely informed that 'fart', 'tits', 'sod', 'sperm', 'arse', 'Jesus!', etc., are illicit expressions, and that 'the Lord Chamberlain cannot accept the word "screwed" in place of the word "shagged"'. It is something of a wonder that no one has lodged a complaint against His Lordship for corrupting and depraving the innocent secretaries to whom this spicy stuff is dictated; at the very least, the Post Office might intervene to prevent what looks to me like a flagrant misuse of the mails.

At the moment, there is nothing we can do about it. The Lord Chamberlain's role as legal censor dates back to 1737, when Sir Robert Walpole's administration—probably the most venal in British history—rushed an Act through Parliament to protect itself from criticism in the theatre. Ever since Tudor times, the Chamberlain (or his subordinate, the Master of the Revels) had been empowered by royal proclamation to regulate dramatic entertainments, but he had mainly confined his cuts to matters of heresy or sedition that might offend the monarch. It was

Walpole's panicky vengefulness that gave statutory recognition and legislative force to the Chamberlain's powers, and established a Court official as the sole dictator of the British theatre. Henceforth, no new plays or additions to old ones could be staged without his approval.

This authority was toughened and extended by the Theatres Act of 1843, a repellent piece of legislation that is still in force. Under its provisions, anything previously unperformed must be submitted to 'the Malvolio of St James's Palace' (Bernard Shaw's phrase) at least a week before opening night; a reading fee of two guineas is charged, so that you pay for the privilege of being banned; licences already granted may be revoked if the Chamberlain changes his mind (or if there is a change of Chamberlain); and any theatre presenting an unlicensed work to a paying audience will be summarily closed down. His Lordship can impose a ban 'whenever he shall be of opinion that it is fitting for the Preservation of Good Manners, Decorum, or of the Public Peace'. He need give no reason for his decisions, from which there is no appeal. Since he is appointed directly by the sovereign, he is not responsible to the House of Commons. He inhabits a limbo aloof from democracy, answerable only to his own hunches. The rules by which he judges plays are nowhere defined in law; to quote Shaw again, and not for the last time, 'they simply codify the present and most of the past prejudices of the class he represents'.

Since he is always recruited from the peerage, he naturally tends to forbid attacks on institutions like the Church and the Crown. He never permits plays about eminent British subjects, living or recently dead, no matter how harmless the content and despite the fact that Britain's libel laws are about the strictest on earth. Above all, he feels a paternal need to protect his flock from exposure to words or gestures relating to bodily functions below the navel and above the upper thigh. This—the bedding-*cum*-liquid-and-solid-eliminating area—is what preoccupies him most, and involves the writers and producers who have to deal with him in the largest amount of wasted time.

The normal procedure is as follows: enclosing the two-guinea fee, you submit your script which is then read by one of three 'Examiners'—anonymous part-time workers, occasionally with some theatrical background. The Examiner passes it on with his comments to the Chamberlain's two Comptrollers—army officers in early middle-age—who add their own observations before referring it to the boss himself. Then begins the salty correspondence, which may go on for months. The Comptroller lists the required cuts and changes; the producer replies, agreeing, protesting or proposing alternatives. (A fine recent protest was penned by the director of John Osborne's *Inadmissible Evidence*: 'We find that the cutting of the words "menstrual periods" is blocking the flow of the scene.')

If postal deadlock is reached, the next stage is a chat with the Comptroller, who usually comes on as a breezy man of the world who knows as much about four-letter words as the next man but somehow feels that the next man should be prevented from hearing them. Insane bargaining takes place: the Comptroller may permit you a 'pee' in Act One so long as you delete a 'Christ!' in Act Three. Discussing a one-line gag about the hero's mother-in-law in Osborne's *Look Back in Anger* ('She's as rough as a night in a Bombay brothel'), the Comptroller roared with laughter and said: 'That's a splendid phrase and I shall use it in the Guards' Club, but it won't do for the theatre, where people don't know one another.' If the author still declines to be slashed and rewritten by strangers, he can apply for an interview with the Chamberlain himself; but unless he has a pretty powerful management behind him, he is unlikely to get one; and it has seldom been known to do any good.

Chamberlains are rarely garrulous. Shaw said of the one who held office in his youth that he made only two recorded pronouncements: 'I am not an agricultural labourer', and 'Who is Tolstoy?' The present incumbent is more of a loose-mouth. In the spring of 1965 he gave an interview to the London *Sunday Times*, in the course of which he said: 'You'd be surprised to see the number of four-letter words and I think I can say obscenities, that are sometimes included in scripts by the most reputable people.' (He meant, of course, 'piss', 'arse' and 'shit' as well as the obvious venereal monosyllables.) 'We normally cut certain expletives, for example, "Christ" and "Jesus" ', he went on, 'which are admittedly used in common parlance . . .but still do give offence to a great number of people.' When asked by the interviewer which subject—sex, religion or politics—raised the most problems, he replied that in terms of quantity, sex was the most troublesome, although: 'I have personally found the religious ones most difficult of all.' He admitted that, if faced with a play that satirised Christianity, 'I would start with a bias against it'. In the six months immediately preceding this colloquy, his office had received 441 scripts, of which sixty-three had been returned for cutting and changing. In eighteen cases the proposed alterations were radical. One of the latter group was John Osborne's *A Patriot for Me*, a play factually based on the career of a homosexual colonel in the Austro-Hungarian army who was blackmailed into spying for the Russians and finally committed suicide. The Chamberlain demanded the excision of five whole scenes. The author refused; and the producers had to turn their theatre into a private club in order to present a major new work by one of Britain's leading dramatists.

Who is the Lord Chamberlain? As I write, he is Cameron Fromanteel, first Baron Cobbold, educated at Eton and Cambridge, and a former Governor of the Bank of England: a cheerful, toothy, soothing chap in his early sixties. His predecessor, who retired in 1963, was the 11th Earl of Scarbrough, educated at Eton and Oxford, and a former Governor of Bombay. Unlike Lord Cobbold, he could boast firsthand experience of artistic endeavour, having written, in 1936, *The History of the Eleventh Hussars*.

These are the men who have exercised absolute power over British drama for the past fourteen years. As a highly respected director once put it: 'Why should a colonial administrator be allowed to put fig leaves on statues? Or a banker to paint out the bits of pictures that he doesn't like?' He is not alone in his bewilderment, which history amply supports. Around the turn of the century, the poet Swinburne declared that the Lord Chamberlain had exposed the English stage 'to the contempt and compassion of civilized Europe'. To cite a few other spokesmen from the same period:

All I can say is that something or other—which probably is consciousness of the Censor—appears to deter men of letters who have other channels for communicating with the public, from writing for the stage. (Thomas Hardy)

The censorship, with its quite wanton power of suppression, has always been one of the reasons why I haven't ventured into playwriting. (H. G. Wells)

I am certain that a dramatic author may be shamefully hindered, and that such a situation is intolerable; a disgrace to the tone, to the character, of this country's civilization. (Joseph Conrad)

There is not perhaps another field so fine in the England of today for a man or woman of letters, but all the other literary fields are free. This one alone has a blind bull in it. (From a protest signed by many writers, including Henry James, J. M. Barrie, Galsworthy, Conan Doyle and Shaw)

All of which suggests that Shaw was right when he argued that the dearth of good English plays between the early eighteenth century and his own début in the late nineteenth was entirely due to the existence of the Lord Chamberlain, a baleful deterrent lurking on the threshold of creativity. After all, why should a firstrate writer venture into a theatre where Sophocles' *Oedipus Rex* was banned? Just before World War One, Sir Herbert Beerbohm Tree wanted to stage this great tragedy of incest; the censor brusquely turned him down, a decision which moved the popular playwright Henry Arthur Jones to publish a suave letter of complaint. It read in part:

> Now, of course, if any considerable body of Englishmen are arranging to marry their mothers, whether by accident or design, it must be stopped at once. But it is not a frequent occurrence in any class of English society. Throughout the course of my life I have not met more than six men who were anxious to do it.

We know very little about the qualities the sovereign looks for when he or she appoints a Chamberlain. According to the current holder of the office, whose opinion may not be wholly disinterested, they include 'wide experience, a knowledge of what is going on in the contemporary world, and the habit of sifting advice, reaching decisions and taking responsibility'. Of the methods employed by the Chamberlain to select an Examiner of plays, we know nothing at all. Shaw wrote in 1899:

> It will be inferred that no pains are spared to secure the services of a very highly qualified and distinguished person to wield this astonishing power—say the holder of a University chair of Literature and Dramaturgy. The inference is erroneous. You are not allowed to sell stamps in an English post office without previously passing an examination; but you may become Examiner of plays without necessarily knowing how to read or write.

This is not to say that a fully qualified Examiner would be an improvement. Rather the contrary: a censor with a firstrate mind, capable of penetrating the elaborate disguises under which contraband ideas are smuggled to the public, and shrewd enough to detect potential nonconformity in the foetal stage, could castrate the drama far more effectively than the present posse of numskulls. All censors are bad, but clever ones are the worst.

In Elizabethan times and throughout the seventeenth century, when censorship was mostly carried out by the Master of the Revels, the chief qualification for the job was greed. The fee for reading a script rose during this period from five shillings to one pound, and in the 1660s a particularly corrupt Master attempted to raise his income by claiming authority over such public pleasures as cockfights, billiards and ninepins. But although the censor was grasping, he was relatively harmless; he did not see himself as the nation's moral guardian, and as long as authors refrained from advocating the overthrow of the monarchy and the established church, their freedom—especially in sexual matters—was virtually complete.

The rot that still plagues the British theatre set in with Walpole, who began to get worried in 1728, when John Gay pilloried the ruling classes with tremendous popular success in *The Beggar's Opera*. Detailed and specific attacks on Walpole's premiership followed in the plays of Henry Fielding; and the result was the crippling, muzzling Censorship Act of 1737. Thereafter Fielding gave up the theatre in favour of the novel: English literature gained the author of *Tom Jones*, but English drama lost the services of a man who might well have developed into the greatest playwright since Shakespeare.

Britain did not at first take kindly to Walpole's encroachment on freedom of speech. Lord Chesterfield argued vainly against it in a majestic and permanently valid speech to the House of Lords:

> If Poets and Players are to be restrained, let them be restrained as other Subjects are, by the known Laws of their Country; if they offend, let them be tried as every Englishman ought to be, by God and their Country. Do not let us subject them to the arbitrary Will and Pleasure of any one Man. A Power lodged in the hands of one single Man, to judge and determine, without any Limitation, without any Control or Appeal, is a sort of Power unknown to our Laws, inconsistent with our Constitution. It is a higher, a more absolute Power than we trust even to the King himself; and therefore I must think we ought not to vest any such Power in his Majesty's Lord Chamberlain.

And Samuel Johnson wrote an essay ironically defending the censorship against a playwright who objected that the Chamberlain had banned one of his works without giving a reason:

> Is it for a Poet to demand a Licenser's reason for his proceedings? Is he not rather to acquiesce in the decision of Authority and conclude that there are reasons he cannot comprehend? Unhappy would it be for men in power were they always obliged to publish the motives of their conduct. What is power but the liberty of acting without being accountable?

Johnson went on to propose that the censor's power should be extended to the press, and that it should be made a felony for a citizen to *read* without the Chamberlain's licence.

But idiocy triumphed and swiftly entrenched itself. The nineteenth century was the censor's paradise and playground. In 1832 the Examiner of plays was quizzed by a royal commission. He said it was indecent for a dramatic hero to call his mistress an 'angel', because angels were characters in Scripture, and Scripture was 'much too sacred for the stage'. When asked why he forbade oaths like 'Damme', he replied: 'I think it is immoral and improper, to say nothing of the vulgarity of it in assemblies where high characters and females congregate.'

The same Examiner had lately banned a meek little play about Charles I, whom the British people had decapitated two centuries earlier. He realised (he said) that its intentions were harmless, 'but mischief may be unconsciously done, as a house may be set on fire by a little innocent in the nursery'. This tone of lofty condescension resounded through the rest of the century. *La Dame aux Camélias* was condemned because it might inflame the public to acts of sexual riot. A stage version of Disraeli's novel *Coningsby* was banned on the eve of its opening. 'You see,' the Chamberlain explained to the baffled adapter, 'you are writing a kind of quasi-political piece, and here you are exhibiting a sort of contrast between the manufacturing people and the lower classes. Don't you think, now, that that would be a pity?' When Henry Irving sought to appear in a poetic play about the life of Mohammed, he was tetchily informed that Queen Victoria's subjects included millions of Mohammedans who would be outraged if the Prophet were represented on stage. The Chamberlain's nervousness about holy metaphysics is notorious; as late as 1912, an extremely godly play was rejected because it contained such blasphemous lines as 'Christ comfort you' and 'The real Good Friday would be that which brought the cure for cancer'.

The arch-fiends, however, were Ibsen and Shaw—social critics who brutally exposed the hypocrisies of official morality and their destructive effect on personal relationships. Both suffered from the censor's gag. 'I have studied Ibsen's plays pretty carefully,' said the Chamberlain's Examiner in 1891, 'and all the characters appear to me morally deranged.' Two years later he ambushed Shaw by banning *Mrs Warren's Profession*; and when he died in 1895, Shaw wrote a cruel and classic obituary:

> The late Mr Piggot is declared on all hands to have been the best reader of plays we have ever had; and yet he was a walking compendium of vulgar insular prejudice. . . . He had French immorality on the brain; he had American indecency on the brain; he had the womanly woman on the brain; he had the divorce court on the brain; he had 'not before a mixed audience' on the brain; his official

career in relation to the higher drama was one long folly and panic.
... It is a frightening thing to see the great thinkers, poets and
authors of modern Europe—men like Ibsen, Wagner, Tolstoy and
the leaders of our own literature—delivered into the vulgar hands of
such a noodle as this amiable old gentlemen—this despised, incapable old official—most notoriously was.

Seventy years have passed since then, but appallingly little has
changed. Less than a decade ago, the Chamberlain stamped on Arthur
Miller's *A View from the Bridge* and Tennessee Williams's *Cat on a Hot
Tin Roof* because he thought them tainted with homosexuality. These
ludicrous bans have now been lifted, but the censor still forbids all
theatrical representations of queer characters who follow their sexual
leanings without being tragically punished or revealing any sense of guilt.
Everything remotely anal, no matter how far removed from sensual enjoy-
ment, is automatically prohibited. In 1964 the Royal Shakespeare Company (Patron: the Queen) put on a French surrealist play of the 1920's in
which a stately Edwardian beauty, symbolising death, was required to
break wind at regular intervals. The stage directions indicated that the
effect could be made by a bass trombone in the wings, but this was not
precise enough for the Chamberlain. He passed the script only when the
director agreed to let the trombonist play the Destiny Theme from
Beethoven's *Fifth Symphony*. This apparently made farting respectable.

John Osborne, probably the most important British dramatist since
Shaw, has naturally been singled out for the censor's special attention.
His first play, an assault on McCarthyism, was presented by a provincial
repertory company in 1951; it contained a scene in which one of the
characters was falsely smeared as a homosexual. The Chamberlain cut
the imputation of queerness and thus crippled the play. 'It's the sheer
humiliation that's bad for the artist,' Osborne said to me not long ago. 'I
know playwrights who almost seem to be *living* with the Lord Chamberlain—it's like an affair. There's a virgin period when you aren't aware of
him, but eventually you can't avoid thinking of him while you're writing.
He sits on your shoulder, like a terrible nanny.'

In 1959 Osborne wrote and directed a musical called *The World of
Paul Slickey*. Before it opened on tour, the usual exchange of letters
with the censor had taken place, including the following concession from
Osborne's lawyer:

> My client is prepared to substitute for:
> 'Leaping from the bridal bed,
> He preferred his youthful squire instead,'

the line:

> 'He preferred the *companionship* of his
> youthful squire instead.'

But while the show was on its way to London the Chamberlain received one or two complaints that prompted him to demand new cuts and revisions. Among several offending lines, there was a lyric that ran:

> And before I make a pass,
> I'll tell her that the sun shines out of her—face.

On this the censor's comment was curt and final. 'If the pause before 'face' is retained, this couplet will be unacceptable.' Osborne sat down in fury to register a general protest:

> Your office seems intent on treating me as if I were the producer of a third-rate nude revue. What I find most bewildering is the lack of moral consistency and objectivity which seems to characterise your recent decisions—decisions which seem to be reversed and changed because of the whim of any twisted neurotic who cares to write to you and exploit his own particular sexual frustration or moral oddity. In paying attention to what is without question an infinitesimal and lunatic minority, you are doing a grave injustice not only to myself but to the general public and your own office.

I sympathise with Osborne's rage, while regretting that he let it trap him into implying that special privileges should be granted to serious drama and withheld from 'third-rate nude revues'. Erotic stimulation is a perfectly legitimate function of bad art as well as good, and a censor who bans a stripper is behaving just as illiberally and indefensibly as one who eviscerates a masterpiece.

Osborne returned to the attack in 1960, when the Chamberlain blue-pencilled eighteen passages—many of them entire speeches—from his chronicle play, *Luther*, in which Alberty Finney was to conquer the West End and Broadway. Osborne stated his terms in a white-hot letter to the London producer:

> I cannot agree to any of the cuts demanded, *under any circumstances*. Nor will I agree to any possible substitutions. I don't write plays to have them rewritten by someone else. I intend to make a clear unequivocal stand on this because (*a*) I think it is high time that someone did so, and (*b*) ... the suggested cuts or alternatives would result in such damage to the psychological structure, meaning and depth of the play that the result would be a travesty.... I will

not even contemplate any compromise ... I am quite prepared to withdraw the play from production altogether and wait for the day when Lord Scarbrough [at that time the Lord Chamberlain] is no more. . . . I have made up my mind and, in fact, did so long ago.

This blast had its effect. For once, the censor crumpled; and *Luther* went on with only five small verbal changes, three of them involving the substitution of 'urine' or 'kidney juice' for 'piss'. Osborne wrote to the producer congratulating him on an 'astonishing victory'. His present belief, shared by most of his contemporaries in the British theatre, is that censorship is not only offensive but superfluous: The existing laws relating to libel and obscenity are already ferocious enough to warm any bigot's heart, and constitute, in themselves, quite a sizable deterrent to freedom of speech. Would Osborne allow a Black Muslim play to be performed in a community of white supremacists? 'Yes—anything that creates energy and vitality is good for the theatre.' When I posed the ultimate question—would he permit sexual intercourse on stage?—Osborne replied: 'It might make me ill, and I'd like to know beforehand what I was in for. But I'm prepared to be exposed to it—although I might want a seat on the aisle.'

Improvisation—the utterance of words unfiltered by the authorised sin-sieve—is one of the Chamberlain's abiding hates. A few years ago, when the off-Broadway revue called *The Premise* came to London, he forbade the cast to improvise, despite the fact that at least half of the show (according to its publicity) was made up on the moment's spur. On this occasion, mindful perhaps of Anglo-American relations, he took no legal action; but in 1958 there were convictions and fines when the producers of a play entitled *You Won't Always Be on Top* enhanced the text with an unlicensed impersonation of Sir Winston Churchill opening a public lavatory.

With these anomalies in mind, consider an antic sequence of events which unfolded in April 1965. The management of an Australian revue called *Guarding the Change* was instructed by the Chamberlain, three hours before the curtain was due to rise at the New Lyric Theatre in London, that two sketches would have to be omitted. One concerned Scott of the Antarctic, who died half a century ago, and the other was a parody of a characteristically radiant royal address which ended with the words:

Our thoughts /good wishes/carpet salesmen/aircraft carriers are on their way toward you. And so, on this beautiful morning/ afternoon/evening, what is there for us to say but hello/how-do-you-do/goodbye/well done/arise, Sir Robert Menzies.

This, like the bit about Scott, was expunged on the grounds of good taste. The management at once telephoned to ask whether they could fill the gap left in their programme by reading to the audience the letter in which the Chamberlain imposed his ban. The request was refused. 'Without fear or favour,' as a wag later remarked, 'the Lord Chamberlain also banned his own letter.'

That same evening, however, the royal family themselves were rocking with laughter at an inspired Irish clown named Spike Milligan, most of whose gags are famously impromptu. To quote a length the wag cited above (Michael Frayn of *The Observer*):

> They were at the Comedy Theatre, watching *Son of Oblomov*, with Spike Milligan departing from the script to make jokes in which he mentioned their names, like 'Why does Prince Philip wear red, white and blue braces?' (Answer: 'To keep his trousers up.') ... But the point is, what is the Lord Chamberlain going to do about Mr Milligan? Mentioning Prince Philip or his braces on the West End stage is not allowed. ... And what will he do about the royal family? If the reporters saw correctly through their night glasses in the darkness, the whole party seem to have aided and abetted Mr Milligan by providing sensible evidence of appreciation. In other words, they are all accessories after the fact. Will the Lord Chamberlain revoke *their* licences? ...

Mr Milligan has in his files what may well be the strangest single document in the history of theatre censorship. In 1962 he collaborated with John Antrobus on a clearly deranged but maniacally funny comedy called *The Bed-Sitting Room*. In January 1963, the joint authors received a communication from the Lord Chamberlain, from which I quote:

> This Licence is issued on the understanding that the following alterations are made to the script:
>
> Act I
> Page 1:   Omit the name of the Prime Minister: no representation of his voice is allowed.
> Page 16:   Omit ' ... clockwork Virgin Mary made in Hong Kong, whistles the Twist.' Omit references to the Royal Family, the Queen's Christmas Message, and the Duke's shooting. ...
> Page 21:   The detergent song. Omit 'You get all the dirt off the tail of your shirt.' Substitute 'You get all the dirt off the front of your shirt.'

Act II

Page 8: The mock priest must not wear a crucifix on his snorkel. It must be immediately made clear that the book the priest handles is not the Bible.

Page 10: Omit from 'We've just consummated our marriage' to and inclusive of 'a steaming hot summer's night.'

Page 13: Omit from 'In return they are willing...' to and inclusive of 'the Duke of Edinburgh is a wow with Greek dishes.' Substitute 'Hark ye! Hark ye! The Day of Judgment is at hand.'

Act III

Pages 12–13: Omit the song 'Plastic Mac Man' and substitute 'Oh you dirty young devil, how dare you presume to wet the bed when the po's in the room. I'll wallop your bum with a dirty great broom when I get up in the morning.'

Page 14: Omit 'the perversions of the rubber'. Substitute 'the kreurpels and blinges of the rubber'. Omit the chamber pot under bed.

No argument I have yet heard in favour of dramatic censorship is strong enough to withstand the armour-plated case against it, which I can sum up in three quotations:

To purchase freedom of thought with human blood and then delegate its exercise to a censor at £400 a year is a proceeding which must make the gods laugh. (Frank Fowell and Frank Palmer, authors of *Censorship in England*, 1912)

What, then, is to be done with the Censorship? Nothing can be simpler. Abolish it, root and branch, throwing the whole legal responsibility for plays on the author and manager, precisely as the legal responsibility for a book is thrown on the author, the printer and the publisher. The managers will not like this; their present slavery is safer and easier; but it will be good for them, and good for the Drama. (Bernard Shaw, 1909).

The Stage, my Lords and the Press are two of our Out-sentries; if we remove them—if we hoodwink them—if we throw them in Fetters—the Enemy may surprise us. Therefore I must look upon the Bill now before us as a Step, and a most necessary Step too, for introducing arbitrary Power into this Kingdom. It is a Step so necessary, that if ever any future ambitious King, or guilty Minister, should form to himself so wicked a Design, he will have reason to thank us for having done so much of the work to his Hand; but such Thanks I am convinced every one of your Lordships would blush to receive—and scorn to deserve. (Lord Chesterfield to the House of Lords, 1737)

Chesterfield was right when he carried the case against the Lord Chamberlain beyond the boundaries of dramatic art into the broader domain of civil liberties and democratic rights. The fundamental objection to censorship is not that it is exercised against artists, but that it is exercised at all.

Sixty-odd years ago, Shaw was alarmed to hear a rumour that the United States was proposing to censor the theatre. 'O my friends across the sea,' he wrote with a passion I echo today, 'remember how the censorship works in England, and DON'T.'

(1965)

Theatre in Paris

'Ten years ago I read the announcements of Paris theatres with vivid curiosity; now I would hardly cross the street to witness the bepuffed sensation of the hour.'

Frank Harris wrote that in 1924, and there are many who would echo him today. For the first time in my recollection, Paris is facing a crisis of confidence in the drama as a dominant art form. The panic is on, and no one who cares about the health of Western theatre can safely ignore it. Paris, New York, and London are the only great theatrical centres where the box office is still the paramount criterion—where the vast majority of plays must either make money or die. Last season, a hundred and thirty commercial productions reached the Paris stage, of which thirteen ran long enough to show a profit. If Paris can stumble so direly, it seems fair to assume that a trip wire at least as perilous lies in wait for Broadway and the West End. Neither London nor New York, after all, is a theatre town on the same gargantuan scale as Paris, where the thirst for live drama is traditionally so insatiable that fifty playhouses exist to slake it. Four of these are owned and subsidised by the government—the Comédie Française, the Théâtre de France, the Théâtre National Populaire, and the Théâtre de l'Est Parisien. The rest are in private hands, and the hands are trembling.

The slump is artistic as well as commercial. Ten years ago we all stared agog at the French avant-garde and the breakthrough it was making. Samuel Beckett, Eugène Ionesco, and Jean Genet were the commanding trio. Their work crossed frontiers and oceans, and the phrase coined to define it—the Theatre of the Absurd—passed into the vocabulary of international criticism. Nowadays the key names are the same, though their owners are well advanced into middle age. The première of *Les Paravents*, Genet's play about Algeria, caused a resonant scandal last spring at the Théâtre de France, but the text was completed seven years ago, when the political situation was so explosive that nobody dared to put the play on. Since 1959 Genet has written nothing for the theatre. Ionesco's double bill of *La Cantatrice Chauve* and *La Leçon* is in its tenth year at the tiny Théâtre de la Huchette, and—sure proof of cultural canonisation—his latest full-length play is in the repertory of the Comédie-Française. As for Beckett, there's usually a revival of *En Attendant Godot* (first staged in 1952) somewhere on the Left Bank, and one hears talk of a new piece, still awaiting performance. According to rumour, it lasts precisely sixty seconds and, apart from a few recorded moans of inarticulate grief, dispenses altogether with actors. If accurate, this bleak synopsis may be a portent. From the actorless play it is only a short step to the spectatorless theatre.

At all events, the ferment of the nineteen-fifties has subsided, and no new playwrights have come along to challenge the Big Three. These days, to be young, French, and excited by the narrative arts almost inevitably means to be engrossed in movies. In May 1966 a long interview between Jean-Luc Godard and the veteran director Robert Bresson appeared in *Cahiers du Cinéma*. It included this significant exchange:

> BRESSON: It seems to me that the arts—the *fine* arts, if you will —are on the decline and approaching their end. They are in the course of dying.
>
> GODARD: I think so, too.
>
> BRESSON: Already very little remains of them. Soon they will not exist. But, strangely enough, if they are killed by cinema, radio and television, the very arts that kill them will end up by making art anew.

If a vote were to be taken, the intelligent sector of French youth would probably endorse the Bresson–Godard line. The problem is not so much that young people do not go to the theatre (they never did, except in school parties or on family outings) as that they do go, devoutly and repeatedly, to the cinema, which they regard as the art that speaks most directly to their generation. They dislike the expense and inconvenience of playgoing. This was made brutally clear in a recent survey of the leisure habits of Paris teenagers. It revealed that if the theatre hoped to attract them, it would have to carry out a lot of reforms. Among their demands were: (*a*) Cheaper seats. The top theatre price is twenty francs or more than twice the cinema maximum. (*b*) The abolition of tips for cloakroom attendants and usherettes. (*c*) Free programmes. The normal charge is two francs. (*d*) A booking system allowing for last-minute decisions, instead of insisting on reservations weeks in advance. (*e*) Curtains rising not later than 8 p.m. In Paris, as in New York, you eat before the show, which seldom starts earlier than 8.45 p.m. In London and Berlin, the curtain goes up around 7.30 p.m., and you eat afterwards. On this issue my sympathies are all with the teenagers. Theatre is best absorbed on an empty belly; food and drink are great sleep inducers, and numb the critical faculties. A generalisation suggests itself: where curtains rise late, drama tends to languish.

Youthful disaffection is merely a symptom of the French theatre's sickness. The causes lie elsewhere. One of them—often invoked by the commercial producers—is the crippling tax on receipts, which was first imposed in the Middle Ages and is still enforced today. Eight and a half per cent of all box-office takings goes straight to the government, and the percentage increases with the length of the run. A typical victim of this invidious levy was *La Grosse Valise*, a musical extravaganza devised by Robert Dhéry, the director and star of *La Plume de Ma Tante*. When it closed last winter after playing to capacity for a year and a half, it had made a profit of less than eighty-five hundred dollars. Some of the local critics blame censorship for the present state of theatrical stagnation. France has no Lord Chamberlain to whom scripts must be submitted before they can be produced, but the police are empowered to forbid any stage performance that in their opinion is likely to cause a breach of the peace. Although this power is rarely used, the threat is always there, and it is formidable enough to deter anyone from putting on a play that might be construed as a seditious attack on De Gaulle. Whether it deters people from writing such plays is another matter. The characteristic mood of French drama since the war has been one of introspection and solipsistic fantasy, and it seems improbable that playwrights in any great numbers are burning to knock the régime.

The writers, in their turn, blame the critics, whom many of them dismiss as blinkered, bourgeois, and essentially frivolous. My own experience confirms the blinkered part. French critics seldom travel, and when they do, their minds remain home-centred. In 1962, a Paris colleague interviewed me in London. Apart from a formal statement of polite (but unsurprised) regret that modern English plays were mostly flops in Paris, he did not mention the English theatre. He talked almost exclusively of Anouilh, Beckett, Ionesco, and Genet, framing his queries so neatly that he had only to remove the question marks to turn them into answers. For example:

Q. You would agree, would you not, that Anouilh could be described as a theatrical Poujadist?

A. Well, it's an interesting phrase, but I'm not sure that—

Q. Thank you. (*Writes furiously for thirty seconds.*) Now, do you feel, as I do, that there is a tendency on the part of French critics to read too many philosophical implications into plays where the philosophical content, expressed or implied, is either minimal or irrelevant?

A. I see what you mean, but oughtn't we to—

Q. (*Holds up forefinger.*) One moment, please. (*Writes at length, then rises with radiant smile and hand outthrust.*) Thank you again. So generous of you to spare me so much of your time.

The simplest way to dramatise the crisis is to look at the achievements of the 1965–66 season in Paris. I'll group under five headings my notes on the productions I saw.

1. Grade B commercial theatre. This is as prevalent and as glib as ever: farces with titles like *Ta Femme Nous Trompe* and *Quand Épousez-Vous Ma Femme?* still dominate the hoardings. The Concert Mayol, an intimate music hall in Montmartre, offers *Paris Nu . . . York!*, the fiftieth in an unbroken series of nude revues that began in 1934. The atmosphere is that of faded burlesque, lacking the raucous enthusiasm of the real thing. Parasols are twirled to simulate train wheels; an epicene tenor gives us 'Singing in the Rain' in English ('I've a smeel on the face . . .'); and in one of the sketches a doctor is threatened with an enema by a mutinous patient. The smeel freezes on the face.

Enticed by its title, I sample *Les Escargots Meurent Debout* ('Snails Die on Their Feet'), a long-running comedy smash at the Théâtre Fontaine. It turns out to be a one-gag show, parodying publicity techniques through the ages: Napoleon, for instance, is asked to lend his name to a newly invented brandy. The author and star is a plump extrovert named Francis Blanche, whose talent is the only attribute he possesses that could hardly be slimmer. In accordance with Paris custom, the curtain rises impudently late—in this case, seventeen minutes after the advertised time.

2. Grade A commercial theatre. A couple of preliminary observations may be in order. First, one must not expect—either in this category of French theatre or in any other—to find plays about poor people. Paris audiences are predominantly middle-class, and they prefer drama to concern itself with people who, if not actually rich, at least have sound bankers' references. Second, there is virtually no chance of seeing a realistic play about contemporary French problems. The kind of theatre that subjects everyday life to critical analysis goes against the national grain, partly because the French are too patriotic to relish self-criticism on the public stage but mostly because they do not regard everyday life, realistically handled, as a worthy theme for serious drama. The tradition of humanism, which maintains that the proper study of mankind is not just exceptional or representative men but men of all kinds, considered as individuals, has never exerted much influence on French playwrights. The clash of ideas and principles is what mainly excites them. Ordinary human behaviour, in all its irrational variety, strikes them as petty and peripheral: reality is too untidy to suit their notion of art. It should not amaze us that France has produced no Chekhov, no Gorki, no Tennessee Williams, no John Osborne, no Harold Pinter.

Framed by the gilded caryatids of the Palais Royal, Feydeau's *La Dame de Chez Maxim* is a solid popular hit, with Zizi Jeanmaire in the role of a jolly cocotte who is mistaken for someone's respectable wife. She attends a country ball, where everyone accepts her as a Parisian hostess, and her verbal blunders (like Eliza Doolittle's) are thought to be glittering examples of the new small talk. I agree with Marcel Achard that Feydeau, who died in 1921, was the greatest master of French comedy after Molière, but here he is well below his quicksilver best. Jacques Charon's direction is camp in the strict and pristine theatrical sense; that is, effetely flamboyant. Caustic cheers greet the rise of the curtain, twenty-one minutes overdue.

In times of recession, the small-cast play comes into its own. Producers suddenly recognise its artistic virtues, and reinterpret the famous dictum of Mies van der Rohe, 'More is less', so that it takes on a new significance: 'More actors is less art.' This, of course, is their quaintly euphemistic way of saying that more expenditure means less chance of breaking even. *L'Idée Fixe*, at the Michodière, is a perfect example of low-risk theatre with aesthetic pretensions. Written in 1931 by Paul Valéry, and never intended for stage performance, it's a prose duologue between two lonely holiday-makers—a psychiatrist and an artist—who meet on a rockbound Mediterranean shore and discuss their anxieties. It may be true, as the artist declares, that 'l'homme est fait pour causer', but the theatre was not created solely for conversation, and after two hours of abstract chat one longs for something non-cerebral to happen. The ideas are persuasively fleshed out by Pierre Fresnay and Julien Bertheau, All the same, a non-play derived from a book is not calculated to restore anyone's faith in the health of the French drama.

Summing up the season in *Le Monde*, a critic gloomily noted that it was heavily dependent on imports, revivals, and literary adaptations. The commercial theatre, he concluded, had its back to the wall, and he wondered why nothing new had emerged to save it. A possible answer can be found in a lecture that Jean-Paul Sartre delivered at the Sorbonne in 1960. Its subject was the stultifying effect of bourgeois audiences on the drama. The bourgeois (Sartre argued) wants to see people like him-self onstage, in order to identify his troubles with theirs, but he cannot stomach the kind of play in which he is surveyed with scientific ob-jectivity. He likes dramatists whose concept of human nature conforms to his own. To understand what that concept is, you must study his use of the word 'human': it is 'human' to cheat, to lie, to compromise, to envy. That is the condition of our species, and the bourgeois view is that we are stuck with it. But the fulcrum of all good drama (Sartre continues) is pur-poseful human action, and this often implies a desire for change—a desire for a differently ordered environment, in which life can be differently lived. It is here that the bourgeois calls a halt, since his picture of the world precludes the possibility of radical change. Having revolutionised the structure of society in the nineteenth century, he has no wish to see it altered again. To hang on to what he already possesses, he is ready, if pressed, to adapt himself, but further than that he will not go. There is no reason to be surprised by his willingness to tolerate plays like *En Attendant Godot*; they support his conviction that the human predica-ment is immutable. It is permissible for a playwright to condemn the bourgeois as a man but not as a bourgeois. Pessimism is welcome as long as it is total—as long as it blights every prospect and damns every hope. Qualified pessimism, which concedes that things look grim but offers recommendations for improvement, is held not to be art. *'Ça, ce n'est plus le théâtre, n'est-ce pas, c'est de la subversion.'* In Sartre's opinion, drama will not be fully reborn until the bourgeois audience is a dwindling minority.

3. Government-subsidised theatre. This remains the backbone of dramatic activity in Paris. Like the rest of the skeleton however, it lacks the energising marrow that only new writers can supply. In a renovated cinema on the outskirts of the city, near the Père-Lachaise Cemetery, the Théâtre de l'Est Parisien has lately taken root. Although films,

ballets, operas, symphony concerts and jazz recitals are presented in the same auditorium, the resident acting troupe managed to offer seven productions in the 1965–66 season. The seats cost little, the programmes are free, and tipping is forbidden. Moreover, the show begins at 7 p.m. ('Allez au théâtre', says one of the company's handouts, 'et couchez-vous tôt.') The TEP also publishes an outspoken monthly magazine: in a recent editorial it described the offended patriots who pelted the stage of the Théâtre de France with rotten fruit during performances of Genet's *Les Paravents* as intellectual racists with the seeds of Nazism in their hearts.

It is no wonder that the TEP has recruited an audience containing a high proportion of youthful enthusiasts. But what do they see? When I was there, a tame production of a nineteenth-century farce—*Le Voyage de Monsieur Perrichon*, by Eugène Labiche. The hero is a pompous middle-class father whose daughter has two rival suitors. During a holiday in Switzerland, one of them arranges to save Perrichon's life; the other, a craftier type, contrives a situation in which his own life is saved by Perrichon. Papa's favour immediately swings towards the latter. The moral, I gathered from a programme note, is that a bourgeois will always prefer a debtor to a creditor, even if the debt is only one of gratitude. I would never have guessed as much from what I witnessed onstage, which was visually pretty but socially and politically quite innocuous. Labiche revivals are fairly common in Paris, and nothing more sadly reveals the drabness of French theatre than its efforts to put over this lightweight entertainer as a ferocious scourge of the bourgeoisie.

The Théâtre National Populaire, now directed by Georges Wilson, still packs the Palais de Chaillot, which seats 2,600 people, and its policy of making firstrate plays cheaply accessible to mass audiences has not changed since Jean Vilar founded the company, in 1951. Many actors have been discovered and brought to maturity under its auspices, but in fifteen years it has failed to unearth a French playwright of international stature.

At the Théâtre de France, Jean-Louis Barrault finds himself in the same blind alley where new authors are concerned. 'A few years ago,' he told me, 'I saw two plays by an actor named Roland Dubillard—*Naïves Hirondelles* and *La Maison d'Os*. They were funny and weird, and I thought he was a great hope. But he seems incapable of writing any more. I've been running the Théâtre de France since 1959, and this year, for the first time, I haven't read a single new script that was worth considering. All I get are plays by authors who seem to despise the public. It's important to provoke the people you *want* to provoke, but it's equally important to please the people you want to please. Young playwrights should work in the theatre and learn what it means to face an audience. Remember that Molière and John Osborne both started as actors. Destruction for its own sake is all very well, but I think the theatre is due for a return to tenderness.'

Barrault's winter plans include stage adaptations of two famous novels—Raymond Queneau's *Zazie dans le Metro* and Flaubert's *La Tentation de Saint Antoine*. Roger Blin's notorious production of *Les Paravents* will continue to hold its place in the company's repertory. The play is a sprawling mosaic of Algerian life under French colonial rule. Three characters run through it—a young man named Saïd, his mother, and his repellently ugly wife. Genet's text embraces squalor almost as if it were a benediction. Metaphors of filth and putrescence multiply, and violence takes on an aura of sensual exaltation. On the one hand, the occupying army is exhorted to think of itself as 'the mightly phallus of France'. On the other, Saïd's wife implores her husband to 'choose evil and always evil', for 'I want you to know only hatred and never love'. Genet sees the two sides as equal partners in a game of mutual debasement. Ever since the play opened, performances have been interrupted by catcalls, walkouts, vegetable missiles, and exploding firecrackers, although the Algerian war ended long ago. Barrault contributes to the programme a dazzling facing-both-ways essay in which he declares that drama differs from the other arts because it takes place in public. This means that in the theatre 'there is perhaps something more sacred than liberty; namely, respect for human beings'. At the same time, he is careful to point out that a writer must be true to his vision, however outrageous it may be, and that *Les Paravents* is a case of 'legitimate provocation'. My own view of the play is that it resembles a swamp of self-indulgent images from which pinnacles of tough theatricality occasionally protrude—a Sargasso Sea dotted with the wreckage of a potential masterpiece.

As tradition dictates, the Comédie Française houses all that is worth reclaiming from the glorious past of the French theatre. A foreigner cannot help reflecting how little of that past is glorious outside France. Molière, Feydeau, and Giraudoux survive in translation, but it is seldom indeed that Corneille, Racine, Marivaux, Beaumarchais, Musset, Hugo, Rostand, and Claudel justify abroad the holy repute they enjoy at home. As exports, they are generally failures, and I suspect that this is due to central role played in French theatre by pure sound—by strophe and antistrophe, by vocal sonorities demanding specific vocal responses. Strip the lines of their music and you are likely to be stunned by their banality.

Take *Le Prince Travesti*, a minor work by Marivaux, which was neglected for more than two centuries and has now been revived to unanimous critical acclaim. It is a comedy of disguises and romantic equivocations, in which passions are politely concealed beneath veils of verbal nicety. The baroque formality of the décor is echoed in Jacques Charon's direction, and you can bet that the characters in matching costumes are going to end up together. Micheline Boudet gives a tremulously beautiful display of unexpressed love. Otherwise, nothing stays in the mind except a vague aural memory of French actors competitively purring in self-congratulation.

With Ionesco's *La Soif et la Faim*, the house of Molière has opened its doors to the *avant-garde*, and many of its older subscribers have been enraged by the intrusion. I cannot imagine why. Like so much of what passes for experimental drama in the era of de Gaulle, the play is inward-looking, self-pitying, and in no sense subversive. Jean, the hero, lives with his wife in a cellar apartment that is sinking into the mud. (He tells us in the same breath that streets, cities, and entire civilisations are also being sucked under. When Ionesco gets his hands on a symbol, you can't accuse him of keeping it under wraps.) To escape from domesticity, Jean embarks on a journey in search of his true self. He wants to breathe pure air and be reborn. No sooner has he bolted than the back wall of the basement rises to reveal a sun-drenched tropical garden. 'If only he had had a little patience!' his wife sighs. Happiness, it seems, is right there in his own back yard. The message at this point, never subsequently contradicted, is identical with that of *Peer Gynt*. In other words, travel is good but home is better. Arriving on a lofty, arid plateau (and here I must pay tribute to Jacques Noel's scenery—firstrate sets are rare in Paris), Jean spends a whole act waiting for a nebulous girl who fails to turn up. From here he staggers on to a sinister monastery, where a disquieting welcome awaits him. Two captive clowns are made to perform for his amusement; faulty education has deformed their minds, and they must be shown their errors. One is called Brechtoll (or Brecht, if I may rip off his mask), and the other goes by the name of Tripp— a cryptic alias for Samuel Beckett. Both are relentlessly quizzed and brainwashed in order to free them from the deterministic ideas by which they are obsessed. In addition, both are starving. If Brechtoll will accept God, he will be fed, but Tripp will be fed if he will deny God. Thus, they are taught that there is no such thing as absolute truth, and no necessary connection between cause and effect. ('If no one is watching us and obliging me to be good to you, who is to prevent me from letting you die of hunger?' the head monk asks Brechtoll. A powerful question, to which

Ionesco offers no answer.) Jean himself, a baffled onlooker at this double interrogation, is finally conscripted to act as a waiter, forever compelled to serve the monks with plate after plate of the same stew. This may conceivably be a symbol of Ionesco's own plight—that of a writer perpetually condemned to feed his critics the same diet. In any case, it makes a suitably arbitrary end to a totally arbitrary play. Every now and then, a sentence, or even a passage, rises sharp and challenging out of the surrounding muddle, but the work as a whole is a prolonged ecstasy of egocentric doodling. In the taxing role of Jean, Robert Hirsch is tireless but rather too consciously tragic.

4. Low-budget experimental theatre. Here the cupboard is distressingly bare. Beckett is a legend in his own lifetime; one sadly doubts whether his successors will be more than anecdotes in theirs. A strong feeling has spread through the avant-garde that Paris is no longer a place in which adventurous young playwrights can comfortably fledge their wings. I even heard an apprentice dramatist complaining about—of all things—the lack of theatre censorship. 'The government censors films and television, but it doesn't worry about the theatre,' he said. 'And that's a terrible omen. It means that plays aren't considered important enough to be worth banning.' One result of this discontent is a flight to the provinces. A typical migrant is Antoine Bourseiller, who has been hailed by many good judges as the most exciting young director in Paris. At present, he runs the little Théâtre de Poche, in Montparnasse, but after Christmas he is moving to Aix-en-Provence, where he will take control of a theatre with an annual subsidy of more than two hundred thousand dollars. Away from the pressures of the capital, he will have the time and the freedom he needs to develop a company with a style of its own. (Describing the sort of drama he favours, Bourseiller uses words like 'baroque' and 'ceremonial', from which it's easy to deduce that his taste inclines towards Genet rather than towards Brecht.) I asked him to diagnose the current malaise of French theatre. 'It's nothing to do with the government,' he said. 'André Malraux may not be the ideal Minister of Culture, but—for all his quirks—he's better than any alternative I can think of. If he died, we'd probably get a bureaucrat who could equally well have organised the railroads. And I don't believe there's a dearth of writers. The real trouble is that we lack directors—not just *metteurs en scène* but people like Jean Vilar and Roger Planchon, who can take a theatre and give it an artistic identity. I don't put Barrault in that category. He's Malraux's court jester.'

Roger Planchon, who is still in his thirties, chose provincial independence fifteen years ago. A Brechtian and a leftist, he runs the Théâtre de la Cité in Villeurbanne, near Lyon, and has built up a loyal and enormous working-class audience there. Planchon treats the classics not as sacred works of art but as historical documents in need of reinterpretation from a Marxist viewpoint. For him, an old play is a piece of historical evidence submitted by an inevitably biased witness; the dramatist. His habit is to eke out the text with his own radical analysis of the age in which the author lived. Thus, when he is staging Marivaux he constantly draws our attention away from the wellborn folk in the salon to the dingy unpleasantness of life below stairs. Although his actors are sometimes less than top class, he regards this as a small price to pay for artistic liberty. When Paris beckons, as it often does, he responds with a catlike smile and a decisive shake of the head.

A small but dedicated faction insists that the future of French drama lies in 'happenings'. These are still quite common in Paris, where I have even heard them described—by a charter member of the lobby—as 'the *commedia dell' arte* of the H-bomb epoch'. Will they save the French theatre? Not for purists like me, who make a crucial distinction between life, where things happen by accident, and art, where they happen by design. If all the world's a stage, we might as well burn down the theatres. As a writer in *Le Monde* put it: 'At the game of improvisation, theatre is beaten in advance by life itself.'

5. Strip tease. Nothing in Paris is more theatrically inventive than the nightly show at the Crazy Horse Saloon, on the Avenue George V. The comic acts tend to be noisy and atrociously witless. But the girls—the incredibly healthy girls—are superb, beautiful in themselves, and rendered more so by the skill with which they are presented. To the distant tinkling of a vibraphone, Veronica Baum perches on the edge of a marble bath and reverently soaps herself while a Venetian blind casts stripes of shade across her skin. Tracy Tiffany, clad only in Op Art patterns projected onto her swivelling body, dances blithely through the story of her life, accompanying herself with snatches of tape-recorded biography. ('I'm an Aries,' she keeps helplessly wailing, as if that explained anything.) It was at the Crazy Horse that Dodo d'Hambourg, the most accomplished German stripper of modern times, first appeared as 'La Veuve'. In this celebrated routine, she played an all too consolable widow who solemnly sheds her weeds, to a background of organ music, during her husband's funeral. Shortly after Dodo had made her reputation with this macabre act, her husband in real life, who was living in Germany, committed suicide. The Crazy Horse was founded fifteen years ago by Alain Bernardin, a former antique dealer and restaurateur. It was a solo venture from the beginning; Bernardin still recruits the girls, directs the

numbers, and pays the bills. An urbane man on the verge of fifty, he has a keen business sense and no star-making illusions. 'Here the show itself is the star,' he says. 'Very few of the girls get anywhere in show business when they leave the Crazy Horse. Mostly, they marry. Stripping seems to encourage ideas of domesticity. It creates bourgeois aspirations.' He enjoys startling his audience with elegant, offbeat sexual fantasies, but he knows that there are limits to what he can attempt: 'I have to stay respectable, because I dare not offend the wives of Americans on expense accounts.'

At the Dolce Vita, a night club in Montparnasse, the tone is distinctly rougher. 'Keep calm,' says the lady m.c. 'Please try not to panic. Here—direct from Harlem—is Dailly Holliday!' Music pounds, and there bursts onto the floor a bulky Negro girl, breathing heavily. She wears a transparent thigh-length shift, through which a flimsy G string is visible, and she has a rose in her mouth. Her first gesture is to kick offstage a chair left behind by the preceding act. Then, hissing with malevolence, she settles down to her chosen task, which is to affront the audience. In the past, Negro performers have often sought to outdo their white colleagues in charm and sophistication. Dailly Holliday, by contrast, goes out of her way to show how different she is from any white stripper who ever peeled. Picking a customer at a ringside table, she thrusts her bottom directly into his face, and keeps it there, rotating her hips in time with the music. She will not let him escape. It is as if she were daring him to reject her, to react with violence to her provocation. Of course, he does nothing of the sort but merely blushes and wriggles, engulfed in a vast panorama of rump. Meanwhile, she grins at him derisively over her shoulder. When his humiliation is complete, she turns her attention elsewhere, unveiling one of her breasts and offering it for intimate inspection of a woman on the other side of the floor. By the time she withdraws it, her new victim is suffocating with embarrassment. After a few valedictory gyrations of those monumental hips, she rushes off to her dressing room, leaving the audience in a state of abashed shock.

Talking with Mlle Holliday after the show, I discovered that she does not come from Harlem; she was born twenty-seven years ago in the French Caribbean dependency of Guadeloupe. Temperamentally, she is not a militant girl. Indeed, she claimed that her principal trait was timidity. 'Her act used to be quite mild, but now it is very hard,' said the manager of the club. 'Americans sometimes resent her.' Whether she knows it or not, Mlle Holliday is the first black-supremacist stripper, and hers is one of the few performances to be seen in Paris that have any relevance to the world outside the theatre.

In 1876 Henry James began a report on the Paris stage with a sentence that still retains a melancholy aptness:

> If it is true that the country is going to the bad, and that the celebrated 'era of revolution' is again to open, people are beguiling the interval in such fashion as they may.

(1966)

II: CINEMA

Bande à Part; La Peau Douce

I have never met Jean-Luc Godard, but the image I get from his films is that of a young man in a trench-coat with his hands in his pockets; a cigarette droops from one corner of his mouth while he talks in snatches, plentifully interrupted with shrugs, out of the other. He speaks softly and swiftly, in an undertone made eloquent by deadpan wit, superbly timed pauses, audacious changes of tempo and persistent narrative zest: we recognise the born spell-binder who does not need to raise his voice.

Usually he is telling a terse fairy-tale about young people uncommitted to anything but their instincts, non-signatories of the social contract, civilisation's permanent fringe-dwellers. Often the fable ends in violence; but as he sketches in his *tableaux vivants* or *mourants*, the narrator himself remains detached and quizzical, even lighthearted.

It is this forswearing of passion, this refusal to involve himself, this determination to leave the emotions to us, that outrages Godard's opponents: they bristle at the contrasts on which he thrives—blithe tone, bitter content; debonair journey, tragic destination; utterly personal choice of incidents to show us, utterly impersonal manner of showing them. Classical in his conciseness, contemporary in his obsessions, Godard is an aphorist working on celluloid. Nothing in *Bande à Part* is more typically provocative than the English teacher who declares in an early sequence that 'Classique=Moderne'. With artists like this, one had better admit temperamental affinities: of all the Western directors whose movies I see through the white lattice-work of subtitles, none speaks to me more intimately than Godard.

Based on an American novel, *Bande à Part* contains references to Billy the Kid and Loopy the Loop: one of Godard's several Brechtian characteristics is his absorption in transatlantic pop culture. On the grey outskirts of Paris two cool but vulnerably dumb young layabouts are plotting a burglary. At a local language school they woo the niece of their intended victim; while the teacher reads *Romeo and Juliet*, three pairs of eyes make speechless, super-Shakespearean contact. The girl (Anna Karina) is radically ingenuous: when asked what marriage means to a woman, she instantly replies: '*C'est donner ses seins et ses jambes.*'

The robbery is planned with disastrous improvidence. Meeting in a bar, the conspirators can think of nothing to say: one of them suggests a minute's silence, whereat Godard cuts off the sound-track for 60 seconds. Later, with an afternoon to kill before committing the crime, they sprint through the Louvre in less than 9 min. 45 sec., thus smashing the American tourist record. In Godard's world, as *Cahiers du Cinéma* recently said: 'Certains instants de grâce éclairaient l'obscurité quotidienne.'

The felony itself is a fiasco. One of the boys (Claude Brasseur) is shot, dying a convulsive Cagney death, and the surviving couple drive away without the booty. The girl meditatively recites a list of personal pronouns and possessive adjectives: we note that she omits the crucial ones, *nous* and *notre*. For his part, the boy (Sami Frey) wonders why people don't amalgamate, why they are always separate, going different ways. This is Godard proclaiming his theme, which is the indifference (not the inhumanity) of man to man.

His three plotters use one another, but never really know one another. Although fear and cupidity bind them together for a temporary purpose, they are essentially strangers. In the final shot, M. Frey embarks on a cruise with Mlle Karina and puts his arm around her; but a steel handrail eloquently divides them. Music intrudes sparingly, and mainly to parody the kind of melodramatic movie that needs such adventitious aids; the relevant credit title reads: 'For the last time (?) on the screen: music by Michel Legrand.' The director's own credit is a simple, pointblank affirmation: 'Cinéma: Jean-Luc Godard.' The end justifies the arrogance.

La Peau Douce is François Truffaut's bid for the major circuits, and its glossy banality will bring comfort to those beleaguered malcontents who thought *Jules et Jim* an inflated romantic bore. A stodgy and charmless literary man (Jean Desailly) has an affair with a sexy air hostess whom he takes so much for granted that she deserts him—too late, however, to prevent his wife from seizing a rifle and mowing him down in a restaurant. Laced with irony, this anecdote might have been bearable; instead, Truffaut gives it the full sentimental treacle (nobody bats an eyelid without waking up the entire studio orchestra) and pads it to a length of two hours with every cliché in the book, including repeated expositions in close-up of how to start and stop a car and how to make a telephone call. *La Peau Douce* is the sort of picture that Hollywood used to turn out twenty-five years ago. I can see the hoardings now: *They Met in the Clouds*, co-starring George Brent and Ann Sheridan.

Amélie; Les Carabiniers

Give a camera a good, steady look at almost any exterior in less-than-perfect weather with nobody about, put something poignant (preferably a solo wind instrument) on the sound track, and the odds are that what you have in the can is a lyrical comment on the bleakness and aridity of human existence. A stretch of damp beach, a block of flats at dawn, a garden in drizzle, a deserted square with yesterday's papers blowing about—it doesn't matter what the setting is so long as it is more or less depopulated. One or two people may be present (two is the maximum, and one of them had better be a girl who looks plangent in close-up), in which case the comment stands a fair chance of becoming poetic.

The rules for lyrical interiors are slightly different in that the weather is less important and groups of family size are permitted, provided they keep their voices down and their lips substantially buttoned. There is nothing like a camera for capturing the essential unfeelingness of objects, so the thing to do is to emphasise frowning furniture, impassive ash-trays and unfriendly-looking lamp-brackets. One solid, object-featuring pan round a silent dinner-table, and you may even be able to dispense with the wind instrument and make do with a ticking clock. What you will then have is a lyrical comment on the monotony of bourgeois life.

Amélie starts out lyrical and stays that way for the better part of two hours. Its setting is Mont St Michel, that rainily picturesque island that dangles like a pendant from the coast of Normandy: more wet sand and solitude you couldn't wish for. Here in the 1880s live a cold-hearted hosier, his sensitive daughter (who would rather be in Paris), his down-trodden son (who yearns to go to sea) and a glowingly mouselike cousin named Amélie (who longs to marry the son): bourgeois lyricism is there in abundance, with two plangent female faces to back it up. As a clincher, there is music by Bach.

The action, such as it tenuously is, recalls theatrical models—Jean-Jacques Bernard on a bad day, or N. C. Hunter on a good one. Lodgers invade the household: a circus proprietor and his sexy daughter, the former bursting with conjuring tricks and the latter perpetually rippling with laughter. The son falls in love with her ripples; and when the strangers depart, it spells heartbreak for the romantic ambitions of Amélie, who wastes away like the Victorian ingenue she is. In other words, this is the old one about the madcap intruders from the outside world who descend on the provinces and leave tears behind them. Excellent faces—and acceptable acting—by Marie-José Nat as Amélie and Clotilde Joano as the hosier's Paris-loving daughter.

The director is Michel Drach, whose second film this is: I missed his first, which was called *On n'enterre pas le dimanche* and dealt with the colour problem. Using every trick in the *cahier* (as detailed above), *Amélie* deals with—but fails to unknot—the problem of colourlessness. More easily than any other medium, the movies can hide paucity of matter beneath plenitude of style.

Jean-Luc Godard's *Les Carabiniers* begins with a quotation from Juan Borges: 'As time passes I value simplicity more and more....' Coming from Godard, of all complex people, this sounds *faux-naïf*; but the film bears it out. If simplicity implies a stripping-down to essentials, and a chaste yet candid directness of statement, *Les Carabiniers* is probably the simplest study of war in the history of narrative cinema.

Other war films invite (i.e. implore or compel) us to identify ourselves with either the victors or the vanquished; occasionally, with both. But the appeal is always to the emotions—to what Conrad called 'the force of sympathy, which is a form of fear'. Godard will have none of this. He wants our eyes unmisted by tears, our mental stance detached and reflective, uncajoled by emotional blackmail. Hence the film's episodic construction, each fragment of action being followed by a few black frames and a Brechtian caption; hence, too, the grainy World-War-One quality of Raoul Coutard's photography, and its total avoidance of close-ups. The donning of uniforms in which to kill strangers is presented not as a tragic ordeal but as a form of casual labour which people take up because they expect to gain something from it. The result is a picture at once highly personal and broadly generalised: one man's vision of all men in all wars.

The tone of the script (on which Rossellini was one of Godard's collaborators) is deliberately nonchalant. Two military cops in a jeep come bumping across a waste-land to deliver a letter to Ulysses and Michelangelo, a pair of oafish derelicts who live in a shanty with their womenfolk, Cleopatra and Venus. (Why these names? To alienate the characters from the modern setting and to prevent us from regarding them as 'real people'.) The letter is from the King, and summons the men to war.

The M.P.s explain that in battle anything they want will be theirs for the seizing: casinos, cinemas, cigar factories, Hawaiian guitars, elephants, Maseratis, women. Can they break a child's arm? Yes. *Both* arms? Yes. The questions are uttered with childlike curiosity, the replies with dead-pan reassurance.

We now plunge into the military escapades—viewed always from a respectful distance—that make up the body of the film. The two con-scripts burst into an enemy household, where Michelangelo stands a young woman on a chair and stares transfixed at her legs; as they leave, Ulysses casually tosses a hand-grenade into the building. They march a group of hostages through a wood until they reach what Michelangelo considers *un endroit joli,* whereupon the prisoners are shot without a second's hesitation. In these killings there is no ill-feeling; there is merely an absence of feeling. When the heroes capture a girl guerrilla, her face is covered with a handkerchief to ease the task of the firing-squad; from beneath it she recites an anti-war poem by Mayakovsky, and one almost expects a sentimental change of heart. But no: suddenly and briskly, cutting her off, the shots ring out and she crumples. Later Ulysses approaches a car salesman to claim his promised Maserati: informed that money is needed, he goes out and quite impersonally stabs the first rich-looking pedestrian he meets.

The war continues, unlocalised and universal, ranging from Italy through Rostov to the Statue of Liberty. Not for a moment—and this is a point unforgettably made—do the slaughtered betray a flicker of resent-ment, or the slaughterers a twinge of compunction. Killing and being killed are experiences as normal as buying a newspaper. At length the two warriors come home with a trunkful of picture-postcards, all of which—they are solemnly assured—can be exchanged for the glamorous objects they depict as soon as the King wins the war. But the King loses; and in a brief dismissive burst of off-screen gunfire they are shot as war criminals. Thus the film ends, as laconically as it began. It eats into the mind like acid. If this is not a masterpiece, it will do until one comes along.

The Director Cult

On this, the fiftieth anniversary of *Tillie's Punctured Romance,* I should like to apply a tentative pin to a romance that has been ballooning steadily ever since the cinema began. I refer to the impassioned venera-tion in which directors are held by critics.

A trivial escapade like *Man's Favourite Sport?* is rated a master-piece by five out of ten reviewers in *Cahiers du Cinéma*, for no better reason than that its director, Howard Hawks, is one of the magazine's pets. Robert Bresson is acclaimed by *cinéastes* everywhere for *Le Procès de Jeanne d'Arc*, which to my unmesmerised eyes recalled nothing so much as Henry James's comment on a would-be Elizabethan production of *Hamlet*: 'It was like morning prayers in a workhouse.'

Quiz any bright filmgoer about the last half-dozen movies he saw, and he will tell you at once who directed and starred in them; but ask him who wrote them, photographed them and composed their background music, and he is very unlikely to remember. What jars me about the present situation is not that certain directors are over-praised, but that the director's contribution to cinema in general has been grossly over-estimated. Here is Scott Fitzgerald, a poor scenarist but a shrewd observer, writing to a friend in 1938:

> In the old days, when movies were a stringing together of the high points in the imagination of half a dozen drunken ex-news-papermen, it was true that the whole thing was the director. He co-ordinated and gave life to the material—he carried the story in his head. There is a great deal of carry-over from those days, but the situation of 'Three Comrades' [scripted by Fitzgerald], where Frank Borzage had little more to do than be a sort of glorified cameraman, is more typical of today. A Bob Sherwood picture, for instance . . . could be shot by an assistant director or a script girl, and where in the old days an author would have jumped at the chance of becoming a director, there are now many . . . who hate the eternal waiting and monotony of the modern job . . . I should say that in seven out of ten cases, your feeling that the director or producer was the great coordinator no longer applies.

Of course things have changed in a quarter of a century, and exceptional directors have won a fuller measure of autonomy. Yet it remains true that the final shape of most pictures is dictated more by the combined skills of the writer, the composer and the cameraman than by the director. Which is, I believe, as it should be. Except in those rare cases when the director is at once a master of actors, a gifted writer and a wizard in the cutting room, he should be content to receive (and critics to bestow) the title of coordinator rather than creator. Men like Welles, Fellini and Godard—and for those who revere them, Bergman and Antonioni—are genuine creators, whose achievements I salute as unique; but many who aspire to the accolade are frauds and mimics; and the mainstream of good world cinema is peopled still, as it always was, by films that have been collectively planned and collectively executed.

I do not decry the great individualists. I seek merely to dent the legend that cinematic art is dependent on directorial supremacy, and to deplore the religion that has grown up around that falsehood. To name but one of its side-effects: the cult of the great director has left us with a dearth of great performers. (In a movie by Welles, the central performer is Welles himself, even if he does not appear.) Bogart, Tracy, Grant, Cagney, Hepburn: these and their like are the glittering products of old-fashioned, collective filmcraft. In the one-man directorial band of the *cinéma des auteurs*, there is no room for such myth-making soloists— unless they are privately linked (like Anna Karina and Monica Vitti) to the conductors. 'Two stars keep not their motion in one sphere': in the modern cinema, the director's star is absurdly and dangerously dominant.

Sex and the Single Girl; Help!

Warner Brothers' *Sex and the Single Girl* is not an adaptation of Helen Gurley Brown's famous manual for spinsters, despite the fact that it deals with a girl named Helen Gurley Brown who has written a best-seller called *Sex and the Single Girl*. (If Signor Pirandello is in the lobby, will he kindly contact the inquiry desk?) What Miss Gurley Brown actually sold the Brothers amounts to eight words: her name, plus the title of her book. Everything else—including her character and the actions attributed to her—is fictitious. This is exploitation by consent, and may mark a breakthrough.

The false Miss Gurley Brown (perkily played by Natalie Wood) is a best-selling psychologist, consulted by a smut-hawking journalist (Tony Curtis) who wants to know whether she is as virginal as single girls are reputed to be. To gain her confidence, he pretends to be married, using as raw material the domestic in-fighting of his neighbours (Henry Fonda and Lauren Bacall).

A classic formula unfolds: basely motivated boy woos innocent girl, whose eyes are opened to his baseness at the very moment when he has regained his innocence and fallen in love with her. The script has flashes of happy invention. The sumptuous offices of the pseudo-filthy magazine for which Mr Curtis works are greedily equipped with slot-machines for every minor amenity, including the use of the mirror in the men's room; and there is a bright running gag whereby Mr Curtis, clad in a *peignoir*, is mistaken for Jack Lemmon, his transvestite partner in *Some Like It Hot.*

A number of barbed lines pierce the prevalent gloss; but not enough to lessen one's astonishment that part-authorship of the screen-play should be credited to Joseph Heller, who wrote the deathless *Catch 22.* The film's chief merit is as an object lesson, from which we may compile a list of the rules currently governing American sex comedy; viz:

1. During the time covered by the script, nobody may go to bed with anybody. This applies even to people who are married.

2. Male characters must never fall in love with non-virgins.

3. Female characters must never utter the word 'virgin' without stammering, or substituting, where possible, a less disgusting alternative (e.g. 'beginner').

4. Affairs must never be consummated. Even when the people concerned are obviously suited only to a brief liaison, they must be compelled to fall in love and marry.

5. The cast should include at least one prewar character actor to enthuse the nostalgics. (In *Sex and the Single Girl* he is Edward Everett Horton, gamely surviving from the era of Eugene Pallette, Eric Blore, Walter Connolly, James Gleason and irreplaceable hundreds more.)

6. Finally, two crucial problems must be solved. First: how to get the girl wet. In *Sunday in New York*, she is drenched by a cloud-burst; in *Sex and the Single Girl*, she falls off a pier. Nothing short of a soaking is a permissible excuse for a man and a woman to remove their clothes in the same apartment. Second: how to get the girl drunk. Only tipsy heroines allow recent acquaintances to kiss them, and most film acquaintances are recent. To account for her speedy yielding, it should be explained that she has a poor head for liquor. Record for the course: 'I shee what you mean,' uttered by Natalie Wood in *Sex and the Single Girl* after two acorn-sized swigs.

THIS this THIS this THIS is the kind of THING (from outer SPACE?) you can expect from *Help!*, the new (and BAM!! it's new or never) film directed by focus-pulling, prize-winning, gag-spawning, zoom-loving Richard ('The KNACK') Lester, shot (POWWW!) in Eastman-colour but influenced by Observercolour and suggesting whole libraries of colourmags sprung BOING! to instant obsolescent life, complete with COOL gaudy consumer-tailored featurettes (one Lester missed: 'Tread Softly: The Dream-World of Wall-To-Wall Carpeting') and genuine only-connecting ADS (another Lester missed: 'Why not fly to the Aleutians in your custom-built Hammond Organ?'), not to mention FOUR EXPENSIVE TWO-DIMENSIONAL OBJECTS—namely John

Lennon, the snickering heavyweight punster; surly, bejewelled Ringo Starr; George Harrison, the 12-string narcissist; and Paul McCartney, the boy next fibre-glass-electric-eye-operated door (under that wig he's really —GASP!—Anne Rutherford)—who are flung about (URGGHH!), battered (SPLAT!!) and flattened (KER-PLUNK!!!) in a comic-strip chase through tourist-enticing London, the whiter-than-white Austrian Alps and selected sunsoaked Bahamas, pursued by Oriental goodness-gracious villains (' "It's a Sellers' market," quips writer Charles Wood') and guaranteed mad scientists, all plotting to slice (EEK!) a magic ring from surly Ringo's bejewelled finger, while off-beat Lester movie garners harvest of heady hosannas ('LOFTY GROSSES LOOM FOR MOP-HEADS' LATEST—Flicker's Total Sexlessness Augers Wham Family Fare') from notoriously hard-to-please CRITICS (ECCHH!!) in American trade press. . . .

In other words, *Help!* is a brilliant, unboring but ferociously ephemeral movie. Richard Lester's direction is a high-speed compendium of many lessons learned from Blake Edwards, Frank Tashlin, Goon comedy, fashion photography and M.G.M. cartoons. The Beatles themselves are not natural actors, nor are they exuberant extroverts; their mode is dry and laconic, as befits the flat and sceptical Liverpool accent. Realising this, Lester leaves it to his cameraman (David Watkin) to create the exuberance, confining the Beatles to deadpan comments and never asking them to react to events with anything approaching emotion. He capitalises on their wary, guarded detachment. 'There's something been in this soup,' says John, having calmly removed from the plate a season ticket and a pair of spectacles.

The script (by Marc Behm and Charles Wood) is chopped into fragments; hundreds of half-heard gags zip by, of which we are given time to laugh at about two dozen. The best-sustained sequence is the one where Ringo is trapped by an escaped tiger that can be tamed only by a full choral rendering of Beethoven's Ninth. The musical items are superbly shot, and the title song is the most haunting Beatle composition to date.

To sum up *Help!* I must go to Coleridge, who said that whereas a scientist investigates a thing for the sheer pleasure of knowing, the non-scientist only wants to find out whether it will 'furnish him with food, or shelter, or weapons, or tools, or ornaments, or *play-withs*,' *Help!* is a shiny, forgettable toy; an ideal play-with.

Hamlet

Of the two silent-screen Hamlets, Forbes-Robertson was too old, and Asta Nielsen belonged to the wrong sex. The year 1948 brought us Laurence Olivier, bearing too many directorial fardels to give the performance we hoped for; and now, in the new Russian *Hamlet*, we have Innokenty Smoktunovsky, a smouldering blond brooder who leads the field, not because he is anyone's ideal prince (I have seen a dozen better in the theatre) but because he inhabits by far the most convincing Elsinore I have ever witnessed on stage or screen.

Shot in black-and-white by its adaptor-director, Grigori Kozintsev, the film begins with Hamlet dashing home on horseback from Wittenberg to a palace in mourning. The opening lines of Claudius's inaugural speech are declaimed by a herald to the assembled populace; the rest is delivered by the usurper himself to the Privy Council. The 'too, too solid flesh' soliloquy is spoken as interior monologue while Hamlet pushes his way through a mob of courtiers, some bowing and curtseying, others too busy to recognise him; odd phrases in French and German remind us that Elsinore is an international crossroads.

In the theatre—apart from the characters with names and a few extras to tote halberds, serve drinks and express shock when people of rank are insulted or slaughtered—the place is normally deserted. Kozintsev populates it, never letting us forget that a royal castle is like a vast hotel which somebody has to run; hence, in the background of almost every scene, we see servants and court officials going about their business, impervious to the agonies unfolding in the foreground.

Horses in the royal stables quiver and stampede as the ghost appears, striding the battlements in slow motion with a vast black cloak billowing behind him. (Here and throughout, the Shostakovich score is a model of tact and power.) We hear no talk of antic dispositions; this is a practical prince with a practical problem too tough to be solved by affected madness. For once, the incestuous couch actually looks slept-in; and when the players arrive, hens and geese strut in the courtyard behind their rodomontade. Stage convention absurdly decrees that the play takes place at night; by setting it mostly in grey Scandinavian daylight, Kozintsev gains far more in realism than he loses in adventitious mystery. 'O what a rogue', uttered over a close shot of Hamlet's motionless face, begins immediately the Player King has finished his specimen speech; the other members of the troupe look on in stony, offended bewilderment.

For 'To be or not to be,' Kozintsev pointlessly apes Olivier by making his hero overlook the rock-bound sea, but he recovers in the climax of the play-scene, when Claudius rises to *applaud* the actors before collapsing into panic.

Thereafter we get increasingly the sense of a household scared, disordered and dishevelled. Menacing images assert themselves: Polonius, pulling down the arras as he dies to reveal a squad of tailor's dummies, modelling Gertrude's wardrobe; Fortinbras and his army plodding across a windy beach while Hamlet murmurs, 'How all occasions . . . '; Ophelia (Anastasia Vertinskaya) being locked in a steel-ribbed robe of mourning, and going publicly mad in a hall full of embarrassed soldiers and insurgents; and a grinning grave-digger who crowns Yorick's skull with a rusty set of cap-and-bells. Towards the end there are a few sentimental extravagances, among them the seagull that rises from the waves beyond Ophelia's grave, presumably symbolising her soul. For the rest: this may not be Shakespeare's *Hamlet*, but it is the most striking evocation of Hamlet's Elsinore that we are ever likely to see.

Where Love Has Gone; My Fair Lady

There are certain films which defy one's efforts to perform the critical act. For criticism to be feasible, there must be some consensus, however minute, between reviewer and artist—at the very least, a shared assumption that both would like to see the world's store of good art increased. They may have wildly conflicting notions of the nature and purpose of art, but beneath the settling dust of such combats there must be a final complicity: both participants must agree that the one has produced, and the other is assessing, something which is intended to be judged by artistic criteria.

Critics are always being told that their only duty is to decide whether a given work is 'good of its kind'. But there are kinds that were never meant to be 'good', by anyone's definition of art. They are commodities, articles made with no thought of lasting, designed solely to be bought and consumed. *Pace* the supporters of pop art, those panicky propagandists who believe that the only way to give art a place in a profit-based world is to erase the vital boundary between art and commerce, the wrapper around a can of soup cannot be judged on artistic terms. Nor, likewise, can *Where Love Has Gone*, before which criticism retires, yielding place to astounded resumé, with sociological footnotes.

In the words of the song, love walked right in and puked all over the floor; but not as wholeheartedly as in this 'blistering best-seller' by Harold Robbins, brought to the screen (for those who like to be blistered) by the team who cleaned up with *The Carpet-Baggers*, an earlier work from the same pen. Within the first twenty seconds, a teenage girl murders her mother's lover with a chisel. As her lawyer puts it, thinking in instant metaphor like everyone else with featured billing: 'She swung wildly and hit a home run.' Mother is Susan Hayward—'a pro at double-entry house-keeping' (the lawyer again)—and in a voluminous flashback we discover how she and her daughter got that way.

Miss Hayward, a San Francisco sculptress of high talent and brim-ming sensuality ('With you, art and sex go hand in hand', murmurs a critic who has benefited from both), married a war hero with ambitions as an architect. But her power-crazed mother, a widowed tycoon played by Bette Davis with the famous vampire smirk turned up to full voltage, forced the lad to ditch his ideals and join her company as a drinking vice-president. Trapped between two archetypal harpies, he becomes a lush— a familiar progression rendered none the livelier by the fact that the actor in question (Michael Connors) has the expressive flexibility of a brass-rubbing. Miss Hayward, formerly seen in goggles, sculpturing furi-ously away with a welder's blow-torch, falls behind on what she calls her 'production schedule' and starts taking her male models as lovers. Hence the divorce, the daughter lovelessly reared—and the shaping of a poten-tial murderess.

Recovering from the flashback, we learn that the fifteen-year-old slayer has been found guilty of justifiable homicide and placed under psychiatric surveillance. It is here (or hereabouts: who can swear to the time-sequence of events in a nightmare?) that the great lines proliferate. Miss Davis to Miss Hayward: 'You have devoted your life to mud and filth.' Mr Connors to Miss Hayward: 'You're not a woman, you're a disease.' Miss Hayward's daughter (a pouting brat) to a psychologist who confronts her with proof that she has lost her virginity: 'It could have hap-pened horseback riding.' Miss Davis, on hearing that her daughter and grand-daughter are being blackmailed because they slept with the same man: 'To have one hundred years of social standing brought to earth in a mass of feathers!' (That may originally have read 'a mess of feathers'; Miss Davis has been known to lengthen her vowels in moments of emo-tional stress). The picture ends with Miss Hayward disembowelling her-self, and the daughter driving off in a swell of hopeful music to a State institution. Direction by Edward Dmytryk, with dresses by Edith Head. Miss Head deserves congratulations.

The trouble with reviewing commodities like this is that you know in advance that, for all the effect it will have, you might as well fill your column with a relief map of Death Valley. The film has been shot, sold and packaged; it has stars, strident publicity and guaranteed distribution; and there is nothing at all, for good or ill, that a critic can do about it. The same used to apply in the starry days of the commercial theatre, before the State took steps to provide subsidised alternatives. Nowadays the balance has tilted; it is the non-commercial theatres that are sucking the best actors and audiences away from their money-minded rivals.

A state-owned chain of cinemas, fuelled by the output of a subsidised film school, would create a situation in which good commercial and non-commercial films would be able to compete on something more like equal terms; and in which intelligent criticism could influence film-going habits on a national scale. The wider the range of available films, the more discriminating the public becomes. Narrowness of choice springs from monopoly, which also breeds apathetic, incurious audiences. Public money, wisely spent, would give us the chance to open our eyes and ears not only to the most expensively promoted films, but to the best.

People keep telling me that George Cukor, in his direction of *My Fair Lady*, has failed to 'use the medium'. I wish I knew what they meant: if, by way of analogy, a man were to stage *Pygmalion* as Shaw wrote it, without songs and dances, should we therefore condemn him for having failed to use the full resources of the theatrical medium?

It is true that Mr Cukor's visual sense occasionally flags: when he gets his camera out of doors, the Cecil Beaton exteriors at which he points it clash with one another a little too cheekily, ranging in style from the semi-realistic (Covent Garden) to the semi-abstract (Ascot). Nor can I deny that, except in the hate-song, 'Just You Wait', where a squad of visionary guardsmen troops into Eliza's mind to execute Henry Higgins, Mr Cukor has not over-taxed his powers of invention. But such quibbles miss the point, which is that he has 'used the medium' purely and self-effacingly to recreate in the cinema a theatrical experience. *My Fair Lady* must be unique among screen musicals in that most of the action is confined to one house, and much of it to one room; the measure of its success is that we never feel the smallest twinge of claustrophobia.

It is not without flaws—some of them inherent in the Broadway original—and I had better clear my throat of these before proceeding to rhapsody. Two of the credit titles are offensive: 'Screenplay by Alan Jay Lerner', 'From a play by Bernard Shaw'. How much more gracious to have named the play and to have admitted that Shaw wrote most of Mr

Lerner's dialogue! And the miracle of six-track stereophonic sound amplifies a couple of *gaffes* in Mr Lerner's otherwise immaculate lyrics:

> She should be taken out and hung
> For the cold-blooded murder of the English tongue.

Shaw would have hanged Higgins for that. As for:

> I'd be *equally* as willing
> That a dentist should be drilling
> *Than* to ever let a woman in my life

—it is quite an achievement to make Higgins, the defender of pure English, commit two syntactical crimes (compounded by a split infinitive) within the space of three lines. To complete the dossier of disdain: the rather leaden presence of Wilfrid Hyde-White as Pickering deprives 'The Rain in Spain' of the triumphant, explosive abandon it had on the stage, with Robert Coote in the part.

Nobody can play the early, unredeemed Eliza convincingly, for which Shaw is to blame. In the Covent Garden scene, her hysterical wails are out of all proportion to the provocation offered by the fact that Higgins is at hand, taking notes. Like all her predecessors in the role, Audrey Hepburn is compelled to ham gamely away until Mrs Higgins's tea-party (Shaw's peak of pure—as opposed to applied—comedy) gives her a chance to act. Thereafter, the silver bells of her talent ring out a memorable peal, and Mr Beaton clothes her in gleaming sheaths of icing: note, in the ballroom scene, the long white gloves and diamond choker that camouflage her tenuous arms and neck. It is only when she sings (dubbed by an imperfectly matching voice) that one misses the buoyant soprano of Julie Andrews.

Stanley Holloway's Doolittle is juicier in close-up than it was in the theatre, and his 'Get Me to the Church on Time', orgiastically sung in a Covent Garden pub, is the most improved number in the show. Mona Washbourne (Mrs Pearce) and Theodore Bikel (Zoltan Karpathy) solidify parts that were formerly sketches. Mr Beaton's interiors (like Mr Cukor, he is happiest indoors) are dominated by a resplendently panelled library decked out with Pre-Raphaelite trophies and choice Edwardiana: one's only complaint is that Higgins the monastic clubman would never have tolerated a sanctum so exquisite.

Which leaves Rex Harrison. In his first number ('Why Can't the English?') he drags the tempo appallingly, and the heavily italicised snarl with which he tells Eliza that 'the angels will weep for you' makes one suspect that the whole show has been slowed down to accommodate provincial dimwits. Soon afterwards, doubts evaporate. You can name on the fingers of one hand the masters of high comedy in the English-speaking world: they can dictate their terms in any country and any medium. Cary Grant is one of their number, and Mr Harrison is another.

Give him a simple, helpless line like: 'Damn Mrs Pearce, and damn the coffee, and damn you!' and he will make it sound as elegantly yet majestically final as a trio of crashing chords at the end of a symphony. His eyes are mere slits and his stance is preposterously angular; but he exudes that combination of the aggressor and the injured, the school-master and the truant, which adds up in Britain (and elsewhere) to erotic infallibility. From the opening words of a number such as 'A Hymn to Him' ('What in all of heaven can have prompted her to go?') you know that you are in absolutely safe hands; a supreme performer is in charge, steering you as a master helmsman steers his yacht. It is an increasingly rare sensation.

Frederick Loewe's score is as durable as anything in the whole history of operetta. Apart from its other singularities, *My Fair Lady* is the only romantic musical in which neither of the principal characters has a lovesong. The nearest Higgins gets to passion is to concede that he has grown accustomed to Eliza's face: a grudging tribute, surely. Yet we are moved at the end in a profoundly romantic way, thanks in equal part to Mr Loewe, Mr Lerner and the incomparable Rex.

Raven's End: The Yellow Rolls-Royce

Liberal humanism walks a tightrope in the cinema. On one side it topples into the aleatory formlessness of *cinéma-vérité*; on the other, into sentimental rhetoric. Its triumphs are triumphs of restraint, a quality that is endlessly frustrating to would-be eulogists. I faced this problem a few months ago when *Nothing but a Man*, a wonderful group portrait of the modern American Negro, turned up at the 1964 London Film Festival and promptly disappeared; and I face it again with *Raven's End*.

Bo Widerberg, the Swede who wrote and directed this little master-piece ('little' is the obligatory critical epithet for all masterpieces that cost less than the earth to make), was about five years old in 1936, when the action takes place. Yet he gives us the feel of the period as vividly as any hunger-marcher. We focus on a single family in a tenement block in Malmo: mother scrubs floors for a living, father gloomily tipples, and their son Anders quietly buds as a writer. Hitler is at large across the

Baltic and getting larger; we hear talk of local Nazis, and somebody asks how the war in Spain is going. But in all this careful evocation there is no trace of hindsight polemics, no self-conscious immersion in squalor, no equation of poverty with tragedy, and none of the generalised character-drawing that turns individuals into spokesmen. You get the feeling that these people would have behaved in exactly the same way, just as unemphatically and irreplaceably, if the camera had never been invented. They never seem conscripted to suit a thesis, or manipulated to make a glib dramatic point.

The central players are a trio for the anthologies. Mother (Emy Storm) wearily runs the household. Once, because the family could not feed another child, she had an abortion; what scars her memory is not the operation itself but the fact that her husband transferred to her the responsibility of deciding whether or not to have it. She has been too busy to learn much about love: we realise that poverty is above all time-consuming, and that it takes money to buy the leisure in which love can grow. There's an annual treat, for which she gets out her curling-tongs: 'Whenever I smell burnt hair,' says her son, 'we're off to the circus.' As played by Thommy Berggren, Anders is not the conventional neurotic outcast but a sensible young factory-hand whose only abnormal quality is a sharply retentive emotional memory which, coupled with a fierce desire to communicate, inevitably makes him a writer—in this case, school of Wesker and Sillitoe.

A ramshackle man named Keve Hjelm gives the great performance as father, a former salesman now sustaining himself on booze and illusions. This is a character fit to live beside Ibsen's Hjalmar Ekdal, Miller's Willie Loman and the soft-brained derelicts of *The Iceman Cometh*. He does not drink, in so few words: he suffers from a dry throat and gargles with rot-gut, which he swallows. When he eats, the table is laid with napkins he has filched from expensive hotels, from whose wine lists he recites voluptuous roll-calls of cognacs.

Drawing on past experience, he impresses on his son the paramount importance of respecting 'the product'; but when Anders asks what the product is *for*, he forgets to answer. He is capable of social shame, resulting from loss of status, but not of moral shame. Attributing his failure to bad luck, he insulates himself within what he calls 'a diving-bell' of alcohol, from which there emerge increasingly favourable comments on the enviable successes of Nazism. He dwindles eventually into a sandwich-man, and we learn, with a shock, that this eroded patriarch is only thirty-nine years old. Mr Hjelm plays him neither for pathos nor as a swine, but with a glorious indifference to any task other than that of presenting a recognisably human being. Even at sombre moments, fun keeps breaking in. Reproaching his father for extravagance, Anders recalls the time when he brought home so many cream-puffs that the family had to live on them for a week. They gave one to the dog next door, which died of colic. . . . But already both he and his father have dissolved into laughter; the prosecutor is chuckling with the accused.

In the last reel, preparing for Anders's escape to Stockholm as a full-time writer, Mr Widerberg ties up the loose ends a little predictably. Sooner or later there had to be a punch-up between father and son, and one guessed that the boy would get reeling drunk when he found that his mother wasn't morally spotless. Otherwise, no complaints: and special honours to Sven Fahlen for a sound-track that brilliantly combines a foreground of script with a background of unrehearsed reality. Let us now look forward to a film about the embattled formative years of a typical British writer of the thirties. Why not a biography, for example, of the present co-editor of *Encounter*, entitled 'The Last of the Big Spenders'?

There is a smiling, gracious staleness about *The Yellow Rolls-Royce* that gives it the air of some long-forgotten ceremonial occasion—the investiture of Dornford Yates, perhaps, as a Knight of the Garter. The stately blandness of its manner is quite at odds with the fusty triviality of what it has to offer: it condescends from a great depth.

'Let us bring a little glamour into the drabness of their lives,' you can hear its makers saying, as they set before us, with a flourish of *largesse*, individual portions of flyblown trifle. Authentic glamour in the cinema is a rare commodity; a difficult, secret blend of elegance, opulence, charm and wit, achieved sometimes in Paris and Hollywood, but never in Britain, where it usually means yet another dose of secondhand Herbert Wilcox.

Directed by Anthony Asquith from a screenplay by Terence Rattigan, *The Yellow Rolls-Royce* consists of three short stories, any one of which might have made a bad short film in its own right. They have two common factors: sentimentality and an expensive motor-car, gaudily painted. In the first episode, Rex Harrison plays a brusque, plaintively barking peer who buys the Rolls for his wife and finds her snogging in the back seat at the precise moment when his horse is winning the Ascot Gold Cup. In a scarcely credible sequence, he stalks away from the car park and sheds a tear on the horse's neck. As his wife, Jeanne Moreau sounds sulky and looks pallid: the sulks I attribute (fancifully, no doubt) to intensive study of the script, and the pallor to a combination of over-decorated sets and insensitive colour photography that would make any actress look pasty.

Characteristic period touches (we are in the early 1930s) include an awed whisper of 'Look! Their Majesties!' as a disembodied toque sails across the bottom of the screen, and a comic Albanian Ambassador who wears the wrong clothes for Ascot. Evidence that Anthony Asquith was alive and well when the film was made is amply supplied by the fact that, within fifteen minutes of the opening shot, action takes place. 'Fetch me my slippers,' says Mlle Moreau to Mr Harrison, who does just that.

The second chapter of this travelogue with foreground figures is set in Italy, where the Rolls is bought by a Chicago hood (George C. Scott) on vacation with a soft-hearted moll (Shirley MacLaine), who briefly encounters and abandons a man-tanned street photographer (Alain Delon). The gangster describes his doxy as 'the most stupidest, most unfeelingest broad in the world'. This kind of Rattiganesque Runyonese would shrivel the tongue of any self-respecting American actor who tried to speak it, so Miss MacLaine and Mr Scott attempt to lick the script by underplaying it—in Mr Scott's case, to the point of embarrassed inaudibility.

Miss MacLaine is often touching, especially in moments of silence; but when she couples with M. Delon, the director is ready with a thunderous cliché (waves crashing on the rocks) to sabotage her efforts. Mr Rattigan's final novelette shows an American millionairess, snobbishly anti-Red, hiring the Rolls in Trieste and driving across the Yugoslav border with an exiled radical in the boot. Once exposed to his charm, she aids the partisans and becomes a belated anti-Nazi (period: 1941). My immediate reaction to Ingrid Bergman's performance as the spunky *chauffeuse* was to suspect that the part had been written for Katharine Hepburn, and to be absolutely sure that, if such was the case, Miss Hepburn had been right to turn it down.

Dispatch from Prague: 1965

A fortnight ago I flew to Prague for a view of the cultural landscape, from which I returned with a fat dossier of demolished preconceptions.

In less than three years of de-Stalinisation, the Czechs have outpaced their rivals in Poland, where the thaw started earlier and seems lately to have frozen over. Decentralisation was the key: the Czech cinema is now divided into five autonomous production groups, each with its own artistic chief and financial administrator, and each turning out six films a year. The State censor can veto a picture, but not until it is finished; and since all production expenditure comes out of public funds, he is likely to think twice before imposing a ban.

Is commercialism—the dictatorship of the box-office—really less harmful to the art of cinema than political censorship? My Czech experience suggests that this is an open question. All censorship is bad: even so, on stage and screen alike, I saw in Prague more serious criticism of the political Establishment in a week than I had seen in London in a year. It is virtually impossible for a Czech artist to make a statement that has no political resonance; no matter how remote the symbols and metaphors he uses, the audience at once translates them into practical politics and current events.

The great model is Kafka, rehabilitated by the thaw and now inescapable: the lonely, baffled questioner of the status quo is a figure who recurs again and again. He is the hero of *Joseph Kilian* (directed by Jan Schmidt and Pavel Juráček), who hires a cat from a pet shop and, having fulfilled this private and socially useless desire, finds that the shop has mysteriously vanished. Even more obviously, he is Joseph K. in Ivan Klíma's play *The Castle*, which deals with a youthful idealist thrust into a State-run home for corrupt and privileged intellectuals, where his presence disquiets the inmates so deeply that they murder him.

The Fifth Rider is Fear, a coldly brilliant film directed with Wellesian virtuosity by Zbyněk Brynych, ostensibly concerns a Jewish doctor during the German occupation who operates on an injured anti-Nazi, thereby exposing all his neighbours to the scrutiny of the Gestapo; but no Nazis appear, the investigators wear plain clothes, and the exterior shots look strictly contemporary. Again, this is Kafka's Prague; and the theme is the *Angst* that innocent people feel when official strangers invade their homes.

The best new play in Prague—Václav Havel's *The Garden Party*—is Absurdist in form but sharply political in content. One of the characters becomes head of the Liquidation Department in order to inaugurate the liquidation of the Inauguration Department; another is a breezy de-Stalinised bureaucrat who proves by his pronouncements ('I'm glad you have contrary opinions: everyone should have from one to three contrary opinions') that a thaw can be regulated just as firmly as a freeze. A third converses in mock-Khrushchev proverbs, e.g. 'He who argues with a mosquito sieve will never dance with a goat near Podmokly.'

Like everyone else, the Czechs make conventional wartime films: *Attentat* (director: Jiri Sequens) is one such, showing how the assassination of Heydrich achieved nothing but the slaughter of numerous hostages and the extermination of Lidice. But it is to younger films that one looks for the flavour of modern Czech cinema. To Jan Němec's *Diamonds of the Night*, for example, which examines the escape of two Jewish boys from an Auschwitz-bound train in a free-wheeling experimental style owing much to Resnais and something to Bresson; I winced at the film's self-indulgence, while envying the total freedom with which the director had been allowed to indulge himself.

Better still, there is *Peter and Paula* (director: Milos Forman), an affectionate, plotless account of the first wage-earning days in the life of a gloomy teenage boy. Hired as a detective in a supermarket, he follows a suspected thief home but lacks the nerve to accost him. He fumbles privately as well as publicly: girls upset him, his father's lectures embarrass him, and in the local dance hall he alone cannot twist. This tender, hilariously unsentimental picture, shown at last autumn's London Film Festival, deserves much wider distribution.

Vladimir Pucholt, who plays the hero's gangling best friend with the ingenuous aplomb of a holy simpleton out of Dostoevsky, has since become the teenage god of Czechoslovakia by starring in *Hop-Pickers* (director: Ladislav Rychman)—the first Czech musical in colour, and the first to feature motor-bikes, electric guitars, pseudo-Robbins choreography, *bossa nova* and the full paraphernalia of what is locally known as 'big beat'. It is naïve, rather like the Garland-Rooney *Babes in Arms*; but I met one young student who had seen it twelve times, and he was not an exception. As for Pucholt, he is still at drama school, happy so long as he is playing parts he can believe in, and utterly unconcerned by the fact that he is not rich.

The toughest Czech study of youth is Evald Schorm's *Courage for Everyday*. This audacious first feature, which begins symptomatically with a long quote from Kafka, takes more ideological liberties than any other film we have yet seen from Eastern Europe: no wonder its public showing has been postponed until the autumn, when the twentieth anniversary celebrations of the liberation of Prague have died down. Its hero is a sexy young factory worker (and party member) about whom a picture magazine is writing a story. He is asked to interview his fellow-workers, to compère a fearful cultural evening at a village hall, to be photographed smiling at prize agricultural exhibits; and in the course of these propagandist exploits he disgusts his friends and loses his mistress. Marxism says that rational economic relationships create good emotional relationships. Heretically, *Courage for Everyday* implies that devotion to Marxism can actually alienate you from your fellow human beings. A brave and perceptive film.

The best is the last, and also the simplest. *The Shop on Main Street* (directed by Elmar Klos and Jan Kadár) takes place during the war in a sunny Slovakian village where a brass band plays in the square, everyone dresses up on Sundays, and you almost expect Jacques Tati to come jangling along on a bicycle. There isn't a German in sight, though, of course, there are local volunteers who wear Nazi uniform. One of them gives his brother-in-law, an impoverished farmer, the title deeds to a shop owned by an elderly Jewish widow. Spruced up and sure of a windfall (hasn't his wife told him that Jews always keep gold hidden under the floorboards?), he goes to claim his Aryan inheritance: but not without problems, since the widow is deaf and doesn't know there's a war on. We soon learn that she is penniless, kept alive only by charitable contributions from richer Jews; but the farmer grows fond of her, and when there is talk of deporting the Jewish population to rest homes and labour camps, he feels disposed to protect her. The night before the deportation, he tells her she must hide; in her deafness, she thinks he is saying that *he* must hide, and she makes an improvised bed for him on the counter of the shop.

How he later gets drunk, watches the Jews assembling in the square, gets drunker, shrieks at the widow to join them, gets drunker still, and finally faces his guilt—all this I lack space to describe in the detail it deserves. From beginning to end, no violence is done to any Jew; yet this is by far the most moving film about anti-semitism that I have ever seen. It has been entered for Cannes, where the simplicity of its camerawork may well tell against it. 'The people from Cannes may not like it,' said Kadár, the co-director. 'Perhaps it will not be sufficiently *snobbique*.' If so, the loss will be theirs.

The grand theme of the film—as of all good modern drama—can be simply stated: how much of a man belongs to authority and how much to himself? What demands can society legitimately make of a man without requiring him to sacrifice his selfhood? At what point must the individual say 'No'? In any country where artists are trying to answer these questions, you may be sure that the arts are flourishing.

Tokyo Story

For the first time, a film by Yasujiro Ozu has been granted a London run; *Tokyo Story* (1953) has arrived at the Academy Club. I feel we owe its maker, who died two years ago, a posthumous apology. Critical legend has long insisted that, of the three acknowledged giants of Japanese cinema (Mizoguchi and Kurosawa being the others), Ozu was the most impenetrably exotic. Having tested the legend, I pronounce it exploded. Beside the blissful sanity of *Tokyo Story*—Ozu's favourite, by the way, among his fifty-four films—it is the Western cinema that seems opaque and exotic.

A master of cutting, he entirely dispenses with pans, tracking shots, fades and dissolves, and would surely endorse what Ivor Montagu says in his recent Pelican, *Film World*: 'A cut from shot to shot is . . . much more natural as a means of changing the visual attention than a moving shot.' Ozu's habit is to begin a sequence with the camera knee-high, shooting through a door or similar oblong frame to disclose his characters in groupings at once utterly ordinary and extraordinarily beautiful; he then cuts in closer as the action demands.

This, to people brought up on restless camera movement, makes him a 'quietist'. The truth is that he is a pure realist, for whom the concept of realism is not barnacled over with crowd-catching epithets like 'stark' and 'savage'. Films commonly approach life with ulterior motives (e.g. to paint it black and white, to make their chosen slice of it symbolic of something larger); Ozu is content merely to show it.

'The perfection of Zen,' says Alan Watts, 'is to be perfectly and simply human. The difference of the adept in Zen from the ordinary run of men is that the latter are, in one way or another, at odds with their own humanity, and are attempting to be angels or demons.' By this definition, Ozu is a Zen director. His view of life is as concrete and unsentimental as the Japanese poem that begins:

> We eat, excrete, sleep and get up:
> This is our world.

And what story does he tell about Tokyo? It is partly mine; more or less it is everyone's. An elderly couple decide to visit their grown-up children in the big city. Neither their doctor son nor their beautician daughter is doing as well as reports have hinted; and neither can devote much time to entertaining the old folks, who are soon bundled off to a seaside resort. Unhappily lodged in a cheap and noisy hotel, they return unannounced to Tokyo, where the embarrassed beautician passes them off to her clients as 'friends from the country'. Father gets falling-down drunk with a pair of cronies, and next day the old couple go uncomplainingly home. On arrival mother is taken mortally ill, which means that the rest of the family must make the long train journey to her deathbed. The generations have drifted far apart, but a pretence of solidarity is kept up, despite twinges of boredom and flurries of irritation on the part of the children. The funeral over, they depart as quickly as decorum permits, leaving father to face his solitude as best he can, a stoic half-smile politely frozen on his lips.

I have heard it said that the limitations within which Ozu works are narrow; but many enviable kinds of freedom accompany his self-imposed restraints—freedom, for example, to trust the audience instead of having to keep it in a constant state of nervous stimulation; and freedom, above all, from the aggressive need to assert one's individuality in order to be accepted as an artist. The acting is momentously subtle. Nothing is underlined, yet nothing is unobserved: the intimacy is Olympian. On the quality of the dialogue (part-written by Ozu) I hesitate to comment, since subtitles are no substitute for knowledge of Japanese. Which prompts a general question: how much of the artistic hegemony automatically accorded by critics to directors is due to the fact that very few critics are equipped to pass judgment on scripts written in foreign languages?

The Sound of Music; Frustration

The situation that gave us *The King and I* also gives us *The Sound of Music*: a buoyant young governess, hired by a despotic patriarch to cope with his numerous children, ends up by melting and winning his heart.

One notes superficial differences: the girl, for example, is a novice on leave from a nunnery, the tyrant is a widowed naval commander named von Trapp, and the setting is not Siam in the nineteenth century but Salzburg in what the opening caption insensately describes as 'the last Golden Days of the Thirties'. (Golden for whom? Hitler? Ivor Novello?) But on the whole this is Rodgers and Hammerstein devoutly engaged in nostalgic self-plunder: it was the last work they wrote together, and its flavour, on screen as on stage, is like that of a sugary, *spätlese* hock, left so long in the sun that it tastes like syrup.

The nuns, as always in American films, are average American housewives inexplicably veiled in black; a twinkling bunch of good-hearted gossips, healthily unconcerned with sex. They all sing their wimples off, including—strangely enough—the Mother Superior, who bursts into full contralto shortly after informing us that singing in the cloister is forbidden. At one point the heroine lyrically proclaims that her heart wants 'to sing through the night like a lark who is learning to pray': the image of a kneeling, nocturnal lark, its wing-tips reverently clasped, is unforgettable and entirely characteristic. Her story—and that of the seven children she takes in hand—is based on fact: there really was a singing Trapp family who stole out of Austria after the *Anschluss* and entranced America with the Salzburg Sound. Christopher Plummer plays Papa von Trapp with evident embarrassment, relying heavily on arch looks of mock-severity and a *dégagé* bearing reminiscent of Olivier in *The Sleeping Prince*.

The film lasts three hours; I was mostly bored but intermittently, unexpectedly touched. The greens and blues of the landscape, as well as the baroque splendours of Salzburg itself, are thrillingly caught by Ted McCord's free-ranging camera; but it is Julie Andrews of the soaring voice and thrice-scrubbed innocence who makes me, even in guarded moments, catch my breath. The director is Robert Wise: given a task so inherently limiting, I cannot see how he can be faulted. He must forgive his fans if they wanly ask themselves what happened to the man who edited *Citizen Kane* and *The Magnificent Ambersons*, and directed the best of all films about boxing, *The Set-Up*. A final, larger question suggests itself: Whatever happened to *original* Hollywood musicals, as opposed to Broadway borrowings?

'Right here, Martin, man has been put through the purgatory of his passions.' This is the opening line of *Frustration*, uttered by a bland transatlantic faggot to his blond male secretary while both survey an ancient Athenian theatre. (Because of sketchy dubbing, the words fail by a split-second or so to match the speaker's mouth, thus creating a distinct impression that he is not only deviant but drunk.) He turns out to be the American Ambassador to Greece, a libellous identification if ever I heard one.

His wife, with whom he has a name-only arrangement, is played by Ingrid Thulin, a prominent member of the Ingmar Bergman repertory troupe. Out of frustration she takes a working-class lover, played by a Greek, who has a strip-teasing sister, played by a Frenchwoman (Claudine Auger). Hereabouts one begins to suspect that internationalism has run mad, and suspicion becomes certainty when one finds in the cast names like Inge Book, Helena Vita and Gregory von Rezzori, all of them playing Greek characters in Kensington accents.

Of the direction (by Hans Albin and Peter Berneis) let me merely say that it notches up a minor first: never before in a feature film have I witnessed a street scene in which a passer-by violently lurches off course in order to avoid the camera. Skimming through the cast list to see if I have overlooked anyone, I encounter the peerless name of Madelon Truss. Welcome back, Miss Truss, if indeed you have ever been away.

Red Desert; Now About These Women

It is axiomatic in the theatre that authors—with a few majestic exceptions—should never be allowed to direct their own plays; the results are too likely to be blighted by uncritical self-indulgence. In the cinema, by contrast, the author-director is enthroned as an object of veneration. That this kind of one-man-bandsmanship may have its drawbacks was twice demonstrated last week: by Michelangelo Antonioni's *Red Desert* and Ingmar Bergman's *Now About These Women.*

Antonioni is at once an aesthete who likes beautiful images and a Socialist with strong views on the way in which capitalist society alienates human beings from one another. His last film, *The Eclipse,* was full of implicit Marxism: all the characters were non-producers, living on investments and thus at one remove from reality. Hence the sterility of their emotional relationships: witness the pseudo-primitive party at which the hostess, financially dependent on African labour, tried in vain to simulate African exuberance. The Stock Exchange scenes, so far from being irrelevant displays of virtuosity (as some critics suggested), were the heart and core of the picture. I have often found Antonioni tedious, an obsessive. dweller on points thrice-made; but hitherto the aesthete in him has at least worked hand in hand with the social theorist.

In *Red Desert* they move apart. You get the feeling that he started out to make a film about the dwarfing, dehumanising effect of heavy industry on the soul, and then—this being his first excursion into colour —fell in love with the visual *largesse* offered by factory chimneys and oil refineries and industrial garbage. He has said that he intended to 'point out the beauty of this world', but that sounds like a rationalisation: as conveyed in the film, his attitude is thoroughly ambivalent. The socialist in him insists that industrial development is useful and necessary; the bourgeois aesthete at first regards it as a hostile monster, belching clouds of poisonous smoke, but soon realises afterwards that it will make a ravishing background for Monica Vitti. As indeed it does: she wanders distracted through an ominous landscape that any fashion photographer might envy.

Miss Vitti, whose husband works in electronics, is recovering from a car crash—possibly a suicide attempt—that has left her in a state of hysterical depression. Reality fills her with dread. Whenever she enters a shot, her face alone is in focus; everything else is blurred. In the opening sequence she buys a half-eaten sandwich from a worker on strike, presumably to underline her need for human communion, even at the basic level of sharing bread. She attends an abortive afternoon orgy, where sex is debated but not practised. Her son, whose favourite toy is a giant symbolic robot, pretends that his legs are paralysed: she tells him a story about a golden-age, pre-industrial paradise of pellucid sea and pink sands, and he is instantly cured.

Finally, she has a brief and botched affair with a transient mining engineer, in which role Richard Harris is so unconvincingly dubbed as to be beyond the reach of criticism: here, if anywhere in the film, is proof that mechanical devices can produce an effect of total alienation. For a moment, after she has slept with him, the bedroom turns pink, which for her equals peace—a use of colour as naïve and pathetically fallacious as in Hitchcock's clod-hopping *Marnie*, where red equalled guilt.

We return to the two Antonionis. The aesthete evokes a beautiful industrial wasteland, and the intellectual sets against it a highly neurotic woman. The trouble is that they seem to be living in different worlds. No causal connection is established, or even hinted at, between the heroine's neurosis and her environment; she suffers in a vacuum that is quite un-related to the circumstances in which she lives. There is nothing to sug-gest that she would be any different if her home were in Connemara or Madagascar. No attempt is made to trace her problem to its roots. She remains a cipher to the end, and leaves us feeling profoundly cheated. Banquets for the eye are not enough: the mind and heart are hungry too.

The Bergman film—likewise his first in colour—is immeasurably worse, and may well (to pluck a phrase from an emergent African play that I recently read) 'go down to history as an event of abysmal import-ance'. Set in the twenties, it has to do with a 'cellist of genius who lives with his wife and six mistresses in a villa that looks inside the way Brighton Pavilion looks outside. The girls have jocular nicknames like Isolde, Traviata and St Cecilia, and in the garden there's a shooting gallery where the wife takes pot-shots at her husband's effigy.

The central character isn't the maestro himself (whom we never see) but a music critic who turns up to write his biography. The latter, insuffer-ably played by Jarl Kulle, has a long cigarette-holder, a longer quill pen, and relentlessly roguish eyebrows. He dances one of those swooping tangoes that seemed so funny fifteen years ago, and even dresses up as a woman for a few agonising minutes. Between his attempts to seduce the ladies of the house, a trad band plays snatches of 'Yes, We Have No Bananas'. There's a climactic firework display, which is not (a coy cap-tion warns us) to be taken symbolically.

I have never numbered Bergman among the slyer contemporary

wags; all the same, I expected something slightly less elephantine than tinted Norman Wisdom. 'What goings-on! I gape in amazement,' remarks one of the subtitles, and I can't say I blame it.

Une Femme Mariée; The Greatest Story Every Told

'Fragments of a film' is how Jean-Luc Godard describes *Une Femme Mariée*, his latest bulletin on the crisis of contemporary morals. By this he intends no insolence; the phrase implies not that the film is slapdash or unfinished, but that it faithfully records the fragmented vision of a girl who cannot make the disparate splinters of her life add up to a coherent whole. The twenty-four hours through which we follow her are not a smooth dramatic progression, rising to a climax and then achieving resolution. They are a staccato series of impressions—caresses, rebuffs, insights, stupidities, transient ups and downs—as befit a girl who lives entirely in the present.

Her lover, in whose bed the film starts, is an actor; her husband, once loved and still slept with, is a pilot. Both have normal memories; but for her, each new experience erases what happened a moment ago. Which of the two should she choose? Tousled, puzzled and weakly well-meaning, Macha Meril makes her dilemma universal. In what sound like unscripted interviews, she questions people about the purpose of life.

A middle-aged intellectual advises her to inject a little reason into absurdity, which baffles her utterly. Finding herself pregnant, she quizzes a doctor on birth control and the relevance of pleasure to love—getting nothing in return but a suave display of fence-sitting. She asks the actor whether he is acting when he makes love to her; but since he may still be acting when he replies, we are left as much in the dark as she is.

What kind of a world is it that can set her moral signposts so capriciously spinning? The clue is that she works for a fashion magazine; hers is a world of secondhand images. The camera roams over girdle and brassiere ads., zooms in on romantic headlines (so that 'Danger' becomes 'ange'), and plasters the screen with record sleeves and movie hoardings. The heroine worries about her posture, snips her pubic hair, and measures the distance between her nipples because magazines tell her to. In a hilarious, deadpan sequence—we forget how funny Godard can be, with his sleepless eye for banality—her husband describes their flat to a guest in the fulsome terms of an estate agent's brochure.

What Godard wants to show is how ideas and moral concepts are shaped by the very means through which they are received. As Marshall McLuhan has explained in his book, *Understanding Media,* the invention of the printing press created a new sort of human being—the individualist —by making knowledge portable and privately digestible. We are now moving into a new era of continuous assault on all the senses by all the pop media—TV, records, films, advertising and journalism. Godard's heroine is living through the transition: hence her moral numbness and sense of impermanence.

According to McLuhan, the mechanised media will take us beyond 'fragmented, literate and visual individualism' into a deeper, broader, more multi-sensual life. Like most of us, however, Godard at once resents and relishes mass communications; hence his readiness to expose Mlle Meril to their bombardment, and the fascination with which we watch her reactions. The film stings and tickles by turns, and always enlists the mind. As lover and husband respectively, Bernard Noel and Philippe Leroy are casually perfect.

Shot in Utah, Nevada and California ('far more authentic', says the handout, awkwardly hedging its bets, 'than is the modern Holy Land, with its bustling cities, its sacred shrines and its bright hope for the future'), *The Greatest Story Ever Told* is the slowest, safest tribute ever paid to the founder of Christianity. Asked whether he considers wealth a crime, Christ carefully answers: 'Not at all—but it may become a burden.' The director, George Stevens, neatly sidesteps the question of Jewish culpability for the Messiah's death by planting in the crowd a satanic hermit (last seen tempting Christ on a high mountain), who is the first to cry: 'Crucify him!' The Last Supper is filmed as painted, with everyone seated on the same side of the table. For light relief, we have Christ going through customs (with Matthew in receipt thereof) and declaring his father, who is within him. Matthew: 'Has *he* anything to declare?' Jesus: 'Yes—his love for you.'

Nothing in the film comes near to evoking the great Jewish moralist and militant anti-Roman rebel who should be its subject. His Jewishness is underplayed throughout: the metaphoric dismissal of non-Jews as 'dogs' (Mark 7: 26–7) is tactfully omitted, and Mr Stevens seems unaware of the fact—long familiar to scholars—that the phrase 'Son of God' applied not merely to Jesus but to *all* Jews. Apart from his parents, no mention is made of the other members of Jesus's family (four brothers and at least two sisters, according to Mark); and he manages, as usual, to conquer the Temple single-handed—a remarkable feat, considering that it housed 20,000 functionaries and was guarded by 500 Roman soldiers (*vide* Joel Carmichael's *The Death of Jesus*). No one coming to the story for the first time would ever guess that Jesus was in fact condemned and crucified as a political insurgent.

Max von Sydow, on loan from Ingmar Bergman's rep, tackles the desperate task of universalising Christ with lean, eye-blazing energy, like a young John Caradine in training, or Alec Guinness seen from the extreme corner of the front-row stalls. Other stars abound. With its sweeping Western vistas, this is a pretty film; but *Shane*—directed by the same man against similar backgrounds—was much more Christlike.

Fail Safe

It seems to me obtuse to knock *Fail Safe* because it deals with roughly the same subject as Stanley Kubrick's *Dr Strangelove*; after all, nobody holds it against Sophocles that he wrote about the same family as Aeschylus, and you could hardly maintain that thermonuclear war was a theme of less general interest than the misfortunes of the House of Atreus.

In any case, the two films differ markedly, not only in style but in basic postulates. *Dr Strangelove* was a nihilistic satire that demanded and got acting of outsize eccentricity: *Fail Safe* is a dramatised documentary in which understated acting is heightened and magnified—as in the early Orson Welles movies—by low-key camerawork and diamond-sharp sound editing.

Moreover, Kubrick's nuclear holocaust needed a madman to trigger it off, whereas in *Fail Safe* the crucial flaw is not human but mechanical: a minuscule error on the part of a computer creates a situation of irrevocable horror. Though I relished the wit and audacity of *Dr Strangelove*, I never felt personally threatened; *Fail Safe* (directed by Sidney Lumet from a script based on the novel by Eugene Burdick and Harvey Wheeler) makes the logic of catastrophe seem much more intimate and irrefutable. Step by plausible step, we are drawn into an apocalyptic experience.

The action is confined to one day and a handful of settings, mainly the Pentagon, the S.A.C. Headquarters and the President's deep shelter. In a hypnotic pretitle sequence, backed by high-pitched electronic wailing (Mr Lumet dispenses with music throughout), a man watches a slow-motion bullfight, fainting with terror as the sword goes in; we cut to his waking, sweat-beaded face, and realise that this is a recurrent nightmare. He rises, washes, exchanges a few words with his half-slumbering wife, and reaches towards the clothes closet: a reverse shot reveals him taking

off the hook the uniform of a three-star general. This sudden shock pre-
pares us for what is to come: a number of otherwise ordinary people will
shortly be forced—by reason of rank, expertise, elective office or mere
accidental proximity—to make extraordinary, irreversible decisions on
which the future of the human race will depend.

Because of a phoney alert on the radar screen, American bombers
are dispatched to their 'fail-safe' points on the perimeter of the Soviet
Union; all return when recalled except for a wing of six planes which
receives the wrong message and sets its course for Moscow.

What to do? A home-based battle is joined between hawks and
doves. The leading hawk is a civilian adviser (played by Walter Matthau,
conceivably the best character actor in America) who takes the Herman
Kahn line that nuclear war is not different in kind from other wars;
therefore, he argues, let the bombers go through and back them up with
a full-scale missile strike. Among the doves we have the nightmare victim
(Dan Herlihy); the general in charge of S.A.C., who discovers that he and
his Russian opposite number served together during the war; and the
President himself, played with agonised wistfulness by Henry Fonda.

I cannot judge whether the final cataclysmic compromise (New York
destroyed to balance the razing of Moscow) is politically credible; but
everything else rings fearfully true, especially the scenes in which officers
brainwashed to regard Communism as the ultimate evil rebel when the
President orders them to collaborate with the Russians in shooting down
American planes. The unswerving patriotism that fitted them for their
jobs is precisely what unfits them to save the world. As I left the cinema
after seeing this fiercely intelligent film, the first thing to catch my eye
was a news poster. It read: 'VIETNAM: U.S. STEPS UP WAR.'

Woman of the Dunes: Hush . . . Hush, Sweet Charlotte

Peter Ustinov once said, *à propos* of ice-shows, that he expected some
day to see *Nanook of the North* on sand. That day has now dawned.
Hiroshi Teshigahara's *Woman of the Dunes* may not be precisely what
Mr Ustinov had in mind—philosophically, it owes less to Flaherty than to
Samuel Beckett—but it will do to be going on with. Fêted at Cannes last
year, it proves that the art cinema is still capable of beating its parodists
at their own game.

A stranded entomologist seeks overnight shelter with a pretty young
widow who lives in a shanty at the bottom of a cavernous sand-pit. Her

function is to shovel sand for sale to jerrybuilders, in return for which the local villagers lower supplies of food and water. Before dawn they remove the rope-ladder by which her guest has descended; henceforth he is trapped and, like her, must shovel or die. All his escape bids fail, except the last, by which time he has accepted his servitude so completely that he is ready to return to it without compulsion. The film's message, delivered with somnolent monotony, is one of fatalistic togetherness: man can adapt to anything, even sleeping with a sand-caked woman.

The subtitles get fairly wild at times. 'It's more bad-tempered than a gribble,' says the widow, referring to some kind of hostile sandfly; and one blinks, as so often in Japanese movies, when remarks uttered with an expression of leering contempt turn out to mean something like: 'That bowl of salt bream tasted good.' About halfway through, understandably exasperated, the hero asks the widow: 'Are you living to clear sand, or clearing sand to live?' This prompts the thought that Teshigahara may have drawn on a source less esoteric than Beckett, viz:

> They wept like anything to see
> Such quantities of sand;
> 'If this were only cleared away,'
> They said, 'it would be grand!'

Screaming jitters on the old plantation are the theme of *Hush . . . Hush, Sweet Charlotte*, in which Bette Davis plays a sort of Confederate Lizzie Borden, notorious in her neighbourhood for having committed an unsolved axe-murder some thirty years ago, and confined ever since to the ancestral home. She summons a long-lost cousin (Olivia de Havilland, staunchly replacing the mighty Joan Crawford, who withdrew from the role through illness) to help her when the mansion is threatened with demolition; but the new arrival, being the sole heiress and not without greed, creates a situation that may remind older filmgoers of *Gaslight*. Heads roll, thunder crashes, and disembodied hands litter the parquet floor.

Meanwhile, potential suspects throng the footage, among them Mary Astor, Joseph Cotten and the implacable Agnes Moorehead, who skulks around the house with arms akimbo and eyes accusingly rolling. An accomplished piece of Grand Guignol (direction by Robert Aldrich: script by Henry Farrell and Lukas Heller) is yanked up to the level of art by Miss Davis's performance as a raging, ageing Southern belle: this wasted Bernhardt, with her screen-filling eyes and electrifying vocal attack, squeezes genuine pathos from a role conceived in cardboard. She has done nothing better since *The Little Foxes*, twenty-four years ago.

A King's Story; The Satan Bug

Matters small and great are strangely yoked in *A King's Story*—strangely, that is, to anyone who suspects that there may be some difference in scale and magnitude between the major crises of the twentieth century and the private affairs of the Saxe-Coburg-Gotha family, better known since 1917 under the alias of Windsor. I wonder what a young Israeli or Cuban would make of this profoundly parochial film: would it not astound him to be told that when the heir to the Windsor fortune contemplated marrying an American divorcée, it was 'one of the most terrible decisions by which a human being has ever been confronted'? Might he not titter, or even guffaw?

For part of the time this neatly edited documentary is a survey of world history from the 1890s to 1936. For the rest, it is a scrapbook of souvenirs, kept by a prolific family whose scions were filmed and photographed a great deal, and to whose senior members the British people mysteriously gave enormous sums of money, together with a number of large and exceptionally hideous houses. (On the evidence of the film, Sandringham gets the ghastliness prize, with its roomful of furniture made out of deers' antlers.)

Home movies and international earthquakes are blandly juxtaposed, with a jarring effect of which the producer, Jack le Vien, seems raptly oblivious. Lenin addressing the workers of Russia and Mussolini leading the march on Rome are given equal screen time with the stone pelican on which young Prince Edward, in defiance of his nanny's orders, used to place funny hats.

The exiled protagonist appears to be quite a sympathetic fellow, both in the colour interviews recently shot on his French estate, and in the jerky newsreels that show him visiting the trenches during World War One (*sans* medals, since he felt he hadn't earned the right to wear them) and getting his hand injured by too much official shaking in the course of a Commonwealth tour. The film is not without touches of conscious irony, as when a banner welcomes the Prince to India with the words: 'Tell Daddy We Are All Happy Under British Rule.' It also plods through quagmires of *cliché*: only the skilled, sepulchral reverence of Orson Welles's narration prevents us from hooting at lines like: 'The Land of Song (i.e. Wales) gave way to the City of Dreaming Spires.' But the main appeal of this devout compilation is to loyal gossips. If it does nothing else, it may help to seduce the fifty-plus age-group back to the cinemas. Let me add that David Warner mimics to perfection the voice of the Duke of Windsor as a young man, even managing to reproduce the vestigial Saxe-Coburg-Gotha lisp.

The Satan Bug, like nearly everything presented by the Mirisch Corporation, has vivid and enticing credit titles. What follows (produced and directed by John Sturges) is deeply nasty. The villain is a pacifist millionaire who has dedicated his life to preventing the United States from developing biochemical weapons; to this end he breaks into a bacteriological research station and steals a flask of newly created virus that could annihilate all human life. He announces that he will not uncork it if the Government agrees to close down its research station. Bear in mind that this is the villain. The hero (George Maharis) swiftly deduces that the thief belongs to what he calls 'those better-Red-than-dead fanatics'; and by the end of the picture he has reclaimed the death-dealing flask for the Pentagon. Bear in mind that this is the hero.

Someone working on the script must clearly have felt a qualm or two about the moral perversity inherent in this set-up: hence, in an early sequence, the hero is shown to be a hater of war as well as a patriot, and the villain's love of peace is unmasked long before the end as an especially rabid form of paranoia. But these literary afterthoughts do not modify the basic premise, which is unblushing national pride in the possession of world-destroying bacteriological weapons.

By science fiction standards, a mortal virus is the cheapest of gimmicks, since it requires nothing more expensive than a lot of people who can lie down. But even on the level of pop melodrama, the film makes no sense; as so often in recent thrillers, the script fails to explain why the villains don't kill the hero as soon as they capture him.

One speech from this jingoistic fable is worth anthologising. Examining a hole clipped through a wire fence, a security cop dourly observes: 'It's cut right to left. A righthanded man. Or a left-handed man who wants us to think he's righthanded.'

Repulsion; Mister Moses

The heroine of Roman Polanski's *Repulsion* has much in common with Tony Perkins in *Psycho*: a psychotic young virgin, she wants sex, hates herself for wanting it, and hates the opposite sex for making her want it. This distracted waif works in a beauty parlour and shares a Kensington flat with her sister, whose orgasmic moans (in the arms of a married lover) keep her awake, squirming with fascination and disgust.

This may suggest that the film is one of the laborious-lubricious kind that Peter Bull commemorates—in *I Say, Look Here!*, his buoyant new volume of memoirs—with the classically terse synopsis: 'It all took place in Sweden and rightly.' But nothing of the sort: Mr Polanski is a serious student of erotic tension, as we know from *Knife in the Water*, and although he is clearly a Hitchcock fan, he goes deeper than *Psycho* by presenting a double murder from the killer's, instead of the victim's, point of view.

The result is very nearly as shocking and far more clinically intimate, despite the fact that Polanski (unlike Hitchcock) offers no psychiatric explanation for the ghastly exploits of his protagonist. He draws us into Carol's nightmare world, so that we see it through her eyes—the eyes on which, in unblinking close-up, the picture begins and ends. 'One of the things we feel after reading a great work is "I have got out." Or from another point of view, "I have got in"; pierced the shell of some other monad and discovered what it is like inside'; thus C. S. Lewis. *Repulsion* is not a great work; the shell is not wholly pierced; but it is ferociously dented.

Sister goes off to Italy with her lover: when Carol is left alone in the flat, her pent-up fantasies begin a desperate proliferation. In a swinging wardrobe mirror we catch sight, briefly and horrifically, of a man who is not there: Carol's interior world has begun to externalise itself. Real cracks in the plaster now yawn and split the wall; lights blaze at midnight outside her bedroom door, and the imagined man rushes silently in to rape her. Objective reality exists only to fuel her neurosis with appropriate symbols—for example, the convent school next door, the crippled musicians in the street, and the rabbit, intended for the pot, which she leaves out on a plate like an aborted foetus. (Never a man to shrink from phallic symbolism, Polanski perhaps bangs the gong too hard when he makes Carol receive from her sister a picture postcard of the Tower of Pisa.) So nearly cataleptic is the girl's condition that she can walk past a car crash without noticing it. It seems entirely and inescapably logical that, when a would-be boy friend and an intimidating landlord make approaches to her, she should respectively club and slash them to death.

Catherine Deneuve, blonde and impassive, gives the role precisely the zombie quality it requires. Yvonne Furneaux and Ian Hendry shine in the background; and I blame the script (by Polanski and Gerard Brach) for the dim conventionality of John Fraser's performance as the slayer's suitor. Gill Taylor's camera work is beyond praise; note his use of a wide-angle lens to isolate Carol from the familiar surroundings, suddenly distant and cavernous, of her flat. The Compton Group, who financed *Repulsion*, have astutely signed Polanski up for two more pictures. They have nabbed quite a prize: there is no better director in the country than this unnerving Pole.

Mister Moses is the one about the African village that must either quit its ancestral home to accommodate the new dam or stay and get drowned. Like most films, it stars Carroll Baker. The running time is 115 minutes; the walking-out time is much earlier. The weather throughout is excellent.

The Disorderly Orderly; Harlow

Jerry Lewis could well be a stray, black-sheep member of J. D. Salinger's Glass family, a manic imbecile at large in a household of Quiz Kids. Look at his frenziedly speaking body, note his absolute worried certainty that no words, however often repeated in however many increasingly scrambled orders of precedence, can possibly do justice to the floods of panic and outrage and apology that plead within him for expression; above all, watch the electric spontaneity of his response to events, how totally he abandons himself to each leap, swerve, shriek or gurgle— this is exemplary Zen behaviour, in the finest traditions of the Glass menagerie.

Even at his loudest and wildest there is something saintly about Mr Lewis; saintly because vulnerable without pathos; willing to be wounded yet afraid to be struck. In *The Disorderly Orderly* he plays a would-be healer, condemned to remain a hospital errand-boy because of a crippling malady that unfits him for medical advancement: he suffers from empathy with his patients.

Listening, as he wheels Alice Pearce through the grounds, to her voluptuous accounts of multiple fractures and intestines in chaos ('My stomach is like a furnace in August'), he feels every twinge and incision, convulsed with vicarious pain. His guard is congenitally lowered.

Most Glass-like of all is his touching, climactic encounter with the basilisk Nurse Higgins (Kathleen Freeman), in whom his mere presence induces a state of lock-jaw that prevents her from addressing him except through permanently gritted teeth. A plate of oatmeal, flung at Mr Lewis, accidentally strikes her head-on. Motionless, she waits while he plucks fragments of china from her porridge-encrusted face. All at once, she starts to whimper; still plucking, he follows suit; and before long, warming to each other's distress, they are both sobbing in mutual commiseration. In this extraordinary sequence pure farce invades Salinger country; and for a moment one recalls, with no sense of incongruity, what Zooey Glass used to say about every fat woman being Jesus Christ.

Script and direction are by Frank Tashlin, who crams the footage with shiny, ingenious gags. The patient swathed in a plaster cast that crashes downhill and surrealistically proves to be hollow ('Come out!' Mr Lewis yells vainly at the debris); the recourse to silence and subtitles whenever a hospital sign reads 'Absolute Quiet'; the brash, elated exuberance of the car chase and the supermarket smash-up at the end—all these bear Mr Tashlin's stamp, as do the glancing gibes at commercialised medicine. ('No money, no bed' runs the hospital's motto.) The rest is pure Lewis, unbridled and galvanic, self-indulgent at times but never less than a geyser of comedic energy.

Written by John Michael Hayes and directed by Gordon Douglas, *Harlow* is that basest of Californian artifacts, a wholly commercial movie that professes to expose the commercialism of Hollywood. (The old saw holds good: where profit rules, truth abdicates.) Apart from Jean Harlow herself, her mother, her father-in-law and her suicidal husband— all of them dead and powerless to sue—the only historical character on view is the star's agent, Arthur Landau, who is presented as a paradigm of honour and integrity. Mr Landau's disclosures about his former client's private life enabled Irving Shulman to write the exceptionally scabrous biography on which the film is based. Public figures like Louis B. Mayer and Howard Hughes are veiled in opaque disguises, and—final absurdity —none of Jean Harlow's movies is mentioned by name.

This dingy charade spends two hours repeating a message already familiar in the first twenty minutes: 'All they want is my body.' Carroll Baker supplies the body, if not the erotic incandescence that made them want it. 'She didn't die of pneumonia,' says her agent after the girl gasps her last, 'she died of life.' In fact, she died of neither. Nothing reveals the essential mendacity of *Harlow* more clearly than its refusal to admit that a Hollywood sex symbol could die of uremic poisoning. Angela Lansbury, Raf Vallone and Red Buttons are among those who officiate at this shoddy exhumation.

Le Bonheur; Grand Hotel

Ancestor-worship abounds in Agnès Varda's *Le Bonheur*. Its summery, soft-focus colours, its adoring images of sunlit flesh and foliage all pay dazzled homage to Impressionism in general and late Renoir in particular.

Genuflection is also made to Renoir *fils*: the pastoral atmosphere of family outings on the fringes of Paris insistently recalls the master's *Partie de Campagne*. Whiffs of Godard are likewise detectable—first in Mlle Varda's choric use of advertising posters, as when the camera picks out a phrase like 'La Tentation' to hint at impending adultery; and again in the close-ups of intertwined limbs (cf. *Une Femme Mariée*) when the affair is fully launched. More subcutaneously, there are affinities with Jean-Jacques Bernard's 'theatre of quietism': from start to finish no voice is raised, except perhaps to attract the attention of a child.

Mlle Varda has absorbed these influences into her bloodstream. What gives her film its special boldness, its melting but non-cloying lyricism, is the fact that it presents a conventional triangle as two overlapping idylls. We begin with a happy family—a handsome young carpenter (Jean-Claude Drouot), his sweetly doting wife and two healthy children. Their life together is celebrated in frame after frame of glowing sensual fulfilment and domestic felicity.

Then M. Drouot meets and sleeps with a trim telephone operator, who dotes on him not more sweetly but differently; in relation to his wife she is not competitive but complementary. Mlle Varda lavishes the same visual poetry on the affair as on the marriage. Thus she commits herself to making a simple but deeply unpopular statement: that it is possible to love two people simultaneously.

When the hero admits his attachment, his wife offers no protest; indeed, they make love immediately afterwards. Later, he wakes up to find that she has crept away and drowned herself. He goes off on a long holiday with the children and then returns to marry his mistress. The ending is as golden as the beginning: a husband and wife are taking the family out for a picnic.

With unblaming, even rapturous, acceptance, the film tells a story that would normally be treated with a cynical grimace or a tragic frown. Mlle Varda measures the necessity of seeking happiness against the risk of inflicting pain. While lamenting the risk, she cannot help—eventually, on balance, with however many provisos—extolling the necessity. Every shot is a tender glorification of the physical world. By way of spiritual endorsement, the background music is by Mozart; and not a note seems out of place.

Grand Hotel, directed by Edmund Goulding in 1932, was one of the first all-star extravaganzas, with Garbo, Crawford, Wallace Beery and two Barrymores (Lionel and John) confined in a towering honeycomb of cubicles that must have borne more than a passing resemblance to the Metro studios at the time. It was also the precursor of many cross-section-type movies, in which stars from all walks of life are thrown together by chance in the same hostelry, aeroplane, liner, lifeboat, stranded bus, Jap-held island, etc. *Grand Hotel*, which takes place in Berlin, shows its age for a shriekingly obvious reason: not one of the characters is American. I cannot think of a single Hollywood picture set in postwar Europe of which the same could be said.

Beery, as a German industrialist, threatened with bankruptcy, is noisily grating; Crawford plays his secretary ('They call me Flaemmchen') with the ungroomed cockiness of a nervous tyro; and both the Barrymores are incorrigibly stagebound—Lionel as an elderly clerk on the spree, and lordly, seedy, glassy-eyed John as a baron turned jewel thief. Remains Garbo, striding through the lobby cocooned in mink and chinchilla; an emigrée ballerina to whom everything since the fall of St Petersburg seems 'so threadbare', a wailing egomaniac who famously 'wants to be alone'—until she meets the baron, whereupon she magically switches from broad Slavonic satire to pure romantic pathos.

Clasping Barrymore's head like a goblet, she gives the lie to an old maxim; *post coitum*, this rangy Swedish animal is not sad but exultant, whirling around her apartment like an unbroken colt. Her technical skill is unsleeping; note how she keeps her compassionate lips an inch or two higher than Barrymore's, thereby up-screening an actor too wily to be upstaged. In the poetic intensity with which she gives voice to banalities, Garbo has no modern rivals; except possibly Callas.

Two Dispatches from Venice: (1) 4 September 1965

> *It's no go your Bergman, it's no go*
> *Fellini,*
> *All they want is John and Paul,*
> *and a starlet in a bikini. . . .*

Venice in the rain: D. H. Lawrence's 'abhorrent, green, slippery city' can seldom have looked danker. The Lido is a sodden strip of sand, Coney Island without the animation. Film critics slump in the lobby of the Excelsior Palace, like steerage passengers on some nightmare cruise: shipboard romances and feuds strike up, and the hotel itself, huge and stupendously crenellated, grows daily more like a superannuated liner. (Why aren't the chairs bolted to the floor?) One old hand insists that this is the drabbest of all Venice festivals; no, says another, the *second* drabbest.

Word comes that the promised *bonne-bouche*—Fellini's first colour film—will be withdrawn; the director isn't happy with the quality of the print. The gloom thickens. You begin to feel that there is a paradox in the very phrase 'film festival': isn't it perverse and inherently unfestive to go to a seaside resort and spend most of one's day in the dark? Sixteen hours have been devoted to rejected footage from Robert Flaherty's *Louisiana Story*: you get a powerful sense of madness closing in when, after something like forty-eight shots of a tree, the cameraman-commentator pensively remarks: 'We got a bit hung up on that tree.'

Veteran delegates swap nostalgic tales of the old days, when there were fireworks on the beach and the usherettes wore crinolines in honour of Anna Neagle; when Hollywood came to the ball *en masse*, and the first male acting award went to Wallace Beery in *Viva Villa*. 'Oh for a Cary Grant retrospective!' I hear a colleague yearning; and I guiltily know what he means, having just returned from a mute German melodrama whose Swedish sub-titles were translated via loudspeaker into Italian and conveyed to me in French by an adjacent Greek.

The critics may mourn the passing of glamorous gaiety, but they deplored it when it flourished. The festival they sniff at today is the festival they begged for fifteen years ago. 'It used to exist for the public,' a disgruntled Venetian told me, 'now it exists for the critics.' Mussolini created it in 1932 to bring prestige and tourists to Italy, and to keep the latter in Venice after the bad weather had begun. Luigi Chiarini, its director since 1963, is an aesthetic puritan, a Savonarola of the cinema with little time for those who go to the movies for entertainment. Formerly a Fascist supporter, he reappeared after the war as a convert to the extreme Left. Talking to this bald, stocky evangelist, I glean the following opinions:

> You are not here to amuse yourself. You can do that in the cinemas around the Piazza San Marco. This is not a fête, it is an exhibition. We are not interested in stars, and spectacle, but in research and experiment. . . . There are two kinds of audiences I care

about—the students who go to the retrospective shows and the ordinary people of Venice, who see the festival films in our open-air cinema. I don't regard the dignitaries who see the official indoor showings as a serious audience ... There is only one door through which to enter a work of art: the door of form. I am an impenitent formalist. Form reflects the artist's historical need.

Chiarini's choice of films for this year's festival has been characteristically personal. One was beyond all classification: it came from Korea and the synopsis began: *Samyong, who is dumb, has been in the service of the Oh family since Mr Oh was a child, and is devoted to his son, whose bad character and violence have disgusted everybody.*
The rest fell into three categories. I append my notes on each:

1. Films in which life is seen as a hostile jungle, *and irremediably so.* This was by far the largest group. *Mickey One*, the American contender, is Kafka plus Fellini crossed with Nelson Algren and William Saroyan. The hero is a night-club comic on the run, pursued by a mysterious Syndicate that may represent anything from the Mafia to the Hound of Heaven: convinced that he is 'guilty of not being innocent', he dashes through scenes of garish brutality to a final confrontation which implies that the Syndicate does not exist. One's attention slackens as the symbols multiply. Warren Beatty plays the lead: a nervy, indistinct performance, repeatedly falling back on mannerisms remembered from Brando. Arthur Penn directed this exercise in unmotivated hysteria.

Tadeusz Konwicki's *Salto* (Poland) is equally paranoid. A saintly scapegoat arrives in a village claiming that 'they' (unidentified) are after him, and that he has come to keep an appointment with death. All the inhabitants symbolise sins (or neuroses), and the stranger, conceivably meant to be a modern Christ-figure, is finally stoned out of town. The script reeks of the theatre, where it would be only marginally more boring. Only the presence of Zbigniew Cybulski, magnetic and unpredictable, keeps one watching.

From Mexico, *Simon del Desierto*, a caustic forty-minute caprice by Luis Bunuel, its hero a modern version of Simon Stylites who flees the world to commune with God from the top of a pillar. Here Satan tempts him in various guises—as a monk who knocks the sacrament, as a schoolgirl who bares her breasts—until, persuaded that it is cowardly to opt out of life, he joins the fiend on a trip to a nightclub in Greenwich Village. Conclusion: those who twist are the devil's seed. I was mildly amused: to love or hate Bunuel's recent work it is probably necessary to believe in God.

Carl Dreyer's *Gertrud* was shown and received in a spirit of homage to the seventy-five-year-old director of *La Passion de Jeanne d'Arc* and *Day of Wrath*. Taken from a nineteenth-century Swedish play, it exudes a pungent whiff of secondhand Ibsen and Sudermann. A resolute 'new woman' abandons her politician husband in favour of a wild young Bohemian artist and is sadly let down, whereupon she retires into lifelong solitude. (I admit the film to the life-is-a-jungle pigeonhole on the frail pretext of its final statement: that love inevitably leads to loneliness.)

If you relish interminable two-shots in which tight-lipped, well-dressed people seated on sofas go through emotional crises without ever looking at one another, you will adore *Gertrud*. One such scene, between the bolting wife and a former lover, I found moderately moving. Critics fed up with the new orthodoxy of quick cuts and no continuity may hail *Gertrud* as a return to a lost classicism: in fact, it's plain old Victorian theatre in a rather gelid state of preservation.

2. Films in which life is seen as a hostile jungle, *but capable of change*. Only one entrant in this category: *Akahige* (*Red-Beard*), by Akira Kurosawa—a Venetian favourite ever since he won the Golden Lion in 1951 with *Rashomon*, which marked the Japanese cinema's first conquest of the Western world. His new work is something of a disappointment: a hospital drama not intrinsically different from a medical series on television. The period, as so often in Japanese films, is hard to define: all one can say is that it is pre-bicycle, post-Samurai, and probably eighteenth century.

There are several sequences of exotic savagery that would upset Dr Gillespie—a murder attempt by a nymphomaniac armed with a lethal hatpin, an operation on an unanaesthetised girl ('Put her intestines back,' snaps the surgeon), and a brawl in which the head of the hospital (Toshiro Mifune) casually breaks about a dozen arms and legs in order to rescue a feverish twelve-year-old girl from a brothel. For the rest, Mr Mifune is a crusty, twinkling old medico of the Hollywood school, who knows how to cope with recalcitrant interns and displays, in his handling of unloved children, a knowledge of psychiatry altogether startling in feudal Japan.

3. Films in which life is seen as a hostile jungle, *but fun*. Again, a solo entry: Jean-Luc Godard's *Pierrot le Fou*, booed by the festival audience and trampled on by the Italian Press—'Godard the madman,' ran a typical local headline. The film is a *roman policier* in which Jean-Paul Belmondo gets mixed up with Anna Karina, who in turn is mixed up with a quasi-political organisation which chases them both to the South of France, where Belmondo discovers that she has betrayed him, shoots

her out of hand and then commits suicide by wrapping sticks of dynamite around his head.

It's a ragbag of *trouvailles*, a free-wheeling holiday movie, an assault on narrative continuity, a surrender to free association and chance encounters. The unit accidentally bumped into Raymond Devos, the great French comic; the result is an extraneous but enormously funny Devos monologue. Godard happened upon an old lady who seemed ideal casting for the Queen of Lebanon in exile; so he wrote in the part, and there she is, triumphantly playing it.

There are puns, songs, aphorisms, literary allusions, topical gags, quotes from ads, spasms of cruelty, interludes of mime and long, inconsequent conversations in cars. The Belmondo character enjoys the Crusoe-life and would clearly prefer to be in some other film; he cajoles Karina into spending a few idyllic days on the Mediterranean littoral, but before long she whisks him away to his own doom and hers. A wilful, aimless, anarchic movie, but also an act of revelry, dedicated to the art of astonishing us.

At his Press conference, Godard insisted that *Pierrot le Fou* was a realistic film (I remember Alain Robbe-Grillet saying exactly the same thing about *L'Année Dernière a Marienbad*). Later, in a private chat, he elaborated; a darkly balding man in his mid-thirties, intent but not intense, and keen to be precisely understood:

> I make no distinction between art and life. Cinema is halfway between art and life.... 'Pierrot le Fou' has more improvisation than anything else I have made. Most of it came out of my head just before it was shot. I worked without notes, like a painter. Anything I saw might end up in the picture. Perhaps I have carried this method as far as it will go....
>
> I took eight weeks to finish shooting—twice as long as usual. The editing was done in a fortnight. We put the shots together more or less as they happened: I don't do many retakes.... I'm not interested in beautiful images. With Antonioni, the colour seems to be inside the camera. With me, it's simply what is in front of the camera....
>
> Every age has its own way of telling stories. Mine is not that of the thirties and forties. It's more like the silent cinema, where you're always jumping from action to emotion and back again. That's why I call *Pierrot le Fou* the first modern movie *before* D. W. Griffiths.... I'm always hearing that films date. Who cares if *A Bout de Souffle* dates? It sums up 1960. Have you noticed how

people say: 'I've just seen an old Eisenstein film'—and how they never say: 'I've just read an old Stendhal novel'?

I wish Godard would come right out and confess that this flighty, haphazard film was really a toy, an unserious playwith. But no French-man could ever admit to an aim so trivial; some philosophic justification would have to be invented. The French, on the whole, are no good at games; nothing appals them more than the notion of sport for sport's sake.

The seven international jurors will make their decisions on Monday. All the evidence suggests that the Golden Lion will go to Luchino Visconti's *Vaghe Stelle Dell'Orsa* (scheduled for showing tomorrow), if only because of the almighty fuss its director created in 1960, when he failed to win the prize with *Rocco and his Brothers*.

There may be no future for festivals like Venice. The openings for art movies have vastly increased since the war, and the prospect of com-petition tends more and more to discourage all entrants save those with nothing to lose. Why, after all, should a commercial producer take the risk of being turned down by the Venice committee; and of exposing himself, if accepted, to the collective onslaught of the international Press?

> *It's no go the Godard, it's no go the*
> *Flaherty,*
> *All they want is Tuesday Weld and a Zanuck*
> *cocktail party* . . .

(2) *11 September 1965*

As most people (including the victor himself) had expected, Luchino Visconti's *Vaghe Stelle dell'Orsa* carried off the Golden Lion in Venice last week. The result was a triumph of chic. Kurosawa's *Akahige*, despite lapses into sentimentality, was a finer film, and so was the unpretentious Czech entry, Milos Forman's *Loves of a Blonde*; but nothing could with-stand Visconti, who arrived at the Lido with a swarm of courtiers in midnight blue, like a feudal prince on a State visit to some outlying dependency.

Vaghe Stelle dell'Orsa (a phrase lifted from Leopardi: when films borrow their titles from poets, beware of pretentiousness) is a family tragedy loaded with Greek overtones and shot with high fashion-plate gloss by Armando Nannuzzi. The daughter of a great Jewish scientist who died in Auschwitz returns after a long absence to the parental home in Tuscany; here, in a variety of expensive interiors, she encounters her batty mother (Marie Bell) and the latter's wartime lover, both of whom (it is hinted) may have been involved in betraying Papa to the Nazis. More important, she runs into her pretty but penniless brother, in whose presence she gets neurotically edgy—so much so that she locks her bedroom door against him at night.

After many oblique accusations, sealed lips are steamed open and the film yields up its puny central secret: in adolescence she had a fleeting incestuous affair with her brother, who attempts to blackmail her but finally takes an overdose of pills when their guilty relationship is exposed. Claudia Cardinale, a doll-face modelled in puppy-fat, plays Visconti's Electra, while Jean Sorel is the pseudo-Orestes: and two less likely members of a Jewish family I have seldom seen.

The whole set-up is offensively contrived: the Greek parallel is invoked to add tragic profundity, and the Jewish background to lend contemporary relevance. Visconti recently directed a genuine tragedy of incest, *'Tis Pity She's a Whore*, on the Parisian stage, and made a memorably cold-blooded mess of it. His new film is likewise anaemic. It recalls Julian Green's *South*, a play that belied homosexuality by treating it with neoclassical portentousness.

In its dying throes, Venice unveiled two masterpieces. One was the Russian *War and Peace*, shown *hors de concours*; lasting three and a half hours, it leaves two-thirds of Tolstoy's novel still unshot, but already one recognises a cinematic *chef d'oeuvre*. The prime mover is Sergie Bondartchuk, director and co-author of the script, who also plays Pierre.

A pre-title sequence alerts us that something magnificent is toward: swooping aerial shots of rivers and forests, intercut with sudden flashes of battle and accompanied by bubbling electronic music, suck us back to the past as in a time machine. Before long we plunge into an officers' party, with the camera lurching and swaying, while a mascot bear guzzles vodka and dissonant chords are drunkenly banged on a piano. The wide-screen colour camera behaves throughout with the mobility of an eagle. From towering vistas we descend without a cut to close-shots of leaves on a stream: and what could be more Tolstoyan than this synoptic vision, embracing alike the general and the particular?

The battle of Austerlitz is a massive, tumultuous set-piece, crowned by an intimate *tableau* that Géricault might have signed: 'Voilà une belle mort,' says a French officer, surveying a dead Russian standard-bearer. For a climax, look at Natasha's first ball, a dazzling vertiginous gala that makes *My Fair Lady* look like a junior prom. The camera waltzes and pirouettes, brushing obstacles aside; now peering from the ceiling, now skimming at shoulder-height; so that our eyes, as well as Natasha's, are misted with tears of amazement. In the absence of subtitles, I can't judge the dialogue scenes; but if Bondartchuk's Pierre, Ludmilla Savelyeva's Natasha and Vyacheslav Tiksonov's Andrey are far from Tolstoy's intentions, I shall be mightily startled.

The second Venice masterpiece had nothing to do with the festival: a prizewinner at Locarno in August, *I Pugni in Tasca* was privately screened on the Lido to an audience of potential distributors. It cries out for a public showing: scripted and directed by Marco Bellocchio (aged twenty-five), it has a technical finesse and an emotional authority that few first films can ever have surpassed. It concerns a fatherless, precariously well-to-do family in northern Italy, who, at first sight, seem scarcely more than normally belligerent, but who gradually reveal, in the sudden, outlandish violence of their reactions to relatively innocuous stimuli, that there is epilepsy in their blood. Apart from mother, who is blind, there are three sons and a daughter. The middle son, a psychopath bursting with animal energy, decides to kill his mother in order to enrich the family with her legacy. Having succeeded, he goes on to murder his younger brother—whereafter the film becomes a horrific, cautionary tale about a child determined to revenge himself simultaneously on his heredity and his environment.

Lou Castel plays the killer with a light-hearted dynamism, a casual boyish fury, that puts one in mind of an under-age Brando—except that the final desperate scene, in which he plays a record of 'Traviata' and dies miming the soprano's voice as it soars over his terminal convulsions, is uniquely his, and no other living actor could better it. Castel and Bellocchio are names to remember: we will surely hear them again.

The Organizer

Mario Monicelli's *The Organizer* is the kind of film about a strike that could never be made in Britain. It keeps its eyes fixed on a specific dispute in a specific historical setting; it doesn't generalise or sentimentalise, it doesn't try to placate all sections of the audience, and it sees no reason to extend the same sympathy to both sides of a manifestly unfair struggle. It also assumes that the spectacle of people learning, by arduous trial and painful error, how to claim their social rights is exciting in itself, not merely as a background for comic proles and strike-crossed lovers.

The only dishonest thing about Monicelli's film is the title foisted on it by the distributors. They obviously decided that *The Organizer*—individualistic and vaguely criminal-sounding—was more likely to be box-office catnip than 'The Comrades' (a literal translation of the original *I Campagni*) or 'The Strikers' (a tolerable alternative), both of which reek in Britain of Redness. Such is the fruit of indoctrination, and you can see it blooming daily in the headlines of the Western press, where strikers are always the enemy, never the managements.

Films like Monicelli's may help to repair the imbalance. Textile workers in Turin at the turn of the century are campaigning for a thirteen-hour day. Their first gesture of defiance fails; when a volunteer blows the whistle an hour earlier than usual, nobody has the nerve to walk out. There now arrives from Genoa a bearded, myopic young professor who darns his own socks, plays the piccolo and turns out to be a professional agitator, long wanted by the police. It is his combination of unselfish zeal and practical experience that inspires the workers to go on strike. Hardship increases; wives complain; a train-load of imported scabs is repelled in pitched battle, after which a man lies dead. The management agrees to meet the workers' representatives, offering jocular, paternal forgiveness in return for total capitulation. Eventually the army fires on a demonstrating crowd, and another man is killed.

Throughout it all the professor (Marcello Mastroianni's best performance: a latterday saint played with busy, unheroic earthiness) goes on battling for a principle that must eventually win. This is Zola without the melodrama, Galsworthy's *Strife* without the false premise that employers and employees are equally matched and thus equally entitled to our charity. In full middle-age, having spent most of his adult life directing Toto, the Italian clown, Monicelli has made a film that is less flamboyant but far more rational and persuasive than Eisenstein's historic *Strike*. Mastroianni apart, Annie Girardot, Folco Lulli and Bernard Blier are among those memorably present.

Ship of Fools

Katherine Anne Porter wrote the novel, Abby Mann turned it into a screenplay, and Stanley Kramer directed the result. All three are becalmed in *Ship of Fools* which is not *Grand Hotel* afloat but rather *Grand Hotel* aground in the shallows of Mr Kramer's imagination. On the whole I prefer the title bestowed on it by Randolph Churchill, who described in a recent dispatch to the *Evening Standard* how Paris had flocked to the première of what he called—translating back from the French—'The Boat of the Mad'.

Steaming from Mexico to Germany in 1933, the boat numbers among its mad about a dozen well-known actors, several of them blatantly lying about their age. They go in two by two. Penniless young artist (George Segal) pairs off with rich young mistress (Elizabeth Ashley), from whom he learns that social protest is not only bad for his art but a sign of maladjustment. (This at the depth of the Depression!) Jose Ferrer, overplaying the role of an anti-semitic publisher so robustly that you expect him to hold his nose whenever a Jew enters the room, pairs off with a busty Aryan blonde. An ostracised Jewish businessman (Heinz Ruehmann, all dapper worldliness and misplaced optimism) pairs platonically off with a philosophic dwarf (Michael Dunn), who is likewise a pariah, and acts as chorus to the movie.

Vivien Leigh, as a waspish American divorcée, has no one to pair off with: deflecting amorous passes with sleek, misanthropic aplomb, she is eventually reduced to addressing herself in the mirror. Within its Shaftesbury Avenue limits, this is a glittering and not over-glamourised performance. The most effective pairing, winning by a neck from Miss Leigh and her mirror, is that of Oskar Werner and Simone Signoret. Mr Werner is the ship's doctor, a heavy-lidded young cardiac case with a catlike presence, a despondent smile and a voice as precisely sour as vinegar. Mme Signoret is a Spanish countess, many years his senior, who needs the drugs he can provide, and falls genuinely in love with the provider. 'My darling, my love, for once let's kiss in broad daylight': only an actress like Mme Signoret could take a parting line as banal as that, and inform it with such a terrible sense of erotic loss.

This twosome apart, I would barely have winced if Mr Kramer's ark had struck an iceberg; and Jose Greco's flamenco troupe, who occupy the screen for several minutes of irrelevant clamour, would rank exceptionally low on my list of lifeboat priorities.

Lady L; The Heroes of Telemark

For eccentric detail, Peter Ustinov has a dandy's eye and ear. In *Lady L*, which he has scripted and directed, a middle-aged woman bumps into David Niven at a costume ball and brightly remarks: 'We're going to Australia next week—have you any messages for anyone?' We never see her again; she vanishes into the throng as swiftly and inexplicably as she rose from Mr Ustinov's crowded imagination. Or from his memory; for what we call imagination can usually be defined as the ability to make unexpected leaps from one corner of an omniretentive memory to another.

Mr Ustinov's own brief appearance as a deranged Bavarian princeling is an eccentric detail in itself; so short is his attention span that during military march-pasts his saluting hand keeps drifting away from his forehead and needs an equerry to guide it back. The film is studded with turn-of-the-century *trouvailles*—a band of anarchists disguised as priests, a private train whose ducal owner is guarded by karate experts, and a profusion of fantastically ornate interiors, among them a Lautrec brothel where the special amenities include a room designed to simulate a moving railway compartment. Colour heightens the rococo gaiety.

Though based on Romain Gary's novel (which I have not read), the script bears all the trademarks we associate with Mr Ustinov. He has burst through the confines of his English birth to become the *émigré's émigré*, a man to whom every human being is a foreigner. We note his passion for aphorisms about national characteristics (as in *The Love of Four Colonels*, few ethnic groups in Europe go unmentioned); for pompous families with skeletons rattling in the cupboards of their lineage (cf. *The Banbury Nose*); and for episodic structure, held together by running gags—compare the recurrent photographer in *The Moment of Truth* with the recurrent bomb-throwings in *Lady L*.

We also note a familiar Ustinov weakness. Many individual passages are pearls; what they lack is adequate stringing. Mr Ustinov's polyglot fairies showered his cradle with every gift save that of sustaining a narrative; he cannot make us care what happens next. It is no accident that the plot of his most successful play, *Romanoff and Juliet*, was borrowed from Shakespeare. In *Lady L* Sophia Loren plays a Corsican laundress who falls in love with a dashing French thief (Paul Newman) and ends up married to an effete English duke (David Niven, unchallenged seigneur of the comic domain that lies between a smile and a wince). She remains a cipher throughout, at whose motives we can only guess. Nothing drives her from one episode to the next except Mr Ustinov's impatience to move to a new location. Claude Dauphin plays the Peter Sellers part (a fumbling French detective, redolent of *The Pink Panther*) in this procession of glittering tableaux. The director himself, perhaps in a vain attempt at artistic unity, dubs one or two of the supporting roles. Castle Howard, type-cast, makes an imposing guest appearance as itself.

Little acting is involved in *The Heroes of Telemark*, directed by Anthony Mann from a script by Ivan Moffat and Ben Barzman: as members of the Norwegian resistance, Kirk Douglas and Richard Harris are mainly required to run about to music and register controlled apprehension in close-up. (As usual, the music does most of the acting, with the customary distribution of parts: horns for the moments of grandeur, skittish woodwinds for interludes of domestic lyricism, sweeping violins to enliven transitional bits in which nothing much is going to happen, and unresolved chords on any combination of instruments to indicate menace.)

Mr Douglas talks through a grinning rictus of bared and gritted teeth, like a demented ventriloquist. Mr Harris, on the other hand, favours a kind of thunderous calm; gazing meaningfully at Mr Douglas, he plays the Hollywood version of the one-upmanship game, otherwise known as 'I'm cooler than you' or 'I can out-relax any man in the unit'. Together, defying an archetypal Nazi commandant (Eric Porter) who revives nostalgic memories of wartime propaganda movies, they plot the destruction of a factory that is producing heavy water for the Germans. Twice foiled, they eventually succeed in sinking a cargo of the stuff *en route* for the Reich.

Apart from its dramatic merits or shortcomings, the film poses questions of truth or falsehood. It is dedicated to the Norwegian resistance fighters who prevented Germany from getting the atomic bomb and thus saved the world from Nazi domination. But did they? According to Margaret Gowing's authoritative book on *Britain and Atomic Energy 1939–45*, the Allies knew quite early on that the Nazis were interested in heavy water to develop power rather than weapons, and that 'there was no danger of the Germans acquiring an atomic bomb before the Allies'. In other words, the script's pretensions rest on an exploded premise.

Tre Epic that Never Was; The Best of Busby Berkeley

Early in 1937, shooting began at Denham Studios on Alexander Korda's production of *I, Claudius*, which was to have been the mightiest epic that Britain had ever thrown into the balance of world cinema.

Charles Laughton, with Nero, Henry VIII, Papa Barrett, Captain Bligh and Rembrandt already under his steadily expanding belt, was to play Robert Graves's anti-hero, the stuttering, halting, profoundly unwilling Emperor Claudius. Merle Oberon was cast as Messalina and

Emlyn (*Night Must Fall*) Williams as Caligula; Flora Robson and Robert Newton were in prominent attendance; and Josef von Sternberg was hired to direct. Four weeks after the cameras started rolling, Miss Oberon was concussed in a car smash. The production was called off, the insurance company paid up, and people have wondered for twenty-eight years exactly what happened in that fruitless, expensive month.

The Epic That Never Was lifts the veil at last. Brilliantly compiled by Bill Duncalf, it contains all the news of the great fiasco that's fit to print. The surviving participants testify in filmed interviews. Robert Graves airily alleges that the script was written by one of Korda's Hungarian chums. (According to von Sternberg's autobiography, the authors were Carl Zuckmayer and Lester Cohen.) Merle Oberon, sounding like something of a pill, insists that the film was intended as a showcase for her, not Laughton. In a few ponderous, pipe-sucking minutes, von Sternberg reveals all the humourless assertiveness that made it so difficult for Laughton to get on with him. From Korda's former script girl we learn how Laughton, having sweated over his role for weeks in deepening gloom, burst on to the set one day and said: 'Don't you realise—it's Edward VIII!'—after which he would never play a scene without listening to a record of the abdication speech.

Then we watch the rushes, and realise at once that when Miss Oberon's chauffeur crashed into that oncoming car, a great screen performance was still-born. At first Claudius is everyone's butt, a holy simpleton who lurches loose-lipped through the jeering crowd, accepting derision almost as his birthright. He is humble not because he limps and stammers but because he has outgrown the need to feel superior to those who mock him. To convey moral goodness without playing for pathos or selfrighteousness is a high tightrope for any actor; yet Laughton walks it without a single false step. He is a grown-up Piggy out of *Lord of the Flies*.

Later, when he must show the Senate that he is fit to be emperor, the shambling clown grows before our eyes into a ruler, forcing his recalcitrant lips to express his purposes until the corrupt assembly is ready to give him best. The speech in which this transformation takes place could only (as Dirk Bogarde says in the admirable narration) be delivered by an actor kissed with genius.

Another nostalgic pipeline to the 1930s was opened last week, with the presentation of *The Best of Busby Berkeley*—an anthology of production numbers devised and directed by a man summed up in the credit titles as 'the Master Builder of the American Musical Film'. Berkeley's was the era when crooners whistled, wore billowing trousers and were usually Dick Powell; when chorus girls danced on acres of shiny black floor, were constantly caught in the rain, played neon-lit violins, formed jigsaw puzzles of the American flag, wore hooped *tortillas* of satin, waltzed on serpentine staircases, slid down water-chutes like medieval sinners on their way to hell, and—the Berkeley trademark *par excellence* —were shot from above in concentric circles, at once floral and anal in design.

Berkeley's routines were militarily drilled to the verge of dehumanisation; only occasionally does a Cagney, a Joan Blondell or a Ruby Keeler break through the iron-clad choreography. (Looking immensely frisky, Miss Keeler put in a personal appearance last week: 'I feel,' she said, 'that you're laughing with me and not at me.' Mr Berkeley, stolid and silver-haired, was also on hand to answer questions: he astonished the audience by declaring that his numbers had all been shot with only one camera.) The Berkeley technique, though always streamlined and often breathtaking, is seldom lovable. It is a highly mechanised form of visual fun: but we belie it if we call it art.

Life at the Top: The Spy Who Came In From the Cold

Two best-selling anti-heroes (for once, a useful vogueword) turned up last week in two firstrate films: John Braine's Joe Lampton in *Life at the Top* and John Le Carré's Alec Leamas in *The Spy Who Came In From the Cold*. As we shall see, they are brothers under the skin.

Both inhabit a moral landscape where *sauve-qui-peut* is all that remains of the law. Both are prisoners of wrong choices made long ago and now irrevocable. Both are wistfully attracted to idealistic women; and in each case we note that the uncorrupted woman is drawn with less conviction than anyone else in the script. Moreover, both films share the same purpose—namely, to show how social and political pressure erodes individual autonomy. Leamas and Lampton discover, in the bitter course of events, that instead of being free agents they are pawns in somebody else's game. They even frequent the same settings; Lampton clinches his first metropolitan business deal in a Soho strip-club almost identical with the one in which Leamas names his price to a Communist spy-ring.

I'm not forcing these analogies to suit critical convenience; they really exist, and there's an excellent reason why we should expect them to. The two anti-heroes are interdependent, opposite sides of the same pinchbeck coin. Joe Lampton is a product of the compromised society that

Alec Leamas is paid to protect. Their contaminated values spring from the same source.

We meet Joe ten years after his marriage, in *Room at the Top*, to the mill-owner's daughter. He resents being owned by his father-in-law (a sledgehammer performance by Donald Wolfit) and still feels a stranger in the lofty Victorian mansions that overlook the huddled slums where he was born. Ted Kotcheff's direction, at first too spendthrift with shock cuts and zooms, soon sheds the gimmicks and gets down to business. A wife-swapping, log-rolling world of North Country opulence is solidly established, with the aid of a stinging script by Mr Kotcheff's fellow-Canadian, Mordecai Richler.

Perhaps in the interests of audience identification, Joe himself seems less of a bastard than when we last saw him. Though unhappy with his wife (unsentimentally played by Jean Simmons), he stays faithful until he finds her in bed with a slimy neighbour; and when he starts an affair with a high-principled TV reporter (Honor Blackman), it's made clear that he does so because she appeals to his long-anaesthetised integrity. Eventually he goes out into the cold, joining her in London and quitting the family firm; but since he has just been refused a seat on the board of directors, one questions the idealism of his motives. There's an ambiguity here that the script fails to resolve—of which, indeed, it seems blithely unaware.

This quibble apart, Joe's London jaunt—a financial and sexual disaster—is brutally credible. Only towards the end of the film, when flashbacks from *Room at the Top* precede an implausibly swift return to power in Warley, does disbelief once more intrude. Laurence Harvey plays Joe with exactly the kind of gaunt shallowness that would pass, in Joe's mind, for sincerity. I hope this leaves no one in doubt that I admire Mr Harvey's performance.

The Spy Who Came In From The Cold is a strictly loyal screen transfer of Mr Le Carré's book, that grim exposition of the ignoble art of double-bluff. It begins, as it ends, with violence on the frontier between East and West Berlin; between these two explosions, no one is killed and very few blows are struck. This is an exercise in political logic—the bread of espionage, not the circuses of Bondery. Richard Burton gives his best screen performance as Leamas, the weary professional drudge who poses as a defector in order to plant false information that will incriminate the head of East German counter-intelligence. As the film progresses, Mr Burton's dour and expressively ravaged face comes to resemble a bullet-chipped wall against which many executions have taken place.

Claire Bloom, rising above the flabbier pages of an otherwise muscular script (by Paul Dehn and Guy Trosper), plays the fervent young Communist librarian with whom Leamas falls in love and whom he unwittingly endangers. The supporting cast consists mainly of East German spies, carefully observing the rigid pecking order that forbids more than momentary contact between inferiors and superiors in the security chain. Robert Hardy snubs Michael Hordern, Sam Wanamaker brushes off Mr Hardy and Oskar Werner rebuffs Mr Wanamaker. All these players are flawless; and there's a brief but telling intervention by Peter Van Eyck as the Communist boss on whose putative treachery the whole plot hangs.

Perhaps the *dénouement*, here conveyed solely in words, is not as pole-axing as it ought to be; otherwise, Martin Ritt's direction is beyond praise. Although *The Spy* and *Life at the Top* are anti-heroic films, they have a hero in common. His name is Oswald Morris, who was the cameraman on both pictures. They deserve a place of honour among the triumphs of black-and-white photography.

The Difficulty of Being Dull

Given a reasonable budget, it is hard to make an entirely boring movie. This is one of the radical differences between cinema and the other narrative arts. Typeface and binding never redeemed a bad novel, and bad plays are very rarely saved by acting or direction; but even the worst movies employ so many expensive skills that they can seldom be totally dull. (Hence the cult of bad horror pictures; one can't imagine a cult of bad plays.)

Let the script, direction and star performances be never so drab, they still cannot guarantee boredom. A brilliant cameraman, a master of editing or a couple of vivid supporting players can readily come to the rescue. Or a composer: much of contemporary cinema is a musical art form, with illustrative pictures and dialogue interludes. Or a designer: we know what the Bond films owe to Ken Adam's decor.

If all else fails, there is always the cinema's ace of trumps: mobility. Exciting locations are great saviours of drivel. When chopped into fragments, set against constantly changing backgrounds, and shot at varying distances from constantly shifting viewpoints, even the dullest writing and acting can hold one's attention. Seen from one angle in permanent long-shot against the same background—seen (in other words) as in the theatre—they would soon prove unbearably tedious. What theatre exposes, film can conceal

Yet the cinema's advantage is also its pitfall. Where tedium is so easily avoided, there is a terrible temptation to settle for the negative virtue of not being boring. The script may be flat and the star hung-over; but you've got Dmitri Tiomkin to write the score, Walter Matthau in a guest appearance, Oswald Morris behind the camera, and a location in Tahiti, so how can you lose?

My Home is Copacabana

A kite sways in the breeze over Rio de Janeiro. It is held by a small black boy who lives with three other children in a ramshackle hut overlooking the famous bay. All of them are parentless, either orphaned or abandoned; nowhere on earth, perhaps, does extreme poverty command a more spectacular view.

So much we glean from the opening shots of *My Home is Copacabana*, a semi-documentary masterpiece whose author, director, cameraman and editor all bear the same name: Arne Sucksdorff, a brilliant Swede long renowned for his studies of wild life. Here he shows us a human jungle flourishing on the fringe of a prosperous city, and the wild ones are a romping, scavenging, frequently starving quartet of illiterate eleven-year-olds, who range in pigment from deepest jet to palest octoroon. They believe that God must be white, since he so blatantly favours his own; and if one or two whites are unhappy, it must be because the Devil is black.

Sucksdorff's Rio is not the classless carnival town of *Orfeu Negro*; it is a banquet reserved for the bourgeoisie, whose scraps the children avidly swoop down to steal. In one ecstatic sequence, they stick pulverised glass to the string of their kite and cut down all its rivals on the beach. Climbing home with the spoils, they find their hut occupied by bandits—outsiders like themselves, but adult and armed.

For begging purposes, they have to learn how to *look* hungry. Hunger itself is not enough, and neither is honesty: when one of them truthfully declares that he has no name, address or parents, nobody believes him. Thereafter—and far more profitably—he tells lurid lies. As long as they eat, the kids are safe from the authorities. Or so they think until Toninho (Antonio Carlos de Lima), a runaway from reform school, wakes up with a toothache after a night on the beach. His chum Jorghino (Cosme Dos Santos) performs an amateur extraction that only increases the pain. Medical care costs money, so Toninho is forced to give himself up to the police. There is nothing brutal in the script, and nothing sentimental; Toninho's final surrender is a long-shot in sunlight.

The children play themselves with unromantic exuberance, too pre-occupied with survival to worry about the iniquitous society that bore and failed to rear them. Sucksdorff respects them (and our intelligence) too much to make them look winsome, or tragic, or anything but every-day urchins. *My Home is Copacabana* is less savage than Bunuel's *Los Olvidados*, but it told me more about children and poverty, and (by understating its case) left me feeling much angrier. This profoundly trustworthy film is a triumph of hard authenticity over easy melodrama.

Two Notes on Direction

First: Let us beware of abusing the verb 'evoke' when we praise a director's achievement—as in phrases about his masterly evocation of Manhattan or the Italian Riviera or Death Valley. In the narrative arts, only novelists and playwrights really evoke, since they start with nothing but a blank page or an empty stage. The cinema (on location, of course; I am not thinking of studio work) starts with reality itself. It can shoot reality in many ways and from many angles, but it begins with a solid, physical *donnée*; it is spared the basic creative pain of evocation out of nothing. When we applaud the skill with which—say—Renoir evokes the Left Bank in *Boudu*, we must bear in mind that he had a head start: the Left Bank was there already.

Second point: Let's also remember that it is virtually impossible to subject a film to extended critical analysis without recourse to technicali-ties that would bore or baffle the majority of filmgoers. Novels are all words; plays are mainly verbal; but films are all images. Listen to Raoul Coutard, the great French cameraman, talking in *Sight and Sound* about Jaques Demy's *Lola*:

> People often tell me that *Lola* was brilliantly shot. 'Was it due to your own mood?' they ask. 'Or to Demy? Or the light of Nantes? Or the look of Anouk Aimée?' It was partly all of these things, but ... above everything else, the images of *Lola* came from the film stock—Gevaert 36, which the factory has now stopped making. ...

Coutard attributes to Gevaert 36 'at least 70 per cent of the lyricism of *Lola*'. He goes on to say that much of the quality of *A Bout de Souffle* was due to Godard's insistence on using Ilford H.P.S. stock (which was made only for still photography) and on having it developed in a special Phenidone bath. The theatre makes use of technical devices, but film is itself a technical device. It may very well be that an ideal film critic would be unintelligible, for at least half of the time, to all but film technicians.

The War Game; Juliet of the Spirits

The authorities at the BBC still refuse either to show or to sell Peter Watkins's *The War Game*. This is very shortsighted of them, because, having seen it at a private screening, I suspect that it may be the most important film ever made. We are always being told that works of art cannot change the course of history. Given wide enough dissemination, I believe this one might.

It begins with maps, reminding us of this country's unique vulnerability to nuclear attack. It then postulates a crisis. Chinese troops enter South Vietnam; America threatens to use atomic weapons against them; Russia gives notice that she will take over West Berlin unless the weapons are withdrawn. Riots at Checkpoint Charlie provoke the Russians to move. Nato divisions, pushing through East Germany to relieve the city, encounter overwhelmingly superior conventional forces, whereupon it is decided (in accordance with Nato policy) to riposte with tactical nuclear weapons. Once these are launched, Russia strikes back with atomic missiles on Western Europe.

While the stakes are rising, we cut back to Britain; to evacuated mothers and children; to interviews with ordinary people, who tell the camera that in their opinion war is not inevitable. There's a sense that, in any case, the authorities will cope, as they did in the blitz. Then the sirens wail, and down—three minutes or thirty seconds later, depending on whether the source is a distant launching pad or a nearby nuclear submarine—comes the holocaust. As in his TV reconstruction of the battle of Culloden, Mr Watkins confines most of his action to a small area, and the whole of his cast to non-actors. Here the place is Kent, a county that contains less than the average number of targets for annihilation.

What follows is a daytime nightmare, a guide to disaster so honestly documented as to rebuke any charge of sensationalism. (Even in a relatively mild nuclear strike, such as the one presented in the film, between a third and a half of the population of this country would be killed or seriously injured.) Sequence after sequence inscribes itself on the memory. The fire-storm near the point of impact; the trembling walls forty miles away; the beleaguered nurse ('Some of these people are falling apart'); the police dutifully shooting the hopelessly maimed; the bewildered husband incoherently wondering whether and when his family will die of radiation sickness; the civilian raids on military food supplies (a boy gestures obscenely at the prying camera); the raiders executed by firing-squad; and—perhaps most chilling of all—the survivors staunchly insisting that Britain was right to retaliate in kind. There are no close-ups of violence in progress, merely of its aftermath—the burned, the organically eroded, the mentally destroyed, the fortunate dead.

The War Game stirred me at a level deeper than panic or grief. So long as adequate warning is given to depressives and other victims of nervous illness, it should not only be televised but screened in cinemas, not just here but everywhere on earth, especially in countries that possess (or would like to possess) the bomb. In refusing to show it, the BBC is like a doctor withholding the truth from a patient who is suffering from a potentially fatal disease; silence may preclude panic, but it also precludes cure.

The War Game is more than a diagnosis; it is a work of art. It precisely communicates one man's vision of disaster, and I cannot think that it is diminished as art because the vision happens to correspond with the facts. Like Michelangelo's Last Judgment, it proposes itself as an authentic documentary image of the wrath to come—though Michelangelo, of course, was working from data less capable of verification.

The film contains no resonant generalities about the nobility of man; instead, it shows us shattered, astonished specimens of a race that owed its pre-eminence to its adaptability, adapted itself too readily to an insane power structure, and so died. In Mr Watkins's fifty-minute masterpiece, our grave—if and when we are compelled to dig it—will have a living monument.

Beside *The War Game*, Fellini's *Juliet of the Spirits* cannot but seem an ecstasy of chic self-indulgence, a gigantic parcel that conceals, beneath layers of gaudy wrapping, a fragment of old rope. (Homage is due to the colour camerawork of the late Gianni di Venanzo.) Having analysed himself in *8½*—a superb narcissistic film flawed by a sentimental finale— Fellini now turns his attention to his wife, Giulietta Masina, here cast as a well-to-do middle-aged woman who, rightly suspecting that her husband has a mistress, seeks fulfilment in occult religions and subjective fantasies. Some of the latter she consciously invokes; others come unsought to pester her waking life.

When a private detective (symbolically disguised as a priest) supplies evidence of her husband's infidelity, this would-be maenad of the menopause decides to immerse herself in erotic delights. But she daren't take the plunge; her beautiful dominant mother inhibits her, and so does the puritan legacy of her convent school, where she once played the role of a virginally martyred saint. As in $8\frac{1}{2}$, the root of the trouble is Catholic guilt, at which revelation we may permit ourselves a yawn. Eventually Giulietta 'comes to terms with herself' and exorcises her childhood phantoms, while her husband goes off to Milan to think things out. To the end, however, she remains a shallow, virtually uncharacterised creature, in whose flamboyantly photographed hallucinations one's interest is seldom more than optical. You might call her a wife out of *Good Housekeeping* having visions out of *Flair*.

Fellini has made an immensely pretty film of monumental triviality. The supporting characters—gigolos, grotesques and overdressed nymphos —all spring from a world of bourgeois charades. If this is Fellini's world, he is going around with the wrong set. Nino Rota's music, nippy and nostalgic as it skips up and down the Hammond organ, has real distinction; Kurt Weill would not have disowned it.

The Loved One

The great thing about Tony Richardson is that he gets his own way, on a scale to which few other British directors have ever aspired. His films may be wilful, erratic, derivative in technique and outrageously flashy in their handling of the more intimate emotions; but they are made on his own terms, reflecting nobody's taste but his.

'You don't understand the mechanics of power,' he once said to a friend who rebuked him for having gone to Hollywood. In *The Loved One*, he wields power with a baroque extravagance that suggests Ludwig of Bavaria at large in Culver City. The casting has the omnibus capriciousness of a command performance (John Gielgud, Rod Steiger, Margaret Leighton, Tab Hunter and Liberace in the same movie?), and Richardson has obviously dared his writers (Terry Southern and Christopher Isherwood) to get as close as they can to the trip-wire that separates satiric effrontery from embarrassing overstatement. When they tumble over, he seems neither to notice nor care.

To use the kind of corn-fed idiom on which Mr Southern loves to pounce, let's shoot straight pool: I was never a passionate admirer of

Evelyn Waugh's novel, which struck me as a one-joke book that scored repeated bull's-eyes on an undefended target—the burial customs of Southern California. Nor did I relish its manner, which was that of a high-born tourist smirking at morally inferior savages. Richardon's movie is faithful to quite a lot of the original. An English writer arrives in Los Angeles, mingles with the starchy British colony, gets a job in a pet cemetery, and falls in love with a dedicated young female cosmetician at the neighbouring necropolis of Whispering Glades, where corpses are majestically interred for fun and profit. He woos her by passing off poems from the *Golden Treasury* as his own. When she discovers that he is a fraud and that Whispering Glades is a commercial circus, she commits suicide by injecting herself with embalming fluid. By and large, the strictly loyal sequences—especially the romantic ones—are the dullest in the film.

The additions and improvisations are often ghastly and often brilliant; but they are never dull. In (or on the verge of) the ghastly category are the following: the leadenly ironic use of 'America, America' on the sound-track, the unfunny miscasting of Rod Steiger as a fussy blond embalmer, the wild assumption that Campus Champ Robert Morse is capable of playing an English poet, the detachable revue sketch in which Margaret Leighton and Milton Berle bewail the death of Arthur (a dog, as if you hadn't guessed), and the final solution, whereby all the corpses are to be blasted into orbit. This latter wheeze must have sounded much brighter around the conference table than it looks on the screen.

The moments of brilliance, though more numerous, are also more fleeting. I think of Mr Morse, surrounded by classical statuary in Whispering Glades, impulsively kissing a marble nipple. Of Liberace as a coffin salesman, discussing the setting-in of what he calls 'rig-mo'. Of Gielgud, teaching English pronunciation to a cowboy star who gets 'dicey' confused with 'dykey'. Of Jonathan Winters as the Blessed Reverend, bellowing: 'There's got to be a way to get those stiffs off my property!' Of the heroine's ranch-type house, a lofty death trap on cantilevers where every step may produce a terminal creak. Above all, there are the grotesque scenes with Mr Steiger's mother, a vast bedridden object ('every inch a queen', as he describes her) who spends half her time eating and the rest watching food commercials on television. You can trace Mr Southern's footprints on the upper slopes of this mountainously uneven film. But it was Mr Richardson, of course, who gave him a free hand to scale them.

Morgan—A Suitable Case For Treatment; Pierrot le Fou

Two studies of anarchic romanticism: *Morgan—A Suitable Case for Treatment*, written by David Mercer and directed by Karel Reisz, and *Pierrot le Fou*, with script and direction by Jean-Luc Godard. In each case the hero belongs to a family that currently dominates the younger Western cinema: the brotherhood of nonchalant outsiders, carrying their private worlds around with them as defensive carapaces against the vast and hostile public world, which they can never hope to change. ('Western' is too exclusive a word: the same breed has lately sprung up in films like the Czech *Josef Kilian* and the Polish *Walkover*.) Are they maladjusted children, nostalgic for the womb? Or is opting out really the sanest choice—the last refuge of individualism?

One's answers to these questions must depend on whether one accepts the view, implicit in most outsider films, that modern society is a capricious and impregnable conspiracy against personal integrity and love. 'This is an island of sanity in a sea of pain,' says Morgan, the Mercer-Reisz protagonist, who has taken up residence in a car outside the house from which his wife has expelled him. Like Godard's hero, he is victimised by a woman's complicity with the *status quo*. Society would call both men neurotic, but this does not necessarily disqualify them from criticising society. The importance of outsider films is that they force us to remember that neurosis is a relative term.

Morgan is vestigially capable of political revolt. His mother (Irene Handl) is a cheerful, impenitent Stalinist from the East End, and he still inscribes hammers and sickles on all flat surfaces that offend him. But his sense of unease transcends politics: when a policeman says, 'You want to watch it,' he desperately replies: 'I know, but where is it?' He has married a rich Hampstead girl (played with sunflower serenity by Vanessa Redgrave) who doesn't mind his being a penniless artist but cannot stand his obsessions with animals. For Morgan identifies with gorillas: 'I've been born,' as he puts it, 'into the wrong species.' Visions of King Kong and Tarzan flit through his waking dreams, all of them wildly at odds with the moon-calf mien and giraffe-calf gait of David Warner, than whom no funnier anti-hero has reached the screen since the debut of Jacques Tati.

Divorced by Miss Redgrave, he blankly refuses to quit her house and even contrives another session in her bed. The latter sequence, intercut with shots of female zebras in heat and tropical birds rhythmically flapping their wings, is at once ludicrous and lyrical. But his anti-social instincts soon get out of hand: after blowing up his mother-in-law (less than mortally), kidnapping his ex-wife, and breaking up her wedding reception in full gorilla kit, he suffers a persecution nightmare in which he is executed by firing-squad. We last see Morgan in an asylum, where he is visited by Miss Redgrave, pregnant with his child.

The scenes of pure farce work superbly, but the descents into serious pain are strained and embarrassing. Mr Mercer's chosen framework of fantasy is too artificial to express what he wants to tell us about the rabid interrelationship of love and violence. Karel Reisz—a specialist in aggresive pariahs, as we know from *Saturday Night and Sunday Morning* and *Night Must Fall*—handles Morgan with gusto and finesse. He also makes daring and effective use of 'natural sound', which means that instead of post-synchronised flatness we get echoes, street noises and spontaneity.

After Morgan the Fey, *Pierrot le Fou*; after the domesticated outsider, the thing itself. A second viewing of Godard's film leaves me far more impressed than when I saw it last year in Venice. Do not come to it expecting a consecutive plot; listen to the American director Samuel Fuller, who appears early on with the oracular statement that cinema is 'emotion'; and look thereafter for emotional images, linked by the connecting thread of alienation from the accepted norms of society.

Anna Karina plays a Parisian baby-sitter with whom Jean-Paul Belmondo (a married man recently fired from a TV job) runs away on impulse. He's fed up with the adipose, ad-glutted world in which he lives: over a magazine shot of a girdle he mutters: 'On entre dans la civilisation du cul.' It seems that Karina is involved in a gun-running organisation; at any rate, there's a corpse in her flat; and she wants Belmondo to drive her south to the coast, where (she claims) she has a gun-running brother who will give them money.

Godard has said that they embody 'le dernier couple romantique, les derniers descendants de *La Nouvelle Heloïse*'; also that 'Anna représente la vie active et lui la vie contemplative'. In other words, she is destructive, while he is passive: here, perhaps, one discerns a reference to Karina's relationship with Godard himself.

As Belmondo says: 'Allons-y, Alonzo!' The journey is the essence, proceeding in existential episodes. You get the feeling, on his part, of a cool deliberate dive into danger; on hers, that in leading him towards the sea, she is luring him to his death. The images (photographed by Raoul Coutard) are dry and hot, slashed in almost every frame with the colours of flame and blood. I recall one majestic shot of a burning car against a fragment of unfinished motorway, with two figures escaping across a wheatfield, over which gigantic pylons tower.

There are real irrelevances (e.g. Belmondo's sudden impersonation of Michel Simon) and others only apparent—such as the scene in which the two refugees mime a bombing attack on Vietnam to earn a few francs from a group of delighted American tourists.

After a brief idyll by the sea, Karina betrays Belmondo. In return, he kills her, and commits suicide by tying a palisade of blood-coloured dynamite sticks round his head and setting fire to the fuse. The keynote is nonchalance: regrettably but predictably, the anti-human world has won. In *Cahiers du Cinéma* Godard quotes a text by Borges about a man who sets out to create a world of his own, and discovers when he has finished that 'ce patient labyrinthe n'est rien d'autre que son portrait'. *Pierrot* is Godard's portrait, eccentricities, illuminations and all.

Footnote on Cinema

Films always take place in the past tense, plays in the present. A film is a canned event that happened long ago; it is shot, dubbed and finished months before the critic sees it. It cannot be modified by what he says. A play, on the other hand, can; it is still a living organism, capable of change and alteration. In fact, the test of a good play is its ability to respond to different interpretations; the test of a good film is that it cannot be other than what it is.

A film critic can sometimes unearth an audience for a minority movie, but he cannot compete with the vast advertising techniques that ensure a mass audience for a majority movie. Does the critic wish to influence the kind of film that costs more than £250,000? It is as if he were to send a postcard to General Motors explaining that he would like them to make a raft next year, or a helicopter, instead of a car.

III: PEOPLE

Cyril Connolly at Fifty

Cyril Connolly is either a *bon viveur* with a passion for literature, or a littérateur with a passion for high living. He has never quite made up his mind, and his biography will be the story of his indecision. It is a conflict of extremes, because his standards of living and writing are both immensely high, too high for comfortable coexistence within the same very self-critical human being: Brillat-Savarin and a fasting friar might sooner inhabit the same cell. Whenever he revisits the *grand restaurants* a nagging voice keeps reminding him of his own dictum: 'The true function of a writer is to produce a masterpiece; no other task is of any consequence.' Fancifully, one can picture him echoing Ben Jonson's cry; 'O! If a man could restrain the fury of his gullet and groin!' Only the best in food or art is good enough for him; only what he calls 'alpha people' interest him, and nothing depresses him more than an encounter with a thriving, contented, beta-plus, best-selling novelist. Mediocre writing strikes him as several degrees worse than no writing: 'The books I haven't written,' he once said, 'are better than the books other people have.' For over twenty years he has been pressing on his contemporaries the information that art is a ferocious taskmistress, that the Muses do not welcome novices, but (as Cocteau said) simply open the door and silently point at the tightrope.

Immoderate faith in Connolly's pronouncements might persuade any young author that literature was almost an impossibility: his glum, lapidary admonitions produce an effect like that of reading a medical textbook on the use of dangerous drugs, and it has been said that the idea of modern English literature without him is as inconceivable as the idea of *Hamlet* without the Ghost. For him the test of a piece of writing is: 'Would it amuse Horace or Milton or Swift or Leopardi? Could it be read to Flaubert?' Writing under the shadow of these appalling questions is naturally an exacting occupation and it is no wonder that Connolly has been a miser of words, publishing only five books of his own work in a lifetime of fifty years.

Horizon, the literary monthly which he ran from 1939 until 1950, established him as a great editor, carrying on a rearguard action in the service of letters at a time when art and frivolity were all but equated in the public mind. His anthology *The Golden Horizon* contains only one item, a brief questionnaire, written by himself, but the book·bears his trademark on every page. Its flavour is wry, pungent and personal; the choice is that of a man to whom pomp, lushness and slogans are uniformly hateful. In *Ideas and Places*, a collection of his *Horizon* editorials, and in *The Unquiet Grave*, a quotation-peppered stew in which the modern intellectual's predicament is sadly anatomized, Connolly has stated his case against twentieth-century culture. The onlooker sees most of the game, but to Connolly the game is a war, with literature an open city being saturation-bombed by economic stress and betrayed from within by *Angst*—a cult word which he did more than anyone else to popularise. Sometimes one suspects that Connolly the physician is merely diagnosing his own ailment, and that the X-rays have been rigged to show only the cancers of guilt and indolence. He has tried and failed to cultivate what Lamb called 'a brawny defiance to the needles of a thrusting-in conscience'.

'His virtue as a critic,' said one observer, 'has always been the directness that comes from treating all writing as the personal expression of a particular human being in particular circumstances. . . .' How late did Baudelaire lie abed? What was Voltaire's digestion like? How important was sex to La Rochefoucauld? These are the questions which fascinate Connolly: in answering them, he has become the greatest living authority on good reasons for not writing. His lifework is a series of attempts to define the material and spiritual circumstances most propitious to the creation of good art. What pressures and solaces, how much drink, how much money, how much of the hermit's barrel and how much of the marriage bed, conduce to the nourishment of the creative mood? He has spent most of his career in search of the right solution.

'I have always disliked myself at any given moment,' he has written; 'the sum total of such moments is my life.' It began in England on 10 September 1903. Much later, in a completely unautobiographical context, he said, 'Thus astrologers find this love of perfection in those born under the sign of Virgo . . . between the end of August and the end of September.' His father was a soldier, of naval and military ancestry, and a collector of shells, a trait which has reproduced itself in Connolly's abiding love of hoarding exotic objects. His mother sprang from a line of gay Irish squirearchs, and in extreme youth, he says, 'I became a snob. The discovery that I was an earl's great-nephew was important to me. ...' He had a conventional English writer's childhood, which is to say, one that was geographically and genealogically bizarre, involving exposure to good books, the minor aristocracy and outposts of Empire— he visited South Africa twice before he was seven.

From private school, where his best friends were Cecil Beaton ('prettiness') and George Orwell ('intellect'), he went to Eton with a scholarship. He read intensively, became known as a wit, and suffered abominably. The evasiveness, the shrillness, the tendency to blink and stammer, which are to be found in most English intellectuals, can be traced directly to their public schools; and Connolly's account of the cliques and cruelty of Eton is characteristically alarming, as much in what it condones as in what it condemns. 'To this day,' he wrote, 'I cannot bear to be sent for or to hear of anyone's wanting to see me about something without acute nervous dread.' He rejoiced when he was admitted to Pop, the Eton Society, much as he rejoiced when, years later, he was elected to White's Club, the Pop of St James's Street.

He took a degree in history at Oxford, and from this period dates his vision of himself as 'the boy who let the side down, the coming man who never came'. In 1926 he found a patron: the London refugee from Philadelphia, Logan Pearsall Smith, author of *Trivia* and like minor works, apprised of his brightness, offered him a secretarial job which proved to be less than exacting. *Chez* Pearsall Smith, he would rise at ten, spending the morning in a constantly replenished hot bath; at luncheon he would grumble politely if the wine insulted his palate; the afternoon might be occupied with yachting on the Solent; and then dinner, after which he customarily fell into a deep sleep.

He likens his subsequent career to a tree that has its destined shape but takes time to decide which branch is the main artery. He flourished ephemerally as a conversationalist, and more lastingly in the pages of the *New Statesman*, where his mentors were Raymond Mortimer and Desmond MacCarthy, who managed to rouse him from fits of what he calls 'mutinous and iconoclastic sloth'. His thirties' journalism is vivid, erudite, sharply metaphoric and only slightly cliquey: the best of it includes half a dozen lacerating burlesques, one of which, the playful demolition of Aldous Huxley entitled 'Told in Gath', has been described as the most brilliant parody of the twentieth century. He also published a novel, *The Rock Pool*, which encapsulated the seedy, sub-Bohemian side of the French Riviera in the twenties, drably shivering under the blast of the mistral.

In 1930 he had married a not ill-heeled American, and was spared the necessity of sinking to the cheaper varieties of journalism. Analysing the blights afflicting the twentieth-century artist, he said,'... broadcasting, advertising, journalism and lecturing all pluck feathers from the blue bird of inspiration and cast them on the wind'. He more or less resisted all four, achieving instead considerable standing as guest, host, mimic, and Guardian of Values. Even now, it is difficult to leave his company without feeling determined to repel all forms of literary prostitution, a determination which can easily lead to inertia. He travelled, found acolytes, made friends and entertained them in Chelsea on champagne and sucking-pig.

'Favourite daydream' he wrote in 1933, 'to edit a monthly magazine entirely subsidized by self. No advertisements. Harmless title. Deleterious contents.' In 1939 war broke out, and with it, like the rash sometimes produced by vaccination, *Horizon*, backed by Connolly's friend Peter Watson. From a chrysalis of journalism, fiction-writing and marriage (he was separated from his wife in 1939), an editor emerged, with views that were perfectionist without being pontifical, and for ten years the magazine spread its name around the world. In 1950, faced with a diminishing circulation, *Horizon* sank: 'only contributions continued to be delivered, like a suicide's milk,' Connolly wrote recently, 'and keep on coming'. He had lived lavishly during the forties, overspending on furniture, china and food; now he was jobless and in debt. A new self was called for.

'Stoic in adversity, Epicurean in prosperity'; thus he epitomised himself; now, obviously, was the Stoic's chance. Nineteen-fifty was a cashless year. He had just remarried, his new wife being the long, catlike, amazingly slim Barbara Skelton, whose circle of friends had formerly ranged from Peter Quennell to King Farouk. With her companionship, Connolly withdrew from London literary life, took an isolated cottage in Kent, acridly illuminated by oil lamps, and became an ascetic. The Spartan, antiseptic life of Oak Cottage was intended to sharpen his creative wits for the twenty years of literary activity which he believed were left to him: two decades to turn out the masterpiece, to put immortal flesh on the Ghost. 'I am,' he said, 'a refugee from the business lunch and the *couche-tard* principle.'

The fleshed Ghost was and is a baggy, besandalled Buddha, with a pink child's face, slack jowls, a receding fuzz of hair skirmishing across his scalp, and somewhat sour, blank eyes which express the resignation of one who envisaged himself in a sedan chair sucking on a hubble-bubble and was fobbed off with secondhand Sheraton and cigars.

Physically, a part for Charles Laughton at his driest and least expostulatory; intellectually, a logbook of his generation's voyages and discoveries —Freud in the twenties, the Left in the thirties, the preservative artistic Right in the late forties. In 1951 Connolly took a post as literary critic on *The Sunday Times*, a retreat to journalism but a concession to security. His vocation was still 'to make books', but his new job enabled him to vary the hermitage routine by spending one night a week at the Ritz, if only to get his pants pressed.

Last winter he concluded that his programme was 'to shed ballast, to cast off some of my selves—the Editor, the International Journalist, the Romantic Adolescent and the Diner-Out'. This last self was hastened to oblivion partly by Virginia Woolf's reference to him in her notebooks as 'that cocktail critic, C. Connolly', but more by Nancy Mitford's gentle parody of him in *The Blessing*, where he figures as the Captain, with a circle of handmaidens, sudden infatuations, and helplessly expensive tastes. 'I want to write myself out of journalism,' he says, 'as I have journalized myself out of editing.' His publications since his rural retirement have been three anthologies, two from *Horizon* and one of *Great English Short Novels*. 'I have read or reread about sixty or seventy novels for this selection,' he told his publishers. 'It has been a revelation to me and freed me at last from the bondage to French nineteenth-century writers, which has been holding me up for years and prevented me from writing more myself.... I should like those who read this anthology to find all long books rather absurd.' He is now, not unexpectedly, working on a short novel ('form and shape and rapidity') about the murder of a man of letters. 'I write as a rule in the afternoons, using the mornings to rev up the engine,' he explains. 'I can go for long spells without working.' Sir Max Beerbohm has attested, among many others, that no writer enjoys writing. Connolly is reluctant to face the typewriter because, he says, the sheer *jouissance* of creation always burdens him with a profound, hungover sense of guilt. He cites, as a parallel, a fellow-critic who was told by a psychiatrist that his literary blockage was due to a subconscious identification of the desire to write with the desire to sleep with his mother.

Connolly fills the pre-lunch revving-up period with his other interests. He must feed his pet coati (a replacement for the lemurs whose distinctive stench pervaded most of his earlier homes); he must attend to his two Chinese ducks and his lovingly fattened guinea fowl. He gardens assiduously and adventurously, and next year he plans a 'Poison Corner'. His own list of hobbies runs: 'READING, travelling, talking, eating, drinking, motoring, gardening, thinking, planting shrubs and watching fishes, architecture, china, silver, paintings, furniture, reading, READING, READING.' His acquisitiveness is violent and endless: 'I am,' he once said, 'one of nature's Rothschilds.' His afternoon bouts of creativeness produce the same concise, elegant, informal results as ever, laced with nodules of venom: he recently dismissed a volume of expendable memoirs with the phrase: 'wanly recommended'. He dines out seldom, but when he does he is ruthlessly critical of the food ('But the mashed potatoes were the best I've ever tasted,' or 'When will X learn that the champagne should *keep on coming*?') and more anxious than of old to get back home and read. Horace, Catullus, Flaubert, Lucretius, Stendhal, Molière, Firbank, Rabelais and Lamb are all within arm's length of his bed, the beloved collaborators on his 'culture picture'. 'A writer has to construct his shell, lik the caddis worm, from the debris of the past.' The French finality of Connolly's style, at once supple and bleak, is one of the most glittering of English literary possessions, among which it shines like a crown jewel in a pawnbroker's shop.

It is hard to explain his influence to anyone who has not felt the impact of his personality. One might say that Alexander Woollcott was a vulgar, eunuchoid, ragtime caricature of Connolly, except that Connolly's earlier waspishness has mellowed with time. Nowadays, he says, 'things do not annoy me unless they are very badly made'. It is the making that worries him, the solitary toil of turning out a perfect sentence: but the hedonist in him forever militates against the anchorite. He wants to move up 'from the cottage class to the country-house class'; and thus, when his American publishers sent him a questionnaire with a final request for 'any other information about yourself... please do not be modest', his response was immediate: 'I could use a million dollars.' He loathes hearty, county people, but relishes the food they can afford. He is a journalist, but takes no newspapers. He detests easy fame, but wants to get rich quick. A fair description of Horace, Connolly's idol, might almost be a description of the idolater himself, but there is something irremediably comic about an English Horace in the 1950s. It conjures up a picture I cannot expunge from my mind: a drafty old Sunbeam Talbot being driven across country at breakneck speed in a rainstorm, Mrs Connolly furiously at the wheel, moodily grinding her teeth, and Connolly himself squatting in the back seat on what appeared to be a spare tyre and murmuring to me, in his fussy, tentative voice, 'By habit, of course, I am an Epicurean,' as the needle touched seventy, the car lurched on a bend and an ominous banging was heard, as I remember, from the neighbourhood of the back axle.

(1954)

George Cukor and the Girls

What films, over the last thirty years, epitomise Hollywood at its most stylish? I do not mean the greatest films, or the most powerful; I mean, rather, the wittiest, the most sumptuously romantic, the most opulently sophisticated. Put this question to a moviegoer with a long memory, and it is likely that his list will include such pictures as *The Philadelphia Story, Camille, Born Yesterday, The Women, Dinner at Eight* and the Judy Garland version of *A Star Is Born*—to which his wife might add *A Bill of Divorcement, Gaslight* and the Katharine Hepburn version of *Little Women.* Both of them, I imagine, would be surprised to learn that all these films were directed by the same man—a sixty-one-year-old New Yorker named George Dewey Cukor, who left the Broadway theatre for Beverly Hills just over thirty years ago.

At that time the movies were in dire need of people who could teach them to talk as well as move. Seeking a coach, they summoned Cukor; and he succeeded in imposing on Hollywood high comedy and Hollywood high romance an acting style that combined cinematic intimacy with theatrical polish and precision. For this achievement he has neither demanded nor received much credit. Ingrid Bergman, Judy Holliday, Shelley Winters, James Stewart and Ronald Colman all won Academy Awards in films of his making; but no Oscar gleams in Cukor's home, although he has four times been nominated for the prize. Outside the industry, he is almost unknown. Even within it, he is often overlooked. Some months ago I asked a reputable screen writer to name the leading Hollywood directors. 'Billy Wilder, William Wyler, George Stevens,' he began. 'Then Ford, Huston, Zinnemann and maybe Kazan.' And what about Cukor? 'Oh, Cukor doesn't make movies,' he continued, 'Cukor just makes actors.'

This relative neglect does not bother him; whatever spurs him, it is not fame. He delights in the company of beautiful things and intelligent people, and he prefers to enjoy it behind the high walls of the rambling, miniature palace in which he lives—a bachelor pleasure-dome, scented with sandalwood, hidden in the hills above the raffish squalor of Sunset Strip. The terraced garden is peopled with Italian statues that are picked out, when the occasion is festive, by tinted rays from concealed spotlights. Inside, the rooms glow with pictures—half a dozen Picassos and as many Toulouse-Lautrecs, together with works by Braque, Rouault, Matisse, Renoir, Buffet, Sutherland and Henry Moore, not to mention a superb

Rodin bronze and a gracious Sargent drawing of Ethel Barrymore, bequeathed to Cukor by the sitter. He loves baubles and bibelots. 'George is galvanized by objects,' says one of his friends. 'They perpetually astonish him. He adores possessing them, and if he catches you looking covetously at something he owns, he'll grasp it almost vengefully. Then, as like as not, he'll give it to you for Christmas.'

Three servants maintain the household, which consists, apart from Cukor himself, of two sleek dachshunds and a myopic, venerable poodle named Sasha. Socially, he is outranked by nobody in the Hollywood hierarchy. At dinner, which is candle-lit and invariably Lucullan, the guests are likely to include Aldous Huxley, Somerset Maugham, or at least one Sitwell; it pleases Cukor to bring literary and cinematic celebrities together. (It was at a Cukor party that a famous English writer was introduced to Joan Crawford, of whom he afterward said: 'She reminds me of an unnamed Du Pont product.') The host himself eats sparingly, to his considerable discomfort. He relishes good food, but some time ago he became dangerously portly, whereafter he put himself on a Spartan regime, and would turn up to dinner *chez* somebody else with a meal of his own, dietetically approved and neatly packed in a basket.

He practices moderation in everything but reading and rising: he consumes books omnivorously and—even when not working—habitually gets up at dawn. Physically, he is now in enviable trim, dapper in build, and full of bristling energy that flows out through his voluble finger tips, his blazing eyes and his eager, piscine mouth, which has been compared to that of a big-game fish snapping at a hook. A tribute to his fitness hangs outside his private gymnasium—a diploma in which his physical instructor, a Frenchman, congratulates him on 'sa plastique impeccable'. It is symptomatic of Cukor's modesty that very few people see the document. The photographs in his house are of the stars—most of them female—with whom he has most happily worked; there are none of Cukor alone. Conversationally, he dwells always on the people he admires; it is a rare evening with Cukor that does not include an anecdote or two about Nazimova, Yvette Guilbert, Isadora Duncan, Mrs Patrick Campbell, or Sarah Bernhardt—the outrageous, beplumed goddesses before whom he eternally goggles.

The writer Lesley Blanch once described him, in a letter to me, as 'a voluptuary in the true classical sense—able to enjoy the greatest luxuries and the smallest toys; finds exquisite pleasures in many ways; which is probably the secret of living. I think he has this. And I think he has not, or has passed, *ambition*, in the destructive sense. This makes him utterly free. And being perfectly sure of who he is, what he is, he does not envy—is not eaten up by competition.'

Mention a performer he knows or worships, and instantly the anecdotes start to pour out. His voice whirrs and buzzes, like an engine that, once revved up, cannot be switched off until it reaches its destination. Two deep lines of concentration bisect his forehead like a highway; and his conductor's fingers begin their dance, sometimes caressing the air or stabbing it for emphasis, and sometimes upheld, with thumb and index joined, to retain one's attention while their owner scans the ceiling in search of the right word. Meanwhile, as Cukor warms to his story, his lower jaw comes swooping forward, revealing seven sharp teeth that gnaw, between phrases, at his upper lip. 'Whenever George gets excited,' somebody once remarked, 'he suddenly acquires four sets of teeth.'

Of Marilyn Monroe, with whom he worked on *Let's Make Love*, he says: 'Her face *moves*—it catches the light—it's genuinely photogenic. And she *thinks boldly*. She thinks as a dog thinks. *Au fond*, her mind is wonderfully unclouded—she doesn't censor her thoughts. She's like Elvis Presley, like all the great performers—whenever she enters, it's an occasion. Maybe I sound like an old hambola, but I love Presley—I think he has *enormous* taste and *enormous* distinction.' (While unquestionably sincere, Cukor's admiration for Miss Monroe does not prevent him from being playful at her expense. Once, in a party game, he was asked what food she most reminded him of. He immediately replied: 'A three-day-old Van de Kamp Bakery angel cake.')

Cukor's background, like that of many people prominent in movies, is Hungarian; it is surprising how much of the history of film-making in the West could be written under the title: *Strictly from Hungary*. Though his parents met in New York, they both belonged to immigrant households and had come to America as adolescents. George's father, Victor, carved a modest niche for himself in American real estate, but the dominant voice in the family counsels was that of Uncle Morris, a prosperous Manhattan lawyer. Almost as soon as George was born, in 1899, it was assumed that he would follow in his uncle's professional footsteps. In his early teens, however, he took to attending the theatre at least twice a week, and the idols he cherished then he cherishes still—Mrs Fiske, Emily Stevens, Ethel Barrymore, Nazimova and the rest.

In 1918, on the verge of entering law school, he momentously decided to accept a job as assistant stage manager in Chicago. His relatives were appalled: 'They acted,' he recalls, 'as if I'd said I was going to become a bookie.' Undeterred, he pushed on; by 1920 he was directing a summer-stock company in Rochester, where he engaged young players like Miriam Hopkins, Bette Davis and Robert Montgomery, endearing himself to all of them except Miss Davis, with whom he never could get on. He also employed a pretty Broadway ingénue named Frances Howard, on whom he exerted so marked an influence that she consulted him before accepting a proposal of marriage from a fledgling movie producer called Samuel Goldwyn.

Mrs Goldwyn remembers Cukor as 'this great big fat wonderful man. He loved to make actors comfortable. He would bother them, but he would bother them quietly. Whenever he was worried about a show, he would eat—fill himself with cakes and go to sleep. Years later, when Selznick fired him from *Gone With the Wind*, he didn't yell or scream, but he ate a great many cakes.'

Cukor began his Broadway career in 1926 by staging *The Great Gatsby*, one of the stars of which was Florence Eldridge. 'We became fast, fast, fast, *fast* friends,' Cukor told me à propos Miss Eldridge, thereby corroborating the theory of Charles Brackett, the eminent screen writer and producer, who holds that you can never be sure that Cukor means what he says until he has repeated it four times. 'He would look at a page of dialogue,' says Mr Brackett, 'and tell us it was phony, phony, phony, *phony*. We used to count the phonies. When he got to the fourth, we knew he was serious.' By 1929 Cukor had directed people like Dorothy Gish, Laurette Taylor and Louis Calhern. His reputation, though small, was solid, and he went into films as an authority on spoken dialogue, in which capacity he was assigned to *All Quiet on the Western Front*. Since 1930, his name has appeared on the directorial credits of forty-two movies—a vast output that represents a vast expenditure, for Cukor is not a cheap director. He demands a peerless cast and a cast-iron script; and these are costly items.

'There are lots of creative directors,' he says, 'who can *seize* a script and make it part of their world—like Lubitsch, or Ford, or Hitchcock. And there are others who try to become part of the script's world. Like me.' Cukor's pictures are always obsequious to their subjects; he never obtrudes himself. There are, naturally, limits to the kind of script he will accept. Temperamentally, he shuns violence, and is probably the only Hollywood director whose celluloid record is completely free of gang warfare. He prefers movies that depend on personal relationships and permit him to evoke what he calls 'the climate of comedy'. This may be why actors revere him. 'The understatement of great screen acting,' Charles Brackett declares, 'was mostly George Cukor's invention. He was one of the first to understand the difference between acting for the theatre and acting for the camera.'

Early in his Hollywood career, Cukor tested a New York actress for an important part. She had 'an odd, barking way with her', but he hired her because he liked her gawky self-confidence, and gave her the female lead in *A Bill of Divorcement*. Even today, one cannot watch Katharine Hepburn's performance in the film without marvelling at the assurance with which she takes command, easily outplaying the seasoned professionals—among them John Barrymore—who surround her. Cukor and Hepburn have made eight pictures together, and become the closest of friends and neighbours. 'He makes you trust yourself,' she said to me. 'He maintains your illusion of yourself—out of the ebullience of his energy and the immense generosity of his spirit.'

Miss Hepburn reminded me that in 1936 she had appeared in a Cukor movie called *Sylvia Scarlett*, opposite a young actor of stodgy reputation who had been christened Archie Leach, though his Hollywood pseudonym was Cary Grant. He played a Cockney confidence trickster, and the film changed the course of his career. 'George taught him how to be funny,' said Miss Hepburn. 'He brought out the Archie Leach in Cary Grant.'

Of all his pictures, Cukor's favourite is *Little Women*, in which Miss Hepburn played Jo. Tallulah Bankhead saw it and sobbed uncontrollably, but it cannot be said that Cukor was overwhelmed by this demonstration of empathy. 'She wasn't moved by the picture,' he commented. 'She was weeping for her lost innocence.'

Judy Holliday shares the Hepburn passion for Cukor, though she phrases it differently: 'He didn't *maintain* my illusion of myself—he *gave* me an illusion of myself. Before I met him, I never thought of myself as an actress. Boy, he sidetracked me in a giant way!' And why did he impress her so much? 'Because he doesn't compete. He'll take suggestions from anybody—the actors, the cameraman, even the prop man—and he never resents it. He has a really healthy ego. And another thing I like. After every take he says, "Wonderful, wonderful, wonderful, wonderful—do it again!"' (For the results, see *Adam's Rib, Born Yesterday, The Marrying Kind* and *It Should Happen to You*.)

Shelley Winters, who made her screen debut in a Cukor picture and won an Academy Award, is equally agog with gratitude: 'When I met him for the first time, I was hiding myself. I'd assumed the personality of an idiot girl, with pink hair and false eyelashes and a sexy girdle. He took one look at me and said, "Damn it, girl, take off those eyelashes and that girdle." He told me I had a perfectly good intelligence, and why insult my mind that way? It never occurred to me until then that acting meant exposing yourself, not hiding yourself. I never knew anything about the intellectual side of being an actor before. While we were working on the picture I followed him around like he was my daddy.'

The voice of Marilyn Monroe is worth adding to the chorus. 'He cherishes the actor,' she said to me, her pink, vulnerable face reflecting hard thought. 'He and John Huston are directors who honestly respect actors. The first day on the set, he told me not to be nervous. I said I was born nervous. He told me, "If I don't sleep tonight, it'll be because I'm worrying about *you* not sleeping."'

Because of Cukor's success with Hepburn, Garbo, Shearer, Crawford, Garland, Gardner, Magnani, and so on, a legend has grown up to the effect that he is exclusively a 'woman's director'. Jack Lemmon, who gave his first screen performance in Cukor's *It Should Happen to You*, emphatically disagrees. 'Cukor,' he says, 'is the greatest actor's director I've ever worked with.' It was Cukor who taught Lemmon to scale down his flamboyant acting style to screen dimensions. About a week after shooting began, Lemmon played an important scene somewhat listlessly, as he thought, and was horrified to hear Cukor say: 'Print it.' Lemmon protested: 'But I didn't feel as if I was acting.' 'Unfortunately,' replied Cukor, 'you were.' Lemmon brooded over this for a couple of days, and then said: 'You mean—you don't want me to act at all?' Cukor beamed. 'You're beginning to get it,' he said.

Another sequence required Lemmon to fly into a rage with Judy Holliday. It went well enough, but Cukor felt something was missing. He pondered, his internal motor whirring, and suddenly fired a question at Lemmon: 'How do you feel when you're really mad at somebody?' 'I get a stomach ache,' said Lemmon truthfully. 'Play it that way,' said Cukor, and the result was one of the picture's pleasantest moments; halfway through his row with Miss Holliday, Lemmon clutched his belly and collapsed doubled up with colic.

Cukor rejoices in such tiny pieces of inspiration—'things you pick out of the air'. When he was directing Garbo in *Camille*, he kept remembering details of his mother's death, which was then fresh in his mind—how she had whimpered toward the end, and turned her face resolutely toward the wall. He used these memories in Marguérite's death scene, a small miracle of acting, and the crown of Garbo's finest performance. 'In Cukor's movies,' according to Lemmon, 'each separate scene is beautifully polished, like a pearl. The only trouble is that sometimes the string holding the pearls together is a little weak.' Cukor himself confirms this. 'I'm not desperately interested in storytelling,' he says, contrasting himself with someone like Cecil B. DeMille, whose pictures he describes as 'preposterous, illiterate, ludicrous, *but*—what a master storyteller!'

Another star who confesses a large debt to Cukor is Rosalind Russell, whose career as a comedienne was launched when he cast her in the film version of Clare Boothe's *The Women*. It featured Norma Shearer, Joan Crawford, Joan Fontaine, Paulette Goddard and a flock of white telephones; Miss Russell, then comparatively unknown, had the role of Sylvia, the professional bitch. 'Don't play Sylvia high-comedy,' he instructed her. 'Play her like a freak.' They were rehearsing a scene set in a hotel powder room; Cukor told Miss Russell to behave with exaggerated prissiness while the other girls were present—'but as soon as they leave, *pick your teeth.*'

The atmosphere on the set of *The Women* was electric with competition; to ease the tension, Cukor would begin each morning's work by giving his own impartially mischievous impressions of the ladies' demeanour on the previous day. He refused to allow Norma Shearer (whom he had directed in M.G.M.'s leadenly ornate production of *Romeo and Juliet*) to queen it over her colleagues. One of the key sequences took place at a couturier's, with Miss Russell subjecting Miss Shearer to a barrage of gossip while the latter was being fitted for a dress. 'Norma just had to stand there doing the Jack Benny bit,' as Miss Russell puts it, 'while I yakked away.' Cukor wanted her in close-up, hissing her malice directly into Miss Shearer's ear; but when the time came, Miss Russell found it impossible to get near the lady, who had thoughtfully changed into a voluminous black crinoline. Cukor accepted the challenge. After a moment's deliberation, he arranged a three-faced mirror in front of Miss Shearer, altered the camera angle and peered through the lens. 'That's much better, Norma dear,' he crooned villainously. 'Now there are *four* Rosalind Russells.' Miss Russell became a Cukor addict on the spot.

He calls her 'that society girl from Connecticut', in allusion to her patrician background, which he never tires of mocking. She once turned up wearing jodhpurs at one of his formal Sunday luncheons. He said nothing but that evening he telephoned her. 'Next week,' he said, 'don't come in costume. Except maybe as a maid—we need some extra help, because I've got some pretty classy people coming. But don't use any bad language, and for God's sake don't push yourself into the pictures, because they're photographing the lunch for *Harper's Bazaar*.'

Here and there one meets mild dissenters from the Cukor cult— Gene Kelly, for example, who tolerates his 'endless chatter' and enjoyed collaborating with him on *Les Girls*, but feels that basically Cukor is a theatre man who neither cares about nor understands the camera. This view is warmly contested by Cukor's old friend and *éminence grise*, the photographer George Huehne, whose pictorial *expertise* made a notable contribution to the success of *A Star Is Born*—Cukor's first colour movie, and the first on which he and Huehne worked together. Nowadays, according to Huehne, Cukor is vitally interested in the cinema *per se*, in composition and design, and not merely in photographing plays. Cukor shot *A Star Is Born* in a semi-impressionist style, boldly splashing his colours about, and taking what for him were fantastic visual risks. The film broke few box-office records, but it triumphantly rebuilt the career of Judy Garland, who regards Cukor as 'the most underrated, underappreciated director alive'.

It was at Miss Garland's home, quite a while ago, that an informal weekly dining club used to meet, consisting of the hostess, Fanny Brice, Katharine Hepburn, Ethel Barrymore and Cukor. One evening Miss Garland surveyed her guests and wondered, aloud: 'What on earth do you suppose we all have in common?' 'That's easy, my dear,' said Miss Barrymore. 'We've all been on the brink of disaster all our lives!' In Cukor's case, at least, the exaggeration concealed more than a grain of truth. For much of his early Hollywood career, he followed David Selznick from studio to studio, turning out a glittering procession of pictures such as *A Bill of Divorcement*, *Dinner at Eight*, *Little Women*, *David Copperfield* and *Camille*. Disaster struck in 1939, when Selznick formed his own company to produce *Gone with the Wind* with Cukor directing. 'Basically,' says Selznick, 'George was a transplanted stage director. He didn't know about cutting. I knew he wouldn't want to be bothered with the spectacular side of the picture, the military stuff.' So Selznick himself undertook to supervise the sets, the lighting and the camera work, excusably determined to keep fingertip control over what was, after all, the supreme gamble of his life—the most expensive and deafeningly publicised movie ever made. The late Clark Gable, as Rhett Butler, found Cukor's delicacy and fastidiousness a trifle disconcerting, but he made no overt complaint; and the ladies adored Cukor's methods—especially Olivia de Havilland and Vivien Leigh.

After a month's shooting, friction grew intense between director and producer. Cukor objected to Selznick's interference; there was a showdown; and Cukor was removed from the picture, which was finished by Victor Fleming. The Misses Leigh and De Havilland threatened to walk out in sympathy, but the gesture was bootless. Cukor was vanquished, and the blow to his pride was thunderous.

Yet he survived; and one understands why he sometimes gets impatient with actors who bring him stories about summary dismissals that wrecked their careers. 'Oh *Ga-aa-ahd*, will you *sta-aaa-rp* about being fired?' he cried on one such occasion. 'We've all been fired, for

Ga-aaa-ahd's sake!' Since *Gone with the Wind*, however, he has fought shy of head-on conflicts with the front office; that shocking plunge into insecurity taught him caution. When executives seek to tamper with his work, he will argue and cajole, but he evades the violence of a show-down. A case in point is *Bhowani Junction*, the most politically conscious of his films, which was brutally cut, but not over Cukor's dead body. He stayed alive. There are those who reprove him for playing safe; for re-maining a studio employee—picking up $4,000 a week when he was with Metro, and now earning around $150,000 a picture—instead of braving the hazards of independent production. 'George ought to have got away,' says Selznick. 'He stayed in Hollywood too long, sitting up there in his castle behind that big wall.' Happily immured in his fancy fortress, Cukor had no intention of being dislodged. And anyway, he hated travelling.

He spent 1942 and most of 1943 as a private in the Signal Corps, working on training films; released by the Army when he reached its age ceiling, he went home to Metro and made *Gaslight*, in which Ingrid Bergman, as the wife, was driven almost insane by Charles Boyer, and won for her pains an Academy Award.

Since then, his prestige has remained steadily high, with several ups and very few downs. In 1955 the name of Selznick cropped up once more to plague him; Irene Selznick, David's ex-wife, invited Cukor to return to Broadway and direct her production of Enid Bagnold's *The Chalk Garden*. He accepted, but extricated himself from the show before it arrived in New York (where, by the way, it was a notable hit). Holly-wood had accustomed him to delegating authority, and he found his patience unequal to the task of supervising all the minutiae of a stage production. 'I got quite discombobulated,' he says (he has a passion for dated slang). 'In the movies I just had to say the word, and seven thousand people would rush in and burn down Lahore. And here were these two dames—Irene and Enid—arguing with me for days on end about a seventy-five dollar table.'

This transient mishap had no effect on his spirits, or on his appetite for work, which for him is a form of play therapy. Pictures like *Adam's Rib*, *Born Yesterday* and *It Should Happen to You* reflect his inimitable ear for the patterns of everyday speech. He treats actors like eccentric children, alternately to be pampered and chided, and propounds theories to account for their behaviour: 'They get more uppish the farther away they are from Hollywood. In England, for example, they're pretty arrogant—but that may be because English studios are kind of inefficient. Everybody's over-employed. I probably sound like a terrible Fascist but believe me, when you're working in England it's happy days in Dixie, with everyone sitting around all day eating Tootsie Rolls. Actors are bad enough when they get to England, but in India they're *unbearable.*' Yet he always forgives them, and discreetly concerns himself with looking after them if they fall on bad times. It was Lesley Blanch, not Cukor, who told me about his generosity to long-forgotten small-part players, 'ghosts who linger on in obscure hospitals'.

I am not sure what kind of artist he is; in fact, I am not sure he would like to be regarded as an artist at all. If art has to do with the expression of a heartfelt and consistent attitude towards life, then Cukor scarcely qualifies. He has no profound emotional commitments; and as an ideologue he hardly exists. Politically, he is an instinctive Democrat. Once, in the course of a presidential campaign, the studio dispatched an emissary to remind him that it was his duty to do all he could to help the Republican cause. 'You're barking up the wrong tree,' said Cukor, and sent the man away. But one cannot say that his political convictions, or indeed any of his convictions, have found embodiment in his work; and for this reason history will probably exclude him from the ranks of the very greatest directors. He has always been interested less in the statement he is making than in the actors through whom he is making it. He is the trainer who sends the players in fighting; he is not fighting for anything himself.

From the great issues of the day, the vast determining factors of our lives, Cukor has generally remained aloof—'up there in his castle behind that big wall'. Yet he is still in demand; his tiptoe enthusiasm has not waned, and his methods have not grown dated. By cutting himself off from his time, he may well have rendered himself timeless.

(1960)

Miles Apart

Now, when the talk is all of free-form jazz and 'action blowing' and 'after third-stream music, what?', may not be a bad time to pay tribute to Miles Davis, who discovered in the arduous course of the 1950s how to make a unique sound with a trumpet. He based a style on that sound; rose to the height of his profession with that style; and is already in danger—such are the quicksands on which jazz reputations are built—of being written off as a reactionary. Miles found himself as a musician some seven or eight years ago; and those who find themselves are seldom objects of affection to those who are still seeking.

'Talent,' said Delacroix, 'does whatever it wants to do. Genius does only what it can.' Miles can make his sound; 'deathly,' as one critic said, 'in its purity'; piercing and orphaned, and so devoid of vibrato that it recalls to one's inner ear the virginal clarity of a Sistine choirboy. With this sound he composes spare, discreet, elliptical solos, avoiding fast *tempi*—which are inimical alike to his temperament and technique—as strictly as he avoids flamboyant emotionalism. To borrow a phrase applied by George Jean Nathan to the ideal critic, he is like a Thermos bottle, suggesting the presence of heat without radiating it.

The modern movement in jazz has many mansions, but only four architects: the late Charlie Parker, Thelonious Monk, Dizzy Gillespie and Miles, the junior partner. These were the four horsemen of the jazz apocalypse that began in the 1940s and ended by transforming the music; new complexities replaced old naïvetés, and in the process jazz grew up.

Yet despite the sophistication of his style, Miles still speaks in a musical idiom to which children can respond; and English children, at that. A few months ago my nine-year-old daughter came in to be kissed while I was playing his most haunting LP, *Kind of Blue*. She listened for a moment and then said: 'That's Miles Davis.' I asked her how she could tell. 'Because,' she replied, 'it sounds like a little boy who's been locked out and wants to get in.'

Miles in the flesh is not always as dependably superb as he is on records. In public, he sometimes displays the kind of diffidence that conceals (and often protects) enormous private egotism. I first saw him perform in the mid-fifties, at the opening of a shortlived jazz club in Greenwich Village; he turned up more than an hour late, and backed on to the stand with his horn under his jacket. Apprehensively, he unveiled it, heavily muted, and blew about eight notes into the mike, after which he withdrew, shaking his head; it was as if Einstein had been asked to lecture on the quantum theory to a class of backward teenagers.

In 1960 he toured Britain for the first time with his quintet and I followed him from date to date. Musically he gave his audiences full measure, but he irked them, too, by his obstinate reluctance to fraternise. In public, Miles is always alone. He never announces numbers, introduces himself or makes jokes; nor, for that matter, do Oistrakh or Menuhin. Less defensibly, he never takes bows, arguing that his responsibility to the audience ends as soon as the last note has been played. The argument is specious. The truth is that Miles loathes being beholden to anyone, even to the extent of acknowledging applause. He leads a life of rigidly limited obligations. Outside his work, his family and a few close friends, he is committed to nothing. A few years ago he turned down an invitation to pose for the camera of Richard Avedon, not because he disapproved of Avedon but because the record company to which he was under contract had specifically asked him to accept. 'When people *ask* you to do something,' he explained to me, 'all you can say is no.' He spoke as if it were self-evident.

In Britain Miles was at his most isolated, performing in provincial concert halls and metropolitan movie-houses to vast assemblies of ethnic strangers. A dapper, tapering figure in evening dress of black Italian silk, he would take the stage like a fawn in a fairground, or a hermit poet thrust against his will into a populous market place. He had always jibbed at visiting England, because, he once told me, 'I can't stand to hear English spoken that way'; only high financial rewards persuaded him to change his mind. Unidentified, and with no preliminary foot-tapping, the first number would start; Miles and the tenor player stating the theme, with the rhythm section working behind them; then Miles alone leaning back with his trumpet aimed at the footlights, composing bleak, illuminating footnotes to what the ensemble had stated, each note hanging in the air like ripe fruit—plump Moselle grapes when his horn was open, and bottled plums when it was muted.

One thought, as with the best performers one often thinks, of a matador, raptly and serenely defying the audience (which in show business is always the bull), and ending up by hypnotising it. Miles has other affinities with Spain; though he has never been there. The Moors fascinate him: were they not the only coloured people to have left a durable mark on European civilisation? He loves the music they bequeathed—*cante flamenco, cante hondo*—and has tried, in albums like *Sketches of Spain*, to make his trumpet reproduce the flexible wailing of Spanish song. 'That music has enough space in it,' he says. 'You can go on for hours. And you don't just *attack* a note. You can change the whole sound of it.' For medical reasons, matadors eat sparingly on workdays; for psychological reasons, Miles does the same. 'Food,' he declares, 'makes my mind sluggish.'

His solo completed, his meditations made audible, Miles wanders into the wings, leaving the limelight to the man on the tenor sax. This habit of casual departure tended to worry the British, although, as Miles would remark with mock bewilderment: 'What do they want me to do? Stand around and bug the guy?' Later, he would make spectral re-entrances from unexpected corners of the stage, just in time for the last chorus of each number. Then the curtains would swing together, cutting off the applause in its prime.

Offstage, he would bustle past the assembled admirers, murmuring vaguely in the hoarse, gurgling undertone that is all that remains of his voice; a botched operation nine years ago not only sliced nodes from his vocal cords but the cords themselves. (In fairness to the surgeon, I should add that some people blame Miles's croak on a shouting match in which he indulged too soon after the operation.)

In London he rarely emerged from his hotel room except to be driven to a concert date. 'I don't need to see places I've read about,' he said to me, explaining his lack of curiosity. Conversations with strangers would resolve themselves, when the stranger had run out of small talk, into lengthy silences, broken only by abrupt, staccato irrelevancies from Miles. One night, driven to apology by a particularly sustained bout of taciturnity, I said that by his standards English people must seem very dull. He coughed and chuckled. 'You don't mind people being dull,' he said, 'if you aren't dull yourself.'

He hates to be touched, physically as well as emotionally. Four years ago he had his skull cracked by a cop who saw him outside Birdland, taking the air, and told him to move on. It was not so much the order that Miles resented as the fact that the cop grabbed him in the course of enforcing it. When that happened, Miles lashed out; and headlines blazed.

Similarly, he resents any encroachment on his artistic privacy. Apart from Ralph Gleason and Nat Hentoff, he has no time for critics. An English reviewer of some repute came up to him after a concert and remarked, politely if a trifle uppishly: 'I've just been listening to that first LP you made, back in 1948, and I'd like to tell you that I think you've improved out of all recognition since then.' Miles stared at him gnomishly and said: 'When did you first hear that LP?' 'About a year ago,' said the critic. 'Man,' said Miles, with a broad, emphatic grin, *'you should have heard it in 1948!'*

The remark was unanswerable, and it sent the critic into a fit of explanation and apology. When he had left, Miles suavely observed: 'That guy's so nervous, *he* fixes *my* tie.' After witnessing a number of similar encounters, I realised that Miles had an innate grasp of the basic English art of one-upmanship. As Lena Horne said to me a year or two ago: 'Miles is a potentate. He's also a puritan, and the combination can be pretty sadistic.'

The potentate was born in Alton, Illinois, in the late spring of 1926. Miles is that new and still relatively rare phenomenon in jazz, a Negro musician who has never known poverty. His father was a prosperous bourgeois dentist, and his mother was a prominent and respected figure in East St Louis, to which the family moved when Miles was a baby. He liked jazz as soon as he heard it, and when he was thirteen his father gave him a trumpet, to what he now suspects was his mother's deep disapproval. It was only at her urgent request that he refrained from leaving high school to go on the road with Tiny Bradshaw's orchestra; but he drew the line when she tried to send him to Fisk University. The Billy Eckstine band was in St Louis, starring Charlie Parker and Dizzy Gillespie, and providentially lacking a third trumpet player. The ensuing tableau is one that recurs throughout jazz history: the band in rehearsal, the empty chair, the shy neophyte nursing his instrument case, the invitation to sit in, and finally the offer of a temporary job. Overnight, the seventeen-year-old gained admittance to the heartland of modern jazz.

In 1945, with his father's support, he went to New York and studied at Juilliard. Befriended and overawed by Charlie Parker—the sweet Bird who came, not many years later, to a sour end, destroyed by narcotics and alcohol—he was rushed into the front line of modernism, then fighting its crucial battles with traditional jazz, and he can be heard on many Parker recordings of the period, straining the limits of his technique to keep pace with the master's baffling flights of invention. From Parker and Thelonious Monk he learned new chord progressions; from the late Freddie Webster he learned a sound—the pure, vibratoless tone that was to become his hallmark. At the same time he taught himself not to imitate the high-register coruscations of Dizzy Gillespie.

Once, according to Nat Hentoff, he asked Dizzy: 'Why can't I play high like you?'

'Because you don't hear up there,' Gillespie told him. 'You hear in the middle register.'

In the late 1940s, Miles met the arranger Gil Evans, a diffident, aquiline man more than ten years his senior, and a restless experimenter with new tonal colourings in jazz. Of these experiments Miles became the centrepiece; the jewel had found its appropriate setting. The first fruits of their collaboration are to be heard in a celebrated series of recordings made in 1949–50 and since reissued under the collective title of *The Birth of the Cool*; led by Miles and guided by Evans, the nine-piece group assembled for these sessions included Gerry Mulligan and John Lewis as player-composers, and its instrumental line-up featured a French horn and a tuba. The results, lightly and elegantly swinging, set a new standard of sophisticated lyricism in modern jazz. Since then Miles and Gil Evans have frequently worked together: some of the finest LPs of recent years— among them *Miles Ahead*, *Porgy and Bess* and *Sketches of*

Spain—are those on which Miles swoops and soars like a kingfisher above the swirling, kaleidoscopic eddies of an Evans orchestration. Their recording dates are concentrated orgies of perfectionism. Evans tends to be the calmer of the two; Miles gets ulcerously edgy. During *Porgy*, he told me, 'I felt like I'd been eating nails.' Few of Miles's close friends are white, and of these Evans is by far the most intimate. 'Gil,' he says, 'is like my thumb.'

For a jazz musician, Miles is nowadays comparatively affluent. He receives between $3,500 and $4,500 a week in clubs, but will play only in clubs of which he approves (i.e. whose owners are untouched by the Jim Crow tarbrush, and respect his refusal to play requests or chat with the clients). He has not always been able to dictate his terms so securely. In 1949—perhaps the high point of drug addiction in jazz history—he took desperately to heroin, that last refuge of the outsider in an over-competitive world; and four years of failing income and increasing unreliability went by before pride drove him to kick the habit. By 1955 he had recovered his balance and more than restored his reputation, coming back with the stripped simplicity of utterance that has marked all his subsequent work.

In this simplicity some critics have found only meagreness. 'He just uses fewer notes,' one of them said to me. 'Since he made his comeback, he doesn't play better, he just plays safer. Except when he's following a Gil Evans score, he sticks to the melody. All he does is play it slowly, with a few unexpected notes thrown in to prove that he's modern.' It is true that Miles seldom takes one by storm or surprise; and it is also true that he sometimes under-exerts himself; but as I listen to the marvellous spate of recorded sound that poured out of the Miles Davis Quintet in the late 1950s, I cannot help recalling a definition that Jean Cocteau once made of art. For some people, he said, art was a complicated way of saying very simple things; 'for us,' he continued, 'it is a simple way of saying very complicated things.' So with Miles Davis in his best period. I need hardly add that the simplicity is only apparent.

Miles lives in a noisy, rambling, duplex apartment on West 77th Street in New York. With its marble-tile floors, leopard-skin rugs, abstract paintings, white brick walls and proliferating electronic gadgets, it might be the hunting lodge of some preternaturally hip Swedish grandee. An Italian greyhound named Milo prances around the place, and upstairs there are turtles. There are also children, four in number. Three of them derive from Miles's first marriage, an early error committed in Illinois and since erased by divorce. Cherry Anne, at eighteen the eldest, enjoys singing, and Gregory, a year younger, used to play the drums;

otherwise the family is resolutely unmusical. After Miles Junior, aged thirteen, we come to a seven-year-old named Jean-Pierre who belongs to his second wife, Frances, from a former marriage. Sly, petite and sparkling, Frances moves with the physical elation of a pedigree pony, as befits a onetime member of the Katherine Dunham company; it was for her that Miles composed the skipping little melody called *Fran-Dance*.

When not working, driving his smart grey Ferrari or keeping his body in trim at a local gymnasium, Miles spends most of his time at home, relaxing in a desultory chaos of family small talk behind which, from some hidden loudspeaker, one can usually hear the faint, appealing cry of the paternal trumpet. Talking to semi-strangers like myself, he is willing to discuss music, but always at a distance, with beady eyes and a disenchanted smile. 'A melody is enough,' he may say; 'I can live on a melody for the next three months. I don't know about third-stream music; it's interesting, but that's all. It's like a woman I don't like, walking naked in front of me.' As he speaks, he is dialling his stockbroker's number; Miles is a dedicated investor. 'Music is like an affair with a woman. If you like her, you like her. But always—no violins. . . . Look, this is Miles. When that other stock goes up to twenty, sell it. Fine. Good-bye. . . . My favourite composers? Debussy, Khachaturian, Bloch and Ravel—*he* was born in the right place, between Spain and France.'

Portentously, I asked him to name the five most important people alive. 'Me and Harold,' he promptly began, meaning Harold Lovette, his lawyer and confidant. 'And Gil, and Fran. And any American Negro over fifty years old. I think every Negro over fifty should get a medal for putting up with all that crap.' He rose and gave me a farewell grip, coupled with a husky salutation. The amplifier played pure Spain, the plangent sound of an Andalusian *saeta*; a woman's lament, reproduced by Miles's horn in all its pain and glottal sobbing.

Bullfighting and jazz are two minor arts with much in common. At the beginning of the century they were national and special; and both depended on collective improvisation. In New Orleans, the trumpet, trombone and clarinet improvised on a given melody; in Spain, the picador, banderillero and matador improvised on the theme of a given fighting bull. Suddenly, in the twenties, there arose in both countries a revolutionary performer who not only changed the course of the art he was practising but made it for the first time internationally renowned. In Spain, Juan Belmonte, and in America, Louis Armstrong. Outside their countries of origin, both were predictably reviled as harbingers of fiendish moral depravity.

In the thirties commercialism takes over. We hear on one side that bullfighting has been ruined by the mechanical, crowd-pleasing efficiency of Domingo Ortega; and on the other that jazz has been killed by the popular triumphs of Benny Goodman. The first hints of resurrection appear in 1939; at Minton's, in Harlem, a nucleus of venturesome musicians inaugurates the modern movement in jazz; and in Spain, a lean young rebel named Manolete takes the *alternativa* and becomes a full matador. There follows, in both countries, a ferocious struggle between the supporters of modernism and the adherents to tradition. The arrival of the LP permits a favoured soloist to improvise for fifteen minutes without interruption; at the same time, bullfighters develop the habit of prolonging the *faena*—the series of passes that precedes the kill—until it becomes the focal point of the spectacle. Traditionalists love teamwork; modernists love soloists; and the battle in both countries remains unresolved for more than a decade. An armistice is ultimately achieved.

In jazz as in bullfighting, there arises a modern classicist, one who combines the best of both worlds. In Spain, his name is Antonio Ordóñez, the *Número Uno* of living matadors. In America it is Miles Davis.

The Spanish have a word, *duende*. It has no exact English equivalent, but it denotes the quality without which no flamenco singer or bullfighter can conquer the summit of his art. The ability to transmit a profoundly felt emotion to an audience of strangers with the minimum of fuss and the maximum of restraint: that is as near as our language can get to the full meaning of *duende*. Laurence Olivier has it; Maurice Evans does not. Billie Holiday had it, and so did Bessie Smith; but Ella Fitzgerald never reached it. It is the quality that differentiates Laurette Taylor from Lynn Fontanne, Ernest Hemingway from John O'Hara, Tennessee Williams from William Inge. Whatever else he may lack, Miles Davis has *duende*.

(1961)

Orson Welles

Some eighteen years ago, in the pages of an English school magazine, there appeared a brief and sickeningly lush essay, entitled 'The New Playboy of the Western World'. It read, in part:

> There is a man flourishing now and being mighty on the other side of the Atlantic. He has a lovely wife and twenty-odd years of

flamboyant youth, but his accomplishments do not end here. He has burst on the American scene with a heavy gesture of ineffable superiority; he is the artistic saviour of a broad land, and he knows it. For Orson Welles is a self-made man, and how he loves his maker. . . . He moulds art out of radio, the scourge of art; he is a wit as only Americans can be wits; and he is a dandy among impromptu speakers. He is a director of plays in kingly fashion, independent as a signpost in all he does; and he has carved out of a face of massy granite the subtle lineaments of a great actor. He is a gross and glorious director of motion pictures, the like of which we have not seen since the great days of the German cinema; he reproduces life as it is sometimes seen in winged dreams.

He is all these things, vastly exaggerated and blown up into a balloon of bold promise and brash achievement. Yet with all his many-sidedness he has no dignity. 'I have,' he once said, 'the dignity of a nude at high noon on Fifth Avenue.' One requisite of greatness he lacks: artistic integrity. Perhaps he has burgeoned too soon and too wildly; but it will come with praise and age, and then we shall behold a gorgeous, patriarchal figure, worthy of the Old Testament. Until then, watch him, watch him well, for he is a major prophet, with the hopes of a generation clinging to his heels.

I was sixteen when I wrote that. I wince today at its alliterations, its borrowed sonorities, and its tone of midget exhortation. Even more, I wince at the calmness of my assertion that Welles was deficient in 'artistic integrity', since that is one kind of integrity he has seldom been accused of wanting; perhaps I meant 'integration', which would make a little more sense.

I quote from the piece not out of vainglory but merely to establish my credentials. In 1943 I was committed to Welles as to nobody else then active in the performing arts; and I am sure there were thousands like me, young people in their teens and twenties for whom Welles was Renaissance man reborn. He seemed to have shortened, almost to vanishing point, the distance between ambition and achievement; no sooner did he approach an art than it surrendered to him. Theatre was the first to fall. We had read of the Negro *Macbeth* he directed in Harlem, and of his two audacious seasons at the helm of the Mercury Theatre. In his spare time he had conquered radio, unhinging America in 1938 with his adaptation of H. G. Wells's *The War of the Worlds*. Then he had gone to Hollywood and subjected the film industry to its first major upheaval since the advent of sound.

Nobody who saw *Citizen Kane* at an impressionable age will ever forget the experience; overnight, the American cinema had acquired an adult vocabulary, a dictionary instead of a phrase book for semiliterates. I first saw it on a Monday afternoon in the English provinces, and was lastingly dazzled by its narrative virtuosity, its shocking but always relevant cuts (do you remember that screeching cockatoo?), its brilliantly orchestrated dialogue, and its use of deep focus in sound as well as in vision. About a dozen other people, scattered throughout the theatre, shared the revelation with me. By the end of the week I had seen the film five times, once with my eyes shut in order to prove to myself that the sound track was expressive enough to be listened to in its own right. That was in 1941; and when *The Magnificent Ambersons* came along, a year or so later, my capitulation was complete. Sceptics had told me that Welles was a technical maestro, incapable of feeling; to confound them, I had only to point to his handling of Booth Tarkington's family saga, in which there were scenes of a naked emotional intimacy rarely matched in the history of Hollywood. Agnes Moorehead's portrait of Aunt Fanny, eaten up with frustrated love for her nephew, seemed to me then (and seems to me still) the best performance of its kind in the English-speaking cinema. At the end of the film came the credit titles, after which a microphone suspended from a boom swung into view. 'I wrote the picture and directed it,' said a serene bass voice. 'My name is Orson Welles.' If my prayer at that moment had been answered, Welles would have written and directed the whole subsequent output of the American film industry. Thus infatuated, I sat down and penned my eulogy.

Time, I am told by many of my friends, has proved me mistaken; if the 'hopes of a generation' ever clung to Welles's heels, they have long since been trampled underfoot. What, I am asked, has the man accomplished in the past eighteen years? A handful of stylish thrillers, a couple of bombastic Shakespeare films, a few hit-or-miss stage productions, a number of self-exploiting television appearances, and several tongue-in-cheek performances in other people's bad epics—what, beyond these, has Welles to show for himself? For one thing, I sometimes reply, he has scars, inflicted by a society which demands that the making of art and the making of money should be yokefellows. For another, he shares with people like Chaplin, Cocteau, Picasso, Ellington, and Hemingway a fixed international reputation that can never wholly be tarnished. Even in eclipse, he remains among the elite, to be judged on their level; the quickest ears prick up and the keenest eyes brighten at the advent of a new Orson Welles production—or rather, manifestation, since one can never predict the form in which his talent will choose to reveal itself.

Apart from writing and directing films and plays, and apart from acting in both, he has tried his hand as a novelist, a painter, a ballet scenarist, a public orator, a magician, a columnist, and a bullfighter.

To understand why he carries with him this permanent aura of expectation, it is perhaps necessary to know him. Last spring I spent a week in Spain at his elbow, listening while he talked about his life and times. In Welles's company, on this occasion as on all previous ones, I automatically assumed the role of stooge. What follow are my memories of what he said, and my comments thereon, which I hope may provide some explanation of why, whenever I find myself bored and wondering whom I would most like to see coming in at the door, the answer is always Orson.

First, a sketch of his physical presence, which is overwhelming. He has the sauntering bulk of a fastidious yet insatiable glutton. Welles is perilously fat, having taken none but the slightest exercise since the time, thirty years ago, when he leapt in to challenge the bulls at every village *corrida* within striking distance of Seville. Jean Cocteau rightly called him 'a giant with the face of a child', adding that he was also 'an active loafer, a wise madman, a solitude surrounded by humanity'. Watch him in repose at a bullfight, lonely in the crowd, his brow contracted above the vast tanned jowls and his eyes bulging with reproach; into such a frame, one feels, the soul of the last American bison might easily migrate. From the pursed lips a tremendous cigar protrudes, and the chin is grimly outthrust; yet in all this dignity there is somehow an element of dimpled mischief. Beneath the swelling forehead a schoolboy winks, and can readily be coaxed into chuckling. Orson amused is an engulfing spectacle, as irresistible as Niagara. The remark (frequently his) is made; a moment of silence ensues, during which his forehead retracts, causing his eyes to pop and his cheeks to sag, turning his face into a tragic mask. For an instant he looks appalled; and then there breaks through the thunderous cachinnation of his laughter. 'A wonderful laugh,' said Tennessee Williams, having listened to it, 'forced and defensive, like mine.' But I think he was wrong: Orson laughs to goad others out of awe into participation. 'I like people to talk to me,' he says, 'What I can't stand is when they talk to Orson Welles.'

Lunch in the garden of the Ritz in Madrid: Orson, surging across the terrace in white shirt and white tie, arouses thoughts of Moby Dick. Spanish decorum has overcome his habitual tielessness. He is in Spain for three reasons: to shoot a documentary for Italian television, to finish off his movie adaptation of *Don Quixote* (with Akim Tamiroff as Sancho Panza and an unknown Mexican as the Don), and to go to the bullfights.

The first two projects are tending to overlap, as Orson intended they should. Last year, dwindling funds forced him to abandon his own picture, with two weeks' shooting still to be done, and when an Italian TV network invited him to direct a series of documentaries, he agreed on condition that the first should deal with Spain. As a title, he suggested *The Land of Don Quixote*. Thus he manages to work for himself while working for somebody else; Orson has spent much of his life in this kind of double harness. As for the bulls, they are his passion; he is one of the very few Anglo-Saxons whose opinions are valued by the Spanish taurine initiates. Among contemporary matadors his favourite is Antonio Ordó-ñez, the graceful young maestro from Ronda, who achieves with the bulls he fights an intimacy so profound, so devoid of arrogance, that it once moved Orson to observe: 'With Antonio, each pass asserts not "how great *I am!*" but "how great *we are!*" ' The remark may stand as a definition of good bullfighting. Though addicted to the bulls, Orson is bored by all other competitive sports; he has no interest in skills he has never practised.

As we eat, he talks about his childhood, and Madrid society pre-tends not to listen—an effort that must be made by all those who find themselves in public places where Orson is conducting a private conver-sation. It is not that he shouts, merely that he cannot help resounding. Except in solitude, a state rare with him, Orson has no private person-ality; everything about him is public, and he is open daily. This has been true as long as he can remember. 'Orson at twenty-six,' it was wickedly said at the height of his Hollywood success 'is still overshadowed by the glorious memory of Orson at six.' He was born in Kenosha, Wisconsin, forty-six years ago last May, and claims to be more English than the English, springing as he does from generations of unmixed colonial stock. 'You can find eighteenth-century Englishmen in the Middle West,' he says, 'just as you can find sixteenth-century Spaniards in Peru.' I begin to see in him an extravagant Whig on the model of Charles James Fox, tinged with more than a hint of Byron, the first of the great romantic ex-patriates. But I remember that Orson hates to be called an expatriate; since the term applies only to people who exile themselves from the country in which they were raised, how can it apply to him, who was not brought up in America? And he has a point: until he was eighteen years old, Orsen spent most of his time abroad.

Both his parents were travellers. His father, Richard Welles, was a Virginian who moved to Wisconsin because he owned two factories there. He was an accomplished gambler, a sedulous globe-trotter, and an unpre-dictable inventor. One of his inventions was a carbide bicycle lamp that made him a great deal of money; others turned out less encouragingly. 'He tried very hard to invent the airplane,' Orson says. 'He thought the Wright brothers were working on the wrong principles, so he designed a steam-driven car with a kind of glider attached to it. He put a Negro servant into the glider and started out, but the steam got into the Negro's eyes and he crashed into a tree. He and my father were photographed afterward, smiling across the wreckage.' Orson's mother was Beatrice Ives of Springfield, Illinois, a gifted pianist, radical in her view of politics and art, and ravishing in her beauty. To this union of playboy and aesthete, at a time when both partners were approaching middle age, George Orson Welles was born, owing his first name to George Ade, the humourist, and his second to a Chicago businessman called Orson Wells. He says he had two remote cousins who later became politically eminent: Sumner Welles and Adlai Stevenson. He also had a brother, Richard, Jr., some ten years his senior, of whose subsequent history little is known; a dreamer and roamer, he was last heard of in Seattle, upholding the family tradition of intelligent dilettantism.

One dwells on Orson's parents because so much about them helped to shape him. He got on splendidly with them both, rather better than they did with each other; where mother had her salon, father favoured the saloon. The child's precociousness was Mozartean. At the age of two he spoke fluent and considered English, and was familiar with the plays of Shakespeare from his mother's readings. The first great wrench came when he was six. His parents separated, and Orson went to live with his mother for two halcyon years, during which he adoringly absorbed her passion for music, poetry, and painting. He hated, however, to practise scales on the piano, and once, at the age of seven, stationed himself on a high window ledge of the Ritz Hotel in Paris, threatening to jump unless his mother told his music teacher to stop badgering him. As always, she complied. The idyll ended when he was eight. Beatrice Welles died, and Orson, already an adult in feeling, was whisked off to share his father's way of life, which revolved round late nights, stage doors, and constant changes of country. 'He was a wandering *bon viveur*,' Orson says, 'and he revelled in theatre people. Before my mother died, painting and music were what interested me most. I'd never thought seriously about the theatre.'

Through his mother he had met Ravel and Stravinsky; through his father he met John Barrymore, together with innumerable circus performers and magicians. He acquired a showman's eye (which later enabled him to act as an unpaid scout for John Ringling North) and an illusionist's dexterity. 'My father loved magic,' he says. 'That's what bound us together.' Such masters as Harry Houdini and Long Tack Sam, the Chinese conjurer who revolutionised card manipulation, were called in to teach him their mysteries. If anything, he improved on what he learned; today Orson is one of the best paid magicians alive. In 1960, at a London hotel, he received more than $1,500 for one performance of a single trick: seizing an axe, he splintered a block of ice within which there was frozen a strongbox, inside which there was locked a scrap of paper, upon which there was inscribed the official registration number of a taxi-driver whom an unbribed guest had brought in from the street just before the axe was lifted. Some years ago Orson agreed to lend his arcane skills to a Hollywood celebration in honour of Louis B. Mayer. So many stars preceded him that by the time his turn came the rabbit concealed in the lining of his suit had urinated 'roughly twenty-seven times'. He has been wary of unpaid performances ever since.

Above all, Orson learned from his father the art of travelling. Who else of his age can declare nowadays, with eyewitness authority, that 'the two great artistic centres of the twenties were Budapest and Peking'? He explored Europe in the care of various tutors, one of whom took him when he was nine to an uncommonly noisy dinner party at Innsbruck, of which he remembers little except the name of the man at the head of the table, one Adolf Hitler. Life with father was more restless and uncertain than it had been with mother. 'How is it,' I suddenly ask Orson, 'that the heroes of your films have no fathers?' I am thinking not so much of Macbeth and Othello as of George in *The Magnificent Ambersons*, who ruins the life of his widowed mother; and especially of Charles Foster Kane, whose father never appears, and who is taken away from his mother as a child and transported into an alien world of men and money, rather like George Orson Welles. In answer to my question, Orson says that there is no reason, that he adored his father; and no doubt he did. All the same, the parallel with Kane is curiously haunting. One recalls the sled named Rosebud, Kane's symbol of maternal affection, the loss of which deprives him irrecoverably of the power to love or be loved. (Mr Bernstein, the lawyer who takes Kane under his wing, is admittedly based on Dr Maurice Bernstein, the family physician who acted as Welles's unofficial guardian after his father died in 1928.) It is not inconceivable, as a perceptive American director once suggested to me, that Orson reached a stage of perfect self-fulfilment just before his mother's death, and that he has been trying ever since to recapture it.

At ten, under heavy persuasion from his father and Dr Bernstein, Orson joined the progressive Todd School for Boys in Woodstock, Illinois, where he flourished for five years, admiringly encouraged by the

school director, Roger Hill, with whom, while still in his teens, he wrote a
fledgling play and edited a popular textbook called *Everybody's Shakespeare*. On principle, however, he disapproves of conventional education
in any form, and will have none of it for Beatrice, his five-year-old
daughter: 'What does it teach you except to show up at the same hour
every morning—and still learn nothing?' In his fourteenth year the death
of his father cast him upon a world from which security, as his parents
had known it, was about to be banished by the Wall Street crash. An
orphaned prodigy, he grew up hoarding nostalgia; in particular, a nostalgia for old-fashioned melodrama, for stock companies, for turn-of-the-
century Americana, which he had imbibed from his father. It persisted
into later life, as many of his stage productions bear witness: *The
Drunkard*, William Gillette's *Too Much Johnson*, *The Green Goddess*,
Around the World in Eighty Days, and *Moby Dick*, which Orson directed
in London as it might have been presented by a touring company in the
nineties. Again and again he has gone back to the flamboyant era of the
actor-manager in the astrakhan collar, the era of Tarkington's Ambersons
and Citizen Kane's infancy. Orson has always secretly thought of himself
as a vagabond rogue.

Just before he graduated from Todd, at the age of fifteen, an ad
appeared in *The Billboard*. It read, in part:

ORSON WELLES—Stock, Characters, Heavies, Juveniles or as
cast . . . Lots of pep, experience and ability. Close in Chicago early
in June and want place in good stock company for remainder of
season.

He was on his own. It is not fanciful to see Orson's life as an
unfinished picaresque novel, each chapter of which is a bizarre adventure
strung like a bead on the thread of the hero's personality; the raw
material, in fact, for a new *Citizen Kane*, different from the old in that the
central character would be a maker of art, not merely a collector.

The lunch is over. Orson insists on paying, and summons his
Italian henchman, a minor but authentic prince, to look after the bill. The
prince sportively doubts whether he has enough cash. 'Very well,' says the
ventripotent Orson, beaming broadly. 'My signature against the world!'

I never cease to be fascinated by the spectacle of a talent so huge
yet so homeless, so vast yet so vagrant. Other people sink roots; but
Orson perpetually wanders, a citizen of no fixed territory save that of art.
I had already heard him on the subject of his upbringing; I wanted now
to discuss his adult life, during which he had spanned the globe in an
effort to recapture the creative security of his childhood.

The next day I lunched with him again, this time at Horcher's, his favourite among the city's great restaurants. Spain has always been one of his chosen countries. Although he is no believer in formal education, he is having his daughter, Beatrice, taught to dance flamenco; when I asked her what she thought about while stamping her feet and flashing her eyes in such precocious frenzy, she pondered and replied, 'I think that I *hate* the *floor*'.

Talking to Orson can be a disquieting experience; one feels one is boring him, wasting his time, especially if the purpose of the meeting is professional. He has so often suffered at the hands of journalists. 'The French are the worst,' he says. 'They ask long questions that *are* the answers. I nod, and the question is printed without the question mark, as my idea.' Having ordered caviare, blintzes, and venison, he tells me that his greatest burden has always been his grandiose physical appearance. 'My trouble is that I exude affluence,' he says. 'I look successful. Whenever the critics see me, they say to themselves: "It's time he was knocked—he's had it too good for too long." But I *haven't* had it so good; I just look that way. I need jobs like anyone else.' He splutters with baritone laughter. 'Every time I bring out a new movie,' he goes on, 'nobody bothers to review it—at least, not until the last paragraph. Instead, they write a long essay on "the Welles Phenomenon and what has become of it". They don't review my work; they review me!'

He left school in 1930, an orphan aged fifteen, and at once set about the task, which proved to be lifelong, of inventing himself. His first parentless years were favoured ones. Thanks to his father's legacy, he never felt the pinch of the Depression. Intended for Harvard, he embarked instead on a painting trip to Ireland, where he gate-crashed the Dublin Gate Theatre and became a professional actor. 'You handle your voice like a singer,' said the director, Hilton Edwards, 'and there isn't a note of sincerity in it.' He was then sixteen. We next hear of him sketching in Morocco, fighting bulls around Seville, and returning unsung to the States in 1933, when Thornton Wilder gave him a letter to Alexander Woollcott, who in turn introduced him to Katharine Cornell. The last lady of the American theatre (as I sometimes think of her) hired him to join her company in a tour of *Romeo and Juliet* and *Candida*. Already, at seventeen, he thought of himself as past the age when he could convincingly play juveniles, and he turned up at the first rehearsal of the Shaw comedy assuming that he had been cast as Morell, Candida's husband. He was surprised to see that Basil Rathbone was also present: 'I took Miss Cornell to one side and told her that I didn't want to interfere, but didn't she think Rathbone was a little elderly to be playing

Marchbanks, the adolescent poet?' It had to be carefully explained to him that that was *his* role; Mr Rathbone had been engaged as Morell.

One of the dates the company played was Atlantic City, where Orson dabbled for the first time in professional magic. He practised palmistry in a booth on the boardwalk, so successfully that he almost unnerved himself. To begin with, he confined himself to simple exercises in applied psychology: 'I would look into the crystal ball and then say to the customer: "You have a scar on your knee"—because in fact most people have. If that didn't work, I would say: "You had a profound emotional experience between the ages of eleven and thirteen." I don't think I ever failed with that one.' But he soon discovered that he was less of a charlatan than he had imagined; too many of his intuitions turned out to be correct. 'I began,' he says, 'to think of myself as Ming the Merciless.' That Orson is capable of insights amounting to prophecy is borne out by a number of stories, the best known of which concerns the occasion when he escorted Eugene O'Neill's daughter Oona to a Hollywood night club and offered, on the strength of two hours' acquaintance, to read her hand. 'Within a very short time,' he declared, 'you will meet and marry Charles Chaplin.' Like so many of her father's heroines, Miss O'Neill obeyed the voice of destiny.

Orson made his Broadway debut in December 1934, playing the Chorus and Tybalt in *Romeo and Juliet*. There ensues the first familiar period of his legend—the four-year battle with the American theatre. 'Paris is the playwright's city,' he says, 'London is the actor's city, and New York is the director's city.' Or if New York wasn't, Orson did much to make it so. In the late thirties, more than at any other time in American history, the development of the theatre seemed intimately bound up with the development of the country as a whole; a radical adventure was under way, and the nation's culture was among the spearheads of the nation's hopes. In 1935 the New Deal sired the Federal Theatre Project, devised not only to alleviate unemployment in the theatre but to bring good drama within the reach of the unemployed audiences. By subsidising the Project, Washington accepted the principle that the fostering of culture was a matter for public as well as private concern. Progressive artists, in a period when nearly all artists were progressives, embraced the scheme; and no one who hopes to understand Orson should forget that his career as a director was launched under its liberal auspices.

The Project set up a Negro branch at the old Lafayette Theatre in Harlem, and it was here, in the spring of 1936, that Orson and John Houseman staged their shattering Negro production of *Macbeth*. 'On

opening night.' Orson recalls, 'the curtain never fell. The audience
swarmed up onto the stage, cheering.' He afterwards went on tour with
the show: 'We had a temperamental Macbeth, and in Indianapolis we
lost him. I blacked myself up about three shades darker than anyone else
in the cast and played the part for two weeks. Nobody in the audience
noticed anything unusual.' Back at the Lafayette, he directed a fiercely
anti-segregationist piece called *Turpentine*, and remembers his horror
when Noble Sissle's pit orchestra played the first-night audience out to
the reactionary strains of 'Is it true what they say about Dixie?'

On Broadway, still for the Federal Theatre, he staged and starred in
Marlowe's *Doctor Faustus*, which ran for six months; but the cultural
euphoria in Washington was being blown away by hot winds from the
right, whose breath Orson felt in the summer of 1937, when government
sponsorship was abruptly withdrawn from his production of Marc
Blitzstein's leftist opera *The Cradle Will Rock* on the eve of its première.
Locked out of the Maxine Elliot Theatre, he found another (the Venice,
later renamed the Century) and led the first-nighters thither on a triumphal march up Sixth Avenue. Confronted by an Actors' Equity ruling
that forbade the actors to appear on the stage, he seated them among the
audience and had them sing their parts from there. It was a great
crusading night. Tom Paine would have enjoyed it; and there is no one in
American history (I have his word for this) Orson would rather have been
than Tom Paine.

In 1939 the Federal Theatre Project was voted out of existence. By
then Orson and John Houseman had spent two seasons in private
enterprise, running the Mercury Theatre on Fortyfirst Street, getting
simultaneously into debt and the history books with a string of productions that included *Danton's Death*, *Heartbreak House*, and the startling
modern-dress version of *Julius Caesar*. They regarded the Mercury
Theatre's broadcasts simply as money-making adjuncts to its theatrical
activities; nobody was more astonished than Orson when, taking a stroll
during a break in the dress rehearsal of *Danton's Death*, he saw his name
travelling in lights around the Times Building, followed by an announcement that he had panicked America with his radio adaptation of H. G.
Wells's *War of the Worlds*. He had intended the programme as a
Halloween joke; not for the first time, and certainly not the last, he had
over-estimated the intelligence of his audience. Such errors are healthy:
what kills art is the assumption that people are stupid. 'About three years
after the Martian broadcast,' Orson says, 'I was reading a Whitman poem
on a patriotic Sunday programme, when someone ran into the studio and
shouted into the mike that Pearl Harbour had been attacked. Nobody

paid any attention. They just shrugged and said, "There he goes again." '
The Mercury Theatre survived on Broadway until the spring of 1939
having demonstrated that a repertory company needs more than critical
applause and intermittently filled houses to keep it alive; it needs the continuity and security that only steady subsidies can provide.

Lunch, the long Spanish lunch, has come to an end. It is time for the
bullfight; and I ask Orson what would have happened if, twenty years
ago, he had been given a theatre of his own and enough money to hold a
permanent company together. 'No question about it,' he says at once;
'I'd be running it today.' Orson's kind of theatre belongs in a tradition
that looks beyond the next flop or the next season's deficit; its affinities
are with the great non-commercial institutions—the Comédie Française,
the Moscow Art Theatre, the Berliner Ensemble. Even as I say that, I
shush myself, realising how much harm it may do to Orson's Broadway
reputation.

His relationship with money requires a brief rubric. The legend
insists that Orson overspends; the truth is that he is a delayed earner.
Citizen Kane was a flop in 1941, but over the years it has returned its
investment many times over, and the same applies to *The Magnificent
Ambersons*. Orson's pictures are long-distance runners in a system dedicated to sprinters. True, *The Lady from Shanghai* was disproportionately
expensive, but against that one must balance *The Stranger* and *Macbeth*,
both of which he brought in on schedule and under budget. Orson's first
large debt was to the United States government, which refused to allow
him tax deductions on personal losses (amounting to $350,000) that were
incurred by his 1946 Broadway production of *Around the World in
Eighty Days*. He moved to Europe, leaving the argument to his lawyers;
and since then his financial problems have affected none but his own productions. They have sometimes lost money and left behind them a trail of
unpaid bills; but this, in our society, is precisely what one would expect
of a man who rates his responsibility to the cause of art above his responsibility to private investment. More subsidy from the state, not less
extravagance on Orson's part, is the answer to the perennial Welles
predicament. He regards art as a social right, not as an accidental
privilege; as a matter for public endowment, not as incentive to private
speculation. That his work should occasionally lose money is not only
inevitable but honourable.

We meet in the bar of the Palace Hotel after the bullfight; it has been
a bad one, but Orson is not depressed, for to the true *aficionado* there are
no dull bullfights. He watches them with the analytical scrutiny of an
initiate, which means that he is never bored and rarely transported. He

watches films in the same way: 'I'm like a vivisectionist. I dissect them shot by shot. I'd give half my kingdom to be able to see a movie and forget what I know about movie technique.' He responds politely to the group that gathers around him in the bar; perhaps too politely, making me wish he would squander less of his energy in a form as perishable as talk. Tennessee Williams, one of the circle, extracts from his mouth a cigarette holder full of cancer-repelling crystals and murmurs to me that no one should ever attack Orson—'a man so vulnerable, and of such magnitude'. Everyone is vulnerable who is at once gifted and gregarious. Orson is fully aware that for him, as for all great talkers, conversation is what Cyril Connolly once called it, 'a ceremony of self-wastage'. I record a few overheard snatches. Of Antonioni, the director of the wildly praised Italian film *L'Avventura*, he says: 'The critics tell me he's a stylist of the cinema. But how can you be a stylist if you don't understand grammar?' Of a famous American actor, generally renowned for his modesty off-screen: 'There is nothing more frightening than quiet vanity.' Of Oscar Wilde's comedies: 'Why don't people realise that they were written to be acted by tweedy, red-faced Victorian squires, not by attractive faggots?' He flies these conversational kites because they are expected of him, and then subsides into heavy, abstracted brooding. The circle disperses, and he generously wastes himself on me.

We talk about his Hollywood epoch, which lasted on and off for roughly seven years. Leaving Broadway in 1939, he brought the Mercury actors—among them Joseph Cotten and Agnes Moorehead—out to work with him for RKO. The trip produced *Citizen Kane*, which stands in no need of eulogy from me. It revolutionised Hollywood rather as the aeroplane revolutionised warfare; it drove William Randolph Hearst, on whom Kane was putatively modelled, to declare war on Orson in his newspapers; and it cost less than $750,000, which seems a reasonable price to pay for a landmark in cinema history. In 1941 Orson started to shoot *The Magnificent Ambersons*, based on Booth Tarkington's story about the decline of a prosperous Southern family. 'I'd finished the rough cut,' Orson says, 'and I needed about two weeks more work to get the picture ready, when Jock Whitney and Nelson Rockefeller, who were both RKO shareholders, asked me to go down to South America and make a film about Latin-American solidarity.' By then the United States had entered the war, and Orson patriotically agreed. The course of shooting was not uneventful; headlines were made in Rio de Janeiro when Orson and the Mexican Ambassador to Brazil protested against an exorbitant hotel bill by carefully throwing a great deal of furniture out of a window of His Excellency's suite.

Meanwhile, in Orson's words: 'RKO had shown *The Ambersons* at a sneak preview, probably in Pomona. The audience laughed at it, so they cut it to pieces, shot a new ending, and released it before I could do anything about it. They called me in Brazil to say they'd broken my contract.' Among the cuts were Agnes Mooreheads's finest moments, many of them improvised during the six-week rehearsal period on which Orson had insisted; and the whole epilogue was lopped off, in which Joseph Cotten visited Miss Moorehead in a shabby rooming house and learned from her how and why the magnificence of the Ambersons had faded. 'Nowadays,' Orson says, 'everybody makes pictures three hours long—it's almost obligatory. There are times when I feel a little bit jealous.' He likes the efficiency of Hollywood studios ('where there's no difference between you and the workers except that they're earning more') and admits that his veneration for the cinema derives from his period at RKO. 'The cinema has no boundaries,' he says. 'It's a ribbon of dream.' He sounds genuinely awed.

His later Hollywood pictures, such as *Journey into Fear, The Stranger*, and *The Lady from Shanghai*, are as different from *Kane* and *The Ambersons* as Graham Greene's 'entertainments' are different from his serious novels; in fact, it may even be that Welles influenced Greene's thrillers by his use of shock cutting, bizarre settings, and eccentric characterisation. The last shot of *The Lady from Shanghai*, completed in 1946, symbolises the end of a phase in Orson's life. The film is socially quite outspoken; Orson plays an ingenuous Irish sailor, once a fighter for the Spanish Republic, who gets involved in what he describes as the 'bright, guilty world' of the rich. He falls for, and is cold-bloodedly deceived by, the wife of a millionaire lawyer. After a horrendous showdown in a deserted fun fair, she is shot by her husband, and appeals to Orson for help. Her injury is mortal; but his decision is moral. He rejects her plea; he has compromised too often, and leaves her, walking out of the fun fair into the grey dawn of a new morning. (The riddled victim was played by his second wife, Rita Hayworth; they were divorced in 1947 after four years together. His first marriage, to a Chicago actress named Virginia Nicholson, had broken up in 1939.)

One tends to forget that his Hollywood days coincide with the Second World War. Orson himself has not forgotten. Flat feet kept him out of the armed forces: 'I'm still suffering,' he says, 'from the traumatic effect of being forbidden to do what all my friends were doing.' He who had addressed innumerable anti-Nazi rallies, who had rabidly supported the fight against Fascism in Spain, now found himself condemned to inactivity when the crucial battle was joined. He pulled what political strings he could, and from time to time he was bundled out of the country under a false name to examine captured Nazi newsreels and other filmic trivia. But his missions were few, and seldom very secret: 'I was flown into Lisbon as Harrison Carstairs, the ball-bearings manufacturer, and there were twenty people waiting at the airport for my autograph.' (On one such errand he met and briefly beguiled himself with an Argentinian radio actress named Eva, who later emerged from obscurity as the wife of Juan Peron.) Meanwhile, the Hearst press regularly printed snide items inquiring why the playboy Welles was lounging around swimming pools when democracy was in danger; and after each new gibe, Orson usually received a draft notice. One of his periodic medical examinations took place when he had just returned from a mission to Latin America, for the purposes of which he had been created a temporary brigadier general. 'Any of you men ever hold rank above a private?' asked the sergeant at the recruiting depot. Orson shuffled forward. 'State the rank you held.' Orson told him. 'O.K., Brigadier General,' said the sergeant enticingly, 'get down on your hands and knees and clean up those cigarette butts.'

Orson has always had a passion for politics. At one time he thought seriously of running for the Senate on the Democratic ticket; had he done so, it would have made a provocative contest, because the Republican candidate in the state of Wisconsin was the late Joseph McCarthy. 'Basically,' Orson says, 'I'm a public orator (as was Charles Foster Kane) and that isn't the same as a television orator, which is what a lot of TV producers keep asking me to be. Television is talking to two or three people through a box, instead of talking to two thousand people and making them *feel* like two or three people.' If Orson were ever to join a party, he would be its first member, and its label would be Liberal Hedonist, or Collective Individualist. Its sympathies would be leftish but it would remain, like its founder, an unaffiliated maverick.

The streets of Madrid have darkened, and drinks have faded into dinner. Orson continues, unfading. After Broadway and Hollywood came his wandering period, which is not yet, and may never be, over. His career since 1946 is a kaleidoscope that baffles chronology. He bids farewell to Broadway with *Around the World in Eighty Days*, the most opulent of his many tributes to the free-wheeling, actor-managing days of the late Victorian era. He departs for Europe, leaving a wake of tax problems behind him, but not before filming a sombre truncation of *Macbeth*— around the Bard in twenty-one shooting days. Later, after numerous halts and hazards due to inadequate finances, he directs and stars in a massively picturesque film of *Othello*, to be described in some quarters as the movie version of Ruskin's *Stones of Venice*. The echoing voices and footsteps, and the sudden cuts from long-shot silence to close-up animation, stamp it as unmistakably Wellesian; so, alas, does the scrambled text, not to mention Orson's own resonantly impassive performance. 'He never acts,' says Eric Bentley; 'he is photographed.' With peerless skill, he plays the mischievously corrupt Harry Lime in *The Third Man*, and improvises a memorable exchange with its producer, the late Alexander Korda.

> ORSON: I wish the Pope would make you a cardinal, Alex.
> KORDA: Why a cardinal?
> ORSON: Because then we'd only have to kiss your ring.

He is also alleged to have improvised Harry Lime's famous observation that after centuries of democracy the Swiss have produced nothing more inspiring than the cuckoo clock; falsely attributed to Orson, the line was actually written by Graham Greene.

In Paris, Orson presents a double bill of his own composition, consisting of a play about Hollywood called *The Unthinking Lobster* and a modern revamping of the Faust legend, with music by Duke Ellington. Between whiles he plays fiends and frauds in other people's films. He flies to New York to appear, outrageously bewhiskered, in Peter Brook's TV production of *King Lear*. For a day's work as Father Mapple in John Huston's film of *Moby Dick* he is paid $20,000, whereafter he makes his own dramatization of the novel and stages it in London, transforming the gilded Duke of York's Theatre into a storm-tossed whaling ship, without benefit of scenery. By now he has remarried, his new wife being Paola Mori, a shrewd, lissome Italian actress of noble birth. In 1956 he returns to Broadway in a production of *Lear*. It flops. During the previews, Orson sprains one ankle and breaks the other, and plays the opening performance from a wheelchair, thereby supplying further fuel for those who think him congenitally self-destructive. His acting ability comes up for reappraisal; Walter Kerr contributes a damaging analysis: 'As an emotional actor, Welles is without insight, accuracy, power, or grace. In short, without talent. The only parts he could ever play were parts that were cold, intellectual, emotionally dead.'

In 1958 Orson is summoned back to Hollywood to play a venal cop in a thriller called *Touch of Evil*. While he is considering the offer in the producer's office, the telephone rings; it is Charlton Heston, who has been approached to play the lead but wants to know who else has been signed. 'Well, we've got Orson Welles—' the producer begins. 'Great!' says Heston, cutting in. 'I'll appear in anything he directs.' 'Hold on a minute,' says the producer, feeling that events are slipping out of his hands. Hastily he asks Orson whether he will direct, to which Orson agrees, on condition that he have full control of script and casting. After a pause: 'Sure,' the producer tells Heston, 'sure Welles is directing.' The result is a picture of enormous virtuosity. Orson demands two weeks of private rehearsal before shooting begins, and gets from his actors performances of fantastic, unguarded intimacy. They are shamelessly themselves, and seem imbued with his own conviction that in show business being inhibited gets you nowhere. Meanwhile, the camera swoops and hovers like a kingfisher, inscribing Orson's autograph on every sequence. Charlton Heston, as a Mexican lawyer, gives the best performance of his life. The film wins prizes in Europe, but is shunned in America. Soon afterwards we find Orson directing Olivier in the London production of *Rhinoceros*.

No one is more fertile than Orson in ideas that, for one reason or another, never get carried out. There was *Monsieur Verdoux*, for which he supplied the original script; and which he was to direct, until Chaplin decided to direct it himself. There was the satire, drawn from the love affair of D'Annunzio and Duse, which he planned for Chaplin and Garbo. There was Homer's *Odyssey*, for which he hired a writer whom he was tardy in paying, and to whose repeated pleas for advice about how to make ends meet he finally replied with a single cable: DEAR ——, LIVE SIMPLY, AFFECTIONATE REGARDS, ORSON WELLES. There were also projects involving Conrad, Dickens, Dostoevski, Rostand, and Tolstoy, of which nothing tangible came.

At dinner we are joined by the Earl of Harewood, who runs the Edinburgh Festival and wonders whether Orson would like to bring a production to it in 1962. In principle, Orson would be delighted. In the course of conversation, Harewood remarks that he was lately in Japan, where he saw the Kabuki Theatre and didn't tremendously like it. Orson rounds on him, mountainously glowering, and observes that anyone who doesn't appreciate Kabuki must be an ignoramus. Harewood nods, adding that he must have seen them on a bad night. Even on a bad night, Orson insists, they are far superior to anything the Western theatre can produce. A firework display, marking the end of the Madrid *feria*, explodes in the park outside the restaurant. Hoping to pacify Orson, Harewood explains that he immensely enjoyed the Kabuki performers Sol Hurok brought to New York. He hopes wrong. 'That,' Orson thunders, 'was a contemptible travesty. If you liked that, you don't like Kabuki.' Yet within minutes he has charmed us out of embarrassment into laughter; and next day I hear from Harewood that the Edinburgh offer still stands, and that Orson and Maria Callas are the only genuine *monstres sacrés* he has ever met.

At times Orson is prey to depressions, onslaughts of gloom, spleen, and sulks that the Middle Ages would probably have ascribed to the cardinal sin of accidie, which induces a sense of futility and a temporary paralysis of the will. 'From *accidie*,' Aldous Huxley once wrote, 'comes dread to begin to work any good deeds, and finally wanhope, or despair. On its way to ultimate wanhope, *accidie* produces a whole crop of minor sins, such as idleness, tardiness, *lâchesse*. . . .' It also means *ennui*, the French brand of philosophic boredom. When *accidie* grips him, you feel that Orson has given up people; that he has already seen everything on earth he will ever want to see, and met everyone he will ever want to meet. Faced with that suggestion, however, he will suddenly revive and deny it; Isak Dinesen, Chou En-Lai, and Robert Graves are three people he venerates and would adore to meet, if only he felt less intimidated by the prospect. Soon his spirits are soaring, and he is telling you that the only hope for American drama lies (as well it may) in theatres outside New York, municipally supported so that every year they can present their best productions for a short season on Broadway. You feel kindled by his presence, by his mastery of rhetoric, by his uncalculating generosity. 'A superb bravura director,' I once called him, 'a fair bravura actor, and a limited bravura writer; but an incomparable bravura personality.' Orson is a genius without portfolio. When he leaves a room, something irreplaceable and life-enhancing goes with him; something that may eventually install him, given luck and our help, in the special pantheon whose other occupants are Stanislavsky, Gordon Craig, Max Reinhardt, Jacques Copeau, and Bertolt Brecht.

(1961)

An Interview with Jean-Paul Sartre

Sartre's apartment in Paris is a working place, small and book-cluttered, on the fourth floor of a corner building in the rue Bonaparte, overlooking the Café des Deux Magots and the church of Saint Germain des Près. Its owner, instead of the bleak, intimidating oracle I expected, is warm, lively, and instantly responsive; a quick, compact figure of a man, with suntanned skin, a condition rare in middle-aged intellectuals. (Or could it have been jaundice?) What follows is a condensation of an interview lasting some ninety minutes.

TYNAN: You once said that *Altona* was not the play you intended to write. You meant it to deal with torture in Algeria, but transposed it because you felt such a play could not be staged in Paris. Now Genet has written a play about Algeria—*Les Paravents*. Do you think it will be put on?

SARTRE: I don't think so. It has been published, and it may win a literary prize, but that is another matter. Strictly speaking, there is no theatre censorship in Paris, but there is self-censorship on the part of theatrical managements. They are afraid that the police may intervene and forbid a production on the grounds that it might cause a public disturbance. That is an economic risk that they can't afford to take.

TYNAN: Have you read Genet's new play?

SARTRE: Yes, and I find it very interesting. It's not the whole truth about Algeria; it's a version of the truth, seen through the prism of Genet's ideas and sensibility. In Genet's mind, one must embrace what is vile in order to achieve what is good. For myself, I don't believe that people should be taught that kind of heroism. But you will notice that it is exactly in keeping with his belief that judges should be as harsh as possible. According to Genet, it is only when man has been reduced to his lowest level—sentenced to death or life imprisonment, despised by the world as a traitor, etc.—that he can begin to rebuild humanity. It's a fascinating theory, but I don't think it really applies to the problem of a colonised people.

TYNAN: Would you say the same thing of *The Blacks*—that it poses a general problem in highly subjective terms?

SARTRE: Yes, I think so. Although many Negroes have found in the play a kind of resonance. I mean the way in which it shows the Negro poised between two cultures. Against his will, and almost as if it were a game, he participates in the culture of the white, and suddenly his own culture begins to take on the aspect of a game.

TYNAN: In your Sorbonne lecture, you condemned bourgeois theatre. Is the bourgeoisie to blame for everything that is wrong with contemporary drama?

SARTRE: The essential fault seems to me to be bourgeois. Look at the plays that are performed nowadays; you will see that the majority are wornout psychological exercises, making use of all the old bourgeois themes—the husband with a mistress, the wife with a lover, the family who don't understand one another. But there is another problem that should be mentioned in connection with the theatre, and that is the cinema. Today many people—not only directors, but ordinary spectators, and especially young intellectuals—think the cinema a better means of expression than the theatre. And under the influence of the cinema, the theatre has tended to withdraw from its own battlefield. It has given in to

Part III: *People*

the enemy; it has multiplied its settings, and has tried, by stressing the visual element, to tell stories in a form that is more cinematic than theatrical. It has thus become easier to destroy. The same thing happens in politics: if a Government shows signs of yielding to the Opposition, in the end the Opposition will seize power.

The theatre is not concerned with reality; it is only concerned with truth. The cinema, on the other hand, seeks a reality which may contain moments of truth. The theatre's true battlefield is that of tragedy—drama which embodies a genuine myth. There is no reason why the theatre should not tell a story of love or marriage, as long as it has a quality of myth; in other words, as long as it occupies itself with something more than conjugal disagreements or lovers' misunderstandings. By seeking truth through myth, and by the use of forms as non-realistic as tragedy, the theatre can stand up against the cinema. Only thus can it avoid being swallowed up.

TYNAN: Isn't it true that there are a number of private symbols in *Altona*—for instance, the tribunal of crabs that Franz addresses?

SARTRE: Yes. Since my childhood I have always had a special aversion to crabs, and all kinds of shellfish.

TYNAN: Including oysters?

SARTRE: I never eat them. For me, the fact that Franz eats oysters means that he is living on extremely unpleasant food. Once, in a moment of fatigue, when I was about thirty-two years old, I had some very disagreeable hallucinations connected with crabs. Since then I have always regarded them as symbols of something inhuman. I can't imagine what these creatures think or feel—probably not very much! For me, theirs is a world completely opposed to the human world.

TYNAN: So this court of crabs is something you regard as frightful?

SARTRE: It is frightful to Franz, not to me. Since Franz is guilty, he makes his judges as frightful as possible. I believe that the tribunal of history always judges men according to standards and values which they themselves could never imagine. We can never know what the future will say of us. It may be that history will consider Hitler a great man— though that would astonish me enormously—and in any case, there is always Stalin! The point is that we know we shall be judged, and not by the rules we use to judge ourselves. And in that thought there is something horrific. Moreover, it has been said that progress is made laterally, in a sideways motion, rather like the movement of crabs. That was also part of my idea.

TYNAN: Jean Genet has said that he can't bear judges who 'lean over amorously towards the defendant'.

SARTRE: I agree in the sense that Genet is speaking from the point of view of the criminal. It is his revenge against society. Instead of saying: 'It's society's fault, not the criminal's! Don't punish him too harshly!' he says the opposite: 'We are enemies of society! Punish us as much as possible. If you don't punish us, you are contemptible. By punishing us you make us live in a harsh world and that makes us the more heroic.' On this point I don't entirely agree with Genet.

On the other hand, there is a world in which I think judges should be wary of 'leaning over amorously towards the defendant'. That is the world of politics. I am opposed to the death penalty; but I think the rebel generals in Algeria should have been condemned to death, and reprieved afterwards. In cases like this the crime is committed against society as a whole.

TYNAN: I recall that in your lecture to the Sorbonne last year, you said that the theatre today had no need of psychology. But isn't the character of Franz full of psychological subtleties?

SARTRE: What I meant was that no situation should be analysed exclusively on the psychological level. Take, for example, the conflict of a man with his wife. Unless we know something about their work, their background, the society that formed them, the situation has no theatrical reality. Franz's problem is the result of many conflicting social circumstances—his father's business, the development of German capitalism, the rise of the Nazis, his father's collusion with Nazism. His problems and inner contradictions are created by historical events.

TYNAN: Talking about Franz's father, do you think his desire for power is purely a bourgeois impulse? Or is it a general human impulse?

SARTRE: I think the desire to retain power comes from already possessing it. Let me put it this way: the authority that a factory owner brings into his family life comes from the factory itself—in other words, from the power that the structure of capitalist society gives to its leaders. The capitalist is not, in himself, an authoritarian. But if one puts him in a position in which he must exercise authority, he will always want to exercise it: he is shaped by his social role.

Now in countries like Germany, and even more in America, we have the phenomenon of capitalist enterprises in which management and ownership are beginning to diverge. Old Gerlach is a man who has had total authority over his business for nearly the whole of his life, and who sees that authority slipping away just at the moment when he is growing old. That is his tragedy. He has created his son in his own image, as a man born to exercise authority. But in reality even if Franz were not cut off from the world, even if he took over the business, he would merely be the owner, not the ruler. Power has passed into the hands of the technocrats.

TYNAN: But isn't it possible that a non-capitalist bureaucrat might seek power for its own sake?

SARTRE: Everything depends on the situation. No one is born with a desire either to seek power or to shun it. It's a man's history that makes him move one way or the other. And even then, he is seldom quite sure. There are many cases of men who thought they wanted power, only to discover when they reached the top of the ladder that they would rather be on the second rung or the third. It's not a question of instincts or inborn tendencies; what counts is a man's relationship with society, with his family, with everything around him.

[My next question gave rise to an interesting confusion. I intended to ask M. Sartre whether he thought it was possible nowadays to create right-wing art. I mispronounced the prase: instead of *la droite*, the political Right, I heard myself referring to *le droit*—the law. Before I could correct myself, M. Sartre had taken the question in his stride, and embarked on his answer. I append it herewith as a tribute to his mental agility.]

SARTRE: By all means, yes. The law *is* theatre. For at the roots of theatre there is not merely a religious ceremony, there is also eloquence. Consider the characters of Sophocles, of Euripides, even of Aeschylus—they are all lawyers; and we must remember that the Greeks loved lawyers. They come forward with a cause to defend. Others take the opposite side and plead against them. At the end, there is a catastrophe in which everyone is judged, and matters return to normal. The stage is the courtroom in which the case is tried. Antigone, for example, has a cause to plead—the cause of the great families, whose traditions and religious obligations are being threatened by the State. Creon, meanwhile, stands for another, newer cause—one which clearly does not appeal to Sophocles, whose sympathies are conservative. Creon is a primitive democrat, who says: 'In a dispute between the State and the family, authority rests with the State.' These are the two positions; and instead of Antigone and Creon, one might just as well have engaged two lawyers to put forward their respective points of view.

TYNAN: A socialist poet named Christopher Logue recently wrote a play about the Antigone legend. His attitude seemed to be that Creon was right.

SARTRE: Naturally. That is the democratic point of view.

TYNAN (*getting back to his original point*): Do you think that nowadays there is such a thing as right-wing art?

SARTRE: I don't think theatre can be directly derived from political events. For instance, I would never have written *Altona* if it was merely a simple question of a conflict between Left and Right. For me, *Altona* is tied up with the whole evolution of Europe since 1945, as much with the Soviet concentration camps as with the war in Algeria. The theatre must take all these problems and transmute them into mythic form. I don't think a playwright's commitment consists simply in stating political ideas. That can be done through public meetings, newspapers, agitation, and propaganda. The playwright who usurps their function may perhaps interest the reading public, but he will not have written a play.

TYNAN: But could an author of extreme right-wing views ever succeed in creating a work of art?

SARTRE: In my opinion, no. Because nowadays although the Right may still be in control of events, to the extent that it still has power, it has lost the ability to understand them. It has surrendered most of its old ideals and has not replaced them; it does not understand the nature of its adversaries. The fact, for example, that Général Challe could declare in court that the army in Algeria was riddled with Communist infiltration —the fact that a man can say that proves to what degree of incomprehension the Right is driven by its inability to face facts.

In the presence of so many accumulated misunderstandings, how can the Right create a work of art? For a work of art, even if it is nonpolitical, must proceed from an understanding of one's era, it must be in harmony with the age. One can't imagine a modern play that could be at the same time right-wing and good.

TYNAN: Which contemporary playwrights do you most admire?

SARTRE: Brecht, incontestably, although he is dead—and in spite of the fact that I do not use his techniques or share his artistic principles. Then, on a different level, there are certain plays of Genet. His work is a game played with mirrors and reflections, very beautiful and very expressive of its era.

TYNAN: You once said that you admired *Waiting for Godot* more than any other play since 1945.

SARTRE: That is true. I have not liked Beckett's other plays, particularly *Endgame*, because I find the symbolism far too inflated, far too naked. And although *Godot* is certainly not a right-wing play, it represents a sort of universal pessimism that appeals to right-wing people. For that reason, although I admire it, I have reservations. But precisely because its content is somewhat alien to me, I can't help admiring it the more.

TYNAN: Are there any English or American playwrights who appeal to you?

SARTRE: Arthur Miller, certainly. And Tennessee Williams clearly has something, although his world is very different from mine, and his work is permeated with subjective myths. One of the troubles with the theatre is that when a play moves from one country to another, it often takes on a completely different meaning. As the audience changes, the play changes.

I am disturbed by this question of transplanting works of art. I remember seeing a remarkable Mexican film: it told of a one-eyed child, who was an object of derision to other children. According to the film, one-eyed people are considered comic in Mexico. The child prays to heaven for a miracle; his mother sends him on a pilgrimage, and they pray together. Meanwhile, a firework display is being held to celebrate the fiesta, and a spark falls into the boy's good eye, blinding him. Even in Mexico, according to the film, blind people are not comic.

Now is this story a savage joke at the expense of religion? Or is the author presenting his belief that, although miracles may be terrible things, they are still miracles? The answer must remain a mystery for those who don't know Mexico.

But in general, films are simple enough to travel freely. American films in particular are more popular here than any others. American plays, by contrast, never get acclimatised in France: they always fail.

TYNAN: Would you like to revisit America?

SARTRE: Frankly, I would rather not. I wouldn't enjoy seeing people in the state of mind that exists in America today. It would grieve me to see people so restless, so uneasy. And to the extent that they were too violent, too full of over-simplifications, I would feel discontented. Nevertheless, I used to like America very much. Very much indeed.

TYNAN: You recently wrote a film script for John Huston about the life of Freud. Could you tell me something about it?

SARTRE: Except in construction, the final script has little resemblance to what I wrote. The fault is partly mine, and partly Freud's. My scenario would have been impossible to shoot; it would have lasted seven or eight hours. As you know, one can make a film four hours long if it has to do with Ben Hur, but a Texas audience won't sit through four hours of complexes. Hence the script was cut down to ninety minutes or so. I haven't seen the final version, and I don't know if I shall leave my name on it; that depends on the contract.

However, what we tried to do—and this was what interested Huston especially—was to show Freud not when his theories had made him famous, but at the time, around the age of thirty, when he was utterly wrong; when his ideas had led him into hopeless error. You know that at one point he seriously believed that what caused hysteria was fathers raping their daughters. We begin in that period, and follow his career up to the discovery of the Oedipus complex.

That, for me, is the most enthralling time in the life of a great discoverer—when he seems muddled and lost, but has the genius to collect himself and put everything in order. Of course, it is difficult to explain this development to an audience ignorant of Freud. In order to arrive at the right ideas, one must start by explaining the wrong ones, and that is a long process: hence the seven-hour scenario.

The other problem was that Freud, like the majority of scientists, was a good husband and father who seems never to have deceived his wife, and even to have been a virgin before he was married. One hears rumours of previous escapades, but I ascribe them to the devotion of his admirers; the psychoanalysts don't want us to think that this man, who knew so much about sexuality, came to marriage utterly unfledged. In short, his private life was not very cinematic.

We therefore tried to blend the internal and the external elements of Freud's drama; to show how he learned from his patients the truth about himself. To take one instance, we show how the memory of the hysterical girls who told him their fathers had raped them provoked in him feelings of violent aggression towards his own father. And finally these two approaches—from the interior and from the exterior—meet in the discovery of the Oedipus complex.

TYNAN: Can one deal with Freud's life from a social viewpoint?

SARTRE: We have tried. There is one great problem that the analysts tend to sidetrack: Viennese anti-semitism. It seems to me that Freud was profoundly aggressive, and that his aggressions were determined by the anti-semitism from which his family suffered. He was a child who felt things very deeply, and probably immediately.

TYNAN: Do you think Freud's discoveries will be of permanent importance?

SARTRE: Unquestionably. Unlike some of my friends, however, I am not convinced that the basis of human activity is sexual. Whether it is or not, I don't believe that this substructure of sexual need reappears intact in the superstructure of the personality. It may reappear, but on a completely new level and in a completely different form; as any believer in the dialectical process must agree. It can no longer be reduced to itself.

One may say that a man's politics reflect his sexual impulses, but one may just as well say that his sexual impulses reflect an underlying sympathy with humanity that may later be translated into political terms. In any event Freud was the first to say something that seems to me of capital importance: that everything which makes a man has meaning.

TYNAN: There are no accidents?

SARTRE: There are no accidents! And Freud's second great discovery was that even in the matter of self-knowledge, human progress derives from human need. I regard Freud as an excellent materialist. He did not single out hunger, because he came from a background where that kind of need did not apply; instead, he chose sexuality, which is equally necessary—not in the sense that a man would die without it, but in the sense that the lack of it may drive him mad.

TYNAN: So you think it is possible to build a bridge between Freud and Marx?

SARTRE: Certainly. I think the Marxists have lost a great deal by cutting themselves off so completely from psychoanalysis, by refusing to accept it. Of course, Freud used his analytic discoveries to bolster up a great many historical theories that hold little interest for any sociologist, least of all for a Marxist. What matters is his demonstration that sexual desire is not simply sexual desire, but something that will encroach upon a man's whole personality, even affecting the way he plays the piano or the violin. That, I think, is a permanent contribution.

TYNAN: Many people, surveying your work as a whole, have remarked that in an age of equality you are the only playwright who creates outsize heroes, gigantic protagonists like Goetz in *Le Diable et le Bon Dieu*, Edmund Kean in your Dumas adaptation, and Franz in *Altona*. Isn't this something of a paradox?

SARTRE: There must be some personal reason; there are always personal reasons—as with the crabs in *Altona*! At bottom, I am always looking for myths; in other words, for subjects so sublimated that they are recognisable to everyone, without recourse to minute psychological details.

Let me give you an example. If I write another play, it will be about the relationship of a husband and a wife. In itself, that would be boring, and so I shall take the Greek myth of Alcestis. If you recall, Death comes to seek out King Admetus. This doesn't please Admetus at all; 'I have things to do,' he says, 'I have my kingdom to rule, I have a war to win!' And his wife Alcestis, who regards herself as utterly superfluous, offers to die in his place. Death accepts the bargain; and then, taking pity on her, sends her back to life. That is the plot. But my version would imply the whole story of female emancipation: the woman chooses the tragic course at a moment when her husband has refused to face death. And when she returns, she is the powerful one, because poor Admetus will always be the man of whom it is said: 'He allowed his wife to die for him!'

TYNAN: But will ordinary people recognise themselves in characters like those?

SARTRE: I think so. I don't remember ever having had difficulties of that sort. *Altona*, for example, was supported by the *petits bourgeois*, not by the rich bourgeoisie who usually keep the theatre alive.

TYNAN: And the proletariat?

SARTRE: That is another matter. In Paris, they never come to the theatre except to see a comic opera or an operetta. Little by little, they were pushed out of the city during the nineteenth century, and they established their life on the outskirts. They hardly ever return; as a theatrical audience, they scarcely exist.

TYNAN: If *Altona* were presented in Moscow, do you think the public would support it?

SARTRE: Yes. Because in Moscow the working-class—even perhaps the peasantry—is much further evolved than ours. Not because of modern Soviet literature, but because of the immense diffusion in Russia of nineteenth-century literature. These people really discuss things in their factories; they make their own choices, and care about the choices they make. They are devoted to educating themselves. Ilya Ehrenburg told me that the soundest criticisms he received came not from the critics but from his readers. That isn't the case here.

TYNAN: Some years ago, I saw *La Putain Respectueuse* in Moscow, very much lengthened and simplified. Were the changes made with your consent?

SARTRE: I didn't see the production, but I agreed to an optimistic ending, as in the film version, which was made in France. I knew too many young working-class people who had seen the play and been disheartened because it ended sadly. And I realised that those who are really pushed to the limit, who hang on to life because they must, have need of hope.

TYNAN: Is it true that you have abandoned your novel about the French Resistance?

SARTRE: Yes. The situation was too simple. I don't mean that it is simple to be courageous and risk one's life: what I mean is that the choice was too simple. One's allegiances were obvious. Since then, things have become much more complicated; much more romantic, in the literary sense of the term. There are many more intrigues and cross-currents. To write a novel whose hero dies in the Resistance, committed to the idea of liberty, would be much too easy. Nowadays, commitment is altogether harder to define.

TYNAN: The era of simplicity has passed: do you think we shall ever arrive at a new simplicity?

SARTRE: If our society can disengage itself from the cold war; if it can manage to shed its colonies in peace; and if there is an evolution of the West under the influence of the East, I see no reason why Soviet Communism need be exported to the West. What I hope is that something will happen akin to the Counterreformation that followed Protestantism—a movement in the other direction. Just as Catholicism has evolved its own kind of Protestantism, I look forward to a day when the West will become Socialist, without ever passing through Communism. At that moment, I seriously believe, simplicity will be reborn.

(1961)

Martha Graham: Holy Acrobat

You do not have to love ballet to admire Martha Graham; all that is necessary is to love the human body and its capacity for expressive movement.

For the merely beautiful, the merely graceful or gymnastic, she has little use. In her dances content struggles to find its appropriate form, and often the struggle is visible in the finished work. Deliberately so; her disciple Agnes de Mille has remarked that where traditional ballet tries to conceal effort, Graham emphasises it, and: 'because effort starts with the nerve centres, it follows that a technique developed from percussive impulses that flow through the body . . . as motion is sent through a whip, would have enormous nervous vitality.'

Graham's dance-language is compressed and angular, as far removed from Fokine's as Oriental ideographs are from Victorian copperplate, and when she began to speak it, more than thirty years ago, the cult that grew up around her confused and baffled the bourgeois balletomanes. The late Stark Young, doyen of American drama critics, was an early fan; but even he used to chide her for being 'ethnic' (which she wasn't), and recalls how he said of her: 'I'm always afraid that Martha's going to give birth to a cube on stage.'

Today there are many who would echo Agnes de Mille's eulogy: 'the most startling inventor, and by all odds the greatest performer that trod our native stage. . . . Technically speaking, hers is the single largest contribution in the history of Western dancing.' And technique is only the beginning. 'I can see technique at Radio City,' she once told Miss de Mille. 'From you I ask something greater than that. From you I ask what cannot be learned in any class. Reaffirmation.' The tone is evangelical and entirely characteristic. Although I have heard her say: 'I am not a high priestess of *anything*,' she has managed to recruit an army of acolytes. They swarm about her, so many moths around her hard, gem-like flame.

In 1954 she played to thin but ecstatic houses at the Saville Theatre. Seeing her then, I was oppressed at first by her iron solemnity, but as her repertoire unfolded, one rapt female archetype succeeding another, I realised that Eric Bentley was right when he said: 'The diagnostic of the dancer Martha Graham is that she is an actress'—and a great one, at that, in the line of Duse. She dwarfed her company, erasing them, even in repose, by the serene authority of her presence; one thought of the late Ruth Draper, another great performer condemned by the uniqueness of her talent to appear only in works of her own creation.

I met Graham briefly in her dressing-room, but awe confined me to monosyllables. I had read too many daunting things about her: that 'in more than one way she resembles Nefertiti' (de Mille), that her beauty was 'of a formidable sort, enigmatic, ambiguous' and her face 'an unnaturally motionless mask' (Bentley). My own first impression was of a woman who looked forty and might be four hundred, and who combined the salient physical qualities of Helene Weigel as Mother Courage and Beatrice Lillie as Kabuki Lil.

With these images colliding in my mind, it is perhaps no wonder that I kept my trap virtually shut. She did the same: what little she said was slowly and precisely articulated, eked out with large, comprehensive gestures that employed the whole arm, from collarbone to finger-tip. I felt that speech, for her, was essentially a foreign language, a Pyrrhic victory over silence.

We did not meet again until last spring, when I spent an afternoon in her New York apartment. It might be the home of a geisha turned puritan. The floor is wall-to-wall wood, polished like ice; on a low coffee-table marigolds float in a shallow bowl; Chinese scrolls speckle the walls; and the centrepiece is an ornately carved Chinese couch, ideal for meditation though not, I should think, for sleep. Small ornaments abound: talismans in jade and ebony, painted sea-shells from Japan, and a tiny bronze ram from Persia, poised for 3,000 years on the brink of attempting a skyward leap.

Her hair stretched back in a high bun, Graham greeted me with both hands. Pensively, and at moments gnomically, she talked about her life and work, sipping brandy between paragraphs, using her whole body to italicise important points, and looking, whenever she paused, as if she were about to disclose some gigantic private sorrow.

She was born in Pittsburgh of Scotch Presbyterian parents, with whom she migrated in childhood to California. Her mother's family were tenth-generation Americans, and there was plenty of Sunday school in her upbringing: 'My great-grandfather would spin in his grave if he knew I was dancing.' Although she is no longer a churchgoer, she thinks of herself as religious and keeps a Bible in her dressing-room.

'I feel the twenty-third Psalm in everything I do. And the nineteenth Psalm, too—"The heavens declare the glory of God, and the firmament showeth his handiwork." And later it says: "There is neither speech nor language." I often hear that when I'm on stage. To my mind there are three sorts of language. First of all, there is the cosmic language, which is movement. Next, there is the language of sound. And finally, the language of particular words. As my father used to tell me: "Movement never lies." '

She was introduced to the pleasures of theatre by an illiterate Irish nurse named Lizzie, who took her to Punch-and-Judy shows. Her father was opposed to dancing as a career, but he died when she was in her teens, and she promptly joined the Denishawn School in Los Angeles, where she was duly enthralled by the preaching and practice of the great dancer-teacher, Ruth St Denis. Her training completed, she moved to New York and taught for a while, but soon decided that she could not meet the demands of her talent without forming a company of her own. By 1931 she had achieved coterie fame on the East Coast, and the coterie has been spreading ever since.

The torments and anxieties of women—biblical, mythological, Victorian and contemporary—stand at the centre of her work. 'All I have ever wanted to do,' she said to me, her lower jaw projecting as she paused in thought, 'was to create a vocabulary that would be adequate to the past and to the twentieth century. Not one or the other, but both. I am a thief. I'll steal from anyone, and any period. But I'm not interested in television or anything two-dimensional. The stage is my area. Theatre used to be a *verb*; it used to be an *act*. But nowadays it is just a noun. It is a place.'

Oriental drama and philosophy have always attracted her: 'I had a Zen master when I was in California. He affected me tremendously, and I've studied Zen on and off ever since. But I don't like what they call in San Francisco "Beat Zen". That's just *talking* about aesthetics, and anyway I hate the word "aesthetic". Real Zen has to do with physical behaviour. I've always been fascinated by Oriental theatre, although I didn't go to Japan until 1956. I met one of their great, ancient female impersonators, and I went down on my knees.' Swinging off her chair, Graham folded the hinges of her body in an illustrative genuflection, so that her forehead brushed the shining floor. Righting herself with equal suddenness, she continued: 'I saw Mei Lan-fang when he came to America. He was the greatest Chinese actor of his time, and he always played female parts. He was that curious creature—a complete man and a complete woman.'

According to rumour, Graham's sense of vocation excludes private emotional allegiances; in the words of de Mille, 'one does not domesticate a prophetess'. I asked her whether rumour was right, and she smiled forgivingly. 'I do not believe in the cloister for the artist,' she said. 'An artist can live a full domestic life. I was married once, but it broke up. I wanted children, but I was told I couldn't have them without a difficult and dangerous operation. The choice I made had nothing to do with art.'

She runs a school of dance in a building owned by her most faithful patron, Bethsabbé de Rothschild, and there she has a family of nearly two hundred, drawn from nineteen countries. Stringently and devotedly, she moulds her pupils in her own durable image: 'Out of this wonderful thing that is man, you make a world. "We did it—you and I": that's what a great artist says to the audience. Look at Fonteyn in *The Sleeping Beauty*—such triumphant exaltation!—and Helene Weigel in *Mother Courage*, and Gielgud in *Hamlet*.'

I reminded her that many of her ballets were concerned with untriumphant, even self-destructive, women. 'Yes, but tragedy is a sort of triumph. Did you ever see Ulanova? She's self-destructive, and that's how she achieves—what is the word?—*illumination*.'

Graham is unimpressed by her reputation as a living legend. 'The works themselves don't matter,' she said as we parted, 'and the legend only matters if it makes other people work. I have no opinion of myself except that I'm glad to be my own master. And if you want to know my philosophy—well, I once knew a man who told his maid that it was her sacred, bounden duty to go on scrubbing his floors. "Mister," she said, "I don't have to do *anything*, except to die." '

(1963)

Joan Littlewood

The most original and unpredictable director in the British theatre today is a stocky middle-aged woman who attended the International Drama Conference at last year's Edinburgh Festival and announced to an audience of two thousand people: 'I'm not a professional director. I don't know what professional directors are.'

She spoke casually but with passion, her perky crumpled face looking, as always, as if tears had lately dried on it. 'I'm an impostor here,' she went on, gesturing toward her fellow-delegates, who included Judith Anderson, Lillian Hellman, Laurence Olivier, Harold Pinter and dozens more. 'I haven't sat through a play in my life since I was fifteen. I spend my time watching the accidents and the courtesies and the hates and the loves and the acting of people in the streets—because that's where I live.' The audience was beginning to be ignited. She held them like an evangelist, but with no oratorical tricks. Her eyes, heavily lidded like those of an ornamental carp, were as non-committal as her tone of voice, their twinkle almost hidden. A few centuries ago, I reflected, such a woman might easily have been burned as a witch.

She continued, this wily holy innocent, in language that bypassed logic, making only emotional sense: 'People ask why I came into the theatre. I didn't come into it. We're all part of it, because theatre is the soul of the people. It's the joy they feel in life. It's the way they express the art of living. Let's set the clowns free, the villains and the nut-cases—and what they make will be theatre.' The Conference had been discussing the relative importance of playwright, actor and director: she waived these formal distinctions. 'When artists or scientists set out, they don't know what the end product will be. It changes. It changes in collaboration, each man trusting and mistrusting the people he works with. That happened in Shakespeare's Globe Theatre, it happened in Greece, it happened in all those times and at all those places under God's sky where men and women have joined together for delight. We must have places where we can eat, drink, make love, be lonely, be together, and share in the theatre of living. That is my theatre.' She wanted a theatre born of spontaneous contact between people, living on the lips and through the limbs of those who created it, not a theatre which practised artificial respiration on printed texts. 'I say to hell with geniuses in the theatre. Let's have the authors by all means, the Lorcas and the Brendan Behans, but let's get them together with their equals, the actors, with all their wit and stupidity and insight. And this clash, this collaboration, this *anti*-collaboration will create an explosion more important than any bomb. Let the bomb be dead, not named. That's all I have to say.'

And with that Joan Littlewood sat down, to wild applause, having made a speech that from any other mouth would have sounded crazily presumptuous. But Joan (I cannot call her Miss Littlewood) is the woman who made Brendan Behan's name with her productions of *The Quare Fellow* and *The Hostage*; who plucked a teenage playwright called Shelagh Delaney from obscurity by directing *A Taste of Honey*; who staged *Fings Ain't Wot They Used t'Be*, the long-running London musical which someone described as '*Guys and Dolls* with its fly open'; and whose greatest success, *Oh What a Lovely War* (a musical version, do you mind, of World War One), has just opened on Broadway after eighteen months in the West End.

Joan is given to talking in visionary riddles, like some latterday William Blake let loose on show business; but she differs from most streetcorner prophets in a couple of vital respects. Firstly, with Joan it is always the beginning of the world that is at hand, not the end. Secondly, although much of what she says sounds like nonsense in theory, it has a way of working in practice. In 1945 she formed her own company of actors, Theatre Workshop, in pursuit of a dream of theatre as a place of communal celebration, a Left-wing shrine of Dionysus dedicated to wiping the puritan frown off the popular image of Socialist art. After two decades of toil, the dream is coming to pass. It now seems quite likely that when the annals of the British theatre in the middle years of the twentieth century come to be written, Joan's name will lead all the rest. Others write plays, direct them or act in them: she alone 'makes theatre'.

She also makes friends and enemies, both of equal intensity. The former concede what the latter complain: that she is a walking paradox, a ragbag of contradictions. She is quiet-spoken, yet outspoken; warm, even gentle, in manner, but in matter abrasive and sometimes obscene. A believer in theatre as a collective art (according to the programme, *Oh What a Lovely War* was 'written by Charles Chilton and the Members of the Cast'), she is a dominating director whose rehearsal methods consist—in the words of one of her playwrights—of 'bellowing instructions through a megaphone in terms that would shame a Fascist traffic cop'. A lifelong Leftist, she has been kicked out of the Communist Party several times for incorrigible independence, and now calls herself 'a Red, which means a Socialist verging toward anarchy'; yet her last permanent address was a sumptuously decorated house in Blackheath, and she often relaxes aboard a yacht owned by her close friend and business manager, Gerry

Raffles. She is also a notable gourmet. Shelagh Delaney, her *protégée* and daughter-figure, regards her as a supreme authority on caviare; and once, in a moment of wry self-scrutiny, Joan summed herself up as 'the synthetic prole'.

Like any good liberal, she admires Negro artists, and three years ago she went to Nigeria to study them at the source. She returned still admiring, but not for reasons that conventional liberals would necessarily endorse: 'They're all thieves and drunks and villains. I used to wonder what people meant when they talked about "the black Irish". Now I know: they meant Nigerians. I'd love to get them into a Shakespeare play, and I know where I'd stage it—in the courtyard of a brothel I went to. It was called "Independence". They'd be marvellous bloody actors because they've never seen European theatre. They've never heard of good taste. They'd have nothing to unlearn. They could start from scratch and be Shakespearean without knowing it.' In Africa as in Britain, Joan is a missionary whose aim is the total destruction of complacent, well-behaved middle-class theatre.

She is coeval with modern warfare. Stockwell, a glum London suburb south of the Thames, was her birthplace in October 1914. When she was born, her mother (who still lives in Stockwell) was sixteen years old and unmarried. Joan has never met her father, though she acquired a stepfather at the age of five, when her mother married a Cockney worker. Joan was a bridesmaid at the wedding. She learned early on to cherish the people she calls 'nuts, clowns and villains'—in other words, outsiders, among whom she has always counted herself. The Socialist habit of idealising 'the simple man' repels her; being a complex proletarian herself, she knows that poverty does not always engender simplicity. She agrees with Ernst Fischer, the venerable Austrian poet and critic, who declares that under Socialism 'the "simple" man gradually turns into a subtle and highly differentiated man'. He is not levelled down; he is levelled up and outwards. Joan's greatest pleasure is to tour the East End pubs, relishing the company of 'my villains' and marvelling at their corrupt, outrageous variety. 'When I was sixteen,' she says, 'I lived in half a bathroom at five shillings a week, and talked mostly to whores. Like everybody else.' She really believes that that is what everybody else does.

Her London resembles the London that Jean Genet—another perceptive outsider—saw and recorded in 1963: a city of people concealing robustly antisocial desires beneath a mask of formality. In Genet's words:

'One might well think you were a nation of neuters, but only at a surface glance.   Because everywhere there is the steady beat of the battened-down impulses, the throbbing of the choked unhappy sexual life force oozing into the streets.

'Nobody touches anyone else. If, by chance, I am introduced to an Englishman, I feel my right hand instantly anxious. I never saw a movement made in your streets just for its own sake, for the sheer pleasure of movement. When you see the English walking, you know they are going somewhere. . . .

'But how can you not want to touch? Touching for me is everything. . . . I find it so strange that you seem not to like to touch; stranger still, that while you will not touch, yet you will brush each other, make no effort to avoid brushing each other, because in that there is no caress. . . .

'God save the Queen, her golden carriage and her horses, her nephews and her navy, though I can't think from what. . . . Delicious ruffians, I must tell you that England has never bored me. Despite your dubious moral sense, your flaccid minds, your uncertain friendliness, the vagaries of your relationships, dressed as your bodies are, overdressed even, to the point of indecency—I was never bored among you, because I had to watch too carefully lest I be robbed or twisted. . . .'

That is Joan's London, a city whose dormant anarchic instincts she has spent much of her life trying to awaken. Like Genet, she 'wants to touch'. And her motive (though she would deride the idea) is partly patriotic: she would like to revive the Elizabethan London of bear-pits and bordellos thronged with 'delicious ruffians'. She has a huge, affectionate knowledge of English local history, and her current obsession is to erect on the banks of the Thames a 'Fun Palace' which would do for the twentieth century what the pleasure gardens of Vauxhall and Ranelagh did for the seventeenth and eighteenth.

Joan's palace would feature and foster all the aspects of life that qualify as 'play'. There would be areas devoted to dancing, eating, electronic games, music-making, love-making, do-it-yourself film-making and do-it-yourself drama; and each activity would be separated from the others not by solid walls but by penetrable barriers of light. (I quote from the prophet herself.) To construct her gigantic, free-form monument to the pleasure principle, Joan hopes to enlist the aid of architects like Buckminster Fuller—'good dome men', as she crisply describes them. There is in her dream a whiff of nostalgia: the Fun Palace may turn out to be nothing more than a flood-lit, jazz-oriented version of a medieval village green. But even that would be a magical achievement in a country where pleasure for its own sake is still a slightly disreputable concept. To live in a Socialist society entirely peopled by individualists: that is the ideal toward which Joan has always steered, and of which the Fun Palace would be a microcosm.

She was educated at a convent school near her home; it was chosen because of proximity, not piety. Neither her mother nor her stepfather is a Catholic, and of her convent upbringing nothing is nowadays discernible, except perhaps her habit of signing letters and telegrams 'Hell'. (This baffled me too, until I realised that 'Hell' is how Cockneys pronounce the initial letter of her surname. Joan the child was a painter and writer. At the age of eleven she directed *Hamlet*, playing all the parts herself. In her teens she saw dozens of classical productions from the gallery of the Old Vic and detested nearly all of them: one of the exceptions was John Gielgud's *Hamlet* in 1930. When she was sixteen she won a working-class scholarship to the Royal Academy of Dramatic Art, and left both school and home for good. She had a chance, a year later, to study theatre in Moscow, with all expenses paid by the Soviet government; she turned it down at the last moment, because 'the other people who were going looked such bloody bores'.

Then began a long spell of wandering. She drifted to Paris, came back to England and migrated to the industrial centres of the north, which she found more congenial than the softer, less militant south. A sharp-eyed nomad, she absorbed on the wing the lessons of the depression and the hunger marches, flitting from one borrowed bed to another. Even today, she refuses to settle down, and is apt, after spending a week in an East End basement, to move into a penthouse at the Hilton Hotel.

The 1930s (which were her teens and twenties) defined her loyalties. She hated those who made profits and befriended those from whose labour profit was made. She wrote film treatments, 'Agitprop' journalism and BBC documentaries. Late in that ominous decade she met and married a folk-singer called Ewan MacColl, who managed a theatre group in Manchester and from whom she is now divorced.

'He didn't like the classics,' she says, 'but that didn't matter, because we were always in touch with the *modern* classics—the contemporary, international plays that the commercial blokes ignored. We knew all about Bertolt Brecht in the thirties. On Broadway and Shaftesbury Avenue he's still a novelty in the sixties. Ewan and I must have founded about fifty revolutionary theatre groups in the north before the war. The feeling was always international. You'd go to a mining village in Yorkshire, and there would be three Poles in top hats performing for the workers.'

When Stalin signed his pact with Hitler in 1939, Joan was frozen out of the BBC, and was not readmitted until the Nazis invaded Russia two years later. Throughout the war she was gathering around herself a nucleus of like-thinking actors, and in 1945 she gave them a name: Theatre Workshop.

Their immediate aim was to be a Leftish living newspaper, presenting instant dramatisations of contemporary history. Ewan MacColl wrote many of the scripts, and the troupe's finances were supervised by Gerry Raffles, whom Joan had met in the late 1930s, when he was a burly schoolboy at Manchester Grammar School. The company was run on a completely egalitarian basis: actors, directors, designers and stage staff all got an equal share of the takings. The classics began to seep into the repertoire, especially those which could be tilted to the Left without undue strain—plays like Lope de Vega's *Fuenteovejuna*, Marlowe's *Edward II* and Jonson's *Volpone*. Theatre Workshop spent eight penniless years on the road, touring Germany, Norway, Sweden and Czechoslovakia as well as Britain, before coming to rest in 1953 at the Theatre Royal, Stratford-atte-Bowe, a shapely Victorian playhouse deep in East London. Here Joan's actors toiled and fasted, many of them so poor that they slept in hammocks slung across the boxes and dressing rooms.

And Joan's beloved Cockney audience failed her. Grudging reviews and thin attendances were her reward until, in 1955, the company appeared at the Paris International Theatre Festival and scored a thunderous success. Suddenly the London critics discovered them, and Joan became *chic* overnight. Legends started to cluster around her, most of them true. There was the story, for instance, of how she interrupted an actor who was auditioning for her and said: 'Let's drop all that and improvise. You want X pounds a week. Argue with me and prove that you need it. Lie as much as you like. If you convince me, you get the job.' (He did.) She enmeshed her actors in tight bonds of family loyalty. Renegades who 'went commercial' (i.e., appeared on television or defected to the West End) had to apologise to the assembled company before being reinstated; but there was justice in her possessiveness, because nearly all Joan's actors were people whom she had personally recruited, trained and moulded. Her brisk, ribald, overwhelmingly candid approach either intimidated you (in which case you fled), or enslaved you (in which case you rapidly learned that the *sine qua non* of good acting was never to be afraid of making a fool of yourself). Inhibitions crumpled beneath Joan's hammer-blows, with results that are joyfully evident in *Sparrers Can't Sing*, the ebullient East End movie she directed two years ago. ('A primitive thing,' she now calls it.) Always she urged her actors to improvise, even when a show had been running for weeks or months. 'As soon as a production's fixed,' she would say, 'it's dead'; anything, she felt, was preferable to the petrified monotony of a commercial run. At Edinburgh last year I chided her for arguing thus. 'Isn't it true,' I demanded, 'that you flew back to London the other day because you'd heard that your latest production was getting out of hand?' 'Oh, no,' she said, gently rebuking. 'It was getting *in* hand.'

In the late 1950s, somewhat against her conscience, she began to transfer her productions to the West End. *The Quare Fellow*, Brendan Behan's savage comedy about the effect of capital punishment on prison inmates, was the first of a flood of Littlewood successes that included *Fings Ain't Wot They Used t'Be* (with lyrics by Lionel Bart), *A Taste of Honey* and *The Hostage*. With the last-named, in 1960, she made her debut as a Broadway director. She became a celebrity and scorned herself for it, because whenever one of her shows moved into the commercial theatre, it hastened the destruction of everything she had fought for. Having coaxed a play to birth, she would see it praised by the critics and whisked off to the West End or Broadway, there to make money for landlords and *entrepreneurs*. It would also make money for Theatre Workshop, of course; but every such transfer meant the loss of a group of actors she had picked, coaches and welded into unity. Each triumph eroded her ideal—a permanent repertory group whose members were all equal contributors. The more her achievements travelled, the more her company dwindled. Lacking a state subsidy, her art was divided and conquered by commerce.

Joan discovered that she had devoted her life to creating a training-ground for other people to poach on. Hence, in 1961, she resigned from Theatre Workshop and announced that she was embarking on a two-year sabbatical. 'I blew my top,' she says, 'and took off for anywhere.'

She went to Africa, returning to make *Sparrers Can't Sing*, and gave innumerable interviews knocking the theatrical set-up; but at last, in the spring of 1963, she succumbed to her old addiction, and came back to the East End playhouse where she had made her name. The bare boards of her home ground were filled once more with the passion of Joan's home team. A radio programme of soldiers' songs from World War One was what fired her: why not, she asked herself, tell the whole story of that repulsive massacre in a single evening of musical theatre? She summoned her actors—by now dispersed in movies, TV series and West End plays—and gave them a reading list of books on the 1914–18 disaster. When they had absorbed the basic facts, she guided them through a maze of improvised scenes designed to explain why the war happened and how it felt to be involved in it. Her method, as always, was what she calls 'the composite mind bit'—whereby everyone in the cast feels responsible for everyone else.

The result was *Oh What a Lovely War*. The programme defined it as 'a group production under the direction of Joan Littlewood', but it was essentially a one-woman show. The big, purposeful heart that beat throughout the evening belonged only to Joan. You felt that her actors had a common attitude toward something larger than acting, a shared vision that extended to life in general; for it is thus, and not by means of rehearsal techniques or new approaches to stagecraft, that true theatrical style is born. After the opening night, I wrote:

The plot is history: nothing less than the First World War. The cast is decked out in the ruffs and white satin suits of a seaside Pierrot show. We are to witness (the M.C. brightly confides) that famous extravaganza, 'the War Game', enacted by the entire company, with musical interludes drawn from songs of the period. The proscenium sparkles with fairy lights; and a terrible counterpoint is soon set up between the romanticism of the lyrics—all gaiety and patriotic gusto—and the facts of carnage in France, illustrated by stills of the trenches and news reports flickering across an electrified ribbon screen.

Between songs, the cast performs a montage of brisk, laconic sketches. . . . We glimpse a bayonet practice, conducted in lightning gibberish; a military ball, rippling with intrigue; a shooting party of international tycoons, blazing away at wildfowl while debating the relative merits of various neutral trade routes for exporting arms to the enemy; and the Christmas truce on the Western front, which Miss Littlewood handles with utter disdain for sentimentality—the Tommies recoil with nausea from a gift of German cheese, and respond by lobbing an inedible Christmas pudding into the opposite trenches.

Meanwhile the songs grow more bitter. The lunatic Haig has taken command, and the dead are rotting in mountains, monuments to his unswerving conceit. And still, indestructibly if not always suddenly, everyone bursts out singing.

In the second half the show tends to repeat itself, as the war so tragically did; but by then Miss Littlewood's passion has invaded one's bloodstream, and after the final scene, in which a line of reluctant heroes advances on the audience, bleating like sheep entering a slaughterhouse, one is ready to storm Buckingham Palace and burn down Knightsbridge Barracks.

Joan is strong meat, and her work is aimed at strong stomachs. 'Emotion is the word,' she once said to me. 'I like emotion in the theatre. Look at its derivation. It means something that moves outward. Towards people. Everything else is dead.'

(1964)

Chaplin on Chaplin

What can one say of the Chaplin memoirs*—transparently un-ghosted—without giving some kind of offence? Perhaps that the book is an essential document, written by a man ill at ease among words and ideas; whose genius was always non-verbal and non-intellectual.

But to say that is to sound superior, and if there is one theme that rings through the volume, it is Chaplin's profound resentment of people who sound—or look, or act—superior. You feel that in his eyes anyone who regards him as a great comedian and nothing more is guilty of condescension, so sharp are his memories of the lowly social status accorded to clowns. The jokes he tells are almost deliberately humour-less. Overhearing a theatre manager saying that Chaplin stinks, he inter-poses: 'Maybe he stinks, but not half as much as your stink-pot theatre.' When a pompous Hollywood barfly warns him that he had better be funny, he retorts: 'Well, if I'm half as funny as you look, I'll do all right.' ('Blimey! A sarcastic wit, eh?' is the crushed barfly's comeback.) Chaplin the mime is a supreme inventor of gags and a master of bodily timing; as he rightly claims, no one before him had blended 'raw slapstick and sentiment'. Chaplin the writer is a simpleton, lost in an alien discipline.

England overwhelmingly made him: she gave him an abiding sense of social, intellectual and emotional inferiority, and he singles out the 'ever-present class tabulation' practised in Britain as the major reason for his decision to live in the United States. The opening chapters, dealing with his life before it became public property, are much the most power-ful: the home in South London, the vaudevillian father who bolted, the stage debut at the age of five, the years in the workhouse with his mother and brother—all this is set down with total recall. The imminence of starvation is chillingly urgent; and the portrait of his mother, a music hall singer who went gently insane, is the book's most rounded achievement. The first trip to Hollywood is likewise vivid. Chaplin describes the suburb of Los Angeles in which the Keystone Studios were situated:

* *My Autobiography*, by Charles Chaplin.

It was an anomalous-looking place that could not make up its mind whether to be a humble residential district or a semi-industrial one. It had small lumber-yards and junk-yards, and abandoned-looking small farms on which were built one or two shacky wooden stores that fronted the road. . . .

Against this setting almost every American silent film I can remember seems to have been shot.

Chaplin's early years left him with three criss-crossing scars—social insecurity, breeding a desire to rise above his background and overawe the bourgeois world; emotional insecurity, breeding a determination to be invulnerable, beyond anyone's power to wound; and psychological insecurity, curable only by massive injections of self-esteem. All three are visible in his films. Note, in his comic *persona*, the nervous fastidiousness and intense superficial gentility of his demeanour; note also the skill with which he sidesteps calamity, usually launching a few fairly vicious kicks at his tormentors; and the monologues of liberal platitude that burden several of his later and lesser screenplays.

The screen Chaplin is usually a character out of his element, thrust by chance into hostile, unfamiliar circumstances (the escaped convict posing as a party guest, the tramp pretending to be Hitler); often an outsider, always a stranger. So with his life. We forget that Chaplin was the first international star of the mass communications era; the first actor to be globally known and mobbed; the first to be threatened with the fate of that Oriental monarch who was literally 'seen' to death. No wonder he withdrew into solitude; no wonder, either, that this sudden and shattering fame, achieved in his twenties, intensified his insecurities. What makes his book fascinating is the way in which, often inadvertently, it reflects them.

Loneliness is omnipresent: 'To a more or less degree,' he says, 'it is the theme of everyone.' Uncertain of who he is, and of his right to be where he is, he feels safest communing with himself—or at least with people who will not presume to interrupt him. He returns to Hollywood after a world trip in the thirties: 'I tried to think of someone whom I knew intimately enough to phone and invite for dinner *without being embarrassed*, but there was no one' (my italics). Later we find him talking to himself. Having heard it rumoured that his house in Beverly Hills is haunted, he sits alone in the dark and asks the spirits to grant him a manifestation. Like many lonely egotists, he is superstitious: we learn of a fortune-teller who assured him that he had 'a money-making hand' and that he would die of pneumonia at eighty-two.

Emotional uncertainties—notably a fear of being exploited by women—quiver beneath the text: stiff, assertive sentences cover up old injuries, like the formal politeness on the face of the rejected tramp at the end of *City Lights*. Seeing a chorus-girl he adored dancing with someone else at a party, he says: 'I could not preclude a feeling that my ardour for her had slightly diminished.' Of his wives before Oona he writes with wincing detachment; and he quotes with approval H. G. Wells's remark that 'the time for sex' is when you have done your work and are bored. Once he fell for a girl on the Côte d'Azur ('propinquity caught me in the meshes of her charm') from whom he hated to part; or, as he puts it in a deeply symptomatic sentence: 'The mere thought of leaving her excited my pity.' The word one expects is something like 'anguish' or 'distress'; but Chaplin will not place himself in a position as vulnerable as that.

Intellectual insecurity—that great provoker of grandiose prose and unsupported assertions—recurs throughout the book. Clichés abound ('a most formidable element in optimism is youth', 'in handling actors in a scene, psychology is most helpful') and we get statements like this, *à propos* of Hollywood in the twenties:

> Celebrated authors came from all parts of the world; Sir Gilbert Parker, William J. Locke, Rex Beach, Joseph Hergesheimer, Somerset Maugham, Gouverneur Morris, Ibanez, Elinor Glyn, Edith Wharton, Kathleen Norris and many others.

Chaplin is 'annoyed' by Whitman and dislikes Shakespeare because his plays are too aristocratic: 'Perhaps it is something psychological within me, possibly my peculiar solipsism . . . I cannot identify myself with a prince's problems.' Nor can he believe that the man of Stratford could have written the plays: 'In the work of the greatest of geniuses humble beginnings will reveal themselves somewhere—but one cannot trace the slightest sign of them in Shakespeare' (as one can, of course, in Chaplin).

His choice and use of words are constantly revealing. As I cite examples, remember that he was plunged, with only two years' schooling behind him, into the company of Shaw, Keynes, Lloyd George, Wells and Einstein. 'Surely a system could be devised,' he says at a Greenwich Village party, 'of lexicographically charting ideas, from abstract words to concrete ones, and by deductive and inductive processes arriving at the right word for one's thought.'

A Negro truck-driver who was present told him that there was such a book: Roget's *Thesaurus*. Internal evidence derived from the autobiography suggests that he went straight out and bought it. A pile of old clothes he offers for sale at Newington Butts is described as 'my ignoble congeries' (Roget lists 'congeries' under 'accumulation'); when Harry Hopkins foresees financial disaster for *The Great Dictator*, Chaplin is not 'frantically ebullient about his prognostications' (Roget lists 'ebullient' under 'excitement'); and the sixteen-year-old Randolph Churchill is 'esurient for intellectual argument' (Roget lists 'esurient' in the same group as 'avid').

Nothing in the book explains how Chaplin came to be so funny; but much of it shows, between the lines, why comedy was the perfect outlet for his feelings of inferiority. The lines themselves show him hardening, chapter by chapter, into a public idol, dogmatic and armourplated. One reveres the comedian; one admires the anti-patriot, the impenitent Socialist and the victim of political harassment. But Chaplin the man remains at arm's length. Apart from its peerless opening pages, *My Autobiography* is the raw material for the real biography that must surely follow.

(1964)

Groucho and Perelman

More than thirty years have passed since Groucho Marx and S. J. Perelman first worked together. According to myth, the classic early quartet of Marx Brothers pictures (*Horse Feathers, Monkey Business, Duck Soup* and *Animal Crackers*) was written single-handed by Perelman; in fact he wrote only the first two, and gets embarrassed when people hail him as the sole literary progenitor of the Brothers and their legend. He saw Groucho in a Broadway show in the late twenties and sent a fervent note backstage; the result was an invitation to Hollywood and a friendship that has survived repeated allegations that Groucho owes everything to Perelman and vice versa.

I met them for lunch at the Connaught Hotel. Side by side, when I entered the lobby, sat two middle-aged men with plenty of head visible through their hair. Both wore tweed suits and striped shirts with button-down collars. Both had toothbrush moustaches, of which Perelman's was straw-coloured and upswept, while Groucho's was close-cropped and grey. At sixty, Perelman is Groucho's junior by nine years and you notice at once that he defers to his elder as a performer. Similarly, Groucho defers to Perelman as an intellectual. They are both New Yorkers and Jewish; Perelman was born in Brooklyn and Groucho on Manhattan's upper East Side.

We move to the restaurant, Groucho leading the way in his low-slung, loping gait (a shell-less tortoise turned biped?), with Perelman in jaunty pursuit. Over Vichysoisse we talk about Jewishness and its enormous formative influence on show business in the United States. Harry Kurnitz, a Hollywood wit respected by both my guests, once went to a crowded theatrical restaurant in Manhattan with a friend who said: 'Do you realise, Harry, that there are two million Jews in New York alone?' Kurnitz looked around him and replied: 'What do you mean— alone?' Why is it that the best comedians are so often Jewish—Eddie Cantor, Phil Silvers, Sid Caesar, Danny Kaye, Jack Benny, Mort Sahl, Lenny Bruce, George Burns, Milton Berle, Bert Lahr, the Marxes, etc.?

'I think it's because the Jews were immigrants,' says Perelman. 'They were wrestling with English as a foreign language. They'd take an Anglo-Saxon cliché—like "I disbursed a goodly sum" and make it funny by pronouncing it in the wrong accent.' In other words, pedantry and polysyllables become comic when uttered by Jews.

Groucho dissents. 'You taught me that,' he says askance to Perelman, 'but then I was trying to be an intellectual.' (He says nearly everything askance.) Groucho doesn't think Jewishness is the vital factor in American comedy; he attributes the Jewish hegemony to the fact that most American comedy is urban, and that most big cities have a large Jewish population.

Many Marx Brothers fans, especially in the early days, refused to believe that Groucho, Chico and Harpo were related to one another. Others insisted that they were a bunch of Italians. American slang for Italian is 'Ginnie' (pronounced 'guinea'), and Groucho recalls a description he overheard in a theatre lobby of himself and his brothers: 'One's a Ginnie, one's a Jew and the other spits on the sidewalk.' Longevity, he thinks, is the quality that makes Jewish performers unique, and he ascribes it to something unconnected with talent: 'It's because Jews don't drink. Or at least, not much. Whenever Jewish comics get together, the bar bill is small. You can imagine how dull our New Years are.' During lunch he drank nothing but water.

Prompted by Perelman, he recalls an occasion when George Burns was touring in vaudeville with a Jewish girl disguised as a Spanish dancer. In the course of the act she would twirl at his fingertips, revealing as she did so a pair of bushily unshaven armpits. After their opening night, the manager called Burns to one side. 'I like your act,' he said, 'but I don't like those two Jews you're dancing with.'

Perelman blames TV for having extinguished the racial (e.g., Jewish) comic: because the sponsors are scared to offend minorities, comedy that has its roots in a particular racial or national idiom tends to get ironed out into anonymity. I ask where it is possible nowadays for a young comic to learn his trade before a live audience as Groucho and his brothers so rigorously did.

'There's no vaudeville now,' Groucho says, 'so it's tough. The main outlet is clubs—small nightspots in places like Cincinnati or Waco, Texas. The big difference is that there used to be "action comics" like me and my brothers. But there's no room for that kind of group comedy on the television screen. So today you get mostly stand-up comics—one man with a microphone.' Perelman adds: 'They're all monologuists now.'

Both eat frugally: pressed beef for Perelman and a ham omelette for Groucho. 'It's thirty years since my brothers and I made our English debut,' says Groucho. 'It was a disaster. The audience threw copper coins on to the stage of the Coliseum. I walked down to the footlights and told them to throw silver, preferably wrapped in banknotes.' Decades of affluence have not banished the spectre of poverty. Groucho sympathises with the Left and disapproves of the monarchy ('why should they live off the people?'); but age has sweetened his attitude towards capitalism. 'I've got to the stage,' he admits, 'where I read the *Wall Street Journal* before I read *Variety*.'

'What are you hawking there?' he bawls suavely at the waiter with the sweet trolley, and orders a fruit salad. Coffee precipitates more reminiscence. Perelman tells me with moist eyes about the West Side Writing and Asthma Club which he and Groucho founded in the thirties. Levy's Tavern on Ninth Street was its headquarters, and the guests who attended its daily lunches included Robert Benchley, Donald Ogden Stewart, the actor Charles Butterworth, and the notoriously eccentric song-writers Bert Kalmar and Harry Ruby (authors of 'Show me a rose —I'll show you a stag at bay').

Groucho, still at large in memory lane, comes up with an account of the most extraordinary vaudeville act he ever saw. It was called 'Swain's Rats and Cats', and it consisted of rats dressed up as jockeys and cats dressed up as horses. Every night they raced around a miniature track. One evening Fanny Brice, who was topping the bill, went into her dressing-room and encountered one of Swain's rats stark naked (the rat, not Miss Brice). She screamed, whereupon the rat was seized and reprimanded. Next week it appeared at the Palace in New York and won every race. The critics congratulated Swain on his new, world-beating rat. 'Not at all,' he said proudly. 'This is a rat who has been in Fanny Brice's dressing-room. This is a self-made rat.' Of Miss Brice herself, Groucho remembers that 'her language was that of Pier Six, and she always carried five sets of teeth—including one for signing autographs in and another for just walking down the street'.

I ask him to name the people who have made him laugh. 'The funniest talkers,' he says, 'the funniest men around a dinner-table would be George Jessel and George Burns. The fastest men with one-line gags would be Oscar Levant and George S. Kaufman. On stage, I would pick W. C. Fields, Willie Howard, Ed Wynn, Bobby Clark and Bert Lahr. But it's hard to laugh at comedians if you're a comedian, especially if they're getting laughs.' Perelman's list of great comics is the same, except that it includes Groucho.

When we parted, Perelman left for the airport, *en route* for the Balkans on some undisclosed errand. Groucho went off to snatch some sleep before dining with T. S. Eliot. Eliot wrote to him several years ago asking for an autographed picture. He sent one, feeling greatly honoured; but Eliot replied insisting on another, in which his cigar was tilted at a more challenging angle. Groucho complied, and was forthwith invited to dinner. What happened when they met I do not know, but there are plenty of Eliot lyrics that would suit the vinegary wryness of Groucho's singing voice to perfection. I should love to hear his recording of 'Under the bam, under the boo'—and what about;

> 'I'll carry you off
> To a cannibal isle . . .
> Yes, I'd eat you!
> In a nice little, white little, soft little, tender little,
> Juicy little, right little missionary stew'?

Groucho is the perfect vocal stand-in for Sweeney Agonistes. And should Eliot be contemplating an EP release of 'O O O O that Shake-speherean Rag' to celebrate the bard's quatercentenary, he need look no further for the ideal minstrel.

(1964)

Papa and the Playwright

There used to be a popular literary pastime called 'Imaginary Con-versations'. The idea was to bring together in imagination great men or women who never met in reality, and improvise dialogue to fit the situa-tion. The more disparate the pair, the better. What, for instance, would St Francis of Assisi have said to the Marquis de Sade? And what would a fly on the wall have gleaned from a chat between Noël Coward and Lenin? I often play the game in my mind, and one of the pairings with which I have toyed is that of Ernest Hemingway and Tennessee Williams. How would the great extrovert react to the great introvert, the big-game hunter to the hot-house plant, the virility symbol to the student of deviation? I never got very far with that confrontation, and usually passed on to something simpler (like Casey Stengel and Sappho); but it persistently nagged at my imagination until a spring day some five years ago, when I was offered a chance of translating my abortive fantasy into accomplished fact.

The time was April 1959, and the place Havana. I had come to Cuba to write a travel article and, hopefully, to meet Fidel Castro, who had then been in power for less than four months. The rift with Washington was still far off: younger readers may not believe me, but there really was a period when it was not thought un-American to approve of Castro's regime. (That was before he began to nationalise American business interests in Cuba.) The city was bursting with libertarian fervour; you felt in the midst of a genuine, do-it-yourself revolution. Although the brothels and blue cinemas were closed, I did manage to attend a private showing, arranged by a young American writer I knew, of a genuine, do-it-yourself erotic film. The secrecy was terrific. We had to lie prone on the floor of an abandoned whorehouse while the movie was projected on to the wall from a distance of less than three feet, producing an image about the size of a credit card. It depicted a teenage boy disastrously failing to make love to a burly, maternal tart. The male star, who also directed the film and worked the projector, apologised to us for his inadequacy, explaining that it was his first picture, and he was not used to the hot lights. Would we not wait for the second reel, in which he actually made it with a Chinese sailor? But we had left.

On my second day in Havana, I went to see Hemingway at his estate in the suburb of San Francisco de Paula, where he settled soon after the end of the Spanish Civil War. NO ADMISSION EXCEPT BY APPOINTMENT, read a sign on the heavy iron gates; but I had an appointment, and pressed on to the ramshackle mansion, full of books, unopened mail and wildlife (stuffed and skinned), which he shared with Miss Mary, the last of his wives. I had met him first in Madrid, several years before. Expecting a booming titan, I had been amazed to shake hands with a gruff, gigantic boy, shy and reticent in manner despite the heroic head and white, Michelangelesque curls. The lips, thin like a student's, belied the massive physique, and would part, at moments of enthusiasm, in an eager, adolescent grin. The blue eyes were moist and plaintive behind the steel-rimmed glasses, though in transports of fury they could become oppressively baleful. I noted that Hemingway was a model of courtesy on his own (or with Miss Mary), but an intolerant boss when surrounded by an entourage of sycophants—unlike the fighting bull, which is dangerous only when isolated from the herd. His voice was a whispering baritone. As I listened to it in Havana, I recalled a phrase from our first Madrid encounter. Describing an Atlantic crossing on the same ship as a notoriously queer English actor, Hemingway had said: 'Whenever he walked into the dining-room, I raised my glass and smashed it on the table, as every gentleman does in the presence of homosexuals.' I had never made up my mind whether he was joking; and if so, how seriously.

Having made a lunch date for the following day, I drove back to central Havana. That evening, I dropped in at the Hotel Nacional for a drink. Leaning against the bar, plumply perched on a stool, his hair darkly coiled with sweat and his bland, fat-cat face smiling out into nowhere, was Tennessee Williams. I flinched; because a few days earlier I had given his latest play, *Sweet Bird of Youth*, an extremely damaging review that included references to dust bowls and sterility. But Tennessee's scars heal swiftly (in public, at least; God knows what private sores continue to suppurate within), and he sauntered over to join me. 'Ken baby,' he said, emitting the thick, bemused snicker by which he hopes to convince you that he is a simpleton; in fact he is as sharp as a tack. He said he was awaiting the arrival of 'a banana millionairess from Key West'; meanwhile, could we meet for lunch tomorrow? I explained that I had a date with Hemingway. Tennessee said he had never met Mr Hemingway, and tentatively wondered whether he might make a third. I said I was sure that Hemingway wouldn't mind. 'But won't he kick me?' said Tennessee, stricken with unease. 'They tell me that Mr Hemingway usually kicks people like me in the crotch.' To silence his qualms, I telephoned Hemingway, who said he would be delighted to meet Mr Williams. We were to foregather at noon the next day, the chosen arena being the Floridita restaurant, Hemingway's favourite eating place.

This was not the first time I had inflicted a brief encounter on Tennessee. Only a year before, at a Mayfair club, I had mischievously introduced him to the renowned ex-madam, Polly Adler. Their conversation had been conducted on parallel lines that never met; Tennessee wanted to talk about brothels, and Miss Adler about literature. She was taking a course in classical poetry at a California college, and urgently solicited Tennessee's views on the passages in Virgil where 'Dido shacks up with Aeneas'. Scant contact was made.

I was the first to arrive at the Floridita. The air-conditioning was so brutal that it blew out my cigarette lighter. Hemingway breasted his way in a few minutes later, wearing a baseball cap, a white T-shirt and tropical trousers: the day was fiercely hot. He ordered a double frozen daiquiri, locally known as a 'Papa *doble*', hugged a few waiters and signed a few autographs. A dramatic bronze bust of him stood in a niche beside the bar. 'We cover it,' he said, 'during Lent.' A trio of Negro musicians saluted him with a song called *Soy Como Soy*—'I am as I am' —about a Lesbian who cannot, however hard she tries, change her appetites to suit Papa's. They next sang a lament for the death of Antonio Maceo, the mulatto general who was killed in Cuba's struggle against Spain. The lyrics were written in Spanish by Hemingway, who embraced the singers and proudly informed me: 'I'm an honorary Negro.'

Twelve-fifteen, and still no Tennessee. I listened to Hemingway's comments on some of his contemporaries. On Scott Fitzgerald: 'He was soft. He dissolved at the least touch of alcohol.' On a popular Southern novelist: 'He's a whisky writer. He can't write without a quart of rye at his elbow. He's a slave to saucedom.' He then made for the men's room, and minutes passed. At twelve-thirty I pursued him and coaxed him out; he had been sparring in the john with an ancient Negro attendant.

Meanwhile, Tennessee had arrived, looking chipper though slightly glazed. He was wearing a yachting jacket with silver buttons, as if to persuade Hemingway that although he might be a decadent, he was at least an *outdoor* decadent. He rather spoiled the effect by flourishing a lengthy cigarette holder. Eleven years separated the contenders: Hemingway aged in at fifty-nine, and Williams at forty-eight. I made the introduction, hands were duly shaken, and I ordered more drinks. Silence fell. Hemingway gazed at the bar. Tennessee beamed at the ceiling. Suddenly: 'What I've always admired about your work, Mr Hemingway,' said Tennessee bravely, 'is that you care about honour among men. And there is no quest more desperate than that.'

Hemingway swivelled his leonine head. 'What kind of men, Mr Williams,' he said, 'did you have in mind?' Tennessee started to shrug, but Hemingway continued: 'People who have honour never talk about it. They know it, and they confer immortality on each other.' That seemed to take care of *that*.

By now the bar was filling up, and so were we. I was beginning to feel slightly drunk, and Tennessee's fixed smile and half-closed eyes did not bode too well. He murmured to me that fear of Hemingway's boot had moved him to start tanking up on martinis at ten a.m. The drink that drives out fear had clearly done its work, for within a few moments he was once again making the running. 'I was in Spain last year for the bullfights,' he said, 'I go every year. I get so disturbed I have to leave after the third bull.' Hemingway sipped and grunted. 'Last summer I met one of the matadors on the beach,' Tennessee went on, 'a lovely boy, very friendly, very accessible. Named Ordóñez—Antonio Ordóñez.' I realised that Tennessee was walking blindfolded into a mine field. Ordóñez was not only the greatest bullfighter in Spain, but one of Hemingway's closest friends: indeed, in the summer that lay ahead, Hemingway seldom left his side, missing none of his *corridas* and later extolling his arts in *Life* magazine. Pedro Romero in *The Sun Also Rises* was modelled on Ordóñez's father. Ignorant of these things, or perhaps forgetful, Tennessee continued: 'He was utterly charming to me, a most enchanting boy. He even showed me his *cogidas*.'

'He showed you his *what*, Mr Williams?' said Hemingway, furrowing his brow and feigning incomprehension.

'His *cogidas*,' Tennessee rattled on, 'his horn wounds. The scars on his thighs. Of course he was wearing a bathing suit.'

'Do you think he would talk to us and show us his *cogidas*?' said Hemingway, all deadpan innocence.

'Oh, I'm certain he would,' Tennessee assured him. 'As I say, he's a most accessible boy.'

At this point a tiresome Commonwealth journalist intervened; and never was bore more welcome. He breezily asked whether I would like to attend an execution that night at Morro Castle across the bay, where one of Batista's bullies was due to be shot. I declined the invitation, explaining that I hated capital punishment and that the idea of death as a spectacle for outsiders disgusted me. Tennessee disagreed: in my place, he said, he would have accepted, since it was a writer's duty to expose himself to any human experience, however loathsome. The bore promptly offered to take him along, and they arranged to meet after dinner. (The plan miscarried: the execution, an open-air event, was postponed because of bad weather.) I asked Hemingway whether he thought I was right to reject the invitation. He nodded. 'There are some refusals,' he said enigmatically, 'that are still permitted us.' He added, however, that he thoroughly approved of Castro. 'This is a good revolution,' he said, 'an *honest* revolution.'

One-fifteen, and still no food; merely a chilling cascade of melting daiquiris. Tennessee, playing it as unsafe as ever, mentioned William Faulkner. 'When I met him,' he said, 'his eyes haunted me. Those terrible, distraught eyes. They moved me to tears.'

Hemingway was not noticeably affected. 'The trouble with Mr

Faulkner,' he said, 'is that he can't *rematar*'—a Spanish taurine verb meaning to round off a sequence of passes with the cape. 'He can give you eighty-nine *naturales*, but he doesn't know how to end the series.' As often, Hemingway not only closed the subject but sat on the lid.

More drinks (we were all still standing, though swaying), and Tennessee plunged in again. 'I used to know your second wife, Mr Hemingway,' he said. 'I believe her name was Pauline. I knew her in Key West when I was young. She was very kind to me when I was poor— a lovely lady, a most hospitable lady. I often wondered what happened to her. They tell me she died. Did she die in great pain?'

Hemingway, who was profoundly attached to his second wife, replied with a stoical sentence that deliberately verged on self-parody; he often used this technique as a mask to avoid direct emotional commitment. 'She died like everybody else,' he said, leaning portentously across the bar, 'and after that she was dead.'

Solid food was obviously out of the question. I went to the lavatory and found, when I returned, that the meeting of minds for which I had hoped had taken place in my absence. The two writers were brow to brow, urgently debating the relative importance of the kidneys and the liver. 'You can survive on one kidney,' Hemingway was arguing, 'but if your liver gives out, you're through.' They were even exchanging the names and addresses of their doctors. I disrupted their communion by announcing that I had a date at two p.m. with Castro, and would have to leave at once. To my slight alarm, Tennessee insisted on accompanying me. He and Hemingway shook hands warmly, linked at last by medicine and mortality.

Just on time, Tennessee and I passed through the gates of the Presidential Palace. Instead of frisking us, the sentry drew our attention to a collection of butterflies owned by one of his colleagues. We admired it, and were escorted to a leather couch outside Castro's anteroom. Here we spent two-and-a-half hours, while soldiers, pregnant women, and men in ice-cream-coloured suits strolled in and out of the leader's presence. Tennessee, growing restive, focused his gaze on a teenage boy in olive-green battle dress who was standing guard at the door. 'Have you noticed,' he mused, 'how everybody touches that boy before they go in? Do you suppose it's for luck? I wonder would he like some American cigarettes. . . .'

Before I could answer his questions, someone identified Tennessee as the famous Yankee playwright, and we were whisked through the anteroom into Castro's sanctum, where a vital cabinet meeting was in session. Castro was on the eve of paying his first visit to the United

States since coming to power. Because of Tennessee, the meeting was suspended; the affairs of the nation ground to a halt while the president paid tribute to the artist in transit. The members of the cabinet, most of them under thirty, rose from their seats around an oval, mahogany table, and Castro strode over to greet us. In clumsy but clearhearted English, he told Tennessee how much he had admired his plays, above all the one about the cat that was upon the burning roof. He hoped that Mr Williams would come to live in Cuba, and write about the revolution. He said he was also grateful to Mr Hemingway. 'We took *For Whom the Bell Tolls* to the hills with us, and it taught us about guerrilla warfare.' Tennessee smiled non-committally, and asked me out of the corner of his mouth whether I thought the boy with a moustache on his left would be willing to run across the square and bring him a hot tamale. I replied that I doubted it, because the boy in question was the minister of education.

We took our leave shortly afterwards. Tennessee has never met Castro since; and he never saw Hemingway again. I offer this account of two accidental meetings simply because they happened. Artistically, nothing came of them; but they may contribute, to future histories of American literature, a bizarre and frivolous footnote.

(1965)

Duke: A Birthday Fanfare

In our teens we make hero-lists of those we worship and intend one day to meet. Mine, when I was thirteen, included a cricketer, a stripper, a painter, a drama critic, several actors, a film director and a jazz musician. I crossed them off as I met them, either socially or professionally, but until recently one name remained unblotted—that of the remote and lordly musician who brought the sound of Harlem chugging and wailing into my Birmingham suburb late in the thirties. On records only, of course; he had visited England with the band in 1933, before I had outgrown hymns and the national anthem; but by 1940 I knew the precise, poignant noise of the Ellington reed section as well as I knew Henry Hall's signature tune, and when a growling trumpet cut across the lyrical brushwork of the saxophones, I could tell you whether it was Bubber Miley or Cootie Williams. I struck the band in what is still regarded by many good listeners as Ellington's most brilliant period (jazz, like bull-fighting—another art then held to be immoral and disreputable outside the racial group that invented it—went through a convulsion of creative replenishment between 1939 and 1942). *Ko-Ko, Jack the Bear, Dusk, Across the Track Blues, Take the A Train, Bojangles* and *Cotton Tail* are among the many three-minute marvels I bought as they were issued. A band of individualists—the throaty lamentations of Joe Nanton's muted trombone, the slippery nostalgia of Johnny Hodges's alto, the bedrock grumbles of Harry Carney on baritone sax—spoke with a general voice, which was Ellington's. I felt a special though spurious kinship with them because the year of their first fame (1927, when they moved into the Cotton Club in Harlem) was also the year of my birth.

When I last saw them—a couple of months ago, playing to a full house in London that ranged in age and ethnic background from infant Trinidadians to sixtyish American professors on sabbaticals—the sixteen-piece band still featured three Cotton Club survivors: Cootie Williams in the rollicking back row of trumpets, and Hodges and Carney in the apparently slumbering front row of reeds. And swaying gently before them, his long back loosely swathed in Italian silk, his lacquered hair and immaculate bandit's smile suggesting a Negro Cesar Romero: the perennial Duke himself, a black prince who should have ruled Haiti in the days of Toussaint l'Ouverture. He conducted us and the band through a retrospective audition of his work from the late twenties to last autumn, pausing between numbers to soothe us with his catch-phrase ('We want you to know that we love you *madly*', delivered in tones of the blandest mockery), and taking several opportunities to demonstrate that those who question his skill as a solo pianist are out of their minds.

Next morning the band flew back to New York. Ellington stayed on at the Dorchester, whither he invited me to talk. We both knew, though neither of us said so, that this might well be his last professional visit to Europe; four decades on the road is enough for anyone, and I offer this account of our meeting as a birthday salute to a diehard nomad who will be sixty-six years old next Thursday.*

He greeted me in sweater, slacks and socks, attended by Ferdinanda, a blonde Frenchwoman of Algerian *colon* origins who acts as his travelling major-domo. Almost the first thing he said was: 'I've been captain of the ship for forty years. I'm like an old Negro conductor who gets fired by the railroad. When a train whistle blows in the middle of the night, that old man's heart is going to break.' He gave a deep, easy chuckle and put his feet up. I asked whether his standards of band discipline had slackened over the years. Not at all, he said; occasionally he had to reprimand a musician who felt 'a spirit of reluctance' and was unable to play, but there was no more to it than that. As for his own

* 29 April 1965.

weaknesses: 'When I was around forty I gave up the juice. Ten years later I went back, and then gave it up again. But even when I was on it, I could never get drunk. One time in Cleveland I acted as referee at a drinking contest between two cats in the band. I took drink for drink with them, and at nine a.m. I wound up carrying them both home. Nowadays I take a glass of wine now and then—Beaujolais or champagne—but ice-cream is the danger. After a concert I order it by the gallon. And caviare: I picked up the caviare habit on tour in Iran.' Ellington dresses sleekly, but without dandyism; during his London stay he astonished Lobb's, the St James's Street bootmakers, by commissioning them to duplicate a favourite pair of shoes he bought thirty years ago in a New York department store for $12.95.

He talked expansively and unpretentiously about his music: 'I used to listen a lot to people like Debussy and Delius, and I admire Britten— especially *The Rape of Lucretia*—but basically I'm a sort of primitive musician. For me the art of writing music is the art of hearing it before you write it. You have to hear it first—cool, fresh, bang, right out of the air. I once played a concert hall in Stockholm, and outside it there was this statue of a girl blowing on Pan-pipes in the middle of a field. I said to myself: "That's me in drag." I take the music seriously, but I hope I don't take myself seriously.' He was the first great jazz musician whose inspiration was urban rather than grass-roots; the first to orchestrate the sound of the big city—a powerhouse pierced from within by the cry of a Negro jungle. When he composed *Sophisticated Lady* in 1933, some critics complained that it wasn't Negro music, by which they meant that it wasn't crude and ingenuous enough to fit their stereotype of the Negro: 'It's the Negro I know,' Ellington told them, 'even if *you* don't.' He has often (though always quietly) been ahead of his time in the field of racial relationships. In 1941 he wrote the score for a revue called *Jump for Joy*: 'a big social-significance show,' he told me. 'Orson Welles saw it, and hired me to work with him on a movie about the history of jazz. I'd written just twenty-eight bars of trumpet solo when RKO cancelled Orson's contract. But I automatically go on accumulating material, and that solo ended up as a forty-minute composition called *A Drum is a Woman*.' In 1947, with lyricist John LaTouche, he wrote *Beggar's Holiday*, a Broadway musical distantly based on *The Beggars' Opera*, in which the white hero (Alfred Drake) fell in love with the daughter of a Negro police chief: 'That was really far-out, but nobody seemed to notice.' He has composed incidental music for Le Sage's classic comedy *Turcaret* at the TNP, and for *Timon of Athens* at Stratford, Ontario. Yet despite the weight and variety of his work, he keeps very few files of band parts

and often finds it impossible to revive a number once it has been recorded. Sometimes it slips his memory altogether: when I played him the
original recording of *Across the Track Blues*, he couldn't remember the
title, which is as if Schönberg were to forget *Pierrot Lunaire*. I had to
remind myself that Ellington lives in a hard-pressed commercial world of
night-club dates, dances, parties and receptions, where fun (for the band
as much as the customers) is the main attraction. 'In other words,' as
Humphrey Lyttelton has written, 'what is bizarre and "out of place" in an
Ellington band show is not the trumpet pyrotechnics, the comic dancing
or the leader's flash clothes, but the surpassing virtue of the music
itself.' I asked Ellington what kind of criticism annoyed him most.
'Critics,' he said, 'who expect you to play what they want you to play.'
Critics, in fact, who expect art instead of high jinks. I understand how he
feels, though I doubt whether devotion to art would deplete his audiences
as much as he fears. Meanwhile he lives smiling behind the walls of his
reputation, securely hemmed in by achievement.

His hobby (he stunned me by saying) is writing plays which nobody
is allowed to read. One of them is called *A Man with Four Sides*—in
other words, a square—and deals with a jazz musician who, oppressed by
the primness of his wife, invents an imaginary girl-friend whom he
addresses in fantasy. 'You have the authority of a thoroughbred,' he tells
her, 'Walk for me, baby'; at which point his wife pops her head round the
door and says: 'Otho, time for bed—it's Tuesday, you know.' The strain
of lush romantic dreaming that runs through Ellington's music positively
stampedes through his dramaturgy. His latest unread play, entitled
Queenie-Pie, concerns a prosperous lady beautician whose looks are
fading. 'An old cat who works for her warns her that the young chicks
are catching up on her. He comes from an island of sunshine, where you
get two summers back to back. On this island there's a man-eating tree
which contains a serum that is the secret of eternal domination of men.
Get that product, he says, and you'll be safe. So she takes a yacht and
goes to the island. The old cat tells her that the tree must be approached
at midnight, because at that time its limbs open to embrace the sky. But
when she's made the grab and got the serum that will make her the
permanent Queenie-Pie, the tree gets mad and causes an eruption. The
yacht sinks, she loses the serum in the sea, there's a great multi-coloured
foam, and she gets washed up on another island. The natives want to
worship her, but all she wants is to be loved. The king is an old way-back
swinger. She teaches his people how to make alcohol and dress well and
get civilised, and they elect her queen. Then a rescue boat arrives. "We
have to get spears and put on skins and be fierce," says Queenie. The cats

on the boat recognise her and want to take her back to New York. But when she decides to go with them, the king tells her that royal women are forbidden to leave the island. So she has to stay. Queenie-Pie has become a *real* queen, and she hates it.' It would be fascinating to see this curious fable staged, especially with Ella Fitzgerald, for whom Ellington wrote the leading part.

A Christian and a Bible reader, he told me with pride that he had just been invited to compose a choral number for a religious concert at a High Episcopalian cathedral in San Francisco. His personal creed is confined to no particular church: 'I have a private religion—a direct line that embraces all faiths. It's a matter of love, unconditional love.' He thinks Britain 'the most civilised country I know, because you make allowances for human weakness. After all, who's going to decide whether it's more damaging and degenerate to be a liar, an adulteress or a dope-fiend? All I know about morality is that too much passion about *anything* is destructive to people.' He dislikes extremists, however just their cause. On tour in India, he met an American lady who insisted that birth control ought to be compulsory in over-populated countries. Offended by her dogmatism and 'feeling plain shitty', he said he thought birth control was a bad idea; rather than spend money on teaching contraception, why not spend it on feeding and healing the children? 'Suppose you've had seventeen children,' he went on, 'and you prohibit the eighteenth, and he happens to be the world's greatest poet? Suppose he flies round the world in limbo for a hundred years? When he finally comes out of someone else's womb, he may find that poetry's gone out of style.'

Some Negroes feel that Ellington regards the struggle for racial equality as a form of extremism; and certainly he has never taken a public stand on the subject. 'Duke doesn't like to be bugged by political things,' says his impresario, Norman Granz, 'they keep him from working.' He even shuts himself off from the fact of poverty: when I mentioned that it was fairly widespread even in the United States, he seemed puzzled and incredulous. His work, of course, reflects the Negro condition —witness the fifty-minute suite *Black, Brown and Beige* (1943), his first attempt at extended composition. ('The title doesn't mean the colour of a Negro's skin, but the colour of his attitudes towards the enemy. Black means he wants to eat them. Brown means he just resents them. Beige means he's happy to integrate.') But neither this nor the show called *My People* which he wrote, composed, directed and part-choreographed in Chicago two years ago evokes much response in the modern, militant Negro. He is a gradualist in a time of lightning change, a black Kerensky overtaken by revolution. When Ellington plays the blues, with whatever sophisticated use of impressionist harmonies, he does so in a spirit of acceptance, as if pain and Negro life were permanently inseparable; whereas the blues that James Baldwin sings are for Mister Charlie, the white oppressor who is soon to be overthrown. When I asked Ellington about the racial situation, he said: 'This is the great playground of international chess. You have to generalise, and I can't do that. I don't know anyone who knows all the Negroes in the United States. I know a lot of them myself, but they're all different. One may have a bend in his nose that makes him different from all the others.' But, as any Jew can testify, there comes a time in the history of a race when one has to generalise or surrender.

Perhaps the truest image of Ellington is that of a blinkered, dedicated musical genius who has spent his life tinkering with a magnificently flexible toy: his orchestra. 'Retire?' he said when I put the final question. 'What could I retire to? What else am I going to play with?'

(1965)

The Bogart I Never Knew

First, the confession. Unlike most journalists, I never got drunk with Humphrey Bogart. I met him only once, at a Mayfair club in 1952, when I had just described his face in print as 'a triumph of plastic surgery'. He called me over to his table, where he was studiously noisy and three parts crocked. We did not love each other at sight, though I happily submitted to what John Crosby once described to me as 'that basilisk authority of his'. He overawed me because he was rich and raucous and because he ate nothing. He looked like 'a great famished wolf', which is how Ellen Terry summed up Irving's performance as Macbeth. I decided later that I preferred the lines his script writers gave him to the ones he ad-libbed that night.

I have now read about eighty-three accounts of him, in magazines or books, and I still cannot find it in me to be mesmerised by Bogart the Man. Successful hard-drinking iconoclasts who can't act frequently express the same opinions as successful hard-drinking iconoclasts (like Bogart) who can. To hate phonies and prize loyalty is a fairly common attribute, even among the untalented. And on every other page of the Bogart dossiers there are tributes from colleagues that bring me out in a sweat of incredulous embarrassment. My favourite comes from Joseph L. Mankiewicz, according to whom: 'He had a kind of eighteenth-century, Alexander Pope nature.' Alexander Pope was a cripple who wrote heroic couplets. There's an eighteenth-century novel called *Humphrey Clinker*: possibly Mankiewicz had got his Humphreys confused.

Perhaps the most irritating thing about Bogart's hagiographers is their failure to agree on basic items of information, beginning with the date of his birth. Ezra (*Bogey: The Good-Bad Guy*) Goodman says it was Christmas Day, 1899. Clifford (*Bogey: The Films of Humphrey Bogart*) McCarty loftily dismisses this as a studio myth, and plumps instead for 23 January, 1899; while in *Bogey: The Man, the Actor, The Legend*, Jonah Ruddy and Jonathan Hill put their money on 25 December, 1900. Similarly, no one seems quite sure how Bogart acquired the scar on his upper lip. One account explains that during his naval service in World War One he was bashed in the face by the handcuffs of a bad-tempered prisoner he was escorting. Another, rather more heroically, insists that the injury came from a splinter of wood, dislodged by an exploding shell.

Writing about his apprenticeship on Broadway in the twenties, Ruddy and Hill claim that he was 'the originator of that famous theatrical line—"Tennis, anyone?"' In the Goodman version, Bogart denies that he ever uttered it. From Alistair Cooke in *The Atlantic Monthly*, we learn that he popularised the phrase: 'Drop the gun, Louie.' Goodman's Bogart is quite categorical: 'I never said "Drop the gun, Louie."' Of all the biographers, Ezra Goodman the Man comes across least adorably in print. He got much of his background material while interviewing Bogart in what is shallowly known as depth for a *Time* magazine cover story in the 1950s. His approach to his subject, alternately sneering and cringing, recalls a famous remark of Max Beerbohm's. A tailor had written to the great essayist, demanding immediate payment in tones that reeked of servility. 'My dear sir,' Beerbohm replied, 'kindly cease from crawling on your knees and shaking your fist.'

Most of the Bogart buffs are content to contradict one another: Goodman breaks new ground by contradicting himself. On page 61 he quotes Bogart as follows:

> 'In John Huston's house, years ago, a group of us played touch football in the living room with a grapefruit. It was high spirits. There were Collier Young, Charley Grayson, John Huston and myself. After the first scrimmage in the second game, I got on the side of the big guy whom I had been opposed to. He played real football. It was exercise, shall we say.'

On page 170, the same incident reappears in a less innocent light, shall we say. It is now an outdoor event, with a cast augmented by the director Richard Brooks. This is Brooks's story:

'There was a fine actress...whose husband nobody could stand. John Huston said: "Let's jump him". Instead, we decided to get a football game rolling.... We got a grapefruit off a tree. Bogey goes on the husband's side with Collier Young (a producer). John and I are on the other side. It's two against three. Together John and I tackled the husband with the grapefruit. Bogey switches sides to join us. Now it's the three of us against Collier Young and the husband. Then Collier Young switches sides and the four of us hit him. We were all wearing tuxedos and we were playing in the mud.'

John Crosby, formerly of the *New York Herald Tribune* and now with the London *Observer*, is one of the few journalists who knew Bogart well. He was and remains an unswerving admirer of Bogart the Man. 'Off screen,' he told me, 'Bogart didn't diminish, which is more than you can say of most movie stars. He was a drinker, but never a wencher. And although he loathed gossip columnists, he liked real newspapermen. Some of us used to meet at a place called Bleeck's on West 40th Street. The sign outside read: BLEECK'S WRITERS AND ARTISTS TAVERN AND FORMERLY CLUB. We called ourselves the Formerly Club, and Bogart was an honorary member whenever he was in New York. If he was buying me a drink, he wouldn't just pass it across—he'd take me by the wrist and screw the glass into my hand as if it was a lamp socket. He'd seen Osgood Perkins—Tony's father—do that in some Broadway comedy in the twenties. Another thing about Bogey: he never went around with hoods and bums. That's pure legend. He was an upper-class boy, and if Jock Whitney or Vincent Astor were giving a party, he'd be there.'

On one point all the biographies agree: that Bogart's physical courage, in the long months of wasting and waiting before cancer finally took his life in January 1957, was tremendous and exemplary. But there are more kinds of courage than one, and it could be argued that Bogart, ten years earlier, had laid himself open to the charge of moral cowardice. In a chartered plane full of movie notables, he flew to Washington to protest against the House Un-American Activities Committee, which had sub-poenaed many Hollywood writers, actors and directors to testify to their political affiliations. In the early hearings, several of the witnesses took the Fifth Amendment when asked whether they were (or had ever been) members of the Communist Party. Ten of them—the so-called Holly-wood Ten—were subsequently held in contempt of Congress and imprisoned. Bogart promptly issued a statement in which he said that his trip to Washington had been 'ill-advised, foolish and impetuous'. No doubt he was upset to find that some of his fellow travellers were in fact fellow travellers, or at any rate holders of views pinker than his own. Whether he should have withdrawn his support quite so publicly and abjectly is another matter. 'Never rat on a rat' was the slogan of the Holmby Hills Rat Pack. For once in his life, Bogart exposed himself to the taunt of being a fink.

If I seem to knock the cult of Bogart the Man, it is because I invented the cult of Bogart the Actor. Not the glib Broadway juvenile who went to Hollywood in 1930 and made nine pictures impressing no one, but the sardonic, close-cropped bandit who flew back to the Coast in 1936 to play Duke Mantee in *The Petrified Forest*. Aged ten, I saw the film when it opened in Britain, and immediately wrote a letter to a movie magazine, begging Warner's to give us more of this untamed man with the warning eyes and the rasping voice. It was my debut in print. Between 1936 and 1941 Warner's heeded my plea in spades; Bogart made twenty-eight films, of which I missed very few.

Already the critics were getting him wrong, as they have ever since. They all said he lisped, whereas I, who could mimic him perfectly, knew that he did nothing of the sort. What he did was to fork his tongue and hiss like a snake. This was new, and so was the sheer bravura of his decision to use his own name. Like all good fans, my schoolmates and I had long been aware that Robert Taylor was Spangler Arlington Brugh, and we wouldn't have been surprised to learn that John Wayne was the pseudonym of Adrian Mumchance III. But Bogart had actually been christened Humphrey DeForest Bogart: which impressed us, because—in Britain, at least—Humphrey was a name with strong associations of pompousness and/or faggotry. We respected Bogart for having the guts to live with it. To us, a heavy named Humphrey was about as bizarre as a flautist named Bugsy.

At that time, the king thug on the Warner lot was Edward G. Robinson, wearing vast lapels like the swept-back wings of a jet. Bogart, lean and hungry, was Cassius to his Caesar. We rooted for Bogart because, although he got second billing, he never said 'Yes, boss' as if he meant it. He was nobody's man but his own. And this extended to his relationship with the audience. You had to take him on his own terms. He never stooped to ingratiation, and though his bullying was silken, it was also icy. In latterday terminology, he was 'inner-directed', steering by a private compass that paid no attention to storm signals from outside. Moreover, if the needle led him (as it usually did) into a hail of bullets, he would die with a shrug: no complaints, no apologies, no hard feelings. Indeed, he rarely displayed strong feelings of any kind. And this, in an age when stars were supposed to emote and be vibrant, was something else we admired. It reflected, in part, the emotional tact of a man who seemed genuinely repelled by sentimentality; and, in part, the professional assurance of an actor who knew damned well that he could get along without it. Either way, it was revolutionary, and we relished it.

The year 1937 was full of vintage Bogart: Turkey Morgan in *Kid Galahad* and—supreme misnomer—Baby Face Martin in William Wyler's *Dead End*, the first of the mother-fixated gangsters, who announced his presence (if memory serves) by flipping a knife into the tree trunk around which Leo Gorcey and his chums were huddled. That was the year we all started wincing, as Bogart did when engaged in any mild form of physical exertion, like loading a gun. To wince correctly, you had to imagine that your upper lip was split, and then try to smile. (We used to wince while filling our fountain pens.) I've sometimes wondered how much of Bogart's appeal in England was due to the fact that he was the first movie hero who literally had a stiff upper lip.

Less propitiously, 1937 was the year of *Marked Woman*, starring Bette Davis, in which Bogart appeared as David Graham, the crusading district attorney. The opinion in my set was unanimous. The film proved not only that Bogart was a rotten D.A. (he gave an equally flat rendering of a similar role in *The Enforcer*, fourteen years later), but that he could never, in any circumstances, play a character named David Graham. Another blotch on *Marked Woman* was that it gave us our first glimpse of Mayo Methot, soon to become Bogart's third wife. (She was the brawling one, subsequently renowned as a zealous fan of General MacArthur and a dead shot with a highball glass across a crowded room.) We disliked her on sight and sent her anonymous letters, pointing out that she was something of a pig and that Bogart deserved better. We all knew—or hindsight tells me we did—that the better girl would be a lean, nonchalant baritone, like himself. But she didn't turn up until 1945, when he made *To Have and Have Not* and whistled for her.

The great Bogart-Cagney confrontation was held in 1938–39. It spanned three movies. I missed the second, a Western called *The Oklahoma Kid*, but the key encounters—the eyeball-to-eyeball stuff—took place in the other two: Michael Curtiz's *Angels with Dirty Faces* and Raoul Walsh's *The Roaring Twenties*. James Cagney was the spruce, ebullient urchin who killed with Irish charm and died in dogged, tenacious spasms of life-loving energy. Ever since *Public Enemy*, in 1931, he had been Hollywood's most dynamic and disarming hood. Murder, as he committed it, seemed like a high-spirited exercise, performed out of pure exuberance. He made vice look spunky and debonair, even funny. No one who saw him in the late 1930s will ever forget the grace of his spring-heeled walk and the rich, elated derision of his voice. Bogart was five years older than Cagney when Warner's sent him into the ring with their most triumphant romantic outlaw. It's easy, when surveying Bogart's career, to overlook the basic fact of his age. He didn't become a star until his late thirties, by which time most aspirants have given up and settled for character parts.

Bogart countered Cagney's agile footwork with unruffled expertise. He was like a laconic Hemingway hero up against Studs Lonigan. Often he out-stared Cagney, so shrewdly and mockingly that he looked like a walking ad for that essential Hemingway prop, that built-in shit detector. The contrast of styles was beautiful to watch. It was Bogart the wily debunker versus Cagney the exultant cavalier. With every punch Cagney threw, Bogart lazily rode. Long afterward I wrote: 'Each had perfected his own version of the fanged killer's smile, and a good deal of *The Roaring Twenties* developed into a sort of grinning contest.' The verdict, on points, went to Bogart's sewage snarl.

Thus far, Bogart's main achievement was to have played George Raft parts better than George Raft had ever played them, and better than Alan Ladd was ever going to play them. There was a significant change in 1941, a subtle modulation that led his career out of what might have been a blind alley. Between 1929 and 1932, in a sudden and strenuous burst of creativity, Dashiell Hammett had written five novels. He never wrote another, nor did he need to: the existing quintet was enough to ensure him a modest but durable niche in American literature. One of them, *The Thin Man*, had been filmed, and so sweetened in the filming that it spawned a series, starring William Powell, Myrna Loy and a lovable dog.

Another, *The Maltese Falcon*, had been waiting on the shelf for the advent of someone like Bogart, who could show the world what Hammett was really about. The Hammett private eye was the first anti-hero. No Batman he: operating in a corrupt society, he was not above using corrupt means. He was a cynic to whom nothing human, however squalid, was alien; a man soured but still amused by the intricate depravity of his fellow creatures; and he could, on occasion, be extremely brutal. In short, he was virtually indistinguishable from the Bogart gangster in every respect but one: he was on the side of the law. From now on Bogart could be ruthless—he could even kill—with no loss of glamour and every appearance of moral rectitude. He could engage in mayhem and emerge untarnished. Still as fascinating as ever, he was no longer reprehensible. This farewell to overt criminality was what enabled Bogart to become a world star and a household god.

Bogart's Sam Spade in *The Maltese Falcon* set the pattern for his maturity, and for my adolescence. With the same director (John Huston) and the same supporting team (including Mary Astor and Sydney Greenstreet), he played a similar role in *Across the Pacific*, this time working for the Government as an undercover agent. Later, in 1946, we saw him as Philip Marlowe, Raymond Chandler's savagely disenchanted outlaw-within-the-law, in *The Big Sleep*. But it was Hammett who fixed and defined the Bogart figure: it all began with Sam.

He looked battered before anything had happened, as if survival at an honourable wage was all he hoped for. There was a dimple on each cheekbone, but you would be unwise to call him cute. He wore his hangover like a long-service medal, and his voice, metallic and nasal, was that of a martyr to drinker's catarrh. You could imagine him demanding a pre-breakfast vodka to cut the phlegm. He was always unsurprised. Wherever he went, you felt that he had been there before and learned nothing he did not already know. Greeting an attractive female customer, he would eye her frankly from shoes to chignon, like the lawyer in Thurber's cartoon who murmurs: 'You're not my client, you're my meat, Mrs Fisk.' And if he took her to bed, that would be that. You could count on the Bogart figure never to utter either of the lines on which romantic melodrama depends: 'I love you' and 'I hate you.' He resisted commitment of this or any other kind. One of his most characteristic moments occurred in *Passage to Marseille* (1944). Playing a Free French journalist, he is asked to declare his nationality. 'Eskimo,' he replies, not batting an eyelid.

The wartime Bogart was mostly a soldier of fortune, typified by Rick in *Casablanca* (1943), the erstwhile idealist who fought against Franco in the Spanish Civil War but now refuses to stick his neck out. Since civilisation is crumbling, he finally abandons his detachment and takes sides. After Bogart's death, Alistair Cooke said that he was 'the romantic democratic answer to Hitler's New Order. . . . He is the first romantic hero who used the gangster's means to achieve our ends.' According to this thesis, we trusted Bogart because he looked deadly enough to face the Nazis and come out on top. But I wonder. Bogart's great money-making years were the late forties and early fifties, and it wasn't until 1954 that Nunnally Johnson singled him out as the only star whose name could go unaided over the title of a movie.

I suspect that the Bogart cult in its present form—classless and international—dates from the Cold War. We trusted him because he was a wary loner who belonged to nobody, had personal honour (that virtue which, as Shaw once said, is nowhere mentioned in the Bible), and would therefore survive. Compared with many of his Hollywood colleagues, he seemed an island of integrity, not perhaps very lovable but at least unbought. His film *persona* was that of a man for whom patriotism was something, but not nearly enough. He was a neutralist at large in Beverly Hills.

In these later years his face, with its slanting planes and wry indentations, had become as complex as a Cubist portrait. As he approached the last of his seventy-five feature films, the highbrows adopted him, most possessively in France. (Jean-Luc Godard's *Breathless*, made in 1960, is a tribute to the Bogart way of life.) I admired him in *The Treasure of the Sierra Madre* and *The African Queen*, but the former was Walter Huston's picture and the latter Katharine Hepburn's; and anyway, I always preferred Bogart indoors. His habitat was the city, not the plain. I don't think we can say he was a great actor, but he remained, to the end, a great *behaver*. Without effort, and with classic economy, he could transfer the essence of himself to a camera and be sure that it would be eloquent on a screen.

And what was that essence? I trace it back to Seneca, of whom Bogart might very well never have heard. He flourished in the first century A.D. and wrote violent tragedies that had an enormous influence on Shakespeare and many other Elizabethan dramatists. (T. S. Eliot composed a celebrated essay about his effect on English literature.) What he preached and put into his plays was the philosophy known as Stoicism. It meant: accept the fact of transience, don't panic in the face of mortality, learn to live with death.

This sums up the Bogart stance. Soon after he died, I reread the letters that Seneca wrote to his friend Lucilius. Certain passages in them seemed to echo and epitomise what I had thought about Bogart during his lifetime. The poet-philosopher might have been writing additional dialogue for the actor's *persona*. 'What is freedom, say you? To be the slave of nothing, of no necessity, of no accident, and to make fortune face you on the level.' Therefore, live close to trouble and care nothing. Live outrageously, if you can carry it off. I remember Richard Burton's story of how he and Bogart were among the guests at a top-level Bel Air party in honour of a visiting foreign diplomat. Bogart, who had been warned in advance to watch his language, sat black-tied and tongue-tied until dinner was over, when he turned to the visitor and said: 'You speak very good English.' 'Thank you,' said the diplomat, 'I had an English governess.' Bogart nodded. Then, with no change of expression: 'Did you fuck her?' he asked civilly, in tones of polite interest.

'Life's like a play,' Seneca tells his friend, 'it's not the length but the excellence of the acting that counts. Where you stop isn't important.... To die soon or die late matters nothing: to die badly or die well is the important point.' Bogart was always dying. It was the thing he knew most about. 'In my first thirty-four pictures,' runs a famous quote, 'I was shot in twelve, and electrocuted or hanged in eight....' 'If a man dies as unconcernedly as he is born,' Seneca continues, 'he has learned wisdom.' People came to see Bogart die, because he did it with such model nonchalance. Raoul Walsh (who directed Bogart in *High Sierra*) knew what was happening when he said: 'You can't kill Jimmy Stewart, Gary Cooper or Gregory Peck in a picture. But you can kill off Bogart. The audience doesn't resent it.'

Back to Seneca: 'This is the moment on which you've been cast. You may perhaps prolong it, but how far? ... Death's one of the obligations of life.' Yet how stunned we were when Bogart finally fulfilled it. We had watched him die so often, had seen him so regularly sacrificed on the altar of the motion-picture code, that we had come to think of him as indestructible. There would always, surely, be another Bogart movie, in which he would be killed again.

'We're wrong in looking *forward* to death,' says Seneca, 'in great measure, it's past already. Death is master of all the years that are behind us.' And Bogart's voice told us as much. Even in the most flippant context, it carried with it a bass note of mortality. The voice was his key attribute, the feature by which we recognised him; and it was cruelly appropriate that when cancer singled him out, it went for his throat.

'Everything's in other hands, Lucilius; time alone is ours.' That would have made a nice encore for Sam. Let it stand as an epitaph for Bogart.

IV: PLACES

Barcelona

It takes all kinds of cities to make Barcelona. It takes, among others, a Roman city, a Gothic city, a maritime city and a city of cosmopolitan pleasure. And the odd thing is that none of them, at first sight, looks particularly Spanish. You do not go to Barcelona for the Spain of the travel brochures, all fans and flamenco: these attributes are an Andalusian monopoly, with head offices in Seville. Nor will you find in Barcelona that other traditional face of Spain, sombre, ascetic and God-bitten: for this you must go to Old Castile, where physical saintliness is as common as undernourishment, of which it is a by-product. The face of Barcelona is a Catalan face, busy and clever, button-holing you with news and noise and argument. It emphatically belongs to an individual. The industrial revolution brought foundries and factories to the city; it did not bring uniformity or anonymity. The Catalans, entrenched in their north-eastern corner of the Spanish peninsula, take an almost tribal pride in being not only as unlike the rest of Spain but as unlike one another as possible.

One of their chief boasts is their intellectual curiosity; there are more bookshops in Barcelona than anywhere else in the country. Moreover, they sometimes act on what they read, as when, in the early days of the civil war, they tried to put into effect, simultaneously and overnight, the teachings of Marx, Engels, Lenin and Bakunin. Everyone who can read does. Once I followed an elderly deliveryman for more than a mile through the intricately enmeshed alleys of Barcelona's Gothic quarter. I was fascinated by his concentration. Not once, despite the rattlesnake snarls of the Lambrettas and the bleating of taxis skidding round blind corners, did he look where he was going; not once did he lift his eyes from the book he was reading. It was called, as I discovered when he stepped backwards on to my feet to avoid being run down by a tram, *The Enigmatic Life of Talleyrand.*

Everywhere in this restless city you can see the past, but what you hear is the present. The clamour of its streets is the sound of people tearing up yesterday—as they literally did in 1936, when the anarchists, always strong in Catalonia, gutted the churches and festooned the town with the red-and-black banners of their movement. Nothing so extreme has happened since, but there is always the chance, in Barcelona, that people may indulge in such un-Spanish activities as coming out on strike, and it is not without significance that General Franco visits the place as seldom, and as briefly, as he decently can.

But the energy of Barcelona is not only, or even mainly, political. What excites me about it is the way in which all its aspects—politics, art, history, commerce, even tourism—seem intermixed and interrelated, all of a tumultuous piece. Barcelona is several cities and an accretion of civilisations, but they all belong together, living in a state of turbulent coexistence. Overlooking the town, and the Mediterranean beyond it, from the west is a hill that may stand as its symbol. Its name is Tibidabo, the Latin for 'I will give to thee', since it was from here, according to a persistent legend, that Satan offered Christ the world. You climb it in a rusty funicular and find, when you reach the top, two things: a deafening amusement park, complete with hair-raising rides out over the abyss, and, bang in the middle of the funfair, a basilica of the Sacred Heart. In Catalonia this is not a paradox.

From Tibidabo all the Barcelonas are visible, spread out in a great teeming bowl, bounded on the south by the hill unpronounceably named Montjuich, and on the north by a muddle of ragged suburbs through which the big cars stream on their way to the Costa Brava, to Tossa, Tamariu and Palamós, and so to the heart of the Salvador Dali country, which is still Catalonia. We are in a region that breeds nonconformist art and artists. Apart from Dali, who once told me that his paintings were in 'the great individualist-anarchist-monarchist tradition of *Espagne*', there are Casals, the master cellist, who refused to play in Franco's Spain, and the fantastic architect Antonio Gaudi. We might also, in this context, remember the long annals of Catalan poetry. Catalan, a rough, abrupt tongue, is a language, not a dialect, and it has defied all the efforts of centralised government to discourage it. It still flourishes, as you may hear every spring, when the annual competition of Catalan poets is held in Barcelona. There are three prizes. The third is a silver rose, the second a golden rose, and the first, by a tradition that is itself poetic, a real rose.

The earliest Barcelona huddles close to the sea, taking its name from the Carthaginian general Hamilcar Barca, for whom it was a military and trading post. The Romans, who followed, behaved according to pattern, circumscribing the city with walls and its inhabitants with laws. Successive occupations by the Visigoths and Moors left behind them little of either beauty or utility, and it was not until the thirteenth century that Barcelona began to build durably. A new wall went up to define the limits of the expanding city, and it is in this area that the vast Gothic monuments stand. Among them the cathedral is dominant, though only in bulk: through a façade of bristling pomp, the work of nineteenth-century restorers, you penetrate into what must surely be the blackest hole in Christendom. Such is the gloom that you can scarcely avoid tripping over the faithful at prayer; deep in their alcoves the saints and virgins dream, smile and bless, dimly gleaming in silver and gold, safe at last from the Reds. It is an oppressive place, and I much prefer the cluster of buildings, royal and holy, that surround it—the arch-deacon's house and cloistered courtyard, the arched hall of the Tinell, where Ferdinand and Isabella welcomed Columbus home from the west, and every vista offered by the Calle de la Piedad, which winds and wanders round the cathedral's massive rump.

Traffic hereabouts is forbidden, which means that it is the only part of the city where one feels entirely safe. Elsewhere in the Gothic quarter the cars are in charge, cleaving through the crowds as arrogantly as ambulances. The streets intersect like straws in a haystack, and the only place I know where it is easier to get lost is the *souk* at Tetuán in Morocco. But the comforts are many; every ten paces brings you to a long, low bar, lined with saucers of sea food to be eaten on toothpicks; and you may, as long as you are not aiming for it, stumble upon the Plaza del Borne. This was the medieval jousting square, at one end of which, like a petrified galleon, stands Santa Maria del Mar, the sailors' church and a formidable tribute to the power of Catalan Gothic. There are exquisite mansions nearby, concealed behind archways on the Calle Moncada, which runs (or rather trickles) into the square; but the rule in this neighbourhood is poverty. Not of the grinding sort: that is left to the south of Spain, by comparison with which Barcelona is a haven of plenty. Thousands of Andalusians move north every year, happy to do the underpaid manual work that most Catalans think beneath them. Although there are few beggars in Barcelona, and few visible cripples, the city is quite poor enough, as you can check by peering along the Calle de las Moscas, Fly Street, which is the narrowest in Spain and arguably the most malodorous. The houses, by leaning together and almost kissing at the sixth floor, form an effective heat trap, and this works on the garbage heaps outside the doors to attract the swarms of insects that give the street its squalor and its name.

Beyond the old city, stabbing out into the ocean, is a second, grimier Barcelona: the port. The Catalans have been building ships since the fourteenth century, among them the fleet that carried Columbus on his second American expedition; there are still people in the province who believe that Columbus himself was a Catalan and point to his statue, high on its pillar overlooking the harbour, with profound fraternal pride. In dusty liveliness, the port of Barcelona resembles Marseilles. Beside the cranes and the itinerant ships there is a shabby, flyblown beach with an adjoining row of exceptional fish restaurants. The best of them is Joanet, where lovers of garlic should insist on clams à la Catalana and/or sea bass served with *aioli*. Tennessee Williams, a summer nomad who adores Barcelona for the privacy it affords him, often basks on this dingy *plage*. It was here that he conceived his play *Suddenly Last Summer*, a grim fable about a poet named Sebastian who is brutally martyred by starving urchins while eating at a fish restaurant alongside a Spanish beach. The name of the beach at Barcelona is San Sebastian.

The third Barcelona is the wildest: a nocturnal city where pleasure can border on riot, and crowds turn into mobs. This is the precinct between (and comprising) two of the loudest streets in the world—the so-called Parallelo, officially the Avenida Marqués del Duero, and the incomparable Ramblas, hymned by Maurice Chevalier in his jauntiest song, À *Barcelone*. This uproarious district clings to the south of the old city like a well-fed leech, of which the Ramblas represent the sucking side. A river, long dried-up, once flowed here, and the Ramblas, whose name derives from the Arabic word for a sandy river bed, follow its course. They are plural because every block of this broad, snaking boulevard has its own separate title—the Rambla de San José, the Rambla de Estudios, the Rambla de Canaletas and so forth. Samuel Johnson declared that the full tide of human existence was at Charing Cross, but he never went to Barcelona. Human existence has been in flood along the Ramblas for five hundred years, and I mean human, not mechanical, because the Ramblas were made for people, not machines. Of course, there are traffic lanes on either side of the street, but the point of it is the wide, tree-girt pedestrian highway down the middle. The hubbub here begins soon after dawn and ends just before dawn, reaching a crescendo around midnight, with knots of impassioned men conducting those competitive monologues that pass in Catalonia for conversation, snatching at each other's arms and jabbing themselves in the breast as they explain why last Sunday's bullfight or last month's lottery was for them a bitter personal defeat. Meanwhile the girls parade, often with other girls, more often with their parents, and never alone if unmarried.

The preferred pattern in clothing is broad candy stripes, and you need not look long to discount the rumour, spread by envious Andalusians, that Catalan women would be pretty if only their bottoms were not underslung.

In the sidewalk cafés enormous wedges of pastry and cream cake are being wolfed, probably washed down with a *granizada*, which is one of Spain's shrewdest answers to heat and aridity. It consists of fruit juice (or black coffee) frozen hard and then smashed into splinters of ice, thus making a semisolid drink cold enough, on a boiling day, to startle anyone's heart. Remarkably enough, the intake of alcohol is low; the Barcelonans are huge eaters but frugal drinkers. Milk is one of their favourite tipples, which accounts for the large number of *lecherias* or dairies. (This word, by the way, is one of the three tests of sophistication formulated by Cyril Connolly for Anglo-Saxon tourists in Spain. You fail if, while passing a *lecheria*, you make a joke about the seven deadly sins. You also flunk if you smile when a Spaniard says he is *constipado*, which simply means that he has a cold, or if you make innuendos about the Hotel Sexy in Almuñecar, which gets its name from a Phoenician word with no carnal implications.)

The great market of San José, half-way down the Ramblas on the right, garishly testifies to the extent of the Catalan appetite; here are skinned kids and sucking pigs, together with the dangling feet and lolling, bloody heads of every animal the region supports. Most of these delicacies can be consumed in the market itself, at a pretty little restaurant called Martí, but preferably not in the heat of noon.

Spanish notes of small denomination, sticky with damp and dirt, are perhaps the most repulsive currency on earth, and the Ramblas are a good place to get rid of them. For a few pesetas you can hire the services of one of the *memorialistas* who sit in their ramshackle sentry boxes behind the market, typing business letters for businessmen without typewriters, and composing letters of all kinds for those, still numerous in Spain, who cannot write at all. The shops on the Ramblas specialise, inevitably, in conventional souvenirs, but there are local oddities, too, including cage birds that sing duets, and monstrous candles of eccentric design, some shaped like Nubian slaves, others like Chinese mandarins, so that you can, if you wish, read by the light of the Queen of Sheba or watch Kubla Khan dwindle to a pool of wax. Art is available at the Liceo, which is one of the most ornate opera houses in Europe, while farther down the street, in the bars near the docks, there is vice, wanly personified by the troupes of elderly girls who were rendered homeless a few years ago, when the government, responding (it is said) to urgent entreaties from harassed commanders of the United States Mediterranean Fleet, ordered the bordellos closed.

But the Ramblas are much more than just a raffish mart and meeting place. They are the pulse of Barcelona, the barometer of the city's mood and temper. When barricades go up, this is where they go up first. George Orwell has described, in *Homage to Catalonia*, the feeling of millennial exuberance that was abroad in the Ramblas at the end of 1936, when Franco's revolt had temporarily united the whole spectrum of leftish parties from Communists to Anarchists. Such was the egalitarianism that everyone, from generals to shoeblacks, called everyone else *tu* instead of the formal *Usted*. It did not, of course, last. The Loyalist government, stiffened increasingly by doctrinaire Communists as the months passed, turned on the Anarchists and their allies in the spring of 1937, and it was at the northern end of the Ramblas that the fighting broke out. Bullets zipped across the great street for days, with the government holding the left side and the Trotskyites the right.

In the quieter cafés you can still meet survivors of that struggle and its aftermath. I chatted with one of them not long ago, a jovial middle-aged businessman who has long since given up politics in favour of a safe family life. Imprisoned in a concentration camp after the civil war, he emerged in good spirits but with a nervous tic that has never left him, a gentle, rhythmical, perpetual shaking of the head, as if he were in a state of quiet, constant disagreement with everything around him. Nowadays, he said, Catalonia was politically apathetic. Most of the intellectuals were exiled after the war and never returned: he came back primarily for his family's sake, but also because he is a proud Catalan who could be happy nowhere else.

He was pleased when I remarked that in Barcelona one saw far fewer men in official uniforms than elsewhere in Spain. 'That will always be so,' he said. 'We have never liked uniforms here.' Outside business and domesticity, I asked, how did he occupy his time? 'I read the papers, like a good citizen,' he said with mock seriousness. 'Every one of them, every day. Just for the crossword puzzles, of course. Everything else in them is the same.' When I asked what he thought of the present government, he smiled broadly. 'We have a true two-party system,' he said. 'One party wants one king, one wants another. That's democracy, isn't it?' He spoke ironically but without bitterness. There are many Catalans like him, who retain an extraordinary buoyancy despite the fact that their lives, if aspiration is life, really ended twenty years ago.

Today, or rather tonight, the biggest single attraction of the Ramblas area is its night life. The great Catalan folk dance is the *sardana*, a complex jig that needs space and numbers and can scarcely be danced indoors, but there is plenty of flamenco for those who want it. My own preference is for the innumerable little *salas de fiestas* in the streets that connect the Ramblas with the Parallelo. Here the prices are low, the customers shirt-sleeved, and the floor shows quite unpredictable. The oddest of the lot is the Bodega Bohemia in the Calle Lancaster, which you enter through a grocery store. At one end of the room, which is suffocatingly smoky, there is a rostrum occupied by a frontless piano, a surly accompanist and a bust of Cervantes. The entertainment, which never varies except when amateurs in the house get up to sing Granada, begins with an elderly gentleman in a frock coat who climbs onto the stage carrying a cardboard box from which he produces two osprey-feather fans. Using these props, and a reedy falsetto, he impersonates Mistinguett for roughly twenty minutes. He is followed by the star attractions, two violently contrasting middle-aged women who dislike each other intensely. One is stocky, flame-haired and facially reminiscent of Charles Laughton as Nero; she sings arias, mostly from Puccini, in a strange cheeping voice that is always a half tone flat. Her rival, lean and deadpan, wears her hair bobbed, but in all other respects is a dead ringer for Virginia Woolf in her later years. Never cracking a smile, she sings tremendously hearty songs about climbing mountains and rowing, which she illustrates with convulsive manual gestures. These performers should be seen as quickly as possible, for they have begun to realise that they are funny, and their art may not long survive this loss of innocence.

The Barrio Chino, as the district is called (for inscrutable reasons, since no Chinese live there), has darkened a little with the passing of the bordellos, but the cabarets remain, and the dark little bars, hung with bulls' heads and sausages and loud with the clatter of dominoes. The southern boundary of the quarter is the Parallelo itself, an ill-lit avenue of inexpensive pleasure that must be rather like the Pigalle of forty years ago. Some of the cheaper saloons have almost a frontier feeling about them, with gaslights, sawdust on the floor and hippy girls high-kicking on a rickety stage. Of the music halls proper, the best is the Molino Rojo (Moulin Rouge), a beautiful old horseshoe auditorium with two balconies, discreet private boxes and drinks served in every seat. Acts are announced on a blackboard whisked on and off at illegible speed from the wings. The standard of the vaudeville is middling to poor, but the spirit of the place is pure theatre. The actors address the audience not just as customers but almost as kinsmen (which in many cases they are), and quite often the audience replies.

A few yards from the Molino, in an amusement arcade, there is a curious signboard. It invites you to ride on an indoor roller coaster, and lists the delights of the trip. You will see: 'The Great Carnivorous Dragon, the Gates of Hell, the Throne of Lucifer, the Cauldron of the Damned, the Gnomes of the Enchanted Wood, the Toilette of the Nymphs, the Temple of Venus and Minerva, Journey to Heaven, Snow White, Airplane Trip.' To get the most out of the jaunt, you would have to be part Christian and part pagan. In fact, you would have to live in the Barrio Chino.

This is the last of the old Barcelonas. The new city, which surrounds them like a wrench gripping a nut, is about six times as large and at first glance immeasurably duller—a palatial, faceless city planned in the nineteenth century and ruled out in blocks as regular as the squares on graph paper. The Plaza de Cataluña, dominated by the neon signs of six banks, is its focal point and symbol. Its opulent stores and arrow-straight avenues sometimes suggest Paris, but a Paris in which the theatres, to take one example, have gone weirdly to pot. The posters outside the Teatro Calderón read like the playbills of a century ago, giving not only the names of the performers but their categories, such as *primerisima vedett, primer actor, otro primer actor, actriz de caracter, galán cantante* (which must mean 'singing gallant'), *actor genérico* (which hardly means anything) and so on down to plain *actor*. The longest and most imposing street, as in most Spanish cities, is known on the map as the Avenida Generalisimo Franco, but since it slashes athwart the prim cubes of the rest of the district, the Barcelonans call it—for brevity's sake, of course— the Diagonal.

It would be a mistake, however, to write off the new town as just another big city. It has marvels of its own, every bit as striking as any-thing in the older Barcelonas. It also has monstrosities. It boasts a bull ring that is the second largest in Spain, beaten only by Madrid, and the first ugliest, a modern travesty of Moorish architecture topped off with blobs of blue-and-white tile. There have been few good Catalan bull-fighters, and Barcelona cannot be regarded as a really serious bullfighting centre. If the Madrid arena is the Old Vic of tauromachy, Barcelona is the Palladium. To the Catalans death is a misfortune, not a mystery, and though they love the bullfight, they come to it for nervous stimulation rather than catharsis. Above all, they appreciate stunts, which the man-agement provides in the form of sixteen-year-old matadors or *corridas* of twelve bulls held at midnight. They also come to let off steam. The sour, deep, thunderous roar with which Barcelona shows its disapproval of a poor bullfight is among the most ominous noises in Spain.

The marvels of the new city are its buildings. There is certainly little in European architecture more totally expressive of a single eccentric vision than the structures scattered across Barcelona by Antonio Gaudi. He flourished, or proliferated, around the turn of the century, at the height of *art nouveau*. His purpose was the reverse of functional. What he propagated was the idea of architecture as the expression in stone, concrete, steel and glass of all natural forms, animal or vegetable, with all the imbalance and luxuriant asymmetry which that implies. His basic approach to art is best described in a story about his childhood. His teacher told him that birds had wings so that they could fly. But cocks have wings, he objected, and *they* can't fly. His buildings sprout similarly useless appendanges. Gaudi was not so much an architect as a brilliant exterior decorator.

His apartment house, nicknamed The Quarry, on the Paseo de Gracia looks like a many-tiered sand castle over which a wave has just washed. Its balconies droop, so that the windows resemble the entrances to caves, and the chimneys, hooded in cloche hats of concrete, might be cottages intended for Disney dwarfs. The corridors within are not carpeted but cobbled, and the rooms are pentagonal, trapezoidal, trian-gular—everything, in short, but square.

Just off the Ramblas is the house Gaudi designed for his patrons, the Güell family; apart from a certain extravagance in the use of wrought iron, and a couple of archways shaped like parabolas, it is relatively tame stuff, and it was not until he conceived the Parque Güell, which is laid out on the slopes leading up to Tibidabo, that Gaudi did full justice to what must have been an extremely rich and generous family. This is the ideal children's playground, with hanging gardens, fairy caverns, arcades of insanely tilting pillars, terraces of multicoloured tiles and rows of giant stone cannonballs—everything unbreakable and suggestive of things to eat, from lollipops to sherbet. Some of the columns, bulging and bristling, still remind me hauntingly of chocolate bars with nut filling.

The most overwhelming of the 'Gaudinian' monuments is unques-tionably the Church of the Sagrada Familia, which was begun in 1881 and is still unfinished. Work goes on by subscription from tourists. 'We con-tinue,' the guide will tell you, 'very smally.' The north façade, crowned by four spires like zeppelins with air vents, is the only one so far com-pleted. It represents the literary idea of art run utterly berserk; pro-gramme music translated into architecture. Turkeys gobble in stone from the portico, and lizards peer; giant columns rest on the backs of turtles; and the site is littered with a battalion of outsize snails, for which, some day, a niche will presumably be found.

To judge Gaudi's quality you must compare his work with that of his contemporary and admirer, Domenechy Montaner, who designed the Palace of Catalan Music, which looks like a Victorian railway terminus in the throes of epilepsy, with a pink façade bursting out in brick boils and hernias, and, inside, balustrades made of saffron-tinted glass and ceilings of blue-and-beige toffee, with vast plaster flowers extruding from every corner. This deformity houses the Orfeo Catalá, one of the finest choirs in Europe, which should be listened to in dark glasses.

The last of the Barcelonas differs from the others in that it is peaceful. Nobody lives on the hill of Montjuich, which stands by the sea to the south of the main city. Its inland slopes are shelved in long terraces, set about with grandiose pavilions that were erected for an International Exhibition thirty years ago. One of them, the topmost, concerns us especially, for it houses the first of the quiet hill's three wonders. The Museum of Antiquities is not, like most of its kind, just a large, echoing building in which fragments of history are hung, mounted or preserved under glass. Many of the rooms are replicas of Catalan interiors, from pre-Roman times to the end of the eighteenth century. The famous collection of early medieval murals, painfully transplanted from the walls of isolated churches high in the Pyrenees, is housed in a series of chambers that are themselves facsimiles of church interiors. Later on, as in most Spanish museums, one gets a fair number of characteristic canvases by the two great Iberian depressants, Zurbarán and Ribera, but not before one has seen, and been transfixed by, the display of fifteenth-century retables. On these painted panels, the cartoon strips of their day, the saints are to be seen suffering astounding rigours, being burned, impaled and even skinned by leering tormentors. One desperate case, after a thorough going-over with an old rake, is depicted being dropped from a rowboat with a gigantic ball-and-chain round his neck. Saint Agatha, smiling serenely, extends towards the spectator a large plate on which repose her breasts, sliced off by infidels, sunny side up. This exhibition of atrocities is a blood-curdling reminder of the insistent and unhealthy emphasis that Spanish Catholicism lays on the physical details of martyrdom. It brings the past horrendously to life.

The second wonder of Montjuich, farther down the slope, is the Pueblo Español, another legacy from the International Exhibition—an entire village made up of life-sized reproductions of houses, gates, fountains and squares chosen from every province of Spain. Somehow, by a miracle of planning, everything fits; the whole design is homogeneous. I can neither explain nor regret the fact that it is usually deserted. The Pueblo Español is Spain without the Spanish, and that, after the tumult of Barcelona, can be profoundly soothing.

On the seaward side of Montjuich is the place where Barcelona ends. The silence here is as deep as any in Spain; a thronged, populous silence, as of innumerable minds halted in mid-thought, uncounted lips frozen on the brink of speech. This is necropolis, where Barcelona accommodates its dead. The hillside is planted with cypresses and climbed by a gently ascending hairpin road, which runs past what appear to be towering walls of lockers cut into the rock, an endless unfolding checkerboard. Some of the niches are protected by panes of glass, behind which you can make out ribbons, necklaces, toys, and now and then a lock of hair. Every locker contains a coffin, every square of the checkerboard; you are passing through canyons of mortality. Some, the fortunate rich, have been able to afford grander resting places, cavelike shrines guarded by magnificent grilles. Others, a few, are buried in the earth in our fashion, with a stone or a statue at their heads. But the majority lie as I have described them, pushed head first into their permanent pigeonholes.

Since the population of a cemetery never decreases, more room is constantly needed to shelter the newcomers. Accordingly, the city fathers have built, in certain open spaces, miniature apartment blocks twenty feet high—housing developments for the dead. To assist the process of mourning, and the placing of flowers and other tributes, they have also provided huge library steps that run on wheels beside the silent panels. There are always a number of unoccupied lockers, and into one such, many years ago, a madman climbed. That same night, as the watchman went by, the maniac uttered from his hiding place a series of agonised cries, begging to be rescued from the tortures of damnation. Next day the watchman, too, was mad.

The graveyard of Montjuich has a sinister, tranquil beauty unlike any other. It is the last of the faces of Barcelona, and it is necessary to complete the picture. Few cities offer such an intensity of life, or such an intensity of death.

(1959)

The Nonconformists of San Francisco

In this bright, free-wheeling, precipitous city—according to the livelier of its eight hundred thousand inhabitants—a new America is being made, far away from the grim imperatives of the Pentagon and Madison Avenue. Eccentricity is cradled here; more extremes of thought and feeling are cherished than anywhere else in the country. Built on a hilly, northward-jutting spur of land, with a blue bay to the east and

Japan to the west, the place is a haven of tolerance after the prestige-ridden insecurity of Los Angeles. To this fact Mr Khruschev might bear witness: on his 1960 tour of America, he was received in Los Angeles with a cautious tartness bordering on incivility. San Francisco, his next stop, greeted him with a relaxed cordiality that prompted Herb Caen, the czar of local columnists, to observe: 'As of today, San Francisco is the safest city in the United States. L.A. goes first.'

Nobody can fully account for this easy acceptance of the odd and the *outré*, though everyone attests to it. Alan Watts, the leading American expounder of Zen Buddhism, describes the Bay area as America's Mediterranean. 'In the Eastern states,' he says, 'you feel two-dimensional. San Francisco reminds you that you have a third dimension as well. I wouldn't live anywhere else.'

This sudden opening of horizons has been felt by a multitude of artists and thinkers; Mark Twain, Robert Louis Stevenson, Bret Harte, Ambrose Bierce, Sinclair Lewis, Maxwell Anderson and William Saroyan are among those who have worked and flourished on the city's hills. But why there? 'Because there's no heavy industry,' one writer told me. 'You can get away from the gloom of factories.' According to another, 'The first reason is topographical: the beauty of the setting is fantastic. And the second reason is the climate: it's never too hot or too cold. There's no conflict between outdoors and indoors. In New York you're always conscious of the seasons, and changes of clothes, and time passing. Here it's as if time didn't exist.'

The city's hospitality to ideas has deep roots in its history. After the abortive liberal insurrections that broke out all over Europe in 1848, many exiles fled to America, which they often preferred to enter by the back door, travelling around Cape Horn to California. They arrived just in time for the Gold Rush; San Francisco became a semi-Europeanised boom town; and its position as the natural landing place for immigrants from China and Japan helped to enrich the mixture. Nowhere else in America were the cultures of Europe and the Orient so closely juxta-posed.

Great ports traditionally welcome strangers: xenophobia is an inland disease; but the internationalism of San Francisco had a special flavour. Its foreign settlers had crossed one or other of the two broadest oceans in the world to get there, and what they found was not only physical beauty but the promise of material plenty. The result was a city of prosperous strangers. Tolerance of national and racial idiosyncrasies was a necessity of everyday living, and it was only natural that this tolerance should be extended to personal idiosyncrasies as well. Nobody, for example, objected to the whims of Joshua A. Norton, who decided, when his plans for cornering the rice market disintegrated in 1854, to adopt the title of Emperor Norton and print his own currency. 'He is perfectly harmless,' wrote one of his contemporaries, 'and, unless his mind be occupied with some more than ordinarily grave question relating to the Empire, is jocular, and disposed to be humorous.'

Among the more recent of Norton's many successors in eccentricity was Tiny Armstrong, beloved by some and a bore to others, who devoted the later days of his life to ambling around the city clad in fancy dress and blowing on a bird whistle. Armstrong died some years ago, but there is still the Fife Man, a skinny old piper who wears a wreath of flowers to mark the advent of spring.

It is not, however, by oddities of garb but by a strange, speculative cast of mind that one recognises the true San Franciscan nonconformist. Consider Gavin Arthur, pink and middle-aged, a student of Jung and a diligent astrologer. One day, if I remember his story correctly, Mr Arthur learned from his horoscope that a fire was imminent in his life. Being then in Chicago, he sped to his home in San Francisco, only to discover that his apartment in New York had burned down. I have heard him greet a guest at his door with the words: 'I believe your grandfather was my grandfather's Secretary of the Navy,' which is scarcely outlandish, since Mr Arthur's grandfather was Chester Arthur, President of the United States.

At one point, feeling that society had denied him the rewards that his lineage deserved, Mr Arthur rather flamboyantly sold newspapers at a street corner; but that episode is now over, and he has found solace in metaphysics. For a year he lived on seaweed, avoiding all sensual pleasures, and the experience convinced him that life was eternal. Once, at a party, he cornered Robert Oppenheimer and asked him sternly whether he did not think it possible that there were other people in the room, invisible and inaudible to human eyes and ears. Doctor Oppenheimer instantly replied: 'I think it not only possible but very, very probable'; which is a demonstration either of Mr Arthur's insight or of Doctor Oppenheimer's tact.

The Beat phenomenon, large though it bulks in the press, is a comparatively recent emanation of the city's artistic energy. An older tradition—the tradition of what he calls 'beautiful letters'—is represented by the gourmet and essayist Lucius Beebe, who commutes to San Francisco from Nevada, making his headquarters in the bar of the Palace Hotel, which frequently resounds with his robust and splendidly articulated laughter. Beebe runs his own newspaper and his own railroad coach and prides himself on living, as he laughs and eats, in the grand manner. He hates to see modern uncouthness encroaching on ancient institutions. A short while ago he was waiting for a friend in the Palace bar when there tumbled through the door a crowd of rumpled and obviously tipsy strangers. His friend followed them in.

'Who are those bums?' cried Beebe in outrage.

'That,' replied his friend, 'is the Champagne Flight from Los Angeles.'

The city abounds in artists, ex-artists and half-artists of all kinds—the hip and the square, the conservative and the radical, the dug-in and the far-out—and the traffic between categories is thick. Yesterday's hipster is tomorrow's square. I wonder where today's arbiters of San Franciscan taste would place Isadora Duncan, who grew up there; or Gertrude Stein, who spent part of her youth in Oakland, the adjoining borough. Asked for her opinion of Oakland, Miss Stein enigmatically stated: 'There is no there there.' On the strength of that remark I think she would still qualify as being moderately hip.

But what about Kenneth Rexroth, the grizzled and acerbic poet-critic, and the rest of the elder group of avant-garde writers whose leader, Henry Miller, now lives down the coast at Big Sur? Perhaps Rexroth's experience is typical; at first the champion of the Beats, he now disowns them as inartistic loafers, and is disowned by them in return. 'We had our renaissance twenty years ago,' he declares; and who can say he is wrong in a town that is in a perpetual state of renaissance? At the heart of the Beat quarter there lives a trim, sixty-year-old Chinese painter named Wing, who has had five wives and is looking for a sixth. Here, where abstract expressionism reigns, Wing paints portraits of a realism so microscopic that they make *Time* magazine covers look like Rorschach tests; yet before you read this he may have been elected the leader of a new cult. The town is full of swinging pendulums, as well as swinging people; sooner or later everybody gets into the pantheon.

The present Square Belt of resident literary successes includes Erskine Caldwell, C. S. Forester and the venerable Kathleen Norris. Another non-Beat author is Barnaby Conrad, whose chosen themes are bullfighting in general and Manolete in particular. Since the great Cordoban matador was fatally gored in 1947, Conrad has bewailed his death in a popular novel, a documentary treatise, a TV programme and several magazine articles; this energetic obituarist even owns a dinghy named *Islero*, after the bull on whose horn Manolete was impaled. In addition to being a littérateur, Conrad is active as *flâneur* and *restaurateur*; he runs two thriving *boîtes*, El Bordell and El Matador, decorated to suggest, respectively, the Barbary Coast and the Costa Brava. He also paints, produces movies, and calls his pet parrot Truman Capote, whether because of its plumage or its accent I cannot say.

Conrad is not the only unusual saloonkeeper in the city; another is Victor Bergeron, the founder of Trader Vic's and conceivably a reincarnation of Long John Silver, with whom he shares a maritime background, a narrative flair and a wooden leg. Then there is Enrico Banducci, in whose celebrated cellar, the hungry i, Mort Sahl held his first professional seminar some eight years ago, at a salary of seventy-five dollars a week. Sahl's comic *persona*, drawn from his student days, was that of a literate, disturbed eager beaver, genuinely anxious to help and be helped; Banducci embraced it, as he has embraced many other off-beat talents. His electrician, Alvah Bessie, was a well-known screen writer until 1950, when he refused to cooperate with the Un-American Activities Committee and went to jail for his recalcitrance, along with the other nine members of the Hollywood Ten.

In this most open of cities, artists and thinkers can experiment in relative peace. West Coast jazz built its fortress in San Francisco, with Dave Brubeck on piano and Paul Desmond on alto; and so did West Coast philosophy, featuring Alan Watts on Zen and the astonishing listener-financed radio station KPFA on almost every subject from logical positivism to homosexuality. On celluloid, one finds innovators like Jordan Belson, who makes abstract shorts and believes that the object of art, as of science, is to translate the lopsided chaos of nature into harmonious symmetry. His films emphasise circles, sometimes inducing a trancelike state in the spectator, who feels as if he were being bombarded with oranges, pool balls and exploding crystals.

In 1957 Belson teamed up with Henry Jacobs, a composer of electronic music who lived (and lives) across the bay in Mill Valley: together they evolved, and performed at the Planetarium in Golden Gate Park, a hallucinating programme of sights and sounds called *Vortex*, which consisted of dissolving patterns projected onto the dome and accompanied by pings, booms and shrieks from dozens of concealed amplifiers. *Vortex* was a huge success, and its inventors subsequently took it to the Brussels World's Fair. Mr Jacobs is a lean, dark, unfathomable man who records under the *nom de disque* of Shorty Petterstein. He specialises in brilliantly faked interviews with such people as a Jewish anthropologist convinced that the roots of Calypso lie in Hebraic myth, and a smug abstainer who chews tobacco, puffs at two cigarettes simultaneously and holds a martini in each hand, just to demonstrate that where habits are concerned he can take them or leave them alone.

In painting and sculpture (and in that order), the city's senior pioneers are Jean Varda and Beniamino Bufano. Varda, a specialist in collage, is white-haired, sunbeaten and robustly Greek. He lives on a creaking barge in Sausalito, the artists' and tourists' colony just across the Golden Gate Bridge, and his manner suggests a retired pagan deity whose hobby is piracy. His becalmed home is full of mystery and hospitality; a Tibetan ghost trap hangs on one wall, and masques are held in honour of spring. Varda creates an atmosphere in which fertility rites would not be out of place, though he once reproved an acquaintance for displaying excessive pride at having become a father: 'Mice, lice, rats, *woodpeckers* can have children,' he declaimed. 'And if herrings weren't so *stupid*, there'd be no sea—just a stinking mass of herrings.' His taste in friendship is extremely catholic, though it tends to exclude the very rich, whom he finds 'unfrequentable' except when they feel tormented by their wealth. One of his neighbours falls into the latter category: 'The man is agonised by his money,' Varda says, 'and we all try to console him. We tell him that things could be worse, he might have general paralysis or syphilis; but it is no use, he still suffers.'

Varda's dicta can be a touch cryptic at times, as when he observes, for example: 'There are two things one must never talk about—digestion and golf', or 'In England the worst insult is to be called "an undesirable". In France, it is "*espèce de photographe*". In America, it is "bulb-snatcher".' For a man as profoundly Mediterranean as Varda, San Francisco is the ideal American setting. He does not regard himself as a European; for him, Greece belongs to the East, not to Europe, and 'the East begins where vulgarity ends'. Varda discovered the purpose of life many years ago: 'It is vision. It is to see.' For those who have mastered the secrets of vision he has designed a special flag. Its emblem is a large, all-seeing eye, and only ten people alive are entitled to fly it.

'Benny' Bufano, Varda's friend and contemporary, is a small, Chaplinesque Italian who sculpts outsized statues in a studio that is part of a sewage reduction plant. Bufano believes in art that has a social function and a social impact; he therefore makes his figures vast to cheat those who might wish to hide them in storage, away from the general public to whom, in his view, they rightfully belong. The massive simplicity of his style recalls Epstein, Diego Rivera and much Buddhist statuary; as with many other San Franciscans, his is a European temperament on to which Oriental influences have been grafted.

When Bufano was twelve years old his mother, who had fourteen other children on her hands, gave him a thousand dollars and told him to go round the world. He obeyed, travelling via China, India, Africa and

Europe, and he was twenty-four when he returned to America. He brought with him a passionate absorption in Eastern philosophy. For San Francisco's Chinatown he designed a stainless-steel statue of Sun Yat-sen; that was one result of the trip. Another was to make him a confirmed pacifist and hater of violence. He had always venerated St Francis; now he worshipped Gandhi as well.

When America entered the First World War, Bufano chopped off half of his right index finger and mailed it to Woodrow Wilson as a protest; forty-three years later, he threatened to paint 'Thou shalt not kill' in his own blood on the walls of San Quentin if Chessman were executed. His dedication to non-violence once won him a nomination for the Nobel Peace Prize; and he served for five years as San Francisco's Art Commissioner, harassing the authorities to spend more on music, painting, sculpture and the general enhancing of the landscape. Always he embodied the causes for which he fought; this doughty little man had irrevocably cast himself in the role of the downtrodden artist. In 1950 a San Francisco restaurant invited him to design a mural. He accepted the commission, but insisted on being paid in food, to be consumed on the premises. 'That way,' he says, 'they couldn't get rid of me. They might not like the mural, but they couldn't starve me out.'

The city's political mavericks have always been numerous. To hold radical views is honourable here, and to grill those who hold them is bad San Franciscan form. Jessica Mitford, the left-wing outrider of the celebrated Mitford sisters—the others being Nancy, the novelist; Diana, the wife of Sir Oswald Mosley; Unity, the late admirer of Adolf Hitler; and Deborah, the Duchess of Devonshire—has settled down happily in Oakland with her second husband, a well-known labour lawyer. (Her first, killed in the last war, was Winston Churchill's nephew, Esmond Romilly.)

The area abounds in union officials with ideas that tend to bring a blush of apoplexy to Republican cheeks. One of San Francisco's most prominent citizens is a fifty-nine-year-old Australian immigrant whom the American Government has been unsuccessfully trying to deport for nearly a quarter of a century. I refer to Harry Bridges, the wiry, wily leader of the longshoremen's union (I.L.W.U.) since its foundation in 1934. Despite his reputation as a leftist firebrand, Bridges is a quiet man to meet, watchfully reposeful as a lizard on a rock, and his sense of humour is extremely sly. Nothing maddens his enemies more than the fact that he is a registered member of the Republican Party. For a comparatively small organisation (it is seventy thousand strong), the I.L.W.U. has attracted a large amount of national attention, not all of which is attributable to Bridges. One of the union's most notable members is Eric Hoffer, who rises at four-thirty in the morning, writes for three hours, and then works all day as a longshoreman. Hoffer had no schooling and was almost blind until the age of fifteen; surmounting these handicaps, he wrote a book of aphorisms called *The True Believer*, which was ardently praised by judges as disparate as Arthur Schlesinger, Jr, and ex-President Eisenhower. He was even compared to La Rochefoucauld, and the analogy does not seem altogether absurd when one considers a remark like: 'There is no doubt that in exchanging a self-centred for a selfless life we gain enormously in self-esteem.'

Something must now be said about the colony of non-political mavericks known as Beats, who inhabit the North Beach area around Grant Avenue. Too much, perhaps, has already been written about them; that bearded young wreck who sits beside you in the Co-existence Bagel Shop, surreptitiously taking notes, is very likely not a Beat at all, but a graduate student in disguise, collecting material for his thesis. The true Beats are a floating (some would say a sunken) population. Kerouac, Ginsberg and Corso, the founding fathers of the postwar years, have long since flown the coop; whenever they return, it is as emissaries from an alien world of royalties, agents and publishers' contracts. They have moved on, and so have many of their successors. Whatever one thinks of the Beat movement, one cannot deny that it is always in motion. Travel is part of its essence, as readers of Kerouac's *On the Road* will be aware; the Beat underground nowadays has international ramifications, with pulsating cells in Venice, Tokyo, Paris, Mexico City, London, Athens and Tangier, apart from Denver, New York and the parent organisation in San Francisco. In each of these cities, the weary or penniless Beat, of any nationality, knows where to find a welcome and a pad in which to curl up.

Many wild claims have been made for Beat writing: it was said, for instance, that it would free American literature from enslavement to European forms and ideas, giving it a fresh, indigenous voice which would bring to poetry the element of spontaneous improvisation that the Beats admired in jazz music and Zen Buddhism. The results have been patchy and self-indulgent; as Kingsley Amis put it, talking off the top of your head is not quite the same thing as spontaneity.

So much for the Beat way of art; but the Beat way of life, at its best, is not so easy to demolish. It is communal and weirdly selfless; a young minister who gave up the cloth to become a full-time Beat writer told me that he had found in North Beach a more genuine dedication to poverty than he had ever seen outside purely religious groups. The subversive fact about the movement is that it is totally uninterested in money except as a means of providing the necessities of food, shelter and clothing. Worse, it openly derides the notion that getting on in the world is of the slightest importance besides getting on with one's friends, one's girl, one's children. The Beats are great lovers of children, and tend to practise a sort of unmarried monogamy. I once heard a Beat rebuking an outsider who had been delivering a coffeehouse lecture on the sexual needs of the American female. 'Talk to me about one chick, and I'll listen,' he said. 'But don't talk to me about chicks in general. That's indecent.'

The Beats reject status-seeking on a national as well as a personal level; one of their recurrent themes is the obscenity of militarism and the bomb. Their relationship to society is one of passive resistance. To participate, they feel, is to connive; hence they have contracted out. If America had a political party that promised to abolish armaments, advertising, and the values that both imply, they might easily take up politics. As it is, they write, make love, contemplate, take marijuana (not heroin or cocaine), and drink cheap wine (not whisky or gin)—doing no harm, except conceivably to themselves.

Who are they? They are not, as a rule, teenagers; in fact, not many of the leading North Beachers are under thirty. According to a survey compiled last year by Dr F. J. Rigney, a young California psychologist, roughly half of the Beat population come from the middle or upper-middle class, and have deliberately chosen to become *declassé*. (The average Beat income is well below the working-class norm.) Dr Rigney also found that a high proportion of Beats were from the eastern states. Many, to my knowledge, are runaways, either from home or from safe jobs; as Oscar Wilde said, 'Everybody who disappears is seen, sooner or later, in San Francisco.' Ex-Catholics are common in Beatdom, and there are even a few ex-Communists, one of whom baffled a board of official investigators by explaining that he had left the Party because it was not revolutionary enough. It seems that if you react sufficiently strongly against your background, the logical place for you to end up is the peninsular haven of North Beach.

An English author who had studied the scene told me that it reminded him of a distinction once made by Sidney and Beatrice Webb between people who were A's (Artistic, Anarchic, Aristocratic), and those who were B's (Bureaucratic, Benevolent, Bourgeois). The Beats, he said, were definitely A's.

And what is the scene like? It is made up of bars, bookshops, art galleries and Spartan pads, all clinging to the steep length of Grant

Avenue. The Vesuvio, advertising 'Booths for Psychiatrists', was the original Beat bar, but the focus last year had shifted to the Coffee Gallery, with its weekly 'Speak Nite' at which Beats meet to compete for a bottle of champagne, awarded by acclamation to the best speech of the evening. 'New York is my homo,' intoned a falsetto young man the last time I was there, 'and Chicago is my hetero.'

The saloons hereabouts are full of gems for shameless eavesdroppers. At the Bread and Wine Mission, Philip Lamantia recites a poem in praise of 'junkies, tricks, dummy poets, mads, holdup men, squares, priests, monks, professional bums, beat Jews, Jew-haters, spade trumpet players, pot-heads, Zen nuts, antispades, super-gigolos . . . and black supremacy, white supremacy and Red Indian supremacy wild ones.'

At the Bagel Shop, somebody muses: 'Kant is to Hegel as hole is to bagel.' A table away I hear the plaint of an ex-Beat ejected from the flock partly because he allowed narcotics to hook him, and partly because he took a full-time job. 'Anxiety is nine-tenths economic,' he insists. 'I'm off the hard stuff now, I'm only on pills. I even have a schedule. Is it three o'clock yet? Time for my amphetamine.' He whips out an ornate pillbox and swallows a blue tablet. 'I wouldn't say I was *interested* in drugs, it's just that they're my pleasure. For ten years I've let the doctors use me as a guinea pig on pills. Why won't they give me marijuana? It's safer than pills and you don't get cancer. But what can I do about it? All I am is just this marvellous yak artist.' At a bookstore I buy a magazine called *Underhound*, and find in it a Beat glossary by one Art Castillo, from which I append excerpts:

BEAT	SQUARE
benzedrine	pornography
Waiting for Godot	*On The Beach*
The Evergreen Review	*The New Yorker*
Dada	*Mad* comics
the Negro	Charles Atlas
death as a necessary evil	obituary
life as a necessary evil	biology

The scene changes swiftly, but a year ago Bob Kaufman was the representative Beat, living in a small apartment, all murals and mattresses, with his wife and a baby son named Parker—after Charlie Parker, the late jazz musician and martyr. Kaufman (who, unlike his wife, is a Negro) spent many years as a sailor before descending on San Francisco in his mid-thirties. He is perhaps the first Beat aphorist, as witness the following extracts from his *Abomunist Manifesto*:

Abomunism was founded by Barabbas, inspired by his dying words, 'I wanted to be in the middle, but I went too far out. . . .'

Abomunists do not write for money, they write the money itself. . . .

Abomunists love love, hate hate, drink drinks, smoke smokes, live lives, die deaths. . . .

Abomunists demand the re-establishment of the government in its rightful home at Disneyland. . . .

We shall demand the right to participate in the population explosion. . . .

We shall demand that the government stop cluttering up our billboards with highways. . . .

We shall demand that Mississippi be granted statehood in some other country. . . .

We shall demand equal time in all churches to answer God's accusations. . . .

We shall demand that World War Three be televised as a public service. . . .

We shall demand that science stop the world from spinning, as some people want to get off now.

In 1959 Kaufman visited Hollywood, returning with a clutch of images that perfectly express the San Franciscan's distaste for Los Angeles:

Plastic Beatniks, in pubic beards, with artistically dirtied feet. . . .

Hindu holymen, with police records clear back to Alabama. . . .

Mondrian-faced drive-ins, featuring hamburger-broiled charcoal. . . .

Two dozen Homos to every Sapiens. . . .

Down at head pot-smokers with down at heel eyes.

Death-faced agents, living on ten per cent of nothing.

Lady painters with three names, having one-man shows of expensive framing.

Unemployed Broadway actors, with nothing to offer but talent, trying to look stupid. . . .

No-coast jazz musicians, uncommitted, waiting to be committed. . . .

Impatient Cadillacs, trading in their owners for more successful models.

I asked this mutinous jester what his next work would be called. He grinned and said: 'Our Man in Nirvana'.

Kaufman's publisher, and the patriarch of the Beats, is a forty-year-old poet named Lawrence Ferlinghetti, who has divided his life between the Bronx, France and San Francisco, where he established the City Lights Book Shop in 1954. Nowhere in America is a wider selection of experimental literature to be found; and a warning against loose intellectual talk hangs in the basement: 'Be sure brain is engaged before setting jaw in motion.' Since 1956, when he started publishing, Ferlinghetti's lists have included Allen Ginsberg's *Howl* (the Beat anthem and best seller), works by Corso, Rexroth, Robert Duncan and William Carlos Williams, and a pirated edition of Ernest Hemingway's *Collected Poems*.

A soft-spoken humanist, sometimes bearded, often not, Ferlinghetti is more conscious of politics than most of his Beat neighbours. His best-known poem, directed against atomic testing, is entitled: *Tentative Description of a Dinner Given to Promote the Impeachment of President Eisenhower*. Last year, while attending a congress of American writers in Chile, he was taken on a tour of the coal mines at Lota. Their squalor appalled him; and when, on departing, he was asked to give his impressions of the congress and its artistic significance, he answered every question with the same phrase: 'The miners in their cages in the mines at Lota.'

The man who epitomises Beatdom, the first folk-hero of the cult, is not a writer at all. He was born in 1926 in Denver, Colorado; as a child he travelled the length and breadth of America with his father, and as an adolescent he developed into a compulsive car thief, which involved him in a number of losing brushes with the law. Shortly after the war he met Ginsberg and Jack Kerouac, who were impressed by his vagabond way of life; and many of his characteristics appear in Dean Moriarty, the protagonist of Kerouac's *On the Road*. His real name is Neal Cassidy, and I talked to him last spring in San Quentin, where he was serving a term for possession and sale of marijuana.

We faced each other across a broad table, beside a window that overlooked the Bay. He was healthily handsome, with fair, close-cropped hair; 'the Johnny Appleseed of marijuana', somebody once called him. He spoke freely about his life and his many wives, using no hipster idioms and no obscenities, but falling at times into oddly old-fashioned forms of speech, among them a trick of always referring to women by their full names. No swell of emotion disturbed the flow of talk.

In 1955, he said, he had broken his leg while employed as a railroad brakeman, and had received $30,000 compensation. In one day at the races he dropped $10,000 of it, to the outraged horror of his wife. 'She was a light-complected Irish girl, and when I looked at her she had suddenly turned black in the face.' She produced a knife and threatened to kill herself, but Cassidy did not take the threat seriously. 'She was always cutting herself.' Next morning, while he slept, she climbed on to the roof of the house and jumped to her death. He was awakened by her screaming as she fell past the bedroom window.

Another of his wives was indirectly responsible for the loss of his left thumbnail. 'She went whoring down the Tenderloin and one day I hit her. I broke her nose, which was all right, but I broke my thumb, too, and the pin they put in to mend it got rusty. I guess from washing diapers. So in the end they took the nail away.' Describing his sex life, Cassidy's voice has the same impersonal lilt with which he recounts his experiences with the police, into whose hands he has so often been led by malice and ill luck. When mimicking a cop's voice, however, he puts on a special growl—the growl that betokens the enemy.

His hobby is philosophy, of which he was San Quentin's keenest student. He believes in reincarnation, and the Buddhist concept of karma, or destiny. 'If you have a good karma, you can go on being reincarnated indefinitely. Mozart and Christ made it twenty times, getting better all the time, always improving. I could tell you about a woman I know who started out as a medieval housewife, which didn't work out, and then became a blood-thirsty pirate in the eighteenth century, which also didn't work out; but finally she achieved the right balance, and today she is the most successful Lesbian in Greenwich Village.'

Cassidy got his first clues to karma from a Southern clairvoyant he met many years ago. 'He'd lie on his bed in Kentucky, take a couple of deep breaths, and tell you what a fellow in Paris was doing at that very moment. He taught me that the five races were created simultaneously, and that each of them represents a different sense. Yellow stands for hearing, red stands for smell, brown stands for taste, black stands for touch, and white stands for vision. What we have to do is bring them together.' San Francisco, it seems to me, is as likely a place as any in which to do it.

(1960)

The Rising Costa del Sol

The Coast of the Sun is a coast of grey beaches and sodden summer heat where it is still possible to spend a Mediterranean holiday that is at once chic and cheap. Rather than Europe's playground, it is Europe's snake pit—an aspect to which I'll return later. It begins at Gibraltar, the drab British fortress that dangles from the Spanish mainland like an uncomfortable earring. As an incitement to Anglophobia, Gibraltar has few rivals in continental Europe; atmospherically it is a successful blend of reform school, naval base and Cornish seaside resort, and thus exemplifies the uncanny skill with which the British contrive to export their least likable features intact. It has fish, chips, and policemen in conical blue helmets; and the fact that it is frequently shrouded in mist provides a final touch of nostalgia for the Englishman abroad. They call it 'The Rock', a nickname it appropriately shares with Alcatraz.

Once out of the stockade, you drive eastward, with the sea on your right, along a road pitted with tiny craters and lined ever more thickly with hoardings that advertise Spanish cognac, bungalows, camping sites, villas for sale, American soft drinks and chances to get in on the ground floor of 'a New Miami in Old Spain'. This is the Costa del Sol, variously known as the Coca-Cola Coast and the Costa Mierda, for which a genteel translation would be the Coast of Dung. Every few miles or so a spit of land pushes out towards the sea, surmounted by one of the crumbling towers, shaped like milk cans, that the Moors erected to warn themselves against attack. Romans and Visigoths, as well as Phoenicians, left their mark on these unlovely shores; but after 1487, when the Moorish battalions were starved out of Málaga, the coastline remained impenetrably Spanish until a dozen years ago, when the tourist invasion began to transform it. As recently as 1955 you could buy plots of land looking toward Africa for a song; today they would fetch the price of a whole Broadway score. The real-estate beachhead, established in and around the village of Torremolinos, now covers fifty-six kilometres, spreading eastward toward Málaga, the leafy provincial capital, and westward towards Marbella, which is the region's nearest approximation to St Tropez. This is the heartland of the most intensive exploitation to which European tourism has lately been subjected. The Duke and Duchess of Windsor have an estate near Marbella, and the seasonal presence of the Windsors has rendered the prettier coastal vantage points unbuyable except by the fantastically rich.

All you get for your money is sea, heat and the companionship of hot, sea-loving outcasts from Britain, America, Germany, France and Scandinavia, in roughly that order of multitude. Ten years ago Torremolinos was a hamlet with two hotels and a handful of *pensiones*; the beach was bare and unpatrolled, and by night you could swim naked without attracting the attention of the guardia civil. Then, as now, you ran the risk of swimming through a salt-flavoured cocktail composed of machine oil and sewage; but at least you were unobserved. Today, you are overlooked not only by policemen, householders and other would-be swimmers, but by three skyscraping hotels—the Pez Espada, the Tritón and the Carihuela Palace—any one of which might have been transplanted from Acapulco. In the village itself, an agglomeration of bars and clubs around a central square, the snake pit writhes; for this is the capital of what has been sourly described as 'Nescafé Society'. Is your marriage about to collapse? Do you seek friends as lost as yourself? Would you bend a law or two for a puff of marijuana, imported from Morocco? Does a barfly life, spiced with amateur orgies, appeal to your notion of holiday? If so, and if you do not mind wading through the debris of broken glass left at dawn by feuding couples, Torremolinos is your place. This is an open township, inbred and amoral, after which the next step is Tangier, followed by a suicidal leap from some high peak in the Canary Islands.

I first visited Torremolinos twelve years ago, when it was merely a thriving fishing village and not (as now) a focal point for playboys from all over the Western world. 'Look at those people!' shouted a British playwright to me as we drove through the square last summer. 'Tories, junkies, Nazis and French militarists from Algeria! You're looking at the fleshpots of Fascism!' He was not as drunk as he sounded; nor are the locals as foul as he represented them. All the same, one finds among the people who live there all the year round a host of moneyed frauds whose wealth enables them to recruit and maintain an entourage of gullible hangers-on—dishevelled English girls expelled from the Côte d'Azur, expatriate American brides deserted by their husbands, expatriate American husbands deserted by their mothers, gaunt Swedish models more interested in sex than in gender—of few human societies could one more aptly say, as Will Cuppy said of the gnus, that first the males come down to the water hole, then the females, and then the others. Except for imported liquor, alcohol is cheap, and thus provides ample opportunities for the great imported game of self-destruction.

Like many ports, Málaga has a foreign cemetery: a local joker suggested that it should be renamed Torremolinos. Property values in this part of the world have risen far more steeply than wages: servants cost ridiculously little, which means that you can destroy yourself in comfort. Up in the hills behind Torremolinos there lives, steadily pickled, an English nobleman who comes down to the village every three months, bursts into the nearest bar and falls flat on his face, to be dutifully driven home by his chauffeur. 'It is closing time in the gardens of the West,' wrote Cyril Connolly as the last war ended. He erred; in Torremolinos it is never closing time. Among the town's more recent casualties was an American widower in his early sixties who gave up drink too late and too suddenly for his blurred brain to stand the shock. Having spent twenty years doing little but watch bullfights, he announced that he was going to become a bullfighter, and that any day now he would make his debut in the ring at Madrid. He trained assiduously, his paunch and jowls shrunken by abstinence, his hands shaking and his eyeballs the colour of daffodils. One winter dawn, not long ago, he went down on his knees beside the swimming pool of a Torremolinos hotel to practise a complicated cape pass. A gust of wind hit the cape and blew him into the pool. His corpse was fished out by the staff just in time to avoid embarrassing the early swimmers.

To say that bullfighting attracts foreigners in whom there is a latent taste for self-slaughter would be to indict myself, for I am a thoroughly hooked *aficionado*; but it is often true, and the obvious place in which to indulge that murderous appetite is southern Spain, where bullfighting was born. During the last few summers of his life Ernest Hemingway spent most of his leisure hours in a house only a few miles from Torremolinos: I remember his watery blue eyes balefully staring at me across a terrace in Málaga as he verbally savaged me for criticising a matador whose skill with the sword he held in high esteem; and I recall how I flinched when, next day, he strode across the same terrace towards me, and how he astounded me by apologising for what he called his unforgivable rudeness. Arrogant one moment, abject the next: such is my last memory of this burly, self-doubting vagabond, whom I never again saw alive. In 1962 one of Hemingway's Spanish idols proved by his own example that suicide had attractions for native bull lovers as well as for foreigners: Juan Belmonte, a great matador appalled by advancing age, killed himself in Hemingway's manner—by his own hand, in his own gun room.

West of Torremolinos, the pace is less frenetic. Fuengirola, the next village of any size, is a quiescent strip of low white houses; and although Marbella, a little further on, is getting smarter and more crowded month by month, it is managing to do so quite graciously. By this I do not mean that it is exactly East Hampton: one of its minor tourist attractions is a bar-cum-nightclub that is run by a man whose fiancée, a svelte and imposing model called April Ashley, was known before her operation, four years ago, as George Mathieson. Not far away there lives (or lived last summer) a comely, unmarried English mother, aged nineteen, who has a talent for attracting minor calamities. Within the short space of three days last August, her bed caught fire and smouldered overnight beneath her; bees nested in her suitcase; she lost her passport, which she always carried with her in case wanderlust should suddenly overcome her; and her hair began to fall out. None of these misfortunes disturbed her except the last, and even for this she had a remedy. 'Restoring hair is easy,' she told me dreamily. 'You just rub into your scalp equal parts of lard and gunpowder.'

Even tourism has its landed aristocracy, and on the Coast of Dung this has its centre in and around Churriana, a steaming pueblo a mile or two inland from the road that links Torremolinos to Málaga. Hereabouts the elder squatters live, underneath the sheltering palms and the equally sheltering income-tax regulations. Some members of this august enclave are genuine expatriates, not just fly-by-night five-year residents: Gerald Brenan, for instance, the greatest English authority on things Spanish, a spry, courteous man who sat in the twenties at the feet of Virginia Woolf, from which he later exiled himself to settle in Andalusia and write such essential books as *The Spanish Labyrinth* and *The Face of Spain*. And on the fringe of the village, behind lofty iron gates that are falsely whispered to be electrified, in a cool, colonnaded villa called 'La Cónsula' (because it was built in the last century for the mistress of a rich German consul), there live Bill and Annie Davis, the reigning American hosts of the Costa del Sol. In its far smaller but similarly impregnable way, 'La Cónsula' is to the Coast of Dung what Hearst's castle of San Simeon was to Lower California—'a place desired by all', as the poet Herrick wrote of his lady's privy parts, 'but got by these/Whom love admits to the Hesperides'.

The Davises offer what is certainly the finest library and probably the best cuisine in the province; they also offer total privacy—the house has no telephone and no mail is delivered. Bill, shrewd and watchful beneath a deceptively mumbling manner that often recalls a retired gun-slinger from the Old West, dispenses the drinks, while Annie, equally bland and no less observant, looks after the food. Expatriates *in excelsis*, they are frankly culture snobs; they love clever people, and guard them jealously, with a kind of informal, unbuttoned hospitality that foreigners always prefer to the stiffer Spanish sort. Hemingway was their guest in his declining years. Hearing that he habitually wrote standing up, they prepared for his advent by hiring a local carpenter to build a number of tall, waist-high desks, which they scattered through the house, thereby convincing the servants (and the neighbourhood at large) that the approaching guest was a monstrous American writer at least ten feet tall. It was at 'La Cónsula' that Hemingway celebrated his sixtieth birthday; the place was *en fête*, and also on fire, since the hosts arranged a display of fireworks that accidentally set the sheltering palms aflame. Men with hoses and helmets were summoned and stayed to get drunk. Hemingway, meanwhile, was engaged in a playful duel with his favourite (and Spain's best) bullfighter, Antonio Ordóñez, who was born in the neighbouring city of Ronda. They were shooting cigarettes out of each other's mouths with rifles.

It is a marvel that the party ended without bloodshed. The life of man, according to André Gide, is divided between the need for pleasure and the need for rest; we must assume that rest supervened. Since Hemingway's death, the Davises have been seeking a replacement with comparable charisma; an invitation has been issued to Ezra Pound, and may by now have been accepted. For the time being, they make do with occasional visits from Orson Welles, who spent last summer in Málaga, because (like Hemingway) he admires the serene, imperturbable art of Antonio Ordóñez, and because he knows that there is no better place to see Ordóñez at his finest than Málaga during the August festivities. These occupy the first two weeks of the month, and entail something like ten bullfights on consecutive days, plus a nightly, noisy fair in the Paseo del Parque. Here, in one of the open-air *boîtes* that skirt the tree-hung central avenue, you may be lucky enough to see Beatrice Welles, Orson's small daughter, stamping her way through a flamenco routine so fiercely and proudly that her Spanish coevals scatter in panic.

Málaga itself has three hundred thousand inhabitants and very little personality, apart from its time of *feria*. Ships berth in its harbour, and the Moors built a fortress on one of its hills; its seafood is fair (though not as good as it ought to be), and it boasts a stately Edwardian hotel— the Miramar—with a commissionaire who sports a half-inch nail on his little finger to prove that he does not belong to the labouring class. Conveniently, the city prefers to forget its principal claim to fame: the fact that it gave birth to Pablo Picasso. Today there is a Picasso museum in Barcelona, and even General Franco seems disposed to welcome back his politically errant compatriot; but when I tried, last year, to hunt down Picasso's birthplace in Málaga, I ran up against shrugs, silence and affectations of ignorance. 'Do you mean the *house* painter?' I didn't. 'Was his name Pablo Ruiz y Picasso?' It was. 'Ah, then, he died in child-hood. It was very sad.' I finally discovered that the artist was born in a middle-class apartment block overlooking the Plaza de la Merced; but no one would reveal which flat his family occupied.

Art is the great absentee from this stretch of the Mediterranean coast. Nowhere else on the shores of this art-spawning sea is there so little to look at; aesthetically speaking, it is a wasteland. The most beautiful sight on the Costa del Sol lies underground, and is not manmade. It was accidentally discovered by a couple of shepherds who fell down a pothole four years ago and climbed to their feet in a wonderland. They had stumbled on the gargantuan, subterranean caves of Nerja, on the coast road from Malaga to Almeria. You reach them by a narrow stairway, and at first you are disappointed; the anteroom is scarcely larger than a middle-sized Paris nightclub; but then you stoop to pass through a smaller tunnel, and suddenly a gigantic vault opens before you, vaster than the volume of St Paul's Cathedral, damper than the deepest dungeon, and thronged with mineral towers, enormous clusters of stalagmites and stalactites, hundreds of feet high and millions of years old—a prehistoric necropolis that imparts an authentic Wordsworthian *frisson*. One re-emerges, blinking, into a sweat-stained world of coach tours and car parks: the pullulating reality of the Coast of Dung.

(1963)

The Three-Star Tour

A human being is a collection of loosely affiliated greeds. Third, in my own make-up, to sexual and intellectual is visceral. To glut it I planned and carried out, not long ago, a six-day gastronomic tour of France, starting in Paris and taking in ten of the twelve three-star restaurants listed in the *Guide Michelin*. For a couple of lunches I descended to two-star level; but apart from these interludes of slumming, I exposed my palate only to high kitchen at its reputed highest. These fragmentary notes, jotted down in fleeting moments of wakefulness as my chauffeur-driven car sped from one temple of the gut to the next, record my progress through a sea of truffles. They are reproduced here in the hope that they may be of use to people seeking information on how to get bloated in the shortest possible time at the greatest possible expense.

Day 1
Paris, where five of the top twelve tables cluster. Lunch at the Grand Vefour, shabbily gilded in its corner of the Palais Royal courtyard. The

exterior still looks as if it hadn't had a lick of paint since Feydeau's funeral; and I wish the head waiter would depart, when taking orders, from his unctuous, unvarying formula of '*Je suis suspendu à vos lèvres, monsieur*'; but the food lives up to my happiest memories. *Toast de crevettes*—shrimps ensauced in a house of pastry—is succeeded by a quartet of ortolans. Wolfing these minuscule birds, which are forcibly fed until their bones are splinter-thin, I feel conscience-qualms, and often end up a vegetarian for several hours afterwards. The Vefour has fewer than twenty tables, and booking ahead in a royal-sounding voice is imperative.

Dinner at Lasserre in the Avenue Franklin-Roosevelt. Suavely gracious eating, which you mount in a lift to savour; and the prices have become suavely more gracious since the place gained its third star in the 1963 Michelin. After a superb and gargantuan truffle, served *en feuilleté* with sauce *Périgourdine*, I am downcast by a flabby steak Dumas. My companion, an American liberal, snidely wonders how I can embark on a tour like this and still call myself a Socialist. I reply, curtly but sincerely, that good food should be available to everyone; Socialism which denies the pleasures of the gullet is Socialism disfigured by the English puritan tradition.

Apropos, I lately dined in a London restaurant with a Left-wing gourmet for host. We shared a moussaka, which tasted like shredded goat immersed in cheesy yoghourt. When the proprietor asked him whether he had enjoyed the meal, my friend replied: 'The only tolerable thing about it was the temperature of the coffee.' He worried me, however, by leaving only a half-crown tip, remarking as he did so: 'One must keep the workers mutinous.'

Day 2

Lunch on the Left Bank at Lapérouse, all panels and mirrors and creaks on the stairs. Distinct sensation of being treated like a gaping tourist, despite the excellence of the *poulet docteur*. Wines are forced on one, as a conjuror forces cards. I confirm an earlier impression that this is a place best visited in the company of Parisian habitués. Why should a chef exert himself when he knows that most of his clientèle would rather be eating an underdone T-bone steak?

Dinner at Maxim's: my first acquaintance with this pleasure-dome of the *Belle Epoque*. A brisk little orchestra plays gems from *My Fair Lady*, and unordered champagne, iced in its bucket, is already on the table: one gets the feeling of a night-club rather than a restaurant. The *sole Albert* is so vast and immaculately sauced that I can only peck at its successor, a *filet de boeuf* in an undistinguished *sauce Périgueux*. Surely the room is too large, too thronged with dancers, to permit that devout concentration on taste and after-taste which high kitchen demands? It is like staging Oscar Wilde in the Coliseum. A disillusioning day.

Day 3

A two-star lunch at the Relais Bisson, Quai des Grands Augustins. To begin with, a crisp vegetable hors d'oeuvre, named *Coeur de Bisson* and blighted by tinned palm-tree hearts; and then *loup au fenouil*, a speciality which I choose at the waiter's insistence and am scarcely equipped to judge, being no fan of this heavy white fish or of the herb that ubiquitously shadows it.

The evening, however, is an expected pinnacle. Whatever one says of the Tour d'Argent, however one gibes at its over-dressed customers and its touristic, cineramic view of Notre Dame, one has to concede the unique virtue of its *canard à la presse*. That thick dark sauce, squeezed out of the duck to anoint its meat, has no rival in France or anywhere else; it is blood and spice indissolubly mingled, toughness and grace combined. I prefaced it with *quenelles de brochet*, light as shuttlecocks. A flawless meal, discreetly enhanced by an expert *sommelier*: his face a network of broken capillaries, he proffers hints instead of applying pressure, and one never gets the feeling that he is pushing the expensive wine in preference to the most suitable one.

Day 4

We quit Paris, aiming south-east on National Cinq. After seventy miles we stop for lunch at Sens, which has a spectacular, lopsided cathedral and a solid, roomy two-star restaurant, the Paris et Poste. I choose a rich *saucisson chaud*, followed unwisely by too much *volaille à la broche*. Hereabouts wine begins to take its toll. Together with my companion, I start to giggle at small fancies; after two bottles of Sancerre and a couple of Armagnacs, we decide that the great unrecognised merit of *haute cuisine* (as of beer in Kingsley Amis's imaginary ad) is that it makes you drunk. After lunch we slumber; you will realise why the car is chauffeur-driven. Switching to National Six, we travel just over a hundred kilometres to Avallon, meeting almost no one on the way; Burgundy is oddly deserted this year.

At Avallon, a quiet little fortified town looking down on a curling river valley, we rise again to three-star heights. The Hôtel de la Poste is a coaching inn at which Napoleon stayed on his return from Elba. Passing through an archway, you reach a courtyard leading to a garden in which a fountain splashes. My bedroom has blue walls and a modern four-poster.

The sense of peace is total. Dinner, in the narrow, placid dining-room, is an unhurried affair. First course: *Les Amusettes de la Poste*, which unfold in three episodes—a slice of feathery *brioche* with a circle of *pâté de foie* in the middle; a square of veal terrine; and a plate of assorted mushrooms and artichokes. Second course: *poulet en civet*, as heavily sauced as it is light on the palate. The wine waiter startles me by decanting our Richebourg '49 into six empty glasses, 'to let it breathe more quickly'. The palate rejoices and the stomach relaxes: this is not far from perfection. 'What a place,' murmurs my friend, 'to write that novel!'

Day 5

We roll on to Saulieu, a smaller, uglier town barely half an hour away. Here, they say, is the innermost sanctum of French gastronomy: the Hôtel de la Côte d'Or, a polished, unpretentious tavern right on the beaten track of National Six, run by Alexandre Dumaine, the acknowledged doyen of French chefs. I order the *pâté de foie*, and find that I have lost my taste for frozen liver ice-cream. But I recall the guide's daunting rebuke to the tourists in the Uffizi Gallery ('It is not the pictures that are on trial here'), and gallantly persevere with the *timbale de fruits de mer*. After one mouthful, I feel sure enough to bet my companion that Dumaine is not in the kitchen. We quiz the waiter, who satisfyingly replies that Dumaine is out of town. Later, I read that he intends to retire this autumn, handing over his culinary kingdom to a twenty-nine-year-old contender named Minot. In course of time, Minot may rise to the occasion. Meanwhile, gourmets had better beware.

Then a long haul down to Lyon, where we change to National Sept for seventeen southerly miles in order to reach the city of Vienne. Our goal here is the Pyramide, founded by M. Point a hundred yards from the swirling Rhône, and owned since his death by his indomitable widow. A rainstorm greets us, battering the garden as we eat a tripartite first course that is a pale imitation of its counterpart at Avallon. Course two: *truite farcie braisée au porto*, the great speciality, and worthy of all the praise it has received. Four or five different flavours meet in peaceful coalition, each of them honouring the trout while retaining their separate identities. Course three: a guinea-hen that should never have been asked to follow an act like course two. N.B. the Pyramide closes on Tuesdays. Gastronomically, Vienne is the turning-point of a trip like this. You can either continue south to Provence, where there are three-star restaurants at Noves (La Petite Auberge) and Lex Baux (the Baumanière); or you can double back north to Lyon and points east. We chose the latter route, spending the night at the Royal Hotel in Lyon.

Day 6

A climbing road takes us a few miles out of Lyon to a baffling disappointment. Mère Brazier's restaurant is a lofty pavilion overlooking the backside of a profoundly unlovely city. The site is high, but nothing in the kitchen justifies an award as regal as three stars. A nice bit of salmon is followed by a nice bit of chicken; both come sweetly and easily off the bone; but is it for this that I have crossed half a country? I discover in myself a mounting resentment towards the pretensions of *haute cuisine*. For one thing, I object to its uninventiveness: French high cooking is mainly dedicated to reproducing the dishes that satisfied high bourgeois taste in the latter part of the nineteenth century. Next, I regret its xenophobia: France refuses pointblank to learn from the culinary traditions of any other country. Finally, I deplore its snobbism: it regards garlic as a plebeian herb whose presence in a dish should never be detectable. No restaurant serving *bouillabaisse* could ever arrive at three-star status. My last memory of Mère Brazier is her ashtray, which is thrust into my hand by a dutiful waitress. It depicts a bulky matron holding at arm's length a saucepan from which an enormous cloud of smoke is escaping. Possible captions suggest themselves: 'Back to the old cookery-book' or: 'Mother Brazier bombs again'.

After lunch, an easterly drive of sixty-odd miles to the lake of Annecy, in the foothills of the French Alps. The sun lances across the water, which is scored by the trails of speedboats. The snow leaves white fingerprints on the mountains. Why, you wonder, are there not more people? Skirting the lake, we make a hairpin descent and reach the preposterous village of Talloires. According to Michelin, it has 659 inhabitants. It also has three restaurants with one star apiece, and one restaurant with three—a higher score than Marseilles. We dine at the latter: l'Auberge du Père Bise, with a wooded terrace against which the water irregularly laps. Like all its fellows outside Paris in the triple-stellar bracket, it is barely half-full. I order *mousse de truite*, garnished with crayfish, followed by *poularde à l'estragon*; and at once I respond to a knowledge of herbs, a mastery of fire (which is the key to great cooking) and a glowing freshness of raw materials which I have not encountered since Avallon. I decided to stay for a recuperative day or two at the adjacent Hôtel de l'Abbaye, a quondam monastery with plushy rooms, a one-star kitchen and instant access to the lake.

Day 7 and after

After testing the six-star gastronomic resources of Talloires, I explore the other restaurants that dot the shores of this matchless lake.

They add up to four more stars. I then return to Père Bise, where I dine on *pâté chaud* (sweetbreads whipped up in pastry), *poularde de Bresse* with an audaciously vinegary *sauce diable*, and a multi-flavoured *gâteau marjolaine*. When I inquire about the latter the waiter says disdainfully: 'Vous ne le trouverez pas dans le commerce.' I chat with M. Bise, beaming and golden-toothed, who has owned the restaurant ever since his father died in 1924. His younger brother Georges runs a less successful but still one-star establishment across the road. (Every little Bise gives your liver a *crise* ...) Speaking of his brother, the elder Bise says: 'Il a tombé deux étoiles. C'est dommage!' There is no pity in his voice. Food in France is a fiercely competitive game. If Hollywood stars are only as good as their last picture, French restaurateurs are only as good as their last star.

The menu, *chez* Bise, does not vary much. It usually begins with a *pâté de foie* (or a *mousse* or a *terrine*); continues with a *gratin d'écrevisse* (or *quenelles de brochet*, or *omble chevalier*); and rises to a climax with *poularde à l'estragon* (or meat in some kind of truffled sauce). The three-star shrines, it occurs to me, are all aiming at the same Platonic ideal—a perfect meal based on standards, and combinations of dishes, that were immutably laid down not less than half a century ago. At its best, it makes superlative eating, but even its best is somewhat limited. Like the Catholic Church, it excludes new formulae, and cannot admit the possibility of improvement.

(1963)

A Memoir of Manhattan

In 1626 a Dutch administrator named Peter Minuit, who was employed by the Dutch West India Company, bought Manhattan Island from the Mana-Hatta Indians in exchange for a parcel of trinkets, said to have been worth twenty-four dollars. And that will do for historical fact. I do not mean to sound flippant or cavalier. The rest of New York's history can be found in the guidebooks; it is not to be found in New York. Or not, at least, in the New York I know and of which I am writing; a city whose living immediacy is so urgent that when I am in it I lose all sense of the past. The twenties, so near when I am in Europe, become in New York a Golden Age of antiquity, remote beyond recapturing, and anything that happened before Prohibition seems downright antediluvian.

First, then, the arrival. Flying over New England on a clear day you look down and see the sun. It pursues you like a golden gopher, bursting up through lakes and rivers, flaming a trail to New York. The city looks its best from the air, or by night, or when you are drunk; in any circumstances, in fact, except those of stone-cold sobriety, by day, at street level. Abnormal itself, a many-fingered gesture of defiance at the sky, it demands an abnormal approach. So fly in by sunlight. Manhattan tilts as your plane banks, the whole carnival of concrete sways, then rights itself; peering down, you pick out the great bridges, Triborough and Brooklyn, Washington and Queens, around which the traffic whorls and loops before straightening out like mercury in a hot thermometer. They connect the rocky, fish-shaped island with the rest of the subcontinent of which—we are always being told—it is so laughably unrepresentative.

Coming to New York from the muted mistiness of London, as I regularly do, is like travelling from a monochrome antique shop to a technicolor bazaar. Colours assert themselves, pure and violent in the perspicuous air. The canyons are alive with plumage, the shop windows are rainbow gay, and the taxis challenge them in brightness as they snuggle, fat-jowled, up to the traffic lights. Neon signs blink at the sun, chasing their tails around the marquees of Times Square; the newsstands, laden with *Hush-Hush*, *Inside Story* and a dozen others, shout confidences in purple and gold. 'Castro Raped My Teenage Daughter', one magazine wildly complains; 'Is Ava Gardner a Secret Hedonist?' asks a second; and a third: 'Is Frank Sinatra a Secret Narcissist?' A patina of grime softens the glaring tints.

To no metropolis on earth do I return more certain that I have not been missed. In Rome and Paris I am needed, as doffed caps and low bows testify; but New York can get along without me very well. Its profile changes from visit to visit; here a face lift, there a nose bob. 'Let's meet for a drink at the Trianon,' says someone; and when I arrive, nothing remains of the place but a hole in the ground; only rats drink down there, or maybe the descendants of those baby alligators, gifts from Florida, that ungrateful children flush down into the sewers, thereby occasioning rumours that the city's subterranean ganglia are inhabited by scaly monsters. 'Why not let's lunch at the Chaumière?' says someone else; but the building that houses that excellent restaurant proves to be a gap in the skyline, a tooth pulled from the grey smile of the street. Did he mean the Chambord, or perhaps the Chauveron? And are they still standing?

Across the street from your hotel room, an office block, possibly made of pre-stressed celery, is going up with a chattering, daylong clamour. Hoping to escape the noise, you demand a loftier room, but by the time your luggage has been moved, the construction gang opposite has overtaken you, and high-level workers—many of them Mohawk Indians, who are immune to vertigo—saunter cat-footed along the slim girders. Architectural novelties are taken for granted. Only hicks now goggle at the site on Fifth Avenue where the Manufacturers' Trust Company erected its glass bank—the most poetic practical joke in financial history. The Lever Building, a transparent matchbox poised on shining stilts, merged long ago into the landscape; and few New Yorkers waste a second glance on the looming, coppery tower of the Seagram Building. Park Avenue, across which these two monuments to commerce confront each other, is the most vulnerable of the world's great streets. Within a decade or less, it will probably have developed into a deep, glass-walled, Gargantuan trench; and I seriously suggest that at Christmas the buildings should be flooded with water and filled with luminous tropical fish, including—for jocularity's sake—a small school of sharks.

And the European will marvel still, as he does today, at the rectangularity of the whole cityscape. Block succeeds block, oblong looks down on cube, compelling the tourist to long, as he moves through the diced monolith of Manhattan, for a street that curves, an architectural line that is not straight. In this world of rightangles your eye rests almost with pleasure on Frank Lloyd Wright's whirligig Guggenheim Museum, an inverted helterskelter fashioned in fudge. Only in Central Park, where roads twist and coil at random, can you escape from the singleminded arrow-straightness of streets and avenues.

But this insistence on travelling between two points by the shortest distance has its rewards, among them the many intersections from which you can see four separate horizons, one for each point of the compass, giving you an exhilarating sense of the spaces outside the city's labyrinth. All roads led to Rome, but all roads lead out of New York. They are perilous for pedestrians, according to an American friend of mine exiled in Britain. 'Those parked cars,' he said to me. 'You think they're empty, but they're not. There are men inside them, crouched down with *steel hooks*. They grab at you with the hooks and pull you in and mug you. Not for money, just for kicks. So stay away from the curbs. *Hug the walls*.' A fantasy, no doubt; but only a New Yorker could have dreamed it up.

Manhattan is a place for coming and going; for raising up and pulling down; for making money and for spending it. It is a port, a bank and a fleshpot. It has the largest population in the country, yet the country's laws are not made there; it produces the nation's plays, plans its television shows, advertises its goods, publishes its books, shapes its opinions and looks after its investments, but it does not govern the nation. Hence its curious air of irresponsibility. Hence, too, its lack of a centre. Where

London has the Houses of Parliament, and Washington the Capitol, New York has—what? City Hall? There is something about Red Square, Trafalgar Square and the Place de la Concorde that calls the mind to order, reminding the individual that he is also a citizen. I cannot say that I feel this in Times Square or Union Square; and the U.N. building hardly counts, since it stands on international soil. Geographically, the centre of New York is occupied by Central Park. It is disputed territory, containing, among other things, a restaurant, a police station, a museum, a zoo and a skating rink. Teenagers battle by night on its fringes in the name of honour; love is made at all hours in its quieter recesses. But what dominates the park is nobody and no building; it is the island rock, thrusting unmanageably up through the coverlet of grass; the island's jagged core, a menace to thin skins and no friend of flowers.

Lacking a true centre, the city is centrifugal, split up into self-contained fragments. To call it a melting pot is not only a cliché but an error; many of the fragments refuse to melt, so stern is their loyalty to racial or national identity. There is Chinatown, celebrating its New Year with gaudy lions and jigging dragons in the streets, and firecrackers frightening the sidewalks; Little Puerto Rico, the city's newest ghetto, frowned on by less recent immigrants (one thinks wanly of the joke about the Indian chief sighing to one of his braves that property values are sure to go down now that the white men have arrived); Kosher New York, downtown on Second Avenue, where I pause to pay tribute to the fertile energies of Jewish writers, composers and actors, without whom the American theatre would scarcely exist; and Harlem, spread out north of the park, a once-stoic community now humming with confident impatience, claiming its place in the American sun. The texture of Harlem's laughter is tough and often baffling to outsiders.

Let me give three examples. Pearl Bailey returns to the Apollo Theater (New York's only vaudeville house), making her entrance down the aisle, attended by four violinists and a pair of lackeys who snootily spray the audience with scent. Next: on Lenox Avenue, a Negro woman, arguing with a white cab driver who is demanding a bigger tip, silences him in five brisk, acidulated words: 'Stop behaving like a nigger!' This I overheard; and a reliable friend tells me of the following exchange, the night after Patterson regained his heavyweight title from Johannson, be-between a Park Avenue matron and a Negro actor:

MATRON (*benignly*): You must be feeling very happy about the result of the fight.
ACTOR: I'm afraid not.

MATRON: But it's such a great victory for your people.

ACTOR: You see, I'm Swedish.

MATRON (*thrown*): Oh. . . .

ACTOR: But *you* must be very happy—after all, it's a great victory for the *American* people.

MATRON: Oh, yes. Yes, of course.

ACTOR (*roguishly*): But you'd better watch out! Because *we* may beat *you* next time!

There is Italy in New York, and also Germany; and on every block, swinging a truncheon, there is Ireland. When the novelist J. D. Salinger last visited the city, to polish a short story, he pinned to *The New Yorker* bulletin board a card on which he explained that he was looking for a small apartment 'in a good Zen Buddhist neighbourhood'. I have no doubt that he found one.

Smart New York—for here, as everywhere else, the real distinctions are not racial or national but economic—is the noontime traffic jam on Park Avenue in the East Fifties; it is also the neat pyramids of dog excrement on the sidewalks outside the grander apartments. ('How do you know it's dogs?' Charles Addams once said to me, and the hair rose on my scalp). It is the whistles of liveried doormen, cab-hunting on rainy corners; and it is that unique phenomenon, the sexually segregated lunch. In other cities, men and women lunch freely together; in New York, where daylight means business, the general rule is *apartheid*. (There are exceptions, of course, but mainly among the decadents.) The custom can best be seen at the Plaza Hotel. At midday, the Plaza's Oak Room is a male preserve, all steaks, horn rims and bloody Marys; the women, all hats, chatter and Camparis, crowd into the Palm Court at the opposite end of the building. In some of New York's pricier French restaurants, one room is set aside, by unspoken law, for business, and another for gossip; eating with a girl, I feel positively androgynous.

What else is plush New York? It is dry Martinis with lemon peel, not olives; it is sailing paper boats in the pool at the restaurant of the Four Seasons; it is ordering larks for dinner at the Forum of the Twelve Caesars (whose slogan, according to a local joker, is: 'All you can eat for two hundred dollars'); it is the Knickerbocker Club, where I have heard a Princeton man say to a waitress, '*Donnez-moi, s'il vous plait, le* corned-beef hash'; and it is living as a certain movie producer lives, in a marble penthouse that suggests the men's room at the Taj Mahal. Above all, it is staying out of New York as much as possible, especially during high summer.

The city has two dominant seasons. One is icy, with the wind splitting your lips and slicing through your kidneys, and the trees in Central Park shrieking in spidery silhouette; the other is molten and miasmic, turning summer into a furnace beyond the vilest imaginings of Nebuchadnezzar. New York also has two Bohemias—Upper and Lower. Upper consists of a bright, competitive in-group that lives on its wit, which has carried it to the ulcerous heights of celebrity that Broadway, television, Hollywood and cabaret make readily accessible to those who are young in years and heart, and old in mind and skill. This is a Bohemia entirely peopled by Christian names; by Gloria and Sidney and Adolph and Betty and Mike and Elaine and Lennie and Steve and Truman and Gore and such; and it has a thick fringe of hangers-on, sitters-in at the sessions, who preserve their equanimity and their bland, knowing smiles by constant recourse to ego-bolstering pills—notably the green, heart-shaped Dexamils, emblems of the insecure and saviours of the shaken.

Lower Bohemia is downtown in Greenwich Village, the internment camp of Manhattan nonconformity. Its official motto is Flaubert's dictum: 'Un homme qui s'est institué artiste n'a plus le droit de vivre comme les autres.' The district still attracts artists, but for every artist it attracts a hundred civilians, so that the secret garden is ridden with vagabond neurotics and trampled underfoot by tourism. Desperately, it retains a distinct local personality. The Village is the Italian quarter of the city, where houses stop soaring and behave like dwelling places, and streets have names instead of numbers. Fittingly, they balk at normality; rather than intersect at right angles, they wander obtusely or acutely and run together into little squares and triangles. Poe lived hereabouts, and so did Henry James, but in their day the Village was still respectable.

It became Bohemian around the turn of the century, and it was not until the twenties, during the residence of Willa Cather, Eugene O'Neill, Thomas Wolfe and Edna St Vincent Millay, that it gained its reputation as a stronghold of protest against mechanised living, as a hiding place where you ignored the lure of safe employment and did instead all the things that can most fruitfully be done with the hands—writing, painting, sculpting, drinking and love-making among them. In the thirties the Village went progressive; along with little theatres and film societies, it bred study groups and recruits for the International Brigade. The clash of political extremes is seldom heard there today. The place is softer, more rueful and twilit, emphatic only in its tolerance of eccentricity. This latter is the basic rule of Village life, and, as Mary McCarthy once said, 'it is plainly not one that will build cities or cathedrals; on the other hand, neither will it destroy them, and this, in the present era, is a thought fraught with pleasure'.

The Village is ready for anyone; for lost boys—some of them resembling Peter Pan, others verging on Wendy—and for stout, curt, hard-drinking girls, clicking their heels with the military finesse of Erich von Stroheim; for anti-social hipsters and beats, and for all-too-social editors and publishers making their homes within the citadel they have pillaged; for junkies, Ivy Leaguers, ascetics and strippers. The walls of the coffeehouses and the paperback bookshops rustle with posters announcing a Pirandello play, a jazz concert, a screening of *Earth*, a lecture demonstration of Dianetics. To quote Miss McCarthy again, 'a sense of the American possibility suddenly becomes very strong'. At the lowest estimate, life in the Village is life without a deadline, a ruin in course of construction, a rhetorical gesture against the affluent society; at its best, it is an experiment in feeling, reading, watching, reflecting and writing that can define and direct the personality, giving it free flight (as good universities do) and a chance to come to rest either in fecundity or inertia.

It is at night that a Londoner is most aware of missing New York. London, on the whole, closes down soon after eleven p.m., but New York is open twenty-four hours a day. It is a nocturnal city, constructed to look more enticing as darkness envelops it. Times Square, a dusty obscenity by day, is a whirlpool of temptation by artificial light; and to survey the midtown spires at night is to feel a gregarious hunger for human companionship, so many and so inaccessible are the lives that are flourishing, or fading, or crashing to disaster inside those pillars of gleaming windows. Perhaps because of my job, I know New York best as a night town, and its people as night people. Some wipe bars, sweep streets, or serve late plates of young tom turkey to customers with ashen, over-entertained faces. Others take me downtown to hear jazz, whose beat is that of the railway wheels that once bore the Negro north, away from his past, on which he looks back in bitter nostalgia. New York is as far as he can go, the end of the line, where he explodes in fluent, sophisticated protest—Charlie Parker ten years ago, and today Ornette Coleman, another master of the alto sax, whose asthmatic virtuosity staggers the clientele at the Five Spot Cafe. At Birdland, Parker's old domain, there may be Miles Davis, the musical embodiment of a lonely-hearts ad with carefully phrased undertones of sex; or Dizzy Gillespie, who smiles and blows at the same time; or Gerry Mulligan, who blows first and smiles later.

My host on this escapade is a buoyant young writer nicknamed

Mack, who epitomises intellectual New York for me as no one else does. He works at night and often when asleep; roused by his wife in the early afternoon, he frequently mumbles: 'Let me alone, I'm writing.' He is a voluminous reader, an adept in nuclear science, economics and cosmogony, a would-be Renaissance man, and a profound student of pot. By no one else have I ever been invited to brunch at six in the evening; and from no other lips have I heard a rebuke to a rival driver, trying sloppily to park, as brutally effective as: 'Man, where's your elementary physics?'

We may have dropped in at a literary party—over-furnished minds in an under-furnished room—full of ex-Trotskyites who shun Stalinism, ex-Stalinists who shun Trotskyites, Socialists who shun both, and liberals who are shunned by all three. The novelist Norman Mailer, an ex-almost-everything, was probably present, needling the male guests about their virility and advocating hand-to-hand combat as the solution of all global problems. Such *soirées* unsettle me, partly because New York intellectuals can always overawe and out-talk me from a standing start, and partly because their talk is mostly aimed at proving that it is naïve to believe, as they once did, that political ideals can ever be translated into healthy, concrete, human achievement. At my request, very likely, Mack whisks us away to the less cynical world of jazz.

Our next move is to a studio on Lower Broadway, where a newly fashionable action painter is riotously At Home. Since he took to trundling a giant garden roller across his canvases, smoothing out the blobs of paint into suave horizontal panels, the critics have declared that his art has acquired a new sense of peace and maturity, and his prices have soared in consequence. He has no great illusions about his artistic abilities, as he demonstrates by urging his guests to throw bottles of New York State champagne at his latest unfinished picture. Indoors, he is habitually naked except for jeans; outdoors, even when going to the drugstore for a bar of soap, he makes a point of wearing full evening dress. He is naturally talented and naturally funny, but until recently he was poor, and he has discovered that his talent sells best when most unnaturally (i.e. unverifiably, irrelevantly) employed. He remains immensely funny.

We leave him, again at my whispered behest, to look in at a midtown clip joint where the main attraction is a robust Armenian stripper who expresses herself in exact accordance with her talents and predilections, compromising with nobody and curling her lip at those who find her art offensive. Planting herself four-square, her legs astride and her back to the audience, she swivels, jackknifes and gyrates for upwards of twenty minutes, during which time each of her buttocks takes on a separate muscular identity, almost as if they had never been introduced.

Smilingly but savagely clipped, we emerge. Events thereafter become telescoped and confused. A few sights and sounds stay clear in the memory. People talking like Jules Feiffer characters in late-night delicatessens: a Broadway actor, clad in a wing collar and a morning coat, buying drinks for the musicians at the Central Plaza on Second Avenue; myself cursing the black fingermarks on my lavender tie, which I had adjusted immediately after reading a morning paper; and the lean, droll cab driver who, having announced: 'I am about to do a sneaky and a swinish thing,' shot through a red light and complacently explained: 'As Baudelaire would have said, the hunters and the hackies have pleasures of their own.' Finally, a gigantic sandwich at Reuben's, where a lady novelist in our group pockets a swizzle stick to take home to her cat: 'Damn creature hasn't eaten in days.'

The streets are flooded with the blue of dawn and the crawling whine of the garbage-disposal trucks. I suddenly remember the mythical, imperturbable Broadway character who stepped off the sidewalk and nearly had his toes amputated by a truck, whereupon he remarked with the faintest of shrugs: 'That's show business.' The boom of an early (or late) plane resounds through the city; and the day's first helicopter, a dangling fly in the sky, newly risen from the heliport at West 30th Street on its way to La Guardia, passes over the grey, awakening towers.

Day has broken now. The streets have lost their echoes; before long they will be filled with early New Yorkers. I look at their faces as I ride back to my apartment. And there, unmistakably, it is: the familiar Manhattan look; a pettish, slightly resentful frown, as if a great promise had somehow not quite been fulfilled. In the midst of prosperity, people look as if they had been robbed. But I am speaking mostly of the middle-aged. My cab passes the United Nations building, glaucous beside the river, and at once I brighten, thinking of the young.

(1960)

V: COMMENTS AND CAUSERIES

The Critic Ad Lib
(With apologies to Frank Sullivan)

Q. I understand you are a seasoned broadcaster on the BBC radio programme called 'The Critics', Mr Minim. What kind of an experience is that?

A. Rewarding. Thoroughly rewarding.

Q. And what is it worth?

A. While. Thoroughly worth while.

Q. Let's begin by considering books. How does the author of a serious book take himself?

A. Much too seriously.

Q. Is that all?

A. By no means. He brings to his subject a rare sense of responsibility.

Q. Does he bring anything else to it?

A. Yes. An imposing display of erudition. Also a well-stocked mind.

Q. What about his novel?

A. It is novelettish in treatment. Its characterisation is skindeep.

Q. What does it lay itself open to?

A. The charge of sentimentality. Conversely, it is charmingly ingenuous, engaging and endearing.

Q. How endearing?

A. Altogether endearing.

Q. For whom did it come off?

A. It came off for me.

Q. To change the subject, Mr Minim, how do you feel about musical films?

A. Antipathetically.

Q. Aren't we being a trifle literary, Mr Minim?

A. Forgive me. I'm not much of a one for musicals.

Q. In spite of anything?

A. In spite of their honest sentimentality. Their bold use of colour. Their enchanting brashness. I cannot help feeling that they are striving.

Q. For what?

A. For effect. But I liked the girl enormously.

Q. What do you think?

A. I think we're all agreed on that point, aren't we?

Q. How about Loddington's new play? Did you find it rooted in anything?

A. Yes, indeed. In a closely observed reality. Its method is documentary.

Q. But enlivened, I hope?

A. Certainly. With touches of fantasy. I enjoyed the club-swinging episode in the Turkish bath.

Q. How did you enjoy it?

A. I particularly enjoyed it. I would like to single it out.

Q. And what happens to the fantasy?

A. It seems to me to get bogged down in documentary realism.

Q. Is it Rotherham?

A. Yes. It is Rotherham important, isn't it, for us to define our terms. What do we mean by realism?

Q. What *do* we mean?

A. We mean the poetry of fact. We mean a sober assessment of life as these people live it. We mean Loddington's almost clinical analysis of their environment.

Q. That strikes a note, doesn't it?

A. It does. A note of quite unsentimental pity, don't you agree?

Q. Do I agree?

A. You won't go all the way with me. You don't mind admitting that in that sense you're an escapist. You are old-fashioned enough to go to the theatre to be entertained.

Q. What is a play, after all?

A. It is a play, not a psychiatric treatise.

Q. And as for the satirical scene in the newspaper office?

A. It seemed to you, though of course you want to hear what Raresby Humpage has to say about it, rather *fun-poking*.

Q. What might it be Rotherham?

A. It might be Rotherham a good idea if we moved on to Art.

Q. What were your reactions to Sam Saddlesby's retrospective exhibition?

A. I found his style a little too lush. Alternatively, I found it not quite lush enough. He is too much preoccupied with paint.

Q. How were his symbols?

A. Valid. On the other hand, his style is overlaid with pseudo-symbolism.

Q. Did you find that Rotherham?

A. Yes. In Rotherham bad taste. A Littleham vulgar.

Q. Did you go to the exhibition with anything?

A. With profound misgivings. I think Humpage hit the nail on the head when he said.

Q. What did he say?

A. That plastically. That sensuously. That in terms of sheer paint.

Q. Am I to mind anything?

A. Oh, yes. Mind you, I don't want to set the cat among the pigeons. Mind you, I'm open to correction there. Mind you, I'm fully prepared to be shot down.

Q. Did you listen to the Third Programme feature, *Pindar's Mistresses*?

A. Yes. I was quite bowled over. I thought it was quite prilliantly done.

Q. What was it full of?

A. Comic invention and a real feeling for its subject.

Q. Was it seen in anything?

A. A true historical perspective.

Q. Where had the writer brought it?

A. Triumphantly off. On its own level, of its kind, and as such, it was perfectly prilliant.

Q. How had the writer seen it?

A. In terms of humour, not only in terms of wit. But in terms of what kind of wit? That's my point.

Q. What sort of point?

A. My whole point.

Q. How was it performed?

A. Admirably. Unpretentiously. Most sensitively, within the context of its terms of reference. It was really very fine.

Q. And in what way was it moving?

A. In a curious way. But it was a bit.

Q. A bit what, Mr Minim?

A. A bit much.

(1953)

Punctuation as an Aid to Loose Thinking

Punctuation is more powerful than we think. I have reached this conclusion after many hours spent staring nervously at the gay little hieroglyphs on my typewriter keyboard; and, more especially, after re-reading Ronald Firbank, whose characters conduct whole colloquies in punctuation. Some tourist princess, eyeing a garage mechanic, will idly wonder '...?...': to which her duenna will respond with a bristling and appalled '!!!!': and so on, indefinitely. Firbank's virtuosity set me thinking. Punctuation, I have since discovered, can not only talk; it can help you to make friends and influence people. What follows is a preliminary guide, designed to show how a working knowledge of dots and dashes can disguise almost any lameness of brain and make it look as stylish as all get out.

1. The Exclamation Mark. Unfashionable nowadays, and essential only to hyperthyroid types, such as sub-editors who seek to liven up one's copy with cheery interpolations like: 'Strange state of affairs!' or 'What a funny coincidence!' Nevertheless, the E. Mark can still occasion-ally do good service by infusing a shot of bright astonishment into the greyest platitudes. 'Aha,' by itself, is dull news; but by adding an E. Mark ('Aha!') you evoke a circle of raised eyebrows and a whole penumbra of fascinated incredulity. The margins of borrowed books are true E. Mark territory. '!' is the correct comment on hanging participles in the test. Reserve '!!' for such statements as 'Shelley was the first anarchist' or 'I never finished *War and Peace.*'

2. The Question Mark. Two principal usages: (*a*) to build up sus-pense. Not recommended, except in such crude forms as the epistolary: 'And then we played the Truth Game and *what* do you suppose Madge came out with? ? ?' Variations of this are in frequent journalistic use, hopefully following up a limp and quite pointless anecdote: 'The little boy's name? Mahatma Gandhi.' (*b*) More advanced: the rhetorical question which the writer cannot be bothered to answer. On these occasions a Q. Mark saves no end of trouble. Example: 'Who will deny that Bankhead's Camille outshone Bernhardt's?'

3. The Semicolon. Here we arrive at the prize-winning supporting crutch of English prose. Its proper function (now outmoded) is to trans-form a sentence into a see-saw, along which the mind ambles, balancing for a moment before the slow swoop into the final clause. Since Sir Thomas Browne's day, the semicolon has been accepted as a valid

adjunct to literary choreography. Unfortunately Browne's style is almost inimitable (without the Demon Skill), and he is as misleading a model to the writer as Chekhov is to the dramatist.

But do not lose heart. The semicolon remains a boon to the weary; a hammock in which any sick sentence (this one, for instance) can convalesce and start afresh. It enables you to snuff out a statement and begin again without recapitulation or apology; e.g. 'Everything he did stripped strength of its arrogance; his pride forswore cruelty; it mingled iron will with mercy; he had, it might be said, compassion.' Four sentences for the price and sense of one, and a splendid tribute to the semicolon's genius for extending a half-thought into a paragraph.

4. The Comma. Particularly helpful to novelists working against time; e.g. 'Nobody noticed she was there, and nobody stared at her, and nobody laughed, but everyone sensed her, sensed her special chill, and felt a pang, and everyone shifted a little, and changed the subject, and was suddenly ashamed.' Here the comma has come to the rescue with a posse, like the cavalry at the end of a Western.

Note: the difference between the comma and the semicolon is Pride.

5. The Three Dots (...). Another haven for the tired novelist, in which connection it should not be confused with the American gossip-writer's usage: 'Drayton Draight gifted ex-wife Mabs with platinum spoon. Could be Sir Stork has taken up that option...' If, having begun to write a novel, you keep falling asleep at the foot of page six, simply add three dots and sell it as a short story. The dots will have given you 'mood' and 'an indefinable flavour of your own'. For instance; 'As night left the sky, an odd thing happened to Louisa May. The pallor vanished from her cheeks. The sad small eyes ripened. The nose perked up, questing. And once or twice, oh! so tentatively, Louisa May chuckled...' This represents the Pen-Dropped-From-Nerveless-Fingers school of fiction.

6. Quotes. These are unrivalled as receptacles for (*a*) opinions you are chary of admitting to, and (*b*) little epigrams of your own whose brilliance genuinely frightens you, since they stand out like obelisks from the desert of your normal style. But quotes demand toil. Their use involves the invention of fictional characters. Any writer of profiles will testify, however, that the results are well worth the labour. Suggestions: when writing about a theatrical personality, invent an omniscient and picturesque stagehand. Keep using him. He can help you round off a paragraph like this one: 'One of the mannerisms Bibber never quite shook off was his habit of resorting to a shrill falsetto in moments of extreme passion. On one occasion a stagehand, listening in the wings, is

reputed to have murmured to a colleague: "'E thinks 'e's back in the choir at the ruddy Sistyne Chapple!" '

Again, many a pun has passed into legend when fathered on what is usually called 'a jaded voice'. Example: 'Several critics have pointed out that Rokesby's style would have been improved if he had borrowed from the best writers, instead of the secondraters. At one cocktail party given in his honour a jaded voice was heard to remark: "Rokesby? He's just a wagon-load of manqués!"' You will note, as a point of technique, that the author had to get his mouthpiece a little sloshed before he got that one off.

7. Parentheses. In expert hands these are identical with quotes. Use them as a shroud for unsupported opinions you want to throw in without being challenged, e.g. 'His much underrated speech at Toronto (superior in many respects to the Gettysburg Address) caused a sensation in what was then a prairie township.'

8. Italics. Never fail to act like a tonic on a moribund paragraph. Italicise any word (*any* word) in the last sentence, and your worries are over. What had been numb with inanity will look fresh and sensitive. Literary critics should pay special attention: 'His work communicates, from first to last, an impression of having been lived through and suffered with. Although it treads the rigid paths of logic, there is anguish between the lines. It has the *ravaged* look of all great polemic.' Or, to take a more complex instance: 'Wordsworth was not only a good *poet*, but also—and in a very real sense—a *good* poet.'

Vocal italics, of course, are the heart and backbone of TV oratory, to which they can often lend the appearance of deliberate, consecutive thought: 'The *kind* of thing I'm getting at isn't really very *new*. It's *old*; as old as *time*. I'm looking for a *basis*—a basis of *endeavour*—on which, in a spirit of *co-operation* . . .' This will later be described as 'a bold but considered declaration of faith in the workings of democracy'.

9. The Hyphen. Seen at its best in such triumphantly cryptic phrases as 'the new-old sophistication of baroque' or 'the curious classical-romantic quality of Fiesole'. (If queried, explain that you didn't have space enough to develop the idea.)

10. The Capital Letter. Old friends are best: this still comes in handy for the writer wishing to imply enormous respect for certain jumbo-size abstractions (e.g. Death, Nation, Dark Gods) which he would prefer not to define. Here is an opportunity well taken: 'The poet's task is to disentangle the frail, perishable sinews of Beauty, and to plait them into the durable vine that is called Art.' In a limited edition you might even get away with 'Poet'.

Note: the difference between pride and Pride is pride.

That seems to cover most of the ground. Quite intentionally, I have left one gaping omission. It concerns the least versatile symbol of all. There is no joy in discussing the single, unalterable function of the full stop.

(1953)

Confessions of a Bayswater Playboy

(We are printing this article as a public service. It is not for the squeamish, nor the complacent. It is the uncensored story of an addict. It DOESN'T *pull its punches. It* DOESN'T *shirk issues with mealy-mouthed hypocrisy.* BUT IT *DOES* REVEAL THE EXISTENCE OF A DEEP-ROOTED SOCIAL EVIL WHICH WILL SHOCK THE CONSCIENCE OF EVERY DECENT MAN AND WOMAN.)

Until I reached the age of six they were just a phrase to me. A healthy, contented child, how could I know, as I played in the nursery, that they would soon come to dominate my whole waking life? My first 'contact' was my governess, who left one of them unguarded in the bathroom, no doubt imagining that if I found it I would tear it up or make a hat of it. But instead, such is human frailty, I read it. I recall to this day the mingled horror and fascination with which I opened *my first Sunday paper.*

It seemed so harmless at first. There, above a photograph of a wrecked air-liner, ran my first headline: 'IT WAS OH-SUCH-A-HEAVENLY DAY!' But almost at once the drug began to work. A warm, impersonal glow suffused my being. Avidly, uncontrollably, I read on, through 'WE ARE MAKING A MESS IN SIAM: A WARNING,' through 'FLOORS CLEANER, SOONER, THE WAXOLITE WAY,' feeling a new sensation of power and certainty with every page. I began to walk on air; I seemed to be patting life on the head, as if it were a pet dog. By the time I had got to the letter signed ' "Lacing-'Em-Up," Broadstairs', I had become, in the jargon of the traffickers, 'a loyal reader'. I was 'real gone'. *The air around me, the very words I spoke, seemed to be made entirely out of Sunday papers.*

When next Sunday came round I was already beyond all moral restraints. I stole the thick, folded wads of telltale grey-flecked newsprint from the breakfast-table before my parents were awake, and devoured them, par by par, in my playpen. Other narcotics meant nothing to me. Gone was all interest in toys and games. When the 'kick' had subsided I hung listlessly about the house, mouthing half-remembered phrases: 'LOST LEG AT OMDURMAN, NOW WASHES BOTTLES'. But inside me was a growing sense of superiority to the rest of men. No secret was hidden from me. 'I Knew 'Em All! Behind-the-Scenes Revelations of the Model Railway Racket'. I was borne up on clouds of god-like common sense. 'Turn It Up, Pablo! An Open Letter to an Exhibitionist'.

Courage was mine: nothing shocked or surprised me. 'IT ISN'T PRETTY, IS IT? This picture, showing Assyrian bandits impaled on shashliks (native scythes), isn't meant to be. We publish it as a reminder. The arm in the foreground was left rotting for days while jungle dogs sniffed at it. It couldn't happen here . . . Or could it?' It could, it could, I exulted. Nothing was impossible, because everything was a public service. Curled up on the nursery carpet, peering nervously over my shoulder at the door, I marched breast forward and faced the future unafraid. 'Let this much be said. The men of Harwell may take heart. Theirs is a heritage fraught with glory. They have pulled us through before. And in spite of the appeasers, the cowards and the worry-mongers, they will do so again.' Again I had the old 'glow', the old 'floating' sensation, the old, unreal 'lift'.

By the time I left school I was needing more than just the mild 'bounce' of two or three Sunday prints. I went out to a peddler on the corner to buy more and more of the stuff, always in tabloid form. Soon I knew how it felt to be, as the vipers say, 'in touch'. 'Eyebrows were raised at the £4,000 romp given by Prince Ahmed of Dhan in honour of the Serbian Ballet when noted Mayfairite Glynn Eastern showed up in tartan trews. He should have known better. My sympathy was with the cove who hauled off and kicked him in the seat of his much-publicised pants. I invite readers of this column to join my Politesse Club, and put the weirdies where they belong, in the pillory. Postcards only, please, to Good Taste, Sunday ——, E.C.4.' After reading that, I felt good inside, almost as if I had been flattered. I felt like E. R. Shrewsbury, whose skin had been cleansed the Pore-Salvo Way. I was 'right-thinking, man'!

As long as I could procure my weekly injections I did not even mind if they came wrapped up in culture: all sense of shame was gone. 'The Week's Reviews: *Month in the Country*—wordy, overlong playlet about rustic goings-on in old Russia, which even the combined talents of Athene Swift and Pallas Yatterley can't rescue from boredom.' With a dazed stare in my eyes I would bury my head in the text, the better to savour its aroma. Feebly, I basked in illusions of authority. It was at this period that I began to lose my memory: time became a meaningless blur. 'Screen bad-girl Robina Pale wolfed a lunchtime bite of lobster at an exclusive Mayfair restaurant and wailed: "I want to be good!" ' Years (or was it hours?) later I read: 'Robina Pale, filmland's favourite good-girl, uncrossed her eyes at a Knightsbridge party last week and pertly confessed: "I'm tired of being goody-good!" ' All names, any name, would do to give me my 'take-off' into bliss. 'Up-and-coming 32-year-old starlet Vanessa Vore had the shock of her life when she returned to her Earl's Court flatlet last Tuesday night to find Mum and Dad, whom she hadn't seen for twenty-three years, sitting down to a champagne supper. Occasion was Vanessa's birthday. Footnote: the shapely, green-eyed ex-waitress later confided: "I wept buckets".' I began to identify myself with the middlemen who purveyed the drug. When Bibberley Nibbles said 'I'M SICK TO DEATH OF MAGDA'S MARRIAGES', I too felt real physical nausea.

At this stage I noticed in myself another symptom of addiction. *I seemed to be writing the Sunday papers as well as reading them.* I used to recite them aloud. 'Do not be deceived by surfaces,' I would croon, 'the true man is beneath, and it may be he who is the companion you and your heart are seeking for. This impetuousness of which you speak is mere dross and show. Give him time and let him have his knife back.' Wisdom was mine, as well as courage. 'Aries: Too much borrowing on no security will get you into debt. Leo: Bad judgment may cause mistakes later in the week. Virgo: A clear head will be a valuable asset. Pisces: Financial matters will be more or less important. Gemini: Do not cross roads blindfold.'

Even when cut off from his regular supply, the true 'reader' can achieve the same, if not greater, euphoria by means of a letter to the editor. I shall never forget the voluptuous exhilaration of seeing my first effort in print: 'Thanks for your exposé on the so-called sport of kings, bullfighting. There has been enough nonsense about this degrading subject. Your picture shows clearly that the self-styled "bull" is no bigger than a large cocker spaniel.' I signed myself 'Soccer Fan, Leeds.' I knew, then, that I had crossed the border and become an initiate, or 'writer', as they are sometimes known. After that I could not stop. Under another alias ('Chin-Up', Stepney) I wrote: 'I collect pictures of people with smiles on their faces. I have three thousand six hundred to date, neatly pasted into seventeen albums. I find my strange hobby a great comfort.'

Life by now was just one orgiastic Sabbath after another. Unable to distinguish between fact and fiction, truth and fantasy, news and advertisements, I read the serials as if they were real-life narratives. 'What has Happened: Fleeing from ill-treatment at the hands of her Moorish masters, the slave-girl Mazeppa journeys to Samarkand, bearing on her slim shoulders a barrel of Thuf, priceless dye. Exhausted, she arrives at Kubal where the station-master sees that her finger-nails have been burned off, caste-mark of the Chosen Ones of Fear. In an instant, careless of convention, she is astride the Khan's heavy, bejewelled charger.' In my poor, whirling brain, Mazeppa was mixed up with the luxury flatlets of Lancaster Gate, with Vanessa Vore (heavy, bejewelled starlet), with the Mess in Siam; and she liked Phoon because she liked her hair, and because Phoon knew *how* she liked it—soft, sure of itself, and sun-kissed. Behind all those 'dubious adverts that have crept back into a certain shop window near Cambridge Circus' I saw Mazeppa's face, covered in Thuf, rioting in profusion . . . I began to feel dizzy. Hallucinatory dreams, as ghastly in their way as The Ghastly Story of Hull, obsessed me day and night. On a weekly outlay of less than two shillings I had sold my life into servitude.

Voluntarily, I committed myself to a rest home. Since then I have come face to face with reality. Deprived of access to the stuff and forbidden to 'write', I have no feelings, no opinions, no capacity for consecutive thought. In my delirium, they tell me, I occasionally scream 'Footnote!' or 'Now mark this!'; and at the height of the fit I toss from side to side, sobbing: 'King Zog—A Vicious Smear!' But when conscious I am not even capable of a frank and outspoken statement of the facts about timber. I have become a burden to society.

In my case the 'cure' has proved to be more terrible than the disease. After six months' incarceration I have lost everything—my unswerving regard for the truth, my sensible impatience with the long-haired crew, my conviction that now is the time for plain speaking. I am a pitiful spectacle, a wreck of a man. I behave like a child, laughing when things amuse me, weeping when they depress me. I spend hours alone in the open air, and I have developed an irrational love of bridge. I even enjoy the conversation of friends. I HAVE BECOME, IN SHORT, A MODERN SAVAGE.

(1953)

Lady Chatterley's Trial (*The Old Bailey, 20 October–2 November 1960*)

'My sex is me as my mind is me, and nobody will make me feel shame about it.'—*D. H. Lawrence.*

Now that the case is over, and Lady Chatterley's adventures are speeding two-hundred-thousand-fold to every outpost of literacy in the country, it seems suddenly unthinkable that the jury could have brought in any other verdict. But it was desperately thinkable right up to three o'clock on Thursday afternoon, as anyone knows who sat through the six days of the trial, and sweated out the dragging hours of the jury's retirement; more than most people, Gerald Gardiner knew it, and looked the reverse of optimistic as he prowled up and down like a wounded lion, waiting for those twelve inscrutable citizens to come to their conclusion.

How we had all stared at them, seizing on each smile, each sniffle, each sign of inattentiveness as evidence of sympathy or hostility to Lawrence's cause! The lean, middle-aged man at the righthand end of the back row seemed prematurely grey: did this betoken sensitivity or hyper-sensitivity? And the quietly eccentric behaviour of the woman upstage right left many of us baffled; she was given to strange, secret smiles, and would take notes at inexplicable moments; a quick, intense burst of scribbling, for instance, followed the information that one of the witnesses had been educated at Tonbridge School.

In front of her sat a younger woman, sedate and pretty, perhaps a teacher; some of us pictured her as the Henry Fonda character whose gentle persistence would finally win over her colleagues, as in *Twelve Angry Men*.

But against this hope, and against the waves of pro-Lawrence partisanship that flooded the court from the public gallery, stood the unanimous opinion of the professional crime reporters that acquittal was impossible: 'They'll never swallow those words,' as one of them put it, with a kind of cynical smugness that seems, even in memory, peculiarly detestable.

Nor, as we waited, could we forget the summing-up of a judge who, throughout the trial, had displayed no uncontrollable impatience to get the book into the shops. A slight old gentleman with a mild, dry voice, resembling beneath the scarlet weight of his robes some relict of feudal Japan, Mr Justice Byrne could not be accused of having loaded the dice in favour of the defence.

One remembered the tone, discreetly incredulous, of his interjections; as when he had asked Richard Hoggart to repeat the phrase 'virtuous, if not puritanical', and had written it down with eyebrows eloquently raised; or when he had put to another witness the question: 'Is there really anything else in this book except adultery?' And his summing-up, with its reminder to the jury (it was almost a sigh that the world today seemed to be full of academic experts, struck the same note of weary bewilderment that must have been heard from the bench when first the psychologists and psychiatrists strode into the courts to confuse plain men with their theories.

Here were professors, critics, editors and poets, standing up in the box to deliver lectures on the nature of literature, clouding the air with semantic evasions, expressing opinions instead of stating facts, and thus dissolving the fabric of concrete truth on which the world of law was founded when it first began. No sooner had one witness dubbed Lawrence a puritan than another would claim him for Catholicism, only to see someone else haul him back, minutes later, into the Protestant camp. Nothing was simple any more; at the Old Bailey, where matters of indecency and obscene behaviour had traditionally been settled by police-men and doctors, respectable men and women were talking about sex as if it were something sacred.

It must have seemed to Mr Justice Byrne that chaos was come again; no wonder he felt the need to recall the jury to sanity, to tell them that their views counted for more than those of the experts, to remind them that this was a Christian country, and to ask them rhetorically whether they perceived 'any spark of affection' between Lady Chatterley and her lover. He urged them not to get lost 'in the higher realms of literature', but to think of factory girls, reading the book in their lunch hour—a social group for whom he, like the prosecuting counsel, showed a tender, recurrent regard.

This protectiveness overflowed into his exposition of the new obscenity laws. The jury had first to decide whether or not the work tended 'to deprave and corrupt'; if they concluded that it did, they must go on to consider whether its publication could be justified as being 'for the public good' on the grounds of its literary and other merits. It was hereabouts, perhaps, that the vision of those corruptible factory girls, those hitherto innocent lunch hours, passed once more across the judge's mind, prompting him to impress on the jury that, while the expert testi-mony should be given due weight, the essence of the Act was contained in four words: 'for the public good'. He detached the phrase from its context, dwelling on it with affectionate iteration, so that one almost forgot that this emphasis, if heavily enough applied, would tilt the new Act towards meaningless fantasy; for a few mad moments, it seemed as if the only point at issue were whether it would be 'for the public good' to publish books that tended 'to deprave and corrupt'.

These and other passages from the summing-up haunted us as we waited; we recalled, for example, the judge's failure to mention, in his survey of the defence witnesses, a name that had echoed thrillingly down the corridors of the Old Bailey on the trial's third morning—Edward Morgan Forster, who had bowed most courteously to the bench before declaring, in prose of the greatest fastidiousness, that certainly Lawrence belonged in the puritan tradition, where his fellows were Bunyan and Blake.

We also remembered the persistence with which both judge and prosecutor had hammered it home that Lady Chatterley was an immoral woman, that she had had sexual relations before marriage, that she had committed adultery under her husband's roof; as if these charges somehow disqualified her from participation in serious literature. Indeed, there were long periods of the trial during which an outsider might well have assumed that a divorce case was being heard; and it often seemed that the Crown was labouring under the same misapprehension, intensified by spasms of uncertainty as to whether the defendant was Constance Chatterley or Frieda von Richthofen. Over much that we heard hung the ancient fallacy that a book whose characters behave 'immorally' is therefore an immoral book; and the further fallacy that an immoral book is by definition an obscene book.

These confusions were inadvertently compounded by some of the defence witnesses, who went rather far in their eulogies of the book's ethical value; and by others who, while confining themselves to its literary merit, seemed unaware that the stress nowadays laid on the moral content of literature is something imperfectly understood by the average legal mind, to which morality means only Victorian morality. It is significant of the modern critical climate that not once in the trial was the word 'aesthetics' mentioned.

We consoled ourselves, as we kept our vigil outside the jury-room, by concentrating on the good, encouraging episodes, and banishing the bad ones. Apart from Mr Forster, we singled out Helen Gardner, bright-eyed and downright, who briskly explained that since the act of sex was not shameful, neither was the word that described it; and Rebecca West, surely a potent name, although the lady's manner, at once firm and rambling, did not always make for perspicuous communication.

We had Walter Allen and Raymond Williams, both splendidly unflappable; Stephen Potter, impressive in the unaccustomed role of Lawrence scholar; and Cecil Day Lewis, as dapper in mind as in bearing. We had the Bishop of Woolwich and the Headmaster of Alleyn's; from the latter pair of witnesses alone, must it not have seemed to the official custodians of our morals that the whole world was ganging up on them?

And there was always, indomitably, Gerald Gardiner, that rock among silks and monument to unassertive sanity, whose final address had left no weakness in the Crown's case unprobed, from its implicit snobbism in the matter of factory girls to its total lack of supporting testimony. Mr Gardiner had coined phrases, too; there was, he said, 'a high breathlessness about beauty that cancels lust'; and he had managed to restate, without boring us, the novel's twin themes—the danger that industrialisation would destroy human relationships, and the consequent need to affirm the supremacy of instinct over intellect.

Yet had he, perhaps, presented his case with too little passion? For in all our ears there still rang the voice of Mervyn Griffith-Jones, counsel for the prosecution, high-cheek-boned and poker-backed, a veteran of Eton, Trinity Hall, the Coldstream Guards and many previous obscenity cases; a voice passionate only in disdain, but barbed with a rabid belief in convention and discipline; a slow, scaly voice, listening to which one almost felt that if Penguin Books were acquitted, the prostitutes would dance in the streets, as they did after Oscar Wilde's conviction.

On Lawrence as a literary artist, the voice (for so I think of Mr Griffith-Jones, since from where I sat only his head was visible)—the voice had done some dedicated homework. 'Is that expert, artistic writing?' it would ask, having cited a passage in which a phrase was several times repeated. The mind's eye saw a man holding up one brick after another and demanding: 'Is that expert, artistic architecture?' The voice marked Lawrence as if he were an examination paper, and its interrogations had much in common with *vivas*.

It exhaled class-consciousness as effortlessly as air. Would the jury wish their servants to read Lawrence's novel? And was it natural for the lady of a great house to 'run off and copulate with her husband's game-keeper'? The voice took on a positively vengeful rasp when cross-examining people who distinguished between sex as Lawrence saw it and sex as a trivial diversion. Wasn't it true that by 'tenderness' the book actually meant tenderness towards the genital organs? (One wondered how else the voice would want them treated.) And could anyone deny that in the 'bouts' of love-making the emphasis was on the 'pleasure and satisfaction' involved? Leisurely and deadly, the voice hounded Connie Chatterley, a traitress to her class in that she not only enjoyed sex, but enjoyed it with a quasi-peasant. Apropos of a passage in which she removes her nightdress before making love, the voice enquired why this 'strip-tease' was necessary; one assumed, charitably, that the question had been carelessly phrased. Throughout the trial, one longed for a witness who might challenge Mr Griffith-Jones in Lionel Trilling's words:

I see no reason in morality (or in aesthetic theory) why literature should not have as one of its intentions the arousing of thoughts of lust. It is one of the effects, perhaps one of the functions, of literature to arouse desire, and I can discover no ground for saying that sexual pleasure should not be among the objects of desire which literature presents to us, along with heroism, virtue, peace, death, food, wisdom, God, etc.

But nobody made that answer; and we, anxious in the corridors, had all but persuaded ourselves that no jury could withstand the impact of Mr Griffith-Jones (whom Roland Culver should play in the movie), when the verdict was returned and Lawrence exonerated.

Looking back, I think I can isolate the crucial incident, the exchange wherein the case was psychologically won. It occurred on the third morning during the testimony of Richard Hoggart, who had called Lawrence's novel 'puritanical'. Mr Hoggart is a short, dark young Midland teacher of immense scholarship and fierce integrity. From the witness box he uttered a word that we had formerly heard only on the lips of Mr Griffith-Jones; he pointed out how Lawrence had striven to cleanse it of its furtive, contemptuous and expletive connotations, and to use it 'in the most simple, neutral way: one fucks'. There was no reaction of shock anywhere in the court, so calmly was the word pronounced, and so literally employed.

'Does it gain anything,' asked Mr Gardiner, 'by being printed "f——"?' 'Yes,' said Mr Hoggart, 'it gains a dirty suggestiveness.'

Rising in cross-examination, Mr Griffith-Jones wanted to know what Mr Hoggart meant by 'puritanical', receiving an answer to the effect that a puritan was a man who felt a profound sense of responsibility to his own conscience. Counsel then read out a series of excerpts from the novel. It must have been by chance that he chose the most impressive passages, the most solemnly ecstatic, the ones about 'the primeval roots of true beauty' and 'the sons of men and the daughters of women'; but slowly, as he recited them, one realised that he genuinely thought them impure and revolting. With every defiling inflection he alienated some part of his audience, seemingly unaware that what he had intended for our scorn was moving us in a way he had never foreseen; yet still he continued, bland and derisive, utterly unconscious of his increasing loneliness. Having finished, he triumphantly asked the witness whether a puritan would feel such 'reverence for a man's balls'. 'Indeed, yes,' said Mr Hoggart, almost with compassion.

I remembered his earlier reply to the suggestion that Lady Chatterley's affairs with Mellors was due solely to her husband's impotence. '*It is not*,' he said: and in those words we heard, for the first time in the trial, the stubborn, uncompromising voice of the radical English moralist. Its volume and assurance grew as the cross-examination proceeded; and before long both jury and audience knew that the real battle had at last been joined—between all that Hoggart stood for, and all that Griffith-Jones stood for; between Lawrence's England and Sir Clifford Chatterley's England; between contact and separation; between love and death.

Command Performance

On 5 May 1960 I paid my first visit to Washington, D.C. It was long overdue; I remember chiding myself as I stepped off the early plane from New York, for although I had been working as an English journalist in America for more than eighteen months, I had somehow never found time for a trip to the Capital. I was glad of a chance to repair the omission, the more so because I planned to return to my London home at the month's end, and the opportunity might not repeat itself. The day was hot and blue, and the city looked green and gracious through the windows of the airport taxi. Fairer weather could not be imagined for sightseeing; and, my wits contentedly numbed by a tranquillising tablet, I had almost forgotten the purpose of my journey when my lawyer, who had travelled with me from New York, leaned forward and told the driver to pull up at the main entrance of an imposing, characterless office block that lay just ahead of us.

'That's the new Senate Office Building,' he said. We entered it together. I straightened my tie and buttoned my jacket, in the breast pocket of which was a subpoena I had received, about eight days before, instructing me to present myself for questioning before the Internal Security Sub-committee of the United States Senate.

Since November 1958 I had been employed as the Broadway drama critic of *The New Yorker*—a post that had been offered me, to my flattered amazement, shortly after the lamented death of its former occupant, Wolcott Gibbs. At that time I was reviewing plays for the London *Observer*, whose editor generously allowed me to accept the offer and spend two theatre seasons in New York. I was no stranger to America; annually, since 1951, I had crossed the Atlantic to inspect the current Broadway crop and report on its merits in the English press.

When I responded to *The New Yorker*'s summons, I brought with me to Manhattan a profound and sympathetic curiosity about America, an American wife, and a small daughter bearing an American passport. Also, and inevitably, I brought with me a bundle of convictions about life in general, and the chances of its continued existence on this endangered planet. I was (and am) a supporter of the British Labour Party; I endorsed (and endorse) the Campaign for Nuclear Disarmament; and I took part in the inaugural trudge of protest to the Atomic Weapons Establishment at Aldermaston. Halfway across the Atlantic, aboard the *Ile de France*, a Midwesterner who was one of my table companions asked me almost rhetorically whether I believed in 'socialised medicine'; and, when I said I did, inquired much less rhetorically whether I had told that to the editor of *The New Yorker*, and whether I didn't think somebody ought to inform him. He was not smiling; but I am afraid I smiled, rightly judging that the editor would consider my private opinions none of his business. During my stay with the magazine, many minor changes in my copy were suggested. Nearly all of them had to do with grammar, syntax, and redundancies; none was political.

To turn out a weekly theatre piece is not, unless you are Flaubert, a full-time job; and I was delighted when Associated Television—one of the largest organisations in British commercial TV—invited me to produce for them a programme on the general topic of American nonconformity. What especially allured me about the project was that it might enable me to crack, if not splinter, a fallacious image of American life that had become rooted in many good English minds during the McCarthy era—namely, the idea that America was a monolithic stronghold of sameness, peopled by faceless organisation men. My own experience had taught me that this notion was absurd; I knew that the country abounded in dissidents of all kinds; and this was as it should be in a nation that was founded, after all, on the right to dissent.

Hence I embraced the job, and flew to London in the summer of 1959 to compile, after exhausting debates with my employers, a list of articulate and representative American nonconformists. The programme was filmed that fall—in New York, San Francisco, and Los Angeles— with an exiguous budget, a crippling schedule, and a cast necessarily restricted to people who were both willing and available at the time of shooting. In January of this year the show was transmitted in England under the title of *We Dissent*; a late-night, ninety-minute cultural gesture, it consisted of statements made by twenty-odd lively American mavericks on the state of nonconformity in general and the nature of their own nonconformity in particular.

Dissent in the arts was supported by Norman Mailer, Jules Feiffer, Alexander King, Mort Sahl, and a clutch of Beat Generation boys, including Allen Ginsberg, Bob Kaufman, and Lawrence Ferlinghetti. Norman Cousins excoriated the nuclear arms race; Kenneth Galbraith summarised his qualms about the affluent society; the Reverend Maurice

McCrackin explained why he chose imprisonment rather than pay income tax for military purposes; and there were cogent contributions from Norman Thomas, Robert Hutchins, and C. Wright Mills.

America being by definition the greatest capitalist country on earth, it followed that Socialism and dissent would frequently be allied. Accordingly, I also included one admitted member of the Communist party (Arnold Johnson); and four speakers reputedly linked with the extreme Left—Clinton Jencks, of the Mine, Mill, and Smelter Workers' Union; the Reverend Stephen Fritchman of the Unitarian Church; Dalton Trumbo, the Hollywood screen writer; and Alger Hiss, to demonstrate that even a man who had been imprisoned for giving perjured testimony about alleged espionage activities could still speak his mind freely in America. Apart from Mr Trumbo, none of them came out with any specifically Socialist opinions, unless you count Mr Jencks's suggestion that the formation of a labour party, on the English model, would be a good thing for American politics. After lengthy discussions with the production staff of Associated Television, we decided to exclude American dissenters of the extreme right, such as Senator Barry Goldwater, William F. Buckley, Jr, and the Imperial Wizard of the Ku Klux Klan. Their participation, it was felt, might have caused British viewers to construe the programme as a slanted piece of anti-American propaganda.

The British press reaction to the show was generally enthusiastic, though a few critics animadverted on the camera work, and several more expressed their amazement at the distressing mildness of American dissent. The response in America, where the show had not been seen, was much more emphatic. A number of Southern newspapers dubbed it subversive, and the New York *Daily News*, in an editorial headed 'Here are Your Hats, Gentlemen', charged the participants with fouling their own nests, and urged them to hop aboard the next boat to England, Russia, or China. Immediately afterward, Messrs Cousins, Hutchins, and Thomas wrote to me, protesting against the context in which I had placed them; and I received a letter from Benjamin Mandel, formerly the business manager of the *Daily Worker* and now the research director of the Senate Internal Security Sub-committee, asking for a full transcript of the programme.

I told Mr Mandel that the transcript belonged to Associated Television, whither I advised him to direct his request. I assume that it was granted, because on 25 February 1960 a fully documented attack on the programme was delivered on the floor of the Senate by Senator Thomas J. Dodd, the Vice-Chairman of the Internal Security Sub-committee and an ex-employee of the FBI. To say that the Senator spoke with feeling would be to do him less than justice; he spoke with the fiercest sort of retributory zeal. He described *We Dissent* as 'a fraud' and 'a prime example of the kind of irresponsible criticism that undermines the Western alliance'; he also condemned its 'outrageously one-sided nature', and a condensed version of the script was reprinted, at his petition, in the Congressional Record. A copy of his speech was sent to me (by whom I know not), and I foolishly consigned it, duly read, to the wastepaper basket. It nettled me, of course, but I took it in a spirit of fair comment, and assumed that there the subject would end. I could not, as it turned out, have been wronger.

Later in the spring of 1960 I received a letter from a fledgling organisation called 'The Fair Play for Cuba Committee', asking me whether I would lend my name to a forthcoming advertisement in the *New York Times* that was intended as a rebuttal of the incomplete and frequently inaccurate accounts of the Cuban revolution that were then appearing in the American press. (I had written, for the January issue of a national magazine, an article about Havana that mentioned Fidel Castro sympathetically; hence, I imagine, the appeal for my signature.) The ad cited, and factually disputed, a number of tendentious remarks about Castro's regime that had been printed in *Newsweek*, *U.S. News and World Report*, and the New York *Journal-American*. It went on to state that Castro's purpose was 'to give Cuba back to the Cubans', and concluded by emphasising the need for full and unbiased reportage. Having assured myself that the factual points made in the ad were valid, I appended my autograph to the list, which included Jean-Paul Sartre, Simone de Beauvoir, Truman Capote, Norman Mailer, James Baldwin, and half-a-dozen others, of whom I had not heard.

Soon afterward the ad hit print. I do not think it gave much aid or comfort to America's enemies, although I have no doubt that it offended a great many American companies whose Cuban interests were being imperilled by Castro's social upheaval. *Time* magazine took a swift and lofty swipe at the signatories; but I noted with pleasure a quotation in the same publication from a speech by Herbert L. Matthews, a senior member of the *New York Times*' editorial board. 'I have never,' said Mr Matthews, 'seen a big story so misunderstood, misinterpreted, and badly handled as the Cuban revolution.' Consoled by Mr Matthews, I stopped fretting and returned to the familiar task of explaining to the readers of *The New Yorker* the nature and quality of the live entertainment available in the immediate neighbourhood of Times Square.

I was leaving my apartment *en route* for the theatre (the date was 27 April) when a little man emerged from the elevator and thrust into my hand an envelope containing a subpoena from the Senate Internal Security Sub-committee. It commanded me to appear in Washington about forty hours later, and it was blank in the section that called for a statement of the subject matter with which the investigation was concerned.

My first response was bewilderment, and my second dread—the kind of nebulous chill that besets all of us when the finger of officialdom points straight in our direction. Economic fears swelled up; supposing I was publicly smeared, would my American earnings be jeopardised? And how could I answer the committee's questions without fatally compromising my integrity? I cancelled the theatre and phoned a lawyer, who wired the committee and successfully demanded a postponement of eight days. They were, without question, the strangest and shakiest eight days of my life. I put through a call to the British Embassy in Washington, and asked whether a Senate committee was entitled to subpoena a visiting foreign journalist; I was told that anyone—of whatever nationality—could be summoned to Washington as soon as he set foot on American soil. It was just my bad luck, I gathered, that I happened to be the first non-resident alien ever to have been Congressionally subpoenaed. I then called an English correspondent, stationed in Washington. He was scarcely more encouraging.

'They've never done this to a European journalist before,' he said, 'but there's no reason why they shouldn't. They could subpoena the *Pravda* man if they wanted to. And frankly, old chap, it's hard enough to be liberal out here without people like you coming along and sticking your necks out.'

Had I been, perhaps, prematurely international in my approach? I talked to the editor of *The New Yorker*, who was superficially unperturbed, though below the surface he was clearly a little rattled, as I gathered from his pleasure when I told him that my hearing was to be held *in camera*. Private interrogations are like auditions; if the performer shows signs of star quality (i.e., if his leanings towards Communism are distinct and provable), he is usually recalled for a public session. Finally, I telephoned Norman Mailer to find out if he had received a subpoena. He hadn't, and was somewhat irked that he hadn't. At his request, I asked my lawyer why he had been overlooked. 'Well, for one thing,' he replied, 'Mailer isn't employed by anyone.' In other words, he had no job to lose.

On 3 May, two days before my appearance in Washington, George Sokolsky of the *Journal-American* devoted his whole column to excerpts from my television show, linked by comments expressive of his puzzlement and disgust. He did not mention me by name; nor have I any idea how he gained access to the transcript. Twenty-four hours later he returned to the assault, quoting from C. Wright Mills and Alger Hiss, and professing never to have heard of Jules Feiffer. His last sentence was: 'Whoever picked this gang did not know America, but I shall give you more of this.' But he never did. The next day was May 5, the date of my trip to Washington. Instead of naming and blasting me, as I had anticipated, he wrote a piece about college girls and their place in society. I cannot escape the suspicion that, in some crucial, irreparable way, I let Mr Sokolsky down.

Before I ventured into the room in which I was to be quizzed, I had learned a little about the habits, procedures, and history of the Internal Security Sub-committee. I knew that it was ten years old, that its anti-Leftism was virulent, and that it had been prominent in the abortive investigations of Owen Lattimore and the Institute for Pacific Relations. I also knew that it accepted only the Fifth (or self-incrimination) Amendment as a legitimate excuse for refusing to answer its questions; to be mum for any other reason could lead to a citation for contempt of Congress. Not at all idly, I wondered if any other Western democracy had ever entrusted such extraordinary powers to the politicians in its legislature. This sub-committee can call anyone in America to question without stating in advance what the questions are to be about. It can punish lies with charges of perjury, and silence with the threat of imprisonment, unless the witness is willing to declare that, by answering, he might be branding himself a criminal. That such authority should exist outside a court of law struck me at the time (and strikes me still) as highly unconstitutional. Throughout the session, I had to keep reminding myself that I was not in England. The task was not overwhelmingly difficult.

The room in Washington was cool and oblong, abutting onto the resonant public chamber. A slim table ran down the middle. When I arrived, with my lawyer, there were assembled the sub-committee's attorney, a florid, genial man named Jules Sourwine; a couple of secretaries; a records clerk; an official stenographer; and the research expert, Mr Mandel. Senator Dodd had not yet arrived, and there were some jocular conversational preliminaries, mainly concerned with the wonderful efficiency of the Senate Office Building's new intercom system. 'The only people we have trouble hearing,' said Mr Sourwine slyly, 'are the witnesses.'

Finally, with no apology, and the most perfunctory greeting, Senator Dodd turned up thirty minutes late and took his place as acting chairman, flushed, frowning, and silver-haired. I identified myself, and was duly sworn in; whereupon the hearing began. The questioning was done mainly by Mr Sourwine, beaming with encouragement, though Senator Dodd leaped in from time to time with supplementaries of his own. We started off on my TV show: Was it not, said Mr Sourwine, expressly designed to hold the United States up to ridicule and contempt? (I should like to quote verbatim, but since I have been forbidden access to the transcript, I must resort to *oratio obliqua*.) I explained that that was not the aim of the programme; that it had been intended to combat the false idea, common in Europe, that America was a land of intellectual conformity. I was then asked how I had contacted such people as Arnold Johnson, Clinton Jencks, and Dalton Trumbo, all of whom, Mr Sourwine said, had been named by sworn witnesses as past or present members of the Communist party (Jencks in testimony before this sub-committee, Trumbo in testimony before this sub-committee, Trumbo in testimony before the House Committee on Un-American Activities). By means of the telephone, I said, and by means of addresses supplied in England. With whom, in England, had I discussed the programme?

This stunned me; it had not occurred to me that the authority of an American committee might extend to England. I replied that I had discussed it with the production staff that had been assigned to me by Associated Television. But what were their names? (Thus Mr Sourwine.) Their names, I pointed out, were listed on the credit titles. In consequence, every one of them was entered into the record; even the cutter of the show may have some very rough questions to answer should he ever apply for an American visa. Again, I was asked to confirm that the show had been slanted in the direction of anti-Americanism. I replied by drawing the subcommittee's attention to the testimony of Professor Eugene Rostow of the Yale Law School, who had been present in the studio throughout the transmission. When it was over, the narrator had asked him whether he thought America should demand a right to reply.

'Oh, not at all, not at all,' he had told the viewers. 'I don't think this programme was unfavourable to America. Of course, it doesn't present the whole story, but it didn't purport to do that. It presented a very interesting and very significant part of the story of American life. . . .'

At this point Senator Dodd broke in, and inquired how I had got on to 'Gene Rostow', who was a friend of his. As untriumphantly as I could, I said that we had telephoned the U.S. Embassy in London and asked them if they could recommend to us a visiting American intellectual whose comments on the show would be informed and impartial. Professor Rostow had been their first choice.

We then moved on to the Cuba advertisement. Hilarity, hereabouts, began to displace dread; such was the calibre of the inquisition that astonished amusement became the only possible response. Had I received money for signing the ad? No. Did I know any of the other signatories? Sartre and de Beauvoir by reputation; Mailer, Baldwin, and Capote, socially. Was I—and it was here that my fear melted into a deep intestinal chuckle—was I aware that President Eisenhower had made a speech in which he stated that the Castro regime was a menace to the stability of the Western hemisphere? No, I was not. And did I think myself justified in holding opinions that openly defied those of the President of the United States? I brooded over this for a long, incredulous moment, and then replied that I was English, and that I had been forming opinions all my life without worrying for a second whether or not they coincided with those of the President of the United States. (Had my wits been active enough, I might have pointed out that Senator Dodd himself, as a Democrat, must sometimes have found himself in the heretical position of having to defy President Eisenhower.)

Utterly unperturbed, Mr Sourwine then flung me a curve ball. Had I or had I not contributed an article to a certain quarterly magazine (which he named, though to avoid libel I had better not)? I said I had. Was I aware that it was notorious as a Communist-front publication? I was not. How had I come to write for it? The editor had called me up, told me that he ran a small-circulation organ of culture and liberal opinion, and invited me to contribute; ever ready to assist embattled little magazines at no inconvenience to myself, I had offered him a thousand words on the current Broadway season. They had previously appeared, I added, in the impeccably non-Communist pages of the London *Observer*; nor had I received (or demanded) any payment for the reprint.

Here, I think, the session would have ended, had I not urged my lawyer to request that there be entered into the record a statement that I had prepared the night before. It ran as follows:

> As an English journalist, I have paid regular annual visits to the United States for the past nine years. I have spent the past two winters here as guest drama critic of *The New Yorker*; during this period I have also been employed by *The Observer*, a London weekly newspaper. I am a visitor to the United States, not an immigrant or a resident alien; nor have I done anything during my stay to belie the statement I made when my visa was first granted —namely, that I am not and never have been a member of the Communist party or of any affiliated organisation. It may be worth

adding that the only organisations to which I pay dues are the Royal Society of Literature, the Critics' Circle, and the Diners' Club. In answering the questions that the committee may put to me, I am perfectly willing to reply to any queries about my activities in the United States; and I have no intention of invoking any of the Amendments to the Constitution. I should like, however, to express my regret that the committee should have seen fit to employ its authority to subpoena a visiting journalist. It has not done so before, to the best of my knowledge; and I respectfully suggest that there may be better ways of demonstrating to the world this country's traditional regard for freedom of speech. Constitutionally, of course, it is within the committee's power to subpoena whom it chooses; I merely submit that governmental grilling of foreign newspapermen is not a practice that one instinctively associates with the workings of Western democracy. It is true that the Soviet government has frequently censured—and sometimes expelled—visiting journalists with whose opinions it disagrees. I can think of several American correspondents to whom this has happened. I leave it to the committee to decide whether this is a wholly desirable precedent.

As I understand it, the function of a Congressional committee is to gather information on the basis of which new legislation may be recommended. I cannot help finding it anomalous that a foreign visitor should be compelled to contribute to the legislative processes of a country not his own. I am profoundly interested in the making of English law; but I am modest enough to feel that the making of American law is none of my business.

After that, I was allowed to quit the chamber. A clerk trotted after me, and asked me to sign a form that would entitle me to claim a witness fee of twelve dollars. His pen contained bright red ink—'No political connotation, of course,' he said tactfully, and was gone. I left the building and lunched with a peppery liberal journalist who has been covering the Washington scene since the thirties. He told me that things had loosened up a lot since McCarthy died, and I think he wondered why I looked so quizzical.

I flew back to New York and to a new hazard, not unconnected (I somehow suspect) with the sub-committee's investigation. The Immigration authorities had discovered a technical oversight in my passport; my permit to work in the United States had accidentally been allowed to expire, and there was a distinct chance that I might be deported. After a lot of effort, inconvenience, and legal consultation, I managed to leave

New York in my own time, on my own terms, and of my own volition. I even contrived to pay my lawyer's bill, which amounted to close on $1,500. On the credit side, I had twelve dollars, plus what Milton called a 'new acquist of true experience from this great event'. I am not sure, however—to pursue the quotation—that I had 'calm of mind'; nor can I say, with any truth, that all my passion was spent.

(1960)

Mencken on Language

To demoralise a bogus highbrow, interview him about bingo and foolproof American gadgets; he will belittle them in lengthy and often influential editorials, whose reliability is jeopardised because we have all progressed far beyond the standpoint he advocates. Apart from *is*, *American* and *gadget* (a British corruption of the French *gachette*, meaning a piece of machinery), every verb, adjective and noun in the foregoing sentence is of American coinage; and most of them were originally denounced as barbaric innovations.

By pointing out facts like these, H. L. Mencken sought to rout the linguistic snobs who regarded American English as a secondclass language, separate from but not equal to British English. In one enormous work (formerly published in three parts, but now compressed into a single volume)*, he set out to define and extol a language that seemed to him not only separate but superior. Against Sydney Smith's ludicrous taunt: 'In the four quarters of the globe, who reads an American book? Or goes to an American play?' he quotes John Adams, second President of the United States: 'England will never more have any honour, except now and then that of imitating the Americans.'

Mencken demolishes the traditional English argument that most Americanisms are good old English expressions that can be traced back to Chaucer and even the Venerable Bede; and he is even more scornful of those American Anglophiles who clung (and still cling) to English usage as a badge of social supremacy. Mencken's heroes are the men who bravely legitimised colloquial American and turned it into literature: Abraham Lincoln, Mark Twain and Ring Lardner. His criterion is always the language as it is spoken, not as it is drilled and disciplined by grammarians and lexicographers. He repeatedly blames the schoolmarms of America for stunting the growth of American English. With tacit endorsement, he cites a dictum of Finley Peter Dunne's famous

* *The American Language*, by H. L. Mencken.

comic character, Mr Dooley: 'When we Americans are through with the English language, it will look as if it had been run over by a musical comedy.'

Today, nearly eight years after Mencken's death, the collision has long since taken place, but neither side can claim a victory. Since the U.S. became a dominant world power, English journalism has been increasingly reluctant to admit transatlantic imports; *sucker, graft* and *cinch* are old and respectable American words, but you will not find them in *The Observer*'s leader columns. At the same time, serious American journalism has become much stricter than ours in its adherence to ortho-dox grammar and syntax. No purer Fowlerian prose exists than that which appears in the *New Yorker*, on whose staff I was carefully instructed that '*which* is appropriate to non-defining and *that* to defining clauses'.

Mencken started to compile his study of American English during the First World War; convinced that the U.S. should remain aloof from European politics, he also felt that the American language should stand apart from its European progenitors. He championed linguistic chauvin-ism in a manner that tended to encourage political isolationism; witness the contemporary Middle West, a profoundly conservative area that has a much greater reverence for 'native American speechways' than the inter-nationally minded Eastern seaboard. Now that American has become an accepted literary language, Mencken has begun to sound brash and parochial, a pamphleteer rather than a historian.

Yet his prose has a crisp, prophetic ring that makes one resent the fussy interventions of Raven McDavid, the Chicago scholar who has—according to the blurb—'performed the double task of updating and condensation'. Mike Nichols, the American comedian, tells me that what irks him most about spoken English is its penchant for blurred, super-fluous words like 'actually' and the last two syllables of 'Can I help you at all?' For my part, I shrink from mass-communication American, where thought is delivered in gift-wrapped parcels, untouched by human mind. And in any language I deplore the whimsical campus pedant. American-isms, says Mencken, 'seldom get anything properly describable as a welcome [save from such small sects of iconoclasts as the Angry Young Men]'. That is Professor McDavid, inside the square brackets. He is a bold editor, unafraid to contradict his author. Mencken defines a *keister* as a suitcase; McDavid, six pages earlier, has no doubt that it means 'a woman's anus'.

Though hired as a condenser, McDavid vastly expands Mencken's notes on the argot of juvenile delinquency and jazz. His errors hereabouts have a wonderful assurance. Cool, he says, is an adjective that chiefly refers 'to restraint in manner of dress'; in fact, it means relaxed or detached in demeanour. 'Sex and drugs', he declares, 'are the main side-interests of the true *cool cats*. . . . Many *cats* have a *hustle* which they *push*.' *Hustle* is an intransitive verb which means to be a whore; *push* is transitive, meaning to sell, and it takes as its object dope.

On jazz, the Professor writes like any ignorant Englishman. A man who plays '*guts* piano' (phrase unknown in jazz circles) is one who 'may make audible visceral grunts. . . .' People who *dig* something are merely 'picking over their own psychic junkpiles in order to salvage some bits of emotional experience unattainable by *squares*'; less romantically but more accurately, to *dig* simply means to relish or appreciate.

Debased etymology of this kind reminds me of an imaginary interview with a jazz musician, recorded some years ago by the San Franciscan wit, Henry Jacobs: 'Well, *dig* is coming from the funerals in New Orleans—the musicians would have to *dig* the graves, because those musicians were poor, you know? . . . And a *kick*, getting a *kick*, is coming again from the old spirituals and blues down South. Sometimes the man who ran the plantation would *kick* the people working there, because they were singing when they should be working in the fields. And that was a *kick*, you know? . . .'

Mencken was fighting a dour and necessary battle. His editor almost loses it for him by a smirk.

(1963)

Fischer on Art

'Art is almost as old as man. It is a form of work, and work is an activity peculiar to mankind.' Thus begins a challenging new paperback* in which Ernst Fischer, the Austrian poet and critic, surveys the whole history of artistic achievement through Marxist eyes.

People have always needed art: but why have they needed it? And what shaped the forms whereby they satisfied their need? Fischer's answers to these questions should be as voraciously studied and debated here as they have been on the Continent.

Art begins as an extension of work; primitive man seeks to master nature by means of tools and magic. Language evolves as a by-product of work, since 'only in work and through work do living beings have much

* *The Necessity of Art*, by Ernst Fischer.

to say to one another'. Magic is the mental equivalent of a tool: a means of influencing and controlling the outside world. The clay figures of beasts found in Middle Stone Age caves exist 'to propitiate the animal world—i.e., to acquire mastery over reality by means of an image.'

Division of labour breaks up tribal society, and class conflict comes into being: the function of the artist-magician, now shared with the priest, is 'to guide individual life back into collective life, the personal into the universal, to *restore the lost unity of man*'.

With the rise of seafaring traders—sovereign adventurers responsible only to themselves, judging products as commodities rather than as objects of use—individualism makes its appearance in the arts: 'The new "I" emerged from the old "we". The individual voice broke away from the chorus.' The process starts with the Greeks and leads up to the full, magnificent blossoming of bourgeois art in the Renaissance and after.

The shock of the Industrial Revolution, presaging a new society, produces the Romantic movement, which shrinks from the machine age and extols the 'organic' as the antithesis of the 'mechanical'. Capitalism takes full control; and Fischer points out that 'only under capitalism has *all* art above a certain level of mediocrity always been an art of protest, criticism and revolt'.

Next we have naturalism, social comment reinforced with documentary detail; but 'there comes a moment of decision when naturalism must either break through to socialism or founder in fatalism, symbolism, mysticism, religiosity and reaction'. Nihilism is likewise suspect:

> We must not overlook the fact that it helps many uneasy intellectuals to reconcile themselves to iniquitous conditions—that its radical nature is often only a form of dramatised opportunism ... [It] can channel revolt into purposelessness and create a passive despair.

Hence it is tolerated by authority, which never objects to the idea that human unhappiness is 'eternal' and irremediable by social change: *vide* Beckett and his school.

As for the relationship between form and content:

> Any ruling class which feels threatened tries to hide the *content* of its class domination and to present its struggle to save an outdated *form* of society as a struggle for something "eternal." ...

In the arts, form tends to be conservative, and content to be revolutionary; it is novelty of content that precedes, demands and imposes novelty of form. As Brecht said: 'Without introducing innovations of a formal kind, literature cannot bring new points of view before the new strata of the public. We build our houses differently from the Elizabethans, and we build our plays differently.'

Fischer sums up in italics: *"Form is social experience solidified."*

This is no monolithic Marxist. He briskly rejects the idea that history and art are wholly governed by economics, quoting Engels to support him:

> According to the materialist view of history, production and reproduction of real life are, *in the last instance*, the determining factor in history. Neither Marx nor I have asserted more than that. If anyone twists this into a claim that the economic factor is the *only* determining one, he transforms our statement into a meaningless, abstract, absurd phrase.

Again, while Fischer prefers art that is consonant with Socialist aims, he concedes that working-class taste has been ruinously blighted by decades of exposure to mass-produced *Kitsch*, and he deplores the Socialist habit of idealising the 'simple' man: 'It is part of the irresistible advance of Socialism,' he says, 'that the "simple" man gradually turns into a subtle and highly differentiated man.'

And what will art be like in a fully Communist world—'when the individual and the collective are no longer in conflict' (as in capitalism), and art is no longer 'a simple means of enlightenment and propaganda' (as in contemporary Socialism)? Fischer predicts the emergence of an infinite variety of styles: 'The differentiation will be between personalities, not classes; between individuals, not social masks. Everything will encourage the interplay of the intimate and the universal. . . .' In the classless community, the individual will be reborn:

> . . . the permanent function of art is to recreate *as every individual's experience* the fullness of *all that he is not*, the fullness of humanity at large. . . . All art has to do with this identification, with this infinite capacity of man for metamorphosis, so that, like Proteus, he can assume any form and lead a thousand lives without being crushed by the multiplicity of his experience. . . . Art as the means of man's identification with his fellow-men, nature and the world, as his means of feeling and living together with everything that is and will be, is bound to grow as man himself grows in stature.

I endorse Fischer's diagnosis of our modern sickness in the arts, though I do not share his conviction that Communism (rather than democratic Socialism) is the only cure. But the book abounds in signs that Fischer is an empirical rather than a doctrinaire Marxist; you never feel that he is tailoring his reactions to fit a thesis. 'A new art,' he says, 'does not come out of doctrines but out of works. Aristotle did not precede . . . Homer, Hesiod, Aeschylus and Sophocles; he derived his aesthetic theories from them.' Marxism has long needed an Aristotle; and in Ernst Fischer I suspect it has found its man.

Meditations on Basic Baroque

The essence of life is the smile of round female bottoms, under the shadow of cosmic boredom. (Guy de Maupassant)

At the age of twelve I saw a trio of *adagio* dancers in a Christmas pantomime at the Prince of Wales Theatre, Birmingham. The girl in the act was nude except for a G-string and a coat of green paint that covered the rest of her body. Her whole get-up transfixed me, but when she turned her back I was hypnotised. In memory, I still am. It was a moment of traumatic pleasure. What follows is no more (but no less) than an attempt at aesthetic rationalisation.

I

Looked at simply as form, as relationship of plane and protuberance, it might be argued that the back view of the female body is more satisfactory than the front. (Sir Kenneth Clark)

I have paid homage on that living altar where the back changes name. (James Joyce: *Ulysses*)

Nowadays the breasts come first in conventional assessments of female beauty; and thus it has been for the last century and a half. Shocked by the vogue for skirts designed to emphasise the rear, the pioneer feminist Mary Wollstonecraft exclaimed in 1792: 'How can a decent woman obtrude that vulgar part of her anatomy on the eye?'

Echoes of her outrage have come ringing down to us across the years. The English language, richer in synonyms for that part of the body than for any other, scarcely named it in print while Victoria was alive; and for a long time after her death euphemisms were preferred to plain speaking. 'Arse' was too plebeian, while 'bottom' (still the right, neutrally descriptive expression: 'the common word exact without vulgarity', in

Eliot's phrase) was too bold for comfort. Instead, we got the arch 'posterior', the evasive 'behind', the breezy 'backside', the coy 'derrière', the anatomical 'buttocks' and the facetious 'fanny'.

Prudery shrank from the bottom because of its proximity to the genital area: the breasts, being well out of the danger zone, remained acceptably aesthetic. When the cinema started to celebrate bottoms (most prominently, those of Marilyn Monroe and Brigitte Bardot), we were told by psychologists that this was merely a case of 'displacement downwards': in other words, the attention normally paid to the breasts had been temporarily switched to a place that happened to have a comparable cleft. Nobody pointed out that the breast-cult might equally well be a case of displacement upwards. The suddenly outswelling downcurve from slim waist to full bottom, its arcs swerving inwards to meet at a peerless erotic crossroads ('ce double trésor,' says a modern French poet, 'au sourire vertical si troublant'), is a uniquely female attribute, in which artists and philosophers as well as lechers have traditionally rejoiced. It is time the tradition was revived.

II

> . . . plump hips for play,
> Set high, well-made, the proper size
> For the jousts of love to utilize.
>> (Francois Villon, translated by Hubert Creekmore)

> How brave a prospect is a broad backside!
> (Henry Vaughan)

First, let us define the subject coolly. My authority is *A Handbook for Art Students* by Arthur Thomson, published in London in 1896.

Hip-width in women, says Thomson, is greater than in man because the female pelvis is broader; moreover, it is tilted forward, thus producing a marked rearward thrust. The major features of the bottom itself are (*a*) the Gluteus Maximus, twin muscular bulges rounded with fat, (*b*) the Great Trochanters, not a high-wire act but the hollows that flank the gluteal muscles, growing deeper when the latter are contracted, and (*c*) the Gluteal Fold, which is the transverse line that separates bottom from thighs. Thomson continues:

> Superiorly, the disposition of the fatty layer over the Gluteus Maximus is different in the two sexes. In women the fat forms a thick pad . . . and thus becomes continuous with the fatty layer which covers the back and side of the flank. In this way the surface forms of the flank and buttocks are blended in one uniform contour.

Anteriorly, the fat of the buttock is distributed in a very characteristic way in the female. It tends to accumulate in considerable quantity on the outer side of the thigh, just below the Trochanters. When in the female fat is present here in undue amount it imparts a clumsy and ungainly appearance. . . . This is particularly liable to occur in female models past their prime, and lends a grossness to the form at variance with the delicacy and refinement displayed in earlier life.

This last comment is a welcome smack in the eye for Rubens, whose galumphing nymphs with overblown rumps I have never been able to cherish. Thomson signs off with a couple of tips on female proportion. Ideally, the length of 'the furrow between the buttocks' should equal half the height of the head from chin to crown, and the width of the hips should be the same as the distance from armpit to armpit, plus the thickness of one arm.

In 1756, at the age of twenty-seven, Edmund Burke brought out his *Philosophical Enquiry into the Origin of our Ideas of the Sublime and the Beautiful.* It has an odd, unintended relevance to our theme. Burke sets out to define the essential qualities of beautiful objects. The first of these is comparative smallness, as opposed to the grandeur of awe-inspiring objects like mountains or cathedrals. The second is smoothness: 'I do not now recall anything beautiful that is not smooth.' The third he calls 'gradual variation', meaning that the shape must avoid straight lines as far as possible, and this leads him into a fourth stipulation: that 'any ruggedness, any sudden projection, any sharp angle' is destructive of beauty. Colours, he adds, should be mild and unglaring, such as 'weak whites' and 'pink reds'.

Later in the treatise he dwells on the tactile pleasure to be derived from globes—especially more than one at a time, so that 'the hand gently rises to one and falls to another; and this pleasure is greatly increased if the globes are in motion, and sliding over one another'. Hail to Edmund Burke, first writer to praise the bottom (which he never mentions) without knowing what he was doing.

III

But shall I tell thee what more thy suit advances?
Thy fair smoothe words? no, no, thy fair smoothe haunches.
(Sir John Harington)

Bottom-worship, according to Krafft-Ebing, is 'among the commonest forms of fetishism'. Its roots belong to that ancient and fortunate era before men learned to separate the erotic impulse from the religious. Primitive idols of femininity usually have a spectacular rearward thrust. Look at the stone-age Venus of Willendorf, whose most imposing feature —to lift a line from Congreve—is 'a jut to her bum would stir an anchorite'. Exaggerated juts are still prized among the Hottentot tribesmen of the Kalahari desert in South-West Africa, who like their women steatopygous—i.e. swollen-buttocked—on a grandiose scale.

History is on their side. 'These two hemispheres,' says the German anthropologist Schertel, 'comprise virtually everything a sexual symbol could contain': they swell, like the male organ, yet are indented, like the female. Schertel then goes off on an etymological rampage. He states (correctly) that the bottom has often been compared to the moon: *la lune* is a euphemism long current in French poetry. He next argues that the Greek *pyge* (buttock) comes from the same root as the Roman god Picus, who represented the moon. Gathering momentum, he claims that the Latin *nates* (buttocks) is linguistically related to *natura* (nature), and the German *Popo* (bottom) to the Russian *popu*, meaning spiritual father, from which we get the word 'Pope'.

By now Schertel is almost airborne. In a final burst of conjecture, he takes off, declaring that the German *Arsch* (arse) has family connections with the Latin *ars* (art), the Greek *arche* (origin) and such remote, impressive ancestor-figures as Iris, the messenger of Zeus, and Eros, the god of love. He concludes: 'One can almost put forward the proposition that all ancient gods of sex and fertility are also gods of the bottom.'

That the Greeks felt that way we know from the moralist Athenaeus, writing in the second century A.D. about the voluptuous habits of former ages. 'So dependent on sensual pleasure were the men of those days,' he says, 'that they actually dedicated a temple to Aphrodite of the Beautiful Buttocks.' He tells of a poor farmer whose two daughters could not decide which of them had the lovelier bottom. To settle the question, they exposed their rumps on the public highway, where a rich young traveller from Syracuse fell in love with one of them so passionately that he came home ill and exhausted. His brother, having heard the story, dashed to the farm and instantly fell in love with the other sister. Despite objections from the boys' father, a double marriage took place, and the girls gratefully spent a slice of their new wealth on building a temple in honour of Aphrodite Callipygos—fair-buttocked Venus.

A statue in Naples bears that name, although there is no evidence to link it with the original tale. It shows a girl raising the rear panel of her robe and peering backwards over her shoulder. 'To conceive of this statue as the object of a religion,' said the German critic and fan Maximilian Ahrem, 'one must think oneself back into a state of simultaneous innocence and lasciviousness. Its curves seem to press themselves into one's hand. What other boon could an acolyte ask of this goddess, as she candidly offers her exquisite rear, than the granting of sensual delight?'

There are potent physical reasons for the bond between bottoms and fertility cults, as anyone can confirm who has read Dr Kinsey's *Sexual Behaviour in the Human Female*. Describing muscular behaviour during sexual play, the report says: 'The most prominent of these muscular activities effect rhythmic movements of the buttocks and of the whole pelvis.... Without the capacity to make these rhythmic movements, mammalian coitus could not occur.' Later we find: 'Movements of vertebral muscles in conjunction with contractions of the gluteal muscles are the chief means by which the pelvis is thrown forward in rhythmic thrusts during copulation'. I.e., the bump and the grind. Finally: 'Not a few females have ... learned that voluntary contractions of their buttocks and movements of the pelvis may develop their erotic reactions and even effect orgasm.'

In passing, I once knew a Polish-American stripper who cracked peanuts between her gluteal muscles as an encore, for all I know effecting orgasm as she did so. Where are you now, sauce-box of West 49th Street?

IV

Your bum is a gorgeous basket brimming with fruits and meat
(from *The Peasant declares his Love* by Emile Roumer,
translated by John Peale Bishop)

In recent years bottoms have made a decisive comeback. You can publicly state, without being stoned or scorned, that they are almost as expressive as faces. There are jubilant bottoms (a French art critic, discussing one of Toulouse-Lautrec's favourite models, recently spoke of 'les fesses riantes de la Goulue'). There are melancholy bottoms, punily sagging; cauliflower bottoms, bulging with muscle and Olympic ambition; impertinent bottoms, up-tilted like breasts; tight-lipped bottoms, puritanically pursed as if denying their identity; gleaming cornucopian bottoms ('Cover her *fesses*; mine eyes dazzle', to pervert Webster's famous line); bottoms flabby as swansdown pillows; and, twice or thrice in a lifetime, assured yet demure, the perfect bottom, that ripe twin pearl or essence of bisected peach. It is nowadays accepted that age withers the bottom much later than the breasts: buttocks are born survivors. And pygophiles everywhere can meet in free assembly to condemn the imprisoning blasphemy of the girdle, which is to the bottom what Stalin was to Communism.

These liberties are new and hard-won. In the last century, Aphrodite Callipygos was forced underground. Her lovers were labelled subversives, and their attempts at guerrilla warfare (flanking movements, perhaps) were branded pornography. One of the last propagandists for pygophilia before Victoria clamped down was T. Bell, M.D. (first name unknown, medical degree doubtful), a forgotten British partisan who published in 1821 *Kalogynomia, or The Laws of Female Beauty*.

A true patriot, Bell begins by insisting that 'the English are the most beautiful people on the globe', citing as his authority Professor Blumenbach of Göttingen ('whose profound science and perfect impartiality no one can doubt'). He is also much-travelled. In France, he says, the prettiest girls come from Marseilles and Avignon; in Spain, from the district near Cadiz; in Portugal, from the town of Guimanarez; and in India, from Lahore and Benares.

Having presented his sensual credentials, Bell moves on to his real purpose, which is to divide women into three groups:

1. Those in whom 'the locomotive organs' (bones, muscles, ligaments) are most highly developed. Type One Woman has a tapering neck, broad shoulders and 'moderately expanded haunches'. It is essential for the thighs to match the haunches in fullness, since otherwise 'a disagreeable vacuity is left between them, and the male loses that smooth and elastic support which is as necessary to the success as to the pleasure of the sexual embrace'. Type One tends to be athletic, and is usually favoured by young men.

2. Those in whom 'the vital organs' (concerned with circulation and secretion, and mostly encased in the trunk) are predominant. Type Two has a luxuriant bosom, and 'THE HAUNCHES are greatly expanded, owing to the vital organs they contain'. This expansion is due to the size of her pelvis. Wide pelvic capacity, according to Bell, is indispensable for 'all those functions which are most essentially feminine—impregnation, gestation and parturition'. Thus a blossoming bottom is an emblem of femininity. In this Type: 'It is a defect, if a REMARKABLE FULLNESS exist not *behind the upper part of the haunches*, and on each side of the lower part of the spine.' Mature men go for Type Two, who walks with 'a soft lateral rolling of the body' (cf. Monroe in *Niagara*).

3. Those ruled by 'the intellectual system'. Type Three has a high forehead, and lacks 'the general embonpoint of the second species'. She has no bottom worth mentioning, and appeals mainly to old men. She walks with a 'a perpendicular rising of the head, at every impulse to step'.

Bell insists that his ideal woman is a mixture of all three types, but his description of the Venus de Medici as a model of female beauty leaves little doubt where his true sympathies lie. In it he focuses on:

> ... the gradual expansion of the haunches, those voluptuous characteristics of the female ... commencing as high as the waist and terminating in the still greater swell of the distinctly separated hips; the flat expanse between these and immediately over the fissure of the hips being relieved by a considerable dimple on each side ...

For more than a century after Bell's work appeared, Anglo-Saxon texts in praise of the bottom were few and clandestine. Like Malcolm in *Macbeth*, though in a slightly different sense, Victorian England firmly declared that: '... there's no bottom, none,/In my voluptuousness.'

In recent decades the ban has been lifted; but although the bottom has now regained much of its old prestige as a sexual target, little has been written about its claim to aesthetic (as distinct from erotic) charisma.

Why *is* the bottom beautiful? In search of a contemporary answer, I ploughed through dozens of books before finding a fertile clue. It turned up at last in *The Second Sex*, by Simone de Beauvoir. 'When woman is given over to man as his property,' says the authoress, 'he demands that she represent the flesh *purely for its own sake*.' (The italics, here and in subsequent quotes from the book, are mine.) This demand, she goes on, is seen at its most naïve in the big-bottomed Venus adored by the Hottentots, 'for the buttocks are the part of the body with fewest nerves, where the flesh seems *an aimless feast*'. And even in civilisations where concepts of form and harmony are cherished, 'the breasts and the buttocks remain favoured objects, because of *their unnecessary, gratuitous blooming*'.

I don't see how the blooming of the breasts can be regarded as unnecessary or gratuitous, since they have a maternal function to perform. But the bottom is another matter. Those tumescent cheeks serve no practical purpose at all; they are a physiological bonus, a pure, gratuitous adornment. (To say that bottoms exist because the human race needs something to sit on is a confusion of cause and effect. It would be truer to say that human beings sit because they have bottoms. After all, the higher apes, who lack our built-in cushions, contentedly squat, and there is no reason why we should not do the same.) The conclusion is obvious. The buttocks are the most aesthetically pleasing part of the body precisely because they are non-functional. Although they conceal an essential orifice, those pointless globes are as near as the human form can ever come to abstract art.

V

The idealisation of the buttocks runs through the whole history of art, which teems with pygophilic representations.

(Schertel)

> Then swing—the round and shining rump
> Like silvern lump she showed me.
> I cried: 'Well done, O mistress mine!
> No more am I in pain for thee!'
>> (from *The Arabian Nights Entertainment*, translated by Sir Richard Burton)

Even a selective guide to bottoms in the arts would occupy a book. All I can offer are a few preferences, and one or two inferences.

1. The dance. Don't be misled by the Black Bottom. Its title refers to the mud of the Mississippi River and has nothing to do with our theme. The Can-Can, which ends with up-flung skirts and out-thrust bottoms, is in the great tradition. Night-club facsimiles that shirk the true finale deserve cat-calls and a point-blank refusal to tip.

2. The movies. Monroe once queened it in a field that has been taken over since her death by Bardot (*vide* Jean-Luc Godard's *Le Mépris*). The most inept and myopic comment on Bardot's bottom comes from Simone de Beauvoir: 'Seen from behind, her slender, muscular dancer's body is almost *androgynous*.' Peripheral attention should be paid to the starlet Vikki Dougan and her rearward-plunging dresses—a style described by her publicists as 'reverse décolletage'.

3. Painting and sculpture. Apart from works already mentioned, I think of the recumbent Hermaphrodite, unearthed in seventeenth-century Rome, restored by Bernini and at present in the Louvre—a perpetual challenge, with its breasts, penis and flamboyantly female bum, to homo and hetero alike. The Rokeby Venus of Velasquez is an irreplaceable act of homage.

We now reach the eighteenth century, and I turn to Sir Kenneth Clark, prince of art historians:

> The Venus of the *dix-huitième* extends the range of the nude in one memorable way: far more frequently than any of her sisters, she shows us her back. ... That the beauty of this aspect was appreciated in antiquity we know from such a figure as the Venus of Syracuse. But the Hermaphrodite and the Venus Callipygos suggest that it was also considered symbolic of lust, and before the eighteenth century the number of female nudes depicted from behind solely on

account of their plastic possibilities was remarkably small. . . . It was Rubens who inspired both Watteau and Boucher. He was a master of the Baroque, and the bottom is a baroque form, harmonising with the clouds and garlands of late baroque decoration.

For the bottom at its most baroque, robustly displayed as a central bispherical feature, consult Watteau's 'Judgment of Paris' and Boucher's nude study of Miss Murphy, prone and plump as she awaits her lover, Louis XV. Many triumphs of the *genre* are either lost or inaccessible, among them Boucher's erotic panels for the royal bedroom, one of which —'L'Attente du Clystère'—was described by Aldous Huxley as 'the most terrific pin-up of the century, perhaps of all time'. For bottom-celebrating sculpture of a slightly later date, visit the Victoria and Albert Museum and gaze at 'The Sleeping Nymph', the last work of Antonio Canova, who died in 1822.

The past hundred years yield an endless list. Bonnard, Degas, Maillol and Rodin spring at once to mind, together with the neglected surrealist primitive, Clovis Trouille. And Picasso, of course: there are several pygophile gems in the famous series of sex-war sketches he drew in the winter of 1953/4. Nor can I omit the great quartet of bronze reliefs, depicting a female nude seen from behind, on which Matisse worked between 1910 and 1930.

4. Poetry. A multitude of sources, from which I choose one. The author is Robert Herrick:

> Now love invites me to survey her thighes,
> Swelling in likeness, like to Chrystall skyes,
> With plump softe flesh, of metall pure and fine,
> Resembling scheildes, both pure and christalline.
> Hence rise those two ambitious hills, that looke
> Into the middle, sweet, sight-stealing Crooke,
> Which, for the better beautifying, shrowds
> Its humble selfe 'twixt two aspiring cloudes.

5. The novel. In modern times I begin with D. H. Lawrence, whose instincts in *Lady Chatterley's Lover* incline rearwards at many crucial moments. Next comes Aldous Huxley, whose later works bear increasingly flagrant marks of pygophilia. In *Ape and Essence* (1949), a science-fiction account of life after World War Three, women are compelled to wear an apron with the word 'NO' on it, a similar patch on either breast, and 'a pair of somewhat larger patches on the seat of their trousers'. A girl engaged in digging a grave bends over, observed from behind by a male fellow-worker:

Close shot of the two prohibitory patches. NO and again NO, growing larger and larger the more longingly he looks. Cupped already for the delicious imagined contact, his hand goes out, tentative, hesitant; then, with a jerk, as conscience abruptly gets the better of temptation, is withdrawn again. . . .

There squirms the puritan sense of guilt at its most acute. In *The Genius and the Goddess* (1955), the shame has died a little, and we have sentences like:

She yawned and, rolling over on her side, turned her back on me . . . the infinitely eloquent back (if you perused it in the dark, like Braille, with your fingertips), of Aphrodite Callipyge.

But of all latterday writers, James Joyce is the most unabashed adorer:

Look. Her beam is broad. She is coated with quite a considerable layer of fat . . . while on her rere lower down are two additional protuberances, suggestive of potent rectum and tumescent for palpation which leave nothing to be desired save compactness. Such fleshy parts are the product of careful nurture.

And what does Leopold Bloom, the protagonist of *Ulysses*, feel as he contemplates the rich panorama of human life?

Satisfaction at the ubiquity in eastern and western terrestrial hemispheres, in all habitable lands and islands explored and unexplored . . . of adipose posterior female hemispheres, redolent of milk and honey and of excretory sanguine and seminal warmth, reminiscent of secular families of curves of amplitude, insusceptible of moods of impression or of contrarieties of expression, expressive of mute immutable mature animality.

If you think pygophilia could go no further, you are wrong. On the same page the master surpasses himself. He deserves the last word:

He kissed the plump mellow yellow smellow melons of her rump, on each plump melonous hemisphere, in their mellow yellow furrow, with obscure prolonged provocative melonsmellonous osculation.

(1966)

The Charleroi Adventure

The more one hears about the forthcoming Charleroi Arts Festival (3–16 July), the more one wonders why a concept so daring yet so simple has never occurred to anyone before. Over the years, we have grown accustomed to the idea that festivals of the arts should only be held in places of great natural beauty, preferably with lengthy cultural pedigrees —such as Salzburg, Bayreuth, Venice or Edinburgh. The assumption seems to be that art is a vile-tasting pill that needs extrinsic sugaring to make it digestible.

Charleroi thinks otherwise. Its Board of Festival Patrons (backed by several American foundations) made it perfectly clear in their first brochure last autumn that they would have no truck with a notion so dated and sentimental. 'If people do not want their art neat,' said the opening paragraph, 'it is surely reasonable to suspect that they do not want it at all.'

Situated in the midst of Belgium's industrial belt, Charleroi is a town of 26,000 inhabitants with few (or rather no) amenities to distract attention from the artistic fare on display. It is frankly ugly; yet this— from the Board's point of view—is precisely its virtue. You need only glance at the official Charleroi travel leaflet (available on request from the Belgian Embassy) to realise that the Festival Board could hardly have chosen a venue less tainted with touristic gimmickry. The front page shows the city by night, a twinkling carpet of blast furnaces spreading out to the horizon and beyond. 'Heart of the Black Country,' the caption runs, 'land of labour and of stern beauty.... Powerful metropolis of the coal, glass and steel industries.' Inside there are colour pictures of the Technical University, the Queen Astrid Maternity Hospital, the Municipal Stadium and the Intercity Slaughterhouses. All the evidence uncompromisingly concurs: here, if anywhere, is a city of here and now, a blank sheet of urban paper awaiting the imprint of culture.

But it is not only Charleroi's topographical bleakness that sets it apart from the general ruck of festivals. Its true uniqueness and audacity lie in the artistic policy it intends to promote. For centuries we have been bombarded with propaganda to the effect that art must be 'entertaining', 'stimulating', 'provocative', 'swinging', 'a gas', or whatever the current cultword happens to be. The implication is that art in itself is not enough; it must also be its own salesman with its own built-in commercials. Against this myth Charleroi has resolutely set its face.

The festival brochure is boldly headed with two quotations. The first is by Susan Sontag, the incisive young American literary critic: 'Is it the obligation of great art to be continually interesting? I think not. We should acknowledge certain uses of boredom as one of the most creative stylistic features of modern literature.' The second quotation comes from Nigel Gosling, the art critic of the London *Observer*: 'There is an element of boredom in all great art.'

It is this revolutionary element that the planners of the Charleroi experiment have made the central plank of their aesthetic platform. 'Our aim,' a member of the Board has said, 'is to show that art, *no matter how boring it may be*, can still be art. And this is true of many popular works as well as those that appeal to minorities. A faint quality of boredom may in fact be what they have in common. Let me put it another way and extend the argument: anything that is profoundly boring *yet still art* may conceivably be the most durable art. We don't know for sure, but Charleroi is the crucible where we'll find out.'

At this stage, the organisers are not particularly concerned about whether people will come to the crucible or not. 'In a sense,' the spokesman added blithely, 'we might even be pleased if nobody showed up. Because if Charleroi exists to achieve anything, it's to isolate and define the kind of art you wouldn't cross the road to see—which is yet art!' 'Yet' is a word often on the lips of the Charleroi brains-trusters. With their evangelistic zeal and constant recourse to italics, they are a breed on their own.

Nineteen experts from twenty-six countries make up the Charleroi Board. Lady Clark (Chairwoman of the Board and wife of Sir Kenneth), Stephen Spender, Anthony Powell and Bryan Forbes comprise the British contingent. Among the other members are Alberto Moravia, Gian Carlo Menotti, Lionel Trilling, Susan Sontag and André Malraux. Hopes are running high that M. Malraux may have the Municipal Stadium cleaned and commission Chagall to paint a floor for the cafeteria of the Technical University. At all events, he and his colleagues have studied the cultural scene of five continents, and come up with a programme that fits what they informally call 'the Gosling bill' (*le projet Gosling*)—i.e., it is at once unmistakable as boredom, yet recognisable as art.

Let me list the provisional schedule of events, which is here published for the first time.

Opening Ceremony

This will be performed outside the Queen Astrid Hospital by Mrs Richard Nixon. In case of rain, Madame Chiang Kai-Shek will officiate.

Gala Première

The Navajo Rain Dancers, flown over from America, will present their famous ritual dance in which, stricken by drought, the tribe prays to the gods for rain. In case of rain, the performance will be held in the Municipal Stadium.

Thereafter, the major arts will be represented as follows:

Drama

During the mornings, there will be demonstrations of mime by members of the Jean-Louis Barrault Company from the Théâtre de France. Great emphasis will be laid on audience participation and the miming of animals. Spectators will be asked, 'Quel est votre animal préféré?' and shown how to mime it.

Afternoons:
Sixteenth Century Puppetry Through the Ages—a series of historical reconstructions by the Drama Department of Iowa State University. We do not know too much about this yet, except that it is the fruit of donkeys' years of research.

Evenings:
Throughout the first week there will be performances on alternate nights of the Helsinki and Oslo productions of *Dear Liar*, Jerome Kilty's dramatisation of the correspondence between George Bernard Shaw and Mrs Patrick Campbell. A panel discussion on *The Irish Drama in Scandinavia* will be held after the last performance. The main feature of the second week's drama will be a production by Herbert Blau of Thomas Hardy's *The Dynasts*, conceived in terms of mainstream jazz. 'Although he died in 1928,' Mr Blau says, 'Hardy was basically a phenomenon of the thirties. He subsumed jazz. We hope to make a few rhetorical connections by following up this clue.' By way of a late-night change of pace, the celebrated Fliegerabwehrgeschutz Klub (Anti-air-craftgun Club) cabaret of Stuttgart will present its bitterly satirical revue, *Hoppla! Wir Fahren Gegen Leipzig!*

At midnight on weekdays a Royal Military Tattoo will take place in the Municipal Stadium. Its theme is *Gallant Little Belgium—1914–1940*.

Film

A crowded list of off-beat attractions has been arranged, among them a tribute to Anthony Asquith (including the rejected sequences of *The*

Yellow Rolls-Royce), a George Brent memorial programme (introduced by Robert Siodmak), a compilation of *films maudits* adapted from the novels of A. J. Cronin, and an anthology of documentaries (never before screened in chronological order) on the world of small boats. There will also be what is mysteriously billed as 'A Confrontation' with Nicholas Ray.

The first Charleroi Festival Lecture on Film will be delivered by Sessue Hayakawa, its subject being the influence of the East on the Western cinema. (Mr Hayakawa's skittish title for his address is: *Anna May Wong or Again She May Not*.) Lastly, it is hoped that the veteran director Henry Hathaway (voted sixth in the *Sacred Monsters of the Classic Screen* poll held by *Borzage*, the new Belgian film magazine) will allow Charleroi to hold the première of his latest movie, *Might On Main Street*.

Opera

A general invitation has been issued to all the leading European companies. Nineteenth-century operas will be especially welcome.

Dance

The Royal Ballet in *Giselle*. This was Charleroi's first choice, and a proud one for Britain. In addition, there will be performances by the National Folkloric Ensemble of Formosa, with a preliminary lecture by the indefatigable Mrs Nixon.

Music

From Trad to Leningrad—a series of concerts given by New Orleans groups from behind the Iron Curtain. One of the featured performers will be K. R. Vinescu, the great Roumanian bass and blues shouter, with his notorious version of *Vranci o Jonic*. We are also promised *Aleatory Grab-Bag*—a catch-all title for an evening of chance (or 'if/if not') music, devised by John Cage and members of the Greek gambling syndicate. Five years after his non-playing recital at London's Wigmore Hall, Gabor Cossa—the silent pianist and antique dealer—will make his comeback at Charleroi. He has been coaxed out of not not-playing by his friend and partner, Harvey Geronimo, the one-armed 'cellist.

Campanology—a full double chime of the Nine Tailors (*Les Neuf Couturiers*) will be rung by l'Ensemble Quasimodo, the Belgian National Society of Bell-ringers.

Son et Lumière—a musical pageant based on the early days of the great Flemish weaving company, Jean-Jacques Lumière and Son.

Graphic Arts

An exhibition of flag designs for newly emergent countries. A Bernard Buffet Retrospective. The Beaverbrook Collection of Canadian Primitives. At the Palace of Fine Arts—*The Raphael Story*.

Literature

A display of autographed first editions of the works of C. P. Snow, together with a lecture by the author on the early novels of Pamela Hansford Johnson, his lady wife.

Zest will be added to this brew by 'folkloric manifestations' indigenous to Charleroi and its suburbs. These will include samples from the rich storehouse of Walloon liturgical drama; the traditional game of *Fall Down, Farmhouses!* which is annually played to mark the beginning of the open-cast mining season; and a Pudding Bee for local chefs. The Charleroi leaflet, I should add, speaks glowingly of the region's 'gastronomic specialty, the Carolo, a delicious cake steeped in kirsch and surmounted with a marzipan shield bearing the city's coat of arms'. Sold in a cellophane carton, it retains its full flavour for up to three weeks. A monster Carolo, fifteen metres in diameter and weighing half a ton, will be consumed in the Town Hall on the last night of the Festival. The traditional Charleroi International Cocktail Competition will be judged by the winner of last year's contest. On that occasion, drinkers will recall, the laurels went to a blend of vodka, bourbon and crème de menthe, entitled 'Force de Frappe Frappée.'

A word on travelling arrangements. It is no joke to get to Charleroi. If one thing is certain, it is that this will be a festival for pilgrims rather than casual trade. There is no airport: you fly to Brussels and take a train. When you arrive, it is likely to be raining. Over the past three decades, Charleroi has averaged an annual 34·4 inches of rain, evenly spread throughout the year. On rainless days a recurrent menace is *smudjstykke* (a sort of tangible smog); one is strongly advised not to bring white dinner-jackets or indeed anything pale.

Much as I hate trend-setting, let me hazard a guarded prediction. It is not unimaginable that the Charleroi adventure may usher in a whole new approach to the arts, based on the hypothesis that *ennui* is not a drawback but a boon. Normally we approach a work of art expecting to be swept off our feet, and discover to our dismay that we are bored. At Charleroi things will be different: expecting to be bored, we may be surprised by joy. Will this unlikely city become the Baden-Baden of the festival circuit—the smart place at which to recuperate from the fleshpots of 'interesting' art? By the middle of July (rainfall 3·4 inches), we shall know.

(1966)

The Coldest of Blood

One Saturday in November 1959 two young men drove 400 miles across the State of Kansas to an imposing white house in the lonely village of Holcomb. There they killed—at pointblank range, with a shotgun—four people whom, until that day, they had never seen. The victims were a prosperous farmer named Herbert Clutter, his wife, Bonnie, and their teenage children, Nancy and Kenyon. The murderers (though this was not known until weeks later) were Dick Hickock and Perry Smith, former cell-mates in the Kansas State Penitentiary.

Hickock, aged twenty-eight at the time of the crime, was a petty thief of bright, cruel intelligence. Since 1950, when his head was battered in a car accident, he had shown increasing evidence of what a psychiatrist was later to call 'severe character disorder'. Perry Smith, thirty-one years old, had a record of arrests that began when he was eight, shortly after his vagabond Irish father parted from his mother, an alcoholic Cherokee Indian. He had been confined in many institutions, among them a Catholic orphanage where the nuns thrashed him for bed-wetting. It was here, for the first of many times, that he dreamed of a giant yellow parrot that would swoop down, destroy his persecutors and lift him up to paradise.

His brother and one of his two sisters had committed suicide. He had amorphous artistic yearnings, and hotly resented his lack of schooling. Like his partner, Dick, he had suffered on the public highway: his legs were dwarfish, the aftermath of a motor-cycle crash in which they had been broken in five places. It was this classic paranoid who fired the shots that obliterated a family.

Dick (who planned the expedition to Holcomb) had been told by a fellow-prisoner, once employed on the Clutter farm, that Mr Clutter kept thousands of dollars at home in a safe. But there was no safe; in spite of which the two intruders proceeded to kill, and departed the richer by less than fifty dollars. They took a trip to Mexico, where (though not queer themselves) they briefly accepted the hospitality of a rich German homosexual in Acapulco. Having hitch-hiked back to the States, they were arrested in January 1960, seven weeks after the crime.

Trial, conviction and sentence to death followed in April. George Docking, Governor of Kansas from 1957 to 1961, opposed capital punishment throughout his term of office; but his successors were less liberally inclined, and after a series of appeals and postponements, lasting five years in all, Smith and Hickock were hanged in April 1965.

What took place in Holcomb was a nightmare collision of two incompatible Americas: the land of hearth-loving, God-fearing families and the land of vengeful, anarchic outcasts. In the end, they annihilated each other.

Truman Capote arrived in Kansas towards the end of November 1959 to cover the case for the *New Yorker*. When Smith and Hickock were brought back in custody, they refused at first to see him; by offering them fifty dollars each for an interview he managed to change their minds. Before long all three were on first-name terms, and by the time Perry and Dick reached the scaffold, Capote had spent hundreds of hours in their company. He had also consulted everyone living, traceable and willing to talk who had ever been closely acquainted with them or their victims.

In all this prodigious research, spread over five years, he neither took notes on the spot nor employed a tape-recorder. Instead, he relied on his memory, which he had sedulously trained until it could retain 95 per cent (or 92 per cent or 97 per cent: his interviewers differ) of total recall.

In Cold Blood, the result of these unique and protracted exertions, is certainly the most detailed and atmospheric account ever written of a contemporary crime. Sometimes, you suspect that Capote's vision of Kansas is over-sentimental (cf., too many phrases like 'the well-loved piece of prairie where he had always hoped to build a house'); often, that he bowdlerises out of deference to the *New Yorker*'s well-known primness. At one point (p. 240) Perry says 'shit': this is the only four-letter word used by any of the characters, criminal or law-abiding, and it was omitted from the *New Yorker* serialisation.

Again, how can we verify events and statements that only the hanged men could corroborate? Driving towards Mexico, Dick deliberately swerves to run over a dog and says: 'Boy! We sure splattered him!' Capote adds that 'it was what he always said after running down a dog'. But did he get that from Dick, or is it Perry trying to make Dick look bad? We are given no clue, here or in many similar dilemmas.

Even so, the book is by any standards a monumental job of editing and a most seductive piece of writing: the first section, cutting back and forth between the unsuspecting Clutters and the approaching killers, is agonisingly well constructed. That said, we must pose the two central questions: Is it art? and is it morally defensible?

The first is easier to answer. Capote calls the book a 'non-fiction novel', by which he means a documentary tale handled with the psychological insight of a novelist. He believes that much of modern fiction is merely a device to evade the libel laws; thus, a breezy, adipose Londoner absurdly appears in print as a tight-lipped, skeletal Scot. If I remember him correctly (my median percentage of recall is in the high sixties), Capote feels that unless you are a Joyce or a Kafka, able to create a world of your own, you are likely to find your richest artistic opportunities in the world of fact. This will be news only to those who (perhaps like Capote himself) were brought up to despise journalism; or who never heard John Grierson's famous definition of documentary—'the creative treatment of actuality'. Like any other art, of course, creative journalism can be abused: witness *Time* magazine, that weekly anthology of non-fiction short stories.

The question of morality is tougher and (for me) more personal. Early in 1960, when I was in New York, upper-Bohemian dinner-guests were already full of 'Truman and his marvellous bit about Perry and Dick'. I attended one such party, which Capote regaled with a dazzling account of the crime and his friendship with the criminals. I said they seemed obviously insane, and he agreed they were 'nuts'. And what would happen to them? 'They'll swing, I guess,' he said.

When I asked whether he thought insane people should be hanged, he said I couldn't understand unless I had read Nancy Clutter's diary: Perry and Dick had destroyed 'such a lovely, intelligent girl'. 'You mean it would have mattered less if she'd been ugly and stupid?' I said.

I don't recall his answer to that, but I do remember several subsequent disputes—one in which I failed to persuade him that he (or the *New Yorker*) ought to provide Perry and Dick with the best available psychiatric testimony; and another in which I convinced him, much against his will, that if he was writing a book about death in cold blood he owed it to his readers to be present at a really cold-blooded killing— the legal strangulation of his friends.

Capote's references in the book to the mental state of the murderers are confused and ambiguous. Early on, we learn that, in Dick's opinion, Perry was 'that rarity, "a natural killer"—*absolutely sane* but conscienceless . . .' (my italics). Later, Capote cites the belief of Dr Joseph Satten, a veteran psychiatrist working at the Menninger Clinic in Kansas, that when Perry killed Mr Clutter (the first and hence the crucial murder, since the other three had the rational purpose of eliminating witnesses), he was 'under a mental eclipse, deep inside a schizophrenic darkness'. The phrase is Capote's and it has the same fanciful vagueness as something he afterwards said to an interviewer: 'Perry never meant to kill the Clutters at all. He had a brain explosion.'

In essence, the only explanation Capote offers for the gratuitous slaughter of Mr Clutter—the *raison d'être*, after all, of his book—is a single remark of Perry's: 'It wasn't because of anything the Clutters did. They never hurt me. . . . Like people have all my life. Maybe it's just that the Clutters were the ones who had to pay for it.' And maybe not: the woolliness is contagious. Nowhere does Capote commit himself to stating that the killers were technically insane, and therefore ought not to have been executed. Indeed, he goes out of his way to stress that Dick was a supporter of capital punishment: 'I'm not against it. Revenge is all it is, but what's wrong with revenge?' 'Essentially,' Capote told *Life* magazine, 'I'm on the side of the victim, not the murderer.'

The accused men received only the most perfunctory psychiatric examination: so much is brutally obvious. The day before the trial began a young psychiatrist named Mitchell Jones volunteered to interview them without payment. He asked them to write out autobiographical statements, which they did in the courtroom while the jury was being selected. And that was all.

In Dr Jones's view, Dick might have been suffering from 'organic brain damage', and Perry showed 'definite signs of severe mental illness'. But he was not allowed to say this in court. Kansas follows the ancient McNaghten Rules, whereby a man is held to be sane and legally responsible for his actions if he knows that what he is doing is wrong. Dr Jones testified that Dick *did* know, and, when asked about Perry, said he had no opinion. He was dismissed at once from the stand. Had he been a psychiatrist of national repute, more skilled in courtroom niceties, would his evidence have been heard? We shall never know.

What we do know, however, is that when the verdict was appealed, three Federal judges declared: 'There was no substantial evidence then, *and none has been produced since*, to substantiate a defence of insanity' (my italics). And they were right; none was produced; although Capote, who investigated so much else, had five years in which he might have unearthed it. He could surely have faced the expense. In cold cash, it has been estimated that *In Cold Blood* is likely to earn him between two and three million dollars.

Had Perry and Dick been reprieved, the book might have been rather different. George Plimpton, in an interview for the *New York Times Book Review*, asked Capote whether his 'artistry' would have suffered if clemency had been granted: he hedged, and changed the subject. He also told Plimpton that neither Perry nor Dick saw the manuscript *in toto*; that Perry's 'greatest objection' was to the title; that Dick wanted changes made ('to serve his purposes legally') and expressed the opinion that 'what I had written wasn't exactly true'.

In the same interview Capote says that someone suggested the break-up of a marriage as a possible theme for a future 'non-fiction novel'; he rejected the idea because 'you'd have to find two people . . . who'd sign a release'. Perry and Dick did sign a release after reading 'three-quarters of the book' (Capote's words). This shows a remarkable degree of tolerance in them since in the course of the book Capote alleges (*a*) that Dick frequently tried to rape pubescent girls, (*b*) that he intended (but failed) to kill a fellow-prisoner in a Kansas jail, and (*c*) that he and Perry were prevented only by chance from carrying out the premeditated murder of a travelling salesman who gave them a lift. (In his chat with Plimpton, Capote adds: 'They had two other murders planned that aren't mentioned in the book.') There is no evidence to substantiate these charges outside the killers' graves, to which Capote contributed the cost of the headstones.

A prominent Manhattan lawyer has given me the following opinion: 'I would doubt whether the book would have been released prior to the decease of the accused.'

We are talking, in the long run, about responsibility; the debt that a writer arguably owes to those who provide him—down to the last autobiographical parenthesis—with his subject-matter and his livelihood. And we are not discussing a thirdrate crime reporter or professional ghoul; one does not waste space on condemning trash. For the first time, an influential writer of the front rank has been placed in a position of privileged intimacy with criminals about to die, and—in my view—done less than he might have to save them.

The focus narrows sharply down on priorities: does the work come first or does life? An attempt to help (by supplying new psychiatric testimony) might easily have failed: what one misses is any sign that it was even contemplated. It is irrelevant to say that Capote writes with genuine pity of his dead friends, and gives them a fraternal quatrain from Villon by way of epigraph. Compassion is the least we expect of an obituarist.

In a recent letter to a former colleague, Dr Satten of the Menninger Clinic (mentioned above) agrees that Capote didn't try to help the condemned men, but sees nothing wrong in this: 'In the conversations I have had with Mr Capote over the years, I think he saw his task as that of an observer and recorder rather than that of an active participant.' By this reasoning, a writer who befriended Timothy Evans at the time of his conviction would have been under no obligation to tell society that it was executing a probably innocent half-wit. Where lives are threatened, observers and recorders who shrink from participation may be said to betray their species: no piece of prose, however deathless, is worth a human life.

The colleague to whom Dr Satten addressed his letter (and who showed it to me) is a woman psychiatrist who knows the Clutter case well. For professional reasons I will not divulge her name. She worked in Kansas, mainly with criminal patients, in 1963–64, and has no doubt that if the Clutter murderers could have been shown to be paranoid schizophrenics, they would have won their appeal. On their relationship with Capote she takes a firm and original line. In her view, he set himself up— consciously or not—as their analyst and confessor; not, however, to bring them comfort but to gain their trust and obtain information.

In a letter to me she reconstructs the situation. She writes: 'The same dependence and fascination that Dick once evoked in Perry is now expanded in both of them towards Capote. In a sense they are telling him what Perry told Dick: "I'm going to put myself in your power. I'm going to tell you something I never told anybody." We know what Dick did with this confidence: he used Perry to kill the people he had in mind. And what did Capote do with their trust?'

Perry, she hazards, came to identify Capote with his father, with whom he had spent many of his few contented days. And at the same time, Capote may have begun to see aspects of himself in Perry: the diminutive stature, perhaps, and the voice that Capote describes as 'both gentle and prim—a voice that, though soft, manufactured each word exactly, ejected it like a smoke ring issuing from a parson's mouth'.

She continues: 'The situation now becomes chaotic. Who's who? Who is the criminal? Who is the interviewer? . . . Is it possible that Capote was gaining satisfaction out of acting as "confessor" to the criminals because of an intense identification with them? At some time or other all of us feel like killing; but now Capote can avoid the real situation, since someone with whom he strongly identifies has done the killing instead.'

Whether Capote identified or not, it seems to me that the blood in which his book is written is as cold as any in recent literature.

The foregoing piece appeared on the front page of *The Observer* Review Section on 13 March 1966. Two weeks later—also on the front page—Mr Capote replied as follows:

The Guts of a Butterfly

Ah, and so at last we know! Mr Kenneth Tynan's chief literary concern is the integrity and responsibility of the writer. But how very surprising—when one considers that these are the particular qualities most notably absent from his article about my book, *In Cold Blood*, which *The Observer* printed two Sundays ago.

Without quoting the piece virtually word by word, I scarcely know how to disentangle this knotted cat's-cradle that Tynan's egocentric ignorance has created. My only choice is to indicate, before tackling the larger issues, a few of the distortions so general to the infested whole.

Certainly the following is typical of Tynan's lazy inaccuracy: '... in the course of the book Capote alleges (*a*) that Dick frequently tried to rape pubescent girls, (*b*) that he intended (but failed) to kill a fellow prisoner in a Kansas jail, and (*c*) that he and Perry were prevented only by chance from carrying out the premeditated murder of a travelling salesman who gave them a lift.... There is no evidence to substantiate these charges outside the killers' graves, to which Capote contributed the cost of the headstones.'

No evidence?

Clearly Tynan's reading of the book is as haphazard as his prose-style; otherwise he could not have failed to notice that Richard Hickock himself describes, in a statement for Dr W. Mitchell Jones, the defence psychiatrist, his sexual interest in pubescent girls, and how, on a number of past occasions, he had implemented that interest. The text of this statement is printed in Part Four. Moreover, is there any *question* that Hickock intended to rape Nancy Clutter? Not only is that a part of the trial record, not only did he never deny it, but he describes the matter at length in an article he himself wrote and published in an American magazine (*Male*, November, 1961).

And now to items (*b*) and (*c*). In a brief preface to my book there appears this sentence: 'All the material in this book not derived from my own observation is either taken from official records or is the result of interviews with the persons directly concerned. ...' Perhaps Tynan thinks this a mere idle phrase. It is not. Almost all the substance of the book can be verified in one form or another, as Tynan would have soon discovered had he taken his work seriously. Yes, the stories involved in (*b*) and (*c*) were told to me by Smith and Hickock; but these particular anecdotes were also told at separate times to four different agents of the Kansas Bureau of Investigation (Clarence Duntz, Harold Nye, Alvin Dewey, and Roy Church—unlike Tynan, I name my sources), and are a part of the official Kansas Bureau dossier.

That's three factual errors in one paragraph; and as for the final reference to my having contributed to the cost of Hickock and Smith's gravestones, Tynan seems to be scornful of this action. Why? If I had not done it no one else would; I was their sole financial support during the entire time of their imprisonment.

Later on, when quoting a remark of mine made in an interview ('Essentially I'm on the side of the victim, not the murderer'), Tynan implies that it is morally wrong of me to have a greater sympathy for victims than criminals; and he *even*, heaven help us, tries to twist the statement into meaning that I am a devoted proponent of capital punishment! Again, in the same grotesquely censorious spirit, the gentleman chastises me for the fact that the book contains only one four-letter word —which only demonstrates how *derrière-garde* this fading hipster has become: doesn't he know that four-letter words are nowadays unrequired everywhere except on television?

Now, to approach the lower slopes of the major contention: that I did not do all I might have done to aid Smith and Hickock in their appeals against execution, and hints that the underlying reason for my (unproved) behaviour was that I could not have published the book as long as Hickock and Smith were alive.

He writes: 'A prominent Manhattan lawyer has given me the following opinion: "I would doubt whether the book would have been released prior to the decease of the accused." ' Mr Tynan is *so* fond of quoting anonymous persons; indeed, he is very like Senator McCarthy, and his whole piece, riddled with ghostly accusators, has the atmosphere of an old-time McCarthy hearing. And so may I say this: I don't believe Tynan ever consulted 'a prominent Manhattan attorney' or obtained any such statement. And I will back my belief with the following offer: if the name and address of this person can be produced, along with a sworn affidavit that he expressed such an opinion to Tynan, I will hand over a cheque for $500 to Tynan's favourite charity (if so uncharitable a spirit *has* a favourite charity).

What I am about to tell illustrates perfectly the quantity, as well as the beyond-contempt quality, of the research the languorous Mr Tynan accomplished before sitting down to type his pious tirade. A few days before *The Observer* published this piece, the literary editor of the paper, Mr Terence Kilmartin, sent me a copy of the manuscript, then later telephoned to ask what I thought of it. I pointed out a major error in the article—which the editor duly corrected. But it's very important, this error: a good portion of Tynan's case depended on it. Because, in the original article, Tynan claimed I could not have published my book because I could never have obtained legal releases from the two murderers —that is, a release exonerating me from any possible libel action.

But what is the truth of the matter? This: I had legal releases, drawn by lawyers and signed before witnesses and notarised, from almost every person who appears in the book—*including Smith and Hickock*. Legally, there was nothing to have prevented me from publishing the book at any time.

The sole deterrent was that no one could judge with any certainty whether my book would help or hinder the case as it was being appealed through the Federal courts, and I was not willing to risk publishing anything that might have proved detrimental to Smith and Hickock's chances for a reversal, especially because both they and the man who was their chief defence counsel during the last three years, Mr Joseph P. Jenkins, were more than hopeful that a new trial would eventually be secured by way of reversal of a verdict in the Federal courts. This hope went undiminished until the very day of the execution, at which time Mr Jenkins still had an action before the Supreme Court. If Mr Tynan doubts that, then all he has to do is write to Mr Jenkins, a lawyer who *does* exist, and whose address is: The Huron Building, Kansas City, Kansas.

However, to move on (though certainly not upward) to the principal area of Tynan's uninformed criticism: 'Nowhere does Capote commit himself to stating that the killers were technically insane, and therefore should not have been executed.' Please remember that I was not writing a polemic but, as far as possible, an objective work of reportage. And, in the role of reporter, why on earth should I have committed myself to a view I feel to be quite untrue? I'm not at all sure that both Smith and Hickock were not a mite saner than Kenneth Tynan (that's not a joke; I mean it). The latter, by slyly alluding to Timothy Evans, seems to suggest that Smith and Hickock were (*a*) half-wits like Evans, and (*b*) perhaps even innocent, like Evans; the full implication is that I let two possibly innocent half-wits go to their death without stirring up a storm! Wow! It really takes one's breath away (as Mr Welch said to Senator McCarthy: 'Have you *no* shame, sir?')

Okay, let's get down to brass tacks. Despite Tynan's entirely ludicrous claims to acquaintance with a third psychiatric expert on the Clutter case (this is another anonymous person who doesn't exist, at least not in the role of expert that Tynan assigns her), there are only *two* psychiatrists who know at firsthand anything about it whatever.

One of them is Dr Joseph E. Satten of the Menninger Clinic in Topeka, Kansas, Dr Satten is one of the most distinguished forensic psychiatrists in the United States, and a universally accepted authority on criminal psychology. The other is Dr W. Mitchell Jones, a *protégé* of Dr Satten's and, at present, the director of the Prairie View Clinic in Newton, Kansas. Dr Jones, whom Tynan, arrogant and ill-informed as ever, attempts to discard as some inexperienced young incompetent, examined Smith and Hickock prior to their trial and remained in *continuous contact* with them throughout the five and a half years spent on Death Row.

Now, neither Dr Satten nor Dr Jones ever thought either Smith or Hickock was more than a severely pathological personality; neither they nor any other competent observer considered them 'insane' in the sense Tynan means. On the contrary, both Smith and Hickock had unusually high intelligence quotients, were super-alert and possessed a wide range of information (see Dr Jones's Written Report: Part Four).

No one, not Dr Jones, nor Dr Satten, or any of the numerous lawyers who worked on the case (names supplied on demand), *ever* thought that a successful appeal could be made in Kansas courts (which abide by the McNaghten Rule) on the basis of insanity or 'diminished responsibility'.

The unpardonable thing is that Tynan was well aware of this fact when he wrote his article. How so? Because Dr Satten himself had told him that I was correct, and that no appeal of this nature could have succeeded in a Kansas court. But Tynan ignores Dr Satten's opinion, he does not mention it at all, for had he done so it would have entirely demolished that little guillotine of an essay he was constructing. To suppress vital information that does not serve one's critical purposes—is *that* an act of integrity, the response of a responsible writer?

And while we're on the subject of ethics, here's a footnote to chew on: Dr Satten specifically told Tynan that he could not quote from any of his (Dr Satten's) letters without my expressed permission, and yet Tynan went right ahead and did it without a fare-you-well. A very scrupulous lad. Very.

But now the moment has come to turn to the matter of the Third Psychiatrist. If you have become bored, and are beginning to doze, please wake up because we are now going to discuss something of truly eerie interest.

The manner in which Tynan introduces this character, and his reasons for introducing her at all, are McCarthy-technique at its serpentine suavest. He tells us only, and of course without providing any name, that she is a woman psychiatrist who at one time worked in Kansas, and who, he assures us, 'knows the Clutter case well'. But why has Tynan suddenly led this veiled and mysterious lady stage-front, and how does he intend to use her? He means to use her the same way a ventriloquist uses a dummy. Why? Because Tynan is a bully; and, true to tradition, he is also a coward. There are some very rotten things he wants to say about me, but he hasn't the guts to come right out and say them himself.

And so, hiding behind the skirts of the female psychiatrist, this fair-fighting, very sporting fellow allows her to speak for him, lets her analyse and fancify on the relationship between me and the two condemned men (though she never knew any one of us), make accusations that range from the gravely unjust ('In her view, he [Capote] set himself up, consciously or not, as their analyst and confessor: not, however, to bring them comfort but to gain their trust and obtain information'), to frivolous libel ('Is it possible that Capote was gaining satisfaction out of acting as "confessor" to the criminals because of an intense identification with them? At some time or other all of us feel like killing; but now Capote can avoid the real situation since someone with whom he strongly identifies has done the killing instead').

Even a man with the morals of a baboon and the guts of a butterfly could not do anything sneakier or more cowardly than that; it would bring a blush to the cheeks of Uriah Heep.

On the surface of it, the most plausible-seeming of Tynan's recriminations is that I did not help these men sufficiently in their legal struggle to avoid execution; in his opinion I should have hired an eminent psychiatrist to 'unearth evidence' of their insanity; he tells us that his friend, the shadowy woman psychiatrist, has 'no doubt that if the Clutter murderers could have been shown to be paranoid schizophrenics, they would have won their appeal'.

Well, if the lady really believes that, then she must be every bit as ignorant of American jurisprudence, and particularly the laws of Kansas, as our chum Tynan (and, as Perry Smith used to often say, that is about as 'ignorant as a day-old nigger'). Although this subject was treated in detail in my book, I will spell it out once more for inattentive readers like Mr Tynan.

The courts of Kansas are under *no obligation* to admit psychiatric testimony, and very seldom do. If fifty world-famous psychiatrists had trooped into court prepared to swear that Smith and Hickock were 'paranoid schizophrenics' (which they weren't, though apparently that point is irrelevant to Tynan) it still would not have done a damn bit of good, because Kansas courts abide by the McNaghten Rule and would not have allowed any testimony that deviated from its confines. In the final portion of the book, I described at length the case of Lowell Lee Andrews, a multiple murderer who was *definitely* schizophrenic, and for whom the staff of the Menninger Clinic, led by Dr Satten, conducted a famous crusade; yet Andrews was hanged, his defenders having been defeated for the reasons stated above.

One last point: supposing Tynan is right, supposing, as a friend of these two men, I ought to have sought out a renowned psychiatrist— where in the U.S. would I have found anyone more renowned or better qualified than Dr Satten, who was already right there on the scene and involved in the case from the start?

It is not for me to estimate how much I aided these pitiful friends of mine, or how much 'comfort' I brought to them; but I feel confident in predicting that, if queried, those closest to the situation, honest and reputable men like Dr Jones and attorney Jenkins and the prison chaplain, James Post, would express opinions poles apart from Tynan's.

As they say around the courthouses, a man who acts as his own lawyer has a fool for a client. And perhaps the artist who defends himself against a critic has one, too. I don't believe in artists replying to criticism, and I have never done so myself, for I think it shows lack of pride and really serves small purpose. But this bullyboy chicanery concocted by Tynan is one over the odds.

On 3 April *The Observer* published the following letter:

Sir,—On the strength of his article last Sunday, Truman Capote seems to have invented yet another new art form: after the Non-Fiction Novel, the Semi-Documentary Tantrum. Ignoring the tone of the piece, let's look at the points he raises.

First, the minor ones. I wasn't suggesting that Dick Hickock never tried to rape pubescent girls; merely that Capote's allegations could not have been substantiated in court. A confidential statement to a psychiatrist is not evidence in the legal sense; and Nancy Clutter, aged nineteen, can hardly be called pubescent.

As to Capote's disclosure that Hickock and Smith had told the cops as well as himself about other murders they had contemplated: I took it for granted that if the police had possessed such damning information, the fact would somewhere be mentioned in the book. Here, as elsewhere, it's impossible to deduce from the text which statements are corroborated and which are not.

A couple of months ago I asked my friend Aaron Frosch, partner in the well-known Manhattan law firm of Weissberger and Frosch (120 East 56th Street, New York City), whether Capote's allegations—if based solely on unsupported hearsay—would have been actionable, had the killers lived to deny them. Founding his answer on this assumption, he said: 'I would doubt whether the book would have been released prior to the decease of the accused.' He continued: 'References in the book to the personal habits of the deceased, unless these were part of the charges against him or were true or were reported in newspapers, would be a basis for action if the accused were still alive.'

Mr Frosch, of course, is the 'prominent Manhatten lawyer' whose existence Capote insultingly denies. His letter is on my desk, in lieu of 'a sworn affidavit'; but unless Capote still believes that I am concocting fictitious quotes from a fictitious source, I shall expect his cheque for $500 within a few days. It should be made out to the Howard League for Penal Reform.*

To get to more serious matters: the fact that Perry and Dick signed legal releases is quite irrelevant to my central point, which was (and is) that Capote could have done more than he did to save his friends by means of psychiatric evidence.

The day before the trial began, they were examined by Dr Mitchell Jones, a psychiatrist who volunteered his services to the defence lawyers. When asked in court whether Perry knew right from wrong at the time of the offence, he said he had no opinion. According to Dr Joseph Satten of the Menninger Clinic in Kansas, a psychiatrist highly esteemed by Capote: 'This possibly was a tactical error or a misunderstanding on Mitchell Jones's part in the heat of testifying.' (I must pause here to nail a wild misstatement of Capote's part—viz: 'Dr Statten specifically told Tynan that he could not quote from any of his (Dr Statten's) letters without my expressed permission.' I have never been told anything of the sort, nor have I ever written to Dr Satten or received a letter from him.)

Capote maintains that there were '*two* psychiatrists' who knew the case 'at firsthand', the other being Dr Satten. But the truth is that Dr Satten never met either Perry or Dick. He merely discussed them with Mitchell Jones, *who was the only psychiatrist ever to interview the murderers.* I won't bother to refute Capote's naïve assumption that they must have been sane because they had high I.Q.s; but I must challenge his blithe assertion that neither was a paranoid schizophrenic. On page 245 we read of Perry: 'His present personality structure is very nearly that of a paranoid schizophrenic.' This opinion is expressed by Mitchell Jones and endorsed by Satten.

Capote speaks of my 'entirely ludicrous claims to acquaintance with

---

* Mr Capote, still apparently sceptical, declined to settle his bet until he had seen an affidavit from Mr Frosch. This was duly provided, and shortly afterwards the Howard League received Mr Capote's cheque for $500, of which a framed photostat now hangs on my study wall.

a third psychiatric expert on the Clutter case ... another anonymous person who doesn't exist. ...' The psychiatrist's name is Dr Estela D'Accurzio; a friend of Dr Satten's. She worked with criminal patients at the Topeka State Hospital and the Kansas Reception and Diagnostic Centre in 1963–64, and believes that the Clutter murderers could have won their appeal if psychiatric testimony had shown them to be paranoid schizophrenics. Capote, on the other hand, contends that 'fifty world-famous psychiatrists ... would not have done a damn bit of good', because Kansas abides by the McNaghten Rule.

He protests too much; and his plea is demonstrably frail. The McNaghten Rule can be overthrown (and often has been) by any psychiatrist prepared to state that the accused did not know the nature of his act. A typical McNaghten case was that of Ronald True, who was sentenced to death for murder at the Old Bailey in 1922, after two defence psychiatrists had pronounced him insane: he was later reprieved on the evidence of three more medical men who simply reinforced their colleagues' findings.

There are many such borderline cases in British law. American examples are just as numerous: consider the trial of Kenneth Chapin (Massachusetts, 1955), who murdered a fourteen-year-old girl, pleaded insanity and got the death penalty. It was commuted to life imprisonment after the intervention of a celebrated psychiatrist, who declared the condemned man a schizophrenic.

Where Capote is concerned, I see no reason to modify my original judgment: 'An attempt to help (by supplying new psychiatric testimony) might easily have failed: what one misses is any sign that it was even contemplated.' The three Federal judges who turned down the appeal rightly said that no evidence had been produced to substantiate a defence of insanity. But it might have been: in which case it is not inconceivable that one or both of Capote's confidants might now be alive.

In his preface to the book, Capote expresses his thanks to the people who helped him—such as the citizens of Finney County, the staff of the Kansas Bureau of Investigation, and many others. From this roll of honour there are two notable absentees. I hope Capote will not object if I repair the omission by paying tribute, on his behalf, to Perry Smith and Dick Hickock, without whose cooperation, garrulity and trust *In Cold Blood* would never have been written.

Kenneth Tynan

On 24 April, under the heading 'Tynan attacked by lawyers', *The Observer* printed the following letter:

Sir,—As one of the attorneys who represented and fought for Richard Eugene Hickok and Perry Edward Smith to the very end, I resent the literary tantrums indulged in by Mr Tynan, not only because his critique of Truman Capote's 'In Cold Blood' was written without any apparent knowledge of the facts or the law, but also because, by innuendo and implication, he has cast an imputation of legal inadequacy upon the lawyers who were closest to the situation.

Mr Tynan says that the 'central point' of his theme is that Capote could have done more than he did to save his friends by means of psychiatric evidence. As I understand Tynan, psychiatric evidence that Hickok and Smith were some sort of "paranoid schizophrenics" might have unlocked their cells on death row and saved them from the gallows. Hedging, however, Tynan then states that even if such testimony were unsuccessful, Capote was to be censured because he did not at least *try* to obtain such testimony.

In the first place, it was no concern of Mr Capote's. A writer has no business interfering with the orderly procedure and processes in a court of law. I happen to know, however, that Capote *did* feel an obligation to help, but after some rather bad experiences with the lawyers, he kept his distance. If the lawyers didn't want Capote's help, what was he to do?

But, back to the central point. We attorneys who worked without one cent of compensation or reimbursement of expenses for almost three years, and who are impeccably cognizant of every factual detail and legal point involved, did everything we could to reopen the case. A great number of legal points were raised, of which the insanity issue was only one. At the habeas corpus hearing in the federal court, which spanned a week including night sessions, *we did present top-notch psychiatric testimony.* Dr Herbert Modlin, a renowned Menninger Foundation neuropsychiatrist, testified at length on the inadequacy of the examination given Hickok and Smith prior to the State trial, and sought to establish either that they were mental defectives or at least that there was enough evidence to warrant a complete psychiatric examination, and that the lack of such examination was a denial of due process of law.

Tynan, however, indicates no knowledge of the procedural problems of using belated psychiatric testimony. He says in his reply to Capote: 'She (Dr Estela D'Accurzio) worked with criminal patients at the Kansas reception and Diagnostic Center in 1963–64 and believes that the Clutter murderers could have won their appeal if psychiatric testimony had shown them to be paranoid schizophrenics' (even if such testimony were presented at the original trial, a jury would not have to believe it). Where would we have integrated such testimony? There is no provision in our

Federal Rules of Criminal Procedure permitting us to hire top psychiatrists for the purpose of conducting a lengthy psychoanalysis of Hickok
and Smith and then eliciting such testimony from the witness stand.

Apparently Mr Tynan or Dr D'Accurzio do not know that the purpose of the federal habeas corpus proceeding in the United States is to
determine if error of constitutional magnitude has been made. The federal
judge is bound by what did or did not take place in the State court. He
is not permitted to open new avenues; otherwise litigation would never
end, and State convictions would rest on shaky foundations. The federal
judge who heard this case ignored Dr Modlin's testimony and fell back on
the McNaghten Rules when he stated in his order: 'A review of the trial
record of this hearing and an observation of their actions during the hearing reveals that both petitioners demonstrate a complete comprehension
of the issues and matters at stake before the court.'

Tynan then points out that three Federal judges on appeal declared:
'There was no substantial evidence then, *and none has been produced
since*, to substantiate a defence of insanity' (Tynan's italics). The court
did say this, but did not volunter any method to get such testimony before
it. But Tynan fails to add the next sentence, which clearly reflects this
court's view: 'The attempt to establish insanity as a defence because of
serious injuries in accidents years before, and headaches and occasional
fainting spells of Hickok, was like grasping at the proverbial straw.'

What about a complete psychiatric examination at Garden City prior
to trial? The original lawyers did try to obtain a court order directing such
a psychiatric examination at the Larned State Hospital. The State, however, vigorously contested the application. The court was in complete
agreement. Now, what could Capote have done that the lawyers could
not do?

Mr Tynan relies heavily upon the professional opinion of Dr
D'Accurzio. He points out that he had never written to Dr Joseph E.
Satten, the renowned Menninger Foundation psychiatrist, nor had he
ever received a letter from him. Why should he? Dr D'Accurzio wrote
for him.

Dr Satten's reply to her is never mentioned by Tynan in his articles.
Dr Satten in substance points out that Capote helped Hickok and Smith
more as an impartial observer and recorder than by actually becoming an
advocate for them. 'I do not think anything more could have been done
for these two men with regard to the issue of capital punishment, or with
regard to the issue of mental illness. By being a neutral observer, I think
Mr Capote helped as much as anyone could have helped under the circumstances that existed.'

While this is not Mr Tynan's 'central point,' he is apparently of the opinion that the book would not have been published if we had been successful and had saved the pair from the gibbet. He even wrote to a Manhattan lawyer and quoted him thus: 'I would doubt whether the book would have been released prior to the decease of the accused.'

The implication is clear. Hickok and Smith had to die to insure publication. However, I would be interested in the Manhattan lawyer's answer if he had been told by Tynan that Capote had valid and legally binding releases from the pair. I personally know that Mr Capote did not want Hickok and Smith to die. The artistic purpose of his book had been accomplished—it would be published whether Hickok and Smith were alive or dead. But it would not be until the case had been appealed through the courts.

Truman was not impatient, as Tynan has charged. After he discovered I was friendly to him, he called me offering advice, as a layman familiar with the facts in Garden City and Topeka, the State capital. *His approach to me was aimed solely at clemency.* Furthermore, Dr Satten agrees with me that Capote didn't want them to die when he says in his letter to Dr D'Accurzio: 'One satisfactory resolution would have been for the Supreme Court to commute sentence, and I'm sure that Mr Capote would have preferred that to the fact of their execution. Either would have ended the case satisfactorily from the point of view of publication of the book.'

Lastly, Mr Tynan makes an incredible and certainly naïve statement in his reply (April 3), when he asserts that the McNaghten right or wrong test can be 'overthrown (and often has been) by any psychiatrist prepared to state that the accused did not know the nature of his act.' Surely, he doesn't mean that a psychiatrist should testify to such a state of facts unless they actually exist. If they do exist, then the expert is staying legally, morally and ethically within the McNaghten rule, and his oath. But if he cannot say that the accused was ignorant of the difference between right and wrong, *then he must not say it.* No psychiatrist can 'overthrow' the rule unless the court goes along with him. In Kansas, as well as the great majority of American jurisdictions, the courts will not go along with him.

Joseph P. Jenkins

Kansas City.

On 1 May, I replied as follows:

Sir,—Before answering the questions raised last Sunday by Joseph P. Jenkins, I'd like to deplore the false and flashy heading that *The*

Observer ran above his letter. 'Tynan attacked by lawyers,' it said across four columns, thus conveying the impression that I had been ambushed by a mob, whereas in fact Jenkins was my sole assailant.

Readers of 'In Cold Blood' will recall that Jenkins's association with the Clutter case began in 1962—two years after the killers had been tried and convicted—when a Federal judge appointed him as unpaid attorney to the condemned men. I have no doubt at all that he and his colleagues fought for the lives of Perry Smith and Dick Hickock as hard as they knew how.

A longer version of Jenkins's letter appeared last week in the American press, lashing me with phrases like 'utter balderdash' and 'God help journalism!', which I patiently accept as part of the shrill and formalised ritual of American courtroom rhetoric. But since I'm accused of neglecting the facts, I might as well start by pointing out a couple of peripheral blunders on Jenkins's part. He triumphantly claims that I 'never mentioned' the letter written by Dr Joseph Satten of the Menninger Foundation to my psychiatrist friend, Dr D'Accurzio: in fact, there are quotations from it both in my original article and in my reply to Truman Capote. And it's a pity, considering Jenkins's concern for the defendants, that he manages to misspell Hickock's name throughout.

But to move towards matters of importance: Jenkins reveals a sadly tenuous knowledge of (and faith in) psychiatry when he scoffs at the value of evidence tending to prove that Hickock and Smith were 'some sort of "paranoid schizophrenics."' He says that among the legal points he brought up, 'the insanity issue was only one.' In the American text he adds, 'and a minor one at that.' But it was not minor; it was crucial; and this is where I part company with him and Capote, his clients' chronicler.

Let's look first at the pre-trial period, between January 7, 1959, when lawyers were assigned to the accused, and March 22, when court proceedings began. During those 10 weeks Capote could certainly have helped to provide the two men with more adequate psychiatric examination than the hasty two-hour session with Dr Mitchell Jones which they received the day before the trial opened. It's true, as Jenkins says, that the original lawyers failed to obtain a court order directing psychiatric examination in a State hospital; but there is no reason (except lack of funds) why the defendants should not have been examined at length inside the county jail.

Parenthetically, Jenkins remarks that 'even if such testimony were presented at the original trial, a jury would not have to believe it.' Of course; but does that mean that it should not have been proffered? As for the McNaghten Rule: I said that it could be overthrown by 'any psy- ·

chiatrist prepared to state that the accused did not know the nature of his act.' By this I naturally meant an honest psychiatrist. Jenkins seems to imply that I was advocating perjury. I won't comment on this astonishing assumption.

Now for the post-trial period and the appeals. Jenkins initiated a habeas corpus hearing in the Federal court, at which an unpaid neuro-psychiatrist named Dr Herbert Modlin (who never met either Smith or Hickock: from first to last, Mitchell Jones was the only psychiatrist to have that privilege) testified that the accused had not been given adequate psychiatric examination. His evidence cut no ice. 'There is no pro-vision,' says Jenkins, 'in our Federal Rules of Criminal Procedure per-mitting us to hire top psychiatrists for the purpose of conducting a lengthy psycho-analysis of Hickok [*sic*] and Smith and then eliciting such testimony from the witness stand.' But if other psychiatrists had known what Capote knew about the private fantasies and psychotic drives of the two killers, and had taken the stand to support Dr Modlin, the judge could have ordered a full psychiatric examination.

According to Jenkins: 'The Federal judge is bound by what did or did not take place in the State court. He is not permitted to open new avenues.' This is simply untrue. To determine whether a constitutional error has been made, a Federal judge can (and frequently does) admit testimony adducing facts that were not raised at the trial. The Supreme Court ruled in 1963 (case of Townsend versus Sain) that where a consti-tutional point was involved in a habeas corpus hearing, a Federal judge might decide 'to hold evidentiary hearings—that is, to try issues of fact anew.' In other words, the question of sanity could have been reopened. And in any case, irrespective of whether Hickock and Smith were insane at the time of the murders or the trial, psychiatrists could have been hired to interview them in prison, in order to establish whether they were fit for execution. The hanging of insane men is clearly 'a cruel and unusual punishment,' and as such forbidden by the Constitution.

So much for the legal quibbles. We touch on the nerve of my com-plaint when Jenkins says, of the case in general, that: 'it was no concern of Mr Capote's. A writer has no business interfering with the orderly pro-cedure and processes in a court of law.' Really? Had Zola no business interfering in the Dreyfus case? Was it wrong for the late Felix Frank-furter—then a law professor at Harvard—to influence public and legal opinion by writing a famous article in the *Atlantic Monthly* about the Sacco-Vanzetti case? Must we rebuke the many authors and polemicists who tried to prevent the execution of the Rosenbergs and Caryl Chess-man? In matters of life and death, there are no interlopers.

One would feel less uneasy about Mr Capote's role in this sorry affair if he had said—even once, even in an interview—that he did not think his friends deserved to hang. 'I personally know,' says Jenkins, 'that Mr Capote did not want Hickok [*sic*] and Smith to die.' No doubt: but it was an opinion that Mr Capote never saw fit, in the course of five long years, to make public.

Kenneth Tynan

INDEX

461